INTERNATIONAL BIBLIOGRAPHY
OF THE SOCIAL SCIENCES

BIBLIOGRAPHIE INTERNATIONALE
DES SCIENCES SOCIALES

Publications of the ICSSD / Publications du CIDSS

INTERNATIONAL BIBLIOGRAPHY OF THE SOCIAL SCIENCES / BIBLIOGRAPHIE INTERNATIONALE DES SCIENCES SOCIALES.

[published annually in four parts / paraîssant chaque année en quatre parties. Until 1961 / Jusqu'en 1961: UNESCO, Paris].

International bibliography of sociology / Bibliographie internationale de sociologie [red cover / couverture rouge]. Vol. 1: 1951 (Publ. 1952).
International bibliography of political science / Bibliographie internationale de science politique [grey cover / couverture grise]. Vol. 1: 1952 (Publ. 1954).
International bibliography of economics / Bibliographie internationale de science économique [yellow cover / couverture jaune]. Vol. 1: 1952 (Publ. 1955).
International bibliography of social and cultural anthropology / Bibliographie internationale d'anthropologie sociale et culturelle [green cover / couverture verte]. Vol. 1: 1955 (Publ. 1958).

Other series / Autres collections:

INTERNATIONAL POLITICAL SCIENCE ABSTRACTS / DOCUMENTATION POLITIQUE INTERNATIONALE.

[quarterly / trimestriel. Basil Blackwell, Oxford].

CONFLUENCE, Surveys of research in the social sciences / CONFLUENCE, états des recherches en sciences sociales.
[semi-annual / semestriel. Mouton, Paris-La Haye].

DOCUMENTATION IN THE SOCIAL SCIENCES / DOCUMENTATION DANS LES SCIENCES SOCIALES.

[UNESCO, Paris].

Catalogue des sources de documentation juridique dans le monde / A register of legal documentation in the world (2nd Ed. / 2ᵉ édition, 1957).
Liste mondiale des périodiques spécialisés dans les sciences sociales / World list of social science periodicals (2nd Ed. / 2ᵉ édition, 1957).
International repertory of social science documentation centres / Répertoire international des centres de documentation de sciences sociales (1952).
International register of current team research in the social sciences / Répertoire international des recherches collectives en cours dans le domaine des sciences sociales (1955).

INTERNATIONAL BIBLIOGRAPHY
OF THE SOCIAL SCIENCES

BIBLIOGRAPHIE INTERNATIONALE
DES SCIENCES SOCIALES

1970

International Bibliography of
SOCIOLOGY

Bibliographie internationale de
SOCIOLOGIE

VOL. XX

Prepared by the
International Committee for Social Sciences Documentation

Établie par le
Comité international pour la documentation des sciences sociales

LONDON : TAVISTOCK PUBLICATIONS
CHICAGO : ALDINE PUBLISHING COMPANY

Manuscript prepared under the auspices of the International Sociological Association by the ICSSD with the financial support of Unesco (Subvention 1971, DG/3.2/41/53)

Manuscrit préparé sous les auspices de l'Association Internationale de Sociologie par le CIDSS avec l'aide financière de l'Unesco (Subvention 1971, DG/3.2/41/53)

422   80720   6

© ICSSD / CIDSS 1972

Published in 1972 by
Tavistock Publications Limited
11 New Fetter Lane, London E.C. 4

Printed by
Presse Ste-Catherine, Bruges, Belgique

TABLE OF CONTENTS
TABLE DES MATIÈRES

FOREWORD

This *International bibliography of sociology*, one of the four sections of the *International bibliography of the social sciences*, is one item in the general programme of the International Committee for Social Sciences Documentation. This committee was set up in 1950 with the help of Unesco for the purpose of encouraging the development of all bibliographical and documentary activities relating to the social sciences. It is composed of representatives of the various disciplines, elected upon the proposal of the following international scientific associations: International Social Science Council, International Sociological Association, International Economic Association, International Political Science Association, International Association of Legal Sciences, International Union of Scientific Psychology, International Union of Anthropological and Ethnological Sciences, International Union for the Scientific Study of Population, International Federation for Documentation, International Federation of Library Associations.

The committee felt that its most important task was to provide each branch of the social sciences with its basic bibliographical tools. Even before the establishment of the committee, several disciplines had adequate bibliographies at their disposal. This was true with regard to psychology and demography in particular; no new publication, therefore, was required in these fields. On the other hand, it seemed essential to prepare annual international bibliographies for certain disciplines where they were lacking: the four sections of the *International bibliography of the social sciences* were therefore elaborated.

The various bibliographies undertaken by the committee are designed to be truly international and to include the most important publications relating to each discipline, whatever the country of origin or the language in which they are drafted. They are also intended to list the various scientific publications, regardless of the form in which they are published (books, articles in periodicals, duplicated reports, etc.), with the exception of unpublished works (e.g. typewritten theses), articles published in the daily press, etc. Special attention is paid to the official publications of governments.

Each bibliography gives a more or less complete picture of the respective discipline, but only in so far as scientific publications are concerned, which implies some sort of selection of titles. This selection is carried out in two steps: first, by national correspondents, who inform the Editorial Staff of the books and articles which they consider important in their national literature, then by the Staff itself which makes a final selection of titles to be included in the bibliographies from among the total titles received, taking into account the position of the author in his discipline, and the scientific quality of the periodical publishing the article, as well as the comparative value of various studies published on the same topic in any given year.

In particular, national correspondents are advised to systematically exclude all books and articles of a journalistic or simple information nature, as well as those dealing in polemics. In sum, the principal criterion for selection is the true scientific character of a text.

Certain publications are mentioned in these bibliographies simultaneously, since the different social sciences are closely enough related to one another for the same subject to be studied by specialists in several different branches. The listing of a work in more than one bibliography is therefore intentional and is meant to place at the disposal of every reader the handiest possible tool for his work.

In many cases, however, it is also necessary to consult specialized bibliographies. A brief list is therefore given below of the main publications which should be consulted in respect of subjects not covered systematically by the present bibliography.

A. As regards "bibliographical listing" proper, it was necessary to bring out an annual international bibliography for each of the four best defined central disciplines of the social sciences: the *International bibliography of sociology*, the *International bibliography of political science*, the *International bibliography of economics* and the *International bibliography of social and cultural anthropology*, all four drafted in collaboration with the appropriate international associations and published in the form of four sections of the *International bibliography of the social sciences*.

1. This programme leaves out certain branches of the social sciences: demography, for which a special bibliography is published quarterly by *Population index;* social psychology, for which the *Psychological abstracts* can be used instead of monthly bibliographical lists.

2. As regards law, the diversity of national legal systems has prevented us from envisaging an international bibliography. On the other hand, the committee has helped the International Association of Legal Sciences to begin the publication of a series of national bibliographies of the law in the various countries. Anglo-Saxon legal periodical publications are presented in the *Index to legal periodicals* and those of all languages other than English in the *Index to foreign legal periodicals*.

3. Other scientific works, classified according to the geographical and cultural region with any aspect of which they are concerned, and not according to the special branch of study to which they belong, are listed in the bibliographies devoted to these various regions: *Bibliographie africaniste*, *Handbook of Latin American studies*, *Boletín bibliográfico de antropología americana* (partly in the form of abstracts), *Bibliographie américaniste*, *Bibliographie océaniste*, *Abstracta islamica* (partly in the form of abstracts), etc.

4. Finally, certain materials of interest to the social sciences are contained in the bibliographies devoted to history, *International bibliography for historical sciences;* to geography, *Bibliographie géographique internationale;* to philosophy, *Bibliographie de la philosophie;* to linguistics, *Bibliographie linguistique;* to medicine, *Index Medicus*.

B. With regard to "analytical bibliography", the committee helped the International Political Science Association to bring out the *International political science abstracts*.

1. Moreover, various groups of experts publish journals of abstracts devoted to the other basic social sciences: for economics, the *Documentation économique* (Paris), *Economic abstracts* (The Hague); for sociology, *Sociological abstracts* (New York). Social psychology has an important section to itself in *Psychological abstracts*.

2. Among publications covering a definite geographic area, *African abstracts* is devoted to ethnological and linguistic works. Two other publications which are partly in the form of abstracts have already been mentioned.

3. Of the related sciences, the medical sciences are the best equipped, with the *Excerptia medica*, the *Biological abstracts* and several highly specialized collections. For philosophy, there is the *Bulletin signalétique, 3ᵉ partie: philosophie* of the French Centre National de la Recherche Scientifique (which has one section devoted to sociology).

In addition, *Historical abstracts* is published in Vienna, covering works relating to the period prior to 1945, and thus forming a supplement to *International political science abstracts*, which normally covers post-war political questions.

All information and correspondence should be addressed to I.C.S.S.D., International bibliography of the social sciences, 27, rue Saint-Guillaume, Paris 7e.

The International Committee
for Social Sciences Documentation

AVERTISSEMENT

Cette *Bibliographie internationale de sociologie* est une des quatre parties de la *Bibliographie internationale des sciences sociales*, et représente ainsi un des éléments du programme d'ensemble du Comité international pour la documentation des sciences sociales. Ce comité a été constitué en 1950 avec l'appui de l'Unesco, en vue d'encourager le développement de toutes les activités bibliographiques et documentaires intéressant les sciences sociales. Il se compose de représentants des diverses disciplines, élus sur proposition des associations scientifiques internationales suivantes: Conseil international des sciences sociales, Association internationale de sociologie, Association internationale des sciences économiques, Association internationale de science politique, Association internationale des sciences juridiques, Union internationale de psychologie scientifique, Union internationale des sciences anthropologiques et ethnologiques, Union internationale pour l'étude scientifique de la population, Fédération internationale de documentation, Fédération internationale des association de bibliothécaires.

Le comité a considéré qu'une de ses tâches prioritaires était de fournir à chaque discipline des sciences sociales ses instruments bibliographiques. Quelques-unes d'entre elles, comme la psychologie et la démographie, disposaient déjà de publications bibliographiques satisfaisantes; pour les autres, il semblait indispensable de créer des bibliographies annuelles internationales. Les quatre parties de la *Bibliographie internationale des sciences sociales* ont ainsi été mises en chantier.

Les diverses bibliographies entreprises par le comité s'efforcent d'être réellement internationales, et de signaler les publications les plus importantes relevant de chaque discipline, quels qu'en soient le pays d'origine et la langue de rédaction. Elles cherchent à recenser les diverses publications scientifiques, sous quelque forme qu'elles aient paru (livres, articles de périodiques, rapports diffusés sous forme multigraphiée...), à l'exclusion toutefois des travaux qui ne sont pas publiés (par exemple les thèses dactylographiées), des articles parus dans la presse quotidienne, etc. Une attention particulière est accordée aux publications officielles des gouvernements.

Les bibliographies tendent à être complètes, mais seulement en ce qui concerne les publications scientifiques, ce qui implique une sorte de sélection des titres. Cette sélection est opérée à deux degrés: d'abord par les correspondants nationaux, qui signalent au Secrétariat de rédaction les ouvrages et articles qu'ils estiment importants dans la production nationale; ensuite par le Secrétariat lui-même qui dans l'ensemble des titres reçus, détermine ceux qui sont finalement inclus dans les bibliographies, prenant garde notamment à l'autorité dont jouissent les auteurs en la discipline, à la valeur respective des études qui concernent un même domaine ou à la qualité scienei-fique des périodiques publiant les articles.

En particulier il est recommandé aux correspondants nationaux d'exclure systématiquement les écrits de type journalistique ou de simple information et les écrits de caractère polémique, le principal critère de sélection devant être, en définitive, la nature proprement scientifique du texte examiné.

Certaines publications sont citées à la fois dans plusieurs bibliographies. En effet, les différentes sciences sociales sont suffisamment proches les unes des autres pour que le même sujet puisse être étudié par plusieurs spécialistes différents. Ces doubles citations sont délibérées, et elles répondent à la volonté de mettre à la disposition de chaque usager l'instrument de travail le plus commode.

Il n'en reste pas moins nécessaire de consulter aussi les publications bibliographiques consacrées aux disciplines voisines. Aussi trouvera-t-on ci-après une liste sommaire des principales publications auxquelles il conviendra de se référer pour les domaines que la présente bibliographie ne couvre pas systématiquement.

A. Sur le plan du "recensement bibliographique" proprement dit, il a fallu créer une bibliographie internationale annuelle pour chacune des quatre disciplines centrales les mieux définies des sciences sociales: la *Bibliographie internationale de sociologie*, la *Bibliographie internationale de science politique*, la *Bibliographie internationale de science économique* et la *Bibliographie internationale d'anthropologie sociale et culturelle*, toutes quatre rédigées en collaboration avec les associations internationales compétentes et publiées comme les quatre parties de la *Bibliographie internationale des sciences sociales*.

1. Ce programme laisse de côté: la démographie, pour laquelle une bibliographie spéciale est donnée trimestriellement par *Population index;* la psychologie sociale, pour laquelle les *Psychological abstracts* peuvent tenir lieu de listes bibliographiques mensuelles.

2. En ce qui concerne le droit, la diversité des systèmes juridiques nationaux n'a pas permis de prévoir une bibliographie internationale. En revanche, le comité a aidé l'Association internationale des sciences juridiques à commencer la publication d'une série de bibliographies nationales du droit dans les différents pays. D'autre part, la littérature juridique périodique anglo-saxonne est couverte par l'*Index to legal periodicals*, et celle de langues autres que l'anglais par l'*Index to foreign legal periodicals*.

3. D'autres travaux scientifiques, classés non d'après la spécialité dont ils relèvent, mais d'après l'aire géographique et culturelle qu'ils étudient, sont relevés dans les bibliographies consacrées à ces diverses régions: *Bibliographie africaniste, Handbook of Latin American studies, Boletín bibliográfico de antropología americana* (partiellement analytique), *Bibliographie américaniste, Bibliographie océaniste Abstracta islamica* (partiellement analytique), etc.

4. Certaines matériaux intéressant les sciences sociales se trouvent enfin dans les bibliographies consacrées à l'histoire: *Bibliographie internationale des sciences historiques;* à la géographie: *Bibliographique géographique internationale;* à la philosophie: *Bibliographie de la philosophie;* à la linguistique: *Bibliographie linguistique;* à la médecine: *Index Medicus.*

B. Sur le plan de la "bibliographie analytique", le comité a aidé l'Association internationale de science politique à créer la *Documentation politique internationale.*

1. Divers groupes de spécialistes publient par ailleurs des recueils de comptes rendus analytiques consacrés aux autres sciences sociales fondamentales: pour l'économie, la *Documentation économique* (Paris), *Economic abstracts* (La Haye); pour la sociologie, *Sociological abstracts* (New York). La psychologie sociale dispose, de son côté, d'une section importante dans les *Psychological abstracts.*

2. Dans le cadre des publications couvrant un champ géographiquement défini, les *Africain abstracts* sont consacrés aux travaux ethnologiques et linguistiques. On a cité plus haut deux autres publications partiellement analytiques.

3. Parmi les sciences voisines, ce sont les sciences médicales qui sont le mieux équipées avec les *Excerpta medica*, les *Biological abstracts* et plusieurs recueils très spécialisés. La philosophie de son côté dispose du *Bulletin signalétique, 3ᵉ partie; philosophie*, du Centre national de la recherche scientifique français (dont une section est consacrée à la sociologie).

On publie d'autre part, à Vienne des *Historical abstracts* qui couvrent les études relatives à la période antérieure à 1945, et qui ainsi constituent un supplément à la *Documentation politique internationale*, laquelle concerne les travaux sur les problèmes politiques postérieurs à cette date.

Tout renseignement et toute communication doivent être adressés au C.I.D.S.S. Bibliographie internationale des sciences sociales, 27, rue Saint-Guillaume, Paris 7e.

LE COMITE INTERNATIONAL
POUR LA DOCUMENTATION DES SCIENCES SOCIALES

PREFACE

This volume of the *International bibliography of sociology*, specially mentioning works published in 1970 is the twentieth of a series published regularly since 1952. It does not indicate any particular change in trend compared with previous volumes. Neither could it have been completed without considerable help contributed to the editorial board.

We have pleasure in thanking those institutions and sociologists, in many different countries, which have sent us information concerning their publications or helped us by their advice.

Our thanks are due to all who have written to us. As it would however be impossible to give the names of all who have helped, we mention only certain institutions here which have rendered special assistance by supplying information on the sociological publications issued throughout a country or even a region: Athens, Amerikanikon Kollegion Thēleōn; Belgrade, the University; Bogotà, Universidad nacional de Colombia, Facultad de sociología; Brussels, Institut de Sociologie Solvay; Bucharest, Bibliotheca Centrală de Stat; Budapest: Library of the Academy of Sciences; Cape Town: University of Cape Town; Geneva, Centre de recherches sociologiques; Jerusalem, Eliezer Kaplan School of Economics and Social Sciences; London, London School of Economics and Political Sciences; Madrid, Instituto Balmes de Sociología; Mexico City, Instituto de Investigaciones Sociales; Milan, Università Cattolica del Sacro Cuore; Moscow, Akademija Nauk SSSR, Fundamental'naja biblioteka obščestvennyh nauk and Institut Filosofii; Oslo, Universitet i Oslo, Instituttet for Sosiologi; Paris, Fondation nationale des sciences politiques; Rio de Janeiro, Centro latino-americano de pesquisas em ciências sociais; Tokyo, Japanese Sociological Association; Utrecht, Sociologisch Instituut van de Rijksuniversiteit; Warsaw, Polska Akademia Nauk.

We appeal to all scientific or university institutions in other countries which would be prepared to render us a similar service, and we point out that, for inclusion in the forthcoming volume, contributions should reach the editor's office not later than March 1st each year.

The editorial staff also wish to express their gratitude to the following experts who have closely co-operated with them particularly: Professor E. H. J. Akkeringa and Mr. F. Bergsma (Utrecht); Professor E. Batson (Cape Town); Mrs Inessa A. Chodosch (Moscow); Professor S. N. Eisenstadt (Jerusalem); Professor Orlando Fals Borda (Bogotà); Dr. T. Kitagawa (Tokyo); Dr. Z. Gross (Warsaw); Dr. András Hegedüs (Budapest); Professor René König (Cologne); Professor Oleg Mandić (Belgrade); Dr. Manuel Diégues Junior (Rio de Janeiro); Mr. Örjar Öyen (Oslo); Professor Carmelo Viñas (Madrid).

PRÉFACE

Ce volume de la *Bibliographie internationale de sociologie*, qui recense essentiellement les travaux parus en 1970, est le vingtième d'une série régulièrement publiée depuis 1952. Il ne présente guère de changement par rapport aux précédents et n'aurait pu davantage être mené à bien sans les nombreux concours dont a bénéficié la rédaction.

Il nous est agréable de remercier ici les institutions et les sociologues de nombreux pays qui nous ont informés de leurs publications ou aidés de leurs conseils.

Les remerciements s'adressent à tous ceux qui nous ont écrit. Ne pouvant toutefois procéder à une énumération complète, nous nous contenterons de mentionner certaines institutions dont le concours a été particulièrement important, et qui nous ont permis de connaître les publications sociologiques de l'ensemble d'un pays ou même d'une région: Athènes: Amerikanikon Kollegion Thēleōn; Belgrade: Université, Institut des Sciences sociales; Bogotà: Universidad Nacional de Colombia, Facultad de Sociología; Bruxelles: Institut de sociologie Solvay; Bucarest: Biblioteca centrală de Stat; Budapest: Bibliothèque de l'Académie des Sciences; Genève: Centre de recherches sociologiques; Jérusalem: Eliezer Kaplan School of Economics and Social Sciences; Le Cap: Université du Cap; Londres: London School of Economics and Political Sciences; Madrid: Instituto Balmes de Sociología; Mexico: Instituto de Investigaciones Sociales; Milan: Università Cattolica del Sacro Cuore; Moscou: Akademija Nauk SSSR, Fundamental'naja biblioteka obščestvennyh nauk et Institut Filosofii; Oslo: Universitet i Oslo, Instituttet for Sosiologi; Paris: Fondation nationale des sciences politiques; Rio de Janeiro: Centro latino-americano de pesquisas en ciências sociais; Tokyo: Japanese Sociological Association; Utrecht: Sociologisch Instituut van de Rijksuniversiteit; Varsovie: Polska Akademia Nauk.

Nous faisons appel à toutes les institutions scientifiques ou universitaires des autres pays qui seraient disposées à nous rendre le même service, précisant seulement que les différentes contributions, pour figurer dans le volume en préparation, doivent être reçues à la rédaction chaque année avant le 1er mars.

La rédaction tient en outre à exprimer sa reconnaissance à plusieurs personnalités qui ont collaboré avec elle de façon particulièrement étroite, à savoir: le professeur E. H. J. Akkeringa et M. F. Bergsma (Utrecht); le professeur E. Batson (Le Cap); Mme Inessa A. Chodosch (Moscou); le professeur S. N. Eisenstadt (Jérusalem); le professeur Orlando Fals Borda (Bogotà); le Dr Takayoshi Kitagawa (Tokyo); le Dr. Z. Gross (Varsovie); Dr. András Hegedüs (Budapest); le professeur René König (Cologne); le professeur Oleg Mandić (Belgrade); le Dr. Manuel Diégues Júnior (Rio de Janeiro); M. Örjar Öyen (Oslo); le professeur Carmelo Viñas (Madrid).

LIST OF PERIODICALS CONSULTED
LISTE DES PÉRIODIQUES CONSULTÉS

Abbia	*Abbia*	Yaoundé
Academy of Management Journal	*Acad. Manag. J.*	Eugene
Acta archaeologica	*Acta archaeol.*	Budapest
Acta ethnographica	*Acta ethnogr. (Budapest)*	Budapest
Acta geographica. Bulletin officiel de la Société de Géographie	*Acta geogr.*	Paris
Acta juridica	*Acta jur. (Budapest)*	Budapest
Acta juridica	*Acta jur. (Cape Town)*	Cape Town
Acta oeconomica	*Acta oecon.*	Budapest
Acta orientalia	*Acta orient. (Budapest)*	Budapest
Acta politica	*Acta polit.*	Amsterdam
Acta Poloniae historica	*Acta Poloniae hist.*	Warszawa
Acta sociologica	*Acta sociol.*	København
Acta tropica	*Acta trop.*	Basel
Actualité économique	*Actual. écon.*	Montréal
Administration	*Administration (Dublin)*	Dublin
Administration	*Administration (Ibadan)*	Ibadan
Administration	*Administration (Paris)*	Paris
Administrative Science Quarterly	*Adm. Sci. Quart.*	Ithaca, N. Y.
Adult Education	*Adult Educ. (London)*	London
Adult Education	*Adult Educ. (Washington)*	Washington
Adult Leadership	*Adult Leadership*	Washington
Aesculape	*Aesculape*	Paris
Affari esteri	*Aff. est.*	Roma
Africa	*Africa (London)*	London
Africa	*Africa (London)*	Madrid
Africa	*Africa (Milano)*	Milano
Africa	*Africa (Roma)*	Roma
Africa Institute Bulletin	*Afr. Inst. B.*	Pretoria
Africa Quarterly	*Afr. Quart.*	New Delhi
Africa Report	*Afr. Rep.*	Washington
Africa-Tervuren	*Afr.-Tervuren*	Tervuren
Africa today	*Afr. today*	Denver, Col.
African Affairs	*Afr. Aff.*	London
African Arts	*Afr. Arts*	Los Angeles, Calif.
African Forum	*Afr. Forum*	New York
African historical Studies	*Afr. hist. Stud.*	Boston
African Music	*Afr. Music*	Johannesburg
African Studies	*Afr. Stud.*	Johannesburg
African Studies Bulletin	*Afr. Stud. B.*	New York
Africana Bulletin	*Africana B.*	Warszawa
Africasia	*Africasia*	Paris
Afrika Archiv	*Afrika Archiv*	München
Afrika heute	*Afrika heute*	Bonn
Afrika no Kenkyû	*Afrika no Kenkyû*	Tokyo
Afrique Contact	*Afr. Contact*	Paris
Afrique contemporaine	*Afr. contemp.*	Paris
Afrique-Documents	*Afr.-Doc.*	Dakar

Afrique et Asie	*Afr. et Asie*	Paris
Afrique littéraire et artistique	*Afr. littér. artist.*	Paris
Afrique médicale	*Afr. médic.*	Dakar
Afro-Asian economic Review	*Afro-Asian econ. R.*	Cairo
Aggiornamenti sociali	*Aggiorn. soc.*	Milano
Agrarwirtschaft	*Agrarwirtschaft*	Braunschweig
Agricoltura	*Agricoltura*	Roma
Agricultural Economics Research	*Agric. Econ. Res.*	Washington, D.C.
Agricultural Situation in India	*Agric. Situation India*	Delhi
Agronomie tropicale	*Agron. trop.*	Paris
Ajia Keizai	*Ajia Keizai*	Tokyo
Ajia Kenkyû	*Ajia Kenkyû*	Tokyo
Akademia	*Akademia*	Nagoya
Állam-és Jogtudomány	*Állam-és Jogtud.*	Budapest
Allemagne d'aujourd'hui	*Allem. aujourd.*	Paris
Altertum	*Altertum*	Berlin
Aménagement du Territoire et Développement régional	*Aménag. Territ. Dévelop. région.*	St Martin d'Hères
América indígena	*Amér. indíg.*	México
América latina	*Amér. lat.*	Rio de Janeiro
American Anthropologist	*Amer. Anthropol.*	New York
American Antiquity	*Amer. Antiq.*	Menasha, Wisc.
American behavioral scientist	*Amer. behav. Scientist*	Princeton, N. Y.
American economic Review	*Amer. econ. R.*	Menasha, Wisc.
American Economist	*Amer. Economist*	New York
American historical Review	*Amer. hist. R.*	New York
American Journal of agricultural Economics	*Amer. J. agric. Econ.*	Menasha, Wisc.
American Journal of Economics and Sociology	*Amer. J. Econ. Sociol.*	New York
American Journal of international Law	*Amer. J. int. Law*	Washington, D.C.
American Journal of psychiatry	*Amer. J. Psychiatry*	New York
American Journal of Sociology	*Amer. J. Sociol.*	Chicago, Ill.
American political Science Review	*Amer. polit. Sci. R.*	Washington, D.C.
American Review of East-West Trade	*Amer. R. East-West Trade*	White Plains, N. Y.
American Scandinavian Review	*Amer. Scand. R.*	New York
American Scholar	*Amer. Scholar*	Washington, D.C.
American sociological Review	*Amer. sociol. R.*	New York
American Sociologist	*Amer. Sociologist*	Columbus, Ohio
American vocational Journal	*Amer. vocat. J.*	Washington
Amministrare	*Amministrare*	Milano
Amministrazione italiana	*Amm. ital.*	Roma
Anales de Antropología	*A. Antropol.*	Mexico
Anales de Arqueología y Etnología	*A. Arqueol. Etnol.*	Mendoza
Análise social	*Anál. soc.*	Lisbõa
Analyse et Prévision	*Anal. et Prévis.*	Paris
Analyse financière	*Anal. financ.*	Paris
Annales (Économies - Sociétés - Civilisations)	*Annales*	Paris
Annales africaines	*A. afr.*	Dakar
Annales de Droit	*A. Dr.*	Bruxelles
Annales de Géographie	*A. Géogr.*	Paris
Annales de Sciences économiques appliquées	*A. Sci. écon. appl.*	Louvain
Annales de l'Économie collective	*A. Écon. coll.*	Liège
Annales de l'INSÉÉ	*Annales INSÉÉ*	Paris
Annales de l'Université d'Abidjan	*A. Univ. Abidjan*	Abidjan
Annales de l'Université de Madagascar	*A. Univ. Madagascar*	Tananarive

Annales de l'Université de Madagascar. Lettres	*A. Univ. Madagascar Lettres*	Tananarive
Annales de la Faculté de Droit de Liège	*A. Fac. Dr. Liège*	Liège
Annales de la Faculté de Droit et des Sciences économiques	*A. Fac. Dr. Sci. écon. (Lyon)*	Lyon
Annales de la Faculté de Droit et des Sciences économiques	*A. Fac. Dr. Sci. écon. (Toulouse)*	Toulouse
Annales de la Faculté de Droit et des Sciences économiques de Lille	*A. Fac. Dr. Sci. écon. Lille*	Lille
Annales de la Faculté des Lettres et Sciences humaines d'Aix-en-Provence	*A. Fac. Lettres Sci. hum. Aix*	Aix-en-Provence
Annales de la Faculté des Lettres et Sciences humaines de Yaoundé	*A. Fac. Lettres Sci. hum. Yaoundé*	Yaoundé
Annales du Centre d'Enseignement supérieur de Brazzaville	*A. Centre Enseign. sup. Brazzaville*	Brazzaville
Annales du Midi	*A. Midi*	Toulouse
Annales Universitatis Mariae Curie-Skłodowska	*A. Univ. M. Curie-Skłodowska*	Lublin
Annales Universitatis Mariae Curie-Skłodowska. Sectio oeconomica	*A. Univ. M. Curie-Skłodowska oecon.*	Lublin
Annali del Mezzogiorno	*A. Mezzogiorno*	Catania
Annali della Facoltà di Agraria	*A. Fac. Agrar. (Milano)*	Milano
Annali della Facoltà di Economia e Commercio	*A. Fac. Econ. Com. (Bari)*	Bari
Annali della Facoltà di Economia e Commercio dell'Università di Messina	*A. Fac. Econ. Com. Messina*	Messina
Annali della Facoltà di Economia e Commercio dell'Università di Palermo	*A. Fac. Econ. Com. Palermo*	Palermo-Roma
Annali della Fondazione Luigi Einaudi	*A. Fond. Luigi Einaudi*	Torino
Annals of the American Academy of political and social Science	*A. Amer. Acad. polit. soc. Sci.*	Philadelphia, Pa.
Annals of the Association of American Geographers	*A. Assoc. Amer. Geogr.*	Lawrence, Kan.
Année sociologique	*Année sociol.*	Paris
Annuaire des Auditeurs et anciens Auditeurs de l'Académie de Droit international de La Haye	*Annu. A. A. A.*	La Haye
Annuaire français de Droit international	*Annu. franç. Dr. int.*	Paris
Annuaire suisse de Droit international/ Schweizerisches Jahrbuch für Internationales Recht	*Annu. suisse Dr. int./ Schweizer. Jb. int. Recht*	Zürich
Annuaire suisse de Science politique	*Annu. suisse Sci. polit.*	Genève
Anschnitt	*Anschnitt*	Essen
Antaios	*Antaios*	Stuttgart
Anthropologica	*Anthropologica (Ottawa)*	Ottawa
Anthropological Forum	*Anthropol. Forum*	Nedlands
Anthropological Linguistics	*Anthropol. Linguist.*	Bloomington, Ind.
Anthropological Quarterly	*Anthropol. Quart.*	Washington
Anthropologie	*Anthropologie (Brno)*	Brno
Anthropologie	*Anthropologie (Paris)*	Paris
Anthropology. Magazine of the anthropological Club at the London School of Economics	*Anthropol. Mag.*	London
Anticipation	*Anticipation*	
Antiquity	*Antiquity*	Cambridge, Engl.
Antropología e Historia de Guatemala	*Antropol. Hist. Guatemala*	Guatemala City
Antropologiai Közlemények	*Antropol. Közlem.*	Budapest
Antropoloji	*Antropoloji*	Ankara

Anuaria de Sociología de los Pueblos ibéricos	*Anu. Sociol. Pueblos ibér.*	Madrid
Anuario del Instituto de Antropologia e Historia	*Anu. Inst. Antropol. Hist.*	Caracas
Anuario indígenista	*Anu. indíg.*	Mexico
Aportes	*Aportes*	Paris
Applied Economics	*Appl. Econ.*	London
Arbeitsmarktpolitik	*Arbeitsmarktpolitik*	Linz
Arbitration Journal	*Arbitr. J.*	New York
Arbor	*Arbor*	Madrid
Architecture d'aujourd'hui	*Archit. aujourd.*	Paris
Archiv des öffentlichen Rechts	*Archiv öff. Rechts*	Tübingen
Archiv des Völkerrechts	*Archiv Völkerrechts*	Tübingen
Archiv für Geschichte von Oberfranken	*Archiv. Gesch. Oberfranken*	Bayreuth
Archiv für Kommunalwissenschaften	*Archiv Kommunalwiss.*	Stuttgart
Archiv für Kulturgeschichte	*Archiv Kulturgesch.*	Köln-Wien
Archiv für Rechts- und Sozialphilosophie	*Archiv Rechts- u. soz.-Philos.*	Berlin-Neuwied-am-Rhein
Archiv für Völkerkunde	*Archiv Völkerk.*	Wien
Archives de Philosophie du Droit	*Archiv. Philos. Dr.*	Paris
Archives de Sociologie des Religions	*Archiv. Sociol. Relig.*	Paris
Archives européennes de Sociologie	*Archiv. europ. Sociol.*	Paris
Archives internationales de Sociologie de la Coopération	*Archiv. int. Sociol. Coop.*	Gif-sur-Yvette
Archivio finanziario	*Archiv. finanz.*	Padova
Archivos del Instituto de Estudios africanos	*Archiv. Inst. Estud. afr.*	Madrid
Arctic Anthropology	*Arctic Anthropol.*	Madison, Wisc.
Artha Vijñana	*Artha Vijñana*	Poona
Arts asiatiques	*Arts asiat.*	Paris
Arts et Traditions populaires	*Arts Trad. popul.*	Paris
Ašhabad	*Ašhabad*	Ašhabad
Asia Afrika Gengo Bunka Kenkyû	*Asia Afrika Gengo Bunka Kenkyû*	Tokyo
Asia Keizai	*Asia Keizai*	Tokyo
Asian and African Studies	*Asian Afr. Stud.*	Bratislava
Asian economic Review	*Asian econ. R.*	Hyderabad
Asian Outlook	*Asian Outlook*	Taipeh
Asian Survey	*Asian Surv.*	Berkeley, Calif.
Asian Tradeunionist	*Asian Tradeunion.*	New Delhi
Asien Forum	*Asien Forum*	
Assistenza sociale	*Assist. soc.*	Roma
Atlantic Community Quarterly	*Atlantic Community Quart.*	Washington
Atomic Energy Law Journal	*Atomic Energy Law J.*	Boston
Aussenpolitik	*Aussenpolitik*	Stuttgart
Aussenwirtschaft	*Aussenwirtschaft (St Gallen)*	St Gallen
Australian and New Zealand Journal of Sociology	*Austral. New Zeal. J. Sociol.*	Melbourne
Australian economic History Review	*Austral. econ. Hist. R.*	Sydney
Australian economic Papers	*Austral. econ. Pap.*	Adelaide
Australian Journal of agricultural Economics	*Austral. J. agric. Econ.*	Armidale, N.S.W.
Australian Journal of Politics and History	*Austral. J. Polit. Hist.*	Sydney
Australian Outlook	*Austral. Outlook*	Melbourne
Australian Quarterly	*Austral. Quart.*	Sydney
Autogestion	*Autogestion*	Paris
Azija i Afrika segodnja	*Azija i Afr. segod.*	Moskva

Baessler-Archiv	*Baessler-Archiv*	Berlin
Bajkal	*Bajkal*	Čita
Banca nazionale del Lavoro. Quarterly Review	*Banca naz. Lav. quart. R.*	Roma
Bancaria	*Bancaria*	Roma
Bancaria Rassegna	*Bancaria Rass.*	
Banco do Brasil. Boletim trimestral	*Banco Brasil. Bol. trim.*	Rio de Janeiro
Bank of England quarterly Bulletin	*Bank England quart. B.*	London
Bank of Finland monthly Bulletin	*Bank Finland mthly B.*	Helsinki
Bank of Israel Bulletin	*Bank Israel B.*	Jerusalem
Bank of Israel economic Review	*Bank Israel econ. R.*	Jerusalem
Bank of London and South America Review	*Bank London South Amer. R.*	London
Banker	*Banker*	London
Banque	*Banque*	Paris
Banque centrale de Tunisie. Bulletin	*Banque centr. Tunisie B.*	Tunis
Banque française et italienne pour l'Amérique du Sud	*Banque franç. ital. Amér. Sud*	Paris
Banque française et italienne pour l'Amérique du Sud. Études économiques	*Banque franç. ital. Amér. Sud. Ét. écon.*	Paris
Banque marocaine du Commerce extérieur. Bulletin mensuel d'Information	*Banque maroc. Com. ext. B. mens. Inform.*	Casablanca
Bantu	*Bantu*	Pretoria
Bayerische Vorgeschichtsblätter	*Bayer. Vorgesch.-bl.*	München
Bayern in Zahlen	*Bayern in Zahlen*	München
Behavioral Science	*Behav. Sci.*	Ann Arbor, Mich.
Behavioral Science Notes	*Behav. Sci. Notes*	New Haven, Conn.
Behaviour Research and Therapy	*Behav. Res. Therapy*	London
Beiträge zur Musikwissenschaft	*Beitr. Musikwiss.*	Berlin
Belfagor	*Belfagor*	Marina di Petrasanta (Lucca)
Bénélux Bulletin trimestriel économique et statistique	*Bénélux. B. trim. écon. statist.*	Bruxelles
Berkeley Journal of Sociology	*Berkeley J. Sociol.*	Berkeley, Calif.
Betriebswirtschaftliche Forschung und Praxis	*Betriebswirtsch. Forsch. u. Praxis*	Herne-Berlin
Biennal Review of Anthropology	*Bien. R. Anthropol.*	Stanford
Biggmästaren	*Biggmästaren*	Stockholm
Bijdragen tot de Taal-, Land- en Volkenkunde	*Bijdrag. Taal-, Land- Volkenk.*	's-Gravenhage
Biuletyn Instytutu Gospodarstwa Społecznego	*Biul. IGS*	Warszawa
Bohemia. Jahrbuch des Collegium Carolinum	*Bohemia*	München
Boletim	*Boletim (Araraquara)*	Araraquara
Boletim cultural da Guiné portuguesa	*Bol. cult. Guiné portug.*	Bissau
Boletim do Instituto Joaquim Nabuco de Pesquisas sociais	*Bol. Inst. Joaquim Nabuco Pesq. soc.*	Recife
Boletin de Documentacion del Fondo para la Investigación económica y social	*Bol. Docum. Fondo Investig. econ. soc.*	Madrid
Boletín de Estudios económicos	*Bol. Estud. econ. (Bilbao)*	Bilbao
Boletín de la Facultad de Derecho y Ciencias sociales	*Bol. Fac. Der. Cienc. soc. (Córdoba)*	Córdoba
Boletín del Banco central de Ecuador	*Bol. Banco centr. Ecuador*	Quito
Boletín del Centro de Estudios sociales	*Bol. Centro Estud. soc.*	Madrid
Boletín del Museo social argentino	*Bol. Mus. soc. argent.*	Buenos Aires

Boletín ELAS	*Bol. ELAS*	Santiago de Chile
Boletín informativo de Ciencia política	*Bol. inform. Cienc. polít.*	Madrid
Boletín mensual de Estadística	*Bol. mens. Estadíst.*	Bogotá
Boletín mexicano de Derecho comparado	*Bol. mexic. Der. comp.*	Mexico
Boletín uruguayo de Sociología	*Bol. urug. Sociol.*	Montevideo
Bollettino della Società geografica italiana	*Boll. Soc. geogr. ital.*	Roma
Bollettino di Informazioni costituzionali e parlamentari	*Boll. Inform. costit. parl.*	Roma
Bollettino di Psicologia applicata	*Boll. Psicol. appl.*	Firenze
Bremer archäologische Blätter	*Bremer archäol. Bl.*	Bremen
British Journal of industrial Relations	*Brit. J. industr. Relat.*	London
British Journal of Psychology	*Brit. J. Psychol.*	London
British Journal of social and clinical Psychology	*Brit. J. soc. clinical Psychol.*	London-New York
British Journal of social Psychiatry	*Brit. J. soc. Psychiatry*	London
British Journal of Sociology	*Brit. J. Sociol.*	London
British Yearbook of international Law	*Brit. Yb. int. Law*	London
Bucknell Review	*Bucknell R.*	Lewisburg, Pa.
Bulldoc. Centre de Documentation sur l'Urbanisme	*Bulldoc*	Arcueil
Bulletin d'Information et de Liaison des Instituts d'Ethno-Sociologie et de Géographie tropicale	*B. Inform. Liaison Inst. Ethno-Sociol. Géogr. trop.*	Abidjan
Bulletin de Conjoncture régionale	*B. Conjonct. région. (Rennes)*	Rennes
Bulletin de Droit tchécoslovaque	*B. Dr. tchécosl.*	Prague
Bulletin de Liaison et d'Information de l'Administration centrale de l'Économie et des Finances	*B. Liaison Inform. Adm. centr. Écon. Finances*	Paris
Bulletin de Madagascar	*B. Madagascar*	Tananarive
Bulletin de l'École française d'Extrême-Orient	*B. Éc. franç. Extr.-Or.*	Paris
Bulletin de l'Économie agricole en Afrique	*B. Écon. agric. Afr.*	Addis-Abeba
Bulletin de l'Institut fondamental de l'Afrique noire	*B. Inst. fondam. Afr. noire*	Dakar
Bulletin de l'Institut international de l'Administration publique	*B. Inst. int. Adm. publ.*	Paris
Bulletin de l'Institut national de la Santé et de la Recherche médicale	*B. Inst. nat. Santé Rech. médic.*	Paris
Bulletin de la Société d'Études océaniennes	*B. Soc. Ét. océan.*	Papeete
Bulletin de la Société de Pathologie exotique	*B. Soc. Pathol. exotique*	Paris
Bulletin de la Société des Études indochinoises	*B. Soc. Ét. indochinoises*	Saïgon
Bulletin de la Société préhistorique française. Compte-rendus mensuels	*B. Soc. préhist. franç. C.R. mens.*	Paris
Bulletin der schweizerischen Gesellschaft für Anthropologie und Ethnologie/ Bulletin de la Société suisse d'Anthropologie et d'Ethnologie	*B. schweiz. Ges. Anthropol. Ethnol./B. Soc. suisse Anthropol. Ethnol.*	Zürich-Bern
Bulletin des Bibliothèques de France	*B. Bibl. France*	Paris
Bulletin des Instituts de Recherches de l'Université d'Abidjan	*B. Inst. Rech. Univ. Abidjan*	Abidjan
Bulletin du Bureau d'Ethnologie	*B. Bur. Ethnol.*	Port au Prince
Bulletin du Centre d'Études et de Recherches psychotechniques	*Bull. CÉRP*	Paris

Bulletin du Centre européen de la Culture	*B. Centre europ. Cult.*	Genève
Bulletin du Ministère des Finances et du Plan	*B. Minist. Finances Plan*	Alger
Bulletin du Musée de la Ville de Genève	*B. Musée Genève*	Genève
Bulletin du Secrétariat des Missions d'Urbanisme et d'Habitat	*B. Secret. Miss. Urban. Habitat*	Paris
Bulletin économique et social du Maroc	*B. écon. soc. Maroc*	Rabat
Bulletin économique pour l'Afrique	*B. écon. Afr.*	Addis-Abéba
Bulletin for international fiscal Documentation	*B. inst. Fisc. Docum.*	Amsterdam
Bulletin mensuel Économie et Statistique agricole	*B. mens. Écon. Statist. agric.*	Rome
Bulletin of African Studies in Canada/ Bulletin des Études africaines au Canada	*B. Afr. Stud. Canada/B. Ét. afr. Canada*	Edmonton
Bulletin of Indonesian economic Studies	*B. Indones. econ. Stud.*	Canberra
Bulletin of the Africa Institute of South Africa	*B. Afr. Inst. South Afr.*	Pretoria
Bulletin of the international Committee on urgent anthropological and ethnological Research	*B. int. Committee urg. anthropol. ethnol. Res.*	Vienna
Bulletin of the Oxford University Institute of Economics and Statistics	*B. Oxford Univ. Inst. Econ. Statist.*	Oxford
Bulletin of the School of oriental and African Studies	*B. School orient. afr. Stud.*	London
Bulletin of the UNESCO regional Office for Education in Asia	*Bull. UNESCO region. Office Educ. Asia*	Bangkok
Bulletin technique et pédagogique	*B. techn. pédag.*	Genève
Bulletins et Mémoires de la Société d'Anthropologie	*B. Mém. Soc. Anthropol. Paris*	Paris
Bunka-jinrui-gaku	*Bunka-jinrui-gaku*	Tokyo
Business and Government Review	*Busin. Gvt R.*	Columbia, Mo.
Business Economics	*Busin. Econ.*	Washington, D.C.
Business History Review	*Busin. Hist. R.*	Boston, Mass.
Cadernos brasileiros	*Cad. brasil.*	Rio de Janeiro
Cahiers africains de la Sécurité sociale	*C. afr. Sécur. soc.*	Genève
Cahiers congolais de la Recherche et du Développement	*C. congol. Rech. Dévelop.*	Kinshasa
Cahiers d'Archéologie et d'Histoire du Berry	*C. Archéol. Hist. Berry*	Bourges
Cahiers d'Études africaines	*C. Ét. afr.*	La Haye-Paris
Cahiers d'Histoire mondiale	*C. Hist. mond.*	Paris
Cahiers d'Outre-Mer	*C. O.-Mer*	Bordeaux
Cahiers de Bruges	*C. Bruges*	Bruges
Cahiers de Documentation de la Chambre de Commerce et d'Industrie de Marseille	*C. Docum. Ch. Com. Marseille*	Marseille
Cahiers de Droit européen	*C. Dr. europ.*	Louvain
Cahiers de Sociologie et de Démographie médicales	*C. Sociol. Démogr. médic.*	Paris
Cahiers de Tunisie	*C. Tunisie*	Tunis
Cahiers de l'Institut international d'Études sociales	*C. Inst. int. Ét. soc.*	Genève
Cahiers de l'Institut pour l'Aménagement urbain de la Région parisienne	*C. Inst. Aménag. urb. Région paris*	Paris

Cahiers de l'Office de la Recherche scientifique et technique Outre-Mer	*Cah. ORSTOM Sér. Sci. hum.*	Paris
Cahiers des Amériques latines. Série Sciences de l'Homme	*C. Amér. lat. Sér. Sci. Homme*	Paris
Cahiers du Centre d'Études des Coutumes	*C. Centre Ét. Coutumes*	Tananarive
Cahiers du Monde hispanique et luso-brésilien	*C. Monde hisp. luso-brésil.*	Toulouse
Cahiers économiques de Bruxelles	*C. écon. Bruxelles*	Bruxelles
Cahiers économiques et sociaux	*C. écon. soc. (Kinshasa)*	Kinshasa
Cahiers internationaux de Sociologie	*C. int. Sociol.*	Paris
Cahiers Laënnec	*C. Laënnec*	Paris
Cahiers nord-africains	*C. nord-afr.*	Paris
Cahiers Vilfredo Pareto	*C. V. Pareto*	Genève
California Management Review	*Calif. Manag. R.*	Los Angeles, Calif.
Canadian Journal of agricultural Economics	*Canad. J. agric. Econ.*	Toronto
Canadian Journal of Economics	*Canad. J. Econ.*	Toronto
Canadian Journal of political Science	*Canad. J. polit. Sci.*	Toronto
Canadian public Administration	*Canad. publ. Adm.*	Toronto
Canadian Review of Sociology and Anthropology	*Canad. R. Sociol. Anthropol.*	Calgary
Canadian Slavonic Papers	*Canad. Slavonic Pap.*	Ottawa
Caravelle. Cahiers du Monde hispanique et luso-brésilien	*Caravelle*	Toulouse
Caribbean Studies	*Carib. Stud.*	Puerto Rico
Carnets de l'Enfance	*Carnets de l'Enfance*	Paris
Case Western Reserve Journal of international Law	*Case West. Reserve J. int. Law*	Cleveland
Central Asiatic Journal	*Centr. Asiat. J.*	Wiesbaden
Centre de Recherches et d'Études des Chefs d'Entreprise. CRC	*CRC*	Paris
Český Lid	*Český Lid*	Praha
Ceylon Labour Gazette	*Ceylon Lab. Gaz.*	Colombo
China Quarterly	*China Quart.*	London
Chinese economic Studies	*Chinese econ. Stud.*	White Plains, N. Y.
Christianisme social	*Christ. soc.*	Paris
Chronique de l'Unesco	*Chron. Unesco*	Paris
Chronique sociale de France	*Chron. soc. France*	Lyon
Chûdai Bungakubu Kiyô	*Chûdai Bungakubu Kiyô*	Tokyo
Chûô-Kôron	*Chûô-Kôron*	Tokyo
Ciencias administrativas	*Cienc. adm. (La Plata)*	La Plata
Civilisations	*Civilisations*	Bruxelles
Civitas	*Civitas*	Roma
Co-existence	*Co-existence*	Ontario-Chicago, Ill.
Collections de l'INSÉÉ. Série C	*Coll. INSÉÉ Sér. C.*	Paris
Colombo Law Review	*Colombo Law R.*	Colombo
Columbia Journal of World Business	*Columbia J. Wld Busin.*	New York
Columbia Law Review	*Columbia Law R.*	Columbia University, N. Y.
Columbian Essays in international Affairs	*Columb. Essays int. Aff.*	New York
Commentary	*Commentary*	New York
Common Market	*Common Market*	La Haye
Common Market Law Review	*Common Market Law R.*	Leyden
Communautés	*Communautés*	Paris
Communications	*Communications*	Paris
Community and Development Journal	*Community Develop. J.*	Manchester
Comparative Education Review	*Comp. Educ. R.*	Kent, Ohio

Comparative Politics	*Comp. Polit.*	Chicago, Ill.
Comparative Studies in Society and History	*Comp. Stud. Soc. Hist.*	The Hague- Ann Arbor, Mich.
Comprendre	*Comprendre*	Venise
Comptes-rendus mensuels de l'Académie des Sciences d'Outre-Mer	*C.R. mens. Acad. Sci. O.-Mer*	Paris
Comunidades	*Comunidades*	Madrid
Comunità internazionale	*Comunità int.*	Padova
Conflict Studies	*Conflict Stud.*	London
Confronter	*Confronter*	Milano
Congo-Afrique	*Congo-Afr.*	Kinshasa, Congo
Conjonction	*Conjonction*	Port-au-Prince
Conjoncture économique lorraine	*Conjonct. écon. lorr.*	Nancy
Connaissance de l'Afrique	*Connaiss. Afr.*	Paris
Connaissance de l'Économie lyonnaise	*Connaiss. Écon. lyon.*	Lyon
Consommation	*Consommation*	Paris
Construction, Aménagement	*Construct. Aménag.*	Paris
Contemporary Japan	*Contemp. Japan.*	Tokyo
Contributions to Indian Sociology	*Contrib. Ind. Sociol.*	New Delhi
Convergence	*Convergence*	Toronto
Coopération	*Coopération*	Paris
Cooperation and Conflict	*Coop. and Conflict*	Stockholm
Coopération et Développement	*Coop. et Dévelop.*	Paris
Cooperative Information	*Coop. Inform.*	Geneva
Cooperazione di Credito	*Coop. di Cred.*	Roma
Cornell Journal of social Relations	*Cornell J. soc. Relat.*	Ithaca, N. Y.
Correspondance d'Orient. Études	*Corresp. Orient*	Bruxelles
Critica marxista	*Crit. marx.*	Roma
Critica sociologica	*Crit. sociol. (Roma)*	Roma
Critique	*Critique*	Paris
Critique socialiste	*Crit. social. (Paris)*	Paris
Croissance des jeunes Nations	*Croissance jeunes Nations*	Paris
Cuadernos américanos	*Cuad. amér.*	México
Cuadernos de la Corporación Venezolana de Fomento	*Cuad. CVF*	Caracas
Cuadernos hispanoamericanos	*Cuad. hispanoamer.*	Madrid
Cuadernos para el Diálogo extraordinario	*Cuad. para el Diálogo extraord.*	Madrid
Culture et Développement	*Cult. et Dévelop.*	Louvain
Culture vivante	*Cult. viv.*	Québec
Current Anthropology	*Curr. Anthropol.*	Chicago, Ill.
Current History	*Curr. Hist.*	Philadelphia, Pa.
Current Sociology/Sociologie contemporaine	*Curr. Sociol./Sociol. contemp.*	Oxford
Cybernetica	*Cybernetica*	Namur
Dados	*Dados*	Rio de Janeiro
Daedalus. Journal of the American Academy of Arts and Sciences	*Daedalus*	Cambridge, Mass.
De Economia	*De Economia (Madrid)*	Madrid
Delta	*Delta (Marseille)*	Marseille
Democrazia e Diritto	*Democr. e Dir.*	Roma
Demográfia	*Demográfia*	Budapest
Demografía y Economía	*Demogr. y Econ.*	México
Demografie	*Demografie*	Praha
Demography	*Demography (Ann Arbor)*	Ann Arbor
Demography	*Demography (Washington)*	Washington
Demosta	*Demosta*	Praha
Den'gi i Kredit	*Den'gi i Kred.*	Moskva

Dento to Gendai	*Dento to Gendai*	Tokyo
Derecho de la Integración	*Der. Integr.*	Buenos-Aires
Desarrollo administrativo	*Desarr. adm.*	Quito
Desarrollo indoamericano	*Desarr. indoamer.*	Bogotá
Deutsche Aussenpolitik	*Dtsche Aussenpolit.*	Berlin
Deutsche Jugend	*Dtsche Jugend*	München
Deutsche Versicherungszeitschrift für Sozialversicherung und Privatversicherung	*Dtsche Versich.-Z.*	Köln
Deutsche Vierteljahrsschrift für Literaturwissenschaft und Geistesgeschichte	*Dtsche Vjschr. Lit.-wiss. u. Geistesgesch.*	Stuttgart
Deutsche Zeitschrift für Philosophie	*Dtsche Z. Philos.*	Berlin
Deutsches Institut für Wirtschaftsforschung. Vierteljahresheft	*Dtsch. Inst. Wirtsch.-Forsch. Vjh.*	Berlin
Deutschland Archiv	*Deutschland Archiv*	Köln
Developing Economies	*Develop. Econ.*	Tokyo
Development and Change	*Develop. and Change*	The Hague
Développement et Civilisations	*Dévelop. et Civilis.*	Paris
Difesa sociale	*Dif. soc.*	Roma
Diogène	*Diogène*	Paris
Direction	*Direction*	Paris
Diritto internazionale	*Dir. int.*	Milano
Document des Études nigériennes [IFAN]	*Doc. Ét. nigér.*	Niamey
Documentación administrativa	*Docum. adm.*	Madrid
Documentation française illustrée	*Docum. franç. illustr.*	Paris
Documentation sur l'Europe centrale	*Docum. Europe centr.*	Louvain
Documentos políticos	*Doc. polít.*	Bogotá
Documents. Revue mensuelle des Questions allemandes	*Documents (Cologne)*	Cologne
Documents CEPESS. Centre d'Études politiques, économiques et sociales	*Doc. CEPESS*	Bruxelles
Doklady Akademii Nauk Azerbajdžanskoj SSR	*Dokl. Akad. Nauk Azerb. SSR*	Baku
Doklady Instituta Geografii Sibiri i dal'nego Vostoka	*Dokl. Inst. Geogr. Sibiri dal'n. Vost.*	Irkutsk
Doklady i Soobščenija (Vsesojuznyj naučno-issledovatel'skij Institut Ėkonomiki sel'skogo Hozjajstva)	*Dokl. Soobšč. (Vsesojuz. nauč.-issled. Inst. Ėkon. sel'sk.-Hoz.)*	Moskva
Doklady Otdelenij i Komissii geografičeskogo obščestva SSSR	*Dokl. Otdel. Komis. geogr. obšč. SSSR*	[SSSR]
Dokumentation der Zeit	*Dokum. Zeit*	Berlin
Don	*Don*	[SSSR]
Donauraum	*Donauraum*	Salzburg
Dôshisha Hôgaku	*Dôshisha Hôgaku*	Kyoto
Doškol'noe Vospitanie	*Doškol'noe Vospitanie*	Moskva
Dossiers de l'Action social catholique	*Doss. Action soc. cath.*	Bruxelles
Dossiers documentaires	*Doss. docum.*	Alger
Droit bulgare	*Dr. bulg.*	Sofia
Droit et Liberté	*Dr. et Liberté*	Paris
Droit social	*Dr. soc.*	Paris
East Africa	*East Africa*	Nairobi
East Africa Journal	*East Afr. J.*	Nairobi
East African Economics Review	*East Afr. Econ. R.*	Nairobi
East African Journal of rural Development	*East Afr. J. rur. Develop.*	Nairobi
East Pakistan Labour Journal	*East Pakistan Lab. J.*	Dacca

Eastern Anthropologist	*East. Anthropol.*	Lucknow
Eastern European Economics	*East. Europ. Econ.*	New York
EAZ. Ethnographisch-archäologische Zeitschrift	*EAZ*	Berlin
Ebony	*Ebony*	Chicago, Ill.
École et Nation	*École et Nation*	Paris
Econometrica	*Econometrica*	Chicago, Ill.
Economia e Lavoro	*Econ. e Lav.*	Padova
Economia internazionale	*Econ. int. (Genova)*	Genova
Economia internazionale delle Fonti di Energia	*Econ. int. Fonti Energia*	Milano
Economia y Ciencias sociales	*Econ. Cienc. soc.*	Caracas
Economic Activity in Western Australia	*Econ. Activity*	Perth
Economic Age	*Econ. Age*	London
Economic and Business Bulletin	*Econ. Busin. B.*	Philadelphia
Economic and political Weekly	*Econ. polit. Wkly*	Bombay
Economic and social Review	*Econ. soc. R.*	Dublin
Economic Bulletin	*Econ. B. (Athens)*	Athens
Economic Bulletin	*Econ. B. (Oslo)*	Oslo
Economic Bulletin. National Bank of Egypt	*Econ. B. (Cairo)*	Cairo
Economic Bulletin for Latin America	*Econ. B. Latin Amer.*	New York
Economic Development and cultural Change	*Econ. Develop. cult. Change*	Chicago, Ill.
Economic Geography	*Econ. Geogr.*	Worcester, Mass.
Economic History Review	*Econ. Hist. R.*	Utrecht
Economic Journal	*Econ. J.*	London
Economic Record	*Econ. Rec.*	Melbourne
Economic Review	*Econ. R. (Helsinki)*	Helsinki
Económica	*Económica (La Plata)*	La Plata
Economica	*Economica (London)*	London
Economics of Planning	*Econ. Planning*	Oslo
Économie appliquée	*Écon. appl.*	Paris
Économie et Finances des Pays arabes	*Écon. Finances Pays arabes*	Beyrouth
Économie et Humanisme	*Écon. et Human.*	Caluire
Économie et Politique	*Écon. et Polit.*	Paris
Économie et Statistique	*Écon. et Statist.*	Paris
Économie rurale	*Écon. rur.*	Paris
Économies et Sociétés. Cahiers de l'ISÉA	*Écon. et Soc.*	Paris
Economisch en sociaal Tijdschrift	*Econ. soc. Tijds.*	Antwerpen
Economista paraguayo	*Econ. parag.*	Asunción
Ecumenical Review	*Ecumen. R.*	Geneva
Educación	*Educación*	Caracas
Educadores	*Educadores*	Buenos Aires
Éducation et Gestion	*Éduc. et Gestion*	Paris
Éducation et Promotion	*Éduc. et Promotion*	Paris
Éducation permanente	*Éduc. perm.*	Nancy
Educational Thechnology	*Educ. Technol.*	Englewood-Cliffs
Égypte contemporaine	*Égypte contemp.*	Le Caire
Ehe. Zentralblatt für Ehe- und Familienkunde	*Ehe*	Bern
Eichsfelder Heimathefte	*Eichsfelder Heimath.*	Heiligenstadt
Einheit	*Einheit*	Berlin
Ekistics	*Ekistics*	Athens
Ekonomi Journal	*Ekon. J.*	Kuala Lumpur
Ekonomia	*Ekonomia (Helsinki)*	Helsinki
Ekonomický Časopis	*Ekon. Čas.*	Bratislava
Ėkonomika i matematičeskie Metody	*Ėkon. matem. Metody*	Moskva

Ėkonomia sel'skogo Hozjajstva	*Ėkon. sel'sk. Hoz.*	Moskva
Ėkonomika Sovetskoj Ukrainy	*Ėkon. Sov. Ukr.*	Kiev
Ėkonomiko-matematičeskij Obzor	*Ėkon.-matem. Obzor*	[SSSR]
Ekonomisk Revy	*Ekon. R. (Stockholm)*	Stockholm
Ekonomiska Samfundets Tidskrift	*Ekon. Samfund. Ts.*	Helsinki
Ekonomista	*Ekonomista*	Warszawa
Ekonomska Revija	*Ekon. R. (Ljubljana)*	Ljubljana
Encounter	*Encounter*	London
Enfant en Milieu tropical	*Enfant Milieu trop.*	Dakar-Paris
Engineering Economist	*Engin. Economist*	Hoboken, N. J.
Enseignement programmé	*Enseign. programmé*	Paris
Épargne du Monde	*Épargne du Monde*	Amsterdam
Équipement - Logement - Transports	*Équipement*	Paris
Erde. Zeitschrift der Gesellschaft für Erdkunde zu Berlin	*Erde*	Berlin
Erdkunde	*Erdkunde*	Bonn
Esprit	*Esprit*	Paris
Est	*Est (Milano)*	Milano
Est-Orient	*Est-Orient*	Paris
Estadística	*Estadística (Washington)*	Washington
Estrategia	*Estrategia*	Buenos Aires
Estudios andinos	*Estud. andinos*	La Paz
Estudios cooperativos	*Estud. coop.*	Madrid
Estudios de Información	*Estud. Inform.*	Madrid
Estudios empresariales	*Estud. empresar.*	San Sebastian
Estudios internacionales	*Estud. int.*	Santiago de Chile
Estudios sindicales y cooperativos	*Estud. sindic. coop.*	Madrid
Estudos políticos e sociais	*Estud. polít. soc.*	Lisbõa
Estudos sociais e corporativos	*Estud. soc. corpor.*	Lisbõa
ETC. A Review of general Semantics	*ETC Rev. gen. Semantics*	San Francisco, Calif.
Ethnographia	*Ethnographia (Budapest)*	Budapest
Ethnographie	*Ethnographie*	Paris
Ethnohistory	*Ethnohistory*	Bloomington, Ind.
Ethnology	*Ethnology*	Pittsburgh, Pa.
Ethno-Musicology	*Ethno-Musicology*	Middletown, Conn.
Ethnos	*Ethnos (Stockholm)*	Stockholm
Étude mensuelle sur l'Économie et les Finances des Pays arabes	*Ét. mens. Écon. Finances Pays arabes*	Beyrouth
Études	*Études (Budapest)*	Budapest
Études	*Études (Paris)*	Paris
Études africaines du CRISP	*Ét. afr. CRISP*	Bruxelles
Études congolaises	*Ét. congol.*	Kinshasa
Études dahoméennes	*Ét. dahom.*	Porto Novo
Études d'Économie rurale	*Ét. Écon. rur.*	Rennes
Études d'Histoire africaine	*Ét. Hist. afr.*	Louvain
Études de la Région parisienne	*Ét. Région paris.*	Paris
Études économiques	*Ét. écon. (Mons)*	Mons
Études et Documents. Conseil d'État	*Ét. Doc. Conseil d'État*	Paris
Études et Documents (Éducation nationale)	*Ét. et Doc. (Éduc. nat.)*	Paris
Études et Documents du Centre de Recherches économiques et sociales	*Ét. Doc. Centre Rech. écon. soc.*	Paris
Études et Statistiques	*Ét. et Statist. (Rabat)*	Rabat
Études et Statistiques. Bulletin mensuel. Cameroun. Afrique équatoriale. Banque centrale	*Ét. Statist. Cameroun. Afr. équat. Banque centr.*	Paris
Études internationales	*Ét. int. (Québec)*	Québec
Études normandes	*Ét. normandes*	Le Havre
Études rurales	*Ét. rur.*	Paris

Études Tiers-Monde	*Ét. Tiers-Monde*	Paris
Eurafrica et Tribune du Tiers-Monde	*Eurafrica Trib. Tiers-Monde*	Bruxelles
Euromoney	*Euromoney*	London
Europa-Archiv	*Europa-Archiv*	Frankfurt-am-Main
Europarecht	*Europarecht*	Münich
Europe-France Outre-Mer	*Europe-France O.-Mer*	Paris
European economic Review	*Europ. econ. R.*	Bruxelles
Exploration in economic History	*Explor. econ. Hist.*	Richmond, Va.
Fabula. Zeitschrift für Erzählforschung	*Fabula*	Berlin
Faits et Tendances	*Faits et Tendances*	Belgrade
Family Coordinator	*Family Coordinator*	Eugene, Ore.
Fare Scuola	*Fare Scuola*	Firenze
Farm Economist	*Farm Economist*	Oxford
Federal Bar Journal	*Fed. Bar J.*	Washington, D.C.
Federal Probation	*Fed. Probation*	Washington, D.C.
Federal Reserve Bank of New York	*Fed. Reserve Bank New York*	New York
Federal Reserve Bank of St Louis	*Fed. Reserve Bank St Louis*	St Louis
Federal Reserve Bulletin	*Fed. Reserve B.*	Washington, D.C.
Finance and Trade Review	*Finance Trade R.*	Pretoria-Johannesburg
Finances et Développement	*Finances et Dévelop.*	Washington
Finanse	*Finanse*	Warszawa
Finansy SSSR	*Finansy SSSR*	Moskva
Finante şi Credit	*Finante şi Cred.*	Bucureşti
Finanzarchiv	*Finanzarchiv*	Tübingen
Finsk Tidskrift	*Finsk Ts.*	Åbo
Fiscalité du Marché commun	*Fisc. Marché commun*	Paris
Földrajzi Értesítö	*Földrajzi Értes.*	Budapest
Folia oeconomica cracoviensia	*Fol. oecon. cracov.*	Kraków
Folia orientalia	*Fol. orient.*	Kraków
Folk	*Folk*	København
Folk Lore	*Folk Lore (London)*	London
Folklore americano	*Folkl. amer. (Lima)*	Lima
Food Research Institute Studies	*Food Res. Inst. Stud.*	Stanford, Calif.
Foreign Affairs	*For. Aff.*	New York
Formazione e Lavoro	*Form. e Lav.*	Roma
Foro internacional	*Foro int.*	México
Forschungen und Berichte. Staatliche Museen zu Berlin	*Forsch. Ber. staatl. Mus. Berlin*	Berlin
Förvaltningrättslig Tidsskrift	*Förvalt. Ts.*	Stockholm
Frankfurter Hefte	*Frankfurt. H.*	Frankfurt-am-Main
Frühmittelalterliche Studien	*Frühmittelalterl. Stud.*	Berlin
Fuldaer Geschichtsblätter	*Fuldaer Gesch.-bl.*	Fulda
Futures	*Futures (Guildford)*	Guildford
Futuribili	*Futuribili*	Roma
Futurum. Zeitschrift für Zukunftsforschung	*Futurum*	Berlin
Gazette	*Gazette (Amsterdam)*	Amsterdam
Gegenwartskunde	*Gegenwartskunde*	Opladen
Gekkan Rôdô Mondai	*Gekkan Rôdô Mondai*	Tokyo
General Systems	*Gen. Systems*	New York
Genève-Afrique	*Genève-Afr.*	Genève
Geografičeskij Sbornik	*Geogr. Sb. (Moskva)*	Moskva
Geographical Journal	*Geogr. J.*	London
Geographical Review	*Geogr. R.*	New York
Geographische Rundschau	*Geogr. Rdsch.*	Braunschweig

German economic Review	*German econ. R.*	Tübingen
German foreign Policy	*German for. Policy*	Berlin, DR
Giornale degli Economisti e Annali di Economia	*G. Economisti*	Padova
Gledišta	*Gledišta*	Beograd
Gospodarka i Administracja terenowa	*Gosp. Adm. teren.*	Warszawa
Gospodarka planowa	*Gosp. planowa*	Warszawa
Government and Opposition	*Gvt and Opposition*	London
Graduate and Faculty Studies. Contributions to Education, Science, Culture	*Graduate Fac. Stud.*	Quezon City
Grands Aménagements régionaux	*Grands Aménag. région.*	Nîmes
Guinea espanola	*Guinea esp.*	Santa Isabel
Gunma Daigaku Kyôikugakubu Kiyô	*Gunma Daigaku Kyôikugakubu Kiyô*	[Nihon]
Gymnasium	*Gymnasium*	Heidelberg
Hamburg in Zahlen	*Hamburg in Zahlen*	Hamburg
Handai Hôgaku	*Handai Hôgaku*	Toyonaka
Handel wewnetrzny	*Handel wewn.*	Warszawa
Handel zagraniczy	*Handel zagran.*	Warszawa
Harvard Business Review	*Harvard Busin. R.*	Boston, Mass.
Harvard Law Review	*Harvard Law R.*	Cambridge, Mass.
Hawaii medical Journal	*Hawaii medic. J.*	Honolulu
Helderberg Review	*Helderberg R.*	Albany, N. Y.
Herold. Vierteljahrsschrift für Heraldik Genealogie und verwandte Wissenschaften	*Herold*	Berlin
Hikone Ronsô	*Hikone Ronsô*	Hikone
Hiroshime University	*Hiroshima Univ.*	Hiroshima
History and political Economy	*Hist. polit. Econ.*	Durham, N. C.
History and Politics Review	*Hist. Polit. R.*	Nedlands
History of Religions	*Hist. Relig.*	Chicago, Ill.
Hitotsubashi Journal of Economics	*Hitotsubashi J. Econ.*	Tokyo
Hitotsubashi Ronsô	*Hitotsubashi Ronsô*	Tokyo
Hochschulwesen	*Hochschulwesen*	Berlin
Hôgaku Kenkyû	*Hôgaku Kenkyû*	Tokyo
Hôgaku Ronsô	*Hôgaku Ronsô*	Kyoto
Hôgaku Shimpô	*Hôgaku Shimpô*	Tokyo
Hokkaidô Daigaku Bungakubu Kiyô	*Hokkaidô Daigaku Bungakubu Kiyô*	Sapporo
Hokudai Hôgaku Ronshû	*Hokudai Hôgaku Ronshû*	Sapporo
Hô to Seiji	*Hô to Seiji*	Nishinomiya
Homme (L'). Revue française d'Anthropologie	*Homme*	Paris
Homme et Société	*Homme et Soc.*	Paris
Hommes et Migrations	*Hommes et Migr.*	Paris
Hommes et Technique	*Hommes et Techn.*	Paris
Hommes, Terre et Eau	*Hommes, Terre, Eau*	Rabat
Homo	*Homo (Berlin)*	Berlin-Frankfurt-am-Main
Homo	*Homo (Toulouse)*	Toulouse
Hôsei Kenkyû	*Hôsei Kenkyû*	Fukuoka
Hôsôgaku Kenkyû	*Hôsôgaku Kenkyû*	Tokyo
Hudožnik	*Hudožnik*	Moskva
Human Organization	*Hum. Org.*	New York
Human Relations	*Hum. Relat.*	London
Humanisme et Entreprise	*Human. et Entr.*	Paris

Ibadan	*Ibadan*	Ibadan
ICA information	*ICA Inform.*	Jerusalem
Ici l'Afrique	*Ici l'Afrique*	
Idéologie	*Idéologie*	Rome
IDOC international	*IDOC int.*	Paris
IFO-Studien	*IFO-Stud.*	Münich
Impact. Science et Société	*Impact*	Paris
Impuestos de la Hacienda publica	*Impuestos Hac. publ.*	Madrid
Indian economic Journal	*Ind. econ. J.*	Bombay
Indian economic Review	*Ind. econ. R.*	New Delhi
Indian Journal of Economics	*Ind. J. Econ.*	Allahabad
Indian Journal of industrial Relations	*Ind. J. industr. Relat.*	New Delhi
Indian Journal of Labour Economics	*Ind. J. Lab. Econ.*	Lucknow
Indian Journal of political Science	*Ind. J. polit. Sci.*	Lucknow
Indian Journal of public Administration	*Ind. J. publ. Adm.*	New Delhi
Indian Journal of social Research	*Ind. J. soc. Res.*	Baraut
Indian Journal of social Work	*Ind. J. soc. Wk*	Bombay
Indian Labour Journal	*Ind. Lab. J.*	Simla
Indian political Science Review	*Ind. polit. Sci. R.*	Delhi
Indian sociological Bulletin	*Ind. sociol. B.*	New Delhi
Indiana Business Review	*Indiana Busin. R.*	Bloomington, Ind.
Indonesia	*Indonesia (Djakarta)*	Djakarta
Indonesia	*Indonesia (Ithaca)*	Ithaca, N. Y.
Industria	*Industria*	Milano
Industria e Produtividade	*Industr. e Produtiv.*	Rio de Janeiro
Industrial and Labor Relations Review	*Industr. Lab. Relat. R.*	Ithaca, N. Y.
Industrial Gerontology	*Industr. Gerontol.*	New York
Industrial Relations	*Industr. Relat.*	Berkeley, Calif.
Industrial Review	*Industr. R.*	Port Moresby
Industrie	*Industrie*	Bruxelles
Industries et Travaux d'Outre-Mer	*Industr. Trav. O.-Mer*	Paris
Industry of free China	*Industry free China*	Taipei
Información social	*Inform. soc. (Lisbõa)*	Lisbõa
Information géographique	*Inform. géogr.*	Paris
Informations sociales	*Inform. soc. (Paris)*	Paris
Inostrannaja Literatura	*Inostr. Lit.*	Moskva
Institut d'Aménagement et d'Urbanisme de la Région parisienne. Cahiers	*Inst. Aménag. Urban. Région paris.*	Paris
Institut des Belles Lettres Arabes	*IBLA*	Tunis
Inter-American economic Affairs	*Inter-Amer. econ. Aff.*	Washington, D.C.
Internasjonal Politikk	*Int. Polit. (Bergen)*	Bergen
International Affairs	*Int. Aff. (London)*	London
International and comparative Law Quarterly	*Int. comp. Law Quart.*	London
International Archives of Ethnography/ Internationales Archiv für Ethnographie/Archives internationales d'Ethnographie	*Int. Archiv. Ethnogr./Int. Archiv Ethnogr./Archiv. int. Ethnogr.*	Amsterdam
International Banking Summer School	*Int. Banking Summer School*	Dublin
International Conciliation	*Int. Conciliation*	New York
International Development	*Int. Develop.*	New York
International Development Review	*Int. Develop. R.*	Washington, D.C.
International economic Review	*Int. econ. R.*	Osaka
International Journal	*Int. J.*	Toronto
International Journal of comparative Sociology	*Int. J. comp. Sociol.*	Leiden
International Journal of Group Psychotherapy	*Int. J. Group Psychother.*	New York

International Journal of Middle East Studies	*Int. J. Mid. East Stud.*	London
International Journal of social Psychiatry	*Int. J. soc. Psychiatry*	London
International Labour Review	*Int. Lab. R.*	Geneva
International Marketing	*Int. Mkting*	Paris
International Migration/Migrations internationales/Migraciones internacionales	*Int. Migration/Migrations int./Migraciones int.*	La Haye-Genève
International Migration Review	*Int. Migration R.*	New York
International Organization	*Int. Org.*	Boston, Mass.
International Problems	*Int. Probl. (Tel-Aviv)*	Tel-Aviv
International Relations	*Int. Relat. (London)*	London
International Review of Community Development	*Int. R. Community Develop.*	Rome
International Review of History and political Science	*Int. R. Hist. polit. Sci.*	Meerut
International Review of Missions	*Int. R. Missions (London)*	London
International Review of social History	*Int. R. soc. Hist.*	Assen
International Review Service	*Int. R. Serv.*	New York
International social Work	*Int. soc. Wk*	Bombay
International Studies	*Int. Stud.*	New Delhi
International Studies Quarterly	*Int. Stud. Quart.*	Detroit, Mich.
Internationale Spectator	*Int. Spectator*	's-Gravenhage
Internationales Afrika Forum	*Int. Afrika Forum*	München
Internationales Asien Forum	*Int. Asien Forum*	München
Interstages	*Interstages*	Bruxelles
Investigación económica	*Invest. econ.*	Mexico
Inwestycje i Budownictwo	*Invest. i Budown.*	Warszawa
IPA Review	*IPA Rev.*	Victoria
Ipek. Jahrbuch für prähistorische und ethnographische Kunst	*Ipek*	Berlin
Iskusstvo	*Iskusstvo*	Moskva
Islam	*Islam*	Berlin
Israel Law Review	*Israel Law R.*	Jerusalem
Istorija SSSR	*Ist. SSSR*	Moskva
Istoriko-filologičeskij Žurnal	*Ist.-filol. Ž.*	[SSSR]
Izvestija Akademii Nauk Kazahskoj SSR. Serija obščestvennyh Nauk	*Izv. Akad. Nauk Kazah. SSR Ser. obšč. Nauk*	Alma-Ata
Izvestija Akademii Nauk Latvijskoj SSR	*Izv. Akad. Nauk Latv. SSR*	Riga
Izvestija Akademii Nauk Moldavskoj SSR. Serija obščestvennyh Nauk	*Izv. Akad. Nauk Moldav. SSR Ser. obšč. Nauk*	Kišinev
Izvestija Akademii Nauk SSSR. Serija ěkonomičeskaja	*Izv. Akad. Nauk SSSR Ser. ěkon.*	Moskva
Izvestija Akademii Nauk SSSR. Serija geografii	*Izv. Akad. Nauk SSSR Ser. geogr.*	Moskva
Izvestija Akademii Nauk SSSR. Serija Literatury i Jazyka	*Izv. Akad. Nauk SSSR Ser. Lit. Jaz.*	Moskva
Izvestija Akademii Nauk SSSR. Serija obščestvennyh Nauk	*Izv. Akad. Nauk SSSR Ser. obšč. Nauk*	Moskva
Izvestija Akademii Nauk Tadžikiskogo SSR. Otdelenie obščestvennyh Nauk	*Izv. Akad. Nauk Tadž. SSR Otdel. obšč. Nauk*	Dušanbe
Izvestija Akademii Nauk Turkmenskoj SSR. Serija obščestvennyh Nauk	*Izv. Akad. Nauk Turkmen. SSR Ser. obšč. Nauk*	Ašhabad
Izvestija Akademii v Nauk Kirgizskoj SSR	*Izv. Akad. Nauk Kirg. SSR*	Frunze
Izvestija. Čečeno-Ingušskij naučno-issledovatel'skij Institut Istorii, Jazyka i Literatury	*Izv. Čeč.-Inguš. nauč.-issled. Inst. Ist. Jaz. Lit.*	Groznyj

Izvestiga Severo-Osetinskogo naučno-issledovatel'skogo Instituta	*Izv. Sev.-Oset. nauč.-issled. Inst.*	Ordžonikidze
Izvestija Sibirskogo Otdelenija Akademii Nauk SSSR	*Izv. Sib. Otdel. Akad. Nauk*	Novosibirsk
Izvestija Sibirskogo Otdelenija Akademii Nauk SSSR. Serija obščestvennyh Nauk	*Izv. Sib. Otdel. Akad. Nauk SSSR Ser. obšč. Nauk*	Novosibirsk
Izvestija Tomskogo politehničeskij Institut	*Izv. Tomsk. politehn. Inst.*	Tomsk
Izvestija Uzbekistanskogo geografičeskogo Obščestva	*Izv. Uzbek. geogr. Obšč.*	Taškent
Izvestija Voronežskogo pedagogičeskogo Instituta	*Izv. Voronež. pedag. Inst.*	Voronež
Izvestija Vsesojuznogo geografičeskogo Obščestva	*Izv. Vsesojuz. geogr. Obšč.*	Leningrad-Moskva
Izvestija vysših učebnyh Zavedenij. Ministerstva vysšego obrazovanija SSSR. Pravovedenija	*Izv. vysš. učeb. Zaved. Pravoved.*	Leningrad
Jahrbuch der Wirtschaft Osteuropas	*Jb. Wirtsch. Osteuropas*	München
Jahrbuch der Wittheit zu Bremen	*Jb. Wittheit Bremen*	Bremen
Jahrbuch des Gesellschafts für die Geschichte und Bibliographie des Brauwesens e.V.	*Jb. Ges. Gesch. Bibl. Brauwesens*	Berlin
Jahrbuch des öffentlichen Rechts der Gegenwart	*Jb. öff. Rechts Gegenwart*	Tübingen
Jahrbuch des Südasien-Instituts der Universität Heidelberg	*Jb. Südasien-Inst. Univ. Heidelberg*	Wiesbaden
Jahrbuch des Zentralinstituts für Wirtschaftswissenschaften	*Jb. zentr.-Inst. Wirtsch. Wiss.*	Berlin
Jahrbuch für Amerikastudien	*Jb. Amerikastud.*	Heidelberg
Jahrbuch für christliche Sozialwissenschaften	*Jb. christ. soz.-Wiss.*	Münster
Jahrbuch für internationales Recht	*Jb. int. Recht*	Göttingen
Jahrbuch für kritische Aufklärung	*Jb. krit. Aufklärung*	Reinbek-bei-Hamburg
Jahrbuch für Liturgik und Hymnologie	*Jb. Liturgik Hymnol.*	Kassel
Jahrbuch für Ostrecht	*Jb. Ostrecht*	Münich
Jahrbuch für Sozialwissenschaft	*Jb. soz.-Wiss.*	Göttingen
Jahrbuch für Volksliedforschung	*Jb. Volksliedforsch.*	Berlin
Jahrbücher für Nationalökonomie und Statistik	*Jb-r nat.-Ökon. u. Statist.*	Stuttgart
Japan Institute of international Affairs annual Review	*Japan Inst. int. Aff. ann. R.*	Tokyo
Japan Quarterly	*Japan Quart.*	Tokyo
Jewish Journal of Sociology	*Jew. J. Sociol.*	London
Jewish social Studies	*Jew. soc. Stud.*	New York
Jimbungaku	*Jimbungaku*	[Nihon]
Jimbun Gakuhô	*Jimbun Gakuhô (Tokyo)*	Tokyo
Jimbun-ronshu	*Jimbun-ronshu*	[Nihon]
Jogtudományi Közlöny	*Jogtud. Közl.*	Budapest
Jordbruksekonomiska Meddelanden	*Jord.-ekon. Medd.*	Stockholm
Journal asiatique	*J. asiat.*	Paris
Journal de la Planification et du Développement	*J. Planif. Dévelop.*	New York
Journal de la Société de Statistique de Paris	*J. Soc. Statist. Paris*	Paris
Journal de la Société des Africanistes	*J. Soc. African.*	Paris
Journal de la Société des Américanistes	*J. Soc. Américan.*	Paris

Journal de la Société des Océanistes	*J. Soc. Océan.*	Paris
Journal des Caisses d'Épargne	*J. Caisses d'Épargne*	Paris
Journal du Droit international	*J. Dr. int.*	Paris
Journal of Administration Overseas	*J. Adm. Overseas*	London
Journal of African History	*J. Afr. Hist.*	London
Journal of African Languages	*J. Afr. Lang.*	East Lansing, Mich.
		London
Journal of agricultural Economics	*J. agric. Econ.*	Manchester
Journal of American Folklore	*J. Amer. Folkl.*	Richmond, Virg.
Journal of applied and behavioral Science	*J. appl. behav. Sci.*	New York
Journal of Asian and African Studies	*J. Asian Afr. Stud.*	Toronto
Journal of Asian Studies	*J. Asian Stud.*	Ann Arbor, Mich.
Journal of biosocial Science	*J. biosoc. Sci.*	Oxford
Journal of Business	*J. Busin.*	Chicago, Ill.
Journal of Business Finance	*J. Busin. Finance*	London
Journal of Common Market Studies	*J. Common Market Stud.*	Oxford
Journal of Commonwealth political Studies	*J. Commonwealth polit. Stud.*	Leicester
Journal of Communication	*J. Communication*	Lawrence, Kan.
Journal of comparative Administration	*J. comp. Adm.*	Beverly Hills, Calif.
Journal of Conflict Resolution	*J. Conflict Resol.*	Ann Arbor, Mich.
Journal of constitutional and parliamentary Studies	*J. const. parl. Stud.*	New Delhi
Journal of contemporary History	*J. contemp. Hist.*	London
Journal of developing Areas	*J. develop. Areas*	Macomb, Ill.
Journal of Development Studies	*J. Develop. Stud.*	London
Journal of economic History	*J. econ. Hist.*	New York
Journal of economic Issues	*J. econ. Issues*	Austin, Texas
Journal of economic Literature	*J. econ. Liter.*	Menasha, Wis.
Journal of economic Theory	*J. econ. Theory*	London-New York
Journal of educational Psychology	*J. educ. Psychol.*	Washington
Journal of educational Research	*J. educ. Res.*	Madison, Wis.
Journal of Ethiopian Studies	*J. Ethiop. Stud.*	Addis-Abeba
Journal of experimental Child Psychology	*J. exper. Child Psychol.*	New York
Journal of experimental Research in Personality	*J. exper. Res. Personality*	New York
Journal of experimental social Psychology	*J. exper. soc. Psychol.*	New York-London
Journal of Finance	*J. Finance*	Chicago, Ill.
Journal of financial and quantitative Analysis	*J. financ. quant. Anal.*	Seattle, Wash.
Journal of genetic Psychology	*J. genet. Psychol.*	Provincetown, Mass.
Journal of Health and social Behavior	*J. Health soc. Behav.*	New York
Journal of human Relations	*J. hum. Relat.*	Wilberforce, Ohio
Journal of human Resources	*J. hum. Resources*	Madison, Wis.
Journal of industrial Economics	*J. industr. Econ.*	London
Journal of industrial Relations	*J. industr. Relat.*	Sydney
Journal of inter-American Studies	*J. inter-Amer. Stud.*	Coral Gables, Fla.
Journal of international Affairs	*J. int. Aff.*	New York
Journal of Latin American Studies	*J. Latin-Amer. Stud.*	Cambridge
Journal of Law and Economics	*J. Law Econ.*	Chicago, Ill.
Journal of Management Studies	*J. Manag. Stud.*	Oxford
Journal of Marketing	*J. Mkting*	Chicago, Ill.
Journal of Marketing Research	*J. Mkting Res.*	Chicago, Ill.
Journal of Marriage and the Family	*J. Marriage Family*	Minneapolis, Minn.
Journal of modern African Studies	*J. mod. Afr. Stud.*	Cambridge-Dar es-Salam

Journal of Money, Credit, and Banking	*J. Money Cred. Bank.*	Colombus, Ohio
Journal of Near Eastern Studies	*J. Near East Stud.*	Chicago, Ill.
Journal of Negro History	*J. Negro Hist.*	Washington
Journal of Pacific History	*J. Pacific Hist.*	Oxford, Mass.
Journal of Peace Research	*J. Peace Res.*	Oslo
Journal of Personality and social Psychology	*J. Person. soc. Psychol.*	Washington, D.C.
Journal of Philippine Statistics	*J. Philippine Statist.*	Manila
Journal of political Economy	*J. polit. Econ.*	Chicago, Ill.
Journal of Politics	*J. Polit.*	Gainesville, Fla.
Journal of Population Studies	*J. Popul. Stud.*	Seoul
Journal of regional Science	*J. region. Sci.*	Philadelphia, Pa.
Journal of Religion in Africa/Religion en Afrique	*J. Relig. Africa/Relig. Afrique*	Leiden
Journal of Risk and Insurance	*J. Risk Insurance*	Bloomington, Ill.
Journal of School Psychology	*J. School Psychol.*	New Brunswick, N.J.
Journal of social Issues	*J. soc. Issues*	New York
Journal of social Psychology	*J. soc. Psychol.*	Provincetown, Mass.
Journal of Southeast Asian History	*J. Southeast Asian Hist.*	Singapour
Journal of Transport Economics and Policy	*J. Transport Econ. Pol.*	London
Journal of World Trade Law	*J. Wld Trade Law*	London
Journal of the American oriental Society	*J. Amer. orient. Soc.*	New Haven
Journal of the American statistical Association	*J. Amer. statist. Assoc.*	Washington
Journal of the economic and social History of the Orient	*J. econ. soc. Hist. Orient*	Leiden
Journal of the Folklore Institute	*J. Folkl. Inst.*	Bloomington
Journal of the historical Society of Nigeria	*J. hist. Soc. Nigeria*	Ibadan
Journal of the History of Ideas	*J. Hist. Ideas*	New York-Lancaster, Pa.
Journal of the Maharaja Sayajirao University of Baroda	*J. Maharaja Sayajirao Univ. Baroda*	Baroda
Journal of the Royal Anthropological Institute of Great Britain and Ireland	*J. roy. anthropol. Inst.*	London
Journal of the Royal Central Asian Society	*J. roy. Centr. Asian Soc.*	London
Journal of the Royal Statistical Society	*J. roy. statist. Soc.*	London
Journal of the scientific Study of Religion	*J. scient. Study Relig.*	
Journal officiel. Avis et Rapports du Conseil économique et social	*J. off. Cons. écon. soc.*	Paris
Journalism Quarterly	*J-ism Quart.*	Minneapolis, Minn.
Judaism	*Judaism*	New York
Justice dans le Monde	*Justice dans le Monde*	Louvain
Justicia	*Justicia*	México
Kanazaw Daigaku Hôbun-gakubu Ronshû Hôkei-hen	*Kanazawa Daigaku Hôbun-gakubu*	Kanazawa
Kansai Daigaku Bungaku Ronshû	*Kansai Daigaku Bungaku Ronshû*	Osaka
Kansantaloudellinen Aikakauskirja	*Kansantal. Aikakausk.*	Helsinki
Keizai Kagaku	*Keizai Kagaku*	Nagoya
Keizai to Keizaigaku	*Keizai to Keizaigaku*	Tokyo
Khadi gramodyog	*Khadi gramodyog*	Bombay
Kobe economic and Business Review	*Kobe econ. Busin. R.*	Kobe
Kobe University economic Review	*Kobe Univ. econ. R.*	Kobe
Kôhô Kenkyû	*Kôhô Kenkyû*	Tokyo

XXXIII

Kokusai Kirisutokyô Daigaku Gakuhô	*Kokusai Kirisutokyô Daigaku Gakuhô*	Tokyo
Kölner Zeitschrift für Soziologie und Sozialpsychologie	*Kölner Z. Soziol. u. soz.-Psychol.*	Köln-Opladen
Kommunist	*Kommunist (Moskva)*	Moskva
Kommunist Éstonii	*Kommunist Éston.*	Tallin
Kommunist Sovetskoj Latvii	*Kommunist Sov. Latvii*	Riga
Konjunkturpolitik	*Konjunkt.-Polit.*	Berlin
Koreana Quarterly	*Koreana Quart.*	Seoul
Közgazdasági Szemle	*Közgazd. Szle*	Budapest
Kraevedčeskie Zapiski (Kamčatkij Oblast kraevedčeskih Muzej)	*Kraeved. Zap. (Kamčat. Obl. kraeved. Muz.)*	[SSSR]
Kraevedčeski Zapiski (Oblastnyj kraevedčeskij Muzej, Magadan)	*Kraeved. Zap. (Obl. kraeved. Muz. Magadan)*	Magadan
Kroeber anthropological Society Papers	*Kroeber anthropol. Soc. Pap.*	Berkeley
Kultura	*Kultura*	Paryż
Kultura i Społecznestwo. Polska Akademia Nauk. Komitet BadaQ nad Kulturą wspolczesną	*Kult. i Społecz.*	Warszawa
Kunde. Mitteilungen des Niedersächsischen Landesvereins für Urgeschichte	*Kunde*	Hannover
Kurtrierisches Jahrbuch	*Kurtrier. Jb.*	Trier
Kyklos	*Kyklos*	Bern
Kyoto University economic Review	*Kyoto Univ. econ. R.*	Kyoto
Kyoto University of African Studies	*Kyoto Univ. Afr. Stud.*	Kyoto
Kyushu Daigaku Kyoiku-gakuby Kiyo	*Kyushu Daigaku Kyoiku-gakubu Kiyo*	[Nihon]
Labor History	*Labor Hist.*	New York
Labour Education	*Labour Educ.*	Geneva
Lakimies	*Lakimies*	Helsinki
Land Economics	*Land Econ.*	Madison, Wis.
Language. Journal of the Linguistics Society of Baltimore	*Language (Baltimore)*	Baltimore, Md.
Languages	*Languages*	Paris
Latin American Research Review	*Latin Amer. Res. R.*	Austin, Tex.
Law and contemporary Problems	*Law contemp. Probl.*	Durham, N. C.
Law and Society Review	*Law Soc. R.*	New York
Lecciones y Ensayos. Facultad de Derecho y Ciencias sociales	*Lecciones y Ensayos*	Buenos Aires
Liberal	*Liberal*	Bonn
Liberian Studies Journal	*Liberian Stud. J.*	Greencastle
Liiketaloudellinen Aikakauskirja	*Liiketal. Aikakausk.*	Helsinki
Lingua	*Lingua*	Amsterdam
Linguistics	*Linguistics*	Paris-The Hague
Linguistique (La)	*Linguistique*	Paris
Lloyds Bank Review	*Lloyds Bank R.*	London
Loughborough Journal of social Studies	*Loughborough J. soc. Stud.*	Loughborough
Lud	*Lud*	Lublin-Kraków
Maharastra cooperative Quarterly	*Maharastra coop. Quart.*	Bombay
Malayan economic Review	*Malayan econ. R.*	Singapore
Man	*Man*	London
Management Accounting	*Manag. Accting*	New York
Management international Review	*Manag. int. R.*	Wiesbaden
Management Science	*Manag. Sci.*	Baltimore, Md.
Manchester School of economic and social Studies	*Manchester Sch. econ. soc. Stud.*	Manchester

Mankind	*Mankind*	Sydney
Manpower and Unemployment Research in Africa, a Newsletter	*Manpower Unempl. Res. Africa*	Montreal
Manpower Journal	*Manpower J.*	New Delhi
Marxism today	*Marxism today*	London
Masses ouvrières	*Masses ouvr.*	Paris
Material'notehničeskie Snabženija	*Material'notehn. Snabženija*	[SSSR]
Mawazo	*Mawazo*	Kampala
Médecine d'Afrique noire	*Méd. Afr. noire*	Dakar
Méditerranea	*Méditerranea*	Paris
Méditerranée	*Méditerranée*	Aix-en-Provence
Mémoires de la Société royale du Canada	*Mém. Soc. roy. Canada*	Ottawa
Mens en Maatschappij	*Mens en Mij*	Amsterdam
Mens en Onderneming	*Mens en Onderneming*	Leiden-Haarlem
Mercanzia	*Mercanzia*	Bologna
Mercurio (Il)	*Mercurio*	Milano
Merkur	*Merkur*	Stuttgart
Metra	*Metra*	Paris
Metroeconomica	*Metroeconomica*	Trieste
Meždunarodnaja Žizn'	*Meždun. Žizn'*	Moskva
Mezinárodní Vztahy	*Mezin. Vztahy*	Praha
Miasto	*Miasto*	Warszawa
Middle East Forum	*Mid. East Forum*	Beirut
Middle East Journal	*Mid. East J.*	Washington, D.C.
Middle Easter Studies	*Mid. East. Stud.*	London
Midway	*Midway*	Chicago, Ill.
Midwest Journal of political Science	*Midwest J. polit. Sci.*	Detroit, Mich.
Migrations dans le Monde	*Migr. dans le Monde*	Genève
Milbank Memorial Fund Quarterly	*Milbank Memor. Fund Quart.*	New York
Minzokugaku Kenkyu	*Minzokugaku Kenkyu*	Tokyo
Mirovaja Ėkonomika i meždunarodnye Otnošenija	*Mir. Ėkon. meždun. Otnoš.*	Moskva
Missions spéciales d'Afrique des Pères Blancs	*Miss. spéc. Afr. Pères Blancs*	Québec
Mitteilungen des Deutschen archäologischen Instituts Abteilung Kairo	*Mitt. dtschen archäol. Inst. Kairo*	Wiesbaden
Mitteilungen des Direktoriums des Österreichischen Nationalbank	*Mitt. Direktor. österr. nat.-Bank*	Wien
Mitteilungen des Instituts für Orientforschung	*Mitt. Inst. Orientforsch.*	Berlin
Mitteilungen für die Archivpflege in Bayern	*Mitt. Archivpfl. Bayern*	München
Mizan	*Mizan*	Oxford
Modern Age	*Mod. Age*	Chicago, Ill.
Modern Asian Studies	*Mod. Asian Stud.*	London
Modern Law Review	*Mod. Law R.*	London
Modern Review	*Mod. R. (Calcutta)*	Calcutta
Moderne Welt	*Mod. Welt*	Köln
Mois en Afrique	*Mois Afr.*	Paris-Dakar
Molodaja Gvardija	*Molod. Gvardija*	Moskva
Monatsberichte der deutschen Bundesbank	*Monatsber. dtschen Bundesbank*	Frankfurt-am-Main
Monde non chrétien	*Monde non chr.*	Paris
Mondo aperto	*Mondo aperto*	Roma
Moneda y Crédito	*Moneda y Créd.*	Madrid
Moneta e Credito	*Moneta e Cred.*	Roma

Monthly Labor Review	*Mthly Lab. R.*	Washington, D.C.
Monthly Review	*Mthly R.*	New York
Moorgate and Wall Street	*Moorgate and Wall Street*	London
Mulino	*Mulino*	Bologna
Musashi Daigaku Ronshû	*Musashi Daigaku Ronshû*	Tokyo
Museum	*Museum*	Paris
Muslim World	*Muslim Wld*	Hartford, Conn.
Muzykal'naja Žizn'	*Muzyk. Žizn'*	Moskva
Na Severe dal'nem	*Na Severe dal'nem*	[SSSR]
Nada	*Nada (Salisbury)*	London
Narodna Tvorčist' ta Êtnografija	*Nar. Tvorčist' ta Êtnogr.*	Kiiv
Narodnoe Hozjajstvo Gruzii	*Nar. Hoz. Gruzii*	T'bilisi
Narodnoe Obrazovanie	*Nar. Obrazov.*	Moskva
Narody Azii i Afriki	*Narody Azii Afr.*	Moskva
National civic Review	*Nat. civic R.*	New York
National Institute economic Review	*Nat. Inst. econ. R.*	London
National Taiwan University Journal of Sociology	*Nat. Taiwan Univ. J. Sociol.*	Taipeh
National Tax Journal	*Nat. Tax J.*	Lancaster, Pa.
National Westminster Bank Quarterly Review	*Nat. Westminster B. Quart. R.*	London
Natural Resources Journal	*Natur. Resources J.*	Albuquerque, N.M.
Naučnaja Organizacija Truda (Respublikanskij Institut naučno-tehničeskoj Informacii i Propagandy	*Nauč. Org. Truda (Resp. Inst. nauč.-tehn. Inform. i Propagandy gos. plan. Komissi Soveta Ministrov Lit. SSSR)*	Moskva
Naučnye Doklady vysšej Školy. Êkonomičeskie Nauki	*Nauč. Dokl. vysš. Školy êkon. Nauki*	Moskva
Naučnye Doklady vysšek Školy. Filologičeskie Nauki	*Nauč. Dokl. vysš. Školy filol. Nauki*	Moskva
Naučnye Doklady vysšej Školy. Filosofskie Nauki	*Nauč. Dokl. vysš. Školy filos. Nauki*	Moskva
Naučnye Trudy (Taškenskij Universitet)	*Nauč. Trudy (Taškent. Univ.)*	Taškent
Naučnye Zapiski (Leningradskij finančeskij-êkonomičeskij Institut)	*Nauč. Zap. (Leningr. finan.-êkon. Inst.)*	Leningrad
Naučnye Zapiski (Vsesojuznaja Akademija vnešnej Torgovli)	*Nauč. Zap. (Vsesojuz. Akad. vnešn. Torg.)*	Moskva
Nauka i Religija	*Nauka i Relig.*	Moskva
Nauka i Tehnika	*Nauka i Tehn.*	Moskva
Naval War College Review	*Naval War College R.*	Newport, R.J.
Nef	*Nef*	Paris
Nenpô Shakai Shinrigaku	*Nenpô Shakai Shinrigaku*	Tokyo
New Guinea Research Bulletin	*New Guinea Res. B.*	
New Hungarian Quarterly	*New Hungar. Quart.*	Budapest
New Left Review	*New Left R.*	London
New Middle East	*New Mid. East.*	London
New Outlook	*New Outlook*	Tel-Aviv
New South	*New South*	Atlanta, Ga.
New World Review	*New Wld R.*	New York
New York University Law Review	*New York Univ. Law R.*	New York
New Zealand Journal of public Administration	*New Zealand J. publ. Adm.*	Wellington
Nigeria Magazine	*Nigeria Mag.*	Lagos-London
Nigerian Journal of Economics and social Studies	*Niger. J. Econ. soc. Stud.*	Ibadan
Nihon Gakushin Kiyô	*Nihon Gakushin Kiyô*	Tokyo

Nord e Sud	*Nord e Sud*	Milano-Napoli
Nordelbingen	*Nordelbingen*	Heide in Hostein
Nordfriesisches Jahrbuch	*Nordfries. Jb.*	Bredstedt
Nordisk administrativt Tidsskrift	*Nord. adm. Tss.*	København
Norois	*Norois*	Poitiers
Notes africaines	*Notes afr.*	Dakar
Notes d'Information et Statistiques. Banque centrale des États de l'Afrique de l'Ouest	*Notes Inform. Statist. Banque centr. Afr. Ouest*	Paris
Notes et Études documentaires	*Notes Ét. docum.*	Paris
Notes on current Politics	*Notes curr. Polit.*	London
Nouvelle Critique	*Nouv. Crit.*	Paris
Nouvelle Revue internationale	*Nouv. R. int.*	Paris
Nouvelles Tendances dans l'Économie tchécoslovaque	*Nouv. Tendances Écon. tchécosl.*	Prague
Novaja i novejšaja Istorija	*Nov. novejš. Ist.*	Moskva
Novyj Mir	*Novyj Mir*	Moskva
Nowe Drogi	*Nowe Drogi*	Warszawa
Nuestro Tiempo	*Nuestro Tiempo*	Madrid
Nuovo Mezzogiorno	*Nuovo Mezzogiorno*	Roma
Objets et Mondes	*Objets et Mondes*	Paris
Oceania	*Oceania*	Sydney
Oceanic Linguistics	*Oceanic Linguist.*	Honolulu
Offene Welt	*Off. Welt*	Frankfurt-am-Main
Öffentliche Verwaltung	*Öff. Verw.*	Stuttgart
Økonomi og Politik	*Økon. og Polit.*	København
Operations Research	*Operations Res.*	Baltimore, Md.
Optima	*Optima*	Johannesburg
Orbis	*Orbis*	Philadelphia, Pa.
Oriens extremus	*Oriens extr.*	Wiesbaden
Orient	*Orient*	Paris
Oriental Economics	*Orient. Econ.*	Tokyo
Orientamenti sociali	*Orientam. soc.*	Roma
Osaka economic Papers	*Osaka econ. Pap.*	Osaka
Ostbairische Grenzmarken	*Ostbair. Grenzmarken*	Passau
Österreichische Osthefte	*Österr. Osth.*	Wien
Österreichisches Institut für Wirtschaftsforschung. Monatsberichte	*Österr. Inst. Wirtsch.-Forsch. Monatsber.*	Wien
Österreichisches Zeitschrift für Aussenpolitik	*Österr. Z. Aussenpolit.*	Wien
Osteuropa	*Osteuropa*	Stuttgart
Osteuropa Recht	*Osteuropa Recht*	Stuttgart
Osteuropa Wirtschaft	*Osteuropa Wirtsch.*	Stuttgart
Ours	*Ours*	Paris
Overseas Business Reports	*Overseas Busin. Rep.*	Washington
Oxford economic Papers	*Oxford econ. Pap.*	Oxford
Pacific Affairs	*Pacific Aff.*	New York
Pacific sociological Review	*Pacific sociol. R.*	Eugene, Ore.
Pacific Viewpoint	*Pacific Viewpoint*	Wellington
Pakistan Development Review	*Pakistan Develop. R.*	Karachi
Pakistan Horizon	*Pakistan Horizon*	Karachi
Pakistan Management Review	*Pakistan Manag. R.*	Karachi
Pamjatniki Turkmenistana	*Pamjatniki Turkmen.*	Ašhabad
Panorama de la Economía	*Panorama Econ.*	Buenos Aires
Państwo i Prawo	*Pań. i Prawo*	Warszawa
Parliamentarian	*Parliamentarian*	London
Parliamentary Affairs	*Parl. Aff.*	London

Partijnaja Žizn'	*Partijn. Žizn' (Moskva)*	Moskva
Partisans	*Partisans*	Paris
Paysans	*Paysans*	Paris
Penant. Revue de Droit des Pays d'Afrique	*Penant*	Paris
Pensamiento político	*Pensamiento polít.*	Mexico
Pensée (La). Revue du Rationalisme moderne	*Pensée*	Paris
PEP (Political and Economic Planning)	*PEP*	London
PEP Broadsheet	*PEP Broadsheet*	London
Personnel	*Personnel*	New York
Personnel Administration	*Personnel Adm.*	Washington
Personnel Journal	*Personnel J.*	Baltimore, Md.
Personnel Practice Bulletin	*Personnel Practice B.*	Melbourne
Personnel Psychology	*Personnel Psychol.*	Baltimore, Md.
Perspective	*Perspective*	Paris
Perspectives de l'Éducation	*Perspect. Éduc.*	Paris
Perspectives économiques de l'OCDE	*Perspect. écon. OCDE*	Paris
Perspectives polonaises	*Perspect. polon.*	Varsovie
Philippine economic Journal	*Philippine econ. J.*	Manila
Philippine Economy Bulletin	*Philippine econ. B.*	Manila
Philippine Journal of public Administration	*Philippine J. publ. Adm.*	Manila
Philippine Studies	*Philippine Stud.*	Quezon City
Phylon	*Phylon*	Atlanta, Ga.
Planning	*Planning*	London
Planning and Development in the Netherlands	*Planning Develop. Netherl.*	Assen
Planning Outlook	*Planning Outlook*	Newcastle-upon-Tyne
Plánované Hospodarství	*Plán. Hospod.*	Praha
Planovoe Hozjajstvo	*Plan. Hoz.*	Moskva
Polish Review	*Polish R.*	New York
Polish sociological Bulletin	*Polish sociol. B.*	Warsaw
Política	*Política (Caracas)*	Caracas
Politica del Diritto	*Polit. Dir.*	Bologna
Política internacional	*Polít. int. (La Habana)*	La Habana
Politica internazionale	*Polit. int. (Milano)*	Milano
Political Quarterly	*Polit. Quart.*	London
Political Science	*Polit. Sci. (Wellington)*	Wellington
Political Science annual	*Polit. Sci. ann.*	New York
Political Science Quarterly	*Polit. Sci. Quart.*	New York
Political Science Review	*Polit. Sci. R.*	Jaipur
Political Scientist	*Polit. Scientist*	Ranchi
Political Studies	*Polit. Stud. (Oxford)*	Oxford
Političeskoe Samoobrazovanie	*Polit. Samoobr.*	Moskva
Politićka Misao	*Polit. Misao*	Beograd
Politico	*Politico*	Pavia
Politics	*Politics (Kensington)*	Kensington, N.S.W.
Politiikka	*Politiikka*	Helsinki
Politique	*Politique*	Paris
Politique aujourd'hui	*Polit. aujourd.*	Paris
Politique étrangère	*Polit. étr.*	Paris
Politische Meinung	*Polit. Meinung*	Köln
Politische Rundschau	*Polit. Rdsch.*	Bern
Politische Studien	*Polit. Stud. (München)*	München
Politische Vierteljahresschrift	*Polit. Vjhschr.*	Heidelberg-Köln-Opladen
Polity	*Polity*	Amherst, Mass.
Poljarnaja Zvezda	*Poljar. Zvezda*	

Pologne et les Affaires occidentales (La)	*Pologne Aff. occid.*	Poznań
Ponte	*Ponte*	Firenze
Population	*Population*	Paris
Population Bulletin	*Popul. B.*	Washington
Population et Famille	*Population et Famille*	Bruxelles
Population Review	*Popul. R.*	Madras
Population Studies	*Popul. Stud.*	London
Pour la Vie	*Pour la Vie*	Paris
Poverty human Resources Abstracts	*Poverty hum. Resources Abstr.*	Ann Arbor, Mich.
Praca i Zabezpieczenie społeczne	*Praca Zabezp. społecz.*	Warszawa
Practical Anthropology	*Practic. Anthropol.*	New York
Právny Obzor	*Právny Obzor*	Bratislava
Pravovedenie	*Pravovedenie*	Leningrad
Présence africaine	*Présence afr.*	Paris
Prêtres aujourd'hui	*Prêtres aujourd.*	Paris
Preuves	*Preuves*	Paris
Previdenza sociale	*Previd. soc.*	Roma
Providenza sociale nell'Agricoltura	*Previd. soc. Agric.*	Roma
Priroda	*Priroda*	Moskva
Probleme economice	*Probl. econ. (Bucureşti)*	Bucureşti
Problèmes sociaux congolais	*Probl. soc. congolais*	Lumubashi-Bruxelles
Problemi del Socialismo	*Probl. Social. (Milano)*	Milano
Problemi della Sicurezza sociale	*Probl. Sicur. soc.*	Roma
Problemi di Gestione	*Probl. Gestione*	Roma
Problems of Communism	*Probl. Communism*	Washington
Problemy ekonomiczne	*Probl. ekon. (Warszawa)*	Warszawa
Problemy matematičeskih Metodov v ěkonomičeskih issledovanijah i planirovanii	*Probl. matem. Metod. ěkon. issled. planirov.*	Kiev
Problemy Mira i Socializma	*Probl. Mira Social.*	Moskva
Problemy naučnogo Kommunizma (Akademija obščestvennyh Nauk pri CK KPSS)	*Probl. nauč. Kommunizma (Akad. obšč. Nauk pri CK KPSS)*	Moskva
Problemy organizacji	*Probl. organ.*	Warszawa
Problemy Severa	*Probl. Sev.*	Moskva
Proceedings of the Academy of political Science	*Proc. Acad. polit. Sci.*	New York
Proche-Orient. Études économiques	*Proche-Orient Ét. écon.*	Beyrouth
Proche-Orient. Études juridiques	*Proche-Orient Ét. jur.*	Beyrouth
Profil	*Profil*	Zürich
Progrès scientifique	*Progr. scientif.*	Paris
Progrès social	*Progr. soc.*	Liège
Progresele Ştintei	*Progr. Ştin.*	Bucureşti
Projet	*Projet*	Paris
Promotion rurale	*Promotion rur.*	Paris
Przegląd komunikacujny	*Przegl. komunik.*	Warszawa
Przegląd statystyczny	*Przegl. statyst.*	Warszawa
Przegląd zachodni	*Przegl. zachod.*	Poznań
P.S. Newsletter of the American political Science Association	*P.S. Newsletter Amer. polit. Sci. Assoc.*	Washington, D.C.
Psychologia africana	*Psychol. afr.*	Johannesburg
Public Administration	*Publ. Adm. (London)*	London
Public Administration	*Publ. Adm. (Sydney)*	Sydney
Public Administration Review	*Publ. Adm. R.*	Chicago, Ill.
Public Choice	*Publ. Choice*	Blacksburg, Va.
Public Finance	*Publ. Finance*	The Hague
Public Interest	*Publ. Interest*	New York
Public Law	*Publ. Law (London)*	London

Public Opinion Quarterly	*Publ. Opin. Quart.*	Princeton, N. J.
Public Policy	*Publ. Pol.*	Cambridge, Mass.
Publizistik	*Publizistik*	Münster-in-Westfalen
Purpan	*Purpan*	Toulouse
Quaderni di Azione sociale	*Quad. Azione soc.*	Roma
Quaderni di Scienze sociali	*Quad. Sci. soc.*	Genova
Quaderni di Sociologia	*Quad. Sociol.*	Torino
Quality and Quantity	*Quality and Quantity*	Padova
Quarterly Journal of Administration	*Quart. J. Adm.*	Ibadan
Quarterly Journal of Economics	*Quart. J. Econ.*	Cambridge, Mass.
Quarterly Journal of local self-Government	*Quart. J. loc. self-Gvt*	Bombay
Quarterly Journal of the Library of Congress	*Quart. J. Libr. Congress*	Washington, D.C.
Quarterly Review of agricultural Economics	*Quart. R. agric. Econ.*	Canberra
Quarterly Review of Economics and Business	*Quart. R. Econ. Busin.*	Champaign, Ill.
Queen's Quarterly	*Queen's Quart.*	Kingston, Ont.
Questions actuelles du Socialisme	*Quest. act. Socialisme*	Paris
Questitalia	*Questitalia*	Venezia
Race	*Race*	London
Rassegna del Lavoro	*Rass. Lav.*	Roma
Rassegna economica	*Rass. econ. (Napoli)*	Napoli
Rassegna italiana di Sociologia	*Rass. ital. Sociol.*	Firenze
Rassegna sindacale	*Rass. sind.*	Roma
Realtà economica	*Realtà econ.*	Milano
Recherche d'Économie et de Sociologie rurales	*Rech. Écon. Sociol. rur.*	Paris
Recherche, Enseignement, Documentation africanistes francophones, Bulletin d'Information et de Liaison	*Rech. Enseign. Docum. african. francophon. B. Inform. Liaison*	Paris
Recherche sociale	*Rech. soc. (Libreville)*	Libreville
Recherches africaines	*Rech. afr.*	Stuttgart
Recherches économiques de Louvain	*Rech. écon. Louvain*	Louvain
Recht in Ost und West	*Recht in Ost West*	Berlin
Reflets et Perspectives de la Vie économique	*Reflets Perspect. Vie écon.*	Bruxelles
Regional Science Association. Papers and Proceedings	*Region. Sci. Assoc. Pap. and Proc.*	Cambridge, Mass.
Regional Studies	*Region. Stud.*	Oxford
Relations industrielles	*Relat. industr.*	Québec
Religion and public Order. An annual Review of Church and State and of Religion, Law and Society	*Relig. publ. Order*	Ithaca, N. Y.
Res publica	*Res publ.*	Bruxelles
Review of economic Studies	*R. econ. Stud.*	Edinburgh
Review of Economics and Statistics	*R. Econ. Statist.*	Cambridge, Mass.
Review of educational Research	*R. educ. Res.*	Boulder, Colo.
Review of Income and Wealth	*R. Income and Wealth*	New Haven
Review of Marketing and agricultural Economics	*R. Mkting agric. Econ.*	Sydney
Review of Politics	*R. Polit.*	Notre Dame, Ind.
Review of religious Research	*R. relig. Res.*	New York
Review of social Economy	*R. soc. Econ.*	Chicago, Ill.

Review of the economic Conditions in Italy	*R. econ. Condit. Italy*	Rome
Revista brasileira de Cultura	*R. brasil. Cultura*	Rio de Janeiro
Revista brasileira de Economica	*R. brasil. Econ.*	Rio de Janeiro
Revista brasileira de Estatística	*R. brasil. Estatíst.*	Rio de Janeiro
Revista brasileira de Estudos políticos	*R. brasil. Estud. polít.*	Belo Horizonte
Revista brasileira de Folclore	*R. brasil. Folcl.*	Rio de Janeiro
Revista brasileira de Política internacional	*R. brasil. Polít. int.*	Rio de Janeiro
Revista colombiana de Antropología	*R. colomb. Antropol.*	Bogotá
Revista colombiana de Folclor	*R. colomb. Folcl.*	Bogotá
Revista da Escola de Comunicacões culturais	*R. Esc. Comunic. cult.*	São Paulo
Revista de Administração de Empresas	*R. Adm. Emprêsas*	Rio de Janeiro
Revista de Administração municipal	*R. Adm. municip. (Rio de Janeiro)*	Rio de Janeiro
Revista de Administração pública	*R. Adm. públ. (Rio de Janeiro)*	Rio de Janeiro
Revista de Ateneo paraguaya. Suplemento antropológico	*R. Ateneo parag. Supl. antropol.*	Asunción
Revista de Ciência política	*R. Ciênc. polít.*	Rio de Janeiro
Revista de Ciencias sociales	*R. Cienc. soc. (Puerto Rico)*	Puerto Rico
Revista de Derecho	*R. Der. (Quito)*	Quito
Revista de Derecho internacional y Ciencias diplomáticas	*R. Der. int. Cienc. diplom.*	Rosario
Revista de Direito administrativo	*R. Dir. adm.*	Rio de Janeiro
Revista de Economía	*R. Econ. (México)*	México
Revista de Economía latinoamericana	*R. Econ. latinoamer.*	Caracas
Revista de Economía política	*R. Econ. polít. (Madrid)*	Madrid
Revista de Economía y Estadística	*R. Econ. Estadíst.*	Córdoba (Argentina)
Revista de Educación	*R. Educación (Madrid)*	Madrid
Revista de Estudios agro-sociales	*R. Estud. agro-soc.*	Madrid
Revista de Estudios de la Vida local	*R. Estud. Vida loc.*	Madrid
Revista de Estudios políticos	*R. Estud. polít.*	Madrid
Revista de Etnografía	*R. Etnogr. (Lima)*	Lima
Revista de Etnografia	*R. Etnogr. (Porto)*	Porto
Revista de Etnografie si Folclor	*R. Etnogr. Folcl.*	Bucureşti
Revista de Filozofie	*R. Filoz.*	Bucureşti
Revista de Fomento social	*R. Fomento soc.*	Madrid
Revista de Planeacion y Desarrollo	*R. Plan. Desarr.*	Bogotá
Revista de Política internacional	*R. Polít. int. (Madrid)*	Madrid
Revista de Política social	*R. Polít. soc.*	Madrid
Revista de Statistică	*R. Statist. (Bucureşti)*	Bucureşti
Revista de la Facultad de Ciências de la Administración	*R. Fac. Cienc. Adm.*	Santa Fé
Revista de la Sociedad interamericana de Planificación	*R. Soc. interamer. Plan.*	San Juan
Revista de la Universidad. Externado de Colombia	*R. Univ. Externado Colombia*	Bogotá
Revista del Banco de la República	*R. Banco Repúbl.*	Bogotá
Revista del Instituto de Antropología	*R. Inst. Antropol. (Tucumán)*	Buenos Aires
Revista del Instituto de Ciencias sociales	*R. Inst. Cienc. soc.*	Barcelona
Revista del Instituto de Sociologia boliviana	*R. Inst. Sociol. boliv.*	Sucre
Revista del México agrario	*R. México agrar.*	México
Revista española de Derecho internacional	*R. esp. Der. int.*	Madrid

Revista española de la Opinión pública	*R. esp. Opin. públ.*	Madrid
Revista geographica	*R. geogr. (Rio de Janeiro)*	Rio de Janeiro
Revista iberoamericana de Seguridad social	*R. iberoamer. Segur. soc.*	Madrid
Revista internacional de Sociología	*R. int. Sociol. (Madrid)*	Madrid
Revista latino-americana de Ciencia política	*R. latino-amer. Cienc. polit.*	Santiago de Chile
Revista latino-americana de Sociología	*R. latino-amer. Sociol.*	Buenos-Aires
Revista mexicana de Ciencia política	*R. mexic. Cienc. polit.*	México
Revista mexicana de Sociología	*R. mexic. Sociol.*	México
Revista mexicana del Trabajo	*R. mexic. Trab.*	México
Revista paraguaya de Sociología	*R. parag. Sociol.*	Asunción
Revista sindical de Estadística	*R. sind. Estadíst.*	Madrid
Revue administrative	*R. adm.*	Paris
Revue algérienne des Sciences juridiques, politiques et économiques	*R. algér. Sci. jur. polit. écon.*	Alger
Revue belge de Droit international	*R. belge Dr. int.*	Bruxelles
Revue belge de Sécurité sociale	*R. belge Sécur. soc.*	Bruxelles
Revue congolaise d'Administration	*R. congol. Adm.*	Kinshasa
Revue d'Allemagne	*R. Allem.*	Paris
Revue d'Économie politique	*R. Écon. polit. (Paris)*	Paris
Revue d'Histoire économique et sociale	*R. Hist. écon. soc.*	Paris
Revue d'Histoire et de Civilisation du Maghreb	*R. Hist. Civilis. Maghreb*	Alger
Revue de Corée	*R. Corée*	Séoul
Revue de Défense nationale	*R. Déf. nat.*	Paris
Revue de Droit contemporain	*R. Dr. contemp.*	Bruxelles
Revue de Géographie alpine	*R. Géogr. alpine*	Grenoble
Revue de Géographie de Lyon	*R. Géogr. Lyon*	Lyon
Revue de Géographie du Maroc	*R. Géogr. Maroc*	Rabat
Revue de Madagascar	*R. Madagascar*	Tananarive
Revue de Psychologie des Peuples	*R. Psychol. Peuples*	Le Havre
Revue de Science financière	*R. Sci. financ.*	Paris
Revue de l'Économie du Centre-Est	*R. Écon. Centre-Est*	Dijon
Revue de l'Est	*R. Est*	Paris
Revue de l'Institut de Sociologie	*R. Inst. Sociol.*	Bruxelles
Revue de l'Occident musulman et de la Méditerranée	*R. Occident musul. Méditerr.*	Aix-en-Provence
Revue de la Société d'Études et d'Expansion	*R. Soc. Ét. Expans.*	Liège
Revue des Droits de l'Homme	*R. Dr. Homme*	Paris
Revue des Études coopératives	*R. Ét. coop.*	Paris
Revue des Sciences économiques	*R. Sci. écon.*	Liège
Revue des Travaux de l'Académie des Sciences morales et politiques	*R. Trav. Acad. Sci. mor. polit.*	Paris
Revue du Centre d'Études des Pays de l'Est	*R. Centre Ét. Pays Est*	Bruxelles
Revue du Conseil économique wallon	*R. Cons. écon. wallon*	Liège
Revue du Droit public et de la Science politique en France et à l'étranger	*R. Dr. publ. Sci. polit.*	Paris
Revue du Marché commun	*R. Marché commun*	Paris
Revue du Sud-Est asiatique et de l'Extrême-Orient	*R. Sud-Est asiat. Extr.-Orient*	Bruxelles
Revue du Travail	*R. Trav. (Bruxelles)*	Bruxelles
Revue économique	*R. écon. (Paris)*	Paris
Revue économique de Madagascar	*R. écon. Madagascar*	Tananarive
Revue économique et sociale	*R. écon. soc.*	Lusanne
Revue économique franco-suisse	*R. écon. fr.-suisse*	Paris
Revue égyptienne de Droit international	*R. égypt. Dr. int.*	Le Caire

Revue fiduciaire	*R. fiduc.*	Paris
Revue française	*R. franç.*	Paris
Revue française d'Études politiques africaines	*R. franç. Ét. polit. afr.*	Paris
Revue française d'Histoire d'Outre-Mer	*R. franç. Hist. O.-Mer*	Paris
Revue française de Pédagogie	*R. franç. Pédag.*	Paris
Revue française de Science politique	*R. franç. Sci. polit.*	Paris
Revue française de Sociologie	*R. franç. Sociol.*	Paris
Revue française de l'Agriculture	*R. franç. Agric.*	Paris
Revue française de l'Énergie	*R. franç. Énergie*	Paris
Revue française des Affaires sociales	*R. franç. Aff. soc.*	Paris
Revue française du Marketing	*R. franç. Mkting*	Paris
Revue générale	*R. gén.*	Bruxelles
Revue générale de Droit international public	*R. gén. Dr. int. publ.*	Paris
Revue géographique des Pyrénées et du Sud-Ouest	*R. géogr. Pyrénées*	Toulouse
Revue hellénique de Droit international	*R. héll. Dr. int.*	Athènes
Revue internationale de Droit comparé	*R. int. Dr. comp.*	Paris
Revue internationale de la Sécurité sociale	*R. int. Sécur. soc.*	Genève
Revue internationale des Sciences administratives	*R. int. Sci. adm.*	Bruxelles
Revue internationale des Sciences sociales	*R. int. Sci. soc.*	Paris
Revue internationale du Développement social	*R. int. Dévelop. soc.*	New York
Revue juridique et économique du Sud-Ouest. Série économique	*R. jur. écon. Sud-Ouest. Sér.*	Bordeaux
Revue juridique et économique du Sud-Ouest. Série juridique	*R. jur. écon. Sud-Ouest Sér. jur.*	Bordeaux
Revue juridique et parlementaire	*R. jur. parl.*	Paris
Revue juridique et politique	*R. jur. polit.*	Paris
Revue politique des Idées et Institutions	*R. polit. Idées Instit.*	Paris
Revue politique et parlementaire	*R. polit. parl.*	Paris
Revue roumaine des Sciences sociales. Série Philosophie et Logique	*R. roum. Sci. soc. Sér. Philos. Logique*	Bucarest
Revue roumaine des Sciences sociales. Série Sciences économiques	*R. roum. Sci. soc. Sér. Sci. écon.*	Bucarest
Revue roumaine des Sciences sociales. Série Sciences juridiques	*R. roum. Sci. soc. Sér. Sci. jur.*	Bucarest
Revue roumaine des Sciences sociales. Série Sociologie	*R. roum. Sci. soc. Sér. Sociol.*	Bucarest
Revue sénégalaise de Droit	*R. sénég. Dr.*	Dakar
Revue trimestrielle de Droit européen	*R. trim. Dr. europ.*	Paris
Revue tunisienne de Sciences sociales	*R. tunis. Sci. soc.*	Tunis
Rheinisch-westfälische Zeitschrift für Volkskunde	*Rhein.-westf. Z. Volksk.*	Bonn
Rheinische Vierteljahrsblätter	*Rhein. Vjbl.*	Bonn
Ricerce economiche	*Ric. econ.*	Venezia
Rinrigaku Nempô	*Rinrigaku Nempô*	Tokyo
Risparmio	*Risparmio*	Roma
Ritsumeikan Daigaku Jimbun Kenkyûjo Kiyô	*Ritsumeikan Daigaku Jimbun Kenkyûjo Kiyô*	[Nihon]
Rivista del Porto di Napoli	*Riv. Porto Napoli*	Napoli
Rivista di Diritto finanziaro e Scienza delle Finanze	*Riv. Dir. finanz.*	Milano
Rivista di Economia agraria	*Riv. Econ. agr.*	Roma

Rivista di Politica agraria	*Riv. Polit. agr.*	Bologna
Rivista di Politica economica	*Riv. Polit. econ.*	Roma
Rivista di Psicologia sociale e Archivio italiana di Psicologia generale e del Lavoro	*Riv. Psicol. soc.*	Torino
Rivista di Sociologia	*Riv. Sociol.*	Roma
Rivista di Studi politici internazionali	*Riv. Studi polit. int.*	Firenze
Rivista internazionale di Filosofia politica e sociale e di Diritto comparato	*Riv. int. Filos. polit. soc. Dir. comp.*	Bologna
Rivista internazionale di Scienze economiche e commerciali	*Riv. int. Sci. econ. com.*	Milano-Padova
Rivista internazionale di Scienze sociali	*Riv. int. Sci. soc.*	Milano
Rivista italiana di Economia, Demografia e Statistica	*Riv. ital. Econ. Demogr. Statist.*	Roma
Rivista trimestrale di Diritto pubblico	*Riv. trim. Dir. pubbl.*	Milano
Rocky Mountain social Science Journal	*Rocky Mountain soc. Sci. J.*	Fort Collins, Colo.
Roczniki Instytutu Handlu wewnętrznego	*Roczn. Inst. Handlu wewn.*	Warszawa
Round Table	*Round Table*	London
Ruch prawniczy, ekonomiczny i socjologiczny	*Ruch prawn. ekon. socjol.*	Poznań
Rural Africana	*Rur. Afr.*	East Lansing
Rural Sociology	*Rur. Sociol.*	Lexington, Ky.
Sächsische Heimatblätter	*Sächs. Heimatbl.*	Dresden
Saeculum. Jahrbuch für Universalgeschichte	*Saeculum*	Freiburg-München
Saharien	*Saharien*	Paris
Saint Louis Quarterly	*Saint Louis Quart.*	Baguio City, Mo.
Sbornik Muzeja Antropologii i Ětnografii. Institut Ětnografii im. Mikluho-Maklaja	*Sb. Muz. Antropol. Ětnogr.*	Moskva
Sbornik naučnyh Trudov (Sverdlovskij juridičeskij Institut)	*Sb. nauč. Trud. (Sverdlovsk. jur. Inst.)*	Sverdlovsk
Sbornik Trudov Vsesojuznyj zaočnyj politehničeskij Institut	*Sb. Trud. Vsesojuz. zaoč. politehn. Inst.*	Moskva
Scandinavian political Studies	*Scand. polit. Stud.*	Helsinki
Schmollers Jahrbuch	*Schmollers Jb.*	Berlin
Schönere Heimat. Erbe und Gegenwart	*Schönere Heimat*	München
Schweizer Monatshefte	*Schweiz. Mh.*	Zürich
Schweizer Rundschau	*Schweiz. Rdsch.*	Soleure
Schweizerische Hochschulzeitung	*Schweiz. Hochschulztg*	Zürich
Schweizerische Zeitschrift für Volkswirtschaft und Statistik	*Schweiz. Z. Volkswirtsch. Statist.*	Basel
Schweizerisches Archiv für Verkehrs-wissenschaft und Verkehrspolitik	*Schweiz. Archiv. Verkehrswiss. u. -Polit.*	Zürich
Science and Society	*Sci. and Soc.*	New York
Sciences sociales aujourd'hui	*Sci. soc. aujourd.*	Moscou
Scientific American	*Scient. Amer.*	New York
Scottish Journal of political Economy	*Scott. J. polit. Econ.*	Edinburgh
Scuola e Città	*Scuola e Città*	Firenze
Seguridad social	*Segur. soc. (Santiago de Chile)*	Santiago de Chile
Seiji Keizai Ronshû	*Seiji Keizai Ronshû*	Tokyo
Seikei Ronsô	*Seikei Ronsô (Tokyo)*	Tokyo
Seiyôshigaku	*Seiyôshigaku*	Tokyo
Sel'skoe Hozjajstvo Krigizii	*Sel'sk. Hoz. Kirgizii*	Frunze
Sel'skoe Hozjajstvo Moldavii	*Sel'sk. Hoz. Moldavii*	Kišinev

Sel'skoe Hozjajstvo Uzbekistana	*Sel'sk. Hoz. Uzbek.*	Taškent
Semiotica	*Semiotica*	Paris
Service social	*Serv. soc. (Québec)*	Québec
Sever	*Sever*	[SSSR]
Shakai Kagaku Tôkyû	*Shakai Kagaku Tôkyû*	Tokyo
Shakaigaku-hyoron	*Shakaigaku-hyoron*	Tokyo
Shakaigaku Ronsô	*Shakaigaku Ronsô*	Tokyo
Shien	*Shien*	[Nihon]
Shisô	*Shisô*	Tokyo
Shûkyô-Kenkyû	*Shûkyô-Kenkyû*	Tokyo
Signes du Temps	*Signes du Temps*	Paris
Simulation and Games	*Simulation and Games*	Beverly Hills, Calif.
Sinai	*Sinai*	Baghdad
Síntese política economica social	*Síntese polít. econ. soc.*	Rio de Janeiro
Síntesi economica	*Síntesi econ.*	Roma
Sipra	*Sipra*	Torino
SIPRAUNO	*SIPRAUNO*	Torino
Skandinaviska Banken quarterly Review	*Skand. Banken quart. R.*	Stockholm
Skandinavskij Sbornik	*Skandinav. Sb.*	[SSSR]
Slavic Review	*Slavic R.*	New York
Social Action	*Soc. Action*	Poona
Social and economic Studies	*Soc. econ. Stud.*	Kingston
Social Biology	*Soc. Biology*	New York
Social Casework	*Soc. Casewk*	New York
Social Compass	*Soc. Compass*	The Hague
Social Forces	*Soc. Forces*	Chapel Hill, N.C.
Social Problems	*Soc. Probl.*	New York-Rochester, Mich.
Social Research	*Soc. Res.*	New York
Social Science	*Soc. Sci. (Winfield)*	Winfield
Social Science Information/Information sur les Sciences sociales	*Soc. Sci. Inform./Inform. Sci. soc.*	Paris
Social Science and Medicine	*Soc. Sci. Medicine*	Oxford
Social Science Quarterly	*Soc. Sci. Quart.*	Austin, Tex.
Social Service Review	*Soc. Serv. R.*	Chicago, Ill.
Social Work	*Soc. Wk (Albany)*	Albany, N. Y.
Sociale Wetenschappen	*Soc. Wetensch.*	Tilburg
Socialisme	*Socialisme*	Bruxelles
Socialist Revolution	*Social. Revol.*	San Francisco, Calif.
Socialističeskaja Zakonnost	*Social. Zakonn.*	Moskva
Socialističeskij Trud	*Social. Trud*	Moskva
Socialt Tidsskrift	*Soc. Tss.*	København
Société de Banque suisse. Bulletin	*Soc. Banque suisse B.*	Bâle
Société royale d'Économie politique de Belgique	*Soc. roy. Écon. polit. Belgique*	Bruxelles
Society and Leisure	*Soc. and Leisure*	Prague
Socijalizam	*Socijalizam*	Beograd
Socio-economic planning Science	*Socio-econ. plan. Sci.*	New York
Sociologia	*Sociologia (Roma)*	Roma
Sociologia internationalis	*Sociol. int. (Berlin)*	Berlin
Sociologia neerlandica	*Sociol. neerland.*	Assen
Sociologia religiosa	*Sociol. relig.*	Padova
Sociologia ruralis	*Sociol. rur.*	Assen
Sociological Analysis	*Sociol. Anal.*	River Forest, Ill.
Sociological Bulletin	*Sociol. B. (Delhi)*	Delhi
Sociological Focus	*Sociol. Focus*	Akron, Ohio
Sociological Inquiry	*Sociol. Inquiry*	Toronto
Sociological Quarterly	*Sociol. Quart.*	Carbondale, Ill.
Sociological Review	*Sociol. R.*	Keele

Sociologicky Časopis	*Sociol. Čas.*	Praha
Sociologie du Travail	*Sociol. Trav.*	Paris
Sociologie et Sociétés	*Sociol. et Soc.*	Montréal
Sociologische Gids	*Sociol. Gids*	Meppel
Sociologus. Zeitschrift für empirische Soziologie, socialpsychologische und ethnologische Forschung	*Sociologus*	Berlin
Sociology	*Sociology*	London
Sociology and social Research	*Sociol. soc. Res.*	Los Angeles, Calif.
Sociology of Education	*Sociol. Education*	Chicago, Ill.
Sociometry	*Sociometry*	New York
Sondages	*Sondages*	Paris
Soobščenija Akademii Nauk Gruzinskoj SSR	*Soobšč. Akad. Nauk Gruz. SSR*	Tbilisi
Soobščenija gosudarstvennogo Ėrmitaža	*Soobšč. gos. Ėrmit.*	Moskva
Soobščenija Muzeja izobrazitel'nyh Iskusstv im. Puškina	*Soobšč. Muz. izobraz. Isk. im. Puškina*	Moskva
Sosiaalinen Aikakauskirja	*Sos. Aikakausk.*	Helsinki
Sosiaalivakuutus	*Sosiaalivakuutus*	Helsinki
Sosiologia	*Sosiologia*	Helsinki
South African Journal of Economics	*South Afr. J. Econ.*	Johannesburg
South Asian Review	*South Asian R.*	London
South Asian Studies	*South Asian Stud.*	Jaipur
Southern economic Journal	*South. econ. J.*	Chapel Hill, N. C.
Southern Folklore Quarterly	*South. Folkl. Quart.*	Gainesville
Southern Quarterly	*South. Quart.*	Hattiesburg, Miss.
Southwestern Journal of Anthropology	*Southwest. J. Anthropol.*	Albuquerque
Sovetskaja Arheologija	*Sov. Arheol.*	Moskva
Sovetskaja Ėtnografija	*Sov. Ėtnogr.*	Moskva
Sovetskaja Muzyka	*Sov. Muzyka*	Moskva
Sovetskaja Pedagogika	*Sov. Pedag.*	Moskva
Sovetskie Arhivy	*Sov. Arhivy*	Moskva
Sovetskij Dagestan	*Sov. Dagestan*	Mahačkala
Sovetskoe Finno-Ugrovedenie	*Sov. Finno-Ugroved.*	[SSSR]
Sovetskoe Gosudarstvo i Pravo	*Sov. Gos. Pravo*	Moskva
Sovetskoe Slavjanovedenie	*Sov. Slavjanoved.*	Moskva
Soviet and Eastern European foreign Trade	*Sov. East. Europe. for. Trade*	White Plains, N. Y.
Soviet Studies	*Sov. Stud.*	Glasgow
Soziale Sicherheit	*Soz. Sicherheit*	Wien
Soziale Welt	*Soz. Welt*	Dortmund
Sozialistische Politik	*Sozial. Polit.*	Berlin
Soziologisches Institut der Universität Zürich	*Soziol. Inst. Univ. Zürich B.*	Zürich
Spółdzielczy Kwartalnik Naukowy	*Spółd. Kwartal. Nauk.*	Warszawa
Sprawy międzynarodowe	*Spr. międzyn.*	Warszawa
Staat (Der)	*Staat*	Berlin
Staat und Recht	*Staat u. Recht*	Potsdam
Staff Papers	*Staff Pap.*	Washington, D.C.
Stanovništvo	*Stanovništvo*	Beograd
Statistica	*Statistica (Bologna)*	Bologna
Statistika	*Statistika (Praha)*	Praha
Statistiques et Études financières	*Statist. Ét. financ.*	Paris
Statistiques et Études financières. Supplément	*Statist. Ét. financ. Suppl.*	Paris
Statisztikai Szemle	*Statiszt. Szle*	Budapest
Stato sociale	*Stato soc.*	Roma
Statsvetenskaplig Tidskrift	*Statsvet. Ts.*	Lund
Stratégie	*Stratégie*	Paris

Strategisk Bulletin	*Strategisk B.*	Stockholm
Studi economici	*Studi econ.*	Napoli
Studi Emigrazione	*Studi Emigr.*	Roma
Studi parlamentari e di Politica costituzionale	*Studi parl. Polit. costit.*	Roma
Studia albanica	*Stud. albanica*	
Studia demograficzne	*Stud. demogr.*	Warszawa
Studia ekonomiczne	*Stud. ekon.*	Warszawa
Studia ethnographica upsaliensia	*Stud. ethnogr. upsaliensia*	Uppsala
Studia finansowe	*Stud. finans.*	Warszawa
Studia islamica	*Stud. islam.*	Paris
Studies in comparative and local Government	*Stud. comp. loc. Gvt*	The Hague
Studies in comparative Communism	*Stud. comp. Communism*	Los Angeles, Calif.
Studies in Soviet Thought	*Stud. Sov. Thought*	Fribourg
Studii și Čercetări de Antropologie. Tomul	*Stud. Čerc. Antropol. Tomul*	București
Studii și Čercetari economice	*Stud. Čerc. econ.*	București
Studium generale	*Stud. gen.*	Berlin
Sudan Society	*Sudan Soc.*	Khartoum
Südost-Forschungen	*Südost-Forsch.*	München
Survey. A Journal of Soviet and East European Studies	*Survey*	London
Survey of current Business	*Surv. curr. Busin.*	Washington, D.C.
Svensk Juristtidning	*Svensk Juristtidning*	Stockholm
Swedish Economy	*Swedish Econ.*	Stockholm
Swedish Journal of Economics	*Swedish J. Econ.*	Stockholm
Synopsis	*Synopsis*	Bruxelles
Talouselämä	*Talouselämä*	[Suomi]
Tam-Tam	*Tam-Tam*	Paris
Teacher Education in new Countries	*Teacher Educ. new Countries*	London
Technikgeschichte	*Technikgesch.*	Düsseldorf
Technological Forecasting. An international Journal	*Technol. Forecasting*	New York
Technology and Culture	*Technology and Culture*	Chicago
Temas sociales	*Temas soc.*	La Paz
Tempi moderni	*Tempi mod.*	Roma
Temps modernes	*Temps mod.*	Paris
Tendances	*Tendances*	Paris
Tendances de la Conjoncture	*Tendances Conjonct.*	Paris
Tennessee Folklore Society Bulletin	*Tenn. Folkl. Soc. B.*	Murfreesboro, Tenn.
Teorija i Praktika fizičeskoj Kul'tury	*Teorija Prakt. fizič. Kul't.*	Moskva
Teorija in Praksa	*Teorija in Praksa*	Ljubljana
Terra	*Terra*	Helsinki
Terra ameriga	*Terra amer.*	Genova
Terre entière	*Terre entière*	Paris
Terre malgache/Tany malgasy	*Terre malgache/Tany malgasy*	Tananarive
Területi Statisztika	*Területi Statiszt.*	Budapest
Terzo Mondo	*Terzo Mondo*	Milano
Tetsugaku Nenpô	*Tetsugaku Nenpô (Kyûshû Daigaku)*	Fukuoka
Textes et Documents	*Textes et Doc. (Bruxelles)*	Bruxelles
Theologische Quartalschrift	*Theol. Quartalschr.*	München-Freiburg-im-Breisgau
Tiden	*Tiden*	Stockholm
Tidskrift utgiven av juridiska Föreningen i Finland	*Ts. jur. För. Finland*	Helsinki

Tiers-Monde	*Tiers-Monde*	Paris
Tôkai Daigaku Kiyô	*Tôkai Daigaku Kiyô*	[Nipon]
Tôkyô Daigaku Kyôyô-gakubu Shakaigaku Kiyô	*Tôkyô Daigaku Kyôyô-gakubu Shakaigaku Kiyô*	Tokyo
Tokyo Daigaku-shinbunkenkyûshokiyô	*Tokyo Daigaku-shinbunkenkyûshokiyô*	Tokyo
Tonan Asia Kenkyu	*Tonan Asia Kenkyu*	Kyoto
Toshi Mondai	*Toshi Mondai*	Tokyo
Toshi Mondai Kenkyû	*Toshi Mondai Kenkyû*	Ôsaka
Town Planning Review	*Town Planning R.*	Liverpool
Tôyô Bunka Kenkyûjo Kiyô	*Tôyô Bunka Kenkyûjo Kiyô*	Tokyo
Transports	*Transports*	Paris
Travail humain	*Trav. hum.*	Paris
Travaux de l'Institut de Recherches sahariennes	*Trav. Inst. Rech. sahar.*	Alger
Travaux et Jours	*Trav. et Jours*	Beyrouth
Tribus. Veröffentlichungen des Linden-Museums	*Tribus*	Stuttgart
Trierer Zeitschrift für Geschichte und Kunst des Trierer Landes und seiner Nachbargebiete	*Trierer Z. Gesch. Kunst Trierer Land. Nachbargeb.*	Trier
Trimestre económico	*Trim. econ.*	México
Trud i zarabotnaja Plata	*Trud i zarabot. Plata*	Moskva
Trudy Akademii Nauk Litovskoj SSR. Obščestvennye Nauk	*Trudy Akad. Nauk Litovsk. SSR. Obšč. Nauk*	Viln'jus
Trudy Burjatskogo Instituta obščestvennyh Nauk	*Trudy Burjat. Inst. obšč. Nauk*	Novosibirsk
Trudy Dagestanskogo sel'skohozjajst-vennogo Instituta	*Trudy Dagestan. selsk.-Hoz. Inst.*	Mahačkala
Trudy Gruzinzkogo politehničeskogo Instituta	*Trudy Gruz. politehn. Inst.*	Tbilisi
Trudy Instituta Ētnografii im. Mikluho-Maklaja	*Trudy Inst. Ētnogr. im. Mikluho-Maklaja*	Moskva
Trudy Instituta (Moskovskij Institut narodnogo Hozjajstva) Problemy soveršenstvovanija Planirovanija	*Trudy Inst. (Moskovs. Inst. narod. Hoz.) Probl. soversenstv. Planirovanija*	Moskva
Trudy Irkutskogo Universiteta. Serija Jazykoznanie	*Trudy Irkutsk. Univ. Ser. Jazykozn.*	Irkutsk
Trudy Kazanskogo aviacionnogo Instituta. Kafedra obščestvennyh Nauk	*Trudy Kazan. aviac. Inst. Kaf. obšč. Nauk*	Kazan'
Trudy Kievskoj vysšej Školy SSSR	*Trudy Kiev. vysš. Školy SSSR*	Kiev
Trudy (Naučno-issledovatel'skij Institut Jazyka, Literatury, Istorii i Ēkonomiki pri Sovete Ministrov Mordovskoj ASSR)	*Trudy (Nauč.-issled. Inst. Jaz. Lit. Ist. Ēkon. Sov. Minist. Mordov. ASSR)*	Saransk
Trudy naučno-issledovatel'skogo Instituta Muzeevedenija i Ohrany Pamjatnikov Istorii i Kul'tury	*Trudy nauč.-issled. Inst. Muzeeved. i Ohr. Pamjat. Ist. i Kul't.*	Moskva
Trudy Otdelenija drevnerusskoj Literatury (Institut russkoj Literatury Akademii Nauk SSSR)	*Trudy Otdel. Drevneruss. Lit. (Inst. russ. Lit. Akad. Nauk SSSR)*	Moskva
Trudy prepodavatelej politēkonomii Vuzov Povoez'ja	*Trudy prepodav. politēkon. Vuzov Povoez'ja*	Kazan
Trudy (Prževal'skij pedagogičeskij Institut)	*Trudy (Prževal'. pedag. Inst.)*	Frunze
Trudy (Tbilisijskij gosudarstvenno-pedagogičeskoj Institut)	*Trudy (Tbilis. gos. pedag. Inst.)*	Tbilisi

Trudy (Tbilisijskij gosudarstvennyj Universitet) Serija ěkonomičeskih Nauk	*Trudy (Tbilis. gos. Univ.) Ser. ěkon. Nauk*	Tbilisi
Trudy Universiteta Družby Narodov im. Lumumby. Istorija	*Trudy Univ. Družby Nar. im. Lumumby Ist.*	Moskva
Trudy Universiteta Družby Narodov im. Lumumby. Jazykoznanie	*Trudy Univ. Družby Nar. im. Lumumby Jazykozn.*	Moskva
Trudy Ural'noj politehničeskogo Instituta	*Trudy Ural'. politehn. Inst.*	Sverdlovsk
Trudy vostočno-sibirskogo gosudarstvennogo Instituta Kul'tury	*Trudy vostoč.-sibir. gos. Inst. Kul't.*	Ulan-Udě
Trybuna spółdzielcza	*Tryb. spółd.*	Warszawa
Turkish Yearbook of international Relations	*Turk. Yearbook int. Relat.*	Ankara
Učenye Zapiski (Adygejskij naučno-issledovatel'skij Institut Jazyka, Literatury i Istorii)	*Učen. Zap. (Adyg. nauč.-issled. Inst. Jaz. Lit. Ist.)*	Krasnodar
Učenye Zapiski (Azerbajdžanskij gosudarstvennyj Universitet) Serija istoričeskih i filosofskih Nauk	*Učen. Zap. (Azerb. gos. Univ.) Ser. ist. filos. Nauk*	Baku
Učenye Zapiski (Azerbajdžanskij Institut narodnogo Hozjajstva)	*Učen. Zap. (Azerb. Inst. narod. Hoz.)*	Baku
Učenye Zapiski (Azerbajdžanskij Universitet) Serija istoričeskih i filosofskih Nauk	*Učen. Zap. (Azerb. Univ.) Ser. ist. filos. Nauk*	Baku
Učenye Zapiski (Baškirskij Universitet)	*Učen. Zap. (Baškir. Univ.)*	[SSSR]
Učenye Zapiski (Blagoveščenskij pedagogičeskij Institut im. M. I. Kalinina)	*Učen. Zap. (Blagov. pedag. Inst. im. Kalinina)*	Blagoveščensk
Učenye Zapiski (Čečeno-Ingušskij pedagogičeskij Institut) Serija Filologija	*Učen. Zap. (Čečen.-Inguš. pedag. Inst.) Ser. Filol.*	Groznyj
Učenye Zapiski (Čit. gosudarstvennyj pedagogičeskij Institut)	*Učen. Zap. (Čit. gos. pedag. Inst.)*	[SSSR]
Učenye Zapiski (Dal'nevostočnyj universitet)	*Učen. Zap. (Dal'nevost. Univ.)*	Vladivostok
Učenye Zapiski (Gor'kovskij gosudarstvennyj Universitet) Serija istoričeskaja	*Učen. Zap. (Gor'k. gos. Univ.) Ser. ist.*	Gor'ki
Učenye Zapiski (Gor'kovskij gosudarstvennyj Universitet) Serija sociologičeskaja Sociologija vysšej Školy	*Učen. Zap. (Gor'k. gos. Univ.) Ser. sociol. Sociol. vysš. Školy*	Gor'ki
Učenye Zapiski Gor'kovskogo gosudarstvennogo pedagogičeskogo Instituta. Serija obščestvennyh Nauk	*Učen. Zap. Gor'k. gos. pedag. Inst. Ser. obšč. Nauk*	Gor'ki
Učenye Zapiski (Institut Istorii, Jazyka i Literatury Dagestanskogo Filiala Akademii Nauk SSSR)	*Učen. Zap. (Inst. Ist. Jaz. Lit. Dagest. Fil. Akad. Nauk SSSR)*	Mahačkala
Učenye Zapiski (Institut meždunarodnyh Otnošenij)	*Učen. Zap. (Inst. meždun. Otnoš.)*	Moskva
Učenye Zapiski Irkutskogo Instituta narodnogo Hozjajstva	*Učen. Zap. Irkutsk. Inst. nar. Hoz.*	Irkutsk
Učenye Zapiski Kafedr marksistsko-leninskoj Filosofii Vysših Partijnyh Škol	*Učen. Zap. Kaf. marks.-lenin. Filos. Vysš. Part. Škol*	Moskva
Učenye Zapiski Kafedr obščestvennyh Nauk Vuzov goroda Leningrada. Filosofija	*Učen. Zap. Kaf. obšč. Nauk Vuzov g. Leningr.*	Leningrad

IL

Učenye Zapiski Kafedr obščestvennyh Nauk Vuzov goroda Leningrada Filosofija. Filosofskie i sociologičeskie Issledovanija	*Učen. Zap. Kaf. obšč. Nauk Vuzov g. Leningr. Filos. filos. sociol. Issled.*	Leningrad
Učenye Zapiski Kafedr obščestvennyh Nauk Vuzov Leningrada. Problemy naučnogo Kommunizma	*Učen. Zap. Kaf. obšč. Nauk Vuzov Leningr. Probl. nauč. Kommunizma*	Leningrad
Učenye Zapiski Kalmyckogo naučno-issledovatel'skogo Instituta Jazyka, Literatury i Istorii	*Učen. Zap. Kalmyc. nauč.-issled. Inst. Jaz. Lit. Ist.*	[SSSR]
Učenye Zapiski Karelskogo pedagogičeskogo Instituta	*Učen. Zap. Karel. pedag. Inst.*	Petrozavodsk
Učenye Zapiski (Kišinevskij gosudarstvennyj Universitet)	*Učen. Zap. (Kišinev. gos. Univ.)*	Kišinev
Učenye Zapiski (Kišinevskij gosudarstvennyj Universitet) Serija Istorija	*Učen. Zap. (Kišinev. gos. Univ.) Ser. Ist.*	Kišinev
Učenye Zapiski. Kišinevskij Universitet	*Učen. Zap. Kišinev. Univ.*	Kišinev
Učenye Zapiski (Kujbyševskij-pedagogičeskij Institut)	*Učen. Zap. (Kujbyš. pedag. Inst.)*	Kujbyšev
Učenye Zapiski (Kujbyševskij planirovočnyj Institut) Progress v uslovijah kommunističeskih Formacij	*Učen. Zap. (Kujbyš. plan. Inst.) Progress uslov. kommun. Formacij*	Kujbyšev
Učenye Zapiski Kurskogo ii pedagogičeskij Institut	*Učen. Zap. Kursk. pedag. Inst.*	[SSSR]
Učenye Zapiski (Leningradskij gosudarstvennyj Universitet naučno-issledovatel'skij Institut kompleksnyh sociologičeskih Issledovanij)	*Učen. Zap. (Leningr. gos. Univ. nauč.-issled. Inst. kompleks. sociol. Issled.)*	Leningrad
Učenye Zapiski (Leningradskij gosudarstvennyj Universitet naučno-issledovatel'skij Institut sociologičeskih Issledovanij)	*Učen. Zap. (Leningr. gos. Univ. nauč.-issled. Inst. sociol. Issled.)*	Leningrad
Učenye Zapiski (Leningradskij pedagogičeskij Institut)	*Učen. Zap. (Leningr. pedag. Inst.)*	Leningrad
Učenye Zapiski (Leningradskogo gosudarstvennogo pedagogičeskogo Instituta)	*Učen. Zap. (Leningr. gos. pedag. Inst.)*	Leningrad
Učenye Zapiski (Marijskii pedagogičeskij Institut)	*Učen. Zap. (Marijsk. pedag. Inst.)*	Joskar-Ola
Učenye Zapiski (Mordovskij gosudarstvennyj Universitet)	*Učen. Zap. (Mordov. gos. Univ.)*	Saransk
Učenye Zapiski (Moskovskij gosudarstvennyj zaočno-pedagogičeskij Institut)	*Učen. Zap. (Moskovs. gos. zaoč.-pedag. Inst.)*	Moskva
Učenye Zapiski (Moskovskij oblastnoj pedagogičeskij Institut)	*Učen. Zap. (Moskov. obl. pedag. Inst.)*	Moskva
Učenye Zapiski (Moskovskij pedagogičeskij Institut)	*Učen. Zap. (Moskov. pedag. Inst.)*	Moskva
Učenye Zapiski (Moskovskogo gosudarstvennogo pedagogičeskogo Instituta)	*Učen. Zap. (Moskov. gos. pedag. Inst.)*	Moskva
Učenye Zapiski (Moskovskogo gosudarstvennogo pedagogičeskogo Instituta) Osnovy naučnogo Kommunizma	*Učen. Zap. (Moskov. gos. pedag. Inst.) Osnovy nauč. Kommunizma*	Moskva
Učenye Zapiski (Naučno-issledovatelskij Institut pri Sovete Ministrov Čuvaškoj ASSR)	*Učen. Zap. (Nauč.-issled. Inst. Sov. Ministr. Čuvaš. ASSR)*	Čeboksary

Učenye Zapiski (Perm'skij gosudarstvennyj Universitet) Filosofija pograničnyh Problem Nauki	*Učen. Zap. (Perm'. gos. Univ.) Filos. pogran. Probl. Nauki*	Perm'
Učenye Zapiski (Perm'skij Universitet)	*Učen. Zap. (Perm'. Univ.)*	Perm'
Učenye Zapiski Petrozavodskogo Universiteta. Lingvističeskij Sbornik	*Učen. Zap. Petrozavod. Univ. Lingv. Sb.*	Petrozavodsk
Učenye Zapiski (Severo-Osetinskij pedagogičeskij Institut)	*Učen. Zap. Sev.-oset. pedag. Inst.*	Ordžonikidze
Učenye Zapiski (Smolenskij pedagogičeskij Institut)	*Učen. Zap. (Smolensk. pedag. Inst.)*	Smolensk
Učenye Zapiski (Sverdlovskogo gosudarstvennogo pedagogičeskogo Instituta) sociologičeskie Problemy narodnogo Obrazovanija	*Učen. Zap. (Sverdlov. gos. pedag. Inst.) sociol. Probl. narod. Obrazovanija*	Sverdlovsk
Učenye Zapiski (Tartuskij gosudarstvennyj Universitet) Trudy po Filosofii	*Učen. Zap. (Tartus. gos. Univ.) Trudy po Filos.*	Tartu
Učenye Zapiski Tartuskogo Universiteta. Trudy po Vostokovedeniju	*Učen. Zap. Tartus. Univ. Trudy Vostokoved.*	Tartu
Učenye Zapiski (Taškentstkij Institut narodnogo Hozjajstva)	*Učen. Zap. (Taškent. Inst. nar. Hoz.)*	Taškent
Učenye Zapiski Tatarskogo gosudarstvennogo Universiteta. Trudy po Filosofii	*Učen. Zap. Tatarsk. gos. Univ. Trudy po Filos.*	[SSSR]
Učenye Zapiski (Tomskij Universitet)	*Učen. Zap. (Tomsk. Univ.)*	Tomsk
Učenye Zapiski (Tomskij Universitet) Problemy Metodologii i Logiki Nauk	*Učen. Zap. (Tomsk. Univ.) Probl. Metodol. Log. Nauk*	Tomsk
Učenye Zapiski Tomskogo gosudarstvennogo pedagogičeskogo Instituta	*Učen. Zap. Tomsk. gos. pedag. Inst.*	Tomsk
Učenye Zapiski Tomskogo gosudarstvennogo Universiteta	*Učen. Zap. (Tomsk. gos. Univ.)*	Tomsk
Učenye Zapiski (Turkmenskij gosudarstvennyj Universitet) Serija ěkonomičeskih Nauk	*Učen. Zap. (Turkm. gos. Univ.) Ser. êkon. Nauk*	Ašhabad
Učenye Zapiski (Turkmenskij pedagogičeskij Institut im. V. I. Lenina)	*Učen. Zap. (Turkm. pedag. Inst. im. Lenina)*	Čardžou
Učenye Zapiski (Turkmenskij Universitet)	*Učen. Zap. (Turkm. Univ.)*	Ašhabad
Učenye Zapiski Udmurtskij pedagogičeskij Institut Filosofija naučnyj Kommunizm	*Učen. Zap. Udmurtsk. pedag. Inst. Filos. nauč. Kommunizm*	[SSSR]
Učenye Zapiski (Ural'skij Universitet) Serija Filologii	*Učen. Zap. (Ural. Univ.) Ser. Filol.*	Sverdlovsk
Ufahamu	*Ufahamu*	Los Angeles, Calif.
UN. Revista de la Direccion de Divulgación cultural	*UN. Rev. Dir. Divulg. cult.*	Bogotá
Unitas	*Unitas*	Helsinki
United Asia	*United Asia*	Bombay
Universidad	*Universidad*	Santa Fé
Universidad de Antioquía	*Univ. Antioquía*	Medellín
Universitas. Pontificia Universidad católica javeriana	*Universitas (Bogotá)*	Bogotá
Universities Quarterly	*Univ. Quart.*	London
Ural-altaische Jahrbücher	*Ural-altai. Jbr.*	Wiesbaden
Urban Affairs annual Reviews	*Urban Aff. ann. R.*	Beverly Hills, Calif.
Urban Affairs Quarterly	*Urb. Aff. Quart.*	Beverly Hills, Calif.
Urban and rural Planning Thought	*Urb. rur. Planning Thought*	New Delhi
Urban and social Change Review	*Urb. soc. Change R.*	Boston, Mass.

Urban Studies	*Urban Stud.*	Edimburgh
Urbanisme	*Urbanisme*	Paris
Uzbekiztonda ižtimoii Fanlar	*Uzbek. ižtim. Fanlar*	Taškent
Verfassung und Recht in Übersee	*Verfassung u. Recht Übersee*	Hamburg
Verfassung und Verfassungswirklichkeit	*Verfassung u. Verfassungswirklichkeit*	Köln
Verwaltung	*Verwaltung*	Heidelberg
Vestnik Akademii Nauk Kazahskoj SSR	*Vestn. Akad. Nauk Kazah. SSR*	Alma-Ata
Vestnik Akademii Nauk SSSR	*Vestn. Akad. Nauk SSSR*	Moskva
Vestnik Arhivov Armenii	*Vestn. Arhiv. Arm.*	Erevan
Vestnik drevnej Istorii	*Vestn. drevn. Ist.*	Moskva
Vestnik gosudarstvennogo Muzeja Gruzii im. Dzănašia	*Vestn. gos. Muz. Gruzii*	Tbilisi
Vestnik kabardino-balkarskogo naučno-issledovatel'skogo Instituta	*Vestn. kabard.-balkar. nauč.-issled. Inst.*	Nal'čik
Vestnik Karakalapakskogo Filiala Akademii Nauk Uzbekskoj SSR	*Vestn. Karakalp. Fil. Akad. Nauk Uzbek. SSR*	[SSSR]
Vestnik Leningradskogo Universiteta. Serija Ėkonomiki, Filosofii i Pravo	*Vestn. Leningr. Univ. Ser. Ėkon. Filos. Pravo*	Leningrad
Vestnik Leningradskogo Universiteta. Geologii i Geografii	*Vestn. Leningr. Univ. Ser. Geolog. Geogr.*	Leningrad
Vestnik Leningradskogo Universiteta. Serija Istorii, Jazyka i Literatury	*Vestn. Leningr. Univ. Ser. Ist. Jaz. Lit.*	Leningrad
Vestnik Moskovskogo Universiteta. Serija Ėkonomika	*Vestn. Moskov. Univ. Ser. Ėkon.*	Moskva
Vestnik Moskovskogo Universiteta. Serija Filologija, Žurnalistika	*Vestn. Moskov. Univ. Ser. Filol. Žurn.*	Moskva
Vestnik Moskovskogo Universiteta. Serija Filosofija	*Vestn. Moskov. Univ. Ser. Filos.*	Moskva
Vestnik Moskovskogo Universiteta. Serija Geografii	*Vestn. Moskov. Univ. Ser. Geogr.*	Moskva
Vestnik Moskovskogo Universiteta. Serija Istorija	*Vestn. Moskov. Univ. Ser. Ist.*	Moskva
Vestnik Moskovskogo Universiteta. Serija Pravo	*Vestn. Moskov. Univ. Ser. Pravo*	Moskva
Vestnik Moskovskogo Universiteta. Serija Žurnalistika	*Vestn. Moskov. Univ. Ser. Žurnal.*	Moskva
Vestnik obščestvennyh Nauk	*Vestn. obšč. Nauk*	
Vestnik Otdelenija obščestvennyh Nauk (Akademija Nauk Gruzinskoj SSR)	*Vestn. Otdel. obšč. Nauk (Akad. Nauk Gruz. SSR)*	Tbilisi
Vestnik sel'skohozjajstvennoj Nauki	*Vestn. sel'sk.-Hoz. Nauki*	Moskva
Vestnik Statistiki	*Vestn. Statist.*	Moskva
Vestnik Zoologi	*Vestn. Zool.*	Moskva
Vie et Sciences économiques	*Vie Sci. écon.*	Paris
Vie sociale	*Vie soc.*	Paris
Vierteljahresberichte	*Vierteljahresberichte*	Hannover
Vierteljahreshefte für Zeitgeschichte	*Vjh. Zeitgesch.*	Stuttgart
Vierteljahreshefte zur Wirtschaftsforschung	*Vjh. Wirtsch.-Forsch.*	Berlin
Vita sociale	*Vita soc.*	Firenze
Vivant univers	*Vivant univers*	Namur
Vnešnaja Torgovlja	*Vnešn. Torg.*	Moskva
Voprosy Antropologii	*Vopr. Antropol.*	Moskva
Voprosy Ėkonomiki	*Vopr. Ėkon.*	Moskva
Voprosy Geografii	*Vopr. Geogr.*	Moskva
Voprosy Istorii	*Vopr. Ist.*	Moskva
Voprosy Istorii KPSS	*Vopr. Ist. KPSS*	Moskva

Voprosy naučnogo Ateizma. Institut naučnogo Ateizma. Akademii obščestvennyh Nauk pri CK KPSS	*Vopr. nauč. Ateizma*	Moskva
Vozes. Revista católica de Cultura	*Vozes*	Petropolis
Waffen- und Kostümkunde. Zeitschrift der Gesellschaft für historische Waffen- und Kostümkunde	*Waffen- u. Kostümkunde*	München
Washington Monthly	*Washington Mthly*	Washington
Weltwirtschaftliches Archiv	*Weltwirtsch. Archiv*	Kiel
Western economic Journal	*West. econ. J.*	Los Angeles, Calif.
Western political Quarterly	*West. polit. Quart.*	Salt Lake City, Utah
Wiadomości statystyczne	*Wiadom. statyst.*	Warszawa
Więż	*Więż*	Warszawa
Wirtschaft und Recht	*Wirtsch. u. Recht*	Zürich
Wirtschaft und Statistik	*Wirtsch. u. Statist.*	Stuttgart
Wirtschaftswissenschaft	*Wirtsch.-Wiss.*	Berlin
Wissenschaftliche Zeitschrift der Karl-Marx-Universität Leipzig Gesellschafts- und sprachwissenschaftliche Reihe	*Wiss. Z. Univ. Leipzig ges.- u. sprachwiss. R.*	Leipzig
World Politics	*Wld Polit.*	Princeton, N. J.
World today	*Wld today*	London
WWI Mitteilungen	*WWI Mitt.*	Köln
Yale economic Essays	*Yale econ. Essays*	New Haven, Conn.
Yale Review	*Yale R.*	New Haven, Conn.
Yamanashi Daigaku Kyôikugakubu Kenkyûhokoku	*Yamanashi Daigaku Kyôikugakubu Kenkyûhokoku*	Kôfu
Yearbook of agricultural Cooperation	*Yb. agric. Coop.*	Oxford
Yorkshire Bulletin of economic and social Research	*Yorkshire B. econ. soc. Res.*	Manchester
Yritystalous	*Yritystalous*	[Suomi]
Yugoslav Survey	*Yugosl. Surv.*	Belgrad
Zagadnienia Ekonomiki rolnej	*Zagadn. Ekon. roln.*	Warszawa
Zbornik pravnog Fakulteta u Zagrebu	*Zb. prav. Fak. Zagrebu*	Zagreb
Zeitschrift für Archäologie	*Z. Archäol.*	Berlin
Zeitschrift für ausländische Landwirtschaft	*Z. ausländ. Landwirtsch.*	Frankfurt-am-Main
Zeitschrift für ausländische öffentliches Recht und Völkerrecht	*Z. ausländ. öff. Völkerrecht*	Stuttgart
Zeitschrift für Betriebswirtschaft	*Z. Betriebswirtsch.*	Wiesbaden
Zeitschrift für Ethnologie	*Z. Ethnol.*	Braunschweig
Zeitschrift für Geschichtswissenschaft	*Z. Geschichtswiss.*	Berlin
Zeitschrift für Nationalökonomie	*Z. nat.-Ökon.*	Wien-New York
Zeitschrift für Politik	*Z. Polit.*	Köln-Wien-Zürich
Zeitschrift für Religions- und Geistesgeschichte	*Z. Relig.- u. Geistesgesch.*	Köln
Zeitschrift für Slawistik	*Z. Slawistik*	Berlin
Zeitschrift für Volkskunde	*Z. Volksk.*	Stuttgart
Zeitschrift für würtembergische Landesgeschichte	*Z. württemb. Landesgesch.*	Stuttgart
Zeitschrift für den Erdkundeunterricht	*Z. Erdkundeunterricht*	Berlin
Zeitschrift für die gesamte Staatswissenschaft	*Z. ges. Staatswiss.*	Tübingen
Zeitschrift für die neutestamentliche Wissenschaft	*Z. neutest. Wiss.*	Berlin

Zentralasiatische Studien des Seminars für Sprach- und Kulturwissenschaft Zentralasiens der Universität Bonn	*Zentralasiat. Stud. Seminars Sprach- u. Kulturwiss. Zentralasiens Univ. Bonn*	Wiesbaden
Zeszyty naukowe	*Zesz. nauk.*	Warszawa
Zeszyty naukowe Szkoły głównej Planowania i Statystyki	*Zesz. nauk. Szkoły główn. Plan. Statyst.*	Warszawa
Zeszyty naukowe wyższej Szkoły ekonomicznej w Katowicach	*Zesz. nauk. wyższ. Szkoły ekon. Katowic.*	Katowice
Zeszyty naukowe wyższej Szkoły ekonomicznej w Sopocie	*Zesz. nauk. wyższ. Szkoły ekon. Sopocie*	Sopot
Znanie-Sila	*Znanie-Sila*	Moskva
Zukunfts- und Friedensforschung	*Zukunfts- u. Friedenforsch.*	Hannover
Žurnalist	*Žurnalist*	Moskva
Žurnalistika v Sibiri (Irkutskij gosudarstvennyj Universitet)	*Žurnal. Sibiri (Irkutsk. gos. Univ.)*	Irkutsk
Zvezda Vostoka	*Zvezda Vostoka*	[SSSR]

CLASSIFICATION SCHEME
PLAN DE CLASSIFICATION

D   **Social control and communication**
          Contrôle social, communication sociales

A HISTORY AND ORGANIZATION OF SOCIAL STUDIES
HISTOIRE ET ORGANISATION DES ÉTUDES SOCIOLOGIQUES

A.1 HISTORICAL DEVELOPMENT
HISTOIRE DE LA SOCIOLOGIE

[See also / Voir aussi: **B.4**; 24, 61, 357, 1749, 3638, 4046]

1 'ABDEL RAHIM, 'A. M. *Tatawwûr al-fikr al-ijtimâ'i* (Development of sociology). al-Qâhirat Maktaba al-Anjlû al-Miŝrîya, 69, 230 p.

2 Bibl. XIX-1. ABRAMS, P. *The origins of British sociology, 1834-1914; an essay with selected papers.* Cr: J. W. PETRAS, *Amer. sociol. R.* 34(6), dec 69 : 961-962.

3 ALLPORT, G. W. "The historical background of modern social psychology", in: G. LINDZEY, E. ARONSON (eds.). *The handbook of social psychology.* New ed. Vol. I. Reading, Mass., Addison-Wesley, 68 : 1-80.

4 ASPLUND, J. (ed.). *Sociologiska teorier. Studier i sociologins historia* (Sociological theories. Studies on history of sociology). 3rd rev. enl. ed. Stockholm, Almqvist och Wiksell, 70, 306 p.

5 FURUTA, H., SAKUTA, K., IKUMATSU, K. (eds.). *Kindainihon shakaishisô shi* (History of modern Japanese social thought). Tôkyô, Yûhikaku, 68, 340 p.

7 Bibl. XIX-7. MITCHELL, G. D. *A hundred years of sociology.* CR: W. J. CAHNMAN, *Amer. sociol. R.* 35(2), apr 70 : 351-352; B. PYM, *Brit. J. Sociol.* 20(4), dec 69 : 463.

8 PANKOKE, E. *Sociale Bewegung, sociale Frage, sociale Politik; Grundfragen der deutschen Socialwissenschaft im 19 Jahrhundert* (Social movement, social question, social policy; basic problems of 19th century German social sciences). Stuttgart, E. Klett, 70, 288 p.

9 PÉRIGNON, S. "Note sur la sociologie positiviste et le 'socialisme philosophique' au XIXᵐᵉ siècle", *Homme et Soc.* 14, oct-nov-dec 69 : 179-185.

10 SWINGEWOOD, A. "Origins of sociology: the case of the Scottish enlightenment", *Brit. J. Sociol.* 21(2), jun 70 : 164-180.

A.2 TEACHING
ENSEIGNEMENT

[See also / Voir aussi: 30, 2802]

11 ALBORNOZ, O. "Universidad y sociología en Venezuela" (University and sociology in Venezuela), *Apostes* 18, oct 70 : 68-97.

12 CORES TRASMONTE, B. "La planificación académica del saber sociológico" (Academic planning of sociological knowledge), *R. esp. Opin. públ.* 19, jan-mar 70 : 125-163.

13 DROR, Y. "Teaching of policy sciences: design for a university doctorate program", *Soc. Sci. Inform./Inform. Sci. soc.* 9(2), apr 70 : 101-122.

14 "Enseñanza de la demografía en el Paraguay (La)" (Teaching of demography in Paraguay), *R. parag. Sociol.* 6(16), sep-oct 69 : 134-136.

15 FRIEDLAND, W. H. "Making sociology relevant: a teaching-research program for undergraduates", *Amer. Sociologist* 4(2), mai 69 : 104-110.

16 KELLUM, D. F. *The social studies; myths and realities.* New York, Sheed and Ward, 69, 157 p.

17 KNUDSEN, D., VAUGHAN, T. R. "Quality in graduate education: a re-evaluation of the rankings of sociology departments in the Cartter report", *Amer. Sociologist* 4(1), feb 69 : 12-19. [USA.]

18   Krug, M. M.; Poster, J. B.; Gillies, W. B. III. *The new social studies; analysis of theory and materials.* Itasca, F. E. Peacock Publishers, 70, 341 p.
19   März, F. (ed.). *Soziale und politische Erziehung* (Social and political education). Bad Heilbrunn/Obb., Klinkhardt, 70, 224 p. [Germany, BR.]
20   Oromaner, M. J. "A note on analytical properties and prestige of Sociology departments", *Amer. Sociologist* 5(3), 1970 : 240-244. [USA]

A.3   CURRENT TRENDS AND ACTIVITIES
TENDANCES ET ACTIVITÉS

[See also / Voir aussi: 79, 109, 115, 120, 168, 530, 750, 1265, 1267, 1735, 2008, 2187, 2232, 2270, 2685, 2705, 2725, 2990, 3302, 3364, 3407, 3537, 3638, 3652, 4044, 4438, 4486, 4509, 4638, 4865, 5169]

21   Bango, J. F. "Sociology in Central Europe", *Docum. Europ. centr.* 8(1), jan-feb 70 : 3-19.
22   Basharat Ali, M. *Comparative sociology; the study of American, German, Russian and Quranic sociology.* Karachi, Jamiyatul Falah Publications, 69, v-94 p.
23   Behavioral and Social Sciences Survey Committee. *The behavioral and social sciences; outlook and need; a report.* Englewood Cliffs, N. J., Prentice-Hall, 69, xv-320 p. CR: A. Leiserson, *Amer. polit. R.* 64(3), sep 70 : 922-924; P. M. Hauser, W. A. Gouldner, C. P. Loomis, K. Lutterman, *Amer. sociol. R.* 35(2), apr 70 : 329-341.
24   Belvederi, R. "La sociologia in Olanda: origine e sviluppo" (Sociology in the Netherlands: origin and development), *Quad. Sci. soc.* 8(1-2), 1969 : 13-24.
25   Benseler, F. (ed.). Der *Positivismusstreit in der deutschen Soziologie* (The controversy on positivism in German sociology). Neuwied-Berlin, Lucjterhand 69, 347 p.
26   Breznik, D. "Demografska istraživanja u Jugoslaviji i u svetu" (Demographic research in Yugoslavia and in the world), *Stanovništvo* 7(3-4), jul-dec 69 : 149-163.
27   Centro Latino Americano de Pesquisas de Ciencias Sociais. Serviço de Documentação. *Levantamento das pesquisas sociais em curso na América Latina (resultados provisórios)* (Directory of social research in process in Latin America (provisional results). Rio de Janeiro, Centro Latino-Americano de Pesquisas em Ciências Sociais, Serviço de Documentação, 69, 59 l.
28   Cerutti, F. "Marxismo e sociologia nella Repubblica federale tedesca" (Marxism and sociology in the German Federal Republic), *Belfagor* 24(6), 30 nov 69 : 633-652.
29   Chesneaux, J. "Le mouvement des 'radical caucuses' dans les sciences humaines aux États-Unis", *Homme et Soc.* 16, apr-mai-jun 70 : 3-26.
30   Connor, D. M.; Curtis, J. E. *Sociology and anthropology in Canada. Some characteristics of the disciplines and their current university programs.* Montreal, Canadian Sociology and Anthropology Association, 70, vii-92 p.
31   Diegues Júnior, M. "As ciencias sociais e o planejamento nacional na América latina" (The social sciences and national planning in Latin America), *Anu. Sociol. Pueblos ibér.* (4), 1968 : 112-119.
32   Dunn, S. P. *Sociology in the U.S.S.R.—a collection of readings from Soviet sources.* White Plains, International Arts and Sciences Press, 69, v-281 p.
33   Espinosa Zavallos, J. "La sociología en el Ecuador" (Sociology in Ecuador), *Anu. Sociol. Pueblos ibér.* (4), 1968 : 29-46.
34   *Estado de las ciencias sociales en la Argentina (El)* (The state of social sciences in Argentina). Buenos Aires, Instituto Torcuato di Tella, Centro de Investigaciones Sociales, 69, 78 p.
35   Fals Borda, O. "Ciencia propia y colonialismo intelectual" (Native science and intellectual colonialism), *Anu. Sociol. Pueblos ibér.* (4), 1968 : 47-70. [Latin American sociology.]
36   Fox, R. G. "Avatars of Indian research", *Comp. Stud. Soc. Hist.* 12(1), jan 70 : 59-72. [On social change in India.]
37   Friedman, S. "Trends in research: two major surveys", *Soc. Sci. Inform./Inform. Sci. soc.* 9(2), apr 70 : 83-100.
38   Fugedi, E. "A középkori Magyarország történeti demogràfiàjànak mai àllàsa" (Present situation of historical demography of medieval Hungary), *Demografia* 12(4), 1969 : 500-507.

39   GANÓN, I. "La sociología en el Uruguay" (Sociology in Uruguay), *Anu. Sociol. Pueblos ibér.* (4), 1968 : 5-28.

40   GERLACH, H. M.; LÖWE, B. P. "Politik, Philosophie und Soziologie im westdeutschen staatsmonopolistischen System" (Politics, philosophy and sociology of the West German State monopoly capitalist system), *Dtsche Z. Philos.* 18(6), 1970 : 629-653.

41   GODOY, H. H. "El desarrollo de las ciencias sociales en la década de 1970" (Development of social sciences in the 1970 decade), *R. latinoamer. Cienc. polít.* 1(1), apr 70 : 7-19. [Latin Americia.]

42   GOULDNER, A. W. *The coming crisis of Western sociology.* New York, Basic Books, 70, xv-528 p.

43   HARRIS, F. R. (comp.). *Social science and national policy.* Chicago, Aldine Publishing Co., 70, 152 p. [USA.]

44   HERSENI, T. "Noi orientăriiñ ştiinţele sociale industriale" (New orientations in industrial social sciences), *Progr. Ştiin.* 5(9), sep 69 : 388-392. [Rumania.]

45   IANNI, O. "Sociologie et dépendance scientifique en Amérique latine", *Soc. Sci. Inform./Inform. Sci. soc.* 9(4), aug 70 : 95-112.

46   KOLAJA, J. "La sociologia in Cecoslovacchia" (Sociology in Czechoslovakia), *Rass. ital. Sociol.* 11(2), apr-jun 70 : 281-294.

47   KOSCHWITZ, H. "Zur Entwicklung der soziologischen Forschung und Wissenschaft in der Sowjetunion" (On the development of sociological research and science in the Soviet Union), *Kölner Z. Soziol. soz. Psychol.* 22(3), sep 70 : 501-519.

48   KRATOCHWIL, G. "Estado actual de la sociología en Argentina" (Present situation of sociology in Argentina), *R. latinoamer. Sociol.* 6(1), mar 70 : 167-176.

49   KRAUSZ, E. *Sociology in Britain; a survey of research.* London, B. T. Batsford,—New York, Columbia University Press, 69, x-222 p. CR: G. D. MITCHELL, *Brit. J. Sociol.* 21(1), mar 70 : 115-116.

50   LANE, D. "Ideology and sociology in the USSR", *Brit. J. Sociol.* 21(1), mar 70 : 43-51.

51   MAISON DES SCIENCES DE L'HOMME. Service d'Échange d'Informations Scientifiques. "Surveys of research in the social sciences, 1968-1969/États des recherches en sciences sociales, 1968-1969", *Soc. Sci. Inform./Inform. Sci. soc.* 9(1), feb 70 : 197-214.

52   MARKIEWICZ, W. "La sociologie polonaise d'aujourd'hui", *Perspect. polon.* 19(6), 1970 : 23-35.

53   MARKIEWICZ-LAGNEAU, J. "Une sociologie nouvelle ou une sociologie naissante ? Le cas soviétique", *Homme et Soc.* 14, oct-nov-dec 69 : 113-126.

54   MARSAL, J. F. "Sobre la investigación social institucional en las actuales circonstancias de América Latina" (On institutional social research under present circumstances in Latin America), *R. latinoamer. Sociol.* 6(1), mar 70 : 144-157.

55   "Marxistisch-leninistische Soziologie im entwickelten gesellschaftlichen System des Sozialismus in der DDR (Die)" (Marxist-Leninist sociology in the developing social system of socialism in the DDR), *Wirtsch.-Wiss.* 17(12), dec 69 : 1816-1870.

56   MORGAN, G. J. "The development of sociology and social gospel in America", *Sociol. Anal.* 30(1), 1969 : 42-53.

57   OROMANER, M. J. "Comparison of influentials in contemporary American and British sociology: a study in the internationalization of sociology", *Brit. J. Sociol.* 21(3), sep 70 : 324-332.

58   PEPER, B. "Venster op de Noorse sociologie" (A view on Norwegian Sociology), *Sociol. Gids* 17(1), jan-feb 70 : 48-57.

59   QUINTERO, R. "La sociología y la antropología en la Venezuela actual" (Sociology and anthropology in present-day Venezuela), *Econ. Cienc. soc.* 11(3), jul-sep 69 : 5-18.

60   REEVES, S. C.; DUDLEY, M. *New Guinea social science field research and publications 1962-67.* Canberra, New Guinea Research Unit, Australian National University, 69, 215 p.

61   ROACH, J. L. "The radical sociology movement: a short history and commentary", *Amer. Sociologist* 5(3), 1970 : 224-233.

62   RODINGEN, H. "Die gegenwärtige rechts- und sozialphilosophische Diskussion in der Sowjetunion" (The current discussion on legal and social philosophy in the Soviet Union), *Archiv Rechts-u. soz.-Philos.* 56(2), 1970 : 209-244.

63   ROSENMAYER, L.; HÖLLINGER, S. (eds.). *Soziologie Forschung in Österreich; Methoden, theoretische Konzepte, praktische Verwertung* (Sociology research in Austria: methods, theoretical concepts, practical uses). Wien, Verlag Hermann Böhlhaus, 69, viii-631 p.

3

64   Schindeler, F.; Lanphier, C. M. "Social science research and parcipatory democracy
      in Canada", *Canad. publ. Adm.* 12(4), 1969 : 481-498.
65   Stahl, H. H. "L'expérience méthodique et technique de l'école roumaine de sociologie",
      R. roum. Sci. soc. Sér. Sociol. 14, 1970 : 15-28.
66   Stouthard, P. C. "Sociological research in the Netherlands", *Soc. Wetensch.* 13(2),
      1970 : 134-138.
67   Tomovic, V. A. "Historical materialism or sociology in Yugoslavia", *Canad. Slavonic
      Pap.* 11(2), 1969 : 199-211.
68   Unesco. Département des sciences sociales. *Tendances principales de la recherche dans les
      sciences sociales et humaines.* Paris, Mouton, 70, 988 p.
69   Urbanek, R. "Sociology in Czechoslovakia", *Soc. Res.* 37(1), 1970 : 129-146.
70   Wane, Y. "Réflexions sur la recherche sociologique en milieu africain", *C. Ét. afr.* 10(3),
      1970 : 384-406.

A.4   ORGANIZATION OF RESEARCH ACTIVITIES: INSTITUTES, AGENCIES, COUNCILS
ORGANISATION DES RECHERCHES: INSTITUTS, BUREAUX, CONSEILS

[See also / Voir aussi: 54, 94, 148, 161, 912, 3633, 4370]

71   Amann, R. "The Soviet research and development system: the pressures of academic
      tradition and rapid industrialisation", *Minerva* 8(2), 1970 : 217-241.
72   Bernardo, R. M.; Worcester, O. A. "Pour une politique rationnelle des rémunérations
      dans les grandes universités des pays en voie de développement", *R. int. Sci. soc.* 22(2),
      1970 :
73   Bibl. xix-66. Boalt, G. *The sociology of research.* CR: W. O. Hagstrom, *Amer. J. Sociol.*
      75(6), mai 70 : 1047-1048; C. Fisher, *Amer. sociol. R.* 35(2), apr 70 : 354.
74   Boalt, G.; Lantz, H. *Universities and research. Observations on the United States and
      Sweden.* Stockholm, Almqvist and Wiksell, 70, 157 p.
75   Campbell, A. "Problèmes de politique du personnel dans les centres de recherche so-
      ciale", *R. int. Sci. soc.* 22(2), 1970 :
76   Cherns, A. B. "Les rapports entre les institutions de recherche et les utilisateurs de
      la recherche", *R. int. Sci. soc.* 22(2), 1970 : 249-268.
77   "Comité d'organisation des recherches appliquées sur le développement économique
      et social [Cordes]", *R. franç. Sociol.* 11(3), jul-sep 70 : 406-420.
78   "Coopération internationale pour le développement des recherches de sciences sociales
      (La)", *R. int. Sci. soc.* 22(1), 1970 : 166-170.
79   Cornblit, O. "Les facteurs qui influent sur la productivité scientifique: le cas de l'Amé-
      rique latine", *R. int. Sci. soc.* 22(2), 1970 : 269-292. [La recherche sociologique.]
80   Crawford, E. T.; Biderman, A. D. "Paper money: trends of research sponsorship in
      American sociology journals", *Soc. Sci. Inform./Inform. Sci. soc.* 9(1), feb 70 : 51-77.
81   Lécuyer, B. P. "L'apport des sciences sociales à l'orientation de l'activité nationale",
      R. int. Sci. soc. 22(2), 1970 : 293-331.
82   Lefer, P.; Querette, M.; Spindler, J. P. "Aperçu sur les moyens consacrés aux re-
      cherches en sciences sociales et humaines en France", *Progr. scient.* 136, dec 69 : 2-15.
83   Lyons, G. M. *The uneasy partnership; social science and the Federal Government in the
      twentieth century.* New York, Russell Sage Foundation, 69, xvi-394 p. CR: B. Barber,
      Amer. J. Sociol. 76(1), jul 70 : 169-171. [USA.]
84   Maison des Sciences de L'homme. Service d'Échange d'Informations Scientifiques.
      *Répertoire national des chercheurs: sciences sociales et humaines. I. Ethnologie, Linguis-
      tique. Psychologie. Psychologie sociale. Sociologie. II. Démographie. Géographie humaine.
      Science économique. Science politique.* Paris, Documentation française, 69, 252 p.,
      1970, 244 p. [France.]
85   Mareski, S. "Organización y programa de trabajo del Centro Paraguayo de Documenta-
      ción social" (Organization and work plan of the Paraguayan Center for Social Docu-
      mentation), *R. parag. Sociol.* 6(16), sep-oct 69 : 132-133.
86   Meurle-Belfrage, K.; Biderman, A. " 'Trends of research in American sociology
      journals': a critique and a reply", *Soc. Sci. Inform./Inform. Sci. soc.* 9(2), apr 70 : 35-40.

87   ORCUTT, G. H. "Data, research, and government", *Amer. econ. R.* 60(2), mai 70 *Pap. and Proc.*: 132-137.

88   RIPERT, A. "Le Département audio-visuel du Centre d'études sociologiques. Activités de recherche 1969-1970", *R. franç. Sociol.* 11(3), jul-sep 70 : 421-427. [France.]

89   ROY, P.; FLIEGEL, F. C. "La recherche en collaboration dans les pays en voie de développement: éléments nationaux et éléments extérieurs", *R. int. Sci. soc.* 22(3), 1970 : 551-571.

90   SCHILLER, T. *Stiftungen im gesellschaftlichen Prozess; ein politikwissenschaftlicher Beitrag zu Recht, Soziologie und Sozialgeschichte der Stiftungen in Deutschland* (Foundations in the social process; a political science contribution to law, sociology and social history of foundations in Germany). Baden-Baden, Nomos Verlagsgesellschaft, 69, 233 p.

91   TREUNER, P. "Regionalforschung in Nordamerika. Eindrücke von einer Studienreise" (Regional research in North America. Impressions from a study trip), *Jb. soz.-Wiss.* 30(3), 1969 : 342-355.

92   TRIST, E. "Les institutions de recherche sociale: types, structure, envergure", *R. int. Sci. soc.* 22(2), 1970 : 332-360.

A.5   SOCIOLOGICAL MEETINGS, CONFERENCES, CONGRESSES, ASSOCIATIONS
CONGRÈS SOCIOLOGIQUES, COLLOQUES, CONFÉRENCES, ASSOCIATIONS

[See also / Voir aussi: 684, 836, 1266, 1504, 3133, 4048, 4468, 4826, 4940, 4946]

93   "Congrès (VIIᵉ) mondial de sociologie, Varna (Bulgarie), 14-19 septembre 1970" *Homme et Soc.* 16, apr-mai-jun 70 : 357-359.

94   "Congreso (XXII) del Instituto Internacional de Sociología" (XXII Congress of the International Institute of Sociology), *Bol. urug. Sociol.* 8(15-16-17), dec 69 : 183.

95   "Congreso (El IX) Latinoamericano de Sociología" (The IXth Latin American Sociology Congress), *Bol. urug. Sociol.* 8(15-16-17), dec 69 : 35-43.

96   "Congress (Seventh) of the European Society for Rural Sociology", *Sociol. rur.* 10(4), 1970 : 295-396. [Münster/Westfalia, 10-14 aug 1970, GFR.]

97   COQUERY-VIDROVITCH, C. "Congrès international des études africaines. Montréal, 15-18 octobre 1969", *Homme et Soc.* 15, jan-feb-mar 70 : 363-366.

98   KRAMBACH, K.; SCHMIDT, H. "Tage der marxistisch-leninistischen Soziologie in der DDR" (Marxist-Leninist sociology days in the German Democratic Republic), *Wirtsch.-Wiss.* 18(3), mar 70 : 416-446. [25-27 nov. 1969.]

99   SIDDIQUI, M.A.K. "A report on the Seminar on social and cultural profile of Calcutta, January 22-23, 1970", *East. Anthropol.* 23(2), mai-aug 70 : 179-186.

A.6   TEXTBOOKS AND MANUALS
MANUELS ET OUVRAGES DIDACTIQUES

100   ALBERTI, B. M. *Curso de sociología* (Course in sociology). Buenos Aires, Editorial El Coloquio, 1970, 288 p.

101   ANDERSON, C. H. (ed.). *Sociological essays and research; introductory readings.* Homewood, Ill., Dorsey Press, 70, xi-379 p.

102   Bibl. XIX-103. BIESANZ, J.; BIESANZ, M. *Introduction to sociology.* CR: J. T. RICHARDSON, *Amer. sociol. R.* 35(3), jun 70 : 612-613.

103   CASTELLAN, Y. *Initiation à la psychologie sociale.* Paris, A. Colin, 70, 268 p.

104   CAZENEUVE, J.; VICTOROFF, D. *La sociologie.* Paris, Denoël, 70, 544 p.

105   COLLINS, B. E.; ASHMORE, R. D. *Social psychology; social influence, attitude change, group processes, and prejudice.* Reading, Mass., Addison-Wesley Publishing Co., 70, vii-389 p.

106   DEAN, D. G. (comp.). *Dynamic social psychology; toward appreciation and replication.* Consulting ed. P. I. ROSE. New York, Random House, 69, xiv-620 p.

107   DOUGLAS, J. D. (ed.). *The impact of sociology; readings in the social sciences.* New York, Appleton-Century-Crofts, 70, viii-280 p.

5

108   DURAND, G. *Les grands textes de la sociologie moderne. Recueil méthodique.* Paris, Bordas, 69, 322 p. CR: R. PRÉVOST, *R. franç. Sociol.* 11(3), jul-sep 70 : 451-432.

109   DUVIGNAUD, J. (comp.). *Anthologie des sociologues français contemporains.* Paris, Presses universitaires de France, 70, 254 p.

110   ENGELMANN, H. O. *Sociology: a guided study text.* Dubuque, Ia., W. C. Brown Book Co., 69, 430 p. CR: W. C. WEINSTEIN, *Amer. sociol. R.* 35(1), feb 70 : 189-190.

111   FREEDMAN, J. L.; CARLSMITH, J. M.; SEARS, D. O. *Social psychology.* Englewood Cliffs, N. J., Prentice-Hall, 70, xvii-493 p.

112   GALLINO, L. *Questioni di sociologia* (Questions of sociology). 2nd rev. enl. ed. Milano, Edizioni di Comunità, 69, xx-256 p.

113   Bibl. XIX-111. GOLDTHORPE, J. E. *An introduction to sociology.* CR: A. N. COUSINS, *Amer. sociol. R.* 34(6), dec 69 : 1024-1025.

114   HEGEDUS, A. *Études sociologiques.* Paris, Anthropos; Budapest, Corvina, 69, 353 p. CR: J. MARKIEWICZ-LAGNEAU, *R. franç. Sociol.* 11(2), apr-jun 70 : 264-266.

115   JODELET, D.; VIET, J.; BESNARD, P. *Une discipline en mouvement: la psychologie sociale.* Préf. de S. Moscovici. Paris, Mouton, 70, 467 p.

116   LEMAINE, G.; LEMAINE, J. M. (comp.). *Psychologie sociale et expérimentation.* Paris, Mouton, 69, 360 p.

117   LENSKI, G. E. *Human societies; a macrolevel introduction to sociology.* New York, McGraw-Hill, 70, xv-525 p.

118   LINDESMITH, A. R.; STRAUSS, A. L. *Readings in social psychology.* New York, Holt, Rinehart and Winston, 69, ix-367 p.

119   LINDGREN, H. C. *An introduction to social psychology.* New York, John Wiley and Sons, 69, 378 p. CR: R. L. BURGESS, *Amer. sociol. R.* 35(3), jun 70 : 611-612.

120   LINDGREN, H. C. (ed.). *Contemporary research in social psychology: a book of readings.* New York, J. Wiley and Sons, 69, 653 p. CR: S. P. SPITZER, *Amer. sociol. R.* 35(2), apr 70 : 354-356.

121   LINDZEY, G.; ARONSON, E. (eds.). *The handbook of social psychology.* New ed. Reading, Mass., Addison-Wesley, 68-69, Vol. I, xv-653 p.; Vol. II, xv-819 p.; Vol. xiii, xiii-978 p.

122   LOUIS, V. *Einführung in die Individualpsychologie* (Introduction to psychology of the individual). Bern-Stuttgart, Haupt, 69, 86 p.

123   MAHIEU, J. M. DE. *Tratado de sociología general* (A treatise on general sociology). Buenos-Aires, Editorial Sudestata, 69, 412 p.

124   MANN, L. *Social psychology.* Sydney-New York, Wiley, 69, xiii-165 p.

125   Bibl. XIX-117. McKEE, J. B. *Introduction to sociology.* CR: R. P. SESSIONS, *Amer. sociol. R.* 35(3), jun 70 : 613-614.

126   McKINNEY, J. C.; TIRYAKIAN, E. A. (eds.). *Theoretical sociology; perspectives and developments.* New York, Appleton-Century-Crofts, Educational Division, 70, viii-538 p.

127   MERCER, B. E.; WANDERER, J. J. *The study of society.* Belmont, Calif., Wadsworth Publishing Co., 70, xi-515 p.

128   MITCHELL, G. D. (ed.). *Sociology: an outline for the intending student.* London, Routledge and K. Paul, 70, vii-212 p.

129   NISBET, R. A. *The social bond; an introduction to the study of society.* New York, Knopf, 70, xix-425 p.

130   OLSON, P. *The study of modern society: perspectives from classic sociology.* New York, Random House, 70, xi-188 p.

131   SCHELLENBERG, J. A. *An introduction to social psychology.* New York, Random House, 70, vii-324 p.

132   SHAW, M. E.; COSTANZO, P. R. *Theories of social psychology.* New York, McGraw-Hill, 70, ix-414 p.

133   SHERIF, M.; SHERIF, C. *Social psychology.* New York, Harper and Row, 69, 616 p. CR: W. SCOTT, *Amer. sociol. R.* 35(4), aug 70 : 819-820.

134   TERRERA, G. A. *Tratado teórico-práctico de sociología* (Theoretical-practical treatise on sociology). Buenos Aires, Plus Ultra, 69, 448 p.

135   VINE, M. V. *An introduction to sociological theory.* New York, D. McKay Co., 69, 382 p. CR: M. M. WILLEY, *Amer. sociol. R.* 35(3), jun 70 : 531-539.

136   Bibl. XIX-131. WALLACE, W. L. (ed.). *Sociological theory: an introduction.* CR: E. ALLARDT, *Acta sociol.* 13(2), 1970 : 135-136.

137 WILKINS, E. J. *An introduction to sociology*. London, Macdonald and Evans, 70, xiv-416 p.

A.7 **REFERENCE BOOKS AND BIBLIOGRAPHIES, COLLECTIONS**
OUVRAGES DE RÉFÉRENCE, BIBLIOGRAPHIES,
COLLECTIONS

[See also / Voir aussi: 51, 60, 289, 318, 661, 1492, 1803, 2071, 2728, 2913, 3031, 3578, 3630, 3642, 3738, 4036, 4489, 4766, 4780, 5075, 5169, 5238]

138 "Analyses bibliographiques, études et notes critiques", *Année sociol.* 19, 1968 : 171-578. [Bibliographie d'ouvrages, classée par domaines: sociologie générale et sociologie politique, sociologie de la connaissance, sociologie et psychologie, morphologie sociale systèmes sociaux et civilisations, sociologie religieuse, sociologie juridique et morale, sociologie économique, sociologie du travail, linguistique.]

139 ARMOR, D. J. "Developments in data analysis systems for the social sciences", *Soc. Sci. Inform./Inform. Sci. soc.* 9(3), jun 70 : 145-171.

140 BENSON, O.; BONJEAN, C. M. "*The Social Science Quarterly*, 1920-1970 : a case history in organizational growth", *Soc. Sci. Quart.* 50(4), mar 70 : 806-825.

141 BERNSDORF, W. (ed.). *Wörterbuch der Soziologie* (Dictionary of sociology). 2nd rev. enl. ed. Stuttgart, F. Enke, 69, xii-1317 p. CR: H. KIESEWETTER, *Kölner Z. Soziol. u. soz.-Psychol.* 22(3), sep 70 : 597-599.

142 "Bibliographie annotée des publications et documents principaux des Nations Unies, concernant la planification du développement (1955-1969)", *J. Planif. Dévelop.* 1, 1970 : 199-240.

143 BISCO, R. L. (ed.). *Data bases, computers, and the social sciences*. New York, Wiley-Interscience, 70, xiii-291 p. [Based on papers presented at the fourth annual conference of the Council of Social-Science Data Archives held at the University of California in Los Angeles in June, 1967.]

144 CORBIN, D. *Open literature publications of the Social Science Department*, 1966-1968. Santa Monica, Calif., Rand Corp., 69, xv-67 p.

145 CRANE, D. "La nature de la communication et des influences dans le domaine scientifique", *R. int. Sci. soc.* 22(1), 1970 : 30-45.

146 CRAWFORD, E. T. (ed.). "The sociology of the social sciences: an international bibliography", *Soc. Sci. Inform./Inform. Sci. soc.* 9(1), feb 70 : 79-93; 9(4), aug 70 : 137-149.

147 EICHHORN, W. *et al.* (eds.). *Wörterbuch der Marxistisch-Leninistischen Soziologie* (Dictionary of Marxist-Leninist sociology). Köln, Westdeutscher Verlag, 69, 535 p.

148 GARCÍA-BOUZA, J. "Actividades de la Comisión de Trabajo sobre Archivo Latinoamericano de Datos del Consejo Latinoamericano de Ciencias Sociales (CLASCO)" (Activities of the working committee on Latin American Data Archives of the Latin American Social Sciences Council), *Amér. lat.* 12(2), apr-jun 69 : 133-144.

149 GRAY, R. A.; VILLMOW, D. *Serial bibliographies in the humanities and social sciences*. Ann Arbor, Pierian Press, 69, xxiv-345 p.

150 HALE, B. M. *The subject bibliography of the social sciences and humanities*. Oxford-New York, Pergamon Press, 70, vii-149 p.

151 HERRERA, E. R. "Cinco revistas de sociología. Un estudio comparativo" (Five sociology reviews. A comparative study), *R. latinoamer. Sociol.* 6(1), mar 70 : 158-167.

152 "India: note on a data-inventory program", *Soc. Sci. Inform./Inform. Sci. soc.* 9(2), apr 70 : 61-68.

153 IOCHI, R.; MIZUTA, H.; FUJIKAWA, M. *Shakai kagaku dokyumenteishon* (Documentation in social sciences). Tôkyô, Maruzen, 68, 464 p.

154 JACQUEY, M. C.; NIELLON, F. *Afrique noire d'expression française: sciences sociales et humaines; guide de lecture*. Paris, Centre d'analyse et de recherche documentaires pour l'Afrique noire; Club des lecteurs d'expression française, 69, vi-301 p.

155 JOLLES, H. M. "Een monument voor tolerantie" (A monument of tolerance), *Mens en Mij* 45(2), mar-apr 70 : 120-128. [The *International Encyclopedia of the Social Sciences*.]

156 "Latin America: report on data inventories in Chile, Argentina and Venezuela", *Soc. Sci. Inform./Inform. Sci. soc.* 9(2), apr 70 : 69-74.

7

157   MAISON DES SCIENCES DE L'HOMME. Service d'Échange d'Informations Scientifiques. *Études africaines. Liste mondiale des périodiques spécialisés/African studies. World list of specialized periodicals.* La Haye, Mouton, 70, 214 p.

158   MARTIN, D. (ed.). *50 key words: sociology.* Richmond, Va., John Knox Press, 70, 84 p.

159   MATCZAK, S. A. *Philosophy; a select, classified bibliography of ethics, economics, law, politics, sociology.* Louvain, Éditions Nauwelaerts; New York, Humanities Press, 70, xxii-308 p.

160   MEYERS, E. D. Jr. "Interactive systems and social science research and instruction", *Soc. Sci. Inform./Inform. Sci. soc.* 9(3), jun 70 : 157-171. [Computers and data processing.]

161   MEYRIAT, J.; BEAUCHET, M. *Guide for the establishment of National Social Sciences Documentation Centres in developing countries.* Paris, Unesco, 69, 72 p.

162   Bibl. XVIII-146. MITCHELL, G. D. (ed.). *A dictionary of sociology.* CR: R. K. KELSALL, *Brit. J. Sociol.* 20(4), dec 69 : 462-463; K. M. BOLTE, *Kölner Z. Soziol. u. soz.-Psychol.* 22(4), dec 70 : 790-791.

163   MUCCHIELLI, A.; MUCCHIELLI, R. *Lexique des sciences sociales.* Paris, Entreprise moderne d'Édition, 69, 196 p.

164   NEEDHAM, C. D.; HERMAN, E. (eds.). *The study of subject bibliography with special reference to the social sciences.* College Park, School of Library and Information Services, University of Maryland, 70, 221 p.

165   O'NEILL ADAMS, M.; DENNIS, J. "Creating local social science data archives", *Soc. Sci. Inform./Inform. Sci. soc.* 9(2), apr 70 : 51-60.

166   "Our first fifty years", *Soc. Sci. Quart.* 50(4), mar 70 : 802-1073. [On the fiftieth anniversary of the *Social Science Quarterly.*]

167   PULLUM, T. W.; ANDERSON, C. A.; HUSBANDS, C. T. "A comparison of book reviewing by the AJS and the ASR", *Amer. J. Sociol.* 75(4, *Part I*), jan 70 : 550-555.

168   ROGGERO, E. "Il contributo della 'Rivista italiana di Sociologia' alla nascita e allo sviluppo della sociologia in Italia" (The contribution of the *Rivista italiana di Sociologia* to the birth and development of sociology in Italy), *Sociologia (Roma)* 4(3), sep 70 : 89-122.

169   SCHOECK, H. *Kleines soziologisches Wörterbuch* (Small sociology dictionary). Freiburg-im Brisgau-Basel-Wien, Herder, 69, 377 p.

170   STEGEMANN, H. "Spezialbibliotheken für die Sozialwissenschaften. Datenbanken für Umfrageforschung" (Specialized libraries in social sciences. Data banks for survey research), *Kölner Z. Soziol. u. soz.-Psychol.* 21(4), dec 69 : 876-885.

171   "Sweden: Geocode. A computer code system for administrative divisions with a boundary-correcting analysis program", *Soc. Sci. Inform./Inform. Sci. soc.* 9(2), apr 70 : 75-81.

172   TEZCAN, M. *Türk sosyoloji bibliyografyasi, 1928-1968* (Turkish sociological bibliography, 1928-1968). Ankara, Başnur Mathaasi, 69, xxviii-1153 p.

173   THEODORSON, G. A.; THEODORSON, A. G. *A modern dictionary of sociology.* New York, Crowell, 69, viii-469 p.

174   THOMSON, W. D. "*Human Organization:* a three-year review (1967-1969)", *Hum. Org.* 29(3), 1970 : 204-222.

175   WHITLEY, R. D. "The operation of science journals: two case studies in British social science", *Sociol. R.* 18(2), jul 70 : 241-258.

A.8   SOCIAL SCIENTISTS
SOCIOLOGUES

A.81   Professional activities
Activités professionnelles

[See also / Voir aussi: 2769, 4353]

176   BARRY, B. M. *Sociologists, economists and democracy.* London, Collier-Macmillan, 70, vi-202 p.

177   BEALS, R. L. *Politics of social research. An inquiry into the ethics and responsibilities of social scientists.* Chicago, Aldine, 69, viii-228 p.

178   BUSINO, G. "Il mestiere di sociologo" (The profession of sociologist), *Rass. ital. Sociol.* 11(1), jan-mar 70 : 7-28. [Also published in French, *C. Vilfredo Pareto* 20, feb 70 : 77-91.]

8

179 CURTIS, J. E.; CONNOR, D. M.; HARP, J. "An emergent professional community; French and English sociologists and anthropologists in Canada", *Soc. Sci. Inform./ Inform. Sci. soc.* 9(4), aug 70 : 113-136.

180 EFFRAT, A. (ed.). "The craft of sociology", *Sociol. Inquiry* 39(2), 1969 : 115-178.

181 GLENN, D.; VILLEMEZ, W. "The productivity of sociologists at 45 American Universities", *Amer. Sociologist* 5(3), 1970 : 244-252.

182 GLENN, N. D.; WEINER, D. "Some trends in the social origins of American sociologists", *Amer. Sociologist* 4(4), 1969 : 291-302.

183 GOVE, W. R. "Should the sociology profession take moral stands on political issues", *Amer. Sociologist* 5(3), 1970 : 221-223.

184 Bibl. XIX-158. HOROWITZ, I. L. *Professing sociology: studies in the life cycle of social science.* CR: G. SJÖBERG, *Acta sociol.* 12(4), 1969 : 241-242; R. COLLINS, *Amer. J. Sociol.* 76(2), sep 70 : 363-365.

185 NATIONAL CLEARINGHOUSE FOR MENTAL HEALTH. *Sociologists and anthropologists; supply and demand in educational institutions and other settings.* Chevy Chase, Md., National Institute of Mental Health, Washington, United States, Government Printing Office, 69, x-164 p.

186 PERROTTA, A.; SANTOLONI, M.; FASOLA-BOLOGNA, A. "Note critiche sul professionismo sociologico" (Critical notes on the sociological professionalism), *Crit. sociol. (Roma)* 15, 1970 : 88-93.

187 RUBEL, M. "Sociologie et utopie", *Année sociol.* 19, 1968 : 243-252. [Mai 1968 en France, et "pourquoi des sociologues ?".]

188 STRAUS, M. A.; RADEL, D. J. "Eminence, productivity, and power of sociologists in various regions", *Amer. Sociologist* 4(1), 1969 : 1-4.

189 WEITZ, R. "The role of the sociologist in rural development", *Sociol. rur.* 10(3), 1970 : 221-236.

A.82   Biographies, obituaries
Notices biographiques et nécrologiques

[See also / Voir aussi: **B.4**; **572**]

190 BEHRENDT, R. F. "Leopold von Wiese", *Kölner Z. Soziol. u. soz.-Psychol.* 22(4), dec 70 : 667-678.

191 BOGARDUS, E. S. "Leopold von Weise, 1876-1969: a personal tribute", *Sociol. soc. Res.* 54(1), oct 69 : 90-93.

192 BOGARDUS, E. S. "Radhakamel Mukerjee as sociologist", *Sociol. soc. Res.* 54(3), apr 70 : 388-399.

193 BRAUDE, L. "Louis Wirth and the locus of sociological commitment", *Amer. Sociologist* 5(3), 1970 : 233-235.

194 CARBONNIER, J. "Gabriel Le Bras, 1891-1970", *Année sociol.* 19, 1968 : 9-11.

195 CAZENEUVE, J. "Paul Hassan Maucorps, 1911-1969", *R. franç. Sociol.* 11(1), jan-mar 70 : 109-110.

196 CONDOMINAS, G. "Paul Mus, sociologue", *C. int. Sociol.* 17(49), jul-dec 70 : 53-68.

197 DAVIDOVITCH, A. "Victor Zoltowski, 1900-1969", *R. franç. Sociol.* 10(4), oct-dec 69 : 524-525.

198 DESROCHE, H. "Gabriel Le Bras, 1891-1970", *Archiv. Sociol. Relig.* 15(29), jan-jun 70 : 3-5.

199 DESROCHE, H. "Gabriel Le Bras. De la sociologie religieuse à une sociologie des religions", *C. int. Sociol.* 17(48), jan-jun 70 : 173-176.

200 DUVIGNAUD, J. "Pierre Francastel", *C. int. Sociol.* 17(48), jan-jun 70 : 176-178.

201 FAUBLÉE, J. "Victor Zoltowski, 1900-1969", *Année sociol.* 19, 1968 : 12-14.

202 FERRAROTTI, F. "Adorno come sociologo" (Adorno as a sociologist), *Crit. sociol.* (Roma) 14, 1970 : 64-69.

203 GABEL, J. "Victor Zoltowski", *C. int. Sociol.* 17(48), jan-jun 70 : 180.

204 GOLDWAY, D. "Howard Selsam, 1903-1970", *Sci. and Soc.* 34(4), 1970 : 385-386.

205 HILGER, D. "Nekrolog Siegfried Landshut, 7.8.1897-8.12.1968", *Kölner Z. Soziol. u. soz.-Psychol.* 22(4), dec 70 : 835-839.

206 HOUTART, F. "Hommage à Gabriel Le Bras", *Soc. Compass* 16(4), 1969 : 434.

9

207   "In memoriam Antoine Oldendorff", *Mens en Mij* 45(2), mar-apr 70 : 73-74.
208   Isambert-Jamati, V. "Paul-H. Maucorps", *C. int. Sociol.* 17(48), jan-jun 70 : 178-179.
209   Jones, F. E. "Howard E. Roseborough, 1919-1969", *Canad. R. Sociol. Anthropol.* 6(3), aug 69 : 188-189.
210   "Kazimierz Szczerba-Likiernik, 1897-1969", *R. franç. Sociol.* 10(4), oct-dec 69 : 522-523.
211   Kühne, O. "Leopold von Wiese: in memoriam", *Soc. Sci. (Winfield)* 45(4), oct 70 : 198-201.
212   Lengyel, P. "Kazimierz Szczerba-Likiernik, 1897-1969", *R. int. Sci. soc.* 22(1), 1970 : 165-166.
213   Lentini, O. "Lucien Goldmann, Bucarest 1913-Parigi 1970" (Lucien Goldmann, Bucarest 1913—Paris, 1970), *Sociologia (Roma)* 4(3), sep 70 : 169-171.
214   Moore, H. "William Lloyd Warner, 26.10.1898-1.6.1970", *Kölner Z. Soziol. u. soz. Psychol.* 22(3), sep 70 : 655-658.
215   Patterson, S. H. "J. J. Hayden, 1894-1970", *Soc. Sci. (Winfield)* 45(4), oct 70 : 228-230.
216   Raum, O. F. "F. Rudolf Lehmann, 1887-1969", *Sociologus* 20(1), 1970 : 1-2.
217   Read, M. "A tribute to Dr J. H. Oldham, 1874-1969", *Africa (London)* 40(2), apr 70 : 113-114.
218   Rioux, M. "Marius Barbeau, 1883-1969", *Canad. R. Sociol. Anthropol.* 6(1), feb 69 : 62.
219   Sauvy, A.; Bourgeois-Pichat, J. "Jean Sutter", *Population* 25(4), jul-aug 70 : 749-758.
220   Sorokin, P. "Nicholas S. Timasheff: in memoriam", *Sociologia (Roma)* 4(2), mai 70 : 193-198.
221   Thrupp, S. L. "Ian Weinberg, 1938-1969", *Comp. Stud. Soc. Hist.* 11(4), oct 69 : 480.
222   Vance, R. B. "Samuel Huntington Hobbs, Jr. 1895-1969", *Soc. Forces* 48(3), mar 70 : 412.

B THEORIES AND METHODS OF SOCIOLOGY
THÉORIES ET MÉTHODES SOCIOLOGIQUES

B.1 DEFINITIONS AND FUNDAMENTAL PROBLEMS OF SOCIOLOGY
DÉFINITIONS ET PROBLÈMES FONDAMENTAUX DE LA SOCIOLOGIE

[See also / Voir aussi: **B.30, B.4, B.5**]

223 ABEL, T. F. *The foundation of sociological theory*. New York, Random House, 70, 258 p.

224 ADORNO, T. W. "Du rapport entre la théorie et l'empirie en sociologie", *Homme et Soc.* 13, jul-aug-sep 69 : 127-133.

225 BADAWÎ, A. S. M. *Naẓarîyât wa-madhâhib 'ijtimâ'iya* (Social theory and doctrine). al-Iskenderîyat, Dâr al'Ma'ârif biMiṣr, 69, 368 p.

226 BATTAGLIA, F. *Cinque saggi intorno alla sociologia* (Five essays about sociology). Roma, Istituto Luigi Sturzo, 69, 182 p.

227 BECKER, H. S. *Sociological work; method and substance*. Chicago, Aldine Publishing Co., 70, x-358 p.

228 BENDIX, R. *Embattled reason; essays on social knowledge*. New York, Oxford University Press, 70, vi-395 p.

229 BERNARDO, G. D. "Logica deontica e scienze sociali" (Deontology and social sciences), *Rass. ital. Sociol.* 11(3), jul-sep 70 : 355-370.

230 BIERSTEDT, R. (ed.). *A design for sociology; scope, objectives, and methods*. Philadelphia, American Academy of Political and Social Science, 69, viii-152 p.

231 BRYANT, C. G. "In defence of sociology: a reply to some contemporary philosophical criticisms", *Brit. J. Sociol.* 21(1), mar 70 : 95-107.

232 BÜHL, W. "Dialektische Soziologie und soziologische Dialektik" (Dialectical sociology and sociological dialectics), *Kölner Z. Soziol. u. soz.-Psychol.* 21(4), dec 69 : 717-746.

233 BURGESS, R. L.; BUSHELL, D. Jr. *Behavioral sociology; the experimental analysis of social process*. New York, Columbia University Press, 69, xiii-418 p.

234 COLLINS, R. "Sociology-building", *Berkeley J. Sociol.* 14, 1969 : 73-84. With "a reply to Collins", by A. L. STINCHCOMBE, *id.* 84-87; a "Comment on Collins" by N. J. SMELSER, *id.* pp. 88-93; and with a "Rejoinder", by R. COLLINS, *id.* pp. 94-98.

235 CONGRÈS MONDIAL DE SOCIOLOGIE (VIᵉ). *Image de l'homme et sociologie contemporaine*. Bruxelles, Éditions de l'Institut de Sociologie de l'Université libre de Bruxelles, 69, 206 p. [Évian, 4-11 septembre 1966.]

236 CRESPI, P. "Prospettive per una teoria sociologica" (Prospects for a sociological theory), *Riv. Sociol.* 6(17), sep-dec 68 : 5-42; 7(18), jan-mar 69 : 7-42.

237 Bibl. XIX-176. CUZZORT, R. P. *Humanity and modern sociological thought*. CR: J. W. PREHN, *Amer. sociol. R.* 35(2), apr 70 : 373-374.

238 DAWE, A. "The two sociologies", *Brit. J. Sociol.* 21(2), jun 70 : 207-218.

239 DEMO, P. "A sociologia a serviço do status quo" (Sociology at the service of the status quo), *Vozes* 63(1), nov 69 : 963-975.

240 DENZIN, N. K. (ed.). *The values of social science*. Chicago, Aldine, 70, 194 p.

241 DEUTSCH, S. E.; HOWARD, J. (eds.). *Where it's at; radical perspectives in sociology*. New York, Harper and Row, 70, xiii-610 p.

242 DOUGLAS, J. D. (ed.). *The relevance of sociology*. New York, Appleton-Century Crofts, 70, xiii-233 p.

243 ENERSTVEDT, R. T. *Dialektikk og samfunnsvitenskap* (Dialectics and social sciences). Oslo, Ny dag, 69, 231 p.

244 ETZKOWITZ, H. "Institution formation sociology", *Amer. Sociologist* 5(2), mai 70: 120-124.

245   FRIEDRICHS, R. W. *A sociology of sociology.* New York, Free Press, 70, xxiii-429 p.
246   GOLDMANN, L. *et al. Dialektiek en maatschappijkritiek* (Dialectics and social criticism). Meppel, Boom, 70, 136 p.
247   HANNAGEN, R. *Realistic sociology; a study of the requirements of order in society.* London, Regency Publ., 69, 271 p.
248   HELLE, H. J. *Soziologie und Symbol; ein Beitrag zur Handlungstheorie und zur Theorie des sozialen Wandels* (Sociology and symbols; a contribution to the theory of action and the theory of social change). Köln, Westdeutscher Verlag, 69, 118 p.
249   HOCHKEPPEL, W. (ed.). *Soziologie zwischen Theorie und Empirie. Soziologische Grundprobleme* (Sociology between theory and empirism. Basic problems of sociology). München, Nymphenburger Verlagshandlung, 70, 237 p.
250   HOROWITZ, D. "Social science or ideology", *Berkeley J. Sociol.* 15, 1970 : 1-10.
251   HULI, D. L. "Systemic dynamic social theory", *Sociol. Quart.* 11(3), 1970 : 351-362. With a reply by H. O. ENGELMANN : 363-365.
252   HUTCHEON, P. D. "Sociology and the objectivity problem", *Sociol. soc. Res.* 54(2), jan 70 : 153-171.
253   KLAGES, H. *Soziologie zwischen Wirklichkeit und Möglichkeit. Plädoyer für eine projektive Soziologie* (Sociology between reality and possibility. Speech for a projective sociology). Köln, Westdeutscher Verlag, 68, 70 p.
254   KURYLEV, A. K. *et al. Iz opyta konkretnyh sociologičeskih issledovanij* (From the experience of concrete sociological studies). Moskva, Moskovs, Univ., 69, 123 p.
255   LACHENMEYER, C. W. "Reduction in sociology: a pseudo-problem", *Pacific sociol. R.* 13(4), 1970 : 211-217. [The reduction of one theory to another.]
256   LANTZ, P. "Critique dialectique et sociologie", *Homme et Soc.* 13, jul-aug-sep 69 : 135-143.
257   Bibl. XVIII-236. LAZARSFELD, P. F. *et al.* (eds.). *The uses of sociology.* CR: T. S. SIMEY, *Brit. J. Sociol.* 20(4), dec 69 : 454-457.
258   LUKIĆ, R. D. *Formalizam u sociologiji* (Formalism and sociology). Beograd, Prosveta, 69, 214 p.
259   MEISSNER, H. *Konvergenztheorie und Realität* (Convergence theory and reality). Berlin, Akademie-Verlag, 69, 178 p.
260   MONGARDINI, C. "Sociologia e azione sociale" (Sociology and social action), *Sociologia (Roma)* 4(3), sep 70 : 61-74.
261   OFSHE, R. (comp.). *The sociology of the possible.* Englewood Cliffs, N. J., Prentice-Hall, 70, xvii-391 p.
262   PARK, P. *Sociology to-morrow: an evaluation of sociological theories in terms of science.* New York, Pegasus, 69, 176 p. CR: J. M. JOHNSON, *Amer. J. Sociol.* 76(1), jul 70 : 175-177.
263   PODGÓRECKI, A. "Five-functions of sociology", *Polish sociol. B.* (1), 1968 : 65-78.
264   RICHTER, M. (comp.). *Essays in theory and history; an approach to the social sciences.* Cambridge, Mass., Harvard University Press, 70, ix-291 p.
265   RIVIÈRE, C. *L'objet social, essai d'épistémologie sociologique.* Paris, M. Rivière, 69, 380 p. CR: J. L. TRISTANI, *C. int. Sociol.* 17(48), jan-jun 70 : 181-182.
266   RUNCIMAN, W. G. *Sociology in its place, and other essays.* Cambridge, Eng., University Press, 70, 236 p.
267   RUVO, V. DE. *Storia e critica sociologica* (History and sociological criticism). Bari, Editoriale universitaria, 69, 123 p.
268   SCHWANENBERG, E. *Soziales Handeln. Die Theorie und ihr Problem* (The social object. Theory and problem). Bern-Stuttgart-Wien, Hans Huber, 70, 287 p.
269   SHARMA, R. N. *Principles of sociology.* New York, Asia Publishing House, 70, xiii-460 p.
270   SHEPARD, P.; MCKINLEY, D. (eds.). *The subversive science. Essays toward a sociology of man.* Boston (Mass.), Houghton Mifflin, 69, x-453 p.
271   SIERKSMA, R. "Naar een nieuwe sociologie" (Towards a new sociology), *Mens en Mij* 45(4), jul-aug 70 : 233-245.
272   SMELSER, N. J.; DAVIS, J. A. (eds.). *Sociology.* Englewood Cliffs, N. J., Prentice-Hall, 69, ix-178 p. CR: P. M. HAUSER; A. W. GOULDNER; C. P. LOOMIS; K. LUTTERMAN, *Amer. sociol. R.* 35(2), apr 70 : 329-341.
273   "Some radical perspectives in sociology", *Sociol. Inquiry* 40(1), 1970 : 3-166. [A special issue.]

274 SOMERS, R. H. "On problem-finding in the social sciences: a concept of active social science", *Berkeley J. Sociol.* 15, 1970 : 48-63. With a comment on Somers: "Critical or technical sociology ?", by R. S. WARNER, *id.*, 64-72; and a rejoinder to Warner: "Technically convincing and critical social science", by R. H. SOMERS, *id.* pp. 73-74.

275 STATERA, G. *La conoscenza sociologica. Aspetti e problemi* (Sociological knowledge. Aspects and problems). Roma, B. Carucci, 70, 278 p.

276 Bibl. XVIII-253. STINCHCOMBE, A. L. *Constructing social theories.* CR: R. H. TURNER; R. W. HODGE, *Amer. sociol. R.* 34(6), dec 69 : 244-249.

277 TOMBERG, F. *Basis und Überbau; sozialphilosophische Studien* (Basis and superstructure: socio-philosophical studies). Neuwied, Luchterhand, 69, 181 p.

278 VREE, J. K. DE. "Opmerkingen over 'theorie' en 'praktijk' " (Remarks on 'theory' and 'practice'), *Soc. Wetensch.* 13(1), 1970 : 12-36.

279 WINTHROP, H. "Does sociology have to be polarized into 'pure' and 'applied' ?" *Canad. R. Sociol. Anthropol.* 6(1), feb 69 : 54-57.

280 ZIMMERMAN, C. C. "A critique of the philosophy of current sociology", *Soc. Sci. (Winfield)* 45(1), jan 70 : 30-39. Also published in *Rass. ital. Sociol.* 11(2), apr-jun 70 : 261-273.

B.2 SOCIOLOGY, ITS SCOPE AND RELATIONS TO OTHER SCIENCES
DOMAINE DE LA SOCIOLOGIE ET RAPPORTS AVEC LES AUTRES SCIENCES

[See also / Voir aussi: 3640]

281 CHADWICK-JONES, J. K. "Recent interdisciplinary exchanges and the use of analogy in social psychology", *Hum. Relat.* 23(4), aug 70 : 253-261.

282 EMMET, D. M.; McINTYRE, A. (eds.). *Sociological theory and philosophical analysis.* New York, Macmillan, 70, xxiv-232 p.

283 "Focus—human biology and the social sciences", *Soc. Res.* 36(4), 1969 : 497-605.

284 GOLDMANN, L. "Économie et sociologie: à propos du traité d'économie politique d'Oscar Lange", *Homme Soc.* 14, oct-nov-dec 69 : 49-62.

285 GROSSACK, M. M.; GARDNER, H. *Man and men; social psychology as social science.* Scranton, Pa., International Textbook Co., 70, xv-367 p.

286 KLUGER, G.; UNKOVIC, C. M. *Psychology and sociology: an integrated approach to understanding human behavior.* St Louis, Mo., C. V. Mosby Co., 69, 404 p. CR: W. SCOTT, *Amer. sociol. R.* 35(4), aug 70 : 819-820.

287 KULCSÁR, K. "A társadalmi folyamatok a szociologiai és demográfiai kutatásokban" (Social processes in sociological and demographic research), *Demográfia* 13(1-2), 1970 : 9-20. [Hungary.]

288 MAIR, L. *Anthropology and social change.* London, Athlone Press; New York, Humanities Press, 69, 203 p.

289 MAISON DES SCIENCES DE L'HOMME. Service d'Échange d'Informations Scientifiques. "Interdisciplinary relations/Relations interdisciplinaires, 1968-1969", *Soc. Sci. Inform./Inform. Sci. soc.* 9(2), apr 70 : 171-183.

290 PARSONS, T. "Theory in the humanities and sociology", *Daedalus* 99(2), 1970 : 495-523.

291 SCHMOLDERS, G. (ed.). *Wirtschaftstheorie als Verhaltenstheorie* (Economic theory as behavioral theory). Berlin, Duncker und Humblot, 69, 117 p. CR: H. G. KRÜSSELBERG, *Kölner Z. Soziol. u. soz.-Psychol.* 22(4), dec 70 : 814-816.

292 SHAPIRO, D.; CRIDER, A. "Psychophysiological approaches in social psychology", in: G. LINDZEY; E. ARONSON (eds.). *The handbook of social psychology.* New ed. Vol. III. Reading, Mass., Addison-Wesley, 68 : 1-49.

293 Bibl. XIX-223. SHERIF, M.; SHERIF, C. (eds.). *Interdisciplinary relationships in the social sciences.* CR: R. L. HALL, *Amer. sociol. R.* 35(3), jun 70 : 542-543.

294 STEIDL, P. *Soziologie. Bildungsinhalte für Wirtschaft, Erziehung, Sozialdienst und Erwachsenenbildung* (Sociology. Content for economics, education, social service and adult education). Innsbruck, Österreichische Kommissions-buchhandlung in Komm., 69, 171 p.

295   THOMPSON, J. D.; VAN HOUTEN, D. R. *The behavioral sciences; an interpretation.* Menlo
       Park, Calif., Addison-Wesley Publishing Co., 70, xv-268 p.
296   TURKSMA, L. *Sociolog en geschiedenis* (Sociologist and history). Meppel, Boom, 69,
       xvi-287 p.

B.3   METHODOLOGY AND TECHNIQUES OF RESEARCH
       MÉTHODOLOGIE ET TECHNIQUES DE RECHERCHE

B.30   General studies
       Études générales

[See also / Voir aussi: **B.1**, **B.4**; 63, 281, 483, 487, 579, 1733, 2733, 3097, 3281, 3486,
3639, 3644, 4022, 4096]

297   BEAUCHAMP, M. A. *Elements of mathematical sociology.* New York, Random House, 1970,
       ix-110 p.
298   BERNARDO, G. DI. "Previsione e profezia nelle scienze sociali" (Prediction and prophecy
       in the social sciences), *Sociologia (Roma)* 4(2), mai 70 : 74-87.
299   Bibl. XIX-231. BERTALANFFY, L. VON. *General system theory: foundations, development,*
       applications. CR: J. LOPREATO, *Amer, sociol. R.* 35(3), jun 70 : 543-545.
300   BISHIR, J. W.; DREWES, D. W. *Mathematics in the behavioral and social sciences.* New
       York, Harcourt, Brace and World, 70, xiii-714 p.
301   BLALOCK, H. M. Jr. *An introduction to social research.* Englewood Cliffs, N. J., Prentice-
       Hall, 70, 120 p.
302   Bibl. XIX-235. BORGATTA, E. F. (ed.). *Sociological methodology.* CR: H. L. COSTNER,
       Amer. sociol. R. 34(6), dec 69 : 950-951.
303   BUGEDA SANCHIZ, J. *Manual de técnicas de investigación social* (Handbook of social re-
       search techniques). Madrid, Instituto de Estudios Políticos, 70, 546 p.
304   CARLOS, S. "Les cheminements de la causalité", *Sociol. et Soc.* 2(2), nov 70 : 189-
       201.
305   CHAZEL, F.; BOUDON, R.; LAZARSFELD, P. *L'analyse des processus sociaux.* Paris, Mouton,
       70, vii-413 p.
306   "Classification and typlogies in social sciences", *Quality and Quantity* 2(1-2), jan 68 :
       9-123 ?
307   CRESPI, F. "Struttura dell'azione sociale e significato" (The structure of social action and
       its meaning), *R. int. Sociol. (Madrid)* 27(103-104), jul-dec 68 : 31-48.
308   DENZIN, N. K. (comp.). *Sociological methods; a sourcebook.* Chicago, Aldine 70, x-590 p.
309   DENZIN, N. K. *The research act; a theoretical introduction to sociological methods.* Chicago,
       Aldine, 70, xiii-368 p.
310   DEUTSCHER, I. "Looking backward; case studies on the progress of methodology in
       sociological research", *Amer. Sociologist* 4(1), 1969 : 35-41.
311   ETZIONI, A.; DUBOW, F. L. (eds.). *Comparative perspectives; theories and methods.* Boston,
       Little, Brown, 69, xiii-410 p.
312   FLETCHER, C. "On replication: notes on the notions of a replicability quotient and a
       generalizability quotient", *Sociology* 4(1), jan 70 : 51-69. [Replication of studies in the
       development of sociology.]
313   FORCESE, D. P.; RICHER, S. (eds.). *Stages of social research; contemporary perspectives.*
       Englewood Cliffs, N. J., Prentice-Hall, 70, x-422 p.
314   Bibl. XIX-254. GREER, S. *The logic of social inquiry.* CR: W. C. WINSATT, *Amer. sociol. R.*
       35(4), aug 70 : 763-764.
315   HAYES, D. P.; MELTZER, L.; WOLF, G. "Substantive conclusions are dependent upon
       techniques of measurement", *Behav. Sci.* 15(3), mai 70 : 265-268.
316   HEBB, D. O ; THOMPSON, W. R. "The social significance of animal studies", in: G.
       LINDZEY; E. ARONSON (eds.). *The handbook of social psychology.* New ed. Vol. II.
       Reading, Mass., Addison-Wesley, 68 : 729-774.
317   HEINEMANN, K. "Ist die Soziologie mathematisierbar ?" (Is sociology relevant to mathe-
       matics ?), *Z. ges. Staatswiss.* 126(3), jul 70 : 484-495.
318   HOLLAND, J.; STEUER, M. D. *Mathematical sociology; a selective annotated bibliography.*
       New York, Schocken Books, 70, vii-109 p.

319 HOLT, R. T.; TURNER, J. E. (eds.). *The methodology of comparative research.* New York, Free Press, 70, ix-419 p.

320 Bibl. XVIII-316. ISAJIW, W. W. *Causation and functionalism in sociology.* CR: K. PIPPING, *Acta sociol.* 13(2), 1970 : 134-135.

321 KELLEHER, G. J. (ed.). *The challenge to systems analysis; public policy and social change.* New York, Wiley, 70, viii-150 p.

322 KOTTAK, C. P. "Towards a comparative science of society", *Comp. Stud. Soc. Hist.* 12(1), jan 70 : 92-109.

323 KRUSKAL, W. (ed.). *Mathematical sciences and social sciences.* Englewood Cliffs, N. J., Prentice-Hall, 70, viii-83 p.

324 KÜHN, A. *Das Problem der Prognose in der Soziologie* (The problem of forecasting in Sociology). Berlin, Duncker und Humblot, 70, 195 p.

325 KURYLEVA, A. K.; SMOL'KOVA, V. G.; ŠTRAKSA, G. M. *Iz opyta konkretnyh sociologičeskih issledovanij* (From the experience of concrete sociological researches). Moskva, Izdatel'stvo moskovskogo universiteta, 69, 121 p.

326 LANE, M. (ed.). *Introduction to structuralism.* New York, Basic Books, 70, 456 p.

327 LANE, M. (ed.). *Structuralism: a reader.* London, Cape, 70, 456 p.

328 LAZARSFELD, P.; BOUDON, R. *Philosophie des sciences sociales. A propos d'un livre imaginaire.* Paris, Gallimard, 70, 506 p.

329 MACKSEY, R.; DONATO, E. (eds.). *The languages of criticism and the sciences of man; the structuralist controversy.* Baltimore, Johns Hopkins Press, 70, xiii-367 p.

330 Bibl. XIX-268. MAYNTZ, R.; HOLM, K.; HÜBNER, P. *Einführung in die Methoden der empirischen Soziologie* (Introduction to methods of empirical sociology). CR: G. BÜSCHGES, *Kölner Z. Soziol. u. soz.-Psychol.* 22(2), jun 70 : 402-403.

331 MIGUELEZ, R. "La lógica de la prueba en las ciencias sociales. Análisis de una hipótesis sociológica" (The logic of proof in social sciences. Analysis of a sociological hypothesis), *Aportes* 16, apr 70 : 167-176.

332 MOZER, K. *Metody social'nogo issledovanija* (Methods of social research). Moskva, 69, 166 p.

333 MUNDY-CASTLE, A. C. "The descent of meaning", *Soc. sci. Inform./Inform. Sci. soc.* 9(1), feb 70 : 125-141. [Research on developing countries and the development of social research methods and theories.]

334 NEGROTTI, M. "Funzionalismo e cibernetica in sociologia: questioni metodologiche" (Functionalism and cybernetics in sociology: methodological questions), *Sociologia (Roma)* 4(3), sep 70 : 123-135.

335 OLIVER, W. D. "Scientism and sociology", *Berkeley J. Sociol.* 14, 1969 : 99-110. With "a comment on Oliver's Scientism and Sociology", *id.* pp. 111-121. With a comment by E. BECKER, *id.* pp. 122-124 and a "rejoinder", by W. D. OLIVER *id.* pp. 124-129.

336 PARAIN-VIAL, J. *Analyses structurales et idéologies structuralistes.* Toulouse, E. Privat, 69, 239 p.

337 PRZEWORSKI, A.; TENNE, H. *The logic of comparative social inquiry.* New York, Wiley-Interscience, 70, xii-153 p.

338 ROSE, J. D. "The moderate approach to sociological functionalism", *Acta sociol.* 13(2), 1970 : 127-131.

339 SCHOFIELD, M. G. *Social research.* London, Heinemann Educational; New York, Humanities Press, 69, vi-138 p.

340 SCHULTZ, W. *Kausalität und Experiment in den Sozialwissenschaften; Methodologie und Forschungstechnik* (Causality and experimentation in the social sciences; research methodology and techniques). Mainz von Hase und Koehler, 70, 167 p.

341 Bibl. XIX-284. SIMON, J. L. *Basic research methods in social science: the art of empirical investigation.* CR: R. CHILTON, *Amer. sociol. R.* 35(3), jun 70 : 609-610.

342 STACEY, M. (ed.). *Comparability in social research.* London, Heinemann Educational, 69, xvii-134 p.

343 Bibl. XIX-288. STACEY, M. *Methods of social research.* CR: D. L. JANOVY, *Amer. sociol. R.* 35(2), apr 70 : 356.

344 STRAUSS, M. A. "Phenomenal identity and conceptual equivalence of measurement in cross-national comparative research", *J. Marriage Family* 31(2), mai 69 : 233-239.

345 *Strukturno-funkcional'nyj analiz v sovremennoj sociologii* (The structural functional analysis in contemporary sociology). Moskva, 69, 198 p.

15

346	Bibl. XIX-291. TAYLOR, C. L. (ed.). *Aggregate data analysis: political and social indicators in cross-national research.* CR: R. WENCES, *Amer. sociol. R.* 34(6), dec 69 : 955.

347	TAYLOR, K. W. "A paradigm for causal analysis", *Sociol. Quart.* 11(2), 1970 : 169-180.

348	TEULINGS, A. W. M. "Kanonische diskriminant; analyse ofwel de toepassing van de multivariate procedures voor analyse op het messo-niveau" (Canonical discriminants; analysis and application of multivariate analysis procedures to middle range analysis), *Sociol. Gids* 17(1), jan-feb 70 : 19-33.

349	TJADEN, K. H. "Zur Kritik eines funktional-strukturellen Entwurfe sozialer Systeme" (Critique of functional-structural outline of social systems), *Kölner Z. Soziol. u. soz.-Psychol.* 21(4), dec 69 : 752-769.

350	TÜTENGIL, C. O. *Sosyal ilimlerde araştırma ve metod* (Social science research and method). İstanbul, İstanbul Universitesi, İktisat Fakültesi, 69, viii-94 p.

351	VAN BOCKSTAELE, J. *et al.* "Nouvelles observations sur la définition de la socio-analyse", *Année sociol.* 19, 1968 : 279-295.

352	VAN DER ZWAAN, A. H. "Sociotechnisch systeemonderzoek" (Sociotechnical systems analysis), *Sociol. Gids* 17(1), jan-feb 70 : 41-47.

353	WEEDE, E. "Zur Methodik der kausalen Abhängigkeitsanalyse (Pfadanalyse) in der nicht-experimentellen Forschung" (On the method of causal analysis (path analysis) in non-experimental research), *Kölner Z. Soziol. u. soz.-Psychol.* 22(3), sep 70 : 532-550.

354	WHITING, J. W. M. "Methods and problems in cross-cultural research", in: G. LINDZEY; E. ARONSON (eds.). *The handbook of social psychology.* New ed. Vol. II. Reading, Mass., Addison-Wesley, 68 : 693-728.

355	WILD, J. "Probleme der theoretischen Deduktion von Prognosen" (Problems of theoretical deduction of predictions), *Z. ges. Staatswiss.* 126(4), oct 70 : 553-576.

356	ZDRAVOMYSKOV, A. G. *Metodologija i procedura sociologičeskih issledovanij* (Methodology and procedure in sociological research). Moskva, Mysl', 69, 204 p.

**B.31	Historical methods
Méthodes historiques**

[See also / Voir aussi: 659, 662, 792, 814]

357	HANSSEN, B. "Methodological remarks on sociological history", *Acta sociol.* 12(4), 1969 : 224-231.

358	RIEGEL, K. F. "History as a nomothetic science: some generalizations from theories and research in developmental psychology", *J. soc. Issues* 25(4), 1969 : 99-127.

359	SCHMIDT, W. "Geschichtsbild und Persönlichkeit in der sozialistischen Gesellschaft" (Historical image and personality in socialist society), *Z. Geschichtswiss.* 18(2), 1970 : 149-162. [Germany, DR.]

**B.32	Statistical methods
Méthodes statistiques**

**B.320	*General studies
Études générales***

[See also / Voir aussi: **B.34**; 353, 438, 859, 1710, 3641]

360	AITCHISON, J. *Choice against chance; an introduction to statistical decision theory.* Reading, Mass., Addison-Wesley Publishing Co., 70, ix-284 p.

361	BARBAT, A. "Cu privire la legăturile dintre statistică şi sociologie" (On the relations between statistics and sociology), *Stud. Čerc. econ.* (1-2), 1969 : 129-144.

362	BIJI, M.; IVANESCU, I.; BIJI, E. "Preocupari actuale in statistica social-economică" (Current problems of socio-economic statistics), *Stud. Čerc. econ.* 1-2, 1969 : 121-128. [Rumania.]

363	BOYLE, R. P. "Path analysis and ordinal data", *Amer. J. Sociol.* 75(4, *Part I*), jan 70 : 461-480.

364	ERICKSEN, G. L. *Scientific inquiry in the behavioral sciences; an introduction to statistics.* Glenview, Ill., Scott, Foresman, 70, 372 p.

365   Heermann, E. F.; Braskamp, L. A. (eds.). *Readings in statistics for the behavioral sciences.* Englewoods Cliffs, N. J., Prentice-Hall, 70, ix-419 p.

366   Bibl. xix-310. Kolstoe, R. H. *Introduction to statistics for the behavioral sciences.* CR: S. Ito, *Amer. sociol. R.* 34(6), dec 69 : 1025-1026.

367   Kozačenko, I. V. *Statistika* (Statistics). Kiev, Urožaj, 69, 251 p.

368   Labovitz, S. "The assignment of numbers to rank order categories", *Amer. sociol. R.* 35(3), jun 70 : 515-524.

369   Land, K. C. "On the estimation of path coefficients for unmeasured variables from correlations among observed variables", *Soc. Forces* 48(4), jun 70 : 506-511.

370   Maisano, S. "Statistica e scienze sociali" (Statistics and social sciences), *A. Fac. Econ. Com. Messina* 7(1), 1969 : 128-155.

371   Mapes, R. "Dependence analysis", *Sociology* 4(3), sep 70 : 395-400.

372   Mosteller, F. "Data analysis, including statistics", in: G. Lindzey; E. Aronson (eds.). *The handbook of social psychology.* New ed. Vol. II. Reading, Mass., Addison-Wesley, 68 : 80-203.

373   Muir, D. E. "Searching data for predictive variables: a set-theoretical approach", *Sociol. Inquiry* 39(1), 1969 : 27-36. With a comment by R. McGinnis : 37-38.

374   Namboodiri, N. K. "A statistical exposition of the 'before-after' and 'after-only' designs and their combinations", *Amer. J. Sociol.* 76(1), jul 70 : 83-102.

375   Perlina, N. M. "K voprosu o prirode statističeskoj zakonomernosti" (On the question of the nature of the application of statistics in the social sciences), *Vestn. Leningrads. Univ. Ser. Èkon. Filos. Pravo* 24(4), dec 69 : 31-40.

376   Rosenthal, H.; Kies, N. E. "L'inférence des propriétés individuelles à partir de données agrégées: problèmes de collinéarité", *R. franç. Sociol.* 11(1), jan-mar 70 : 65-73.

377   Scolnik, J. "A new methodology for the multivariate analysis of data. Application: of the Argentine model", *Soziol. Instit. Univ. Zürich B.* 16, jan 70 : 31-126.

378   Wortman, P. M. "Cognitive utilization of probabilistic cues", *Behav. Sci.* 15(4), jul 70 : 329-336.

B.321   Sampling
Échantillonnage

379   Althauser, R. P.; Rubin, D. "The computerized construction of a matched sample", *Amer. J. Sociol.* 76(2), sep 70 : 325-346.

380   Anderson, C. L.; Halford, L. J. "A four-state comparison of variable sampling and data collection procedures", *Pacific sociol. R.* 13(3), 1970 : 149-155.

381   Bebbington, A. C. "The effect of non-response in the sample survey with an example", *Hum. Relat.* 23(3), jun 70 : 169-180.

382   Gabaldón Mejía, N. *Algunos conceptos de muestreo* (Some concepts of sampling). Caracas, Instituto de Investigaciones Económicas y Sociales, 69, 61 p.

383   Garza, T. H.; Coronel, J. A. "Un método para la determinación del tamaño de muestra en encuestas sobre poblaciones finitas" (A method for the determination of sample size in surveys on finite populations), *Demogr. y Econ.* 4(1), 1970 : 121-128.

384   Lagay, B. W. "Assessing bias: a comparison of two methods", *Publ. Opin. Quart.* 33(4), 1970 : 615-618.

385   Moore, P. G. "The myth of the percentage sample", *J. Manag. Stud.* 7(2), mai 70 : 149-155.

386   Murdock, G. P.; White, D. R. "Standard cross-cultural sample", *Ethnology* 8(4), oct 69 : 329-369.

387   Pasquier, A. *Éléments de calcul des probabilités et de théorie des sondages.* Paris, Dunod, 69, xiv-239 p.

388   Peel, J.; Skipworth, G. "Sample size: an innovatory procedure in survey analysis", *Sociology* 4(3), sep 70 : 385-393.

389   Rojas, B. A. "Estratificación por tamaño de unidades de muestreo" (Stratification by size of the sample unit), *Demogr. y Econ.* 3(3), 1969 : 328-338.

390   Weksberg, J. "The role of sampling in population censuses—its effect on timeliness and accuracy", *Demography (Washington)* 5(1), 1968 : 362-373.

391   Williams, W. H. "The systematic bias effects of incomplete responses in notation samples", *Publ. Opin. Quart.* 33(4), 1970 : 593-602.

B.322   Quantitative and qualitative analysis
Analyse quantitative et qualitative

[See also / Voir aussi: 2147]

392   FILSTEAD, W. J. (comp.). *Qualitative methodology; firsthand involvement with the social world.* Chicago, Markham Publishing Co., 70, xi-352 p.

393   GAVRILEC, Ju. N. "Nekotorye voprosy količestvennogo izučenija social'no-ěkonomičeskih javlenij" (Some questions on the quantitative study of socio-economic phenomena), *Ěkon. matem. Metody* (5), 1969 : 703-716.

394   THEIL, H. "On the estimation of relationship involving qualitative variables", *Amer. J. Sociol.* 76(1), jul 70 : 104-154.

B.33   Techniques in field work: interviewing, observation, etc.
Techniques d'enquête: interviews, observation, etc.

[See also / Voir aussi: **D.20, D.30**; 314, 601, 916, 1264, 2711, 4064, 5186, 5330]

395   ADERMAN, D.; BERKOWITZ, L. "Observational set, empathy, and helping", *J. Person. soc. Psychol.* 14(2), feb 70 : 141-148.

396   ALUTTO, J. A. "A note on determining questionnaire destination in survey research", *Soc. Forces* 48(2), dec 69 : 251-252.

397   ANDERSON, W. A. "Role salience and social research: the Black sociologist and field work among Black groups", *Amer. Sociologist* 5(3), 1970 : 236-239.

398   CANNELL, C. F.; KAHN, R. L. "Interviewing", in: G. LINDZEY; E. ARONSON (eds.). *The handbook of social psychology.* New ed. Vol. II. Reading, Mass., Addison-Wesley, 68 : 526-595.

399   CAPLOW, T. *L'enquête sociologique.* Paris, A. Colin, 70, 267 p.

400   CATALDO, E. F. *et al.* "Card sorting as a technique for survey interviewing", *Publ. Opin. Quart.* 34(2), 1970 : 202-215.

401   COHEN, E. "Dimensions of bias in an informant network", *Sociologia (Roma)* 4(2), mai 70 : 159-167. Followed by an Italian translation; 167-174.

402   DOHRENWEND, B. "An experimental study of directive interviewing", *Publ. Opin. Quart.* 34(1), 1970 : 117-126.

403   ELLIS, R. A.; ENDO, C. M.; ARMER, J. M. "The use of potential nonrespondents for studying nonresponse bias", *Pacific sociol. R.* 13(2), 1970 : 103-109.

404   Bibl. XIX-337. GORDEN, R. L. *Interviewing: strategy, techniques and tactics.* CR: L. A. DEXTER, *Amer. sociol. R.* 35(1), feb 70 : 186.

405   HARTMANN, H. *Empirische Sozialforschung. Probleme und Entwicklungen* (Empirical social research. Problems and developments). München, Juventa-Verlag, 70, 240 p.

406   HOCHSTIM, J. R.; ATHANASOPOULOS, D. A. "Personal follow-up in a mail survey; its contribution and its cost", *Publ. Opin. Quart.* 34(1), 1970 : 69-82.

407   JACOBS, G. (ed.). *The participant observer.* New York, G. Braziller, 70, xii-302 p.

408   LERG, W. B. *Das Gespräch; Theorie und Praxis der unvermittelten Kommunikation* (The interview; theory and practice of natural communication). Düsseldorf, Bertelsmann Universitätsverlag, 70, 376 p.

409   MAKARCZYK, W. "An experiment on re-interviewing for adoption dates", *Sociol. rur.* 10(1), 1970 : 38-56.

410   Bibl. XVIII-341. MANN, P. H. *Methods of sociological inquiry.* CR: J. P. KOVAL, *Amer. sociol. R.* 35(1), feb 70 : 187-188.

411   MARQUIS, K. H. "Effects of social reinforcement on health reporting in the household interview", *Sociometry* 33(2), jun 70 : 203-215.

412   McFALL, R. M.; SCHENKEIN, D. "Experimenter expectancy effects, need for achievement and field dependence", *J. exper. Res. Personality* 4(2), féb 70 : 122-128.

413   NOELLE-NEUMANN, E. "Wanted: rules for wording structured questionnaires", *Publ. Opin. Quart.* 34(2), 1970 : 191-201.

414   PARKER, S. R.; BYNNER, J. M. "Correlational analysis of data obtained from a survey of shop stewards", *Hum. Relat.* 23(4), aug 70 : 345-359.

415   PHEYSEY, D. G.; PAYNE, R. L. "The Hemphill group dimensions description questionnaire", *Hum. Relat.* 23(5), oct 70 : 473-497.

416 PHILLIPS, J. P. N. "A new type of personal questionnaire technique", *Brit. J. soc. clin. Psychol.* 9(3), sep 70 : 241-256; 9(4), dec 70 : 338-346.

417 ROEDE, H. *Befrager und Befragte. Probleme der Durchführung des soziologischen Interviews* (Interviewed and interviewer. Problems of conducting a sociological interview). Berlin, VEB Deutscher Verlag der Wissenschaften, 68, 250 p. CR: H. ESSER, *Kölner Z. Soziol. u. soz.-Psychol.* 22(2), jun 70 : 404-405.

418 Bibl. XIX-345. ROSENBERG, M. *The logic of survey analysis.* CR: H. SCHUMAN, *Amer. sociol. R.* 34(6), dec 69 : 953-954.

419 SCHWARTZBAUM, A.; GRUENFELD, L. "Factors influencing subject-observer interaction in an organizational study", *Adm. Sci. Quart.* 14(3), sep 69 : 443-450.

420 STANOWSKI, A. "L'analyse secondaire des matériaux sociologiques par la méthode de comparaison des unités territoriales", *Archiv. Sociol. Relig.* 15(29), jan-jun 70 : 93-96.

421 STEBBINS, R. A. "Studying the definition of the situation theory and field research strategies", *Canad. R. Sociol. Anthropol.* 6(4), nov 69 : 193-211.

422 STRECKER, I. A. *Methodische Probleme der ethno-soziologischen Beobachtung und Beschreibung.* (Versuch einer Vorbereitnung zur Feldforschung) (Methodological problems of ethno-sociological observation and description). Göttingen, Institut für Völkerkunde, 69, 98 p.

423 TREINEN, H. "Notes on an experience with secondary analysis of survey data as a teaching device", *Soc. Sci. Inform./Inform. Sci. soc.* 9(2), apr 70 : 123-132.

424 VAN ES, J. C.; WILKENING, E. A. "Response stability in survey research: a cross-cultural comparison", *Rur. Sociol.* 35(2), jun 70 : 191-205.

425 VAN KOOLWIJK, J. "Unangenehme Fragen. Paradigma für die Reaktionen des Befragten im Interview" (Disagreable question. Paradigms for the reaction of responders in an interview), *Kölner Z. Soziol. u. soz.-Psychol.* 21(4), dec 69 : 864-875.

426 WEICK, K. E. "Systematic observational methods", in: G. LINDZEY; E. ARONSON (eds.). *The handbook of social psychology.* New ed. Vol. II. Reading, Mass., Addison-Wesley, 68 : 357-451.

427 WELLER, L.; LUCHTERHAND, E. "Comparing interviews and observations on family functioning", *J. Marriage Family* 31(1), feb 69 : 115-122.

428 WESTPHAL-HELLBUSCH, S. "Methoden und praktische Probleme der heutigen Feldforschung. Aufgezeigt an Beispielen aus Indien" (Methods and pratical problems of today's field research, using by examples from India), *Sociologus* 20(1), 1970 : 3-17.

429 WILLIAMS, A. F.; WECHSLER, H. "The mail survey: methods to minimize bias owing to incomplete response. A research note", *Sociol. soc. Res.* 54(4), jul 70 : 533-535.

430 WISEMAN, J. P.; ARON, M. S. *Field projects for sociology students.* Cambridge, Mass., Shenkman Publishing Co., San Francisco, Canfield Press, 70, vii-264 p.

431 WURR, R. "Die Strategie des Einlebens und die teilnehmende Beobachtung bei der Er forschung fremder Gesellschaften" (The way of life strategy and participant observation in research on foreign societies), *Sociol. int. (Berlin)* 8(2), 1970 : 167-178.

B.34 Experimental methods: tests, models, scales
Méthodes expérimentales: tests, modèles, échelles

[See also / Voir aussi: **C.31, C.40, D.20, D.30**; 516, 603, 650, 655, 893, 909, 1033, 1331, 1455, 1849, 1991, 2230, 2274, 2721, 4907, 5284]

432 ABELSON, R. P. "Simulation of social behavior", in: G. LINDZEY; E. ARONSON (eds.). *The handbook of social psychology.* New ed. Vol. II. Reading, Mass., Addison-Wesley, 68 : 274-356.

433 AGAR, M. "The simulated situation: a methodological note", *Hum. Org.* 28(4), 1969 : 322-329.

434 ALEXANDER, C. N. Jr.; ZUCKER, L. G.; BRODY, C. L. "Experimental expectations and autokinetic experiences: consistency theories and judgmental convergence", *Sociometry* 33(1), mar 70 : 108-122.

435 ARONSON, E.; CARLSMITH, J. M. "Experimentation in social psychology", in: G. LINDZEY; E. ARONSON (eds.). *The handbook of social psychology.* New ed. Vol. II. Reading, Mass., Addison-Wesley, 68 : 1-79.

436 BALTZ, C. "Ordinateur, technique des modèles et société de répression", *Temps mod.* 27 (289-290), aug-sep 70 : 496-506.

437 BERGER, S. M.; LAMBERT, W. W. "Stimulus-response theory in contemporary social psychology", in: G. LINDZEY; E. ARONSON, (eds.). *The handbook of social psychology.* New ed. Vol. I. Reading, Mass., Addison-Wesley, 68 : 81-178.

438 BOLTON, G. M.; GRAY, L. N.; MAYHEW, B. H. JR. "An experimental examination of a stochastic model of dominance", *Soc. Forces* 48(4), jun 70 : 511-520.

439 BREWER, M. B.; CRANO, W. D.; CAMPBELL, D. T. "The use of partial correlations to test hypotheses", *Sociometry* 33(1), mar 70 : 1-11.

440 Bibl. XIX-362. BUCHLER, I. R.; NUTINI, H. G. (eds.). *Game theory in the behavioral sciences.* CR: R. D. LUCE, *Amer. J. Sociol.* 75(5), mar 70 : 885-886.

441 CARDOSO, A. *O teste sociométrico* (The sociometric test). Lisboa, Tipografia Garcia e Carvalho, 69, 66 + 2 p.

442 CLEMENZ, M. *Soziologische Reflexion und sozialwissenschaftliche Methode. Zur Konstruktion und Begründung soziologischen Modelle und Theorien* (Sociological reflexions and social sciences methods. Construction and basis of models and sociological theories). Frankfurt am Main, Suhrkam, 70, 291 p.

443 DAVIS, M. D. *Game theory; a nontechnical introduction.* New York, Basic Books, 70, xii-208 p.

444 DUBIN, R. *Theory building: a practical guide to the construction and testing of theoretical models.* New York, The Free Press, 69, 298 p. CR: N. C. MULLINS *Amer. sociol. R.* 35(2), apr 70 : 352-353.

445 EMSHOFF, J. R. "A computer simulation model of the Prisoner's Dilemma", *Behav. Sci.* 15(4), jul 70 : 304-317.

446 FERNANDEZ DÍAZ, A. "La necesidad del empleo de modelos en las ciencias sociales" (The need to use models in the social sciences), *R. Econ. polít. (Madrid)* 54, jan-apr 70 : 173-184.

447 GORDON, T. J.; ENZER, S.; ROCHBERG, R. "An experiment in simulation gaming for social policy studies", *Technol. Forecasting* 1(3), 1969 : 241-261. [USA.]

448 GULLAHORN, J. E.; GULLAHORN, J. T. "Simulation and social system theory: the state of the union", *Simulation and Games* 1(1), mar 70 : 19-42.

449 HALPIN, S. M.; PILISUK, M. "Prediction and choice in the Prisoner's Dilemma", *Behav. Sci.* 15(2), mar 70 : 141-153.

450 HEINTZ, P. "Preliminary analysis of Scolnik's model", *Soziol. Institut. Univ. Zürich B.* 17, mai 70 : 1-11.

451 HENRY, P. "Quelques modèles mathématiques de processus d'influence sociale", *Bull. CERP* 18(3-4), jul-dec 69 : 203-235.

452 HERNANDEZ, R. A. "The steps from the X's to Y", *Soziol. Institut. Univ. Zürich B.* 17, mai 70 : 21-58. [Data processing method.]

453 HERNES, G. "Markovian approach to measures of association", *Amer. J. Sociol.* 75(6), mai 70 : 992-1011.

454 HOEPF, R. T.; HUBER, G. P. "A study of self-explicated utility models", *Behav. Sci.* 15(5), sep 70 : 408-414.

455 HOLM, K. "Gültigkeit von Skalen und Indizes" (The validity of scales and indicators), *Kölner Z. Soziol. u. soz.-Psychol.* 22(2), jun 70 : 356-386; 22(4), dec 70 : 693-715.

456 JUAN, L. "Construction d'un test de lecture de dessins", *Bull. CERP* 18(3-4), jul-dec 69: 267-277.

457 LABOVITZ, S. "The nonutility of significance tests: the significance of tests of significance reconsidered", *Pacific sociol. R.* 13(3), 1970 : 141-148.

458 LEE, T. C.; JUDGE, G. G.; ZELLNER, A. *Estimating the parameters of the Markov probability model from aggregate time series data.* Amsterdam, North-Holland Publishing Co., 70, 254 p.

459 LEVIN, R. I.; DESJARDINS, R. B. *Theory of games and strategies.* Scranton, Pa., International Textbook Co., 70, xi-132 p.

460 MARTIN, J. D. "Two significance tests for shotgun studies", *Pacific sociol. R.* 13(1), 1970 : 41-46.

461 MINOR, M. W. "Experimenter-expectancy effect as a function of evaluation apprehension", *J. Person. soc. Psychol.* 15(4), aug 70 : 326-332.

462 MORRIS, R. N. "Multiple correlation and ordinally scaled data", *Soc. Forces* 48(3), mar 70 : 299-311.

463 MOSER, U.; ZEPPELIN, I. VON; SCHNEIDER, W. "Computer simulation of a model of neurotic defense processes", *Behav. Sci.* 15(2), mar 70 : 194-202.

464 NOSACHUK, T. A. "Pretesting effects: an inductive model", *Sociometry* 33(1), mar 70 : 12-19.

465 OFSCHE, R.; OFSCHE, S. L. "Choice behavior in coalition games", *Behav. Sci.* 15(4), jul 70 : 337-349.

466 PETRUSEK, M. *Sociometrie. Teorie, metod, techniky* (Sociometry. Theory, methods, techniques). Praha, Svoboda, t. Rudé právo, 69, 262 + 5 p.

467 ROSENBERG, S. "Mathematical models of social behavior", in: G. LINDZEY; E. ARONSON (eds.). *The handbook of social psychology.* New ed. Vol. I. Reading, Mass., Addison-Wesley, 68 : 179-244.

468 SHUBIK, M. "Game theory, behavior and the paradox of the Prisonner's Dilemma: three solutions", *J. Conflict Resol.* 14(2), jun 70 : 181-194.

469 SHUBIK, M. *Games of status.* Santa Monica, Rand Corporation, 69, vii-39 p.

470 ȘILEȚCHI, M.; CURTA, L. "Les modèles mathématiques et la prévision sociale", *R. roum. Sci. soc. Sér. Sociol.* 14, 1970 : 83-95.

471 VAN DEN ENDE, H. W.; VAN ROSSUM, W. "Het beschrijven van causale modellen met behulp van termen uit de informatietheorie" (The elaboration of causal models with the help of information theory terms), *Mens en Mij* 45(3), mai-jun 70 : 204-217.

472 VORONOV, Ju. P. *Izmerenie i modelirovanie v sociologii* (Measurement and model elaboration in sociology). Novosibirsk, Nauka, 69, 174 p.

473 WARTAK, J. "Logio-structure tables: computer oriented method of solving problems", *Behav. Sci.* 15(6), nov 70 : 532-535.

474 WERTS, C. E.; LINN, R. L. "Cautions in applying various procedures for determining the reliability and validity of multiple-item scales", *Amer. sociol. R.* 35(4), aug 70 : 757-759.

475 WHITE, H. C. "Simon out of Homans by Coleman", *Amer. J. Sociol.* 75(5), mar 70 : 852-862. [Simon's linear model for some of Homan's propositions about small groups.]

476 WILSON, R. S.; SCOTT, K. K. "Computer programs for autonomic research", *Behav. Sci.* 15(4), jul 70 : 380-385.

B.4 GENERAL THEORETICAL SYSTEMS
SYSTÈMES THÉORIQUES GÉNÉRAUX

[See also / Voir aussi: 4. 28, 147, 193, 593, 596, 598, 614, 618, 1770, 1805, 2392, 2393, 2415, 3397, 3632, 3798, 3968, 4359, 4487, 4880, 4903, 4922]

477 ABRAHAMSSON, B. "Homans on exchange: hedonism revived", *Amer. J. Sociol.* 76(2), sep 70 : 273-285.

478 AMBARCUMOV, E. "Teoretičeskoe masledie V. I. Lenina i nekotorye problemy sociologii" (The theoretical patrimony of V. I. Lenin and certain sociological problems), *Mir. Ėkon. meždun. Otnoš.* 2, feb 70 : 3-16.

479 ANDRESKI, S. (ed.). *Herbert Spencer, the principles of sociology.* London, Macmillan, 69, xxxvi-821 p. CR: J. D. Y. PEEL, *Brit. J. Sociol.* 21(1), mar 70 : 109-110.

480 ANDREW, E. "Work and freedom in Marcuse and Marx", *Canad. J. polit. Sci.* 3(2), jun 70 : 241-256.

481 ANSART, P. *Marx et l'anarchisme. Essai sur les sociologies de Saint-Simon, Proudhon et Marx.* Paris, Presses universitaires de France, 69, 556 p.

482 ANSART, P. *Sociologie de Saint-Simon.* Paris, Presses universitaires de France, 70, 213 p.

483 ARAMBERRI, J. R. "La obra de Umberto Cerroni (Un intento de reconstrucción de la metodología de la ciencia social)" (The work of Umberto Cerroni, a tentative reconstruction of social science methodology), *Bol. inform. Cienc. polít.* 4, jun 70 : 67-94.

484 BAUMAN, E. "Essai d'une théorie marxiste de la société", *Homme et Soc.* 15, jan-feb-mar 70 : 3-26.

485 BEELING, R. F. *De sociologie van Georg Simmel* (George Simmel's sociology), Amsterdam, De Bussy, 69, 178 p.

486 BELLEBAUM, A. "Ferdinand Tönnies: Analyse und Bewerkung sozialer Konflikte" (Ferdinand Tönnies: analysis and work in social conflicts), *Kölner Z. Soziol. u. soz.-Psychol.* 22(1), mar 70 : 121-128.

21

487   BELOV, L. M. "V. I. Lenin i problema ličnosti" (V. I. Lenin and the problem of personality), *Nauč. Zap. (Leningr. finan. ěkon. Inst.)* (34), 1970 : 200-220.

488   BILOUS, J.; QUIRK, J.-H. "Interest in Pareto's sociology: an essay in the quantitative
history of social science", *C. Vilfredo Pareto* 20, féb 70 : 145-164.

489   BLAIN, R. R. "A critique of Parsons' function paradigm", *Sociol. Quart.* 11(2), 1970 :
157-168.

490   BOKSZAŃSKI, Z. "Florian Znaniecki's concept of social action and the theory of action in
sociology", *Polish sociol. B.* (1), 1968 : 18-29.

491   BOUSQUET, G.-H. "Pareto, l'équilibre social et M. Marrill", *C. Vilfredo Pareto* 20,
feb 70 : 135-143.

492   BYNDER, H. "Émile Durkheim and the sociology of the family", *J. Marriage Family*
31(3), aug 69 : 527-533.

493   CAHNMAN, W. J. "Tönnies und Durkheim: eine dokumentarischen Gegenüberstellung"
(Tönnies and Durkheim: a documentary confrontation), *Archiv Rechts-u. soz.-Philos.*
56(2), 1970 : 189-208.

494   CAILLÉ, A. "L'autonomie du système économique, selon Talcott Parsons", *Sociol. Trav.*
12(2), apr-jun 70 : 187-207.

495   CAUDLE, M. W. "Sir Thomas More's *Utopia:* origins and purposes", *Soc. Sci. (Winfield)* 45(3), jun 70 : 163-169.

496   CERRONI, U. "Il metodo dell'analisi sociale di Lenin" (Lenin's method of social analysis),
Crit. sociol. (Roma) 13, 1970 : 13-33.

497   Bibl. XIX-437. CLARK, T. N. (ed.). *Gabriel Tarde on communication and social influence:
selected papers.* CR: E. CHERTOK, *Amer. sociol. R.* 35(2), apr 70 : 349-350.

498   COWELL, F. R. *Values in human society; the contributions of Pitirim A. Sorokin to sociology.*
Boston, P. Sargent, 70, xii-480 p.

499   DEUTSCH, M. "Field theory in social psychology", in: G. LINDZEY; E. ARONSON (eds.).
The handbook of social psychology. New ed. Vol. I. Reading, Mass., Addison-Wesley,
68 : 412-487. [K. Lewin's theory.]

500   DUBAR, C. "La méthode de Marcel Mauss", *R. franç. Sociol.* 10(4), oct-dec 69 : 515-
521.

501   DUESBERG, H. *Person und Gemeinschaft: philosophisch-systematische Untersuchungen des
Sinnzusammenhangs von personaler Selbständigkeit und interpersonaler Beziehungen an
Texten von J. G. Fichte und M. Buber* (Person and community; systematic philosophi-
cal inquiries in the nature of personal autonomy and interpersonal relations in texts by
J. G. Fichte and M. Buber). Bonn, H. Bouvier, 70, xxviii-362 p.

502   DUVIGNAUD, J. (éd.). *Émile Durkheim, journal sociologique.* Paris, Presses universitaires de
France, 69, 728 p. CR: P. ANSART, *C. int. Sociol.* 17(49), jul-dec 70 : 179-181.

503   DUVIGNAUD, J. *Georges Gurvitch, symbolisme social et sociologie dynamique.* Paris, Seghers,
69, 192 p.

504   ECKSTEIN, P. "On Karl Marx and Max Weber", *Sci. and Soc.* 34(3), 1970 : 346-348.

505   Bibl. XIX-446. EISENSTADT, S. N. (ed.). *Max Weber on charisma and institution building:
selected papers.* CR: R. G. KLIETSCH, *Amer. sociol. R.* 35(2), apr 70 : 346-347.

506   FARBERMAN, H. A. "Mannheim, Colley, and Mead: toward a social theory of mentality",
Sociol. Quart. 11(1), 1970 : 3-13.

507   FILLOUX, J.-C. (éd.). *Émile Durkheim, la science sociale et l'action.* Paris, Presses universitaires de France, 70, 334 p. CR: P. ANSART, *C. int. Sociol.* 17(49), jul-dec 70 : 179-181.

508   FREUND, J. *Max Weber.* Paris, Presses universitaires de France, 69, 132 p.

509   FROMM, E. "Le modèle de l'homme chez Freud et ses déterminants sociaux", *Homme
et Soc.* 13, jul-aug-sep 69 : 111-125.

510   GABAUDE, J. M. *Le jeune Marx et le matérialisme antique.* Toulouse, Privat, 70, 277 p.

511   GIDDENS, A. "Durkheim as a review critic", *Sociol. R.* 18(2), jul 70 : 171-196.

512   GIDDENS, A. "Marx, Weber and the development of capitalism", *Sociology* 4(3), sep 70 :
289-310.

513   GODDIJN, H. P. M. *De sociologie van Emile Durkheim* (Émile Durkheim's sociology).
Amsterdam, De Bussy, 69, 221 p.

514   GOLDMANN, L. "Das Denken Herbert Marcuse" (Herbert Marcuse's thought), *Soz. Welt*
20(3), 1969 : 257-273.

515   GRIGOR'JAN, G. S. (ed.). *Karl Marks i problemy obščestvennyh nauk* (Karl Marx and social
sciences problems). Moskva, 69, 147 p.

516   GUALA, G. "Jung, Durkheim, Lévi-Strauss: dagli archetipi ai modelli" (Jung, Durkheim, Lévi-Strauss: from archetypes to models), *Sociologia (Roma)* 4(2), mai 70 : 101-132.

517   GUELFAT, I. "Aux sources de la marxologie authentique, N. I. Ziber", *Homme et Soc.* 17, jul-aug-sep 70 : 141-148.

518   HAHN, M. *Bürgerlicher Optimismus im Niedergang. Studien zu Lorenz von Stein und Hegel* (Bourgeois optimism on the decline. Studies on Lorenz von Stein and Hegel). München, W. Fink Verlag, 69, 224 p. CR: H. PROSS, *Kölner Z. Soziol. u. soz.-Psychol.* 22(1), mar 70 : 160-161.

519   HALL, C. S.; LINDZEY, G. "The relevance of Freudian psychology and related view points for the social sciences", in: G. LINDZEY, E. ARONSON (eds.). *The handbook of social psychology.* New ed. Vol. I. Reading, Mass., Addison-Wesley, 68 : 245-319.

520   HARTMANN, K. *Die Marxsche Theorie. Eine philosophische Untersuchung zu den Hauptschriften* (Marxist theory. A philosophical examination of the major texts). Berlin, de Gruyter, 70, xii-593 p.

521   HAYES, E. N.; HAYES, T. (eds.). *Claude Levi-Strauss: the anthropologist as hero.* Camridge, Mass., MIT Press, 70, xv-264 p.

522   HOHMEIER, J. "Zur Soziologie Ludwig Gumplowicz' (1838-1909)" (Ludwig Gumplowicz' sociology, 1838-1909), *Kölner Z. Soziol. u. soz.-Psychol.* 22(1), mar 70 : 24-38.

523   HORVÁTH, R. "L'interdépendance des facteurs économiques et démographiques dans la pensée de Grégoire Berzeviczy, 1763-1822", *Population* 25(5), sep-oct 70 : 975-987.

524   HOWARD, D. "Fétichisme, aliénation et théorie critique: réflexions sur un manuscrit de Marx publié récemment", *Homme et Soc.* 17, jul-aug-sep 70 : 97-110.

525   HYPPOLITE, J. *Studies on Marx and Hegel.* New York, Basic Books, 69, 202 p. CR: C. TAYLOR, *Amer. polit. Sci. R.* 64(2), jun 70 : 626-628; M. FAIA, *Amer. sociol. R.* 35(4), aug 70 : 767-768.

526   INTERNATIONAL SOCIAL SCIENCE COUNCIL. *Marx and contemporary scientific thought/ Marx et la pensée scientifique contemporaine.* The Hague, Mouton, 70, xi-612 p.

527   IPOLA, E. DE. "Vers une science du texte social. Le(re)-commencement de la sociologie marxiste", *Sociol. et Soc.* 2(1), mai 70 : 123-143.

528   IZZO, A. "Una vecchia disputa: Hegel critico della società civile ?" (An old controversy. Hegel as a critique of the civil society), *Crit. sociol. (Roma)* 13, 1970 : 34-54.

529   JACOBS, H. "Aspects of the political sociology of Talcott Parsons", *Berkeley J. Sociol.* 14, 1969 : 58-72.

530   JIMENO, V. "El accionalismo, una sociología actual" (Actionalism, a current sociology), *Anu. Sociol. Pueblos ibér.* (5), 1969 : 5-30. [Alain Touraine, France.]

531   KOZYR-KOWALSKI, S. "Weber and Marx", *Polish sociol. B.* (1), 1968 : 5-17.

532   LEACH, E. R. *Lévi-Strauss.* London, Fontana, 70, 127 p.

533   LEFEBVRE, H. "Les paradoxes d'Althusser", *Homme et Soc.* 13, jul-aug-sep 69 : 3-37.

534   *Leninskij analiz imperializma i sovremennyj kapitalizm* (Leninist analysis of imperialism and contemporary capitalism). Moskva, Izdatel'stvo moskovskogo universiteta, 69, 281 p.

535   LEONARD, S. E. *Henri Rousseau and Max Weber.* New York, R. I. Feigen, 70, 94 p.

536   LICHTMAN, R. "Symbolic interactionalism and social reality: some Marxist queries", *Berkeley J. Sociol.* 15, 1970 : 75-94.

537   LÓPEZ CALERA, N. M. "Filosofía de la negación y critica social en Herbert Marcuse" (Philosophy of negation and social criticism in Herbert Marcuse *R. Estud. polít.* 167, sep-oct 69 : 69-101.

538   LOURAU, R. "Marxisme et institutions", *Homme et Soc.* 14, oct-nov-dec 69 : 139-156.

539   LOWY, M. "L'humanisme historiciste de Marx ou relire *Le Capital*", *Homme et Soc.* 17, jul-aug-sep 70 : 111-125.

540   LUCHETTI, M. "I 'sistemi socialisti' di Vilfredo Pareto e i limiti dell'educazione" (Vilfredo Pareto's 'socialist systems' and the limits of education) *Rass. ital. Sociol.* 11(2), apr-jun 70 : 207-230.

541   MARSIGLIA, G. "Classi e potere nell'opera di C. Wright Mills" (Class and power in C. Wright Mills' works), *Rass. ital. Sociol.* 10(4), oct-dec 69 : 569-622.

542   MARTENS, A. "Bijdrage van het actionalisme van A. Touraine tot een organisatietypologie" (Contribution of A. Touraine's actionalism to a typology of organizations), *Mens en Mij* 45(5), sep-oct 70 : 319-331.

23

543   MAYA, C. "Poder y conflicto social: Ralf Dahrendorf y C. Wright Mills" (Power and social conflict: Ralf Dahrendorf and C. Wright Mills), *R. esp. Opin. públ.* 20, apr-mai 70 : 31-56.

544   McGOVERN, A. F. "The young Marx on the State", *Sci. and Soc.* 34(4), 1970 : 430-466.

545   Bibl. XIX-470. McLELLAN, D. *The young Hegelians and Karl Marx.* CR: R. P. HUMMEL, *Amer. polit. Sci. R.* 64(3), sep 70 : 932-933.

546   MERQUIOR, J. G. "Vico et Lévi-Strauss. Note à propos d'un symposium", *Homme* 10(2), apr-jun 70 : 81-93.

547   MITZMAN, A. *The iron cage; an historical interpretation of Max Weber.* New York, Knopf, 70, xii-328-ix p.

548   MORAWSKI, S. "Le marxisme et ses rivages possibles", *Homme et Soc.* 13, jul-aug-sep 69 : 145-168.

549   MOSCOVICI, S. "Le marxisme et la question naturelle", *Homme et Soc.* 13, jul-aug-sep 69 : 59-109.

550   MÜLLER-SCHMID, P.-P. "Die Philosophie des 'kritischen Rationalismus' in K. R. Poppers Konzeption der 'offene Gesellschaft' " (The philosophy of "critical rationalism" in R. K. Poppers' conception of an "open society"), *Archiv Rechts-u. soz.-Philos.* 56(1), 1970 : 123-148.

551   MUSSCHE, G. "Le système de Schumpeter et la sociologie économique", *A. Fac. Dr. Sci. écon. Lille* 1968 : 125-165.

552   NATHANSON, M. "Phenomenology and typification: a study in the philosophy of Alfred Schutz", *Soc. Res.* 37(1), mar 70 : 1-22.

553   NELSON, L. "H. C. Taylor and rural sociology", *Rur. Sociol.* 35(1), mar 70 : 97-98.

554   NOLAND, A. "Proudhon's sociology of war", *Amer. J. Econ. Sociol.* 29(3), jul 70 : 289-304.

555   ONO, O. "Kenryoku no shiten ni motozuku shakai bunseki" (On Bertrand Russell's theory of power), *Dôshisha Hôgaku* 19(4), 1968 : 1-26; 19(5), 1968 : 1-20.

556   ORIDOROGA, M. T. "Voprosy sem'i i braka v trudah Karla Marksa" (Questions on family and marriage in Karl Marx's works), *Trudy Kiev. vysš. Školy SSSR* (2), 1969 : 29-44.

557   PERLINI, T. "A proposito di Korsch" (About Korsch), *Crit. sociol. (Roma)* 15, 1970 : 33-68.

558   PLETNIKOV, Ju. K. *Voprosy istoričeskogo materializma i kritika nekotoryh koncepciji buržuaznoj sociologii* (Questions on historical materialism and critics of some conceptions of bourgeois sociology). Moskva, 69, 396 p.

559   PROTO, M. "Antonio Labriola e la sociologia" (Antonio Labriola and sociology), *Riv. Sociol.* 6(17), sep-dec 68 : 149-160.

560   Bibl. XIX-489. RAISON, T. (ed.). *The founding fathers of social science.* CR: G. W. LOWIS, *Amer. sociol. R.* 35(2), apr 70 : 353-354.

561   Bibl. XIX-491. REISS, A. J. Jr. (ed.). *Cooley and sociological analysis.* CR: A. VAN DER SLICE, *Amer. sociol. R.* 35(1), feb 70 : 127-128.

562   RIGA, P. J. "Herbert Marcuse et la critique sociale", *Justice dans le Monde* 11(3). mar 70 : 348-369.

563   ROELENS, R. "Les avatars de la médiation dans la sociologie de Lucien Goldmann", *Homme et Soc.* 15, jan-feb-mar 70 : 295-316.

564   Bibl. XIX-495. ROGERS, R. E. *Max Weber's ideal type theory.* CR: G. A. DONOHUE, *Amer. sociol. R.* 35(2), apr 70 : 344-345.

565   ROHRER, E. "La sociologie de Theodor Geiger", *Année sociol.* 19, 1968 : 101-131.

566   ROSENTHAL, R. (ed.). *McLuhan: pro and con.* Baltimore, Md., Penguin Books, 69, 308 p. CR: D. Q. BRODIE, *Amer. sociol. R.* 35(2), apr 70 : 387-388.

567   ROUMAINTSEV, A. M.; OSSIPOV, G. B. "La sociologie marxiste et les recherches empiriques", *Homme et Soc.* 14, oct-nov-dec 69 : 99-112.

568   RUSCONI, G. E. "L'ambivalenza di Adorno" (The ambivalence of Adorno), *Crit. sociol. (Roma)* 13, 1970 : 146-160.

569   SCHULTE, L. "Marcuses Kritik an der Gesellschaft" (Marcuse's criticism of society), *Polit. Stud. (München)* 186, jul-aug 69 : 408-414.

570   SHERMAN, H. J. "The Marxist theory of value revisited", *Sci. and Soc.* 34(3), 1970 : 257-282.

571   SIEVERS, B. "Herrschaft und Ungleichheit. Zur Kritik der Dahrendorfschen Ungleichheitstheorien und ihren Deduktion" (Domination and inequality. A critique of Dahrendorfian inequality theories and deductions from it), *Jb. soz.-Wiss.* 20(3), 1969 : 318-341.

572 SILBERMANN, A. "Theodor W. Adornos kunstsoziologisches Vermächtnis" (The cultural sociological testament of Theodor W. Adorno), *Kölner Z. Soziol. u. soz.-Psychol.* 21(4), dec 69 : 712-716.

573 SIMPSON, G. *Auguste Comte, sire of sociology.* New York, Cromwell, 69, xv-114 p.

574 SOULEZ, P. "L'involutionnisme de Platon", *C. int. Sociol.* 17(49), jul-dec 70 : 151-162.

575 SPENCER, M. E. "Weber on legitimate norms and authority", *Brit. J. Sociol.* 21(2), jun 70 : 135-150.

576 STUCK, H. "Wissenschaftssoziologische Kritik an deutschen Technokratie-Theorien: ein Bericht" (A sociological critique of German theories concerning technocracy: a report), *Futurum* 2(3), 1969 : 366-391.

578 TASHJEAN, J.-E. "Interest in Pareto's sociology: reflections on a bibliography", *C. Vilfredo Pareto* 20, feb 70 : 141-143.

579 VAQUERO, P. *Althusser o el estructuralismo marxista (Estudio de una polémica entre marxistas)* (Althusser or Marxist structuralism. Study of a polemic between Marxists). Algorta, Ed. Zero, 70, 159 p.

580 VAZJULIN, V. A. *Logika Kapitala K. Marksa* (Logic in K. Marx' *Capital*). Moskva, Izdatel'stvo moskovskogo Universiteta, 68, 295 p.

581 VODOPIVEC, V. "Marxova misel v sodobni revolucionarni teoriji in praksi" (Karl Marx's thought on contemporary revolutionary theory and practice), *Teorija in Praksa* 7(3), mar 70 : 372-379.

582 WEINGART, P. "Beyond Parsons? A critique of Ralf Dahrendorf's conflict theory", *Soc. Forces* 48(2), dec 69 : 151-165.

583 WIATR, J. J. "Herbert Marcuse: philosopher of a lost radicalism", *Sci. and Soc.* 34(3), 1970 : 319-341.

584 WILBURN, W. V. "Testing Talcott Parsons' theory of motivation", *J. soc. Psychol.* 80(2), apr 70 : 239-240.

585 WRONG, D. H. (comp.). *Max Weber.* Englewood Cliffs, N. J., Prentice-Hall, 70, viii-214 p.

586 ZUIDEMA, S. U. *De revolutionaire maatschappijkritiek van Herbert Marcuse* (Herbert Marcuse's revolutionary criticism of society). Amsterdam, Buijten en Schipperheijin, 70, 205 p.

B.5 ANALYSIS OF BASIC SOCIOLOGICAL CONCEPTS
ANALYSE DES CONCEPTS SOCIOLOGIQUES FONDAMENTAUX

[See also / Voir aussi: 421, 490, 541, 543, 555, 564, 570, 571, 648, 860, 919, 1194, 1734, 1808, 2143, 2372, 2801, 3962, 4335, 4363, 4754]

587 AUBERT, V. "Justice as a problem of social psychology", *Archiv Rechts-u. soz.-Philos.* 56(4), 1970 : 465-483.

588 BARDIS, P. D. "Present relevance of classical conceptions of time", *Sociol. int. (Berlin)* 8(1), 1970 : 55-68.

589 Bibl. XVIII-516. BOUDON, R. *A quoi sert la notion de 'structure'? Essai sur la signification de la notion de structure dans les sciences humaines.* CR: M. VUILLE, *C. Vilfredo Pareto* 20, feb 70 : 165-170.

590 DOS SANTOS, T. "The concept of social classes", *Sci. and Soc.* 34(2), 1970 : 166-193; *Soc. Sci. Quart.* 51(1), jun 70 : 166-193.

591 DUFFIELD, J. "The value concept in *Capital*, in light of recent criticism", *Sci. and Soc.* 34(3), 1970 : 293-302.

592 FEDOROV, K. M. "Interes kak sociologičeskaja kategorija" (Interest as a sociological category), *Učen. Zap. Irkutsk. Inst. nar. Hoz.* (15), 1969 : 55-92.

593 FRIEDMANN, P. "Die Konzeption der Repräsentation bei Mably" (Mably's concept of representation), *Archiv Rechts-u. soz.-Philos.* 56(3), 1970 : 415-441.

594 GLICK, T. F.; PI-SUNYER, O. "Acculturation as an explanatory concept in Spanish history", *Comp. Stud. Soc. Hist.* 11(2), apr 69 : 136-154.

595 HARMS, V. *Der Terminus "Spiel" in der Ethnologie; eine begriffskritische Untersuchung, dargestellt anhand von Berichten über die Kultur der Samoaner* (The term "game" in ethnology. A critical conceptual survey illustrated by relations in the Samoan culture). Hamburg-München, K. Renner, 69, viii-333 p.

596   HERICHON, E. "Le concept de propriété dans la pensée de Karl Marx", *Homme et Soc.*
       17, jul-aug-sep 70 : 163-181.

597   HEYKE, H.-E. "Über den Begriff des technischen Fortschritts" (On the concept of
       technical progress), *Jb. soz.-Wiss.* 21(2), 1970 : 99-126.

598   HODGES, D. C. "Marx's concept of value and critique of value fetishism", *Sci. and Soc.*
       34(3), 1970 : 343-346.

599   ISHIDA, T. "Beyond the traditional concepts of peace in different cultures", *J. Peace
       Res.* (2), 1969 : 133-147.

600   KLONCLAN, G. E.; COWARD, E. W. Jr. "The concept of symbolic adoption: a suggested
       interpretation", *Rur. Sociol.* 35(1), mar 70 : 77-83.

601   LISON TOLOSANA, C. "Operatividad del concepto de estructura en el trabajo de campo"
       (Utility of the concept of structure in field work), *R. esp. Opin. públ.* 20, apr-mar 70 :
       6-20.

602   LOPREATO, J.; ALSTON, L. "Ideal types and the idealization strategy", *Amer. sociol. R.*
       35(1), feb 70 : 88-96.

603   MATEI, T.; HOFFMAN, O. "Valeur cognitive des concepts opérationnels utilisés dans la
       prognose sociologique", *R. roum. Sci. soc. Sér. Sociol.* 14, 1970 : 109-114.

604   McLEMORE, S. D. "Simmel's 'stranger': a critique of the concept", *Pacific sociol. R.*
       13(2), 1970 : 86-94.

605   MEIER, C. *Entstehung des Begriffs Demokratie; vier Prolegomena zu einer historischen
       Theorie* (The birth of the concept of democracy: four prolegomena to an historical
       theory). Frankfurt am Main, Suhrkamp Verlag, 70, 220 p.

606   Bibl. XIX-533. MINAR, D. W.; GREER, S. (eds.). *The concept of community: readings with
       interpretations.* CR: J. R. SHUSTER, *Amer. sociol. R.* 35(3), jun 70 : 588-589.

607   MOYA, C. "Teoría del conflicto versus teoría del consensus" ('Poder' como categoría
       sociológica fundamental)" (Conflict theory versus consensus theory: "Power" as a
       fundamental sociological category), *Bol. Inform. Cienc. polít.* 3, mar 70 : 29-51.

608   RÉVÉSZ, L. "Marxistisch-Leninistischer Demokratiebegriff" (The Marxist-Leninist
       concept of democracy), *Stud. Sov. Thought* 8(1), mar 68 : 33-56.

609   RITSERT, J. "Die Antinomien des Anomie-konzepts" (Antinomies of the concept of
       anomy), *Soc. Welt* 20(2), 1969 : 145-162.

610   ROSARIO, C. "Sobre el concepto de socialización en las sciencias sociales" (On the
       concept of socialization in the social sciences), *R. Cienc. soc. Puerto Rico* 14(1), jan-mar
       70 : 5-25.

611   ROSENAU, J. N. "Intervention as a scientific concept", *J. Conflict Resol.* 13(2), jun 69 :
       149-171.

612   ROUCEK, J. S. "The development of the concept of social change", *R. int. Sociol. (Madrid)*
       27(105-106), jan-jun 69 : 51-88.

613   SCHMIDT-RELENBERG, N. "Über Verantwortung. Ein Beitrag zur Soziologie des Alltags-
       Klischees" (Responsibility. An essay on the sociology of a banal cliché), *Kölner Z.
       Soziol. u. Sozialpsychol.* 22(2), jun 70 : 251-264.

614   SKLAIR, L. "The fate of the 'functional requisites' in Parsonian sociology", *Brit. J.
       Sociol.* 21(1), mar 70 : 30-42.

615   SUSMAN, G. I. "The concept of status congruence as a basis to predict task allocations in
       autonomous work groups", *Adm. Sci. Quart.* 15(2), jun 70 : 164-175.

616   TJADEN, K. H. *Soziales System und sozialer Wandel. Untersuchung zur Geschichte und
       Bedeutung zweier Begriffe* (Social system and social change. Research on the history and
       meaning of two concepts). Stuttgart, Enke Verlag, 69, viii-336 p. CR: N. LUHMANN,
       Kölner Z. Soziol. u. soz.-Psychol. 22(4), dec 70 : 793-795.

617   VASCONI, T. A. "Dependencia y superestructura" (Dependency and superstructure),
       Econ. Cienc. soc. 11(3), jul-sep 69 : 99-131.

618   VEJNGOL'D, Ju. Ju. *K voprosu o 'social'noj vole' kak kategorii marksistskoj sociologii* (On the
       'social will' as a category of Marxist sociology). Frunze, 70, 48 p.

619   WILLER, D.; WEBSTER, M. Jr. "Theoretical concepts and observables", *Amer. sociol. R.*
       35(4), aug 70 : 748-757.

620   WRONG, D. H. "Some problems in defining social power", *Amer. J. Sociol.* 73(6), mai 68 :
       673-681.

C SOCIAL STRUCTURE
STRUCTURE SOCIALE

C.0 GENERAL WORKS
OUVRAGES GÉNÉRAUX

[See also / Voir aussi: 117, 4329]

621 ARDREY, R. *The social contract; a personal inquiry into the evolutionary sources of order and disorder.* New York, Atheneum, 70, 405 p.

622 Bibl. XIX-552. BERRIEN, F. K. *General and social systems.* CR: W. BUCKLEY, *Amer. sociol. R.* 34(6), dec 69 : 958-959.

623 CALLAN, H. *Ethnology and society; towards an anthropological view.* Oxford, Clarendon Press, 70, 176 p.

624 GONZALEZ, N. L. "The neoteric society", *Comp. Stud. Soc. Hist.* 12(1), jan 70 : 1-13.

625 KNEBEL, H. J. *Ansätze einer soziologischen Metatheorie subjektiver und sozialer Systeme* (Addenda to a sociological metatheory of subjective and social systems). Stuttgart, Enke, 70, 100 p.

626 LANDHEER, B. "Die Weltgesellschaft als dynamisches Sozial-System und ihre Kommunikationsmittel" (World society as a dynamic social system and its means of communication), *Jb. int. Recht* 14, 1969 : 188-208.

627 LIPP, W. *Institution und Veranstaltung. Zur Anthropologie der sozialen Dynamik* (Institution and organisation. On the anthropology of social dynamics). Berlin, Duncker und Humblot, 68, 216 p.

628 LUHMANN, N. *Soziologische Aufklärung; Aufsätze zur Theorie sozialer Systeme* (Sociological enlightenment: essays in the theory of social systems). Köln, Westdeutscher Verlag, 70, 268 p.

629 MANNICHE, E. (ed.). *Social struktur of sociale relationer* (Social structure and social relations). København, Fremad, 69, 109 p.

630 McINTOSH, D. *The foundations of human society.* Chicago, University of Chicago Press, 69, x-341 p. CR: M. A. WEINSTEIN, *Amer. polit. Sci. R.* 64(2), jun 70 : 619-620.

631 ORLOV, G. P. "Vremja obščestva kak forma social'nogo bytija i ego struktura (metodologičeskie problemy)" (Social time as a form of social life and its structure; methodological problems), *Sb. nauč. Trud. (Sverdlovsk. jur. Inst.)* (10), 1969 : 272-295.

632 SCHELSKY, H. (ed.). *Zur Theorie der Institution* (The theory of the institution). Düsseldorf, Bertelsmann Universitätsverlag, 70, 162 p.

633 SCHULZ, G. *Das Zeitalter der Gesellschaft. Aufsätze zur politischen Sozialgeschichte der Neuzeit* (The era of society. Essays on the socio-political history of the contemporary era). München, Piper, 69, 480 p.

634 WARRINER, C. K. *The emergence of society.* Homewood, Ill., Dorsey Press, 70, x-163 p.

635 WEISZ, P. B. (ed.). *The contemporary scene; readings on human nature, race, behavior, society and environment.* New York, McGraw-Hill, 70, xxi-349 p.

636 WELLS, A. F. *Social institutions.* London, Heinemann Educational, 70, x-298 p.

637 ZIJDERVELD, A. C. "Rationality and irrationality in pluralistic society", *Soc. Res.* 37(1), mar 70 : 23-47.

C.1   DEMOGRAPHIC FACTORS
         FACTEURS DÉMOGRAPHIQUES

C.10   General studies
         Études générales

[See also / Voir aussi: 251, 287, 390, 776, 4238, 4725, 4989, 5006, 5184]

638   BARBERI, B. *Teoria e politica della popolazione* (Theory and policy of population). Roma, Ceres, 69, 293 p.

639   BECHHOFER, F. (ed.). *Population growth and the brain drain—Proceedings.* Edinburgh, University Press, 69, xvi-236 p. CR: D. G. MARSHALL, *Amer. sociol. R.* 35(4), aug 70 : 786.

640   Bibl. XIX-565. BEHRMAN, S. J.; CORSA, L. Jr.; FREEDMAN, R. (eds.). *Fertility and family planning: a world view.* CR: S. POLGAR, *Amer. sociol. R.* 35(2), apr 70 : 413-414.

641   Bibl. XIX-566. BENJAMIN, B. *Demographic analysis.* CR: Y. KIM, *Amer. sociol. R.* 35(3), jun 70 : 579.

642   Bibl. XIX-567. BERELSON, B. (ed.). *Family-planning programs: an international survey.* CR: O. WALZ, *Amer. sociol. R.* 35(4), aug 70 : 783-784.

643   Bibl. XIX-568. BOGUE, D. J. *Principles of demography.* CR: J. C. RIDLEY, *Amer. sociol. R.* 35(2), apr 70 : 412-413; G. ALBRECHT, *Kölner Z. Soziol. u. soz.-Psychol.* 22(3), sep 70 : 638-640.

644   BOWER, L. G. "The return from investment in population control in less developed countries", *Demography (Washington)* 5(1), 1968 : 422-432.

645   BRONER, D. L.; BELJAEVSKIJ, I. K. *Osnovnye problemy demografičeskoj nauki* (Essential problems of demographic science). Moskva, 69, 198 p.

646   BURMAN, B. K. "Family planning from the point of view of cultural anthropology", *Ind. J. soc. Wk.* 30(4), jan 70 : 343-354.

647   CALDGRAN BELTRAÕ. "Implicações sociológicas de desenvolvimento demográfico" (Sociological implications of demographic development), *R. brasil. Estatist.* 30(119), jul-sep 69 : 277-288.

648   DAVID, A. S.; CHING-JU HUANG. "Population theory and the concept of optimum population", *Socio-econ. plan. Sci.* 3(3), oct 69 : 191-218.

649   DAY, L. H.; DAY, A. T. "Family size in industrialized countries; an inquiry into the social-cultural determinants of levels of childbearing", *J. Marriage Family* 31(2), mai 69 : 242-251.

650   DELVECCHIO, F. "Un modello di sviluppo della popolazione" (A model of population development), *G. Economisti* 28(11-12), nov-dec 69 : 822-830.

651   DOŠIĆ, D. "Demografsko strukture kao osnov za proličavanje društvenih struktura" (Demographic structures as bases for the study of social structures), *Stanovništvo* 7(3-4), jul-dec 69 : 189-195.

652   EBANKS, G. E. "Users and non-users of contraception: tests of stationarity applied to members of a family planning programme", *Popul. Stud.* 24(1), mai 70 : 85-91.

653   EICHER, J. C. *La population, la famille; étude démographique.* Paris, Scodel, 69, 155 p.
654   FEDERICI, N. "A demográfia irányzatai és fejlödésének távlatai" (Trends and development prospects of demography), *Demográfia* 12(3), 1969 : 225-240.

655   FISH, M.; THOMPSON, A. A. "The determinants of fertility: a theoretical forecasting model", *Behav. Sci.* 15(4), jul 70 : 318-328.

656   FORD, T. R.; JONG, G. F. DE (ed.). *Social demography.* Englewood Cliffs, N. J., Prentice-Hall, 70, x-690 p.

657   GEORGE, P. *Population et peuplement.* Paris, Presses universitaires de France, 69, 212 p.
658   GRITTI, J. *La pilule dans la presse, sociologie de la diffusion d'une encyclique.* Tours, Mame, 69, 158 p.

659   GUILLAUME, P.; POUSSON, J. P. *Démographie historique.* Paris, A. Colin, 70, 414 p.
660   HAWTHORN, G. *The sociology of fertility.* London, Collier-Macmillan, 70, v-161 p.
661   HILL, R. "A classified international bibliography of family planning research, 1955-1968", *Demography (Washington)* 5(2), 1968 : 973-1001.

662   HOLLINGSWORTH, T. H. *Historical demography.* London, Hodder and Stoughton, 69, 448 p.

663   IONESCU, C. "Implications socio-économiques des modifications démographiques", *R. roum. Sci. soc. Sér. Sociol.* 14, 1970 : 29-39.

664 JONES, G.; GINGRICH, P. "The effects of differing trends in fertility and of educational advance on the growth, quality and turnover of the labor force", *Demography (Washington)* 5(1), 1968 : 226-248.

665 Bibl. XIX-592. KHALATBARI, P. *Überbevölkerung in den Entwicklungsländern. Ein Beitrag zur marxistischen Bevölkerungstheorie* (Overpopulation in developing countries. A contribution to the Marxist theory of population). CR: D. TOSCHER, *Kölner Z. Soziol. u. soz.-Psychol.* 22(3), sep 70 : 641-643.

666 KOZLOV, V. I. *Dinamika čislennosti narodov. Metodologija issledovanija i osnovnye faktory* (Dynamics of population. Research methodology and fundamental factors). Moskva, Nauka, 69, 407 p.

667 KUNZ, P. R.; BRINKERHOFF, M. B. "Differential childlessness by color; the destruction of a cultural belief", *J. Marriage Family* 31(4), nov 69 : 713-719.

668 LARSEN, T. B.; JØRGENSEN, I. *Befolkningseksplosionen* (The demographic explosion). København, Gyldendal, 69, 120 p.

669 LAURIAT, P. "The effect of marital dissolution on fertility", *J. Marriage Family* 31(3), aug 69 : 484-493.

670 LEDERMANN, S. *Nouvelles tables-types de mortalité.* Paris, Presses universitaires de France, 69, xxi-260 p.

671 LIEBERSON, S. "Measuring population diversity", *Amer. sociol. R.* 34(6), dec 69 : 850-862.

672 MATTELART, A. "Une lecture idéologique de l'*Essai sur le principe de population*", *Homme et Soc.* 15, jan-feb-mar 70 : 183-219.

673 McCORMACK, A. *The population problem.* New York, Crowell, 70, 263 p.

674 MUHSAM, H. V. "Crítica de dos teorías sobre el factor población en el desarrollo" (Critique of two theories on the population factor in development), *Demogr. y. Econ.* 3(3), 1969 : 308-318.

675 MUHSAM, H. V. "Sur les relations entre la croissance de la population et le développement économique", *Population* 25(2), mar-apr 70 : 347-362.

676 NIZARD, A.; VALLIN, J. "Les plus faibles mortalités", *Population* 25(4), jul-aug 70 : 847-867.

677 ORGANISATION DE COOPÉRATION ET DE DÉVELOPPEMENT ÉCONOMIQUES. Centre de développement. *Problèmes démographiques; aide internationale et recherche.* Paris, OCDE, 69, 237 p. [Issued also in English under title: *Population; international assistance and research.*]

678 POTTER, R. G.; JAIN, A. K.; McCANN, B. "Net delay of newt conception by contraception: a highly simplified case", *Popul. Stud.* 24(2), jul 70 : 173-192.

679 POTTER, R. G.; McCANN, B.; SAKODA, M. J. "Selective fecundability and contraceptive effectiveness", *Milbank Memor. Fund Quart.* 48(1), jan 70 : 91-102.

680 PRADERVAND, P. "Les pays nantis et la limitation des naissances dans le Tiers-Monde", *Dévelop. et. Civilis.* 39-40, mar-jun 70 : 4-40.

681 PRESTON, S. H. "An international comparison of excessive adult mortality", *Popul. Stud.* 24(1), mar 70 : 1-20.

682 PRESTON, S. H. "Mortality differentials by social class and smoking habit", *Soc. Biology* 16(4), dec 69 : 280-289.

683 SÁRKÁNY, J. "Az ujszülött-halálozás néhány aspektusáról" (On some aspects of early neonatal mortality), *Demográfia* 13(3), 1970 : 184-211.

684 SHELESNYAK, M. C. (ed.). *Growth of population: consequences and controls; proceedings.* New York, Gordon and Breach, Science Publishers, 69, xvii-458 p. [Conference on Population, Princeton, 1968.]

685 SIMON, J. L. "Family planning prospects in less-developed countries and a cost-benefit analysis of various alternatives", *Econ. J.* 80(317), mar 70 : 58-71.

686 SMITH, T. L.; ZOPF, P. E. Jr. *Demography; principles and methods.* Philadelphia, F. A. Davis Co., 70, 590 p.

687 SZABADY, E. "Népességtudomány és humábniológia" (Demography and human biology) *Demográfia* 13(1-2), 1970 : 21-31.

688 Bibl. XVIII-617. SZABADY, E. (ed.). *World view of population problems.* CR: W. H. WHITNEY, *Amer. sociol. R.* 35(3), jun 70 : 579-581.

689 TAUBER, A. "Population pressure and development strategy", *Int. Develop.* 1968 : 117-126.

690   UNITED NATIONS. Department of Economic and Social Affairs. *Growth of the world's urban and rural population, 1920-2000.* New York, UN, 69, vii-124 p.

691   VAN PRAAG, P. "Enkele opmerkingen over de relaties tussen demografische en politieke variabelen" (Some remarks on the relations between demographic and political variables), *Tijds. soc. Wetensch.* 15(1), 1970 : 3-23.

692   VENTURA, S. J. "Recent trends and differentials in illegitimacy", *J. Marriage Family* 31(3), aug 69 : 446-450.

693   VINCENT, C. E.; HANEY, G. A.; COCHRANE, C. M. "Familial and generational patterns of illegitimacy", *J. Marriage Family* 31(4), nov 69 : 659-667.

694   VOLKOV, A. G. (ed.). *Voprosy demografii* (Demographic questions). Moskva, Statistika, 70, 280 p.

695   WARD, R. J. "Alternative means to control population growth", *R. soc. Econ.* 27(2), sep 69 : 121-138.

696   WINKLER, W. *Demometrie* (Demometry). Berlin, Duncker und Humblot, 69, 447 p.

C.11   Population changes (studies by countries)
Changements de population (études localisées)

C.11(1)   *Africa*
Afrique

[See also / Voir aussi: 4844]

697   BUMBA, A. A. "Étude démographique des populations du district du Bas-Congo", *Congo-Afr.* 10(43), mar 70 : 129-144.

698   CALDWELL, J. C. "The control of family size in tropical Africa", *Demography (Washington)* 5(2), 1968 : 598-619.

699   CALDWELL, J. C.; IGUN, A. "The spread of anti-natal knowledge and practice in Nigeria", *Popul. Stud.* 24(1), mar 70 : 21-34.

700   Bibl. XIX-633. CALDWELL, J. C.; OKONJO, C. (eds.). *The population of tropical Africa.* CR: A. E. OKORAFOR, *Amer. J. Sociol.* 75(6), mai 70; 1064-1066.

701   CANTRELLE, P. *Étude démographique dans la région du Sine-Saloum (Sénégal). État civil et observation démographique, 1963-1965.* Paris, 69, ii-121 p. [Travaux et documents de l'ORSTOM.]

702   CLARKE, J. I. "Population policies and dynamics in Tunisia", *J. develop. Areas* 4(1), oct 69 : 45-58.

703   "Connaissance et pratique du planning familial à Tunis", *R. tunis. Sci. soc.* 7(22), jul 70 : 9-92.

704   DOW, T. E. Jr. "Family planning. Theoretical considerations and African models", *J. Marriage Family* 31(2), mai 69 : 252-256.

705   DOW, T. E. Jr. "Fertility and family planning in Africa", *J. mod. Afr. Stud.* 8(3), oct 70 : 445-457.

706   FORDE, E. R. *The population of Ghana; a study of the spatial relationships of its socio-cultural and economic characteristics.* Evanston, Ill., Dept. of Geography, Northwestern University, 68, x-154 p.

707   FOSSATI, C. "Sull'incidenza della tuberculosi polmonare in Cirenaica. Considerazioni statistiche sulle cause di morte negli ultimi anni" (On the incidence of pulmonary tuberculosis in Cirenaica. Statistical considerations on the causes of death in the last years), *Previd. soc.* 26(3), mai-jun 70 : 799-810.

708   GENDREAU, F. "Quelques aspects de la recherche en démographie à Madagascar", *Cah. Orstom Sér. Sci. hum.* 6(4), 1969 : 93-127.

709   HANCE, W. A. *Population, migration and urbanization in Africa.* New York, Columbia University Press, 70, xiv-450 p.

710   LESTHAEGHE, R. "La fécondité urbaine au Maroc", *B. écon. soc. Maroc* 30(110-111), 1969 : 91-99.

711   MARCOUX, A. "Évolution générale et mouvements saisonniers des naissances en Tunisie de 1956 à 1968", *R. tunis. Sci. soc.* 7(20), mar 70 : 173-214.

712   MARTENSSON, M. "La planification familiale au Maghreb: enquêtes nationales concernant les connaissances, les attitudes et les pratiques", *B. écon. soc. Maroc* 31(112-113), jan-jun 69 : 197-210.

713   "Orientations de la recherche démographique au Sénégal", *Cah. ORSTOM Sér. Sci. hum.* 6(4), 1969 : 3-91.

714   SADIE, J. L. "An evaluation of demographic data pertaining to the non-white population of South Africa", *South. Afr. J. Econ.* 38(1), mar 70 : 1-35; 38(2), jun 70 : 171-191.

715   SAINT-MOULIN, L. DE. "Quelle est la population de Kinshasa ?", *Congo-Afr.* 10(42), feb 70 : 65-77.

716   SASON, H. "Approche socio-démographique de la société algérienne", *R. Occident musul. Méditerr. n° spéc.* 1970 : 327-332.

717   SCOTT, C.; SABACH, G. "The historical calendar as a method of estimating age: the experience of the Moroccan multi-purpose sample survey of 1961-63", *Popul. Stud.* 24(1), mar 70 : 93-109.

C.11(2)   America
Amérique

[See also / Voir aussi: 1780, 4997]

718   AMATO, P. W. "A comparison: population densities, land values and socio-economic class in four Latin American cities", *Land Econ.* 46(4), nov 70 : 447-455.

719   ARRIAGA, E. E.; DAVIS, K. "Las pautas de los cambios de mortalidad en América Latina" (The norms of changes in mortality in Latin America), *R. parag. Sociol.* 6(15), mai-aug 69 : 93-123.

720   BARNETT, L. D. "Population policy: payments for fertility limitation in the United States ?", *Soc. Biology* 16(4), dec 69 : 239-248.

721   BEYNON, T. G.; OSTRY, S.; PLATEK, R. "Some methodological aspects of the 1971 census in Canada", *Canad. J. Econ.* 3(1), feb 70 : 95-110.

722   BIGGAR, J. C.; BUTLER, E. W. "Fertility and its interrelationship with population and socioeconomic characteristics in a Southern State", *Rur. Sociol.* 34(4), dec 69 : 528-536. [USA.]

723   BOURCIER DE CARBON, P. "Précision sur les perspectives de population active. Application au Mexique", *Population* 25(1), jan-feb 70 : 77-96.

724   CHARBONNEAU, H.; LAVOIE, Y.; LÉGARÉ, J. "Recensements et registres paroissiaux du Canada durant la période 1665-1668. Étude critique", *Population* 25(1), jan 70 : 97-124.

725   COFRESI, E. "El control de la natalidad en Puerto Rico" (Birth control in Puerto Rico), *R. Cienc. soc. (Puerto Rico)* 13(3), jul-sep 69 : 379-385.

726   COLLVER, O. A. "Women's work participation and fertility in metropolitan areas", *Demography (Washington)* 5(1), 1968 : 55-60. [USA.]

727   COSTA, O. "O povoamento da Amazônia" (Amazonian population), *R. brasil. Estud. polít.* 27, jul 69 : 151-174.

728   DALT, H. E. "The population question in Northeast Brazil: its economic and ideological dimensions", *Econ. Develop. cult. Change* 18(4. Part I), jul 70 : 536-576. Also published in Spanish, *Demogr. y Econ.* 3(3), 1969 : 279-307.

729   "Demographic aspects of the black community", *Milbank Memor. Fund Quart.* 48(2) apr 70 *Part II:* 11-362. [USA.]

730   EARLY, J. D. "The structure and change of mortality in a Maya community", *Milbank Memor. Fund Quart.* 48(2), apr 70 : 179-202.

731   HALL, M. P. "Male use of contraception and attitudes toward abortion, Santiago, Chile 1968", *Milbank Memor. Fund Quart.* 48(2), apr 70 : 145-166.

732   HAREWOOD, J. 'Recent population trends and family planning activity in the Caribbean", *Demography (Washington)* 5(2), 1968 : 874-893.

733   HENRIPIN, J.; LÉGARÉ, J. *Évolution démographique du Québec et de ses régions, 1966-1986.* Québec, Presses de l'Université Laval, 69, ix-128 p.

734   JAFFE, F. S.; GUTTMACHER, A. F. "Family planning programs in the United States", *Demography (Washington)* 5(2), 1968 : 910-923.

735   KATZ, M. "Legal dimensions of population policy", *Soc. Sci. Quart.* 50(3), dec 69 : 731-741. [USA.]

736   LONG, L. H. "The fertility of migrants to and within North America", *Milbank Memor. Fund Quart.* 48(3), jul 70 : 297-316.

737 MACISCO, J. J. Jr. _et al._ "The effect of labor force participation on the relation between migration status and fertility in San Juan, Puerto Rico", _Milbank Memor. Fund Quart._ 48(1), jan 70 : 51-70.

738 MARINO, A. "Family, fertility and sex ratios in the British Caribbean", _Popul. Stud._ 24(2), jul 70 : 159-172.

739 [MAYONE] STYCOS, J. "Opposition to family planning in Latin America—conservative nationalism", _Demography (Washington)_ 5(2), 1968 : 846-854.

740 MICKLIN, M. "Traditionalism, social class and differential fertility in Guatemala City", _Amér. lat._ 12(4), oct-dec 69 : 59-78 .

741 MINCHAS GEIGER, P.; OXNARD, S. "Aspects of population growth in Brazil", _R. geogr._ _(Rio de Janeiro)_ 70, jun 69 : 7-28.

742 MIRANDA S., E.; ARRETX, G., C. "Análisis de los cambios demográficos en el sistema de seguridad social" (Analysis of demographic changes in the social security system), _Segur. soc. (Santiago de Chile)_ 99, 1968 : 7-41. [Chile.]

743 MORELOS, J. B. "El problema demográfico de México" (The Mexican demographic problem), _Demogr. y Econ._ 3(3), 1969 : 319-327.

744 NARAYANAN, R. "Population control as an aspect of United States policy", _Int. Stud._ 10(1-2), jul-oct 67 : 131-162.

745 NEWCOMBE, H. B.; SMITH, M. E. "Changing patterns of family growth: the value of linked vital records as a source of data", _Popul. Stud._ 24(2), jul 70 : 193-203. [Canada.]

746 "Población en Colombia (La): diagnóstico y política" (Population in Colombia: diagnostic and policy), _R. Plan. Desarr._ 1(4), dec 69 : 19-81.

747 PRESSAT, R. "Fécondité américaine et fécondité européenne", _Population_ 25(4), jul-aug 70 : 814-827.

748 RAWLINGS, S. W. _Population of Chile: estimates and projections, 1961-1991._ Washington, United States Government Printing Office 69, 50 p.

749 ROMERO, H. _Población, desarrollo y control de natalidad en América Latina; prejuicios y controversias_ (Population development and birth control in Latin America; prejudices and controversies). México, Editorial Diana, 69, 156 p.

750 ROTHMAN, A. M. "Desarrollo y estado actual de la demografía en la Argentina" (Development and present state of demography in Argentina), _R. latinoamer. Sociol._ 5(3), nov 69 : 657-662.

751 STOCKWELL, E. G. "A methodological consideration for studying the consequences of population decline", _Rur. Sociol._ 34(4), dec 69 : 552-555. [USA.]

752 VIDAL, J. L. "Paraguay: proyección de la población, por sexo y grupo de edades, 1960-2000" (Paraguay: population projection by sex and age group, 1960-2000), _R. parag._ _Sociol._ 7(17), jan-mar 70 : 80-106.

C.11(3) _Asia_
Asie

[See also / Voir aussi: 1319, 5183]

753 AGARWALA, S. N. "India népességének szerkezete, növekedése, termékenysége és az ezeket befolyásoló tényezök" (Growth, structure and fertility pattern of India's population and the factors associated with them), _Demográfia_ 13(3), 1970 : 165-183.

754 ARNIM, B. VON. _Bevölkerungsentwicklung, Bevölkerungspolitik und Wirtschaftsplanung in Indien_ (Population development, demographic policy and economic planning in India). Stuttgart, G. Fischer, 69, vii-214 p.

755 BOSE, A. "Eleven myths of family planning", _South Asian R._ 3(4), jul 70 : 323-330. [India.]

756 CHANDRASEKHAR, S. M. "Hogyan küzd India népesedési problémájával" (How India fights its demographic problems), _Demográfia_ 12(3), 1969 : 251-262.

757 CHANG, C. T. "Factors influencing the declining birth-rate in Singapore", _Malayan econ. R._ 15(1), apr 70 : 83-100.

758 CHEN, P. C. "China's birth control action programme, 1956-1964", _Popul. Stud._ 24(2), jul 70 : 141-168.

759 CHOW, L. P. "Family planning in Taiwan, Republic of China: progress and prospects", _Popul. Stud._ 24(3), nov 70 : 339-352.

760 DANDEKAR, K. BHATE, V. "Methodology of family planning surveys", *Artha Vijnana* 11(4), dec 69 : 651-661. [India.]

761 DUBEY, D. C. *Adoption of a new contraceptive in urban India.* New Delhi, Central Family Planning Institute, 69, 132 p.

762 EL-BADRY, M. A. "Higher female than male mortality in some countries of South Asia: a digest", *J. Amer. statist. Assoc.* 64(328), dec 69 : 1234-1244.

763 GOLDSTEIN, S. "Religious fertility differentials in Thailand, 1960", *Popul. Stud.* 24(3), nov 70 : 325-337.

764 KOEHLER, J. E. *The Philippine family planning program; some suggestions for dealing with uncertainties.* Santa Monica, Calif., Rand Corporation, 70, xi-25 p.

765 LAL, B. B. "Abridged life tables for rural India, 1966-1967", *Artha Vijñana* 11(3), sep 69 : 420-430.

766 MALHOTRA, S. P.; BHARARA, L. P.; PATWA, F. C. "Population, resources and food situation in various tracts within the arid zone of Rajasthan", *Ind. sociol. B.* 6(4), jul 69 : 213-221.

767 MIGOZZI, J. "La mortalité au Cambodge: ses facteurs", *C. O.-Mer* 23(90), apr-jun 70 : 202-220.

768 NAKAGAWA, M. "Some problems of population movements in China under the T'ang dynasty", *Hitotsubashi J. Econ.* 9(2), feb 69 : 35-42.

769 NITISASTRO, W. *Population trends in Indonesia.* Ithaca, Cornell University Press, 70, xxi-266 p.

770 PEPER, B. "Population growth in Java in the 19th century: a new interpretation", *Popul. Stud.* 24(1), mar 70 : 71-84.

771 POFFENBERGER, T.; POFFENBERGER, S. B. *Husband-wife communication and motivational aspects of population control in an Indian village.* New Delhi, Central Family Planning Institute, 69, 117 p.

772 SIAMPOS, G. S. "The population of Cambodia 1945-1980", *Milbank Memor. Fund Quart.* 48(3), jul 70 : 317-360.

773 TIEN, H. Y. "Marital moratorium and fertility control in China", *Popul. Stud.* 24(3), nov 70 : 311-323.

C.11(4) *Europe*

[See also / Voir aussi: 38, 747, 1434, 1553, 1602, 2599, 2626, 5157, 5250]

774 ACSÁDI, Gy. "Népességpolitikai kerdések a szocialista országok régiojában" (Problems on population policies in the European socialist countries region), *Demógrafia* 12(4), 1969 : 464-479.

775 AGATA, C. D'. "Le diverse misure della popolazione nelle previsioni demografiche regionali" (The different population measures in the regional demographic forecasts), *Riv. ital. Econ. Demogr. Statist.* 21(3-4), jul-dec 67 : 135-150. [Italy.]

776 ANDRÉ, R. "Étude régionale de la natalité et de la fécondité des populations belge et étrangère", *R. Inst. Sociol.* 3, 1969 : 569-586.

777 ANDRÉ, R. *Le vieillissement de la Belgique.* Bruxelles, Éditions de l'Institut de sociologie de l'Université libre de Bruxelles, 69, 143 l.

778 ANDRÉ, R.; GYSELINGS, R. "Variation saisonnière de la mortalité infantile en Belgique", *R. Inst. Sociol.* 3, 1970 : 587-597.

779 ANDRÉ, R.; ROUSSIEAUX, J. P. "Analyse démographique de l'arrondissement de Nivelles", *R. Inst. Sociol.* 4, 1969 : 761-786. [Belgique.]

780 ANIČIĆ, Z. "Neki pokazatelji skorašnjih tendencija fertiliteta stanovništva Jugoslavije" (Some indicators of current fertility trends of the Yugoslav population), *Stanovništvo* 7(3-4), jul-dec 69 : 172-185.

781 BEIRAS, J. M. *Estructura y problemas de la población gallega* (Structure and problems of Galician population). La Coruña, Servicio de Estudios del Banco del Noroeste, 70, 387 p. [Spain.]

782 BELLETTINI, A. "L'analisi della struttura e delle dinamica della popolazione urbana attraverso la gestione automatizzata dell'anagrafe comunale" (The analysis of urban population structure and dynamics through the automatic organization of the communal registry office), *Statistica (Bologna)* 29(4), oct-dec 69 : 535-562. [Italy.]

33

783   BELLINI, L. "Alcune esperienze nelle indagini demografiche per il piano di sviluppo economico regionale dell'Umbria" (Some experiences of demographic researches for the Umbrian regional economic development plan), *Riv. ital. Econ. Demogr. Statist.* 23(1-4), jan-dec 69 : 183-192.

784   BENJAMIN, B. *The population census.* London, Heinemann Educational, 70, ix-170 p. [UK.]

785   BENJAMIN, B. "The 1971 population census and after", *J. roy. statist. Soc.* 133(2), 1970 : 240-256. [UK.]

786   BERENT, J. "Causes of fertility decline in Eastern Europe and the Soviet Union. I. The influence of demographic factors. II. Economic and social factors", *Popul. Stud.* 24(1), mar 70 : 35-58; 24(2), jul 70 : 247-292.

787   BIGGERI, L. "Su un metodo di previsione della popolazione attiva a livello regionale" (On a forecasting method of the working population at a regional level), *Riv. ital. Econ. Demogr. Statist.* 23(1-4), jan-dec 69 : 67-101. [Italy.]

788   BLAYO, C. "Fécondité, contraception et avortement en Europe de l'Est", *Population* 25(4), jul-aug 70 : 829-845.

789   BREZNIK, D. "Demographic trends in Yugoslavia", *Yugosl. Surv.* 11(2), mai 70 : 1-15.

790   CÂNDIDO, L. M. *Aspectos regionais da demografía portuguesa* (Regional aspects of Portuguese demography). Lisboa, Instituto Gulbenkian de Ciência, 69, 246 p.

791   CARTWRIGHT, A. *Parents and family planning services.* New York, Atherton Press, 70, x-293 p. [UK.]

792   CHARBONNEAU, H. *Tourouvre-en-Perche aux XVIIe et XVIIIe siècles; étude de démographie historique.* Paris, Presses universitaires de France, 70, xiv-423 p.

793   COMITE, L. DI. "Sulla stagionalità della mortalità in Francia" (On the seasonal variations of mortality in France), *G. Economisti* 28(11-12), nov-dec 69 : 856-867.

794   COMPTON, P. A. "Aspects of intercommunity population balance in Northern Ireland", *Econ. soc. R. (Dublin)* 1(4), jul 70 : 455-476.

795   DAVID, H. P. *Family planning and abortion in the socialist countries of Central and Eastern Europe.* New York, Population Council, 70, xi-306 p.

796   DIÉZ NICOLÁS, J. "Estructura por sexo y edades de la poblacíon española, 1900-1960" (Structure by sex and age of the Spanish population, 1900-1960), *Bol. Centro Estud. soc.* 9(3), 1969 : 3-65.

797   DIÉZ NICOLÁS, J. "La medida de la concentración provincial de la población en España (1900-1960)" (The measurement of provincial population concentration in Spain, 1900-1960), *R. int. Sociol. (Madrid)* 26(103-104), jul-dec 68 : 137-159. [Voir pour la première partie, Bibl. XIX-713.]

798   DÍEZ NICOLÁS, J. "Tamaño, densidad y crecimiento de la población en España, 1900-1960" (Size, density and population growth in Spain, 1900-1960), *R. int. Sociol. (Madrid)* 28(109-110), jan-apr 70 : 87-123.

799   DOOGHE, G. "La dénatalité récente en Belgique", *R. belge Sécur. soc.* 12(4), apr 70 : 569-583.

800   DRAKATOS, C. G. "The determinants of birth rate in developing countries: an econometric study of Greece", *Econ. Develop. soc. Change* 17(4), jul 69 : 596-601.

801   DRAKE, M. *Population and society in Norway, 1735-1835.* New York, Cambridge University Press, 69, xx-256 p. CR: R. B. LITCHFIELD, *J. econ. Liter.* 8(3), sep 70 : 876-878.

802   DRAKE, M. *Population in industrialization.* London, Methuen, 69, viii-200 p.

803   FEDERICI, N. "La misura degli equilibri demografici regionali e le loro modificazioni in Italia dal 1861 al 1961" (The measurement of regional demographic equilibrium and its modification in Italy from 1861 to 1961), *Riv. ital. Econ. Demogr. Statist.* 22(1-4), jan-dec 68 : 45-71.

804   FESTY, P. "Évolution de la fécondité en Europe occidentale depuis la guerre", *Population* 25(2), mar-apr 70 : 229-274.

805   FESTY, P. "Évolution de la fécondité en Suède depuis la guerre", *Population* 25(3), mai-jun 70 : 644-649.

806   GILI, A. "Popolosità e dinamica demografica di lungo periodo nei comuni dell' Emilia e del Veneto" (Long-term population density and demographic dynamics in the communes of Emilia and Veneto), *Statistica (Bologna)* 29(4), oct-dec 69 : 603-649.

807 HAIR, P. E. H. "Bridal pregnancy in earlier rural England further examined", *Popul. Stud.* 24(1), mar 70 : 59-70. [See also P. E. H. JAIR, "Bridal pregnancy in England in earlier centuries), *ibid.*, 20(2), jul 66 : 233-243.]

808 HEMERY, S. "La population totale", *R. Écon. polit. (Paris)* 79(5), sep-oct 69 : 861-874. [France, 1968.]

809 HENRY, L. "La population de la Norvège depuis deux siècles", *Population* 25(3), mai-jun 70 : 543-557.

810 HUTTEL, B.; BOUSTEDT, O. "Tendenzen der natürlichen Bevölkerungsentwicklung in Hamburg bis 1985" (Natural evolution trends of Hamburg population till 1985), *Hamburg in Zahlen*, apr 70 : 115-125.

811 JOLY, J. "Le recensement de la population française de 1968. Les premiers résultats", *Aménag. Territ. Dévelop. région.* 3, 1970 : 385-440.

812 KELSALL, R. K. *Population.* Revised ed. Harlow, Longmans, 70, ix-119 p. [UK.]

813 KNODEL, J. "Two and a half centuries of demographic history in a Bavarian village", *Popul. Stud.* 24(3), nov 70 : 353-376.

814 LACHIVER, M. *La population de Meulan du XVIIe au XIXe siècle (vers 1600-1870). Étude de démographie historique.* Paris, SEVPEN, 69, 340 p.

815 LASORSA, G. "Sviluppo della popolazione e delle forze di lavoro per gruppi di regioni in Italia" (Development of population and labour forces by groups of regions in Italy), *Riv. ital. Econ. Demogr. Statist.* 23(1-4), jan-dec 69 : 109-120.

816 LOCOH, T. "La population des ménages agricoles. Émigration et vieillissement. Résultats depuis 1962 et perspectives jusqu'en 1975", *Population* 25(3), mai-jun 70 : 497-516. [France.]

817 LUKÁCS, J. "The transmission of life: certain generalizations about the demography of Europe's nations in 1939-41", *Comp. Stud. Soc. Hist.* 12(4), oct 70 : 442-451.

818 LUTZ, H. *Theoretische Grundlagen des österreichischen Mikrozensus* (Theoretical bases of Austria's micro-sensus). Wien, Würzburg, Physica-Verlag, 69, 132 p.

819 MIRANDA, J. D. "A população universitária e a população portuguesa: um confronto da sua composição social" (University population and Portuguese population: a comparison of its social composition), *Análise soc.* 7(25-26), 1969 : 158-166.

820 NADOT, R. "Évolution de la mortalité infantile endogène en France dans la deuxième moitié du XIXe siècle", *Population* 25(1), jan-feb 70 : 49-58.

821 PALOMÄKI, M.; HAUTAMÄKI, L. *Recent population changes in North Carelia, Finland. (A statistical study in areas smaller than rural communes).* Helsinki, Societas geographica Fenniae, 69, 94 p.

822 PENNINO, C. "Previsioni sulla futura popolazione della Sicilia fino al 2.000" (Estimates of the future Sicilian population till 2000), *Riv. ital. Econ. Demogr. Statist.* 21(3-4), jul-dec 67 : 67-92.

823 PÉTERFALVY, A. DE. "Évolution d'une politique démographique socialiste. Un exemple: la Hongrie", *R. Centre Ét. Pays Est* 10(2), 1969 : 59-117.

824 PETRIĆ, N. "Planiranje porodice u Jugoslaviji" (Family planning in Yugoslavia), *Stanovništvo* 7(3-4), jul-dec 69 : 209-219. [Also published in French in *Faits et Tendances* 5(6), 1970 : 27-48.]

825 PETRIOLI, L. "La teoria di Lexis sulla durata normale della vita umana in base alle passate e recenti esperienze italiane" (Lexis theory on the normal life span based on past and recent Italian experiences), *Riv. ital. Econ. Demogr. Statist.* 21(1-2), jan-jun 67: 5-26.

826 PETRIOLI, L. "Tavole di nuzialita della popolazione italiania 1960-63" (Nuptiality tables of the Italian population 1960-63), *Riv. ital. Econ. Demogr. Statist.* 21(3-4), jul-dec 67 : 151-164.

827 PRAIS, S. J.; SCHMOOL, M. "Statistics of Milah and the Jewish birth-rate in Britain", *Jew. J. Sociol.* 12(2), dec 70 : 187-194.

828 PRESSAT, R. et al. "La conjoncture démographique: la France", *Population* 25(2), mar-apr 70 : 373-420.

829 SANTORO, V. *Campania: aspetti economico-sociali della struttura demografica* (Campania : economic and social aspects of the demographic structure). Napoli, Giannini, 69, x-316 p.

830 SCHWARZ, K. "Messzahlen zur Beurteilung der räumlichen Verteilung der Bevölkerung im Bundesgebiet" (Geographical distribution of population of the Federal Republic), *Wirtsch. u. Statist.* 7, jul 70 : 337-342.

831 SELIGMANN-TRIBALLAT, N.; ELIE, P.; BEGUÉ, J. *Résultats préliminaires du recensement de 1968: démographie générale, population active, ménages, logements.* Paris, Institut national de la statistique et des études économiques, 69, 122 p.

832 SIVIGNON, M. "Quelques données démographiques sur la République Populaire d'Albanie", *R. Géogr. Lyon* 45(1), 1970 : 61-74.

833 SZABADY, E. "A csecsemöhalandóságot befolyásoló biológiai, társadalmi tényezök Mayarországon" (Social and biological factors influencing infant mortality in Hungary), *Demográfia* 12(4), 1969 : 492-499.

834 SZABADY, E. "Les effets sociaux et démographiques d'une nouvelle mesure de la politique démographique en Hongrie", *Popul. et Famille* 18, jun-jul 69 : 1-8.

835 SZABADY, E. "Magyar termékenységi és családtervezési vizsgálatok" (Hungarian fertility and family planning studies), *Demográfia* 12(4), 1969 : 417-436.

836 TAYLOR, L. R. (ed.). *The optimum population for Britain.* London-New York, Academic Press, 70, xxiii-182 p.

837 THIRRING, L. "Adatok a termékenység alakulásának város és vidék kôzötti különbségeiröl" (Data on the development of fertility differences between urban and rural areas), *Demográfia* 12(3), 1969 : 307-322. [Hungary.]

838 TREBICI, V.; GÎNDAC, I. D.; HRISTACHE, I. "Aspecte ale fenomenelor demografice pe tipuri de oraşe in România" (Aspects of demographic phenomena by type of city in Rumania), *R. Statist. (Burcureşti)* 18(8), aug 69 : 25-35.

839 WALSH, B. "An empirical study of the age structure of the Irish population", *Econ. soc. R. (Dublin)* 1(2), jan 70 : 259-279.

840 WANNER, R. A. "Population growth and industrialization: the Swedish case", *Cornell J. soc. Relat.* 4(2), aug 69 : 49-56.

C.11(5) **Middle East**
Moyen-Orient

841 AL-SHALASH, 'A. Ḥ. *Dirâsâṯ taḥlîlîyaṯ li-tarkîb al-sukkân al-dîmûghrâfî fîl-Urdan* (An analytical study of the demographic structure in Jordan). al-Baŝraṯ, Maṭba' aṯ Ḥadâd, 68, 46 p.

842 BULUTOĞLU-IRMAK, Y. *La structure par âge et la mortalité de la population de la Turquie. Essai d'analyse démographique.* Istanbul, Fakülteler Matbaasi, 69, xv-202 p.

843 *Ḥa-tekûnat ḥa-demografîyât šel ḥa-ôklûsîyaḥ be-Yiśrael 1965-1967* (Demographic characteristics of the Jewish population in Israel, 1965-1967). Yerušalayîm, Ḥa-liškaḥ ha-merkazît li-sṯaṯisṯiqaḥ, 69, 49 p.

844 SPECKMANN, J. D. "Family planning in Pakistan", *Sociol. Gids* 17(3), mai-jun 70: 213-224.

845 TABET, B. "Démographie et urbanisation", *Trav. et Jours* 33, oct-dec 69 : 5-20. [Liban.]

846 UNITED ARAB REPUBLIC. CENTRAL AGENCY FOR PUBLIC MOBILISATION AND STATISTICS. *The increase of population in the United Arab Republic and its impact on development.* Cairo. CAPHS, 69, 392 p.

847 WANDER, H. *Bevölkerungsprobleme im Wirtschaftsaufbau kleiner Länder—das Beispiel Jordanien* (Demographic problems of the economic development of small countries; the example of Jordan). Tübingen, J. C. B. Mohr, 69, viii-228 p.

C.11(6) **Pacific**
Pacifique

848 LEE, Y. L. *Population and settlement in Sarawak.* Singapore, D. Moore for Asia Pacific Press, The Cellar Book Shop, 70, xv-257 p.

C.11(7) **USSR**
URSS

[See also / Voir aussi: 786]

849 ADEIŠVILI, G. "Socialistiçeskij zakon narodonaselenija i nekotorye osobennosti ego projavlenija v Gruzinskoj SSR" (The socialist law of population and some characteristics of its demonstration in the Georgia SSR), *Nar. Hoz. Gruzii* (12), 1968 : 14-24.

850 ALTYEVA, L. "Dinamika i faktory roždaemosti Turkmenskoj SSR" (Dynamics and factors of the Turkmen SSR birth rate), *Učen. Zap. (Turkm. gos. Univ.) Ser. ěkon. Nauk* 52, 1969 : 69-75.

851 ATABAEV, B. "Rost nasalenija Turkmenskoj SSR za gody sovetskoj vlasti" (Growth of Turkmen SSR population under Soviet power), *Učen. Zap. (Turkm. gos. Univ.) Ser. ěkon. Nauk* 52, 1969 : 61-68.

852 DEMKO, G. J.; CASETTI, E. "A diffusion model for selected demographic variables: an application to Soviet data", *A. Assoc. Amer. Georgr.* 60(3), sep 70 : 533-539.

853 HYDE, G. "Abortion and the birth rate in the USSR", *J. biosoc. Sci.* 2(3), jul 70 : 283-292.

854 LISTENGURT, F. M. "Perspektivnye izmenenija gorodskogo naselenija v SSSR" (Perspective changes of urban population in USSR), *Izv. Akad. Nauk SSSR Ser. Geogr.* (1), 1969 : 59-68.

855 MAKSIMOV, G. "Pervye itogi vsesojuznoj perepisi naselenija 1970 g" (First results of the 1970 general population census), *Vestn. Statist.* 8, aug 70 : 12-22. [USSR.]

856 POD'JAČIH, P. "Programma razrabotki mogov vsesojuznoj perepisi naselenija 1970 g" (The program for processing results of the 1970 national census), *Vestn. Statist.* 2, 1970 : 23-33. [USSR.]

857 RAKOV, A. A. *Naselenie BSSR* (Population in RSS of Belorussia). Minsk, Nauka i tehnika, 69, 221 p.

858 VALENTEY, D. "Les problèmes démographiques de l'Union Soviétique", *Population* 25(2), mar-apr 70 : 363-372.

859 VENECKIJ, I. "Analiz bračnosti metodom ženihov i nevest" (Analysis of nuptiality using the bachelor and married girl method), *Vestn. Statist.* 1, 1970 : 39-44.

C.12 Age groups
Groupes d'âge

C.120 *General studies*
Études générales

[See also / Voir aussi: 693, 1379]

860 BUCHHOFER, B.; FRIEDRICHS, J.; LÜDTKE, H. "Alter, Generationsdynamik und soziale Differenzierung. Zur Revision des Generationsbegriffs als analytisches Konzept" (Age, the dynamism of generations and social differentiations. Towards the revision of the notion of generation as an analytical instrument), *Kölner Z. Soziol. u. Sozialpsychol.* 22(2), jun 70 : 300-334.

861 CARLSON, G.; KARLSSON, K. "Age, cohorts and the generations", *Amer. sociol. R.* 35(4), aug 70 : 710-718.

862 Bibl. XIX-745. FEUER, L.S. *The conflict of generations: the character of significance of student movements.* CR: A. LIEBMAN, *Amer. sociol. R.* 34(6), dec 69 : 1012-1013; A. EHRLICH, *Brit. J. Sociol.* 21(2), jun 70 : 233-234.

863 JOHNSTONE, J. W. C. "Age-grade consciousness", *Sociol. Education* 43(1), 1970 : 56-68.

864 LAQUEUR, W.; MOSSE, G. L. (eds.). "Generations in conflict", *J. contemp. Hist.* 5(1), 1970 : 190 p. [Contents : "Youth and politics in Czechoslovakia, by G. GOLAN.— "Youth movements in France in the 1930s", by A. COUTROT.—"Youth in Britain, 1920-60: detachment and commitment", by A. MARWICK.—"John Hargrave, the green shirts and social credit", by J. L. FINLAY.—"Relations between generations in the Israeli kibbutz", by E. COHEN and M. ROSNER.—"The origins of student radicalism in Japan", by H. D. SMITH.—"Some comments on the Japanese student movement in the sixties", by K. TSURUMI.—"Students and the youth movement in Germany: attempt at as structural comparison", by W. KARL.—"Student politics in the Weimar Republic", by W. ZORN.—"Adolescent status and student politics", by F. PARKIN.— "The international student movement", by P. G. ALTBACH.—"Rites de passage: the conflict of generations in industrial society", by P. ABRAMS.]

866 MEIER, H. C. "Generational differences in value orientations toward higher education", *Sociol. Education* 43(1), 1970 : 69-89.

867 MENDEL, G. *La crise de générations; étude sociopsychanalytique.* Paris, Payot, 69, 254 p.

868 SMITZ, P. *De generatiestrijd in onze Westerse maatschappij* (Conflict of generations in our Western society). Assen, Van Gorcum, 69, viii-188 p.

37

C.121   Infancy and childhood
         Enfance

[See also / Voir aussi: 1801, 1841, 1862, 2629, 2640, 2646, 2719, 2911, 3342, 3783, 3800, 3805, 4151, 4199, 4209, 4251, 4291, 4445, 4463, 5162, 5164]

869   BÉNOS, J. *L'enfance inadaptée et l'éducation psychomotrice.* Paris, Maloine, 69, 178 p.

870   Bibl. XIX-751. BETTELHEIM, B. *The children of the dream.* CR: A. C. KERCKHOFF, *Amer. sociol. R.* 35(1), feb 70 : 172-173.

871   BROEL-PLATERIS, A. A. *Children of divorced couples: United States, selected years.* Washington, United States, Government Printing Office, 70, vi-40 p.

872   CANDIANI MONCALVO, E. "Intorno ad un aspetto del comportamento morale di bambini immigrati" (About an aspect of the moral behaviour of immigrant children), *Riv. Psicol. soc.* 17(1), jan-mar 70 : 53-82.

873   CAPUL, M. *Les groupes rééducatifs.* Paris, Presses universitaires de France, 69, 248 p.

874   COLES, R. *Uprooted children; the early life of migrant farm workers.* Pittsburgh, University of Pittsburgh Press, 70, xxiii-142 p.

875   COUGHLIN, B. J. "Religious values and child welfare", *Soc. Casewk* 51(2), 1970 : 82-90.

876   DANZIGER, K. (ed.). *Readings in child socialization.* Oxford-New York, Pergamon Press, 70, x-377 p.

877   DEVOR, G. M. "Children as agents in socializing parents", *Family Coordinator* 19(3), jul 70 : 208-212.

878   ENTWISTLE, H. *Child-centred education.* London, Methuen, 70, 222 p.

879   FEDDER, R.; GABALDON, J. *No longer deprived; the use of minority cultures and languages in the education of disadvantaged children and their teachers.* New York, Teachers College Press, 70, xii-211 p.

880   GOULART, R. *The assault on childhood.* London, Gollancz, 70, xi-278 p. [Children as consumers in the USA.]

881   GREENBERG, E. S. "Black children and the political system", *Publ. Opin. Quart.* 34(3), 1970 : 333-345. [USA.]

882   GREENBERG, E. S. "Children and government: a comparison across racial lines" *Midwest J. polit. Sci.* 14(2), mai 70 : 249-275. [USA.]

883   HAMM, N. H. "A partial test of a social learning theory of children's conformity", *J. exper. Child Psychol.* 9(1), feb 70 : 29-42.

884   HARTLEY, R. E. "Children's perceptions of sex preference in four culture groups", *J. Marriage Family* 31(2), mai 69 : 380-387.

885   HODGKINS, B. J.; HERRIOTT, R. E. "Age-grade structure, goals and compliance in the school: an organizational analysis", *Sociol. Education* 43(1), 1970 : 90-105.

886   HOLZER, H. "Frükkindliche Entwicklung und politisches Verhalten der Erwachsenen" (The precocious development of children and political behaviour of adults), *Polit. Stud. (München)* 21(193), sep-oct 70 : 576-591. [Germany BR.]

887   HUNDERTMARCK, G. *Soziale Erziehung im Kindergarten* (Social education in the kindergarten). Stuttgart, E. Klett, 69, 138 p.

888   KEARNS, B. J. R. "Childrearing practices among selected culturally deprived minorities", *J. genet. Psychol.* 116(2), jun 70 : 149-156.

889   KHATRI, A. A.; SIDDIQUI, B. B. "A boy or a girl? Preferences of parents for sex of offspring as perceived by East Indian and American children. A cross-cultural study", *J. Marriage Family* 31(2), mai 69 : 388-392.

890   KUROKAWA, M. "Psycho-social roles of Mennonite children", *Canad. R. Sociol. Anthropol.* 6(1), feb 69 : 15-35.

891   LYONS, S. R. "The political socialization of ghetto children: efficacy and cynicism", *J. Polit.* 32(2), mai 70 : 288-304. [USA.]

892   Bibl. XIX-766. MAIER, H. W. *Three theories of child development; the contributions of E. E. Erikson, J. Piaget and R. R. Sears, and their applications.* CR: J. W. MEYER, *Amer. sociol. R.* 35(4), aug 70 : 820.

893   MEDIOLI CAVARA, F. "Espressioni projettive dell'ambiente sociale ed economico nel test della famiglia" (Projective expressions of the social and economic milieu in the family test), *Riv. Psicol. soc.* 17(1), jan-mar 70 : 23-52.

894   MIALL, W. E.; DESAI, P.; STANDARD, K. L. "Malnutrition, infection and child growth in Jamaica", *J. biosoc. Sci.* 2(1), jan 70 : 31-44; 2(2), apr 70 : 133-144.

895 MIDDLETON, J. (comp.). *From child to adult; studies in the anthropology of education.* Garden City, N. Y., Natural History Press, 70, xx-355 p.

896 OPIE, I.; OPIE, P. *Children's games in street and playground; chasing, catching, seeking, hunting, racing, duelling, exerting, daring, guessing, acting, pretending.* Oxford, Clarendon, 69, xvii-371 p.

897 PAGSIBIGAN, G. M. "Attitudes towards working mothers of children in six selected public elementary school in Manila", *Graduate Fac. Stud.* 19, 1968 : 71-85.

898 PERRON-BORELLI, M.; PERRON, R. *L'examen psychologique de l'enfant.* Paris, Presses universitaires de France, 70, 240 p.

899 PHADKE, S. "Children in urban areas of India", *Carnets de l'Enfance* (11), jan 70 : 109-124.

900 SAUNIER, F. *L'enfant et ses droits, commentaire de la "Déclaration" des Nations Unies.* Paris, Éditions Fleurus, 70, 216 p.

901 SCHVANEVELDT, J. D.; FRYER, M.; OSTLER, R. "Concepts of 'badness' and "goodness of parents as perceived by nursery school children", *Family Coordinator* 19(1), jan 70 : 93-103.

902 SMITH, C. P. (ed.). *Achievement-related motives in children.* New York, Russell Sage Foundation, 69, 263 p. CR: H. D. SEIBEL, *Amer. sociol. R.* 35(4), aug 70 : 790-791.

903 TRUBOWITZ, J. *Changing the racial attitudes of children; the effects of an activity group program in New York City schools.* New York, Praeger, 69, xxi-228 p.

904 UNICEF. "L'enfant et l'adolescent dans les groupes marginaux de la population urbaine en Amérique latine", *Carnets de l'Enfance* 11, jan 70 : 57-70.

905 UNICEF. "Problèmes de l'enfance et de la jeunesse dans les zones péri-urbaines des États arabes", *Carnets de l'Enfance* 11, jan 70 : 97-108.

906 UNICEF. "Rural children and youth in Latin America", *Carnets de l'Enfance* 11, jan 70 : 31-56.

907 VAN RIJSWIJK-CLERKK, L. E. *Kind en milieu* (Children and social environment). Assen, Van Gorcum, 69, xii-271 p.

908 WILLIAMS, N. *Child development.* London, Heinemann Educational Books; New York Humanities Press, 69, vii-110 p.

C.122 Adolescence and youth problems
Adolescence et problèmes de la jeunesse

[See also / Voir aussi: **F.151**; 187, 867, 904, 905, 906, 1795, 1804, 1888, 1889, 1956, 2033, 2255, 2386, 2563, 2578, 2598, 2650, 2714, 2720, 2732, 2873, 3214, 3275, 3333, 3342, 3359, 3783, 3796, 3806, 3966, 3970, 3987, 4116, 4173, 4176, 4192, 4195, 4201, 4209, 4210, 4213, 4214, 4225, 4231, 4238, 4243, 4290, 4432, 4921, 5020, 5095, 5132, 5147, 5148, 5160, 5426, 5430]

909 AHLIVININSKIJ, B. V.; LEBEDEV, A. G.; MATŠUK, N. I. "O primenenii idej i metodov teorii informacii v sociologičeskih issledovanijah problem molodeži" (On the application of information theory and methods in sociological studies on youth problems), *Učen. Zap. (Leningr. gos. Univ. nauč.-issled. Inst. kompleks. sociol. Issled.)* (6), 1969 : 35-42.

910 ALTBACH, P. G. (ed.). *The student revolution; a global analysis.* Bombay, Lalvani Publishing House, 70, x-408 p.

911 ALTBACH, P. G. (eds.). *Turmoil and transition: higher education and student politics in India.* New York, Basic Books, 69, viii-267 p. CR: D. A. MARTIN, *Amer. J. Sociol.* 75(6), mai 70 : 1053-1054; D. W. HARPER, Jr. *Amer. sociol. R.* 35(4), aug 70 : 794-795.

912 BADINA, O. "Le cadre institutionnel de l'étude scientifique de la jeunesse en Roumanie", *R. roum. Sci. soc. Sér. Sociol.* 14, 1970 : 97-108.

913 Bibl. XIX-782. BAIER, H. (ed.). *Studenten in Opposition. Beiträge zur Soziologie der deutschen Hochschule* (Students in opposition. Essays in the sociology of the German university). CR: M. KAASE, *Kölner Z. Soziol. u. soz.-Psychol.* 22(1), mar 70 : 193-196.

914 BARTON, A. H. "La crisi a Columbia: campus, Vietnam e ghetto" (The crisis at Columbia University: campus, Vietnam and ghetto), *Quad. Sociol.* 18(1-2), jan-jun 69 : 124-158.

915 BELL, D.; KRISTOL, I. (eds.). *Confrontation: the student rebellion and the universities.* New York, Basic Books, 69, 191 p. CR: H. C. MEIER, *Amer. sociol. R.* 35(2), apr 70 : 361-363. [USA.]

916   BERG, M.; ROTH, H.; BELSER, H. *Die berufstätige Jugend—Untersuchungen mit dem
       Problemfragebogen für männliche Jugendliche* (Working youth—a survey among
       young males, a questionnaire). Hannover, Hermann Schrödel Verlag, 69, 381 p.

917   BLOCK, J. H.; HAAN, N.; SMITH, M. B. "Socialization correlates of student activism",
       J. soc. Issues 25(4), 1969 : 143-177.

918   BONILLA, F.; GLAZER, M. *Student politics in Chile.* New York, Basic Books, 70, xiv-367 p.

919   BORJAZ, V. N. "Metodologičeskie principy opredelenija ponjatija 'molodež' " (Metho-
       dological principles of the determination of the 'youth' notion), *Učen. Zap. (Leningr.
       gos. Univ. nauč.-issled. Inst. sociol. Issled)* (6), 1969 : 23-34.

920   BORK, R. H.; KRANE, H. G.; WEBSTER, G. D. *Political activities of colleges and universities;
       some policy and legal implications.* Washington, American Enterprise Institute for
       Public Policy Research, 70, 60 p. [USA.]

921   BOUDON, R. "Mai 68: crise ou conflit, aliénation ou anomie ?", *Année sociol.* 19, 1968 :
       223-242. [France.]

922   BOUGUEREAU, J. M. "L'intervention des étudiants", *Temps mod.* 25(279), oct 69 : 424-
       434.

923   BRADEMAS, J.; KENNEDY, E. M.; NAMBA, M. "On student unrest", *Soc. Sci. (Winfield)*
       45(1), jan 70 : 3-12.

924   BRICKMAN, W. W.; LEHERER, S. (eds.). *Conflict and change on the campus; the response to
       student hyperactivism.* New York, School and Society Books, 70, 528 p.

925   BURNS, T. "La rivolta dei privilegiati" (The revolt of the privileged), *Quad. Sociol.*
       18(1-2), jan-jun 69 : 159-176.

926   CAIN, A. H. *Young people and revolution.* New York, John Day Co., 70, 153 p.

927   CASACCIA, L. "Problemi e bisogni dei lavoratori studenti" (Problems and needs of student
       workers), *Quad. Sci. soc.* 8(3), 1969 : 316-327.

928   CENTRUL DE CERCETĂRI PENTRU PROBLEMELE TINERETULUI. *Tineretul—object de cercetare
       stiintifică* (Youth—an object for scientific research). Bucuresti, CCPPT, 69,
       xiii-454 p.

929   CHRESTA, H. *Jugend zwischen Konformismus und Opposition. Eine sozialpsychologische
       Untersuchung jugendlicher Selbstausagen* (Youth between conformity and opposition.
       A social psychology survey based upon self-declaration). Zürich-Einsiedeln-Köln,
       Benziger, 70, 228 p. [Germany, BR.]

930   "Crise de l'université, mouvement étudiant et conflits sociaux: étude critique de textes
       sociologiques français et étrangers", *Sociol. Trav.* 11(3), jul-sep 69 : 287-336. [Trois
       contributions: L. MAHEU, "Les approches 'fonctionnalistes' " : 287-308; N. ABBOUD,
       "Les analyses en termes de 'rapports sociaux' " : 308-321; K. RENON, "Les inter-
       prétations de la protestation étudiante et de la crise de l'Université en Allemagne"]

931   DOEHLEMANN, M. "Der Protest der Jungen; soziologische Aspekte" (Youth protest;
       sociological aspect), *Dtsche Jugend* 18(1), jan 70 : 9-20.

932   DORON, R. *La vie affective de l'adolescent inadapté; changement et personne.* Paris, Dunod,
       70, ix-388 p.

933   DOUGLAS, S. A. *Political socialization and student activism in Indonesia.* Urbana, Uni-
       versity of Illinois Press, 70, vi-228 p.

934   DOWSEY, S. J. (ed.). *Zengakuren: Japan's revolutionary students.* Berkeley, Calif., Ishi
       Press, 70, viii-271 p.

935   DUNLAP, R. "Radical and conservative student activists: a comparison of family back-
       grounds", *Pacific sociol. R.* 13(3), 1970 : 171-181.

936   DUNPHY, D. C. *Cliques, crowds and gangs; group life of Sydney adolescents.* Melbourne,
       Cheshire, 69, xi-170 p.

937   Bibl. XIX-811. EMMERSON, D. K. (ed.). *Students and politics in developing nations.* CR:
       M. W. MEYER, *Amer. sociol. R.* 35(3), jun 70 : 563-565.

938   ENCEL, S. "Sociology and student unrest", *Austral. New Zeal. J. Sociol.* 6(1), apr 70 :
       3-9.

939   FIELDS, A. B. *Student politics in France; a study of the Union Nationale des Étudiants de
       France.* New York, Basic Books, 70, viii-198 p.

940   FISH, K. L. *Conflict and dissent in the high schools.* New York, Bruce Publishing Co., 70,
       187 p.

941   FISK, T. "The nature and causes of student unrest", *Polit. Quart.* 40(4), oct-dec 69 :
       419-425.

942 FLACKS, R. "Social and cultural meaning of student revolt: some informal comparative observations", *Soc. Probl.* 17(3), 1970 : 340-357. [USA.]

943 FORACCHI, M. M. "1968 : el movimiento estudiantil en la sociedad brasileña" (1968: the student movement in Brazilian society), *R. mexic. Sociol.* 31(3), jul-sep 69 : 609-620.

944 FREEBERG, N. E. "Assessment of disadvantaged adolescents: a different approach to research and evaluation measures", *J. educ. Psychol.* 61(3), jun 70 : 229-240.

945 FREIOVÁ, E. "The cultural orientation of Czechoslovak youth", *Archiv. europ. Sociol.* 10(2), 1969 : 259-270.

946 FRIEDMAN, H. "Los adolescentes de las villas de emergencia de Buenos Aires" (Adolescents in the squatter settlements of Buenos Aires), *R. latinoamer. Sociol.* 5(1), mar 69 : 80-93.

947 FUNNELL, V. "The Chinese communist youth movement, 1949-1966", *China Quart.* 42, apr-jun 70 : 105-130.

948 FUSE, T. "Il radicalismo degli studenti in Giappone: una 'rivoluzione culturale ?'" (Student radicalism in Japan: a "cultural revolution" ?), *Quad. Sociol.* 18(1-2), jan-jun 69 : 258-289.

949 GANDHI, R. S. "Conflict and cohesion in an Indian student community", *Hum. Org.* 29(2), 1970 : 95-102.

950 *Gendai no gakuseiundô* (Contemporary student movement). Tôkyô, Shinkô Shuppansha, 69, 331 p.

951 GERMANI, G. "La socializzazione politica dei giovani nei regimi fascisti: Italia e Spagna (The political socialization of youth in fascist regimes: Italy and Spain", *Quad. Sociol.* 18(1-2), jan-jun 69 : 11-58. Also published in Spanish, in *R. latinoamer. Sociol.* 5(3), nov 69 : 544-592.

952 GITCHOFF, G. T. *Kids, cops, and kilos: a study of contemporary suburban youth.* San Diego, Calif., Mater-Westerfield Publishing Co., 69, 178 p. CR: E. SAGARIN, *Amer. sociol. R.* 35(4), aug 70 : 808-809. [USA.]

953 GLAZER, N. *Remembering the answers; essays on the American student revolt.* New York, Basic Books, 70, 311 p.

954 GOLDMAN, R. *Angry adolescents.* Beverly-Hills, Calif., Sage Publications, 69, 119 p. CR: E. SAGARIN, *Amer. sociol. R.* 35(4), aug 70 : 808-809.

955 GOLOFAST, V. B. "Élementy sociologičeskoj teorii molodeži" (Elements for a sociological theory of youth), *Učen. Zap. (Leningr. gos. Univ. nauč.-issled. Inst. kompleks. sociol. Issled)* (6), 1969 : 13-22.

956 GREELEY, A. M.; SPAETH, J. L. "Political change among college alumni", *Sociol. Education* 43(1), 1970 : 106-113.

957 GROMOV, I. A.; KONNIKOVA, S. N.; LISOVSKIJ, V. T. "Molodež' v obščestve" (Youth and society), *Učen. Zap. (Leningr. gos. Univ. nauč.-issled. Inst. kompleks. sociol. Issled)* (6), 1969 : 3-12.

958 HEISKANEN, I.; STOLTE HEISKANEN, V. "Oppi- ja ammattikoulunuorten mahdollisuus-rakenteet, osallistumisaktiivisuus ja politiikan tuntemus" (Opportunity structure, social participation, and level of political information of Finnish secondary and vocational school students), *Politiikka* 12(3), 1970 : 205-218.

959 HOLLOWAY, R. "Street boys in Addis Abeba", *Community Develop. J.* 5(3), jul 70 : 139-144.

960 JADOV, V. A. (ed.). *Molodež i trud.* (Youth and labour). Moskva, Molodaja Gvardija, 70, 302 p.

961 JAMESON, J.; HESSLER, R. M. "The natives are restless: the ethos and mythos of student power", *Human Org.* 29(2), 1970 : 81-94. [USA.]

962 JAROVOJ, V. "Nekotorye social'no-èkonomičeskie problemy molodeži razvityh kapitalis-tičeskih stran" (Some socio-èconomic problems of youth in developed capitalist countries), *Nauč. Dokl. vyss. Skoly (èkon. Nauki)* 2, 1970 : 101-108.

963 JOHNSTONE, J. C.; WILLIG, J.-C.; SPINA, J. M. *Young people's images of Canadian society; an opinion survey of Canadian youth 13 to 30 years of age.* Ottawa, Queen's Printer, 69, xvii-152 p.

964 KADRITZKE, U. "La sociologia tedesca di fronte al movimento studentesco" (German sociology faces the student movement), *Quad. Sociol.* 18(1-2), jan-jun 69 : 237-257.

965 KAHN, R.; BOWERS, W. J. "The social context of the rank-and-file student activist: a test of four hypotheses", *Sociol. Education* 43(1), 1970 : 38-55.

966   KANDEL, D.; LESSER, S. G. "Parent-adolescent relationships and adolescent independence in the U. S. and Denmark", *J. Marriage Family* 31(2), mai 69 : 348-358.

967   KAZUKO, T. "The Japanese student movement", *Japan Quart.* 15(4), oct-dec 68 : 430-455; 16(1), jan-mar 69 : 25-44.

968   KING, K. "Adolescent perception of power structure in the Negro family", *J. Marriage Family* 31(4), nov 69 : 751-755.

969   KITAZAWA, Y. "Storia della lotta studentesca in Giappone" (History of the student struggle in Japan), *Ideologie* 4(11), jan-mar 70 : 121-140.

970   KLIGSBERG, B. "La crise de l'identité juive dans la jeunesse juive d'Argentine", *Dispersion et Unité* 10, 1970 : 202-212.

971   KOGAN, L. N. *Rabočaja molodež'. Trud, učeba, dosug* (Working youth; work, studies, leisure). Sverdlovsk, Sred. ural'noe knižnoe izdatel'stvo, 69, 126 p.

972   KON, I. "La sociedad burguesa y la juventud" (Bourgeois society and youth), *R. Inst. Sociol. boliv.* 9, 1969 : 19-32.

973   KOZAKIEWICZ, M. "Industrialization and promotion de la jeunesse", *R. Inst. Sociol.* 3, 1970 : 417-426. [Pologne.]

974   KUBÍČKOVÁ, M. "Poznámky k mezinárodnímu zvláště americkému studentskému knutí" (Remarks on the international student movement, with particular reference to the American one), *Sociol. Čas.* 5(5), sep-oct 69 : 508-523.

975   KUMAR, B. "Effects of authoritarianism upon social adjustment of tribal and non tribal students", *Ind. sociol. B.* 6(4), jul 69 : 230-234. [India.]

976   LESSING, H.; LIEBEL, M. "Bürgerliche Jugendrevolten zwischen Autoritätskonflikt und Klassenkampf" (Bourgeois youth revolts between authority conflict and class struggle), *Dtsche Jugend* 18(6), jun 70 : 255-264.

977   LEVYKIN, I. T. *Sel'skaja molodež: sociolgičeskij očerk* (Rural youth: a sociological study). Moskva, Sovetskaja Rossija, 70, 159 p. [USSR.]

978   LIPSET, S. M. "Riflessi politici dell'attivismo studentesco" (Political implications of student activism), *Quad. Sociol.* 18(1-2), jan-jun 69 : 95-123.

979   LIPSET, S. M.; ALTBACH, P. G. (eds.). *Students in revolt.* Boston, Houghton Mifflin, 69, xxxiv-561 p. [Most of the essays in this volume were first published in the Winter, 1968 issue of *Daedalus*.]

980   LUTTE, G. *et al. Jeunesse européenne d'aujourd'hui; modèles de comportement et valeurs.* Paris, Éditions ouvrières, 70, 246 p.

981   MAFUD, J. *Las rebeliones juveniles en la sociedad Argentina* (Juvenile rebellions in Argentine society). Buenos Aires, S. Rueda, 69, 151 p.

982   MARINI, R. M. "Les mouvements étudiants en Amérique latine", *Temps mod.* 27(291), oct 70 : 718-731.

983   MARTINOTTI, G. "La marginalité positive, statut social et orientation politique chez les étudiants italiens", *Anal. et Prévis.* 9(3), mar 70 : 145-154.

984   MATEJOVSKI, A. "Il movimento degli studenti in Cecoslovacchia: mito o realtà ?" (The student movement in Czechoslovakia: myth or reality ?), *Quad. Sociol.* 18(1-2), jan-jun 69 : 177-194.

985   MCCANDLESS, B. R. *Adolescents: behavior and development.* Hinsdale, Ill., Dryden Press, 70, xii-515 p.

986   MILLER, D. *The age between: adolescents in a disturbed society.* London, Cornmarket Hutchinson, 69, viii-172 p.

987   MIŠIN, V. I.; RUBCOV, I. Ė.; TERENT'EV, A. A. "Problema social'nogo sostava sovremennogo studenčestva" (Problem of the social composition of contemporary student population), *Učen. Zap. (Gor'k. gos. Univ. Ser. sociol. Sociol. vysš. Škola)* 100(2), 1970 : 7-19.

988   MOGILEVSKIJ, R. S. *et al.* "Molodež i disciplina truda" (Youth and labour discipline), *Učen. Zap. (Leningr. gos. Univ. nauč. Issled. Inst. kompleks. soc. Issled.)* (6), 1969 : 152-161.

989   MOOR, R. A. DE. *Studentprotest en universiteit* (Student protest and university). Rotterdam, Universitaire Pers Rotterdam; Antwerpen, Standaard Wetenschappelijke Uitgeverij, 70, 150 p.

990   NEMČENKO, V. S. *et al. Professional'naja adaptacija molodeži* (The professional adaptation of youth). Moskva, Moskovskij Universitet, 69, 128 p.

991   NISHIHIRA, N. "Gendai Nihon seinen no shakai ishiki" (Youth's social consciousness

in contemporary Japan), *Yamanashi Daigaku Kyôikugakubu Kenkyûhokôku* 18, 1968 : 119-128.

992 O'KANE, J. M. "Economic and non economic liberalism, upward mobility potential, and Catholic working-class youth", *Soc. Forces* 48(4), jun 70 : 499-506. [USA.]

993 POLETAEV, V. E.; USTINOV, V. A. "Izmanenie social' nogo oblika kolhoznaj molodeži (1938-1969 gg.)" (Changes in social characteristics of collective farm youth (1938-1969), *Ist. SSSR* 14(4), jul-aug 70 : 3-17.

994 RECA, I. C. "El movimiento estudiantil y el proceso de reforma de la Universidad de Chile" (The student movement and the process of reform in the University of Chile), *R. parag. Sociol.* 6(16), sep-oct 69 : 63-104.

995 REHBERG, R. A.; SCHAFER, W. E.; SINCLAIR, J. "Toward a temporal sequence of adolescent achievement variables", *Amer. sociol. R.* 35(1), feb 70 : 34-48.

996 REICH, C. A. *The greening of America; how the youth revolution is trying to make America liveable.* New York, Random House, 70, 399 p.

997 RICHARDSON, H. J. *Adolescent girls in approved schools.* London, Routledge and K. Paul, 69, xii-297 p. CR: P. WILES, *Brit. J. Sociol.* 21(2), jun 70 : 239.

998 ROCHEBLACE-SPENLÉ, A. M. *L'adolescent et son monde.* Paris, Éditions universitaires, 69, 208 p.

999 ROUCEK, J. S. "Student activism in contemporary politics", *Sociol. int. (Berlin)* 8(2), 1970 : 219-231.

1000 RUBIN, V. D.; ZAVALLONI, M. *We wish to be looked upon; a study of the aspirations of youth in a developing society.* New York, Teachers College Press, 69, xi-257 p.

1001 SAUVY, A. *La révolte des jeunes.* Paris, Calmann-Lévy, 70, 269 p.

1002 SCHEUCH, E. K. "Aspetti sociologici dell'agitazione studentesca" (Sociological aspects of student agitation), *Quad. Sociol.* 18(1-2), jan-jun 69 : 195-236.

1003 SERRANO GÓMEZ, A. "Estudio socio-criminológico de la juventud española" (A socio-criminological study of Spanish youth), *R. int. Sociol. (Madrid)* 113-114, 1970 : 81-99.

1004 SHAPIRA, R.; ETZIONI, E. " 'Individual' and 'collective' values of Israeli students: the impact of youth movements", *Jew. J. Sociol.* 12(2), dec 70 : 165-180.

1005 SHIPPEY, F. A. "Clique structure in religious youth groups", *Sociol. soc. Res.* 54(3), apr 70 : 371-377.

1006 SMITH, D. M. "Adolescence: a study of stereotyping", *Sociol. R.* 18(2), jul 70 : 197-212.

1007 "Sociologie et contestation", *Hommes et Soc.* 16, apr-mai-jun 70 : 1-360. [Notamment chez les étudiants.]

1008 SOUZA, A. DE. "Student participation in university governance, a sociological approach", *Soc. Action* 20(1), jan-mar 70 : 22-34. [India.]

1009 STATERA, G. "L'utopia del movimento studentesco italiano" (Utopia of the Italian student movement), *Crit. sociol. (Roma)* 15, 1970 : 173-195.

1010 STOLTE HEISKANEN, V.; HEISKANEN, I. *Effects of functional and social selectivity of the educational system on the political orientations of youth.* Helsinki, Institute of Political Science, University of Helsinki, 70, 29 p.

1011 "Student competition", *Sociol. Focus* 3(4), 1970 : 1-120.

1012 "Student rebellion", *Polit. Sci. Quart.* 84(2), jun 69 : 169-385.

1013 TOURAINE, A. "Crise et conflit", *C. int. Sociol.* 48, jan-jun 70 : 5-24. [Réponse à R. Boudon à propos de mai 68 en France.]

1014 VALABRÈGUE, C. *La condition étudiante.* Paris, Payot, 70, 192 p.

1015 WASBURN, P. C. "Some political implications of students' acquisition of social science information", *Soc. Forces* 48(3), mai 70 : 373-383.

1016 WEINBERG, I.; WALKER, K. N. "Student politics and political systems: toward a typology", *Amer. J. Sociol.* 75(1), jul 69 : 77-96.

1017 WON, G.; YAMAMURA, D. "Expectations of youth in relating to the world of adults", *Family Coordinator* 19(3), jul 70 : 219-224.

1018 "Youth of the new world", *New Wld* 37(4), 1969 : 183 p.

C.123   Old age
       Vieillesse

[Voir aussi / See also: **F.214**; 2585, 4247]

1019   AMBROŽ, J. "Stárnutí a práce" (Aging and work), *Demografie* 11(4), oct-dec 69: 311-320. [Czechoslovakia.]

1020   BERLINGUER, G. "Gli anziani nella società: previsioni demografiche e programmi regionali" (The aged in society: demographic forecasts and regional planning), *Riv. ital. Econ. Demogr. Statist.* 22(1-4), jan-dec 68 : 149-159.

1021   BOUR, H.; AUMONT, M. *Le troisième âge; prospective de la vie.* Paris, Presses universitaires de France, 69, viii-139 p.

1022   FRANCHER, J. S. "American values and the disenfranchisement of the aged", *East. Anthropol.* 22(1), jan-apr 69 : 29-36.

1023   GRAY, R. M.; KASTELER, J. M. "An evaluation of the effectiveness of a foster grandparent project", *Sociol. soc. Res.* 54(2), jan 70 : 181-189.

1024   LOHMANN, S. *Die Lebenssituation älterer Menschen in der geschlossenen Altersfürsorge* (The living conditions of old people in public assistance old age homes). Hannover, Vincentz, 70, 166 p.

1025   MERTENS, J. "L'intégration sociale des personnes âgées", *R. belge Sécur. soc.* 12(7), jul 70 : 826-836.

1026   Bibl. XIX-896. NEUGARTEN, B. L. (ed.). *Middle age and aging: a reader in social psychology.* CR: R. E. BOYD, *Amer. sociol. R.* 34(6), dec 69 : 1009-1010.

1027   PAILLAT, P.; WIBAUX, C. *Les citadins âgés.* Paris, Presses universitaires de France, 69, xii-281 p.

1028   PIOTROWSKI, J. "Ludzie starzy w Polsce i ich potrzeby" (The old people in Poland and their needs), *Biul. IGS* 13(2), 1970 : 7-36.

1029   PRESTON, C. E. "A cross-national comparison of subjective agedness", *Int. J. comp. Sociol.* 11(1), mar 70 : 54-58.

1030   SCHMELZER, H.; TEBERT, W. *Alter und Gesellschaft; eine soziologische Untersuchung der sozialen Voraussetzungen von Massnahmen der Altenhilfe* (Age and society; a sociological survey on the social principles of professions of assistance to the aged). Bonn, Eichholz-Verlag, 69, 244 p.

1031   SEQUEIRA, M. L. "Condições económicas da existência da população idosa da cidade de Lisboa" (Economic conditions of the existence of the aged population of Lisbon), *Inform. soc. (Lisboa)* 4(16), oct-dec 69 : 5-25.

C.13   Migration

C.130   General studies
       Études générales

[See also / Voir aussi : 639]

1032   BOUSCARAN, A. T. *European Economic Community migrations.* The Hague, Martinus Nijhoff, 69, 155 p.

1033   BUNGE, M. "Four models of human migration: an exercise in mathematical sociology", *Archiv-Rechts-u. soz.-Philos.* 55(4), 1969 : 451-466.

1034   EDUCATION AND WORLD AFFAIRS. Committee on the International Migration of Talent. *The international migration of high-level manpower: its impact on the development process.* New York, Praeger, 70, xxxvi-738 p.

1035   GODFREY, E. M. "The brain-drain from low income countries", *J. Develop. Stud.* 6(3), apr 70 : 235-247.

1036   JACKSON, J. A. *Migration.* Cambridge, University Press, 69, vii-304 p.

1037   JANSEN, C. J. *Readings in the sociology of migration.* Oxford-New York, Pergamon Press, 70, x-402 p.

1038   MANGALAM, J. J.; SCHARZWELLER, H. "Some theoretical guide-lines toward a sociology of migration", *Int. Migr. R.* 4(2), 1970 : 5-22.

1039   PANOV, M. "V. I. Lenin o meždunarodnoj trudovoj migracii pri kapitalizme" (V. I. Lenin on international labour migrations in the capitalist system), *Sociol. Trud* 15(6), jun 70 : 10-15.

1040   TERMOTE, M. *Migration et équilibre économique spatial*. Louvain, Université Catholique, Faculté des Sciences économiques, sociales et politiques, 69, viii-256 p.

1041   TUGAULT, Y. "Methode d'analyse d'un tableau 'origine-destination' de migrations", *Population* 25(1), jan-fev 70 : 59-68.

1042   WEIERMAIR, K. "Economic implications of the international migration of high leval manpower", *Migr. int.* 8(1-2), 1970 : 5-19.

1043   WUNSCH, G. "Le calcul des soldes migrataires par la méthode de la 'population attendue'. Caractéristiques et évaluation des biais", *Popul. et Famille* 18, jun-jul 69 : 49-61.

C.131   *Emigration (local studies)*
         Émigration (études localisées)

[See also / Voir aussi: 1095]

1044   BELLOULA, T. "L'émigration algérienne", *Doss. docum. (Alger)* 6, mai 70 : 3-25; 7, mai 70 : 5-25.

1045   BUI-DANG-HA-DOAN, J. "Quelques aspects démographiques des migrations de 'cerveaux': un exemple français", *C. Sociol. Démogr. médic.* 9(3), jul-sep 69 : 165-167.

1046   CHYLINSKA, K. "Emigracja Polska po 1967 r" (Polish emigration since 1967), *Kultura* (11), nov 70 : 17-55.

1047   COMAY, P. Y. "Déterminants des migrations des savants et des ingénieurs", *Sociol. et Soc.* 2(1), mai 70 : 63-77. [Canada.]

1048   EGLI, D. "Émigration et développement à l'île Maurice", *Migr. dans le Monde* 19(2), apr-jun 70 : 5-10.

1049   FLEMING, D.; BAILYN, B. *The intellectual migration, Europe and America, 1930-1960*. Cambridge, Mass., Harvard University Press, 69, 748 p.

1050   KOIRANEN, V. A. "Emigration of Finns to Sweden—drain or benefit for Finland", *Econ. R. (Helsinki)* 2, 1970 : 47-52.

1051   MACKAY, D. I. *Geographical mobility and the brain drain—a case study of Aberdeen University graduates, 1860-1960*. London, George Allen and Unwin, 69, 216 p.

1052   MOREIRA, A. "Emigração portuguesa" (Portuguese emigration), *Estud. polít. soc.* 7(3), 1969 : 621-638.

1053   MOSTWIN, D. "Polonia amerykanska" (Polish emigration to the United States), *Kultura* (5), mai 70 : 121-134.

1054   NILSSON, F. *Emigrationen från Stockholm till Nordamerika, 1880-1893* (Emigration from Stockholm to North America, 1880-1893). Stockholm, Läromedelsförlaget, 70, 393 p.

1055   PASSIGLI, S. *Emigrazione e comportamento politico* (Emigration and political behaviour). Bologna, Società Editrice Il Mulino, 69, 251 p. CR: S. Z. KOFF, *Amer. polit. Sci. R.* 64(3), sep 70 : 965-966.

1056   SAMUEL, T. J. "Migration of Canadians to USA: the causes", *Migr. int.* 7(3-4), 1969 : 106-116.

1057   SCHRIER, A. *Ireland and the American emigration, 1850-1900*. New York, Russell and Russell, 70, 210 p.

1058   WILLIAMS, R. C. "European political emigration: a lost subject", *Comp. Stud. Soc. Hist.* 12(2), apr 70 : 140-148.

C.132   *Immigration*

C.1320   *General studies*
         Études générales

1059   WILSON, C. *et al. Economic issues in immigration: an exploration of the liberal approach to public policy on immigration*. London, Institute of Economic Affairs, 70, xviii-155 p.

45

C.1321 *Local studies*
Études localisées

[See also / Voir aussi: 575, 736, 872]

1060 "Algériens en France", *Hommes et Migr.* 115, 1970 : 79-90.

1061 ERICSON, A. S. "Impact of commuters across the Mexican border", *Mthly Lab. R.* 93(8), aug 70 : 18-27.

1062 FORTNEY, J. "International migration of professionals", *Popul. Stud.* 24(2), jul 70 : 217-232. [USA.]

1063 *Ḥa-'aliyah li-Yiśrael*, 1966-1968 (Immigration to Israel, 1966-1968). Yerušalayîm *Ḥa-liškah ha-merkazît* li-štatistiqaḥ, 70, 46 p.

1064 "Immigration in Canada", *Int. Migr. R.* 3(4), 1969 : 5-100.

1065 JONES, K.; SMITH, A. D. *The economic impact of Commonwealth immigration*. Cambridge, University Press, 70, ix-177 p.

1066 KALBACH, W. E. *The impact of immigration on Canada's population*. Ottawa, Dominion Bureau of Statistics, 70, xxxiv-465 p.

1067 MACHERET, A. *L'immigration étrangère en Suisse à l'heure de l'intégration européenne.* Genève, Librairie de l'Université, Georg., 69, xx-355 p.

1068 PRÉVOST, G. "Comment et pourquoi les travailleurs sénégalais viennent en France", *Hommes et Migr.* 115, [1970]: 91-119.

1069 RITTERBAND, P. "Law, policy, and behavior: educational exchange policy and student migration", *Amer. J. Sociol.* 76(1), jul 70 : 71-82. [USA.]

1071 RUDČENKO, A. M. "Nemeckie kolonisty v Rossii" (German settlers in Russia), *Učen. Zap. (Inst. meždun. Otnoš)* (2), 1969 : 80-98.

1072 SOLBERG, C. E. *Immigration and nationalism, Argentina and Chile, 1890-1914*. Austin, University of Texas Press, 70, xi-222 p.

1073 "U. S. immigration, 1970: policies, procedures, problems", *Int. Migr. R.* 4(3), 1970 : 1-90.

1074 WEISBERGER, P. "L'imigration en Belgique", *Industrie* 24(2), feb 70 : 61-68.

1075 WILLI, V. J. *Überfremdung. Schlagwort oder bittere Wahrheit?* (Foreign invasion. Slogan or bitter truth ?). Bern, Herbert Lang, 70, x-288 p. [Switzerland.]

C.1322 *Refugee problems*
Problèmes des réfugiés

1076 BROOKS, H. C.; EL-AYOUTY, Y. (eds.). *Refugees south of the Sahara; an Africa dilemma.* Westport, Conn., Negro Universities Press, 70, xviii-307 p.

1077 DAVID, H. P. "Involuntary international migration adaptation of refugees", *Migr. int.* 7(3-4), 1969 : 67-81.

1078 DODD, P.; BARAKAT, H. "Palestinian refugees of 1967: a sociological study", *Muslim Wld* 60(2), apr 70 : 123-142.

1079 GOUNDIAM, O. "La protection juridique des réfugiés en Afrique", *R. sénég. Dr.* 4(8), sep 70 : 5-31; *Migr. dans le Monde* 19(1), jan-mar 70 : 7-13.

1080 MONCARZ, R. "Effects of professional restrictions on Cuban refugees in selected health professions in the United States (1959-1969)", *Migr. int.* 8(1-2) 1970 : 22-27.

1081 PARZEN, H. "The Arab refugees—their origin and projection into a problem (1948-1952)", *Jew. soc. Stud.* 31(4), oct 69 : 292-323.

1082 PERETZ, D. *The Palestine Arab refugee problem*. Santa Monica, Calif. Rand Corp. 1969, ix-74 p.

1083 WEINSTOCK, S.A. *Acculturation and occupation: a study of the 1956 Hungarian refugees in the United States*. The Hague, Nijhoff, 69, x-127 p.

C.1323 *Immigrants: situation and absorption*
Situation et absorption des immigrants

[See also / Voir aussi: 1083, 1692, 3356]

1084 ANTONOVSKY, A.; KATZ, D. "Factors in the adjustment to Israeli life of American and Canadian immigrants", *Jew. J. Sociol.* 12(1), jun 70 : 77-78.

1085 BENSIMON-DONATH, D. "L'intégration économique des immigrants nord-africains en Israël et des Juifs nord-africains en France. Essai d'étude comparative" *R. franc. Sociol.* 10(4), oct-dec 69 : 491-514.

1086 BENSIMON-DONATH, D. "L'intégration sociale des juifs nord-africains en Israel", *Dispersion et Unité* 10, 1970 : 89-120.

1087 BRODY, E. B. (ed.). *Behavior in new environments; adaptation of migrant populations.* Beverly Hills, Calif., Sage Publications, 70, 479 p.

1088 GORDON, D. N. "Immigrants and municipal voting turn-out: implications for the changing ethnic impact on urban politics", *Amer. sociol. R.* 35(4), aug 70 : 665-681.

1089 HILL, G. S. *Immigration and integration; a study of the settlement of coloured minorities in Britain.* Oxford, Pergamon Press, 70, ix-214 p.

1090 JOHNSTON, R. *The assimilation myth. A study of second generation Polish immigrants in Western Australia.* The Hague, Martinus Nijhoff, 69, 117 p.

1091 LANNIE, V. P. "Alienation in America: the immigrant Catholic and public education in pre-Civil War America", *R. Polit.* 32(4), oct 70 : 503-521.

1092 LEE, T. R. "The role of the ethnic community as a reception area for Italian immigrants in Melbourne, Australia", *Migr. int.* 8(1-2), 1970 : 50-62.

1093 LYNCH, P. "Accueil communautaire des immigrants en Australie", *Migr. dans le Monde* 19(2), apr-jun 70 : 1-4.

1094 MUÑOZ ANATOL, J. "La familia española migrante" (The Spanish migrant family) *R. int. Sociol. (Madrid)* 27(107-108), jul-dec 69 : 89-105; 28(111-112), mai-aug 70 : 53-72. [In France.]

1095 PASCUAL, A. "El retorno de los emigrantes conflicto o intégración ?" (The return of emigrants, conflict or integration ?), Barcelona, Ed. Nova Terra, 70, 219 p. [Spain.]

1096 Bibl. XIX-954. PATTERSON, S. *Immigrants in industry.* CR: C. D. KING, *Amer. sociol. R.* 35(1), feb 70 : 184-185.

1097 ROSE, A. M. *Migrants in Europe; problems of acceptance and adjustment.* Minneapolis, University of Minnesota Press, 69, 194 p. CR: W. CONNOR, *Amer. polit. Sci. R.* 64(3), sep 70 : 963-965.

1098 SANDHU, K. S. *Indians in Malaya; some aspects of their immigration and settlement (1786-1957).* London, Cambridge University Press, 69, xxiv-346 p.

1099 SANDHU, K. S. "Some aspects of Indian settlement in Singapore, 1819-1969", *J. South-east Asian Hist.* 10(2), sep 69 : 193-201.

1100 SANDIS, E. E. "Characteristics of Puerto-Rico migrants to, and from, the United States", *Int. Migr. R.* 4(2), 1970 : 22-44.

1101 SHERROW, F. S.; RITTERBAND, P. "An analysis of migration to Israel", *Jew. soc. Stud.* 32(3), jul 70 : 214-223.

1102 THOMAS, C. J. "Projections of the growth of the coloured immigrant population of England and Wales", *J. biosoc. Sci.* 2(3), jul 70 : 265-282.

1103 WILD, R.; RIDGEWAY, C. "The job expectations of immigrant workers", *Race* 11(3), jan 70 : 323-334.

1104 WILLIAMS, G. B. "The Welsh in Patagonia: a geographical perspective", *R. geogr. (Rio de Janeiro)* 69, dec 68 : 121-144.

C.133 *Internal migrations*
Migrations intérieures

[See also / Voir aussi: 709, 737, 874, 1087, 4269]

1105 ADAMS, D. W. "Rural migration and agricultural development in Colombia", *Econ. Develop. Cult. Change* 17(4), jul 69 : 527-539.

1106 ADAMS, N. A. "Internal migration in Jamaica—an economic analysis", *Soc. econ. Stud.* 18(2), jun 69 : 136-151.

1107   ALARÇÃO, A. *Mobilidade geográfica da população da Portugal (continente e ilhas adjacentes);* *migrações internas, 1921-1960* (Geographical mobility of Portuguese population [continental and adjacent islands]; internal migration 1921-1960). Lisboa, Fundação Calouste Gulbenkian, Centro da Estudos da Economia Agrária, 69, 346 p.

1108   ANDRÉ, R. "Géographie des mouvements migratoires intérieurs en Belgique de 1964 à 1968", *R. Inst. Sociol.* 2, 1970 : 383-402.

1109   ASSOR, V. "Les déplacements quotidiens de travail dans l'agglomération parisienne", *Hommes et Tech.* 25(301), nov 69 : 1018-1030.

1110   BALBE, B. C.; ALESSI, N. D'. "Migraciones internas e inserción en el proceso productivo" (Internal migrations and insertion in the productive process), *Aportes* 18, oct 70 : 148-160. [Argentina.]

1111   BARBICHON, G. "Configuration de changements d'emploi. Matériaux pour une connaissance de la mobilité professionnelle en France", *Bull. C. E. R. P.* 18(3-4) jul-dec 69 : 167-202.

1112   BEALS, R. F.; MENEZES, C. F. "Migrant labour and agricultural output in Ghana", *Oxford econ. Pap.* 22(1), mar 70 : 109-127.

1113   BHOWMICK, P. K. *Occupational mobility and caste structure in Bengal: study of rural markets.* Calcutta, Indian Publications, 69, viii-98 p.

1114   BONTRON, J. C. "Migrations et exode rural", *Paysans* 14(80), oct 69-mai 70 : 65-72. [France.]

1115   CALDWELL, J. C. *African rural-urban migration: the movement to Ghana's towns.* Canberra, Australian National University Press; London, C. Hurst; 69, xi-258 p.

1116   CHEVALLIER, M. *Note sur les études de mobilité géographique et professionnelle.* Lyon, Groupe de Sociologie urbaine, 69, 31 p.

1117   COHEN, A. *Custom and politics in urban Africa—a study of Hausa migrants in Yoruba towns.* London, Routledge and Kegan Paul, 69, xii-252 p. CR: E. MAKINEN *Amer. polit. Sci. R.* 64(2), jun 70 : 613-614.

1118   COMPTON, P. "A magyar városok belföldi vándorlási jellemzöinek többváltozós elemzése" (Multivariate analysis of characteristics of migration within Hungarian cities), *Demográfia* 12(3), 1969 : 273-306.

1119   FAIRCHILD, C. K. "Rural disadvantaged mobility", *Labor Law J.* 20(8), aug 69 : 461-473. [USA.]

1120   FLINN, W. L.; COVERSE, J. W. "Eight assumptions concerning rural-urban migration in Colombia: a three shantytown test", *Land Econ.* 46(4), nov 70 : 456-466.

1121   GIUSTI, J.; LA FUENTE, P. DE. "Proceso migratorio y cambio social en América latina" (Migratory process and social change in Latin America), *R. mexic. Sociol.* 31(3), jul-sep 69 : 621-632.

1122   GREENWOOD, M. "The determinants of labor migration in Egypt", *J. region. Sci.* 9(2), aug 69 : 283-290.

1123   GUARINI, R. "Analisi territoriale del movimento migratorio del periodo 1951-67 nel quadro delle previsioni demografiche regionali" (Territorial analysis of the migratory movement in the 1951-67 period in the frame work of the regional demographic forecasts), *Riv. ital. Econ. Demogr. Statist.* 23(1-4), jan-dec 69 : 257-302. [Italy.]

1124   HARLOFF, H. J. *Der Einfluss psychischer Faktoren auf die Mobilität der Arbeit* (The influence of psychological factors in labour mobility). Berlin, Duncker und Humblot, 70, 234 p.

1125   HARRIS, J. R.; TODARO, M. P. "Migration, unemployment and development: a two-sector analysis", *Amer. econ. R.* 60(1), mar 70 : 126-142. [Africa.]

1126   HUNTER, L. C.; REID, G. L. *European economic integration and the movement of labour.* Kingston, Ont., Industrial Relations Centre, Queen's University, 70, xi-38 p.

1127   Bibl. XIX-986. HUNTER, L. C.; REID, G. L. (eds.). *Urban worker mobility.* CR: P. G. MARDEN, *Amer. sociol. R.* 34(6), dec 69 : 998.

1128   IWANICKI, E. "Farmers in Polish towns (an attempt at a typology and classification)", *Polish sociol. B.* (1), 1969 : 83-89.

1129   JAKUBCZAK, F. "Problemy integracje wychodziow ve wsi w spolecznosei unejskiej" (The problems of integration of emigrants in urban society), *Kult. i Społecz.* 13(2), apr-jun 69 : 181-198. [Poland.]

1130   JEGOUZO, G. "Processus généraux de la mobilité professionnelle des agriculteurs", *Rech. Écon. Sociol. rur.* 3, 1970 : 1-21. [France.]

1131 KAKUMOTO, R. "The revolution in commuter transportation—a proposal for solving the housing shortage and commuter congestion in the metropolis by a new Tôkaidô line type high speed railway", *Develop. Econ.* 7(4), dec 69 : 590-616.

1132 KENNEDY, L. V. *The Negro peasant turns cityward; effects of recent migrations to northern centers.* College Park, Md., McGrath Pub. Co., 69, 270 p. [USA.]

1133 KLETT, H. "Veränderungen in der territorialen Verteilung der Negerbevölkerung in den USA-Gesellschaftliche Ursachen und Folgen" (Modifications in the territorial distribution of black population in the United States: causes and social consequences), *Z. Erdkundenungerr.* 22(1), 1970 : 1-10.

1134 KURODA, T. *A new dimension of internal migration in Japan.* Tokyo, Institute of Population Problems, Ministry of Health and Welfare, 69, 38 p.

1135 KURODA, T. *Continuity and transformation of migration behaviour in Japan.* Tokyo, Institute of Population Problems, Ministry of Health and Welfare, 70, 21 p.

1136 LATUCH, M. "Rola migracji we wzroście ludnościowym Warszawy" (The role of migration in the population increase of Warsaw), *Biul. IGS* 13(1), 1970 : 15-39.

1137 LEE, H. S. "A study on migration of population in Korea, mainly concerned with cities", *J. Popul. Stud.* (8), 1969 : 73-113.

1138 LEONE, U. "Il trapianto del lavoratore" (Worker transplantation), *Rass. econ. (Napoli)* 34(4), jul-aig 70 : 1003-1013. [Italy.]

1139 MASNICK, G. "Employment status and retrospective and prospective migration in the United States", *Demography (Washington)* 5(1), 1968 : 79-85.

1140 MASSUCCO COSTA, C. A.; RIZZO, G. "Condizioni oggettive a movimenti soggettivi nelle migrazioni interne" (Objective conditions and subjective movements in internal migrations), *Riv. Psicol. soc.* 16(4), oct-dec 69 : 295-312.

1141 MCDONALD, J. R. "Toward a typology of European labor migration"; *Migr. int.* 7(1-2), 1969 : 5-12.

1142 MCWILLIAMS, C. *Factories in the field—the story of migratory farm labor in California.* Hamden, Conn., Archon Books, 69, 334 p.

1143 MERLIN, P. *La dépopulation des plateaux de Haute Provence.* Paris, Documentation francaise, 69, 182 p.

1144 "Migraciones internas y desarrollo" (Internal migrations and development), *Aportes* 15, jan 70 : 95-155. [Latin America.]

1145 "Migrazioni (Le) interne italiane oggi" (Italian internal migrations today), *Studi Emigr.* 6(16), oct 69 : 225-272.

1146 MIRACLE, M. P.; BERRY, S. S. "Migrant labour and economic development", *Oxford econ. Pap.* 22(1), mar 70 : 86-108.

1148 Bibl. XIX-995. NALSON, J. S. *Mobility of farm families. A study of occupational and residential mobility in an upland area of England.* CR: G. ALBRECHT *Kölner Z. Soziol. u. soz.-Psychol.* 22(2), jun 70 : 408-413.

1149 NELKIN, D. "A response to marginality: the case of migrant farm workers", *Brit. J. Sociol.* 20(4), dec 69 : 375-389. [USA.]

1150 PELLICCIARI, G. *L'immigrazione nel triangolo industriale...* (Immigration in the industrial triangle)... Milano, F. Angeli, 70, 681 p. [Italy.]

1151 PEREZ DIAZ, V. *Emigracion y sociedad en la Tierra de Campos. Estudio de un proceso migratorio y un proceso de cambio social...* (Emigration and society in 'Tierra de Campos'. Study of a migratory process and of social change). Madrid, Escuela Nacional de Administración Pública, 69, 307 p.

1152 PERSKY, J. J.; KAIN, J. F. "Migration, employment, and race in the Deep South", *South. econ. J.* 36(3), jan 70 : 268-276. [USA.]

1153 PETTISS, S. "A study on social consequences of internal migration of youth from rural to urban areas in three African countries—research report", *Manpower Unempl. Res. Africa* 2(2), nov 69 : 39-42.

1154 PIANKA, H. G. "Zur Problematik der Transmigration in Indonesien. Ein Beitrag zur Bevölkerungspolitik" (On migration in Indonesia. A report on demographic policy), *Asien Forum* 1(4), oct 70 : 535-547.

1155 PICQUET, M. "Quelques données rapides sur le problème migratoire à Tunis", *Population* 25(3), mai-jun 70 : 607-612.

1156 POKŠINEVSKIJ, V. V. "Migracii naselenija v SSSR" (Population migrations in the USSR), *Priroda* (9), 1969 : 67-75.

49

1157   PRASADA RAO, C. "Rural-urban migration: a clue to rural-urban relations in India", *Ind. J. soc. Wk* 30(4), jan 70 : 335-342.
1158   PRESTON, D. A. "Rural emigration in Andean America", *Hum. Org.* 28(4), 1969 : 279-286.
1159   RECCHINI DE LATTES, Z. L.; LATTES, A. E. *Migraciones en la Argentina; estudio de las migraciones internas e internacionales, basado en datos censales, 1869-1960* (Internal migrations in Argentina: a study of internal and international migrations, based on census data, 1869-1960). Buenos Aires, Centro de Investigaciones Sociales, Instituto Torcuato di Tella, 69, xix-333 p.
1160   RONALD, C. Y. "Recent internal population movement in Thailand", *A. Assoc. Amer. Geogr.* 59(4), dec 69 : 710-730.
1161   ROSA, G. DALLA. "Les migrations des montagnards basco-béarnais en France", *R. géogr. Pyrénées* 41(1), jan 70 : 43-52.
1162   ROS JIMENO, J. "Las migraciones interiores y el Primer Plan de desarrollo en España" (Internal migrations and the first Spanish development plan), *R. inter. Sociol.* 26(103-104), jul-dec 68 : 91-108.
1163   ROUSSEL, L. "Measuring rural-urban drift in developing countries—a suggested method", *Int. Lab. R.* 101(3), mar 70 : 229-246.
1164   RUTMAN, G. L. "Migration and economic opportunities in West Virginia: a statistical analysis", *Rur. Sociol.* 35(2), jun 70 : 206-217.
1165   SAB, V. "Motifs de la migration intérieure en Tchécoslovaquie", *Demosta* 3-4, 1969 : 269-280.
1166   SALVI, P. V.; BHOITE, M. S. "Role of some family factors in rural migration", *Ind. J. soc. Wk* 29(4), jan 69 : 341-346. [India.]
1167   SANDERS, J. "The depressed area and labor mobility—the eastern Kentucky case", *J. hum. Resources* 4(4), 1969 : 437-450.
1168   SELVARATNAM, V. "Sociological implications of labour migration in Central Africa", *East. Anthropol.* 22(3), sep-dec 69 : 281-306; 23(2), mai-aug 70 : 113-130.
1169   SOKOLOV, L. "Veze izmedu migracije i vrste naseljenih mesta u makedoniji" (Relations between migrations and types of localities in Macedonia), *Stanovništvo* 7(3-4), jul-dec 69 : 195-209. [Yugoslavia.]
1170   SORKIN, A. L. "Some aspects of American Indian migration", *Soc. Forces* 48(2), dec 69 : 243-250.
1171   STEVENS, R. P. "Spatial aspects of internal migration in Mexico, 1950-1960", *R. geogr. (Rio de Janeiro)* 69, dec 68 : 75-90.
1172   STONE, L. O. *Migration in Canada: some regional aspects.* Ottawa, Dominion Bureau of Statistics, 69, xxiv-407 p.
1173   TABAH, L.; COSIO, M. E. "Mesure de la migration interne au moyen des recensements. Application au Mexique", *Population* 25(2), mar-apr 70 : 303-346.
1174   TAISNE-PLANTEVIN, V. "La mobilité résidentielle en région parisienne", *C. Inst. Aménag. Urbanisme Région paris.* 19, mar 70 : 56 p.
1175   THIBAULT, A. "En Picardie: maintien de la population rurale et migrations journalières", *Ét. Région paris.* 44(27), jul 70 : 18-26. [France.]
1176   UCROS, J. "Los trabajadores ambulantes en la caña de azucar" (Migrant sugar cane workers), *R. mexic. Sociol.* 31(3), jul-sep 69 : 547-588.
1177   ZUICHES, J. J. "In-migration and growth of nonmetropolitan urban places", *Rur. Sociol.* 35(3), sep 70 : 410-420.

C.2   **GEOGRAPHICAL AND ECOLOGICAL FACTORS**
         FACTEURS GÉOGRAPHIQUES ET ÉCOLOGIQUES

C.20   **General studies**
         Études générales

1178   ANTOINE, P.; JEANNIÈRE, A. *Espace mobile et temps incertains; nouveau cadre de vie, nouveau milieu humain.* Paris, Aubier-Montaigne, 70, 157 p.
1179   BLACK, J. N. *The dominion of man; the search for ecological responsibility.* Edimburgh, University Press, 70, vi-169 p.
1180   HESSLINK, G. K. "The function of neighborhood in ecological stratification", *Sociol. soc. Res* 54(4), jul 70 : 441-459.

1181 JOHNSON, C. E. (comp.). *Eco-crisis.* New York, Wiley, 70, 182 p.

1182 KAPP, K. W. "Environmental disruption and social costs: a challenge to economics", *Kyklos* 23(4), 1970 : 833-847.

1183 KAPP, K. W. "Environmental disruption: general issues and methodological problems, *Soc. Sci. Inform.* | *Inform. Sci. soc.* 9(4), aug 70 : 15-32.

1184 KNEESE, A. V. "Directions of needed research and international cooperation in the future", *Soc. Sci. Inform.* | *Inform. Sci. soc.* 9(4), aug 70 : 33-52. [Research on man and his environment.]

1185 LOVE, G. A.; LOVE, R. M. (eds.). *Ecological crisis: readings for survival.* New York, Harcourt Brace Jovanovich, 70, VII-342 p.

1186 MENDA, L. "La sfida ecologica" (The ecological challenge), *Nord e Sud* 17(124), apr 70 : 8-20.

1187 MORRILL, R. L. *The spatial organization of society.* Belmont, Calif., Wadsworth Publishing Co., 70, ix-251 p.

1188 NYMMIK, S. Ja. "Vozdejstvie prirody na formirovanie social'no-ekonomičeskih territorial'nyh kompleksov" (Influence of nature on the location of socio-economic territorial complexes), *Vestn. Moskov. Univ. Ser. Geogr.* (1), 1969 : 31-38.

1189 "Pollutions at nuisances", *Inform. soc. (Paris)* 24(8), aug 70 : 5-106.

1190 RAY, M. "The spatial structure of economic and cultural differences: a factorial ecology of Canada", *Region. Sci. Assoc. Pap. and Proc.* 23, 1969 : 7-23.

1191 RIDGEWAY, J. *The politics of ecology.* New York, Dutton, 70, 222 p. [USA.]

1192 "Society and its physical environment", *A. Amer. Acad. polit. soc. Sci.* 389, mai 70 : 1-116.

1193 SOMMER, R. *Personal space: the behavioral basis of design.* Englewood Cliffs, N. J., Prentice Hall, 69, 177 p. CR: McCANN, *Amer. sociol. R.* 35(1), feb 70 : 164-165.

1194 STEPHAN, G. E. "The concept of community in human ecology", *Pacific sociol. R.* 13(4), 1970 : 218-228.

C.21 **Regional and community studies**
Études régionales et monographies

[See also / Voir aussi: 1326, 2065, 2105, 2940]

1195 AGBLEMAGNON, F. N'S. *Sociologie des sociétés orales d'Afrique noire; les Ewe du Sud-Togo.* Paris, Mouton, 69, 216 p.

1196 AL-SHÂ'IR, R. T. *al-Mujtama' al-'Arabî* (Arab society), al-Qâhiraṭ, Dâr al-Naḥdaṭ, al-'Arabîyaṭ, 70, 272 p.

1197 ANISIMOV, A. F. *Obščee i osobennoe v razviti obščestva i religii narodov Sibiri* (General and specific in the development of Siberian society and religion) Leningrad, Nauka, 69, 148 p.

1198 BAJBULATOV, B. B. *Ot kočev'ja k socializmu. Iz istorii osedanija kočevogo i polukočevogo naselenija Kirgizii v 1917-1937 gg* (From nomadism to socialism. History of the settlement of nomadic and semi-nomadic Kirghiz tribes, 1917-1937). Frunze, Kyrgyzstan, 69, 167 p.

1199 BARKATAKI, S. (comp.). *Tribes of Assam.* New Delhi, National Book Trust, India, 69, 167 p.

1200 BARTON, A. H. *Communities in disaster: a sociological analysis of collective stress situations.* Garden City, N. Y., Doubleday and Co., 69, 352 p. CR: C. W. FOGLEMAN, *Amer. sociol. R.* 35(1), feb 70 : 150-151.

1201 BASCOM, W. R. *The Yoruba of Southwestern Nigeria.* New York, Holt, Rinehart and Winston, 69, xvii-118 p.

1202 BASSO, K. H. *The Cibecue Apache.* New York, Holt, Rinehart and Winston, 70, xvi-106 p.

1203 BERNDT, R. M.; BERNDT, C. H. *Man, land and myth in North Australia; the Gunwinggu people.* Sydney, Ure Smith, 70, xviii-262 p.

1204 CAPLAN, L. *Land and social change in East Nepal: a study of Hindu-tribal relations.* London, Routledge and K. Paul, 70, xvi-224 p.

1205 CASTILLO, G. V. DEL. "México visto desde afuera, análisis de cinco estudios" (Mexico seen from the outside, analysis of five studies), *R. parag. Sociol.* 6(15), mai-aug 69 : 83-92.

1206   CASTILLO ARDILES, H. *Pisac; estructura y mecanismos de dominación en una región de refugio*
        (Pisac: structure and mechanisms of domination in a refugee region). México, Instituto
        Indigenista Interamericano, 70, x-192 p. [Peru.]

1207   CHIPETO, H. "The passing of tribal man: a Rhodesian view", *J. Asian Afr. Stud.* 5(1-2),
        jan-apr 70 : 10-15.

1208   DAVIDOVA-TURCINOVA, E. "K vymezeni a specifice současného cikánského problému v
        Československu" (On the subject of the definition and specification of the current
        problem of gypsies in Czechoslovakia), *Sociol. Čas.* 6(1), jan-feb 70 : 29-41.

1209   DORSTON, J. W. "Institutional differentiation in Guatemalan communities", *Develop.
        cult. Change* 18(4), jul 70 : 598-616.

1210   DOWNES, R. M. *The Tiv tribe.* Kaduna, Government Printer, 1933. Farnborough,
        Gregg, 69, 7-105 p.

1211   DOZIER, E. P. *The Pueblo Indians of North America.* New York, Holt, Rinehart and
        Winston, 70, xv-224 p.

1212   Bibl. XIX-1040. EISENSTADT, S. N. *Israeli society.* CR: M. SCHWARTZ, *Amer. J. Sociol.*
        75(5), mar 70 : 891-893; J. T. SHUVAL, *Amer. sociol. R.* 34(6), dec 69 : 987-989.

1213   FERNEA, R. A. *Shaykh and Effendi; changing patterns of authority among the El Shabana of
        southern Iraq.* Cambridge, Mass., Harvard University Press, 70, xi-227 p.

1214   FERRELL, R. *Taiwan aboriginal groups; problems in cultural and linguistic classification.*
        Nankang, Taipei, Institute of Ethnology, Academia Sinica, 69, iv-4444 p.

1215   FONTENELLE, L. F. R. *Rotina e fome em uma região cearense; estudo antropológico* (Habit
        and hunger in a Ceara region; an anthropological study). Fortaleza, Imprensa Universi-
        taria do Ceara, 69, 184 p. [Brazil.]

1216   GABAODÓN MÁRQUEZ, E. *Venezuela, su imagen desvelada (ensayo: sobre el coloniaje, la
        forma societaria peculiar de nuestro país, y de la América Latina)* (Venezuela, its re-
        vealed image: an essay on colonization, the special societal form of our country and
        Latin America). México, J. Ramos Pimentel, 69, viii-192 p.

1217   GROOT, S. W. DE. *Djuka society and social change. History of an attempt to develop a
        Bush Negro community in Surinam 1971-1926.* Assen, Van Gorcum, 69, xvi-256 p.

1218   HANSON, F. A. *Rapan lifeways; society and history on a Polynesian island.* Boston, Little,
        Brown, 70, ix-227 p.

1219   HARDGRAVE, R. L. Jr. *The Nadars of Tamiland: the political culture of a community in
        change.* Berkeley-Los Angeles, University of California Press, 69, xiv-314 p. CR:
        V. JESUDASON, *Amer. J. Sociol.* 76(1), jul 70 : 196-199.

1220   HARGOUS, S. *Les oubliés des Andes.* Paris F. Maspero, 69, 120 p.

1221   HARRISSON, T. H. *The Malays of South-West Sarawak before Malaysia; a socio-eco-
        logical survey.* East Lansing, Michigan State University Press; London, Macmillan,
        70, 671 p.

1222   HAVILAND, W. A. "A note on the social organization of the Chontal Maya", *Ethnology*
        9(1), jan 70 : 96-98.

1223   HELMS, M. W. "The cultural ecology of a colonial tribe", *Ethnology* 8(1), jan 69 : 76-84.
        [Miskito Indians of Eastern Nicaragua and Honduras.]

1224   HICKERSON, H. *The Chippewa and their neighbors; a study in ethnohistory.* New York,
        Holt, Rinehart and Winston, 70, x-133 p.

1225   HUDSON, C. M. *The Catawba Nation.* Athens, University of Georgia Press, 70,
        ix-142 p.

1226   HURAULT, J. "Éleveurs et cultivateurs des hauts plateaux de l'Adamawa; la population
        du Lamidat de Bayo. II. La fécondité et les structures démographiques et leur évolu-
        tion", *Population* 25(5), sep-oct 70 : 1039-1084. [Voir pour la première partie, *ibid.*
        24(5), 1969 : Bibl. XIX-1058.]

1227   HURAULT, J. "Essai de synthèse du système social du Bamiléké", *Africa (London)*
        40(1), jan 70 : 1-24.

1228   KLIMA, G. J. *The Barabaig; East African cattle-herders.* New York, Holt, Rinehart and
        Winston, 70, xii-114 p.

1229   LEBEUF, A. M. D. *Les principautés Kotoko; essai sur le caractère sacré de l'autorité.* Paris,
        Éditions du Centre National de la Recherche Scientifique, 69, 388 p.

1230   LOHMAR, U. "Soziologische Aspekte der Wiedervereinigung Deutschlands" (Socio-
        logical aspects of German reunification), *Jb. soz.-Wiss.* 20(1), 1969 : 283-293.

1231   "Makrosociologisch onderzoek in Suriname door het Sociografisch Instituut" (Macro-sociological research in Surinam by the Sociographic Institute), *Sociol. Gids* 17(3), mai-jun 70 : 201-212.

1232 MATOS MAR, J. "Micro-región y pluralismo" (Micro-region and pluralism), *Bol. urg. Sociol.* 8(15-16-17), dec 69 : 99-118. [Chancay Valley, Peru.]

1233 MILLER, N. N. (ed.). *Research in rural Africa.* East Lansing, Mich., African Studies Center, Michigan State University, 69, 341 p.

1234 MOHI DIN, A. "The Mawlimu", *Civilisations* 19(3), 1969 : 329-346.

1235 NA'IBI, S.; HASSAN, A. *The Gwari, Gade and Koro tribes.* Ibadan, Ibadan University Press, New York, Africana Publishing Corporation, 69, vii-54 p. [Revised and expanded version of *The Gwari tribe in Abuja Emirate*, previously published as a *Nigeria Magazine*, special publication.]

1236 NOGUEIRA SALDANHA, N. "Regionalismo em ciencia social: o caso do Nordeste" (Regionalism in social science: the case of the Northeast), *Bol. Joaquim Nabuco Pesq.soc.* 16-17, 1969 : 63-90. [Brazil.]

1237 OLIVIER DE SARDAN, J. P. *Système des relations économiques et sociales chez les Wogo, Niger.* Paris, Institut d'Ethnologie, Musée de l'Homme, 69, viii-241 p.

1238 POWERS, W. K. *Indians of the Northern Plains.* New York, Putnam, 69, 256 p.

1239 RAMACHANDRA RAO, S. K. *Social institutions among the Hindus.* Mysore, Rao and Raghavan, 69, 85 + 1 p.

1240 Bibl. XIX-1078. RAMSØY, N. R. (ed.). *Det norske samfunn* (Norwegian society). CR: K. SVALASTOGA, *Acta sociol.* 12(4), 1969 : 237-240.

1241 ROHNER, R. P.; ROHNER, E. C. *The Kwakiutl; Indians of British Columbia.* New York, Holt, Rinehart and Winston, 70, xv-111 p.

1242 SALISBURY, R. F. *Vunamami; economic transformation in a traditional society.* Berkeley, University of California Press, 70, xi-389 p.

1243 SAN MARTIN FERRARI, H. *Nosotros los chilenos (tres ensayos antropológicos de interpretacion)* (We the Chileans, three anthropological interpretative essays). Santiago-Chile, Editora Austral, 70, 288-3 p.

1244 SEREBRJANNYJ, L. R. *Islandija: strana, ljudi, hozjajtvo* (Iceland: country, people, economy). Moskva, Nauka, 69, 248 p.

1245 SHEPARDSON, M.; HAMMOND, B. *The Navajo Mountain community; social organization and kinship terminology.* Berkeley, University of California Press, 70, ix-278 p.

1246 SMIRNOV, A. S. "Sovetskij narod kak osobaja social'naja obščnost' " (Soviet people as a specific social community), *Učen. Zap. Kafd. marks.-lenin. Filos. Vysš. Part. Škol.* (7), 1970 : 3-17.

1247 "Sociedade (A) tradicional no Brasil" (Traditional society in Brazil), *Dados* 3(5), 1968 : 3-112.

1248 ŠOLC, V. *Los aymaras de las islas del Titicaca* (The Aymaras of the Titicaca Islands). México, 69, x-194 p. [Bolivia; Peru.]

1249 STOLL, J. A. "A society of primitives in a changing world. The Guajiro Indians: kinship, property, social structure", *Sociologus* 20(2), 1970 : 164-172.

1250 SOVTHAU, A. W. "The illusion of tribe", *J. Asian Afr. Stud.* 5(1-2), jan-apr 70 : 28-50.

1251 STILLER, R.; WARDA, J. *Malezja. Zarys wiedzy o kraju i ludziach* (Malaysia. Study on the country and people). Warszawa, Książka i Wiedza, 70, 237 p.

1252 TANNER, N. "Disputing and dispute settlement among the Minangkabau in Indonesia", *Indonesia* 8, oct 69 : 21-68.

1253 THOMPSON, L. (ed.). *African societies in Southern Africa; historical studies.* London, Heinemann; Lusaka, University of Zambia, 69, xiii-336 p.

1254 "Tsiganes (Les) en Tchécoslovaquie", *Démografie* 11(3), jul-sep 69 : 193-230.

1256 UCHENDU, V. C. "The passing of tribal man: a West African experiences", *J. Asian Afr. Stud.* 5(1-2), jan-apr 70 : 51-65.

1257 VIERTLER, R. B. *Os Kamayurá e o Alto Xingu; análise do processo de integração de uma tribo numa área de aculturação intertribal* (The Kamayurá and the Upper Xingu; analysis of an integration process of a tribe in a region of intertribal acculturation). Sao Paulo, Instituto de Estudos Brasileiros da Universidade de São Paulo, 69, 118 p.

1258 VOGT, E. Z. *Zinacantán: a Maya community in the highlands of Chiapas.* Cambridge, Belknap Press of Harvard University Press, 69, xxix-733 p.

1259 WADDELL, J. O. "Resurgent patronage and lagging bureaucracy in a Papago off-reservation community", *Hum. Org.* 29(1), 1970 : 37-42.

53

1260   WALLMAN, S. *Take out hunger: two case studies of rural development in Basutoland.*
        London, Athlone Press; New York, Humanities Press, 69, xii-178 p.
1261   WANE, Y. *Les Toucouleur du Fouta Tooro (Sénégal)—stratification sociale et structure
        familiale.* Dakar, Institut Fondamental d'Afrique Noire, 69, vii-250 p.
1262   WEITLANER, R. J.; OLIVERA DE VAZQUEZ, M. *Los grupos indígenas del norte de Oaxaca*
        (Indigenous groups of Northern Oaxaca). México, Instituto Nacional de Antropología
        e Historia, 69, 151 p. [Mexico.]
1263   WESOŁOWSKI, W. (ed.). *Struktura i dynamika społeczeństwa polskiego* (Structure and
        dynamics of Polish society). Warszawa, Państwowe Wydawnictwo Naukowe, 70, 326 p.

C.22   Social surveys
           Enquête sociales

[See / Voir: 3260]

C.23   Rural studies
           Sociologie rurale

C.230   *General studies*
            Études générales

[See also / Voir aussi: 96, 189, 553, 1444]

1264   BENNETT, C. F.; LEONARD, R. C. "Field experimentation in rural sociology", *Rur.
        Sociol.* 35(1), mar 70 : 69-76.
1265   BOLDIZZONI, D. "Un filone di ricerca della sociologia rurale americana: la diffusione
        delle innovazioni in agricoltura" (A research field of American rural sociological
        research: diffusion of innovations in agriculture), *Quad. Sociol.* 19(1), jan-mar 70 :
        42-73.
1266   "Congress (Seventh) of the European Society for Rural Sociology", *Sociol. rur.* 10(1),
        1970 : 74-75. [10-14th August 1970 at Münster/Westfalen, GFR.]
1267   CONNOR, D. M.; CURTIS, J. E. "A perspective on rural sociology in Canada and some
        implications", *Rur. Sociol.* 35(2), jun 70 : 267-274.
1268   "Contribution à une sociologie villageoise", *Communautés* 26, jul-dec 69 : 3-188.
1270   DEHENNE, M. "Méthodologie pour des monographies villageoises dans une zone de
        colonisation de terres neuves", *Cah. ORSTOM Sér. Sci. hum.* 6(3), 1969 : 29-72.
1271   MINZ, B. "A conceptual model for analysing community development programmes",
        Soc. Action 20(1), jan-mar 70 : 40-58.
1272   MORABITO, F. "La realtà rurale, problema della società" (Rural reality, a problem of
        society), *Orientam. soc.* 26(3), mar 70 : 180-194.
1273   SMITH, T. L.; ZOPF, P. E. Jr. *Principles of inductive rural sociology.* Philadelphia, F. A.
        Davis Co., 70, 558 p.
1274   STROPPA, C. (comp.). *Sociologia rurale* (Rural sociology). Milano, U. Hoepli, 69, 642 p.
        [Articles previously published in various periodicals.]

C.231   *Rural social structure: villages, communities*
            Structure rurale: villages, communautés

[See also / Voir aussi: 4789]

1275   ALTHABE, G. *Oppression et libération dans l'imaginaire. Les communautés villageoises de la
        côte orientale de Madagascar.* Paris, F. Maspéro, 69, 359 p.
1276   AUGÉ, M. *Le rivage alladian; organisation et évolution des villages alladian.* Paris, ORSTOM,
        69, 264 p.
1277   AVILA, M. *Traditional and growth; a study of four Mexican villages.* Chicago, University
        of Chicago Press, 69, xv-219 p.
1278   BAKULA, B. B. *The effect of traditionalism on rural development; the case of the Omurunazi
        Ujamaa village, Bukoba.* Dar es Salaam, University College, 69, 40 p.

1279   BERGERET, A.; COMBAZ-FAUQUEL, A. "Villages malgaches et développement", *Communautés* 27, jan-jun 70 : 103-138.

1280   BLYTHE, R. *Akenfield. Portrait of an English village.* New York,Pantheon Books 69,287 p.

1281   BOISSEVAIN, J. *Hal-Ferrug: a village in Malta.* New York..., Holt, Rinehart and Winston, 69, xviii-104 p.

1282   BOUDEWEEL-LEFEBVRE, M. A. *La mutation de la campagne française, étude comparative de la transformation de quatre pays agricoles...* Gap, Éditions Ophrys, 69, 227 p.

1283   BOUDOU, A.; KAYSER, B. *et al.* "Les centres ruraux de la région Midi-Pyrénées", *Aménag. Territ. Dévelop. région.* 3, 1970 : 517-534.

1284   BRUNEAU, M. "Un village du Nord de la Thaïlande: Ban Muang Wa", *C. O.-Mer* 23(90), apr-jun 70 : 140-174.

1285   CELLIER, R. "Dans un village du Bas-Vivarais, Le rôle des coopératives et l'évolution des exploitations", *Communautés* 27, jan-jun 70 : 161-180.

1286   CORNELL, J. B.; SMITH, R. J. *Two Japanese villages: Matsunagi, a Japanese mountain community* by J. B. CORNELL; *Kurusu, a Japanese agricultural community* by R. J. SMITH. New York, Greenwood Press, 69, xiv-232 p.

1287   CRESSWELL, R. *Une communauté rurale de l'Irlande.* Paris, Institut d'ethnologie, 69, 573 p.

1288   DAVYDOV, A. D. *Afganskaja derevnja. (Sel'skaja obščina i rassloenie krest'janstva)* (An Afghan village. Agricultural community and differentiation of peasantry), Moskva, Nauka, 69, 262 p.

1289   DOSHI, S. L. "Nonclustered tribal villages and community development", *Hum. Org.* 28(4), 1969 : 297-302.

1290   ERDEI, F. "The changing Hungarian village", *New Hungar. Quart.* 11(38), 1970 : 3-16.

1291   FATHY, H. *Gourna: a tale of two villages.* Cairo, Ministry of Culture, 69, 295 p. [Egypt.]

1292   FOGEL, G. "Programa integrado urbano-rural de desarrollo de la comunidad en Encarnación, Itapúa (Paraguay)" (Integrated rural-urban program for community development of Encarnación, Itapúa, Paraguay), *R. parag. Sociol.* 6(14), mar 69 : 5-69.

1293   GIORIO, G. *Organizzazione di comunità. Con particolare riferimento all'ambiente rurale italiano* (Community organization. With particular reference to the Italian rural environment). Padova, Marsilio, 69, 319 p.

1294   GOSSELIN, G. "Le développement des communautés rurales Gbeya", *Archiv. int. Sociol.* 26, jul-dec 69 : 127-155.

1295   GUILLOT, B. "Le village de Passia. Essai sur le système agraire Nzabi", *Cah. ORSTOM. Sér. Sci. hum.* 7(1), 1970 : 47-88. [Gabon.]

1296   KANTOWSKY, D. "Die Zukunft dichtvevölkerter Agrargebiete Asiens" (The future of densely populated agricultural provinces of Asia), *Sociol. rur.* 10(3), 1970 : 253-257 [Example of a village near Benares.]

1297   KANTOWSKY, D. *Dorfentwicklung und Dorfdemokratie in Indien; Formen und Wirkungen von Community Development und Panchayati Raj detailliert am Beispiel eines Entwicklungsblocks und dreier Dörfer im östlichen Uttar Pradesh* (Rural development and rural democracy in India. Forms and consequences of community and panchayat development based on the example of a development block and three villages in Eastern Uttar Pradesh). Bielefeld, Bertelsmann Universitätsverlag, 70, 170 p.

1298   KEENLEYSIDE, D. "Rural reconstruction—the Canadian experience", *Khadi gramodyog* 15(12), sep 69 : 837-844.

1299   LEWIS, G. J. "A Welsh rural community in transition: a case study in Mid-Wales", *Sociol. rur.* 10(2), 1970 : 143-161.

1300   LORENZO, A. "Employment effects of rural and community development in the Philippines", *Int. Lab. R.* 100(5), nov 69 : 419-444.

1301   MENDRAS, H. "Passé et avenir des collectivités rurales", *Diogène* 69, jan-mar 70 : 123-142. [France.]

1302   MODERNE, F. "Villages communautaires et socialisme tanzanien", *Dévelop. et Civilis.* 39-40, mar-jun 70 : 147-166.

1303   NAIDU, S. B. "La communauté villageoise en Inde", *Communautés* 27, jan-jun 70 : 139-154.

1304   NICOLAS, G. "Dévelopment rural et comportement économique traditionnel au sein d'une société africaine", *Genève-Afr.* 8(2), 1969 : 18-35.

1305   Bibl. XIX-1120. PERISTIANY, J.-G. (ed.). *Contributions to Mediterranean sociology: Mediterranean rural communities and social change.* CR: D. MAKOFSKY, *Amer. sociol. R.* 35(1), feb 70 : 179-180.

1306   RAYMAEKERS, P. "Villages en développement, Congo-Kinshasa (zone occidentale)" *Archiv. int. Sociol. Coop.* 26, jul-dec 69 : 75-110.

1307   RAZA, M. R. *Two Pakistani villages; a study in social stratification.* Lahore, Punjab University Sociologists Alumni Association, Dept. of Sociology, University of the Punjab, 69, 104 p.

1308   SIDDLE, D. J. "Rural development in Zambia: a spatial analysis", *J. mod. Afr. Stud.* 8(2), jul 70 : 271-284.

1309   "Sviluppo di comunità in Italia/Community development in Italy", *Int. R. Community Develop.* 19-20, 1968 : 1-220.

1310   TAKAHASHI, A. *Land and peasants in central Luzon, socio-economic structure of a Bulacan village.* Tokyo, Institute of Developing Economies, 69, x-168 p.

1311   TIRONE, L. "Vitrolles, du village à la ville. Essai d'analyse de l'évolution des structures d'habitat d'une commune de l'étang de Berre", *Méditerranée* 10(4), oct-dec 69 : 409-433.

1312   TONESS, O. "Tobatí: uno pueblo en el Paraguay" (Tobatí: a village in Paraguay), *R. parag. Sociol.* 6(14), mar 69 : 132-137.

1313   VALSAN, E. H. *Community development programs and rural local government; comparative case studies of India and the Philippines.* New York, Praeger, 70, xxviii-485 p.

1314   WEINTRAUB, D. "Rural periphery, societal center, and their interaction in the process of agrarian development: a comparative analytical framework", *Rur. Sociol.* 35(3), sep 70 : 367-376.

1315   WEYAND, H. *Untersuchungen zur Entwicklung saarländischer Dörfer und ihrer Fluren* (Surveys in development of Saarland villages and their lands). Saarbrücken, Institut für Landeskunde des Saarlandes, 70, 217 p.

1316   YOUNG, R. C.; LARSON, O. F. "The social economy of a rural community", *Rur. Sociol.* 35(3), sep 70 : 337-353. [USA.]

1317   ZINK, A. *Azereix. La vie d'une communauté rurale à la fin du XVIIIᵉ siècle.* Paris, SEVPEN, 69, 324 p.

C.232   **Rural living**
         Vie rurale

[See also / Voir aussi: 813, 977, 993, 1128, 1142, 1148, 1149, 1226, 1307, 1898, 2342, 2379, 2441, 2528, 2620, 2733, 3059, 3129, 3130, 3165, 3168, 3333, 3577, 3579, 3782, 3793, 3801, 4160, 4193, 4234, 4286, 4520, 4770, 4950]

1318   ADAMS, J.; WOLTEMADE, U. J. "Village economy in traditional India: a simplified model", *Hum. Org.* 29(1), 1970 : 49-56.

1319   AGARWALA, S. N. *A demographic study of six urbanising villages.* Bombay-New York, Asia Publishing House, 70, 195 p. [India.]

1320   AGUILERA, G. M. "La paradoja del campo mexicano: excedentes agrícolas y miseria rural" (The paradox of the Mexican countryside, agricultural surplus and rural misery), *R. México agrar.* 2(1-2), jan-apr 69 : 111-129.

1321   ALESSIO, N. D'. "Chaco: un caso de pequeña producción campesina en crisis" (Chaco: a case of small rural production in crisis), *R. latinoamer. Sociol.* 5(2), jul 69 : 384-409. [Argentina.]

1322   BARBAN, A. M. *et al.* "A study of Riesman's inner-other directedness among farmers", *Rur. Sociol.* 35(2), jun 70 : 232-243.

1323   BARNABAS, A. P. *Social change in a North Indian village.* New Delhi, Indian Institute of Public Administration, 69, xviii-179 p.

1324   BATCHELOR, P. G. "Faith and farm; community orientated rural training in Nigeria", *Community Develop. J.* 5(2), apr 70 : 79-84.

1325   BECKER, W. L. "Análisis social del primer proyecto piloto integral de desarrollo rural en el eje norte de colonización" (Social analysis of the first integral pilot project for rural development in the Northern colonisation), *R. parag. Sociol.* 6(14), mar 69 : 70-101.

1326　BENOIST, J. "Types de plantations et groupes sociaux à la Martinique", *C. Amér. lat. Sér. Sci. Homme* 2, 1968 : 130-159.

1327　BLAYO, Y. "La mobilité dans un village de la Brie vers le milieu du XIXᵉ siècle", *Population* 25(3), mai-jun 70 : 573-605.

1328　BOCK, P. K. *Peasants in the modern world.* New Mexico, University of New Mexico Press, 69, 173 p.

1329　BOWDEN, E. "A comparison of predictions from static and dynamic models of farm innovation", *Rur. Sociol.* 35(2), jun 70 : 253-260. [Uganda.]

1330　BOWDEN, E.; MORIS, J. "Social characteristics of progressive Bagoude farmers", *East Afr. J. rur. Develop.* 2(1), 1969 : 56-62.

1331　BÜCHLER, H. C. "Modelos dinámicos en el análisis del campesinado boliviano y ecuatoriano" (Dynamic models in the analysis of Bolivian and Equatorian peasantry), *Estud. andinos* 1(2), 1970 : 5-18.

1332　COMBAZ-FAUQUEL, A. "Situation et perspectives associatives de l'animation rurale malgache", *Dévelop. et Civilis.* 39-40, mar-jun 70 : 132-146.

1333　COOLEY, F. L. "Village government in the Central Moluccas", *Indonesia* 7, apr 69 : 139-163.

1334　COSTER, M. DE. "Le phénomène rural en Afrique centrale", *R. franc. Ét. polit. afr.* 54, jun 70 : 85-95.

1335　CRAPUCHET, S. "Populations rurales et développement en Iran", *Archiv. int. Sociol.* 26, jul-dec 69 : 157-172.

1336　DECKER, H. DE. "L'animation rurale féminine à Bukavu", *Congo Afr.* 10(48), oct 70 : 441-453.

1337　DELORME, H.; TAVERNIER, Y. *Les paysans français et l'Europe.* Paris, A. Colin, 69, 153 p.

1338　DESPLANQUES, H. *Campagnes ombriennes; contribution à l'étude des paysages ruraux en Italie centrale.* Paris, A. Colin, 69, 573 p.

1339　ESSER, K. "Agrarreform: ein Machtoproblem—Zum Herrschaftssystem der Landherren in Chile" (Agrarian reform: a problem of power. On the system of domination by landowners in Chile), *Vierteljahresberichte* 39, mar 70 : 33-53.

1340　FEDER, E. "La 'función social de la tierra' y la pobreza rural en la América latina. ¿Es la reforma agraria realmente perjudicial para los campesinos ?" (The social function of land and rural poverty in Latin America. Is the agrarian reform really prejudicial to the peasants ?), *Trim. econ.* 37(145), jan-mar 70 : 3-38.

1341　FEDER, E. "Sobre la impotencia política de los campesinos" (On peasants' political powerlessness), *R. mexic. Sociol.* 31(2), apr-jun 69 : 323-386.

1342　FÉL, E.; HOFER, T. *Proper peasants—tradition life in a Hungarian village.* Chicago, Aldine Publishing Co., 69, xiii-440 p.

1343　FROELICH, J. C. "Le paysan noir et le défi moderne", *Civilisations* 19(4), 1969 : 452-463. [Togo.]

1344　FUNG, T.; MONAL, I. "Estructura agraria e ideología campesina" (Agrarian structure and peasant ideology), *R. mexic. Sociol.* 31(4), oct-dec 69 : 995-1018.

1345　GAMST, F. C. "Peasantries and elites without urbanism: the civilisation of Ethiopia", *Comp. Stud. Soc. Hist.* 12(4), oct 70 : 373-392.

1346　GANGULY, J. B. *Economic problems of the Jhumias of Tripura; a socio-economic study of the system of shifting cultivation in transition.* Calcutta, Bookland 69, viii-129-ivp.

1347　GAUDY, M. *Animation rurale; encadrement et moyens de développement économique et social en pays tropicaux.* Paris, La Maison Rustique, 69, vii-133 p.

1348　GHOSE, K. K. *Agricultural labourers in India; a study in the history of their growth and economic condition.* Calcutta, Indian Publications, 69, xiv-296 p.

1349　GOLDBERG, H. E. "Egalitarianism in an autocratic village in Israel", *Ethnology* 8(1), jan 69 : 54-75.

1350　GOLDFINGER, M. *Villages in the sun; Mediterranean community architecture.* London, Lund Humphries, 69, 224 p.

1351　GOŁEBIOWSKI, B. "Szkoła i wychowanie lo srodowisku wiejskim" (School and education in the rural milieu), *Kult. i Spolecz.* 13(2), apr-jun 69 : 141-166. [Poland.]

1352　GOUSSAULT, Y. "Liens et liaisons entre l'animation rurale et les institutions en Afrique noire francophone", *Dévelop. et Civilis.* 39-40, mar-jun 70 : 90-112.

1353　GRÜNBERG, H. *Die sozialistische Wandlung des Dorfes* (The socialist evolution of the village). Berlin, Deutscher Landwirtschaftsverlag, 70, 103 p. [Germany, DR.]

1354 HASAN, A. "The occupational pattern in a Terai village", *East. Anthropol.* 22(2), mai-aug 69 : 187-206. [Nepal.]

1355 Bibl. XIX-1190. HATHAWAY, D. E.; BEEGLE, J. A.; BRYANT, W. K. *People of rural America.* CR: C. VANLANDINGHAM, *Amer. sociol. R.* 35(1), feb 70 : 183-184.

1356 HEGEDÜS, A. "Soziale Veränderungen im Ungarischen Dorf" (Social changes in the Hungarian village), *Österr. Osthefte* 12(1), 1970 : 1-18.

1357 HILL, P. *Studies in rural capitalism in West Africa.* Cambridge, Eng., University Press, 70, xxiii-172 p.

1358 HINDERINK, J.; KIRAY, M. B. *Social stratification as an obstacle to development; a study of four Turkish villages.* New York, Praeger, 70, xxviii-248 p.

1359 HIRSCHFELD, A. "Développement communautaire, animation rurale et mouvement coopératif", *R. Ét. coop.* 49(160), 1970 : 159-168.

1360 HO, R. "Land ownership and economic prospects of Malayan peasants", *Mod. Asian Stud.* 4(1), jan 70 : 83-92.

1361 HUNTER, G. *Modernizing peasant societies—a comparative study in Asia and Africa.* London-New York, Oxford University Press, 69, 324 p. CR: A. S. BANKS, *Amer. polit. Sci. R.* 64(2), jun 70 : 648-649.

1362 JAY, R. R. *Javanese villagers: social relations in rural Modjokuto.* Cambridge, Mass., MIT Press, 69, 648 p. CR: E. H. VAJDA, *Amer. sociol. R.* 35(4), aug 70 : 784-785.

1363 JOHNSON, R. W. M. "The African village economy—an analytical model", *Farm Econ. (Oxford)* 11(9), 1969 : 359-379.

1364 KHAN, I. H. "Local government in rural India", *Polit. Hist.* 15(3), dec 69 : 11-25.

1365 KIENIEWICZ, S. *The emancipation of the Polish peasantry.* Chicago, University of Chicago Press, 69, xix-285 p.

1366 KRAMBACH, K. "Einige soziologische Aspekte der Rolle der landwirtschaftlichen Produktions Genossenschaften als spezifische soziale Grundeinheiten der gesellschaftlichen Aktivität und Organisiertheit der Klasse der Genossenschaftsbauern" (Some sociological aspects of the role of agricultural production co-operatives as basic units of social activity and class organization of peasant co-operants), *Wirtsch.-Wiss.* 17(22), dec 69 : 1846-1852.

1367 KULP, E. M. *Rural development planning; systems analysis and working method.* New York, Praeger, 70, xxi-664 p.

1368 KUPER, A. *Kalahari village politics; an African democracy.* Cambridge, Eng., University Press, 70, xii-191 p.

1369 LAMBERT, B. *Les paysans dans la lutte des classes.* Paris, Éditions du Seuil, 70, 187 p.

1370 LANDSBERGER, H. A. (ed.). *Latin American peasant movements.* Ithaca, Cornell University Press, 69, xi-476 p. CR: R. J. ALEXANDER, *J. econ. Liter.* 8(3), sep 70 : 871-873.

1371 LANNEAU, G. "Aspects de la mutation psycho-sociologique des paysans français", *Sociol. rur.* 10(2), 1970 : 120-142.

1372 LEANDER, L. *A case study of peasant farming in the Digelu and Yeloma areas, Chilalo Awraja, Ethiopia.* Addis Ababa, Chilalo Agricultural Development Unit, Planning and Evaluation Section, 69, 157 p.

1373 MADDEN, J.P. "Social change and public policy in rural America: data and research needs for the 1970's", *Amer. J. agric. Econ.* 52(2), mai 70 : 308-314.

1374 McCOY, J. L. *Rural poverty in three southern regions: Mississippi Delta, Ozarks Southeast Coastal Plain.* Washington, United States Departmant of Agriculture Economic Research Service, 70, vi-37 p.

1375 MEISTER, A. *Participation, animation et développement à partir d'une étude rurale en Argentine...* Paris, Éditions Anthropos, 69, 383 p.

1376 MENDRAS, H. *La fin des paysans; changement et innovations dans les sociétés rurales françaises.* Paris, A. Colin, 70, 306 p.

1377 MENDRAS, H.; TAVERNIER, Y. *Terre, paysans et politique; structures agraires, systèmes politiques et politiques agricoles.* Paris, SÉDÉIS, 69, v.

1378 MINANGI, A. C. *Continuity and change in local leadership; a Kwaya village in Musoma.* Dar es Salaam, University College, 69, 24 p.

1379 MIRA CASTERA, J. M. "Estratificación, generaciones y cambio social en una comunidad rural" (Stratification, generations and social change in a rural community), *R. esp. Opin. públ.* 19, jan-mar 70 : 39-56. [Spain.]

1380 MOYERNE, F. "Les villages Ujamaa et l'édification du socialisme en Tanzanie", *R. écon. Madagascar* 5, jan-dec 70 : 363-381.

1381 MUDIRAJ, G. N. R. "Rural authority structure and directed social change", *Ind. sociol. B.* 6(4), jul 69 : 275-282. [India.]

1382 MURATORIO, B. "Participación social y política de los campesinos de Nor Yungas, Bolivia" (Social and political participation of peasants in Nor Yungas, Bolivia), *R. mexic. Sociol.* 31(4), oct-dec 69 : 909-945.

1383 MATOS MAR, J. *et al. Dominación y cambios en el Perú rural; la micro-region del valle de Chancay* (Domination and change in rural Peru: the Chancay Valley micro-region). Lima, Instituto de Estudios Peruanos, 69, 377 p.

1384 OLSON, D. F. "Territory, village identity and the modern Eskimo reindeer manager", *Canad. R. Sociol. Anthropol.* 6(4), nov 69 : 248-257. [Alaska, USA.]

1385 OMVEDT, G. "Imperialism and rural modernization", *Berkeley J. Sociol.* 14, 1969: 130-151.

1386 OUEDRAOGO, L. B. "Une expérience d'animation rurale en Haute Volta", *Archiv. int. Sociol. Coop.* 26, jul-dec 69 : 111-125.

1387 PANOFF, M. *La terre et l'organisation sociale en Polynésie.* Paris, Payot, 70, 286 p.

1388 PARRACCIANI, W. "Famiglia contadina ed emancipazione femminile" (Rural family and women's emancipation), *Crit. marx. (Roma)* 8(1-2), jan-apr 70 : 407-413. [Italy.]

1389 "Paysannerie africaine et technique moderne", *Civilisations* 19(4), 1969 : 425-435.

1390 PIETRASZEK, E. *Wies robotnicza zarys problematyki socjologicznej* (Peasant worker villages. A sociological study). Wrocław, Zaklad narodowy imienia Ossolinskich, Wydawnictwo polskiej akademii nauk, 69, 192 p.

1391 POLAK, A. "Enige aspecten van een proces van verandering in een Indonesische gemeenschap" (Some aspects of a process of change in an Indonesian community), *Sociol. Gids* 17(3), mai-jun 70 : 192-200.

1392 POWELL, J. D. "Peasant society and clientelist politics", *Amer. polit. Sci. R.* 64(2), jun 70 : 411-425.

1393 PUGH, R. "Los campesinos venezolanos, organización política, liderazgo y economía" (Venezuelan peasants, political organization, leadership and economy), *R. mexic. Sociol.* 31(4), oct-dec 69 : 947-993.

1394 RAHIMOV, A. *Social'no-ékonomičeskie preobrazovanija v tadžikskoj derevne* (Socio-economic changes in the Tadjik villages). Dušanbe, 68, 231 p.

1395 RAZAFIMPAHANANA, B. "L'adaptation à une technique culturale nouvelle en milieu rural malgache", *Terre malgache* (7), jan 70 : 83-98.

1396 RIEGELHAUPT, J. F.; FORMAN, S. "Bodo was never Brazilian—economic integration and rural development among a contemporary peasantry", *J. econ. Hist.* 30(1), mar 70 : 100-116.

1397 ROHRER, W. "Agrarianism and the social organization of US agriculture: the concomitance of stability and change", *Rur. Sociol.* 35(1), mar 70 : 5-14.

1398 ROLING, N. "Adaptations in development: a conceptual guide for the study of noninnovative responses of peasant farmers", *Econ. Develop. cult. Change* 19(1), oct 70 : 71-85.

1399 ROY, P.; WAISANEN, F. B.; ROGERS, E. M. *The impact of communication on rural development; an investigation in Costa Rica and India.* Hyderabad-Paris, UNESCO, National Institute of Community Development, 69, xvi-160 p. CR: A. L. BERTRAND, *Amer. sociol. R.* 35(4), aug 70 : 780-781.

1400 RUSHING, W. A. "Class, power, and alienation: rural differences", *Sociometry* 33(2)., jun 70 : 166-177. [USA.]

1401 SCHWARTZ, N. B. "Goal attainment through factionalism: a Guatemalan case", *Amer, Anthropol.* 71(6), dec 69 : 1088-1108.

1402 SEKULIC, S. "Desarrollo comunitario en Israel" (Community development in Israel), *Comunidades* 4(11), mai-aug 69 : 52-68.

1403 SIGNORINI, M. "Aspetti e fasi dell'integrazione del contadino nella società urbana" (Aspects and phases of integration of the peasant in the urban society), *Rass. ital. Sociol.* 11(1), jan-mar 70 : 121-140.

1404 SILVERMAN, S. " 'Exploitation' in rural central Italy: structure and ideology in stratification study", *Comp. Stud. Soc. Hist.* 12(3), jul 70 : 327-339. [Mezzadria system.]

1405 SINGH, N. P. "Risk-taking and anxiety among successful and unsuccessful, traditional and progressive agricultural entrepreneurs of Delhi", *Brit. J. soc. clin. Psychol.* 9(4), dec 70 : 301-308.

1406   SINHA, D. *Motivation of rural population in a developing country.* Bombay-New York,
        Allied Publishers, 69, 51 p.
1407   SISSON, R. "Peasant movements and political mobilization: the Jats of Rajasthan",
        Asian Surv. 9(12), dec 69 : 946-963.
1408   SOLANO SAGARDE, N. *Metodología del desarrollo de comunidades rurales bolivianas*
        (Methodology of Bolivian rural community development). Tupiza, Bolivia, Ediciones
        Rico, 69, 181 p.
1409   SORENSON, J. L. "The social bases of instability in rural Southeast Asia", *Asian Surv.*
        9(7), jul 69 : 540-545.
1410   STAVENHAGEN, R. (comp.). *Agrarian problems and peasant movements in Latin America.*
        Garden City, N. Y., Doubleday, 70, xi-583 p.
1411   STAVENHAGEN, R. "Aspectos sociales de la estructura agrária en México" (Social aspects
        of Mexican agrarian structure), *R. México agrar.* 1(4), mai-jun 68 : 35-56.
1412   STAVENHAGEN, R. "Marginalidad y participación en la reforma agraria mexicana"
        (Marginality and participation in the Mexican agrarian reform), *R. latinoamer.
        Sociol.* 5(2), jul 69 : 249-275.
1413   STREIB, G. "Farmers and urbanites: attitudes toward intergenerational relations in
        Ireland", *Rur. Sociol.* 35(1), mar 70 : 26-39.
1415   TREMBLAY, M. A.; CHAREST, P.; BRETON, Y. *Les changements socio-culturels à Saint-
        Augustin; contribution à l'étude des isolats de la Côte-Nord du Saint-Laurent.* Québec,
        Presses de l'Université Laval, 69, 182 p.
1416   WALCOT, P. *Greek peasants, ancient and modern: a comparison of social and moral values.*
        Manchester, Manchester University Press, 70, 8-136 p.
1417   WEINTRAUB, D.; LISSAK, M.; AZMON, Y. *Moshava, kibbutz and moshav. Patterns of
        Jewish rural settlement and development in Palestine.* London, Cornell University
        Press, s.d., xxiii-360 p. CR: D. BENSIMON, *R. franç. Sociol.* 11(3), jul-sep 70 : 438.
1418   WERTHEIM, W. F. "From Aliran towards class struggle in the countryside of Java",
        Pacific Viewpoint 10(2), sep 69 : 1-17.
1419   WHYTE, W. F. "El mito del campesino pasivo: la dinámica del cambio en el Peru rural"
        (The myth of the passive peasant: the dynamics of change in rural Peru), *Estud.
        andinos* 1(1), 1970 : 3-28.
1420   WILKINSON, K. P. "Phases and roles in community action", *Rur. Sociol.* 35(1), mar
        70 : 54-68.
1421   WOLOCH, I. (comp.). *The peasantry in the old regime; conditions and protests.* New York,
        Holt, Rinehart and Winston, 70, 112 p.
1422   ZAMITI, K. "Les obstacles matériels et idéologiques à l'évolution sociale des campagnes
        tunisiennes. L'expérience de mise en coopératives dans le gouvernement de Beja",
        R. tunis. Sci. soc. 7(21), mai 70 : 9-55.
1423   ZGHAL, A. "La participation de la paysannerie maghrébine à la construction nationale",
        R. tunis. Sci. soc. 7(22), jul 70 : 125-161.

C.233   Rural dwellings
Habitat rural

1424   "Maison rurale (La)", *Norois* 16(63), jul-sep 69 : 334-501.
1425   SINGH, S. N. "Rural housing in U.P.: facts and fallacies", *Quart. J. loc. self-Govt*
        40(1-2), jul-sep - oct-dec 69 : 105-108. [India.]
1426   UNITED NATIONS. Department of Economic and Social Affairs. *Rural housing: a review
        of world conditions.* New York, U.N., 69, vi-186 p.
1427   VAN HECKE, E. "Structure agraire et habitat au Bas-Congo", *Ét. afr. CRISP* 106-107,
        apr 70 : 1-62.

C.234 **Rural-urban studies**
Villes et campagnes

[See also / Voir aussi: 709, 837, 845, 1105, 1114, 1115, 1117, 1119, 1120, 1128, 1153, 1157, 1163, 1177, 1403, 1413, 1654, 1694, 2515, 3960, 3981, 4976, 5100]

1428 ARANGO, J. *The urbanization of the earth.* Boston, Beacon Press, 70, xiv-175 p.

1429 ARRIAGA, E. E. "A new approach to the measurement of urbanization", *Econ. Develop. cult. Change* 18(2), jan 70 : 206-218.

1430 BANERJI, S. *The spatial dimension of urbanization in relation to development planning in India.* New Delhi, Associated Publishing House, 69, 104 p.

1431 BLOK, A. "South Italian agro-towns", *Comp. Stud. Soc. Hist.* 11(2), apr 69 : 121-135.

1432 BODJUL, I. I. *Važnaja social'naja problema kommunističeskogo obščestva. Preodolenie suščestvennyh različij meždu gorodom i derevnej v uslovijah Moldavskoj SSR* (An important social problem of communist society: the elimination of differences between town and villages in the Moldavian SSR). Kišinev, Kartja moldovenjaskě, 69, 232 p.

1433 BOJKOV, N. N. *Različija meždu gorodom i derevnej i material'naja osnova ih preodolenija* (Difference between town and village and the material basis of its elimination). Novosibirsk, Nauka, 69, 355 p.

1434 CHIASSINO, G. "Aspetti demografici dell'urbanizzazione in Italia" (Demographic aspects of urbanization in Italy), *G. Economisti* 29(3-4), mar-apr 70 : 213-224; 29(7-8), jul-aug 70 : 628-636.

1435 COORNAERT, M.; MORBIEU, M. "La ville mange-t-elle la campagne ?", *C. int. Sociol.* 17(48), jan-jun 70 : 165-172.

1436 COSTA, L. C. "Política de urbanização" (Urbanization policy), *R. Adm. municip. (Rio de Janeiro)* 97, nov-dec 69 : 637-654.

1437 "Developing patterns of urbanization", *Urb. Stud.* 6(3), nov 69 : 279-453. [UK.]

1438 DOUMENGE, F. "L'urbanisation et l'aménagement de l'espace au Japon", *C.O.-Mer* 22(88), oct-dec 69 : 356-387.

1439 DRAGAN, I. "Rythme de l'urbanisation et intégration urbaine", *R. roum. Sci. soc. Sér. Sociol.* 14, 1970 : 67-82.

1440 FRIEDLANDER, D. "The spread of urbanization in England and Wales, 1851-1951", *Popul. Stud.* 24(3), nov 70 : 423-443.

1441 FRIEDMANN, J. "The future of urbanization in Latin America: some observations on the role of the periphery", *Region. Sci. Assoc. Pap. and Proc.* 23, 1969 : 161-174.

1442 HAMMOND-TOOKE, W. D. "Urbanization and the interpretation of misfortune: a quantitative analysis", *Africa (London)* 40(1), jan 70 : 25-39. [South Africa.]

1443 HARDOY, J.; SCHAEDEL, R. P. (eds.). *El proceso de urbanización en América desde sus orígenes hasta nuestros días / The urbanization process in America from its origins to the present day.* Buenos Aires, Editorial del Instituto, Torcuato di Tella, 69, 364 p.

1444 KAUFMAN, H. F.; SINGH, A. "The rural-urban dialogue and rural sociology", *Rur. Sociol.* 34(4), dec 69 : 546-551.

1445 LEFEBVRE, H. *Du rural à l'urbain.* Paris, Éditions Anthropos, 70, 285 p.

1446 LEWIS, R. A.; ROWLAND, R. H. "Urbanization in Russia and the USSR: 1897-1966", *A. Assoc. Amer. Geogr.* 59(4), dec 69 : 776-796.

1447 MOČALOV, A. M. "Preodolenie protivopoložnosti i suščestvennya različij meždu gorodom i derevnej" (The elimination of contradictions and existing differences between town and village), *Učen. Zap. (Moskovs. gos. pedag. Inst.) Osnovy nauč. Kommunizm* 348(2), 1970 : 37-71.

1448 MUKHOPADHYAY, C. "Trend of urbanization in West Bengal", *Mod. R. (Calcutta)* 124(11), nov 69 : 847-865.

1449 NEWMAN, M.; MARCH, E. P. "Rural areas in an urban economy", *Amer. J. agric. Econ.* 51(5), dec 69 : 1097-1109.

1450 OHADIKE, P. O. "The nature and extent of urbanization in Zambia", *J. Asian Afr. Stud.* 4(2), apr 69 : 107-121.

1451 PALUCH, A. "Rozwöj miast i urbanizacja w Afryce Zachodniej" (The development of cities and urbanization in Western Africa), *Kult. i Społecz.* 13(2), apr-jun 69 : 293-314.

1452 PERVUŠIN, A. S.; REZNIČENKO, A. B. "Nekotorye problemy urbanizacii v Latinskoj Amerike" (Some urbanization problems in Latin America), *Učen. Zap. (Moskov. obl. pedag. Inst.)* 246(14), 1969 : 349-361.

61

1453   PLOTNICOV, L. "Rural-urban communications in contemporary Nigeria: the persistance of traditional social institutions", *J. Asian Afr. Stud.* 5(1-2), jan-apr 70 : 66-82.

1454   RAMÍREZ, T. E. "El proceso de urbanización en Colombia" (The urbanization process in Colombia), *R. geogr. (Rio de Janeiro)* 68, jun 68 : 19-32.

1455   ROOS, L. L. Jr. "Urbanization and modernization—some computer-based experiments", *Behav. Sci.* 15(4), jul 70 : 350-358. [Turkey.]

1456   ROSENTHAL, D. B. "Deurbanization, elite displacement and political change in India", *Comp. Polit.* 2(2), jan 70 : 169-202.

1457   SAXENA, S. *Trends of urbanisation in Uttar Pradesh.* Agra, Satish Book Enterprise, 70, xii-275 p.

1458   SCHNAIBERG, A. "Rural-urban residence and modernism—a study of Ankara province, Turkey", *Demography (Ann Arbor)* 7(1), feb 70 : 71-85.

1459   SEROŠTAN, N. A. *Gorod i derevnaja pri kapitalizme* (Town and village under capitalism). Har'kov, Prapor, 70, 130 p.

1460   SILVANY, A. J. DA S. "Urbanização nos países en desenvolvimento" (Urbanization in developing countries), *R. Adm. municip. (Rio de Janeiro)* 100, mai-jun 70 : 9-50.

1461   SINGH, B. "Some problems of urbanization", *Quart. J. loc. self-Govt* 40(3), jan-mar 70 : 187-206.

1462   STAN, C. "Industrialisation et urbanisation en Roumanie", *Inform. géogr.* 34(2), mar-apr 70 : 71-79.

1463   SVANIDZE, S. A. "V. I. Lenin o likvidacii protivo-položnosti meždu gorodom i drevnej" (V. I. Lenin on the elimination of contradictions between towns and villages), *Trudy Gruz. politehn. Inst.* (7), 1969 : 28-41.

1464   TÖRNQVIST, G.; RHENMAN, E. *The process of urbanization in the perspective of organization theory.* Stockholm, Stiftelsen Företagsadministrativ Forskning, 69, 1-26 l. [Sweden.]

1465   "Urbanisation: politiques et plans de développement", *R. int. Dévelop. soc.* 1, 1969 : 3-149.

1466   WEEKS, J. R. "Urban and rural natural increase in Chile", *Milbank Memor. Fund Quart.* 48(1), jan 70 : 71-89.

1467   WEITZ, R. "The rural-urban relationship in the development process", *Int. Develop.* 1968 : 221-230.

1468   YASA, I. "The impact of urbanization on the occupational and expenditure patterns of an agricultural village within the last 25 years", *Develop. and Change* 1(2), 1969-1970 : 51-63. [Turkey.]

1469   YOSHITOMI, S. "Toshika to toshi no miraizô" (Urbanization and the future of a city), *Toshi Mondai Kenkyû* 20(1), 1968 : 3-15. [Japan.]

C.24   Urban studies
Sociologie urbaine

C.240   *General studies*
Études générales

[See also / Voir aussi: **C.234**]

1470   "Application of computers to the problems of urban society", *Socio-econ. plan. Sci.* 4(1), mar 70 : 186 p. [USA.]

1471   BAALI, F.; VANDIVER, J. S. (eds.). *Urban sociology: contemporary readings.* New York, Appleton-Century-Crofts, 70, xiv-428 p.

1472   BERRY, B. J. L.; HORTON, F. E. (eds.). *Geographic perspectives on the urban systems; with integrated readings.* Englewood Cliffs, N. J., Prentice-Hall, 70, xii-564 p.

1473   BESSON, J. F. *L'intégration urbaine.* Paris, Presses universitaires de France, 70, 312 p.

1474   CESARETTI, C. M. "Appunti per una ricerca sulla città" (Notes for a research on the city), *Questitalia* 13(147), apr 70 : 9-19.

1475   CHENOT, L.; BEAUNEZ, R. *Villes et citoyens. Méthode d'enquête pour la connaissance et l'analyse d'une ville.* Paris, Éditions ouvrières, 69, 216 p.

1476   COMMITTEE ON SOCIAL AND BEHAVIORAL URBAN RESEARCH, NATIONAL RESEARCH COUNCIL. *A strategic approach to urban research and development: social and behavioral considerations.* Washington, D.C., National Academy of Sciences, 69, 100 p. CR: P. J. HENRIOT, *Amer. polit. Sci. R.* 64(3), sep 70 : 946-949.

1477   COUSINS, A. N.; NAGPAUL, H. *Urban man and society; a reader in urban sociology.* New York, Knopf, 70, xi-486-viii p.

1478   CULLINGWORTH, J. B.; ORR, S. C. (eds.). *Regional and urban studies; a social science approach.* London, Allen and Unwin, 69, 282 p. [UK.]

1479   DONALDSON, S. *The suburban myth.* New York, Columbia University Press, 69, 272 p. CR: A. KIRSCHENBAUM, *Amer. sociol. R.* 35(4), aug 70 : 789-790.

1480   DOWNS, A. *Urban problems and prospects.* Chicago, Markham Publishing Co., 70, 293 p.

1481   Bibl. XIX-1297. FORRESTER, J. W. *Urban dynamics.* CR: A. G. FELDT, *Amer. sociol. R.* 35(2), apr 70 : 364-365.

1482   FORTE, F. *Sviluppo urbano. Teorie ed esperienze...* (Urban development. Theories and experiences . . .). Padova, Marsilio, 69, 200 p.

1483   FRIEDEN, B. J.; NASH, W. W. Jr. (eds.). *Shaping an urban future: essays in memory of Catherine Bauer Wurster.* Cambridge, Mass., MIT Press, 69, 222 p. CR: R. FEDERICO, *Amer. sociol. R.* 34(6), dec 69 : 967-968.

1484   Bibl. XIX-1298. GANS, H. J. *People and plans: essays on urban problems and solutions.* CR: R. DEWEY, *Amer. sociol. R.* 35(2), apr 70 : 365-367; R. E. PAHL, *Brit. J. Sociol.* 20(4), dec 69 : 460-461.

1485   HELLMAN, H. *The city in the world of the future.* New York, M. Evans; Philadelphia, Lippincott, 70, 186 p.

1486   JAMOTTE, C.; PAELINK, J. H. P. "Un modèle de simulation dynamique pour une région urbaine", *Rech. écon. Louvain* 35(5), dec 69 : 371-400.

1487   JUPPENLATZ, M. *Cities in transformation; the urban squatter problem of the developing world.* St. Lucia, University of Queensland Press, 70, xiv-257 p.

1488   KILBRIDGE, M. D.; O'BLOCK, R. P.; TEPLITZ, P. V. *Urban analysis.* Boston, Division of Research, Graduate School of Business Administration, Harvard University, 70, xv-332 p.

1489   LEAHY, W. H.; McKEE, D. L.; DEAN, R. D. (eds.). *Urban economics; theory, development and planning.* New York, Free Press, 70, viii-339 p.

1490   LEFEBVRE, H. *La révolution urbaine.* Paris, Gallimard, 70, 248 p.

1491   LEINWAND, G.; SCHEETZ, R. E. *The city as a community.* New York, Washington Square Press, 70, 192 p.

1492   MEYER, J. K. *Bibliography on the urban crisis; the behavioral, psychological and sociological aspects of the urban crisis.* Chevy Chase, Md., Washington, United States, Government Printing Office, 69, vii-452 p. [USA.]

1493   MEYERSON, M. (ed.). *The conscience of the city.* New York, G. Braziller, 70, xv-397 p.

1494   MICHELSON, W. M. *Man and his urban environment: a sociological approach.* Reading, Mass., Addison-Wesley Publishing Co., 70, xiii-242 p.

1495   Bibl. XVIII-1558. MORRIS, R. N. *Urban sociology.* CR: G. SABAGH, *Amer. sociol. R.* 34(6), dec 69 : 964-965.

1496   MUMFORD, L. *The culture of cities.* New York, Harcourt, Brace, Jovanovich, 70, xviii-586 p.

1497   NETZER, R. *Economic and urban problems; diagnoses and prescriptions.* New York, Basic Books, 70, vi-213 p.

1498   PAGE, J. K. "Possible developments in the urban environment", *Futures (Guildford)* 2(3), sep 70 : 215-221.

1499   RODWIN, L. *Nations and cities; a comparison of strategies for urban growth.* Boston, Houghton-Mifflin, 70, xvi-395 p.

1500   SANTOS, M. "Mecanismos de crescimento urbano nos países em vias de desenvolvimento" (Mechanisms of urban growth in developing countries), *Amér. lat.* 12(4), oct-dec 69 : 134-148.

1501   SANTOS, M. "Une nouvelle dimension dans l'étude des réseaux urbains dans les pays sous-développés", *A. Géogr.* 79(434), jul-aug 70 : 425-445.

1502   SIMONCINI, G. *Il futuro e la città. Urbanistica e problemi di previsione urbana* (The future and the city. Urbanistics and the problem of urban prevision). Bologna, Il Mulino, 70, 303 p.

1503   Bibl. XIX-1315. THOMLINSON, R. *Urban structure: the social and spatial character of cities.* CR: J. N. EDWARDS, *Amer. sociol. R.* 35(3), jun 70 : 584-585.

1504   TRYSTRAM, J. P. (éd.). *Sociologie et urbanisme; colloque des 1, 2 et 3 mai 1968.* Paris, Éditions de l'Épi, 70, 188 p.

1505   "Urban issues", *Management Sci.* 16(12), aug 70 : 711-799.
1506   VAN CLEEF, E. *Cities in action.* New York, Pergamon Press, 70, xiii-235 p.
1507   VAPNARSKY, C. A. "On rank-size distributions of cities: an ecological approach", *Econ. Develop. soc. Change* 17(4), jul 69 : 584-595.
1508   WALLIS, A. "Status and hierarchy of the cities", *Polish sociol. B.* (1), 1969 : 49-58.
1509   ZISCH, W. E.; DOUGLAS, P. H.; WEAVER, R. C. *The urban environment: how it can be improved.* New York, New York University Press, 69, xxi-107 p.

C.241   Urban structure: towns
Structure urbaine: villes

[See also / Voir aussi: **C.234**; 792, 838, 1174, 1458, 2901, 3351]

1510   Bibl. XIX-1319. ADAM, A. *Casablanca. Essai sur la transformation de la société marocaine au contact de l'Occident.* CR: M. COORNAERT, *C. int. Sociol.* 17(48), jan-jun 70 : 184-186; D. BENSIMON, *R. franç. Sociol.* 11(1), jan-mar 70 : 115.
1511   ALONSO, W. "The mirage of new towns", *Publ. Interest* 19, 1970 : 3-17. [USA.]
1512   ALONSO, W. "What are new towns for ?", *Urb. Stud.* 7(1), feb 70 : 37-55. [USA.]
1513   BARBIER, B. *Villes et centres des Alpes du Sud. Étude de réseau urbain.* Gap, Éditions Ophrys, 69, 423 p.
1514   BLEUCHOT, H. "Une ville minière marocaine: Khouribga", *R. Occident musul. Méditerr.* 6, 1969 : 29-52.
1515   BRAUN, P. *Die sozialräumliche Gliederung Hamburgs* (The socio-territorial structure of Hamburg). Göttingen, Vandenhoeck und Ruprecht, 68, 206 p. CR: G. ALBRECHT, *Kölner Z. Soziol. u. soz.-Psychol.* 22(2), jun 70 : 436-442.
1516   CHESNAIS, M. "Villes et agglomérations normandes: évolution de leur population entre 1954 et 1968", *Ét. normandes* 73, 1969 : 1-10.
1517   CLARKE, J. I.; CLARK, B. D. *Kermanshah: an Iranian provincial city.* Durham, University of Durham, Dept. of Geography, 69, 6-137 p.
1518   *Concentración (La) urbana en España* (Urban concentration in Spain). Madrid, Anales de Moral Social y Económica, 69, 245 p.
1519   CORNU, M. "Villes nouvelles ou les incertitudes de l'urbanisme", *Pensée* 148, nov-dec 69 : 17-34. [France.]
1520   DELER, J. P. "Croissance accélérée et formes de sous-développement urbain à Lima", *C.O.-Mer* 23(89), jan-mar 70 : 73-94.
1521   ELAZAR, D. J. *Cities of the prairie; the metropolitan frontier and American politics.* New York, Basic Books, 70, xiv-514 p.
1522   FITCH, L. C.; WALSH, A. H. (eds.). *Agenda for a city; issues confronting New York.* Beverly Hills, Calif., Sage Publications, 70, 718 p.
1523   FONDATION NATIONALE DES SCIENCES POLITIQUE. *L'expérience française des villes nouvelles.* Paris, Armand Colin, 70, 214 p. [Journée d'étude sur les villes nouvelles, Paris, 1969.]
1524   HABENSTREIT, B. *The making of urban America.* New York, Messner, 70, 189 p.
1525   HANNA, W. J.; HANNA, J. L. *Urban dynamics in black Africa.* Washington, American University, Center for Research in Social Systems, 69, xxiii-356 p.
1526   HARRIS, C. D. *Cities of the Soviet Union; studies in their functions, size, density, and growth.* Chicago, Rand McNally, 70, xxviii-484 p.
1527   HOSS, J.-P. *Communes en banlieue: Argenteuil et Bezons.* Paris, A. Colin, 69, 136 p. (Travaux et recherches de science politique, n⁰ 4). [France.]
1528   HUET, J. P. "La croissance de l'agglomération de Nancy: l'expansion démographique", *Conjonct. econ. lorr.* 10(3), nov 69 : 11-26.
1529   JOSSE, R. "Croissance urbaine au Sahara: Ghardaïa", *C.O.-Mer* 23(89), jan-mar 70 : 46-71.
1530   KERBLAY, B. "La ville soviétique entre le possible et l'imaginaire", *Annales* 25(4), jul-aug 70 : 897-911.
1531   KRAPF-ASKARI, E. *Yoruba towns and cities. An inquiry into the nature of urban social phenomena.* Oxford, Clarendon Press, 69, xii-195 p.
1532   KURASAWA, S. "Japanese city: a study on its structural changes", *Develop. Econ.* 7(4), dec 69 : 527-543.

1533 LAMBETH, E. B. "New towns: can they work ?", *Washington Mthly* 1(9), oct 69 : 2-20. [USA.]

1534 LAZZAROTI, R. "Limoges, capitale régionale, peut-elle devenir une métropole d'équilibre ?", *Norois* 17(65), jan-mar 70 : 57-80.

1535 LEBON, J. H. G. "The Islamic city in the Near-East; a comparative study of Cairo, Alexandria and Istanbul", *Town Planning R.* 41(2), 1970 : 179-194.

1536 LEVALLOIS, M. *Villeneuve-sur-Lot, étude d'économie urbaine...* Bordeaux, Bière, 69, 72 p.

1537 MARCILLO, M. L. *La ville de São Paulo: peuplement et population (1750-1850) d'après les registres paroissiaux et les recensements anciens.* Rouen, Université de Rouen, 69, 248 p.

1538 MARTHELOT, P. "Aggression démographique et développement urbain. Variantes sur le thème: villeneuves et médinas", *R. Occident musul. Méditerr.* n° spéc. 1970 : 297-309. [Casablanca et Le Caire.]

1539 MARTHELOT, P. "Le Caire, nouvelle métropole", *Acta geogr.* 3(1), 1970 : 3-8.

1540 McPHELIM, M. "Manila: the primate city", *Philippine Stud.* 17(4), oct 69 : 781-789. [Philippines.]

1541 MOHL, R. A.; BETTEN, N. (eds.). *Urban America in historical perspective.* New York, Weybright and Talley, 70, vii-426 p.

1542 OSBORN, F. J.; WHITTICK, A. *The new towns: the answer to megalopolis.* Completely revised and reset ed. London, Leonard Hill Books, 69, 456 p. [UK.]

1543 PANDEYA, P. *Impact of industrialisation on urban growth: a case study of Chhotanagpur.* Allahabad, Central Book Depot, 70, 258 p.

1544 PENFOLD, A. "Caracas: urban growth and transportation", *Town Planning R.* 41(2), 1970 : 103-120.

1545 PONCET, E. "Note sur l'évolution récente de l'agglomération du Caire", *A. Géogr.* 79(431), jan-feb 70 : 78-111.

1546 PRAKASH, V. *New towns in India.* Detroit, The Cellar Book Shop, 69, x-149 p.

1547 PRESTON, D. A. "New towns. A major change in the rural settlement pattern in highland Bolivia", *J. Latin Amer. Stud.* 2(1), mai 70 : 1-27.

1548 "Projet original (Une): la ville nouvelle de Vaudreuil", *Administration (Paris)* 23(68), 1970 : 67-73. [France.]

1549 RUPPERT, H. *Beirut; eine westlich geprägte Stadt des Orients.* (Beirut; an oriental city encircled on the West). Erlangen, Palm und Enke, 69, 140 p.

1550 SATO, L. "La mégalopolis du Tokaido", *Projet* 46, jun 70 : 744-751. [Japon.]

1551 SCHAFFER, F. *The new town story.* London, MacGibbon and Kee, 70, xv-342 p. [UK.]

1552 SHIBBE, S. J. *al-Numû al-hâdith lil-madinat al-'Arabiyat* (Recent Arab city growth). Kuwait, Kuwait Government Printing Press, 69, 832 p.

1553 STONE, P. A. *Urban development in Britain; standards, costs and resources, 1964-2004.* I. *Population trends and housing.* Cambridge, Cambridge University Press, 70, xxii-411 p.

1554 STRASZEWICZ, L. "La trasformazione e lo sviluppo delle funzioni urbane di Lodz (Polonia)" (The transformation and the development of the urban functions of Lodz (Poland), *Boll. Soc. geogr. ital.* 11(1-3), jan-mar 70 : 74-88.

1555 TAGER, J.; GOIST, P. D. (eds.). *The urban vision; selected interpretations of the modern American city.* Homewood, Ill., Dorsey Press, 70, x-310 p.

1556 THOMAS, R. "Aycliffe to Cumbernauld—a study of seven new towns in their regions", *P.E.P. Broadsheet* 35(516), dec 69 : 801-962. [UK.]

1557 VAUJOUR, J. *Le plus grand Paris; l'avenir de la région parisienne et ses problèmes complexes.* Paris, Presses universitaires de France, 70, xi-202 p.

1558 VEYRET-VERNER, G. "Essai de définition et de classification des petites villes: leur insertion dans un réseau urbain", *R. géogr. alpine* 58(1), 1970 : 51-66. [France.]

1559 VIDYARTHI, L. P.; LAL, R. B. *Cultural configuration of Ranchi; survey of an emerging industrial city of tribal India, 1960-62.* Calcutta, J. N. Basu, Bookland, 69, x-412 p.

1560 WOOLMER, H. "Grantown-on-Spey; an eighteenth-century new town", *Town Planning R.* 41(3), 1970 : 237-249.

C.242   Urban living
Vie urbaine

[See also / Voir aussi: 710, 715, 718, 782, 814, 899, 904, 905, 946, 952, 959, 1027, 1031, 1088, 1109, 1127, 1136, 1137, 1155, 1169, 1413, 1439, 2007, 2067, 2351, 2464, 2487, 2539, 2540, 2547, 2613, 2692, 2739, 2821, 2837, 2838, 2844, 2847, 2872, 2884, 2921, 3420, 3622, 3962, 4127, 4237, 4539, 4554, 5213, 5228, 5229, 5232, 5286]

1561   ADEPOJU ONIBOKUN, G. "Sociocultural constraints on urban renewal policies in emerging nations: the Ibadan case", *Hum. Org.* 29(2), 1970 : 133-139.

1562   AIKEN, M. "Community power and community mobilization", *A. Amer. Acad. polit. soc. Sci.* 385, sep 69 : 76-88.

1563   AIKEN, M.; MOTT, P. E. (eds.). *The structure of community power.* New York, Random House, 70, xi-540 p.

1564   ALFORD, R. R. "Bureaucracy and participation in four Wisconsin cities", *Urb. Aff. Quart.* 5(1), sep 69 : 5-30.

1565   ALFORD, R. R. "Data resources for comparative studies of urban administration", *Soc. Sci. Inform./Inform. Sci. soc.* 9(3), jun 70 : 193-203.

1566   ANTON, T. "Incrementalism in utopia. The political integration of metropolital Stockholm", *Urb. Aff. Quart.* 5(1), sep 69 : 59-82.

1567   ANTUNES, A.; DURAND, C. *Contribution à une sociologie des groupes urbains. Groupes typiques, groupes de transition, groupes leaders. Vocation et rôles urbains à Poitiers.* Paris, Ministère de l'Équipement et du Logement, Publications des Recherches urbaines, s.d., 65-iii p. CR: J. BOUCHET, *R. franç. Sociol.* 11(2), apr-jun 70 : 269-272.

1568   AUSTIN, A. G.; LEWIS, S. *Urban government for metropolitan Lima.* New York, Praeger Publishers, 70, xv-186 p.

1569   BALAN, J. "Migrant-native socio-economic differences in Latin American cities; a structural analysis", *Latin Amer. Res. R.* 4(1), 1969 : 3-26.

1570   BALBO, L. "Struttura del potere e processi di decisione a livello di comunità" (Power structure and decision process at the community level), *Quad. Sociol.* 18(4), oct-dec 69 : 466-494.

1571   BANFIELD, E. C. *Urban government—a reader in administration and politics.* Rev. ed. New York, Free Press, 69, xvii-718 p. [USA.]

1572   BERKOWITZ, M. I.; BRANDAUER, F. B.; REED, J. H. *Folk religion in an urban setting; a study of Hakka villagers in transition.* Hong Kong, Christian Study Centre on Chinese Religion and Culture, 69, xi-167 p.

1573   BERNARD, G. "Analyse d'un réseau social en milieu urbain", *C. Ét. afr.* 10(4), 1970 : 632-639.

1574   BOULARD, F.; REMY, J. "Villes et régions culturelles: acquis et débats", *Archiv. Sociol. Relig.* 15(29), jan-jun 70 : 117-140. [Sur la pratique religieuse.]

1575   BOUMA, D. H. "The issue-analysis approach to community power: a case study of realtors in Kalamazoo", *Amer. J. Econ. Sociol.* 29(3), jul 70 : 241-252. [USA.]

1576   BUTLER, J. E.; FUGUITT, G. V. "Small-town population change in distance from larger towns: a replication of Hassinger's study", *Rur. Sociol.* 35(3), sep 70 : 396-409.

1577   CAVALLI, L. "Ritorno a Middletown" (Return to Middletown), *Quad. Sociol.* 18(4), oct-dec 69 : 446-465.

1578   CHAMBOREDON, J. C.; LEMAIRE, M. "Proximité spatiale et distance sociale. Les grands ensembles et leur peuplement", *R. franç. Sociol.* 11(1), jan-mar 70 : 3-33.

1579   CLARK, I. N. "Structure communautaire, prise de décision, dépenses budgétaire et rénovation urbaine dans 51 communautés américaines", *Aménag. Territ. Dévelop. région.* 3, 1970 : 179-219.

1580   COLLOQUE NATIONAL DE DÉMOGRAPHIE. *Grandes villes et petites villes; démographie et croissance urbaine, démographie et scolarisation.* Paris, Éditions du Centre national de la recherche scientifique, 70, 573 p.

1581   CONNERY, R. H.; CARALEY, D. *Governing the city: challenges and options for New York.* New York, Frederick O. Praeger, 69, 230 p. CR: R. D. HORTON, *Amer. polit. Sci. R.* 64(2), jun 70 : 642-643.

1582   COUTURIER, M. *Recherches sur les structures sociales de Chateaudun, 1525-1789.* Paris, SEVPEN, 69, s.p.

1583   CRAIN, R. L.; KATZ, E.; ROSENTHAL, D. B. *The politics of community conflict: the fluoridation decision.* Indianapolis, Bobbs-Merrill Co., 69, xx-269 p. CR: R. D. CORWIN, *Amer. J. Sociol.* 76(1), jul 70 : 182-186; R. EYESTONE, *Amer. polit. Sci. R.* 64(1), mar 70 : 215-216; P. WEHR, *Amer. sociol. R.* 35(4), aug 70 : 775-776.

1584   Bibl. XIX-1413. DALAND, T. *Comparative urban research: the administration and politics of cities.* CR: W. O. WINTER, *Amer. polit. Sci. R.* 64(2), jun 70 : 646-648.

1585   DOUGHTY, P. L. "La cultura del regionalismo en la vida urbana de Lima, Perú" (The culture of regionalism in urban life in Lima, Peru), *Amér. indíg.* 29(4), oct 69 : 949-981.

1586   DYE, T. R. "Community power studies", *Polit. Sci. Ann.* 2, 1969-70 : 35-70.

1587   ECKERT, E. H. "Die Medina-Gesellschaft; Versuch einer Rekonstruktion des Sozial-strukturen" (The Medina-society; research on the reconstruction of social structure), *Kölner Z. Soziol. soz. Psychol.* 22(3), sep 70 : 473-500.

1588   FARLEY, R. "The changing distribution of Negroes within metropolitan areas: the emergence of Black suburbs", *Amer. J. Sociol.* 75(4, Part I), jan 70 : 512-529.

1589   FATTINNANZI, E.; PETRALIA, S. "Sviluppo urbano e conflitti sociali" (Urban development and social conflicts), *Probl. Social. (Milano)* 12(45), mar-apr 70 : 253-269. [Italy.]

1590   FEIT, E. "Urban revolt in South Africa: a case study", *J. mod. Afr. Stud.* 8(1), apr 70 : 55-72.

1591   FELDMAN, L. D.; GOLDRICK, M. (eds.). *Politics and government of urban Canada: selected readings.* Toronto, Methuen, 69, xiii-382 p.

1592   "Fenomeno urbano e desenvolvimento social na região de Lisboa" (Urban phenomenon and social development in the Lisbon region), *Inform. soc. (Lisboa)* 5(19), jul-sep 70 : 3-191.

1593   FERRARESI, G. "Appunti sul ruolo politico della grande città in Italia" (Notes on the political role of the big city in Italy), *Questitalia* 13(146-147), mai-jun 70 : 30-42.

1594   FROLIC, B. M. "Soviet urban political leaders", *Comp. polit. Stud.* 2(4), jan 70 : 443-464.

1595   GOODMAN, J. S. (ed.). *Perspectives on urban politics.* Boston, Allyn and Bacon, 70, xi-558 p.

1596   GÖRGEN, H. P. *Düsseldorf und der Nationalsozialismus. Studie zur Geschichte einer Grosstadt im 'Dritten Reich'* (Dusseldorf and National Socialism. A study of the history of a large city under the IIIrd Reich). Düsseldorf, Schwann, 69, 254 p.

1597   "Governing megacentropolis", *Publ. Adm. R.* 30(5), sep-oct 70 : 473-520. [USA.]

1598   GRÉMION, P. "Introduction à une étude du système politico-administratif local", *Sociol. Trav.* 12(1), jan-mar 70 : 51-73.

1599   HAMPTON, W. A. *Democracy and community: a study of politics in Sheffield.* London, New York, Oxford University Press, 70, xxv-349 p.

1600   HAWLEY, A. H.; ZIMMER, B. G. *The metropolitan community; its people and government.* Beverly Hills, Calif., Sage Publications, 70, 154 p.

1601   HEINBERG, J. D. "Economic and social disparities between central cities and their suburbs: a reply", *Land Econ.* 46(3), aug 70 : 345-349. [See M. C. BRAZER's article, Bibl. XVII-1552.]

1602   JANICKA, S. (ed.). *Ludność i stosunki społeczne w konurbacji górnośląskiej: Bytom-Chrozów-Gliwice-Zabrze* (Population and social relations in urban complex in Upper-Silesia: Byton - Chrozów-Gliwice-Zabrze). Katowice, Śląski Instytut Naukowy, 69, 288 p.

1603   JOHNSON, K. M. *Urban government for the Prefecture of Casablanca.* New York, Praeger, 70, xxiv-251 p.

1604   JONES, F. L. *Dimensions of urban social structure: the social areas of Melbourne, Australia.* Canberra, Australian National University Press, 69, xii-149 p.

1605   JONES, G. W. *Borough politics; a study of the Wolverhampton Town Council, 1888-1964.* London, Macmillan, 69, 418 p. [UK.]

1606   KRAVITZ, S.; KOLODNER, F. K. "Community action: where has it been ? Where will it go ?", *A. Amer. Acad. polit. soc. Sci.* 385, sep 69 : 30-40.

1607   MADGWICK, P. J. *American city politics.* London, Routledge and Kegan Paul, 70, x-117 p.

1608   MARSTON, W. G. "Social class segregation within ethnic groups in Toronto", *Canad. R. Sociol. Anthropol.* 6(2), mai 69 : 65-79.

1609   MARSTON, W. G. "Socio-economic differentiation within Negro areas of American cities", *Soc. Forces* 48(2), dec 69 : 165-176.

1610   MÉDARD, J.-F. *Communauté locale et organisation communautaire aux États-Unis.* Paris, A. Colin, 69, 336 p. (Cahiers de la Fondation nationale des Sciences politiques, n° 172).

1611   MEISTER, A. "Trasformazione sociale nella periferia delle grandi città dell'America Latina. Modello e piano di ricerca" (Social transformation in the suburbs of big cities in Latin America. Model and research plan), *Int. R. Community Develop.* 21-22, dec 69 : 45-76.

1612   MICHETTI, H. H.; PARAHYBA, M. A. DE A. G. "O jôgo das fôrças politicas na vida de Araraquara" (The interplay of political forces in the life of Araraquara), *Cienc. polit.* 2(3), jul-sep 68 : 59-78. [Brazil.]

1613   MILLER, D. C. *International community power structures; comparative studies of four world cities.* Bloomington, Indiana University Press, 70, xx-320 p.

1614   MITCHELL, J. C. (ed.). *Social networks in urban situations: analyses of personal relationships in Central African towns.* Manchester, Manchester University Press; New York, Humanities Press, 69, x-378 p. CR: K. BOHM, *Acta sociol.* 13(3), 1970 : 205-206.

1615   NELSON, J. "The urban poor: disruption or political integration in Third World cities ?", *Wld Polit.* 22(3), apr 70 : 393-414.

1616   NEYMAN, E.; TYSZKA, A. "Cultural differentiation and social stratification of a small town", *Polish sociol. B.* (1), 1969 : 89-96.

1617   NIX, H. L. *Community social analysis of Athens - Clarke County.* Athens, Ga., University of Georgia Institute of Community and Area Development and the Department of Sociology and Anthropology, 69, 143 p. CR: J. A. BEEGLE, *Amer. sociol. R.* 35(3), jun 70 : 587-588.

1618   ORBELL, J. M. "An information-flow theory of community influence", *J. Polit.* 32(2), mai 70 : 322-338. [Columbus, Ohio, USA.]

1619   ORR, J. B.; NICHELSON, F. P. *The radical suburb; soundings in changing American character.* Philadelphia, Westminster Press, 70, xix-201 p.

1620   PAHL, R. E. *Patterns of urban life.* London, Longmans; New York, Humanities Press, 70, x-152 p.

1621   PETERSON, P. E. "Forms of representation: participation of the poor in the community action program", *Amer. polit. Sci. R.* 64(2), jun 70 : 491-507. [USA.]

1622   POZAS, A. "Los grupos urbanos marginados: nuevo intento de explicación" (Urban marginal groups: a new attempt to explain them), *Aportes* 18, oct 70 : 131-147. [Chile.]

1623   *Problemática (La) de la marginalidad social en Barcelona* (The problem of social marginality in Barcelona). Barcelona, Instituto de Reinserción Social, 70, 156 p.

1624   "Quality of urban life (The)", *Urb. Aff. ann. R.* 3, 1969 : 580 p.

1625   RABINOVITZ, F. F. "Data resources for cross-national urban research on administration and politics: a proposal", *Inform. Sci. soc./Soc. Sci. Inform.* 9(3), jun 70 : 173-191.

1626   RANDLE, P. H. "Structuras urbanas pampeanas" (Pampean urban structures), *C. Amér. lat. Sér. Sci. Homme* 3, 1969 : 87-123. [Argentina.]

1627   RHODES, G. *The government of London: the struggle for reform.* London, London School of Economics and Political Science, 70, xv-320 p.

1628   ROBERTS, B. "Urban poverty and political behavior in Guatemala", *Hum. Org.* 29(1), 1970 : 20-28.

1629   RODGERS, H. R. Jr. *Community conflict, public opinion and the law: the Amish dispute in Iowa.* Columbus, Charles E. Merrill Publishing Co., 69, 154 p. CR: K. M. DOLBEARE, *Amer. polit. Sci. R.* 64(2), jun 70 : 609-611.

1630   RUCHELMAN, L. I. (ed.). *Big city mayors; the crisis in urban politics.* Bloomington, Indiana University Press, 70, xi-371 p.

1631   RUCK, S. K.; RHODES, G. *The government of Greater London.* London, Allen and Unwin, 70, 3-198 p.

1632   SAINT-MOULIN, L. DE; DUCREUX, M. "Le phénomène urbain à Kinshasa", *Ét. congol.* 12(4), oct 69 : 117-142.

1633   SCHOENFELD, E. "Small town Jews' integration into their communities", *Rur. Sociol.* 35(2), jun 70 : 175-190.

1634   SEBASTIANI, C. "Marginalità politica e integrazione manipolata: sondaggio in tre borgate romane" (Political marginality and manipulated integration: a survey in three Roman suburbs), *Crit. sociol. (Roma)* 14, 1970 : 89-134.

1635 SEIDLER, M. "Some participant observer reflections on Detroit's community action program", *Urb. Aff. Quart.* 5(2), dec 69 : 183-205.

1636 Bibl. XIX-1460. SHANK, A. (ed.). *Political power and the urban crisis.* CR: S. NOHARA, *Amer. sociol. R.* 35(4), aug 70 : 774-775.

1637 ŠKARATAN, O. L. "Problemy social'noj struktury sovetskogo goroda" (Problems of the social structure of the Soviet city), *Nauc. Dokl. vysš. Skoly filos. Nauki* 5, sep-oct 70 : 22-31.

1638 SMITH, R. G. *Public authorities in urban areas.* Washington, National Association of Counties Research Foundation, 69, xxvii-426 p. [USA.]

1639 SOUSA BETTENCOURT, J. DE. "O problema de integração social na cidade de Luanda" (The problem of social integration in Luanda City), *Anu. Sociol. Pueblos ibér.* (4), 1968 : 203-226. [Angola.]

1640 SWEETSER, F. L. (ed.). *Studies in American urban society.* New York, Crowell, 70, viii-272 p.

1641 TALLMAN, I.; MORGNER, R. "Life-style differences among urban and suburban blue-collar families", *Soc. Forces* 48(3), mar 70 : 334-348. [USA.]

1642 TURK, H. "Interorganizational networks in urban society: initial perspectives and comparative research", *Amer. sociol. R.* 35(1), feb 70 : 1-19.

1643 WALTON, J. "Development decision-making: a comparative study in Latin America", *Amer. J. Sociol.* 75(5), mai 70 : 828-851. [Guadalajara, Mexico; Cali, Colombia.]

C.243 Housing and town planning
Logement et urbanisme

[See also / Voir aussi: 1131, 1519, 1553, 2610, 4558, 5100]

1644 AIKEN, M.; ALFORD, R. R. "Community structure and innovation: the case of public housing", *Amer. polit. Sci. R.* 64(3), sep 70 : 843-864.

1645 AIKEN, M.; ALFORD, R. R. "Community structure and innovation: the case of urban renewal", *Amer. sociol. R.* 35(4), aug 70 : 650-665. [USA.]

1646 ALESHIRE, R. A. "Planning and citizen participation. Costs, benefits and approach", *Urb. Aff. Quart.* 5(4), jun 70 : 369-393. [USA.]

1647 ANDREWS, F. W.; PHILIPPS, G. W. "The squatters of Lima: who they are and what they want", *J. develop. Areas* 4(2), jan 70 : 211-225.

1648 BAIR, F. H. Jr. *Planning cities; selected writings on principles and practice.* Ed. by V. CURIS. Chicago, American Society of Planning Officials, 70, xi-499 p.

1649 BARNETT, A. S.; PICKVANCE, C. G.; WARD, R. H. "Some factors underlying racial discrimination in housing: a preliminary report on Manchester", *Race* 12(1), jul 70 : 75-87.

1650 BELL, C.; BELL, R. *City fathers: the early history of town planning in Britain.* London, Barrie and Rockliff, The Cresset Press, 69, 216 p.

1651 BELUSZKY, P. "Néhány adat a tanyás településrendszer mai helyzetéröl" (Some data on the current "tanya" housing system), *Földrajzi Értes.* 18(1), 1969 : 116-124. [Hungary.]

1652 BIAREZ, S.; BLANCHET, C.; KUKAWA, P.; MINGASSON, C. "L'urbanisme concerté: les ambiguïtés grenobloises", *Sociol. Trav.* 12(4), oct-déc 70 : 449-468.

1653 BONAZI, R. "Les résidences secondaires dans le département de la Haute-Savoie", *R. géogr. alpine* 58(1), 1970 : 111-134.

1654 Bibl. XIX-1483. BREESE, G. (ed.). *The city in newly developing countries: readings on urbanism and urbanization.* CR: G. C. MYERS, *Amer. sociol. R.* 35(2), apr 70 : 367-368; B. ROBERTS, *Brit. J. Sociol.* 20(4), dec 69 : 461-462.

1655 BRT, F. "Potřeba a možnosti řešení bytového problému" (Necessity and possibilities for a solution of the housing problem), *Plán. Hospod.* 22(11), nov 69 : 58-69. [Czechoslovakia.]

1656 BRT, F. "Společenské a ekonomické aspekty" (Social and economic aspects), *Plán. Hospod.* 23(4), apr 70 : 60-70. [Of housing policy in Czechoslovakia.]

1657 BULLOUGH, B. *Social-psychological barriers to housing desegregation.* Los Angeles, Uni-

69

versity of California, Housing, Real Estate, and Urban Land Studies Program, 69, x-134 p. [USA.]

1658 CASASCO, J. A. "The social function of the slum in Latin America: some positive aspects", *Amer. lat.* 12(3), jul-sep 69 : 87-111.

1659 CASTRO, R. G. "El problema de la vivienda en Colombia" (The housing problem in Colombia), *Doc. polít.* 85, jan-feb 70 : 40-52.

1660 CHERRY, G. E. *Town planning in its social context.* London, Leonard Hill, 70, x-182 p.

1661 CHVIDKOVSKI, O. "L'esthétique de la ville de demain", *Pensée* 148, nov-dec 69 : 3-16.

1662 "City of the future", *Ekistics* 29(175), jun 70 : 366-377.

1663 COTTEREAU, A. "Les débuts de planification urbaine dans l'agglomération parisienne", *Sociol. Trav.* 12(4), oct-dec 70 : 363-392.

1664 DENNIS, N. *People and planning: the sociology of housing in Sunderland.* London, Faber, 70, 392 p. [UK.]

1665 DIETZ, H. "Urban squatter settlements in Peru—a case history and analysis", *J. inter-Amer. Stud.* 11(3), jul 69 : 353-370.

1666 DUKER, J. M. "Housewife and working-wife families: a housing comparison", *Land Econ.* 46(2), mai 70 : 138-145.

1667 "Favelas do Rio de Janeiro (Las)" (The "favelas" of Rio de Janeiro), *Amér. lat.* 12(3), jul-sep 69 : 1-200.

1668 GALIENNE, C. "Urbanisme et circulation", *R. Trav. Acad. Sci. mor. polit.* 121(4), 1968 : 53-72. [France.]

1669 GAZZANI, D. "Il problema della casa oggi" (The problem of the home today), *Riv. Sociol.* 7(18), jan-mar 69 : 189-220.

1670 GLASS, R. "Housing in Cambden", *Town Planning R.* 41(1), 1970 : 15-40. [UK.]

1671 GRISON, C. "Politique du logement et amélioration de l'habitat", *J. Caisses Épargne* 89(6), jun 70 : 355-364. [France.]

1672 GROUPE DE SOCIOLOGIE URBAINE DE NANTERRE. "Paris 1970: reconquête urbaine et rénovation-déportation", *Sociol. Trav.* 12(4), oct-dec 70 : 488-514.

1673 HERLYN, U. *Wohnen im Hochhaus; eine empirisch-soziologische Untersuchung in ausgewählten Hochhäusern der Städte München, Stuttgart, Hamburg und Wolfsburg* (Living in an apartment: an empirical sociological study of apartments chosen in the city of Munich, Stuttgart, Hamburg and Wolfsburg). Stuttgart, K. Krämer, 70, 275 p.

1674 HOWREY, E. P. "Simulation and projection of metropolitan housing conditions", *Socio-econ. plan. Sci.* 3(3), oct 69 : 219-228.

1675 HUBER, P. "Basic information for urban planning in Latin America", *R. geogr. (Rio de Janeiro)* 69, dec 68 : 145-156.

1676 ION, J. "La promotion immobilière: du logement à l'habitat", *Sociol. Trav.* 12(4), oct-dec 70 : 416-426.

1677 JOBERT, B. "Organisations décentralisées d'étude et de planification en Allemagne: étude du cas de Stuttgart", *Aménag. Territ. Dévelop. région.* 3, 1970 : 535-582.

1678 KAMRANY, N. M.; CHRISTAKIS, A. N. "A systems approach to public policy estimation: urban planning at the country level", *Socio-econ. plan. Sci.* 3(3), oct 69 : 229-244.

1679 KARKAL, G. L. "Problems of urban housing and slums", *Ind. J. soc. Res.* 11(1), apr 70 : 34-41.

1680 KULESZA, H. "Pozion czynszów i wydatków na mieszkanie w krajach socjalistycznych" (The level of rents and expenditure on housing in socialist countries), *Biul. IGS* 13(2), 1970 : 63-78.

1681 LACOUR, C. "Quelques récents résultats de recherches en matière d'armature urbaine", *Metra* 9(1), mar 70 : 13-56. [France.]

1682 LAQUEUR, W. *et al.* (eds.). *Urbanism: the city in history.* London, Weidenfeld and Nicolson, 69, 204 p.

1683 LAUMANN, E. O.; HOUSE, J. S. "Living room styles and social attributes: the patterning of material artifacts in a modern urban community", *Sociol. soc. Res.* 54(3), apr 70 : 321-342.

1684 LAUTMAN, J.; MOULIN, R. "La commande publique d'architecture", *Sociol. Trav.* 12(4), oct-dec 70 : 393-415.

1685 LEAN, W. *Economics of land use planning - urban and regional.* London, Estates Gazette, 69, x-266 p.

1686 LEE, T. "Urban neighborhood as a socio-spatial schema", *Ekistics* 30(177), aug 70 : 119-129.

1687 LEVY-LAMBERT, H. "Un modèle de politique du logement: 'Poho' ", *B. Liaison Inform. Adm. centr. Écon. Finances* 50, jan-mar 70 : 100-123.

1688 LICHFIELD, N.; CHAPMAN, H. "Cost benefit analysis in urban expansion: a case study, Ipswich", *Urb. Stud.* 7(2), jun 70 : 153-188. [UK.]

1689 LULLO, O. DI; GARAY, L. G. B. *La vivienda popular de Santiago del Estero* (The popular dwelling in Santiago del Estero). Tucumán, Universidad Nacional de Tucumán, Facultad de Filosofía y Letras, 69, 88 p. [Argentina.]

1690 MARIÉ, M. "Sociologie d'une rénovation urbaine", *Sociol. Trav.* 12(4), oct-dec 70 : 469-487.

1691 MAUNDER, W. F. *Hong Kong urban rents and housing.* Hong Kong, Hong Kong University Press, 69, xiv-192 p.

1692 MAYER, E. *Die Wohnungsversorgung der Einwanderer als Sozial-problem des Staates Israel* (Immigrant housing as a social problem of the State of Israel). Bonn, Domus-Verlag, 69, 276 p.

1693 McLOUGHLIN, J. B. *Urban and regional planning: a systems approach.* London, Faber; New York, Praeger, 69, 331 p.

1694 Bibl. XIX-1306. MEADOWS, P.; MIZRUCHI, E. H. (eds.). *Urbanism, urbanization, and change: comparative perspectives.* CR: D. G. BROMLEY, *Amer. sociol. R.* 35(3), jun 70 : 583-584; F. L. SWEETSER, *Acta sociol.* 13(3), 1970 : 201-202.

1695 MELENDRES-SUBIRATS, M.; LENTIN, F. "La planification urbaine face au marché du logement: trois projets de villes nouvelles en France", *Sociol. Trav.* 12(4), oct-dec 70 : 427-448.

1696 MESSNER, S. "Urban redevelopment in Indianapolis: a benefit-cost analysis", *J. region. Sci.* 8(2), 1968 : 148-158.

1697 MICHEL, J. "Expérience de participation dans les coopératives d'habitation", *Communautés* 25, jan-jun 69 : 112-130.

1698 MOLES, A. A. "Sociodynamique et politique d'équipement culturel dans la société urbaine", *Communications* 14, 1969 : 137-149.

1699 MOORE, W. Jr. *The vertical ghetto: everyday life in an urban project.* New York, Random House, 69, 265 p. CR: E. WORKS, *Amer. sociol. R.* 35(4), aug 70 : 799-800.

1700 MOYER, L. N.; KAPLAN, S. J.; KLEIN, T. A. "Model cities: a design for evaluation", *Soc. Sci. (Winfield)* 45(2), apr 70 : 84-92. [USA.]

1701 MOYNIHAN, D. P. *Toward a national urban policy.* New York, Basic Books, 70, xiv-348 p. [USA.]

1702 Bibl. XIX-1524. MUTH, R. F. *Cities and housing: the spatial pattern of urban residential land use.* CR: F. S. KRISTOF, *J. econ. Liter.* 8(2), jun 70 : 493-495.

1703 NELISSEN, N. J. M.; KROPMAN, J. A. "Sociologie van het wonen" (Sociology of housing), *Soc. Wetensch.* 12(2), 1969 : 90-105.

1704 OLIVEIRA, F.; BOLAFFI, G. "Aspectos metodológicos do planejamento urbano no Brasil" (Methodological aspects of urban planning in Brazil), *R. Adm. Emprêsas* 10(1), jan-mar 70 : 155-162.

1705 OTTINO, P. "Les *fare tupuna* ou 'maisons de famille' en Polynésie orientale", *Homme* 10(2), apr-jun 70 : 45-58.

1706 PAHL, R. E. *Whose city? and other essays on sociology and planning.* Harlow, Longman, 70, 10-273 p.

1707 PARISSE, L. "Les favelas dans la ville: le cas de Rio de Janeiro", *R. geogr. (Rio de Janeiro)* 70, jun 69 : 109-130.

1708 PIETRI, J.; BERGER, M. "Les densités résidentielles en zone urbaine", *C. Inst. Aménag. Urban. Région paris.* 19, mar 70 : 28 p.

1709 "Planification et urbanisme en Pologne", *Inst. Aménag. Urban. Région paris.* 20, jun 70 : 104 p.

1710 POISSON, J. P. "Pour une sociologie statistique des acquisitions d'appartements neufs", *J. Soc. Statist. Paris* 111(7-8-9), jul-aug-sep 70 : 177-184.

1711 "Power, poverty and urban policy", *Urb. Aff. ann. R.* 2, 1968 : 597 p.

1712 RIBOUD, J. "Le développement urbain", *R. Trav. Acad. Sci. mor. polit.* 121(4), 1968 : 17-31. [France.]

1713   RICHARDSON, H. W.; VIPOND, J. "Housing in the 1970's", *Lloyds Bank R.* 96, apr
        70 : 1-14. [UK.]
1714   RICHMOND, A. H. "Housing and racial attitudes in Bristol", *Race* 12(1), jul 70 : 49-59.
1715   ROCHEFORT, R. "Grands ensembles et mutations des banlieues lyonnaises", *R. Géogr.*
        Lyon 45(2), 1970 : 201-214. [France.]
1716   RO CHUNG-HYUN. "Housing problems in urban Korea", *Koreana Quart.* 11(2), 1969 :
        51-62.
1717   ROFFE, A. *Un método de análisis del problema de la vivienda en zonas urbanas, aplicable*
        en Venezuela (A method for analysing the problem of housing in urban zones applicable
        in Venezuela). Caracas, Banco Obrero, Oficina de Programación y Presupuesto,
        Centro de Información y Documentación, 69, vii-197 p.
1718   SCHUSSHEIM, M. J. "Housing in perspective", *Publ. Interest* 19, 1970 : 18-30. [USA.]
1719   SCOTT, A. "Spatial equilibrium of the central city", *J. region. Sci.* 9(1), 1969 : 29-45.
        [London.]
1720   SCOTT, M. *American city planning since 1890. A history commemorating the fiftieth*
        anniversary of the American Institute of Planners. Berkeley, University of California
        Press, 69, 747 p. CR: B. D. HARMAN, *Amer. polit. Sci. R.* 64(3), sep 70 : 944-945.
1721   SHADE, P. A. *The economics of city planning: a case study of Indianapolis.* Bloomington,
        Ind., Bureau of Business Research, Indiana University, 70, vii-184 p.
1722   SIEGAN, B. H. "Non-zoning in Houston", *J. Law Econ.* 13(1), apr 70 : 71-147.
1723   SMITH, W. F. *Housing: the social and economic elements.* Berkeley, University of California
        Press, 70, xiv-511 p.
1724   SPENCER, K. M. "Older urban areas and housing improvement policies", *Town Planning*
        R. 41(3), 1970 : 250-262.
1725   STAPLES, J. H. "Urban renewal: a comparative study of twenty-two cities, 1950-1960",
        West. polit. Quart. 23(2), jun 70 : 294-304. [USA.]
1726   "Vivienda y explosión urbana" (Housing and urban explosion), *Nuestro Tiempo* 17(193-
        194), jul-aug 70 : 3-156. [Spain.]
1727   WELFELD, I. H. "Toward a national housing policy", *Publ. Interest* 19, 1970 : 31-43.
        [USA.]
1728   WELSH-BONNARD, S. "Les équipements collectifs dans les grands ensembles résiden-
        tiels", *Doss. Action soc. cath.* 47(4), aug-sep 70 : 301-313. [Belgique.]
1729   WHEATLEY, P. "The significance of traditional Yoruba urbanism", *Comp. Stud. Soc.*
        Hist. 12(4), oct 70 : 393-423.
1730   WILHEIM, J. *Urbanismo no subdesenvolvimento* (Urbanism in underdevelopment). Rio
        de Janeiro, Editora Saga, 69, 425 p.
1731   Bibl. XIX-1476. WOLF, E. P.; LEBEAUX, C. N. *Change and renewal in an urban com-*
        munity. CR: R. T. ASH, *Amer. J. Sociol.* 76(2), sep 70 : 347-349.
1732   WRIGHT, C. D. *The slums of Baltimore, Chicago, New York and Philadelphia.* New
        York, Negro Universities Press, 69, 620 p.

C.3   **CULTURE AND PERSONALITY**
        CULTURE ET PERSONNALITÉ

C.30   **General studies**
        Études générales

        [See also / Voir aussi: 572, 599, 2434, 2567, 4382, 4451, 4921]

1733   ALUAS, I. "Sociilogia culturii—considerații metodologice" (Sociology of culture—
        methodological considerations), *R. Filoz.* 16(10), 1969 : 1185-1194.
1734   ANDREEV, É. M. "Problema ličnosti kak sociologičeskoj kategorii" (Problem of personality
        as a sociological category), *Učen. Zap. (Moskovs. gos. Pedag. Inst.)* 361, 1969 : 5-35.
1735   AYME, A. "Sociologie de la culture", *Nouv. Crit.* 31, feb 70 : 24-30. [France.]
1736   BALLER, É. A. *Preemstvennost' v razvitii kul'tury* (Heritage in the development of
        culture). Moskva, Nauka, 69, 294 p.
1737   BEHRENDT, R. F. "Entwicklung als gezielter Kulturwandel" (Development as an object
        of cultural change), *Off. Welt* 99-100, 1969 : 76-85.
1738   BOWDEN, E. "A dimensional model of multilinear sociocultural evolution", *Amer.*
        Anthropol. 71(5), oct 69 : 864-870.

1739 BOWDEN, E. "Indices of sociocultural development and cultural accumulation: an exponential cultural growth law and a 'cultural surgency' factor", *Amer. Anthropol.* 71(6), dec 69 : 1112-1115.

1740 CHOUNGOURIAN, A. "Lebanese and American aspects of personality: a cross-cultural comparison", *J. soc. Psychol.* 81(1), jun 70 : 117-118.

1741 COHEN, R. A. "Conceptual styles, culture conflict, a nonverbal test of intelligence", *Amer. Anthropol.* 71(5), oct 69 : 828-856.

1742 "Cultural innovation", *Comp. Stud. soc. Hist.* 11(4), oct 69 : 369-475. [Spec. issue.]

1743 FREYRE, G. "Importãcia dos estudos transnacionais" (Importance of cross-national studies), *R. brasil. Cultura* 1(1), jul-sep 69 : 77-92.

1744 GERGEN, K. J.; MARLOWE, D. (eds.). *Personality and social behavior.* Reading, Mass. Addison-Wesley Publishing Co., 70, 228 p.

1745 GILBERT, G. M.; MURPHY, G. *Personality dynamics; a biosocial approach.* New York, Harper and Row, 70, vii-365 p.

1746 GOLINO, E. *Cultura e mutamento sociale* (Culture and social change). Milano, Edizioni di Comunità, 69, 324 p.

1747 Bibl. XIX-1567. GREY, A. L. (ed.). *Class and personality in society.* CR: R. H. LAUER, *Amer. sociol. R.* 35(1), feb 70 : 139.

1748 HAČATURJAN, A. B. "K voprosu o kul'turnom nasledii i kul'turnoj revoljucii" (On cultural heritage and cultural revolution), *Učen. Zap. (Moskovs. gos. zaoč. pedag. Inst.)* (25), 1969 : 13-46.

1749 Bibl. XIX-1569. HARRIS, M. *The rise of anthropological theory: a history of theories of culture.* CR: J. P. GILLIN, *Amer. sociol. R.* 34(6), dec 69 : 962; P. LOIZOS, *Brit. J. Sociol.* 21(1), mai 70 : 114-115.

1750 HERRMANN, T. *Lehrbuch der empirischen Persönlichkeitsforschung* (A treatise on empirical research on personality). Göttingen, Verlag für Psychologie, 69, 467 p.

1751 HURH, W. M. "Imitation: its limitations in the process of inter-societal culture diffusion", *Int. J. comp. Sociol.* 10(3-4), sep-dec 69 : 263-285.

1752 KELLE, V. Ž. et al. *Filosofsko-sociologičeskie problemy teorii ličnosti. I. Problema ličnosti v trudah K. Marksa i V. I. Lenina. II. Problema ličnosti v klassičeskoj i sovremennoj buržuaznoj filosofii* (Philosophical and sociological problems of the theory of personality. I. Problem of personality in K. Marx and V. I. Lenin's works. II. Problem of personality in classical and contemporary bourgeois philosophy). Moskva, 69, 181 p. + 204 p.

1753 KLIMPEL, P. *Erziehung und Entwicklung der Persönlichkeit* (Education and personality development). Berlin, Volk und Wissen Volkseigener Verlag, 69, 216 p.

1754 KLOSKOWSKA, A. "The semiotic criterion of culture", *Polish sociol. B.* (1), 1968 : 47-58.

1755 KUČINSKIJ, V. A. *Ličnost', svoboda, pravo* (Personality, liberty, law). Minsk, Nauka i tehnika, 69, 198 p.

1756 LEVY, L. H. *Conceptions of personality; theories and research.* New York, Random House, 70, ix-492 p.

1757 LIEBERT, R. M.; SPIEGLER, M. D. *Personality; an introduction to theory and research.* Homewood, Ill., Dorsey Press, 70, xi-426 p.

1758 MARKARJAN, É. S. *Očerki teorii kul'tury* (Aspects of the theory of culture). Erevan, 69, 228 p.

1759 MUENSTERBERGER, W. (comp.). *Man and his culture: psychoanalytic anthropology after 'totem' and 'taboo'.* London, Rapp and Unsing, 69; New York, Taplinger Publishing Co., 70, 411 p.

1760 PERETTI, A. DE. *Les contradictions de la culture et de la pédagogie.* Paris, Éditions de l'Épi, 69, 301 p.

1761 PERLMAN, F. "La reproduction de la vie quotidienne", *Homme et Soc.* 15, jan-feb-mar 70 : 345-362.

1762 PERVIN, L. A. *Personality; theory, assessment, and research.* New York, Wiley, 70, xiv-632 p.

1763 PETTITT, G. A. *Prisoners of culture.* New York, Scribner, 70, xii-291 p.

1764 "Politique culturelle (La)", *Communications* 14, 1969 : 210 p.

1765 SADLER, W. A. Jr. (ed.). *Personality and religion; the role of religion in personality development.* New York, Harper and Row, 70, 245 p.

1766 SANFORD, N. *Issues in personality theory.* San Francisco, Jossey-Bass, 70, xiii-176 p.

73

1767   SÈVE, L. *Marxisme et théorie de la personnalité.* Paris, Éditions sociales, 69, 511 p.
1768   SIEGEL, B. J. "A formal analysis of power relations and culture change", *Int. J. comp. Sociol.* 11(2), jun 70 : 115-129.
1769   SINGH, S. "Creative abilities: a cross-cultural study", *J. soc. Psychol.* 81(1), jun 70 : 125-126.
1770   SPASIBENKO, S. G. "K. Marks i metodologija issledovanija ličnosti" (K. Marx and research methodology on personality), *Učen. Zap. (Moskov. gos. pedag. Inst.)* (361), 1969 : 36-62.
1771   SPASIBENKO, S. G.; SPASIBENKO, N. P. "Ličnost'pri socializme" (Personality under socialism), *Učen. Zap. (Moskovs. gos. pedag. Inst.) Osnovy nauč. Kommunizm* 348(2), 1970 : 155-185.
1772   SPITZER, S. P. (ed.). *The sociology of personality; an enduring problem in psychology.* New York, Van Nostrand Reinhold Co., 69, xiv-207 p.
1773   ten HAVE, P. "Emancipation and culture", *Mens en Mij* 45(4), jul-aug 70 : 246-257. [The cultural activities of groups involved in a process of emancipation.]
1774   THOMPSON, L. "Cultural homeostasis: a heuristic concept in understanding culture process", *East. Anthropol.* 22(1), jan-apr 69 : 1-12.
1775   WILLENER, A. *L'image-action de la société; ou La politisation culturelle.* Paris, Éditions du Seuil, 70, 350 p.
1776   ZIJDERVELD, A. C. *The abstract society; a cultural analysis of our time.* Garden City, N. Y., Doubleday, 70, xvi-198 p.

C.31   Individual and society
Individu et société

C.310   *General studies*
Études générales

[See also / Voir aussi: 122, 501, 524, 609, 610, 921, 1091, 1400, 1412, 1932, 2691, 3449, 3757, 4065, 4172, 4188, 4200, 4213, 4258, 4453, 4710, 4806, 4935, 5252]

1777   ALBERONI, F. "Il costo della socializzazione" (The cost of socialization), *Sociologia (Roma)* 4(2), mai 70 : 5-15.
1778   ANDERSON, C. H. "Marginality and the academic", *Sociol. Inquiry* 39(1), 1969 : 77-84.
1779   BALDAMUS, W. *Alienation, anomie and industrial accidents; an essay on the use of sociological time series.* Birmingham, Eng., University of Birmingham, Faculty of Commerce and Social Science, 69, 44 + iii p.
1780   BARNETT, L. D.; GRIFFITH, J. J. "Anomia and achievement values and attitudes toward population growth in the United States", *Pacific sociol. R.* 13(1), 1970 : 47-52.
1781   Bibl. XVIII-1899. BECKER, H. S. *et al.* (eds.). *Institutions and the person: essays presented to Everett C. Hughes.* CR: M. LANE, *Brit. J. Sociol.* 21(2), jun 70 : 235-236.
1782   BERKOWITZ, L. "Social motivation", in: G. LINDZEY, E. ARONSON (eds.). *The handbook of social psychology.* New ed. Vol. III. Reading, Mass., Addison-Wesley, 68 : 50-135.
1783   BLOCK, G. H. "Alienation—Black and White, or the uncommitted revisited", *J. soc. Issues* 25(4), 1969 : 129-141.
1784   BUCHER, R.; STELLING, J.; DOMMERMUTH, R. "Differential prior socialization: a comparison of four professional training programs", *Soc. Forces* 48(2), dec 69 : 213-223.
1785   BURROWS, D. J.; LAPIDES, F. R. (eds.). *Alienation; a casebook.* New York, Crowell, 69, x-287 p.
1786   CALDAROLA, C. "La natura umana e il problema della socializzazione" (Human nature and the problem of socialization), *Riv. Sociol.* 6(17), sep-dec 68 : 43-56.
1787   CENTRO PARA EL DESARROLLO ECONÓMICO Y SOCIAL PARA AMÉRICA LATINA. *Marginalidad en América Latina—un ensayo de diagnóstico* (Marginality in Latin America—a tentative diagnosis). Santiago de Chile, CDESAL, 69, 418 p.
1788   Bibl. XIX-1594. DAWSON, R. E.; PREWITT, K. *Political socialization.* CR: J. V. TORNEY, *Amer. J. Sociol.* 75(6), mai 70 : 1056-1058; M. L. LEVIN, *Amer. sociol. R.* 35(1), feb 70 : 134-135.
1789   DIMOV, V. M. "K voprosu o dialektike vzaimootnošenij ličnosti i obščestva" (On the dialectics of interrelations of individual and society), *Učen. Zap. (Moskovs. gos.-pedag. Inst.)* 361, 1969 : 85-104.

1790 Durou, B.; Rimailho, A. *Les "Vagueux" dans la société industrielle.* Toulouse, Éditions Privat, 70, 240 p.

1791 Égorovo, V. S.; Ivanov, R. V. "Čelovek kak sub'ekt obščestevennyh otnošenij" (Man as a subject of social relations), *Probl. nauč. Kommunizma (Akad. obšč. Nauk pri CK KPSS)* (3), 1969 : 232-250.

1792 Fend, H. *Sozialisierung und Erziehung. Eine Einführung in die Sozialisierungsforschung* (Socialization and education. An introduction to research on socialization). Weinheim-Berlin-Basel, Beltz, 70, 264 p.

1793 Fishburn, P. C. "The irrationality of transitivity in social choice", *Behav. Sci.* 15(2), mar 70 : 119-123.

1794 Gabel, J. *Sociologie de l'aliénation.* Paris, Presses universitaires de France, 70, 216 p.

1795 Gallo, P. J. "L'alienazione degli studenti in una università americana" (Students' alienation in an American university), *Rass. ital. Sociol.* 11(2), apr-jun 70 : 295-310.

1796 González Trejo, H. *Formas de alienación en Argentina* (Forms of alienation in Argentina). Buenos-Aires, C. Pérez, 70, 101 p.

1797 Heinemann, K. "Zur Soziologie des Interesses" (About sociology of interest), *Sociol. int. (Berlin)* 8(1), 1970 : 79-95.

1798 Hoppe, R. A.; Milton, G. A.; Simmel, E. (eds.). *Early experiences and the processes of socialization.* New York, Academic Press, 70, xi-220 p.

1799 Klapp, O. E. *Collective search for identity.* New York, Holt, Rinehart and Winston, 69, 383 p. CR: M. C. Kennedy, *Amer. sociol. R.* 34(6), dec 69 : 1014-1015.

1800 Kulcsár, K. *Az ember és társadalmi környezete* (Man and social environment). Budapest, Gondolat Kiadó, 69, 371 p.

1801 Bibl. xix-1617. Langton, K. P. *Political socialization.* CR: R. A. Pitts, *Amer. sociol. R.* 35(4), aug 70 : 773-774.

1802 Lyman, S. M.; Scott, M. B. *A sociology of the absurd.* New York, Appleton-Century-Crofts, 70, xi-221 p.

1803 Lystad, M. H. *Social aspects of alienation; an annotated bibliography.* Chevy Chase, Md. Washington, United States Government Printing Office, 69, 92 p.

1804 Mahov, F. S. "Svoboda individual'nosti ee rabstvo stereotipa ? Zametki o socializacii molodeži v SŠA" (Freedom of individuality or stereotype serfdom ? Remarks on the 'socialization' of youth in the USA), *Sov. Pedag.* (10), 1969 : 125-134.

1805 Mandel, E.; Novack, G. *The Marxist theory of alienation.* New York, Pathfinder Press, 70, 63 p.

1806 Marlowe, D.; Gergen, K. J. "Personality and social interaction", in: G. Lindzey, E. Aronson (eds.). *The handbook of social psychology.* New ed. Vol. III. Reading, Mass., Addison-Wesley, 68 : 590-665.

1807 Matza, D. *Becoming deviant.* Englewood Cliffs, N. J., Prentice-Hall, 69, ix-203 p. CR: M. K. Opler, *Amer. J. Sociol.* 75(6), mai 70 : 1055-1056.

1808 Napoleoni, C. "Sul concetto di alienazione" (On the concept of alienation), *Futuribili* 3(13-14), aug-sep 69 : 22-36.

1809 Negro Pavón, D. "Individualismo y colectivismo en la ciencia social" (Individualism and collectivism in the social sciences), *R. int. Sociol. (Madrid)* 113-114, sep-dec 70 : 5-31.

1810 Nun, J. (ed.). "La marginalidad en América latina" (Marginality in Latin America), *R. latinoamer. Sociol.* 5(2), jul 69 : 174-409.

1811 Ofshe, L.; Ofshe, R. *Utility and choice in social interaction.* Englewood Cliffs, N. J., Prentice-Hall, 70, ix-202 p.

1812 Palma, G. di. "Alienazione e partecipazione nelle democrazie occidentali" (Alienation and participation in Western democracies), *Rass. ital. Sociol.* 11(3), jul-sep 70 : 471-496.

1813 Pereira, L. "Poblaciones 'marginales' " (Marginal populations), *R. parag. Sociol.* 7(17), jan-mar 70 : 107-122.

1814 Perroux, F. *Aliénation et société industrielle.* Paris, Gallimard, 70, 192 p.

1815 Razin, V. I. *et al. Ličnost' i obščestvo* (Personality and society). Moskva, 69, 255 p.

1816 Reeder, L. G.; Reeder, S. J. "Social isolation and illegitimacy", *J. Marriage and Family* 31(3), aug 69 : 451-461.

1817 Regin, D. *Sources of cultural estrangement.* The Hague, Mouton, 69, 157 p.

1818 Schacht, R. *Alienation.* Garden City, N. Y., Doubleday, 70, lxv-286 p.

75

1819 SIEGRIST, J. *Das Consensus-Modell. Studien zur Interaktionstheorie und zur kognitiven Sozialisation* (The consensus model. Studies on interaction theory and cognitive socialization). Stuttgart, Enke, 70, viii-154 p.

1820 SPASIBENKO, S. G.; SPASIBENKO, N. P. "Vzaimotnošenija ličnosti i obščestva pri socializme" (Interrelations of personality and society in socialism), *Učen. Zap. (Moskov. gos. pedag. Inst.)* 361, 1969 : 63-84.

1821 STONE, G. P.; FARBEMAN, H. A. *Social psychology through symbolic interaction.* Waltham Mass., Ginn-Blaisdell, 70, x-783 p.

1822 STROLL, C. S.; INBAR, M. "Games and socialization: an exploratory study of race differences", *Sociol. Quart.* 11(3), 1970 : 374-380.

1823 SUNDIN, B. *Individ, institution, ideologi* (Individual, institution, ideology). Stockholm, Aldus/Bonnier, 70, 240 p.

1824 SURIE, H. G. "De marginale mens" (Marginal man), *Sociol. Gids* 17(4), jul-aug 70 : 306-319.

1825 TAJFEL, H. "Social and cultural factors in perception", in: G. LINDZEY, E. ARONSON (eds.). *The handbook of social psychology.* New ed. Vol. III. Reading, Mass., Addison-Wesley, 68 : 315-394.

1826 THIELBAR, G. "Localism-cosmopolitanism: prolegomenon to a theory of social participation", *Sociol. Quart.* 11(2), 1970 : 243-254.

1827 THURLINGS, J. M. G. "Het sociologisch geweten" (The sociological conscience), *Sociol. Gids* 16(4), jul-aug 69 : 214-227.

1828 TOMEH, A. K. "Empirical considerations on the problem of social integration", *Sociol. Inquiry* 39(1), 1969 : 65-76.

1829 TORDAI, Z. *Az elidegenedés mítosza és valósága* (Reality and myth of alienation). Budapest, Kossuth Könyvkiadó, 70, 305 p.

1830 WARR, P. B.; COFFMAN, T. L. "Personality, involvement and extremity of judgement", *Brit. J. soc. clin. Psychol.* 9(2), jun 70 : 108-121.

1831 ZIGLER, E.; CHILD, I. L. "Socialization", in: G. LINDZEY, E. ARONSON (eds.). *The handbook of social psychology.* New ed. Vol. III. Reading, Mass., Addison-Wesley, 68 : 450-589.

1832 ZOHNER, D. "Environmental discontinuity, stress, and sex effects upon susceptibility to social influence", *J. genet. Psychol.* 116(2), jun 70 : 211-218.

C.311 *Interpersonal relations*
Relations interpersonnelles

[See also / Voir aussi: 501, 1990, 2214, 2220, 2608, 4403]

1833 ALEXANDER, C. N. Jr.; EPSTEIN, J. "Problems of dispositional inference in person perception research", *Sociometry* 32(4), dec 69 : 381-395.

1834 AMES, R. G.; SAKUMA, A. F. "Criteria for evaluating others: a re-examination of the Bogardus social distance scale", *Sociol. soc. Res.* 54(1), oct 69 : 5-24.

1835 ARGYLE, M.; WILLIAMS, M. "Observer or observed ? A reversible perspective in person perception", *Sociometry* 32(4), dec 69 : 396-412.

1836 ARNTZ, J. "Agressie en taboe" (Aggression and taboo), *Soc. Wetensch.* 13(2), 1970 : 118-133.

1837 BACH, G. R.; DEUTSCH, R. M. *Pairing.* New York, P. H. Wyden, 70, xii-241 p.

1838 BALES, E. F. *Personality and interpersonal behavior.* New York, Holt, Rinehart and Winston, 70, xiv-561 p.

1839 BLAKE, B. F.; TESSER, A. "Interpersonal attraction as a function of the other's reward value to the person", *J. soc. Psychol.* 82(1), oct 70 : 67-74.

1840 BOYLE, R.; BONACICH, P. "The development of trust and mistrust in mixed-motive games", *Sociometry* 33(2), jun 70 : 123-139.

1841 BRAGINSKY, D. D. "Machiavellianism and manipulative interpersonal behavior in children", *J. exper. soc. Psychol.* 6(1), jan 70 : 77-99.

1842 Bibl. XIX-1643. CARSON, R. C. *Interaction concepts of personality.* CR: R. A. HARDERT, *Amer. sociol. R.* 35(4), aug 70 : 818-819.

1843 CARTWRIGHT, D.; HARARY, F. "Ambivalence and indifference in generalizations of structural balance", *Behav. Sci.* 15(6), nov 70 : 497-513.

1844 CURRY, T. J.; EMERSON, R. M. "Balance theory: a theory of interpersonal attraction ?", *Sociometry* 33(2), jun 70 : 216-238.

1845 EISENSTADT, J. W. *Personality style and sociometric choice.* Washington, NTL, Institute for Applied Behavioral Science, 69, 51 p.

1846 ETTINGER, R. F.; NOWICKI, S. Jr.; NELSON, D. A. "Interpersonal attraction and the approval motive", *J. exper. Res. Personality* 4(2), feb 70 : 95-99.

1847 GALLO, P. S. Jr.; FUNK, S. G.; LEVINE, J. R. "Reward size, method of presentation, and number of alternatives in a prisoner's dilemma game", *J. Person. soc. Psychol.* 13(3), nov 69 : 239-244.

1848 GOFFMAN, E. *Strategic interaction.* Philadelphia, University of Pennsylvania Press, 69, x-145 p.

1849 GROVES, P. H. "A computer simulation of interaction in decision-making", *Behav. Sci.* 15(3), mai 70 : 277-285.

1850 GUYER, M.; RAPOPORT, A. "Threat in a two-person game", *J. exper. soc. Psychol.* 6(1), jan 70 : 11-25.

1851 KAPLAN, M. F.; OLCZAK, P. V. "Attitude similarity and direct reinforcement as determinants of attraction", *J. exper. Res. Personality* 4(3), jun 70 : 186-189.

1852 KELLEY, H. H. *et al.* "A comparative experimental study of negotiation behavior", *J. Person. soc. Psychol.* 16(3), nov 70 : 411-438.

1853 KELLEY, H. H.; STAHELSKI, A. J. "Social interaction basis of cooperators' and competitors' beliefs about others", *J. Person. soc. Psychol.* 16(1), sep 70 : 66-91.

1854 KERSHENBAUM, B. R.; KOMORITA, S. S. "Temptation to defect in the prisoner's dilemma game", *J. Person. soc. Psychol.* 16(1), sep 70 : 110-113.

1855 KING, M. G. "Sex differences in the perception of friendly and unfriendly interactions", *Brit. J. soc. clin. Psychol.* 9(3), sep 70 : 212-215.

1856 KIPNIS, D.; GOODSTADT, B. "Character structure and friendship relations", *Brit. J. soc. clin. Psychol.* 9(3), sep 70 : 201-211.

1857 KOLB, D. A.; BOYATZIS, R. E. "On the dynamics of the helping relationship", *J. appl. behav. Sci.* 6(3), nov 70 : 267-289.

1858 KOMORITA, S. A.; BARNES, M. "Effects of pressures to reach agreement in bargaining", *J. Person. soc. Psychol.* 13(3), nov 69 : 245-252.

1859 LEVENTHAL, G. S.; WEISS, T.; LONG, G. "Equity, reciprocity, and reallocating rewards in the dyad", *J. Person. soc. Psychol.* 13(4), dec 69 : 300-305.

1860 LIEBLICH, A. "Reaction to the frustrations of the other", *Hum. Relat.* 23(4), aug 70 : 335-344.

1861 LINDZEY, G.; BYRNE, D. "Measurement of social choice and interpersonal attractiveness", in: G. LINDZEY, E. ARONSON (eds.). *The handbook of social psychology.* New ed. Vol. II. Reading, Mass., Addison-Wesley, 68 : 452-525.

1862 LOTT, A. J.; LOTT, B. E. "Some indirect measures of interpersonal attraction among children", *J. educ. Psychol.* 61(2), apr 70 : 124-135.

1863 LOWE, G. R. *Personal relationships in psychological disorders.* Harmondsworth, Penguin, 69, 143 p.

1864 LUBOW, B. K. *et al.* "An empirical approach to work behavior, interaction and rehabilitation", *Hum. Org.* 28(4), 1969 : 303-321.

1865 LUMSEN, E. A. Jr. "Person perception as a function of the deviation of the visual axes of the object-person", *J. soc. Psychol.* 80(1), feb 70 : 71-78.

1866 MALHOTRA, S. *Interpersonal relationship; psychological, sociological and educational study.* Allahabad, United Publishers, 69, xiii-197 p.

1867 MAYHEW, B. H. Jr.; GRAY, L. N.; RICHARDSON, J. T. "Behavioral measurement of operating power structures: characterizations of asymmetrical interaction", *Sociometry* 32(4), dec 69 : 474-489.

1868 McCLINTOCK, C. G.; NUTTIN, J. M. Jr.; McNEEL, S. P. "Sociometric choice, visual presence, and game-playing behavior", *Behav. Sci.* 15(2), mar 70 : 124-131.

1869 McMARTIN, J. A. "Two tests of an averaging model of social influence", *J. Person. soc. Psychol.* 15(4), aug 70 : 317-325.

1870 MELTZER, L.; RUSSO, N. F. "Interpersonal evaluation as a function of social attention", *J. soc. Psychol.* 81(1), jun 70 : 79-86.

1871 MURDOCH, P. "Norm formation in an interdependent dyad", *Sociometry* 33(3), sep 70 : 264-275.

1872 OSGOOD, C. E. "Speculation on the structure of interpersonal intentions", *Behav. Sci.* 15(3), mai 70 : 237-254.

1873 OSKAMP, S.; KLEINKE, C. "Amount of reward as a variable in the prisoner's dilemma game", *J. Person. soc. Psychol.* 16(1), sep 70 : 133-140.

1874 PAINE, R. "In search of friendship: an exploratory analysis in 'middle-class' culture", *Man* 4(4), dec 69 : 505-524.

1875 PALMER, J.; BYRNE, D. "Attraction toward dominant and submissive strangers: similarity versus complementarity", *J. exper. Res. Personality* 4(2), feb 70 : 108-115.

1876 PILIAVIN, I. M.; RODIN, J.; PILIAVIN, J. A. "Good samaritanism: an underground phenomenon ?", *J. Person. soc. Psychol.* 13(4), dec 69 : 289-299.

1877 PODD, M. H.; MARCIA, J. E.; RUBIN, H. M. "The effects of ego identity and partner perception in a prisoner's dilemma game", *J. soc. Psychol.* 82(1), oct 70 : 117-126.

1878 PRUITT, D. G. "Motivational processes in the decomposed prisoner's dilemma game", *J. Person. soc. Psychol.* 14(3), mar 70 : 227-238.

1879 PRUITT, D. G.; JOHNSON, D. F. "Mediation as an aid to face saving in negotiation", *J. Person. soc. Psychol.* 14(3), mar 70 : 239-246.

1880 ROSENTHAL, T. L.; ROGERS, C.; HURT, M. Jr. "Magical child-care beliefs and sequence and recall effects in social perception", *Hum. Relat.* 23(3), jun 70 : 191-199.

1881 SCHMITT, D. R.; MARWELL, G. "Reward and punishment as influence techniques for the achievement of cooperation under inequity", *Hum. Relat.* 23(1), feb 70 : 37-45.

1882 SERMAT, V. "Is game behavior related to behavior in other interpersonal situations ?", *J. Person. soc. Psychol.* 16(1), sep 70 : 92-109.

1883 SIEGEL, B. J. "Defensive structuring and environmental stress", *Amer. J. Sociol.* 76(1), jul 70 : 11-32.

1884 SIGALL, H.; ARONSON, E.; VAN HOOSE, T. "The cooperative subject: myth or reality ?", *J. exper. soc. Psychol.* 6(1), jan 70 : 1-10.

1885 SMITH, W. P.; LEGINSKI, W. A. "Magnitude and precision of punitive power in bargaining strategy", *J. exper. soc. Psychol.* 6(1), jan 70 : 57-76.

1886 STALLING, R. B. "Personality similarity and evaluative meaning as conditioners of attraction", *J. Person. soc. Psychol.* 14(1), jan 70 : 77-82.

1887 STEBBINS, R. A. "Social network as a subjective construct: a new application for an old idea", *Canad. R. Sociol. Anthropol.* 6(1), feb 69 : 1-14.

1888 STENSAASEN, S. *Interstudent attraction and social perception in the school class. An inquiry into the operation of preference for the balanced state among members of the natural classroom group.* Oslo, Universitetsforlaget, 70, 282 p.

1889 SUHANOV, I. V. "Dinamika ocenočnyh otnošenij v kollektive studenčeskoj gruppy" (Dynamics of relations of esteem in a student community), *Učen. Zap. (Gor'k. gos. Univ.) Ser. sociol. Sociol. vysš. Škola* 100(2), 1970 : 138-158.

1890 SUMMERS, D. A.; TALIAFERRO, J. D.; FLETCHER, D. J. "Judgment policy and interpersonal learning", *Behav. Sci.* 15(6), nov 70 : 514-521.

1891 SWINGLE, P. G. "Exploitative behavior in non-zero-sum games", *J. Person. soc. Psychol.* 16(1), sep 70 : 121-132.

1892 TAGIURI, R. "Person perception", in: G. LINDZEY, E. ARONSON (eds.). *The handbook of social psychology.* New ed. Vol. III. Reading, Mass., Addison-Wesley, 68 : 395-449.

1893 TAYLOR, D. A.; OBERLANDER, L. "Person-perception and self-disclosure: motivational mechanisms in interpersonal processes", *J. exper. Res. Personality* 4(1), jul 69 : 14-28.

1894 TAYLOR, M. "Influence structures", *Sociometry* 32(4), dec 69 : 490-502.

1895 TEGER, A. I. "The effect of early cooperation on the escalation of conflict", *J. exper. soc. Psychol.* 6(2), apr 70 : 187-204.

1896 THIAGARAJAN, K. M.; DEEP, S. D. "A study of supervisor-subordinate influence and satisfaction in four cultures", *J. soc. Psychol.* 82(2), dec 70 : 173-180.

1897 Bibl. XIX-1675. TOCH, H. *Violent men—an inquiry into the psychology of violence.* CR: F. FERRACUTI, *Amer. J. Sociol.* 75(6), mai 70 : 1052-1053; S. E. WALLACE, *Amer. sociol. R.* 35(2), apr 70 : 361.

1898 VAN DEN BAN, A. W. "Interpersonal communication and the diffusion of innovations", *Sociol. rur.* 10(3), 1970 : 199-220.

1899 VITZ, P. C.; KITE, W. R. "Factors affecting conflict and negotiation within an alliance", *J. exper. soc. Psychol.* 6(2), apr 70 : 233-247.

1900 WEBBER, R. A. "Perception of interactions between superiors and subordinates", *Hum. Relat.* 23(3), jun 70 : 235-248.

1901 WEINSTEIN, E. A.; BLACK, C. R. "Factors mediating the effects of others' responses on the self", *Sociol. Inquiry* 39(2), 1969 : 189-194.

1902 WHEELER, L. *Interpersonal influence.* Boston, Allyn and Bacon, 70, viii-119 p.

1903 WICHMAN, H. "Effects of isolation and communication on cooperation in a two-person game", *J. Person. soc. Psychol.* 16(1), sep 70 : 114-120.

1904 WILSON, T. P. "Conceptions of interaction and forms of sociological explanation", *Amer. sociol. R.* 35(4), aug 70 : 697-710.

1905 WINTHROP, H. "Social interaction underlying the professional evaluation of teachers", *Sociol. int. (Berlin)* 8(1), 1970 : 1-22.

1906 WOLMAN, R. N. "Early recollections and the perception of others: a study of delinquent adolescents", *J. genet. Psychol.* 116(2), jun 70 : 157-164.

1907 WYER, R. S. Jr. "Prediction of behavior in two-person games", *J. Person. soc. Psychol.* 13(3), nov 69 : 222-238.

1908 WYER, R. S. Jr. "A quantitative comparison of three models of impression formation", *J. exper. Res. Personality* 4(1), jul 69 : 29-41.

1909 ZAJONC, R. B. "Cognitive theories in social psychology", in: G. LINDZEY, E. ARONSON (eds.). *The handbook of social psychology.* New ed. Vol. I. Reading, Mass., Addison-Wesley, 68 : 320-411.

C.312 Individual and group
Individu et groupe

C.3120 General studies
Études générales

[See also / Voir aussi: **C.40, C.42, D.22**; 451, 2206, 4252]

1910 JABLOKOVA, É. A. "Izučenie ličnosti v uslovijah maloj social'noj gruppy" (The study of personality in the conditions of a small social group), *Sb. Trud. Vsesojuz. zaoč. politehn. Inst.* 57, 1969 : 99-113.

1911 RICE, A. K. "Individual, group and intergroup processes", *Hum. Relat.* 22(6), dec 69 : 565-584.

1912 Bibl. XIX-1684. TIGER, L. *Men in groups.* CR: F. M. MARTINSON, *Amer. sociol. R.* 35(4), aug 70 : 803-805.

C.3121 Authority and leadership
Autorité et leadership

[See also / Voir aussi: **C.55**; 505, 1213, 1594, 1969, 2150, 2450, 2469, 2693, 3011, 3781]

1913 AIRAN, J. W. *The nature of leadership; a practical approach.* Bombay, Lalvani Publishing House, 69, xxii-186 p.

1914 BERGER, J.; FISEK, M. H. "Consistent and inconsistent status characteristics and the determination of power and prestige orders", *Sociometry* 33(3), sep 70 : 287-304.

1915 CHEMERS, M. M. "The relationship between birth order and leadership style", *J. soc. Psychol.* 80(2), apr 70 : 243-244.

1916 COLMAN, A. M.; LAMBLEY, P. "Authoritarianism and race attitudes in South Africa", *J. soc. Psychol.* 82(2), dec 70 : 161-164.

1917 DENHARDT, R. B. "Leadership style, worker involvement and deference to authority", *Sociol. soc. Res.* 54(2), jan 70 : 172-180.

1918 EDWARDS, J. N. "Organizational and leadership status", *Sociol. Inquiry* 39(1), 1969 : 49-56.

1919 EISENMAN, R.; CHERRY, H. O. "Creativity, authoritarianism and birth order", *J. soc. Psychol.* 80(2), apr 70 : 233-235.

1920 FABIAN, J. "Le charisme et l'évolution culturelle: le cas du mouvement Jamaa au Katanga", *Ét. congol.* 12(4), oct 69 : 92-116.

1921   FIEDLER, F. E.; O'BRIEN, G. E.; ILGEN, D. R. "The effect of leadership style upon the
       performance and adjustment of volunteer teams operating in stressful foreign environ-
       ments", *Hum. Relat.* 22(6), dec 69 : 503-514.

1922   FOX, D. M. "The identification of community leaders by the reputational and decisional
       methods: three case studies and an empirical analysis of the literature", *Sociol. soc.
       Res.* 54(1), oct 69 : 94-103.

1923   GIRARD, J. *Genèse du pouvoir charismatique en Basse Casamance (Sénégal).* Dakar,
       IFAN, 69, 372 p.

1924   HARTFIEL, G. (ed.). *Die autoritäre Gesellschaft* (The authoritarian society). Opladen,
       Westdeutscher Verlag, 69, 215 p. CR: H. SCHMID, *Acta sociol.* 13(3), 1970 : 203-204.

1925   HINCKLEY, B. "Congressional leadership selection and support: a comparative analysis",
       J. Polit. 32(2), mai 70 : 268-287.

1926   HOGAN, H. W. "A symbolic measure of authoritarianism: an exploratory study", *J.
       soc. Psychol.* 82(2), dec 70 : 215-219.

1927   JOHNSON, H. H.; IZZETT, R. R. "Relationship between authoritarianism and attitude
       change as a function of source credibility and type of communication", *J. Person.
       soc. Psychol.* 13(4), dec 69 : 317-321.

1928   KATZELL, R. *et al.* "Effects of leadership and other inputs on group processes and
       outputs", *J. soc. Psychol.* 80(2), apr 70 : 157-169.

1929   KIPP, H. "Autoritätsbeziehungen in der Ehe" (Authority relationships in marriage),
       Sociol. int. 8(1), 1970 : 23-54.

1930   LAMOUNIER, B. "Explorações sôbre a teoria da liderança e elites tecnocraticas" (Ex-
       ploratory thoughts about the theory of leadership and technocratic elites), *Dados* 3(4),
       1968 : 40-67.

1931   LIEBMAN, C. S. "Dimensions of authority in the contemporary Jewish community",
       Jew. J. Sociol. 12(1), jun 70 : 29-37.

1932   LUTTERMAN, K. G.; MIDDLETON, R. "Authoritarianism, anomia, and prejudice", *Soc.
       Forces* 48(4), jun 70 : 485-492.

1933   MERTON, R. K. "Ambivalencia de los lideres de las organizaciones: un ensayo inter-
       pretativo" (Ambivalence of leaders in organizations: an interpretative essay), *Bol.
       urug. Sociol.* 8(15-16-17), dec 69 : 184-202. [Translation of an original article which
       will be published in the work: *The contradictions of leadership: selected speeches of
       J. F. Oates, Jr.* Ed. by B. BILLINGS. New York, Appleton Century Crofts, 70.]

1934   MITCHELL, T. R. "Leader complexity and leadership style", *J. Person. soc. Psychol.*
       16(1), sep 70 : 166-174.

1935   MITCHELL, T. R. "The construct validity of three dimensions of leadership research",
       J. soc. Psychol. 80(1), feb 70 : 89-94.

1936   MORRIS, C. G.; HACKMAN, J. "Behavioral correlates of perceived leadership", *J. Person.
       soc. Psychol.* 13(4), dec 69 : 350-361.

1937   ORPEN, C. "Authoritarianism in an 'authoritarian' culture: the case of Afrikaans-
       speaking South Africa", *J. soc. Psychol.* 81(1), jun 70 : 119-120.

1938   PRESTON, J. D. "A comparative methodology for identifying community leaders",
       Rur. Sociol. 34(4), dec 69 : 556-562.

1939   PRESTON, J. D. "The search for community leaders: a re-examination of the reputational
       technique", *Sociol. Inquiry* 39(1), 1969 : 39-48.

1940   PREWITT, K. "From the many are chosen the few", *Amer. behav. Scientist* 13(2), nov-
       dec 69 : 169-187.

1941   ROSEN, M. A. *Leadership change and work-group dynamics. An experiment.* Ithaca (N. Y.),
       Cornell University Press, 69, xx-261 p.

1942   ROSSEL, R. D. "Instrumental and expressive leadership in complex organizations",
       Adm. Sci. Quart. 15(3), sep 70 : 306-317.

1943   SCARR, S. "How to reduce anthoritarianism among teachers: the human development
       approach", *J. educ. Res.* 63(8), apr 70 : 367-372.

1944   SCHNEIDER, B. "Relationships between various criteria of leadership in small groups",
       J. soc. Psychol. 82(2), dec 70 : 263-268.

1945   SINGH, A. "A reassessment of action approach to community leadership", *Sociol. rur.*
       10(1), 1970 : 3-20.

1946   STEINER, J. M.; FAHRENBERG, J. "Die Ausprägung autoritärer Einstellung bei ehe-
       maligen Angehörigen der S.S. und der Wehrmacht" (The determination of the

authoritarian structure among veterans of the S.S. and the Wehrmacht), *Kölner Z. Soziol. soz. Psychol.* 22(3), sep 70 : 551-565.

1947 TEDESCHI, J. T. *et al.* "Social power and credibility of promises", *J. Person. soc. Psychol.* 13(3), nov 69 : 253-261.

1948 YANG, K.-S. "Authoritarianism and evaluation of appropriateness of role behavior", *J. soc. Psychol.* 80(2), apr 70 : 171-181.

C.3122 *Role studies and theory*
Rôle : études et théorie

[See also / Voir aussi: 397, 1948, 2026, 2150, 2773, 2975, 3329, 3788, 5191]

1949 ALDOUS, J. "Occupational characteristics and males' role performance in the family", *J. Marriage Family* 31(4), nov 69 : 707-712.

1950 ARNOTT, C.; BENGTSON, V. L. "Only a homemaker: distributive justice and role choice among married women", *Sociol. soc. Res.* 54(4), jul 70 : 495-507.

1951 BALSWICK, J. O.; ANDERSON, J. A. "Role definition in the unarranged date", *J. Marriage Family* 31(4), nov 69 : 776-778.

1952 BEZDEK, W.; STRODTBECK, F. L. "Sex-role identity and pragmatic action", *Amer. sociol. R.* 35(3), jun 70 : 491-502.

1953 BRENNAN, W. C.; KHINDUKA, S. K. "Role discrepancies and professional socialization: the case of the juvenile probation officer", *Soc. Wk* 15(2), apr 70 : 87-94.

1954 CATTON, W. R. "What's in a name ? A study of role inertia", *J. Marriage Family* 31(1), feb 69 : 15-18.

1955 DeFLEUR, M. L. *et al.* "The departmental chairmanship: an analysis of a changing social role", *Pacific sociol. R.* 13(1), 1970 : 5-18.

1956 DORN, D. S. "Idealized sex roles among young people", *J. hum. Relat.* 18(1), 1970 : 789-797.

1957 EISENSTADT, S. N.; WEINTRAUB, D.; TOREN, N. *Analysis of processes of role change.* New York, D. Davy and Co., 69, 43 p. CR: W. BENNIS, *Amer. J. Sociol.* 75(6), mai 70 : 1058-1060.

1958 FREEDMAN, J. L. "Role playing: psychology by census", *J. Person. soc. Psychol.* 13(2), oct 69 : 107-114.

1959 HASTINGS, A.; HININGS, C. R. "Role relations and value adaptation: a study of the professional accountant in industry", *Sociology* 4(3), sep 70 : 353-366.

1960 HOCHSCHILD, A. "The role of the ambassador's wife: an exploratory study", *J. Marriage Family* 31(1), feb 69 : 73-81.

1961 HOLTER, H. *Sex roles and social structure.* Oslo, Universitetsforlaget, 70, 298 p.

1962 JOHNSON, D. W.; DUSTIN, R. "The initiation of cooperation through role reversal", *J. soc. Psychol.* 82(2), dec 70 : 193-203.

1963 LANE, M. "Publishing managers, publishing house organization and role conflict", *Sociology* 4(3), sep 70 : 367-383.

1964 LARSON, R. F. "The influence of sex roles and symptoms on clergymen's perceptions of mental illness", *Pacific sociol. R.* 13(1), 1970 : 53-61.

1965 LUDWIG, E. G.; COLLETTE, J. "Disability, dependency and conjugal roles", *J. Marriage Family* 31(4), nov 69 : 736-739.

1966 MARTIN, J. D. "Suspicion and the experimental confederate: a study of role and credibility", *Sociometry* 33(2), jun 70 : 178-192.

1967 McDANIEL, C. O. Jr. "Dating roles and reasons for dating", *J. Marriage Family* 31(1), feb 69 : 97-107.

1968 MOWRER, E. R. "The differentiation of husband and wife roles", *J. Marriage Family* 31(3), aug 69 : 534-540.

1969 PAPANEK, M. L. "Authority and sex roles in the family", *J. Marriage Family* 31(1), feb 69 : 88-96.

1970 PETRONI, F. A. "Social class, family size, and the sick role", *J. Marriage Family* 31(4), nov 69 : 728-735.

1971 RIZZO, J. R.; HOUSE, R. J.; LIRTZMAN, S. I. "Role conflict and ambiguity in complex organizations", *Adm. Sci. Quart.* 15(2), jun 70 : 150-163.

1972   RUDDOCK, R. *Roles and relationships*. London, Routledge and K. Paul; New York, Humanities Press, 69, x-117 p.

1973   SARBIN, T. R.; ALLEN, V. L. "Role theory", in: G. LINDZEY, E. ARONSON (eds.). *The handbook of social psychology*. New ed. Vol. I. Reading, Mass., Addison-Wesley, 68 : 488-567.

1974   SEWARD, G. H.; WILLIAMSON, R. C. (eds.). *Sex roles in changing society*. New York, Random House, 70, xii-419 p.

1975   STEBBINS, R. A. "Role distance, role distance behaviour and jazz musicians", *Brit. J. Sociol.* 20(4), dec 69 : 406-415.

1976   STEWART, E. C.; DANIELIAN, J.; FOSTER, R. J. *Simulating intercultural communication through role-playing*. Alexandria, Va., George Washington University, Human Resources Research Office, 69, viii-57 p.

1977   STRODTBECK, F. L.; BEZDEK, W.; GOLDHAMER, D. "Male sex-role and response to a community problem", *Sociol. Quart.* 11(3), 1970 : 291-306.

1978   TOBAN, E. V. "Relationship of socio-economic status and preference for symptoms in a role-playing situation", *J. soc. Psychol.* 80(1), feb 70 : 59-62.

1979   TOWERS, J. M. *Role playing for supervisors*. Oxford, Pergamon Press, 69, xii-295 p.

1980   WILLIS, R. H.; WILLIS, Y. A. "Role-playing versus deception: an experimental comparison", *J. Person. soc. Psychol.* 16(3), nov 70 : 472-477.

1981   WYER, R. S. Jr. "The prediction of evaluations of social role occupants as a function of the favorableness, relevance and probability associated with attributes of these occupants", *Sociometry* 33(1), mar 70 : 79-96.

C.3123   *Status experience and self-perception*
              Expérience du statut et perception de soi

[See also / Voir aussi: 615, 1914, 2018, 2903, 3329]

1982   BALKWELL, J. W. "A structural theory of self-esteem maintenance", *Sociometry* 32(4), dec 69 : 458-473.

1983   CALLARI GALLI, M. "Per una scienza che definisca il 'se stesso' e l'altro' " (For a science which defines the self and the other), *Rass. ital. Sociol.* 10(4), oct-dec 69 : 537-568.

1984   COLLINS, J. J. "Transformations of the self and the duplication of ceremonial structure", *Int. J. comp. Sociol.* 10(3-4), sep-dec 69 : 302-307.

1985   COOPER, J.; JONES, R. A. "Self-esteem and consistency as determinants of anticipatory opinion change", *J. Person. soc. Psychol.* 14(4), apr 70 : 312-320.

1986   EVAN, W. M.; SIMMONS, R. G. "Organizational effects of inequitable rewards: two experiments in status inconsistency", *Adm. Sci. Quart.* 14(2), jun 69 : 224-237.

1987   FISEK, M. H.; OFSHE, R. "The process of status evolution", *Sociometry* 33(3), sep 70 : 327-346.

1988   GORDON, M.; WILSON, S. R. "Status inconsistency and satisfaction with sorority membership", *Soc. Forces* 48(2), dec 69 : 176-183.

1989   HAMM, B. C.; CUNDIFF, E. W. "Self-actualization and product perception", *J. Mkting Res.* 6(4), nov 69 : 470-472.

1990   JONES, S. C.; SHRAUGER, J. S. "Reputation and self-evaluation as determinants of attractiveness", *Sociometry* 33(3), sep 70 : 276-286.

1991   KITAHARA, M. "An axiomatic model of self", *Acta sociol.* 13(1), 1970 : 30-39.

1992   KOLB, D. A.; BOYATZIS, R. E. "Goal-setting and self-directed behavior change", *Hum. Relat.* 23(5), oct 70 : 439-457.

1993   LANDECKER, W. S. "Status congruence, class crystallization, and social cleavage", *Sociol. soc.* 54(3), apr 70 : 343-355.

1994   LEHMAN, S. "Personality and compliance: a study of anxiety and self-esteem in opinion and behavior change", *J. Person. soc. Psychol.* 15(1), mai 70 : 76-86.

1995   LEYENS, J.-P. "Influence de la distance psychologique et de l'éducation sur l'identification", *Bull. CERP* 18(3-4), jul-dec 69 : 255-266.

1996   LOWIN, A.; HRAPCHAK, W. J.; KAVANAGH, M. J. "Experimental investigation of consideration and initiating structure", *Adm. Sci. Quart.* 14(2), jun 69 : 238-253.

1997   LUDWIG, D. J. "Evidence of construct and criterion-related validity for the self-concept", *J. soc. Psychol.* 80(2), apr 70 : 213-223.

1998 MORSE, S.; GERGEN, K. J. "Social comparison, self-consistency, and the concept of self", *J. Person. soc. Psychol.* 16(1), sep 70 : 148-156.

1999 NAHRENDORF, R. O. "The professional self in an academic community", *Soc. Sci. (Winfield)* 45(3), jun 70 : 149-156.

2000 ORCUTT, J. D. "Self-concept and insulation against delinquency: some critical notes", *Sociol. Quart.* 11(3), 1970 : 381-390.

2001 RULE, B. G.; REHILL, D. "Distraction and self-esteem effects on attitude change", *J. Person. soc. Psychol.* 15(4), aug 70 : 359-365.

2002 SEGAL, D. R.; SEGAL, M. W.; KNOKE, D. "Status inconsistency and self-evaluation", *Sociometry* 33(3), sep 70 : 347-357.

2003 SÉVIGNY, R.; GUIMOND, P. "Psycho-sociologie de l'actualisation de soi: quelques problèmes de validation", *Sociol. et Soc.* 2(2), nov 70 : 249-264.

2004 SMITH, J. R. "Perception of self and other (mate) as motivation for marriage counseling: an interactional approach", *Sociol. soc. Res.* 54(4), jul 70 : 466-476.

2005 SMITH, T. S. "Structural crystallization, status inconsistency and political partisanship", *Amer. sociol. R.* 34(6), dec 69 : 907-921.

2006 SPADY, W. G. "Lament for the letterman: effects of peer status and extra-curricular activities on goals and achievement", *Amer. J. Sociol.* 75(4, *Part II*), jan 70 : 680-702.

2007 STEINMANN, A.; FOX, D. J. "Specific areas of agreement and conflict in women's self-perception and their perception of men's ideal woman in two South American urban communities and an urban community in the U.S.", *J. Marriage Family* 31(2), mai 69 : 281-289.

2008 STERN, C. "La investigación norteamericana sobre las consecuencias de la incongruencia de status: revisión y crítica" (North American research on the consequences of status incongruency: review and critique), *R. mexic. Cienc. polít.* 15(57), jul-sep 69 : 337-357.

2009 STIMPSON, D. V. "The influence of commitment and self-esteem on susceptibility to persuasion", *J. soc. Psychol.* 80(2), apr 70 : 189-195.

2010 TALLEY, R. W. "Dissonance and expectations on a shop floor", *Hum. Relat.* 23(4), aug 70 : 361-369.

2011 WAHRMAN, R. "Status, deviance, and sanctions", *Pacific sociol. R.* 13(4), 1970 : 229-240.

2012 WALSTER, E. "The effect of self-esteem on liking for dates of various social desirabilities", *J. exper. soc. Psychol.* 6(2), apr 70 : 284-253.

2013 WILLIAMS, R.; BYARS, H. "The effect of academic integration on the self-esteem of Southern negro-students", *J. soc. Psychol.* 80(2), apr 70 : 183-188.

2014 ZELLNER, M. "Self-esteem, reception, and influenceability", *J. Person. soc. Psychol.* 15(1), mai 70 : 87-93.

2015 ZWEIGENHAFT, R. L. "Signature size: a key to status awareness", *J. soc. Psychol.* 81(1), jun 70 : 49-54.

C.3124 *Group adjustment and conformity*
Adaptation au groupe et conformité

[See also / Voir aussi: 975, 1921, 4107]

2016 CLOUD, J.; VAUGHAN, G. M. "Using balanced scales to control acquiescence", *Sociometry* 33(2), jun 70 : 193-202.

2017 COLLINS, B. E.; HELMREICH, R. L. "Studies in forced compliance: contrasting mechanisms of attitude change produced by public-persuasive and private-true essays", *J. soc. Psychol.* 81(2), aug 70 : 253-264.

2018 COSTANZO, P. R. "Conformity development as a function of self-blame", *J. Person. soc. Psychol.* 14(4), apr 70 : 366-374.

2019 CRANO, W. D. "Effects of sex, response order and expertise on conformity: a dispositional approach", *Sociometry* 33(3), sep 70 : 239-252.

2020 FLINN, W. L. "Influence of community values in innovativeness", *Amer. J. Sociol.* 75(6), mai 70 : 983-991.

2021 FRAGER, R. "Conformity and anticonformity in Japan", *J. Person. soc. Psychol.* 15(3), jul 70 : 203-210.

2022 GLICK, O. W.; JACKSON, J. "Effects of normative similarity on group formation among college freshmen", *Pacific sociol. R.* 13(4), 1970 : 263-268.

2023   HALL, D. T.; SCHNEIDER, B.; NYGREN, H. T. "Personal factors in organizational identification", *Adm. Sci. Quart.* 15(2), jun 70 : 176-190.

2024   HERZ, L. "A note on identificational assimilation among forty Jews in Malmö", *Jew. J. Sociol.* 11(2), dec 69 : 165-173.

2025   HORNE, W. C. "Group influence on ethical risk taking: the inadequacy of two hypotheses", *J. soc. Psychol.* 80(2), apr 70 : 237-238.

2026   HOROWITZ, I. A.; ROTSCHILD, B. H. "Conformity as a function of deception and role playing", *J. Person. soc. Psychol.* 14(3), mar 70 : 224-226.

2027   HOSTETLER, J. A. "Socialization and adaptations to public schooling: the Hutterian Brethren and the Old Order Amish", *Sociol. Quart.* 11(2), 1970 : 194-205.

2028   JOHNSON, D. W.; NEALE, D. C. "The effects of models, reference groups, and social responsibility norms upon participation in prosocial activities", *J. soc. Psychol.* 81(1), jun 70 : 87-92.

2029   KENNEDY, J. J.; COOK, P. A.; BREWER, R. R. "The effects of three selected experimenter variables in conforming judgment", *J. soc. Psychol.* 81(2), aug 70 : 167-175.

2030   LEMAINE, G.; DESPORTES, J.-P.; LOUARN, J.-P. "Rôle de la cohésion et de la différenciation hiérarchique dans le processus d'influence sociale", *Bull. CERP* 18(3-4), jul-dec 69 : 237-253.

2031   LONDON, H.; MELDMAN, P. J.; LACKTON, A. C. "The jury method: some correlates of persuading", *Hum. Relat.* 23(2), apr 70 : 114-121.

2032   LONG, H. B. "Relationships of selected personal and social variables in conforming judgment", *J. soc. Psychol.* 81(2), aug 70 : 177-182.

2033   MEYER, J. W. "High school effects on college intentions", *Amer. J. Sociol.* 76(1), jul 70 : 59-70.

2034   MOSCOVICI, S.; LAGE, E.; NAFFRECHOUX, M. "Influence of a consistent minority on the responses of a majority in a color perception task", *Sociometry* 32(4), dec 69 : 365-380.

2035   MYERS, M. T.; GOLDBERG, A. A. "Group credibility and opinion change", *J. Communication* 20(2), jun 70 : 174-179.

2036   NINANE, P.; FIEDLER, F. E. "Member reactions to success and failure of task groups", *Hum. Relat.* 23(1), feb 70 : 3-13.

2037   O'LEARY, C. J.; WILLIS, F. N.; TOMICH, E. "Conformity under deceptive and non-deceptive techniques", *Sociol. Quart.* 11(1), 1970 : 87-93.

2038   PALMER, S. H. *Deviance and conformity; roles, situations and reciprocity.* New Haven, Conn., College and University Press, 70, 208 p.

2039   PAPAGEORGIS, D. "Effects of disguised and persuasion contexts on beliefs", *J. soc. Psychol.* 80(1), feb 70 : 43-48.

2040   PEDERSEN, E.; ETHERIDGE, K. "Conformist and deviant behaviour in high school: the Merton typology adapted to an educational context", *Canad. R. Sociol. Anthropol.* 7(1), feb 70 : 70-82. [USA.]

2041   PURNELL, R. F. "Socio-economic status and sex differences in adolescent reference-group orientation", *J. genet. Psychol.* 116(2), jun 70 : 233-240.

2042   SCHIAVONE, M. "Correlazioni ed influenze tra ambiente e quoziente d'intelligenza" (Correlations and influence between milieu and intelligence quotient), *Quad. Sci. soc.* 9(1), 1970 : 46-55.

2043   SISTRUNK, F.; CLEMENT, D. E. "Cross-cultural comparisons of the conforming behavior of college students", *J. soc. Psychol.* 82(2), dec 70 : 273-274.

2044   SMITH, K. H. "Conformity as related to masculinity, self, and other descriptions; suspicion, and artistic preference by sex groups", *J. soc. Psychol.* 80(1), feb 70 : 79-88.

2045   STRICKER, L. J.; MESSICK, S.; JACKSON, D. N. "Conformity, anticonformity, and independence: their dimensionality and generality", *J. Person. soc. Psychol.* 16(3), nov 70 : 494-507.

2046   TOMEKOVIC, T.; STAJNBERGER, I.; SULEJMANOVIC, G. "Mutual rating among workers as a measure of their merit to their work group", *Hum. Relat.* 23(2), apr 70 : 153-164.

2047   WALLACH, M. A.; MABLI, J. "Information versus conformity in the effects of discussion on risk taking", *J. Person. soc. Psychol.* 14(2), feb 70 : 149-156.

2048   WARREN, D. I. "The effects of power bases and peer groups on conformity in formal organizations", *Adm. Sci. Quart.* 14(4), dec 69 : 544-557.

2049   WEAVER, T. "Use of hypothetical situations in a study of Spanish American illness referral systems", *Hum. Org.* 29(2), 1970 : 140-154.
2050   WEICK, K. E.; PENNER, D. D. "Discrepant membership as an occasion for effective cooperation", *Sociometry* 32(4), dec 69 : 413-424.
2051   WITT, R. E. "Informal social group influence on consumer brand choice", *J. Mkting Res.* 6(4), 1969 : 473-476.
2052   ZIMMERMAN, S. F.; SMITH, K. H.; PEDERSEN, D. M. "The effect of anticonformity appeals on conformity behavior", *J. soc. Psychol.* 81(1), jun 70 : 93-103.

C.32   Civilizations and national characteristics
Civilisations et caractéristiques nationales

[See also / Voir aussi: 431]

2053   BASTIDE, R. "Systèmes sociaux et civilisations", *Année sociol.* 19, 1968 : 359-376.
2054   CLARK, K. McK. *Civilization: a personal view.* London, British Broadcasting Corporation, 69, xviii-359 p.
2055   JOFFE, J. A. *Studies in the history of civilization.* New York, Philosophical Library, 70, xv-331 p.
2056   RICHTA, R. "La dialectique de l'homme et de son œuvre dans la civilisation moderne", *Homme et Soc.* 13, jul-aug-sep 69 : 39-57.
2057   TERHUNE, K. W. "From national character to national behaviour: a reformulation", *J. Conflict Resol.* 14(2), jun 70 : 203-264.
2058   WISH, M.; DEUTSCH, M.; BIENER, L. "Differences in conceptual structures of nations: an exploratory study", *J. Person. soc. Psychol.* 16(3), nov 70 : 361-373.

C.32(1)   *Africa*
Afrique

[See also / Voir aussi: 89, 1195, 1937, 4476]

2059   'ABDAL-'AZIZ, M. B. A. *Taṭawwur al-fikr wal-lughaṭ fîl-maghreb al-ḥadîth* (Development of thought and language in present-day Morocco). al-Qâhiraṭ, Jâmi 'ât-al-Dawla al-'Arabîyaṭ, Mu'aḥad al-Buhûth, al-Dirâsât al-'Arabîyaṭ, 69, 240 p.
2060   BUGNICOURT, J. "Flux culturels et action administrative dans l'espace africain", *B. Inst. int. Adm. publ.* 13, jan-mar 70 : 76-113.
2061   COHEN, R.; MIDDLETON, J. (eds.). *From tribe to nation in Africa; studies in incorporation processes.* Scranton, Chandler Publishing Co., 70, xi-276 p.
2062   DAVIDSON, B. *The African genius; an introduction to African cultural and social history.* Boston, Little, Brown, 70, 367 p.
2063   DAVIDSON, B. *The Africans: an entry to cultural history.* Harlow, Longmans, 69, 367 p.
2064   DEBBASCH, C. *et al. Mutations culturelles et coopération au Maghreb.* Paris, Éditions du Centre national de la recherche scientifique, 69, 263 p.
2065   GULLIVER, P. H. (ed.). *Tradition and transition in East Africa; studies of the tribal element in the modern era.* Berkeley, University of California Press, 69, 378 p.
2066   JACKSON, J. G. *Introduction to African civilisations.* New York, University Books, 70, 384 p.
2067   JACOBSON, D. "Culture and stratification among urban Africans", *J. Asian Afr. Stud.* 5(3), jul 70 : 176-183.
2068   MAZRUI, A. A. "Africa and the crisis of relevance in modern culture", *Présence afr.* 72, 1969 : 9-20.
2069   MIDDLETON, J. *Black Africa; its peoples and their cultures today.* New York, Macmillan, 70, 457 p.
2070   MOORE, C. D.; DUNBAR, A. (eds.). *Africa yesterday and today.* New York, Praeger, 69, viii-394 p.
2071   OLAFIOYE, A. O. (comp.). *Social life and customs in Nigeria: a selective bibliography.* Lagos, National Library of Nigeria, 69, 25 p.
2072   ROTHCHILD, D. "Kenya's africanization program: Priorities of development and equity", *Amer. polit. Sci. R.* 64(3), sep 70 : 737-753.

85

2073　SMITH, E. W. *The golden stool; some aspects of the conflict of cultures in modern Africa.* Chicago, Afro-Am Press, 69, xvi-328 p.

2074　STAEVEN, C.; SCHÖNBERG, F. *Kulturwandel und Angstentwicklung bei den Yoruba West-afrikas* (Cultural change and development of anxiety among the West African Yorubas). München, Weltforum, 70, 434 p.

2075　VIEYRA, P. S. "Centres culturels et politique de la culture en Afrique", *Présence afr.* 74, 1970 : 185-190.

C.32(2)　America
Amérique

[See also / Voir aussi: 4469, 5028]

2076　CAVE, A. A.; CLAYTON, J. L. *American civilization: a documentary history.* Rev. ed. Dubuque, Iowa, Kendall/Hunt Publishing Co., 69, xv-367 p.

2077　FERREIRA REIS, A. C. "As escolas de direito na formação da cultura brasileira" (The schools of law in the formation of Brazilean culture), *R. brasil. Cultura* 2(3), jan-mar 70 : 131-146.

2078　FORD, J. A. *A comparison of formative cultures in the Americas; diffusion or the psychic unity of man.* Washington, Smithsonian Institution Press; United States Government Printing Office, 69, xvi-211 p.

2079　KELLY, C. "A ecologia na interpretação da cultura fluminense" (Ecology and the understanding of culture in river areas), *R. brasil. Cultura* 1(2), oct-dec 69 : 69-82. [Brazil.]

2080　KÖHLER, U. *Gelenkter Kulturwandel im Hochland von Chiapas; eine Studie zur angewandten Ethnologie in Mexiko* (Directed cultural change in the highlands of Chiapas. A study in applied ethnology in Mexico). Bielefeld, Bertelsmann Universitätsverlag, 69, 294 p.

2081　MITCHELL, D. D. *Resource units in Hawaiian culture; a series of studies covering sixteen important aspects of Hawaiian culture.* Honolulu, Kamehameha Schools, 69, 219 p.

2082　OSWALT, W. H. *Understanding our culture, an anthropological view.* New York, Holt, Rinehart and Winston, 70, xv-160 p. [USA.]

2083　QUESADA, M. "Réalité et possibilité de la culture latino-américaine", *Tiers-Monde* 10(39), jul-sep 69 : 487-507.

2084　RÓZSA, G. "La organización de la ciencia y la cultura en Cuba" (The organization of science and culture in Cuba), *R. mexic. Sociol.* 31(3), jul-sep 69 : 633-642.

2085　SEDA BONILLA, E. "La despersonalización del puertorriqueño. La función de la cultura en los procesos políticos" (The depersonalization of the Puerto Rican. The function of culture in the political process), *Aportes* 15, jan 70 : 77-94.

2086　WEAVER, C. N. "Accidents as a measure of the cultural adjustment of Mexican-Americans", *Sociol. Quart.* 11(1), 1970 : 119-125.

C.32(3)　Asia
Asie

2087　AUBIN, F. "Traditions et mutations: sociologie actuelle de la Mongolie", *C. int. Sociol.* 17(49), jul-dec 70 : 83-110.

2088　AZIZ, A. *An intellectual history of Islam in India.* Edinburgh, Edinburgh University Press, 69, x-226 p.

2089　BELO, J. (comp.). *Traditional Balinese culture; essays.* New York, Columbia University Press, 70, xxvii-421 p.

2090　BUSSAGLI, M. *Culture e civiltà dell'Asia centrale* (Culture and civilization in Central Asia). Torino, ERI, 70, x-319 p.

2091　CASAL, J. M. *La civilisation de l'Indus et ses énigmes.* Paris, Fayard, 69, 225 p.

2092　DUTT, G.; DUTT, V. P. *China's cultural revolution.* New York, Asia Publishing House, 70, viii-260 p.

2093　Bibl. XIX-1828. FRASER, T. M. Jr. *Culture and change in India: the Barapali experiment.* CR: V. JESUDASON, *Amer. J. Sociol.* 76(1), jul 70 : 196-199; O. R. GALLAGHER, *Amer. sociol. R.* 34(6), dec 69 : 991.

2094   ITS, R. F. (ed.). *Kul'tura narodov zarubežnoj Azii i Okeanii* (Culture of non Soviet Asian and Oceanian peoples). Leningrad, Nauka, 69, 364 p.

2095   IVANOVA, E. V. *Tajskie narody Tailanda* (Thai people in Thailand). Moskva, Nauka, 70, 197 p.

2096   MARUYAMA, M. *Thought and behavior in modern Japanese politics.* Expanded ed. Ed. by I. MORRIS. London-New York, Oxford University Press, 69, xvii-407 p.

2097   MEYER, C. "Mutations sociologiques, continuité culturelle ?", *Projet* 46, jun 70 : 752-765. [Japon.]

2098   RAGHUNATHAN, N. *Reason and intuition in Indian culture.* Madras, University of Madras, 69, 86 p.

2099   RAHIM, M. A. *Cultural evolution in East Pakistan.* Dacca, Mullick Bros., 69, 29 p.

2100   SINOR, D. *Inner Asia; history, civilization, languages; a syllabus.* Bloomington, Indiana University, 69, xvi-261 p.

2101   VIDYARTHI, L. P. (ed.). *Conflict, tension, and cultural trend in India.* Calcutta, Punthi Pustak, 69, viii-312 p.

C.32(4)   *Europe*

[See also / Voir aussi: 5249]

2102   AMENDOLA, G. "La situazzione culturale nella provinzia di Brindisi" (The cultural situation in the Brindisi province), *Crit. sociol. (Roma)* 15, 1970 : 125-169. [Italy.]

2103   BOLDIZSÁR, I. "A new relation between culture and democracy", *New Hungar. Quart.* 11(37), 1970 : 45-55. [Hungary.]

2104   DULOUP, V. *La civilisation française.* New York, Harcourt, Brace and World, 70, xiii-327 p.

2105   FOOTE, P. G.; WILSON, D. M. *The Viking achievement; the society and culture of early medieval Scandinavia.* London, Sidgwick and Jackson, 70, xxv-473 p.

2106   HARDRÉ, J. *La France et sa civilisation.* New York, Dodd, Mead and Co., 69, xii-592 p.

2107   MUSIO, G. *La cultura solitaria. Tradizione e acculturazione nella Sardegna arcaica* (Solitary culture. Tradition and acculturation in archaic Sardinia). Bologna, Il Mulino, 69, 343 p.

2108   TUÑON DE LARA, M. *Medio siglo de cultura española (1885-1936)* (A half-century of Spanish culture [1885-1936]). Madrid, Ed. Técnos, 70, 293 p.

C.32(5)   *Middle East*
Moyen-Orient

2109   BOUHDIBA, A. "Der Hammam: Beitrag zu einer Psychoanalyse des Islam" (The hammam: contribution to a psychoanalysis of Islam), *Kölner Z. Soziol. soz.-Psychol.* 22(3), sep 70 : 463-472.

2110   HILAN, R. *Culture et développement en Syrie et dans les pays retardés.* Paris, Éditions Anthropos, 69, xv-388 p.

2111   JACOBSEN, T. *Toward the image of Tammuz and other essays on Mesopotamian history and culture.* Ed. by W. L. MORAN. Cambridge, Harvard University Press, 70, x-507 p.

2112   LUTFIYYA, A. M.; CHURCHILL, C. W. (eds.). *Readings in Arab Middle Eastern societies and cultures.* The Hague, Mouton; New York, Humanities Press, 70, xvii-733 p.

2113   MARDIN, S. "Power, civil society and culture in the Ottoman Empire", *Comp. Stud. Soc. Hist.* 11(3), jun 69 : 258-281.

2114   SWEET, L. E. (ed.). *Peoples and cultures of the Middle East; an anthropological reader.* 2 vols. Garden City, N. Y., Natural History Press, 70, 2 vols.

C.32(6)   *Pacific*
Pacifique

[See also / Voir aussi: 2094]

2115   HARDING, T. G.; WALLACE, B. J. (comps.). *Cultures of the Pacific: selected readings.* New York, Free Press, 70, xv-496 p.

2116   LARDIZÁBAL, A. S.; TENSUAN-LEOGARDO, F. (eds.). *Readings on Philippine culture and social life.* Manila, Rex Book Store, 70, vii-295 p.
2117   MARTIN-ROQUERO, C. T. "The culture of the central Mindanao Manobos", *Graduate Fac. Stud.* 19, 1968 : 33-47.
2118   MEAD, S. M. *Traditional Maori clothing; a study of technological and functional change.* Wellington-Auckland, Reed, 69, 238 p. [New Zealand.]

C.32(7)   USSR
URSS

2119   DUNN, S. P.; DUNN, E. "Kulturentwicklung und Integration nichtrussischer Völkerschaften in der Sowjetunion" (Cultural development and integration of non Russian peoples in the Soviet Union), *Osteuropa* 20(4), apr 70 : 262-275.

C.33   Culture contact
Contacts entre cultures

[See also / Voir aussi: 594, 2107, 2268, 2885, 4102, 4227, 4665]

2120   CHEMERS, M. M. "Cross-cultural training as a means for improving situational favorableness", *Hum. Relat.* 22(6), dec 69 : 531-546.
2121   KIMMEL, P. R.; PERLMAN, D. "Psychosocial modernity and the initial accommodation of foreigners visiting the United States", *J. soc. Psychol.* 81(1), jun 70 : 121-123.
2122   Bibl. XIX-1855. REDEKOP, C. *Japanese Americans: the evolution of subculture.* CR: C. REDEKOP, *Amer. sociol. R.* 35(2), apr 70 : 379-380.

C.4   SOCIAL COMPLEXES AND SOCIAL GROUPS
COMPLEXES ET GROUPES SOCIAUX

C.40   General and theoretical works
Ouvrages généraux et théoriques

[See also / Voir aussi: **C.312**; 415, 419, 542, 1933, 2261, 2978, 2993, 3366]

2123   AGERSNAP, T. (ed.). *Contributions to the theory of organization.* 2 vols. New York, Humanities Press, 69, 154 p., 118 p. CR: D. G. CHANDLER, *Amer. sociol. R.* 35(4), aug 70 : 810-811.
2124   ALLEN, V. L. "La doctrine de l'empirisme et l'étude des organisations", *Homme et Soc.* 15, jan-feb-mar 70 : 221-239.
2125   ARGYRIS, C. *Intervention theory and method; a behavioral science view.* Reading, Mass., Addison-Wesley, 70, x-374 p. [Organizational change.]
2126   BANNESTER, E. M. "Multiorganization", *Hum. Relat.* 23(5), oct 70 : 405-429.
2127   BAUTZ, R.; HELD, T. "Interaction analysis: structural mobility chances of societal units", *Soziol. Instit. Univ. Zürich B.* 16, jan 70 : 1-30.
2128   BECKER, S. W.; BALOFF, N. "Organization structure and complex problem-solving", *Adm. Sci. Quart.* 14(2), jun 70 : 260-271.
2129   BEENSEN, R. *Organisationsprinzipien; Untersuchungen zu Inhalt, Ordnung und Nutzen einiger Grundaussagen der Organisationslehre* (Organization principles: researches on the context, arrangement and utility of some basic statements of organization theory). Berlin, Duncker und Humblot, 69, 236 p.
2130   BELLI, C.; GUALA DUCA, R. (comps.). *Sociologia dell'organizzazione. Sviluppi ed applicazioni* (The sociology of organization. Developments and applications). Milano, F. Angeli, 69, 385 p.
2131   BLAU, P. M. "A formal theory of differentiation in organizations", *Amer. sociol. R.* 35(2), apr 70 : 201-218.
2132   BREUER, F. J. L. I. "De organisatiekundige actie" (Practice in organizational sciences), *Mens en Mij* 45(2), mar-apr 70 : 104-119.
2133   BROWN, M. E. "Identification and some conditions of organizational involvement", *Adm. Sci. Quart.* 14(3), sep 69 : 346-356.

2134 Buchanan, P. C. "Laboratory training and organization development", *Adm. Sci. Quart.* 14(3), sep 69 : 466-480.

2135 Clark, P. A.; Ford, J. R. "Methodological and theoretical problems in the investigation of planned organisational change", *Sociol. R.* 18(1), mar 70 : 29-53.

2136 Corwin, R. G. "Patterns of organizational conflict", *Adm. Sci. Quart.* 14(4), dec 69 : 507-521.

2137 Cyert, R. M.; Maccrimmon, K. R. "Organizations", in: G. Lindzey, E. Aronson (eds.). *The handbook of social psychology.* New ed. Vol. I. Reading, Mass., Addison-Wesley, 68 : 568-611.

2138 Dalton, G. W.; Lawrence, P. R.; Greiner, L. E. (eds.). *Organizational change and development.* Homewood, Ill., R. D. Irwin, 70, x-393 p.

2139 Driver, M. J.; Streuffert, S. "Integrative complexity: an approach to individuals and groups as information-processing systems", *Adm. Sci. Quart.* 14(2), jun 69 : 272-285.

2140 Dunham, A. *The new community organization.* New York, Crowell, 70, xiv-605 p.

2141 Elbing, A. O. *Behavioral decisions in organizations.* Glenview, Ill., Scott, Foresman, 70, xvi-879 p.

2142 Ghorpade, J. "Study of organizational effectiveness: two prevailing viewpoints", *Pacific sociol. R.* 13(1), 1970 : 31-40.

2143 Giannotti, G. "Ancora sul concetto-problema della comunità" (Again on the concept-problem of community), *Rass. ital. Sociol.* 11(1), jan-mar 70 : 49-80.

2144 Goodman, R. A. "Organizational preference in research and development", *Hum. Relat.* 23(4), aug 70 : 279-298.

2145 Grochla, E. "Systemtheorie und Organisationstheorie" (Systems theory and organisation theory), *Z. Betriebswirtsch.* 40(1), jan 70 : 1-16.

2146 Grusky, O.; Miller, G. A. (eds.). *The sociology of organizations: basic studies.* New York, Free Press, 70, x-592 p.

2147 Harasawa, Y. "Soshikiron no sûryôteki kenkyû no kokoromi ni tsuite" (Toward the quantitative analysis of organization), *Musachi Daigaku Ronshû* 15(5), 1968 : 1-34.

2148 Harrison, R. "Choosing the depth of organizational intervention", *J. applied behav. Sci.* 6(2), apr-mai-jun 70 : 181-202.

2149 Hickson, D. J.; Pugh, D. S.; Pheysey, D. C. "Operations technology and organization structure: an empirical reappraisal", *Adm. Sci. Quart.* 14(3), sep 69 : 378-397.

2150 House, R. J. "Role conflict and multiple authority in complex organizations", *Calif. manag. R.* 12(4), 1970 : 53-60.

2151 House, R. J.; Miner, J. B. "Merging management and behavioral theory: the interaction between span of control and group size", *Adm. Sci. Quart.* 14(3), sep 69 : 451-465.

2152 Inkson, J. H. K.; Pugh, D. S.; Hickson, D. J. "Organization context and structure: an abbreviated replication", *Adm. Sci. Quart.* 15(3), sep 70 : 318-329.

2153 Jenks, R. S. "An action-research approach to organizational change", *J. applied behav. Sci.* 6(2), apr-mai-jun 70 : 131-150.

2154 Bibl. xix-1884. Jones, G. N. *Planned organizational change: a study in change dynamics.* CR: W. Bennis, *Amer. J. Sociol.* 76(6), mai 70 : 1058-1060; C. K. Warriner, *Amer. sociol. R.* 35(4), aug 70 : 813.

2155 Kelly, J. *Organizational behaviour.* Homewood, Ill., R. D. Irwin, 69, 653 p. CR: D. Podmore, *Brit. J. Sociol.* 21(1), mar 70 : 119-120.

2156 König, R. "Soziale Gruppen" (Social groups), *Geogr. Rundsch.* 21(1), 1969 : 2-14.

2157 Landsberger, H. A. (ed.). *Comparative perspectives on formal organizations.* Boston, Little, Brown, 69, vii-290 p.

2158 Lehtovuori, J. "Organisaatioteorian osa-alueista" (On sub-areas of organizational theory), *Liiketal. Aikakausk.* 18(3), 1968 : 477-489.

2159 Lipovec, F. "Kaj je organizacija podjetja ?" (What is organization ?), *Ekon. R. (Ljubljana)* 20(2), 1969 : 164-178.

2160 Lynton, R. P. "Linking an innovative subsystem into the system", *Adm. Sci. Quart.* 14(3), sep 69 : 398-417.

2161 Mahoney, T. A.; Weitzel, W. "Managerial models of organizational effectiveness", *Adm. Sci. Quart.* 14(3), sep 69 : 357-365.

2162 Øien, F. *Quantitative concepts and definitions in organization theory.* Oslo, Bedrifstøkonomisk Institutt, 69, 85 p.

2163   PALISI, B. J. "Some suggestions about the transitory-permanence dimension of organi-
        zations", *Brit. J. Sociol.* 21(2), jun 70 : 200-206.

2164   PERROW, C. *Organizational analysis: a sociological view.* London, Tavistock Publications,
        70, xiii-192 p.

2165   PONDY, L. R. "Varieties of organizational conflict", *Adm. Sci. Quart.* 14(4), dec 69 :
        499-506.

2166   ROSENGREN, W. R.; LEFTON, M. (eds.). *Organizations and clients; essays in the sociology
        of service.* Columbus, Ohio, Merrill, 70, x-222 p.

2167   SEXTON, W. P. (comp.). *Organization theories.* Columbus, Ohio, Merrill, 70, x-433 p.

2168   SHULL, F. A. Jr.; DELBECQ, A. L.; CUMMINGS, L. L. *Organizational decision making.*
        New York, McGraw-Hill, 70, xvi-320 p.

2169   SILVERMAN, D. *The theory of organizations: a sociological framework.* London, Heine-
        mann Educational, 70, ix-246 p.

2170   SUMMERS, G. F.; CLARK, J. P.; SEILLER, L. H. "The renewal of community sociology",
        Rur. Sociol. 35(2), jun 70 : 218-231.

2171   WALTON, R. E.; DUTTON, J. M.; CAFFERTY, T. P. "Organizational context and inter-
        departmental conflict", *Adm. Sci. Quart.* 14(4), dec 69 : 522-543.

2172   WEICK, K. E. (ed.). "Laboratory studies of experimental organizations", *Adm. Sci.
        Quart.* 14(2), jun 69 : 155-304.

2173   WHITE, H. C. *Chains of opportunity; system models of mobility in organizations.* Cam-
        bridge, Mass., Harvard University Press, 70, xv-418 p.

2174   WILKINSON, K. P. "The community as a social field", *Soc. Forces* 48(3), mar 70 : 311-
        322.

2175   ZWERMAN, W. L. *New perspectives on organization theory; an empirical reconsideration of
        the Marxian and classical analyses.* Westport, Conn., Greenwood Publishing Corp.,
        70, xx-219 p.

C.41   Communities and associations
          Communautés et associations

[See also / Voir aussi: **C.7, C.822, C.9214;** 936, 949, 1005, 1366, 1417, 1422, 2554,
2745, 4344]

2176   AKERS, R. "Framework for the comparative study of group cohesion: the professions",
        Pacific sociol. R. 13(2), 1970 : 73-85.

2177   AKERS, R.; CAMPBELL, F. L. "Size and the administrative component in occupational
        associations", *Pacific sociol. R.* 13(4), 1970 : 241-251.

2178   ANGUEIRA MIRANDA, M. A. *Hacia la comunidad cooperativa libre—por une revolución
        social al margen del poder y la violencia* (Towards a free cooperative community—for a
        social revolution at the limits of power and violence). Buenos Aires, Editorial Proyec-
        ción, 69, 206 p.

2179   BLAKE, J. A. "The organization as an instrument of violence: the military case", *Sociol.
        Quart.* 11(3), 1970 : 331-350.

2180   BOLLE DE BAL, M. "Psychosociologie de l'assemblée libre", *R. Inst. Sociol.* 4, 1969 :
        663-670.

2181   BOOTH, A.; BABCHUK, N. "Personal influence networks and voluntary association
        affiliation", *Sociol. Inquiry* 39(2), 1969 : 179-188.

2182   BOOTH, A.; BISZTRAY, G. "Value orientations, member integration and participation in
        voluntary association activities", *Adm. Sci. Quart.* 15(1), mar 70 : 39-46.

2183   CARDEN, M. L. *Oneida: utopian community to modern corporation.* Baltimore, Md.,
        Johns Hopkins Press, 69, 228 p. CR: B. YORBURG, *Amer. sociol. R.* 35(4), aug 70 :
        770-771.

2184   COATS, A. W.; COATS, S. E. "The social composition of the Royal Economic Society
        and the beginnings of the British economics 'profession', 1890-1915", *Brit. J. Sociol.*
        21(1), mar 70 : 75-85.

2185   DAVIS, J. R.; PALOMBA, N. A. "The National Farmers Organization and the prisoner's
        dilemma: a game theory prediction of failure", *Soc. Sci. Quart.* 50(3), dec 69: 742-748.

2186   EITZEN, D. S. "A study of voluntary association memberships among middle-class
        women", *Rur. Sociol.* 35(1), mar 70 : 84-91.

2187 ERLANGER, H. S. "Jury research in America: its past and future", *Law Soc. R.* 4(3), feb 70 : 345-370.

2188 FROSINI, V. "Mitologia e sociologia della mafia" (Mythology and sociology of the Mafia), *A. Mezzogiorno* 9, 1969 : 367-383. [Italy.]

2189 JONES, R. K. "Sectarian characteristics of Alcoholics Anonymous", *Sociology* 4(2), mai 70 : 181-195.

2190 SCHILT, T. "Muziekkorps en band, twee vormen van sociale participatie" (Orchestra and band, two forms of social participation), *Sociolog. Gids* 16(4), jul-aug 69 : 228-237.

2191 SHEPHER, J. "Familism and social structure: the case of the kibbutz", *J. Marriage Family* 31(3), aug 69 : 567-573.

2192 SHEPHER, J. "Organizational effectiveness in kibbutz society in the light of a new theory", *Sociol. rur.* 10(1), 1970 : 21-37.

2193 SINGH, M. *Co-operatives in Asia.* New York, Praeger, 70, xvii-489 p.

2194 SWATEZ, G. M. "The social organization of a university laboratory", *Minerva* 8(1), 1970 : 36-58.

2195 TATON, R. "Naissance et développement de quelques communautés scientifiques nationales au XIXᵉ siècle", *R. int. Sci. soc.* 22(1), 1970 : 105-122.

2196 TONDL, L. "Les situations de conflit dans les communautés scientifiques", *R. int. Sci. soc.* 22(1), 1970 : 123-142.

2197 TOURNIAC, J. *Vie et perspectives de la franc-maçonnerie traditionnelle.* Paris, Gedalge, 69, 192 p. [France.]

2198 VINCENT, J. "Local cooperatives and parochial politics in Uganda: problems of organization, representation, and communication", *J. Commonwealt polit. Stud.* 8(1), mar 70 : 3-17.

2199 WARREN, R. L. "Toward a non-utopian normative model of the community", *Amer. sociol. R.* 35(2), apr 70 : 219-227.

2200 WINICK, C.; WINICK, M. A. "A social-therapeutic jazz-club in England", *Int. J. soc. Psychiatry* 15(3), 1969 : 197-202; *Brit. J. soc. Psychiatry* 3(4), 1969-70 : 276-281.

C.42 Small groups
Petits groupes

[See also / Voir aussi: **C.312, C.40;** 475, 1537, 1910]

2201 BEDNAR, R. L. "Group psychotherapy research variables", *Int. J. Group Psychotherap.* 20(2), apr 70 : 146-152.

2202 BERGER, J.; CONNER, T. L. "Performance expectations and behavior in small groups", *Acta sociol.* 12(4), 1969 : 186-198.

2203 BLEANDONU, G. *Les communautés thérapeutiques.* Paris, Éditions du Scarabée, 70, 125 p.

2204 BOYD, W. H.; BOLEN, D. W. "The compulsive gambler and spouse in group psychotherapy", *Int. J. Group Psychother.* 20(1), jan 70 : 77-90.

2205 BURNSTEIN, E. "An analysis of group decisions involving risk (The 'risky shift')", *Hum. Relat.* 22(5), oct 69 : 381-395.

2206 CANNAVALE, F. J.; SCARR, H. A.; PEPITONE, A. "Deindividuation in the small group: further evidence", *J. Person. soc. Psychol.* 16(1), sep 70 : 141-147.

2207 Bibl. XIX-1949. CAPLOW, T. *Two against one: coalitions in triads.* CR: J. N. PORTER, *Amer. sociol. R.* 35(1), feb 70 : 133-134; M. COORNAERT, *R. franç. Sociol.* 11(1), jan-mar 70 : 117.

2208 CECIL, E. A.; CHERTKOFF, J. M.; CUMMINGS, L. L. "Risk-taking in groups as a function of group pressure", *J. soc. Psychol.* 81(2), aug 70 : 273-274.

2209 COHEN, G. B. *The task-tuned organization of groups.* Amsterdam, Swets and Zeitlinger, 69, 212 p. CR: C. D. WARD, *Amer. sociol. R.* 35(4), aug 70 : 816-817.

2210 DAVIS, J. H. *Group performance.* Reading, Mass., Addison-Wesley Publishing Co., 69, x-115 p.

2211 DAVIS, J. H. "Individual-group problem solving, subject preference and problem type", *J. Person. soc. Psychol.* 13(4), dec 69 : 362-374.

2212 EDELSON, M. *The practice of sociotherapy: a case study.* New Haven, Yale University Press, 70, 345 p.

2213   "Encounter and T-groups—the current use of the group for personal growth and development", *Int. J. Group Psychother.* 20(3), jul 70 : 263-355.

2214   FELDMAN, R. A. "Group integration and intense interpersonal disliking", *Hum. Relat.* 22(5), oct 69 : 405-413.

2215   FRY, C. L.; HOPKINS, J. R.; HOGE, P. "Triads in minimal social situations", *J. soc. Psychol.* 80(1), feb 70 : 37-42.

2216   GALPER, J. "Nonverbal communication exercises in groups", *Soc. Wk* 15(2), apr 70 : 71-78.

2217   GRADA, E. DE. *Elementi di psicologia di gruppo* (Elements of group psychology). Roma, Bulzoni, 69, 396 p.

2218   GRAY, L. N.; MAYHEW, B. H. Jr. "The stability of power structures in small groups: a regression analysis", *Pacific sociol. R.* 13(2), 1970 : 110-120.

2219   Bibl. XIX-1955. GREENBERG, I. A. *Psychodrama and audience attitude change.* CR: E. F. SHAW, *Amer. sociol. R.* 35(1), feb 70 : 163-164.

2220   HACKER, S. L.; GAITZ, C. M. "Interaction and performance correlates of Machiavellianism", *Sociol. Quart.* 11(1), 1970 : 94-102 [Machiavellian approach to human relationships in small groups.]

2221   HACKMAN, J. R.; VIDMAR, N. "Effects of size and task type on group performance and member reactions", *Sociometry* 33(1), mar 70 : 37-54.

2222   HALL, J.; WATSON, W. H. "The effects of a normative intervention on group decision-making performance", *Hum. Relat.* 23(4), aug 70 : 299-317.

2223   HELLER, F. A. "Group feed-back analysis as a change agent", *Hum. Relat.* 23(4), aug 70 : 319-333.

2224   HELLER, G. C. "Existentialist group psychotherapy and culture pattern", *Brit. J. soc. Psychiatry* 3(4), 1969/70 : 258-264.

2225   HOOPER, D.; SHELDON, A.; KOUMANS, A. J. R. "A study of group psychotherapy with married couples", *Int. J. soc. Psychiatry* 15(1), 1968-69 : 57-68.

2226   JOYNER, R. C.; GREEN, C. J. "Demonstration of computer-augmented group problem solving", *Behav. Sci.* 15(5), sep 70 : 452-462.

2227   KEMP, C. G. *Foundations of group counseling.* New York, McGraw-Hill, 70, xii-321 p.

2228   KOLAJA, J. "Variables de pequeños grupos y variables sociales" (Small groups variables and social variables), *R. esp. Opin. públ.* 20, apr-mai 70 : 115-124.

2229   KROGER, R. O.; BRIEDIS, I. "Effects of risk and caution norms on group decision-making", *Hum. Relat.* 23(3), jun 70 : 181-190.

2230   LEWIS, G. H. "Bales' Monte Carlo model of small group discussions", *Sociometry* 33(1), mar 70 : 20-36.

2231   LIMA, L. DE O.; LIMA, F. L. S. O. *Treinamento em dinámica de grupo; no lar, na emprêsa, na escola* (Training in group dynamics; at home, in the firm, in the school). Petrópolis, Editôra Vozes, 69, 432 p.

2232   LOURAU, R. "Où en est la dynamique des groupes ?", *Temps mod.* 26(287), jun 70 : 2084-2097. [États-Unis.]

2233   MADRON, T. W. *Small group methods and the study of politics.* Evanston, Northwestern University Press, 69, xxx-218 p.

2234   MARKOWITZ, J. *The psychodynamic evolution of groups.* New York, Vantage Press, 69, xvi-193 p.

2235   MILLS, T. M.; ROSENBERG, S. *Readings on the sociology of small groups.* Englewood Cliffs, N. J., Prentice-Hall, 70, viii-247 p.

2236   MORRIS, C. C. "Changes in group interaction during problem-solving", *J. soc. Psychol.* 81(2), aug 70 : 157-165.

2237   MÜLLER, P. *Die soziale Gruppe im Prozess der Massenkommunikation* (The social group in the mass communications process). Stuttgart, Enke, 70, viii-261 p.

2238   NIJKERK, K. J.; VAN PRAAG, P. H.; HULSWITH, J. F. *Groepswerk. Begrippen, velden, methoden* (Group work. Concepts, fields, methods). Alphen aan den Rijn, Samsom, 70, 242 p.

2239   NITZ, L. H.; PHILLIPS, J. L. "The effects of divisibility of payoff on confederative behaviour", *J. Conflict Resol.* 13(3), sep 69 : 381-387. [Coalition formation in the triad.]

2240   PINNEY, E. L. Jr. *A first group psychotherapy book.* Springfield, Ill., Thomas, 70, xiii-204 p.

2241 RAVEN, B. H.; SHAW, J. I. "Interdependence and group problem-solving in the triad", *J. Person. soc. Psychol.* 14(2), feb 70 : 157-165.

2242 REEVES, E. T. *The dynamics of group behavior.* New York, American Management Association, 70, 399 p.

2243 SAMUELS, F. "The intra- and inter-competitive group", *Sociol. Quart.* 11(3), 1970 : 391-396.

2244 SAMUELS, F.; O'ROURKE, J. F. "The ambiguity of negative social-emotional behaviour as an index of group cohesion", *Canad. R. Sociol. Anthropol.* 6(1), feb 69 : 47-53.

2245 SLAVSON, S. R. "Eclecticism versus sectarianism in group psychotherapy", *Int. J. Group Psychother.* 20(1), jan 70 : 3-13.

2246 SMITH, G. F.; MURDOCH, P. "Performance of informed versus noninformed triads and quartets in the 'minimal social situation' ", *J. Person. soc. Psychol.* 15(4), aug 70 : 391-396.

2247 STEIN, A. "The nature and significance of interaction in group psychotherapy", *Int. J. Group Psychother.* 20(2), apr 70 : 153-162.

2248 TAYLOR, H. F. *Balance in small groups.* New York, Van Nostrand Reinhold Co., 70, x-321 p.

2249 TAYLOR, M. "The problem of salience in the theory of collective decision-making", *Behav. Sci.* 15(5), sep 70 : 415-430.

2250 TEMPERLEY, S. R. "A study of a self-governing work group", *Sociol. R.* 18(2), jul 70 : 259-281.

2251 VIDMAR, N. "Group composition and the risky shift", *J. exper. soc. Psychol.* 6(2), apr 70 : 153-166.

2252 VIDMAR, N.; McGRATH, J. E. "Forces affecting success in negotiation groups", *Behav. Sci.* 15(2), mar 70 : 154-163.

2253 VINACKE, W. E.; CHERULNIK, P. D.; LICHTMAN, C. M. "Strategy in intratriad and intertriad interactions", *J. soc. Psychol.* 81(2), aug 70 : 183-198.

2254 VINOKUR, A. "Distribution of initial risk levels and group decisions involving risk", *J. Person. soc. Psychol.* 13(3), nov 69 : 207-214.

2255 VOLKOV, I. P. "Opyt sociometričeskoj diagnostiki social'no-psihologičeskoj organizacii studenčeskih grupp" (Experience of a sociometric diagnostic of the socio-psychological organization of student groups), *Učen. Zap. (Leningr. gos. Univ. nauč.-issled. Inst. kompleks. soc. Issled.)* (6), 1969 : 99-108.

2256 VOS, K.; DOESBECKER, C.; BRINKMAN, W. "Succes en cohesie in kleine groepen; een replicatie" (Success and cohesiveness in small groups; a reply), *Mens en Mij* 44(6), nov-dec 69 : 493-509.

2257 WARD, D. J. "Group therapy and discussion topics", *Brit. J. soc. Psychiatry* 3(4), 1969/70 : 273-275.

2258 WILSON, S. R. "Some factors influencing instrumental and expressive ratings in task-oriented groups", *Pacific sociol. R.* 13(2), 1970 : 127-131.

2259 ZAJONC, R. B. *et al.* "Social facilitation and imitation in group risk-taking", *J. exper. soc. Psychol.* 6(1), jan 70 : 26-46.

2260 ZIMMERMANN, D. *Estudios sobre psicoterapia analítica de grupo* (Studies on analytical group psychotherapy). Buenos Aires, Ediciones Hormé; distribución exclusiva, Editorial Paidós, 69, 250 p.

C.44   Intergroup relations
Relations entre groupes

[See also / Voir aussi: **C.33, C.71, C.83**; 486, 543, 554, 582, 607, 611, 1911, 2171, 2304, 2337, 2381, 2389, 2400, 2465, 2628, 2807, 3048, 3105, 4307]

2261 ASSAEL, H. "Constructive role of interorganizational conflict", *Adm. Sci. Quart.* 14(4), dec 69 : 573-583.

2262 CARROLL, B. A. "How wars end: an analysis of some current hypotheses", *J. Peace Res.* 4, 1969 : 295-320.

2263 COLTON, T. "The 'new biology' and the causes of war", *Canad. J. polit. Sci.* 2(4), dec 69 : 434-447.

2264 CROZIER, B. "The study of conflict", *Conflict Stud.* 7, oct 70 : 1-24.

2265   DECHMANN, H.; DECHMANN, M. "Alliances as forms of organization in the international system", *Soziol. Instit. Univ. Zürich B.* 18, jul 70 : 46-71.

2266   FINKBEINER, B. "Towards developing a mathematical model of the international system: some preliminary questions", *Sociol. Instit. Univ. Zürich B.* 17, mai 70 : 12-20.

2267   GINSBERG, R. *The critique of war: contemporary philosophical explorations.* Chicago, Henry Regnery Co., 60, 360 p. CR: G. L. SNULL, *Amer. polit. Sci. R.* 64(3), sep 70 : 930-931.

2268   GLENN, E. S. *et al.* "A cognitive interaction model to analyse culture conflict in international relations", *J. Conflict Resol.* 14(1), mar 70 : 35-48.

2269   GLUCKSMANN, A. *Le discours de la guerre.* Paris, Éditions de l'Herne, 69, 378 p. CR: B. DE PEYRET, *R. franç. Sociol.* 10(4), oct-dec 69 : 540-541.

2270   GORDEEV, Ju. V. "O koncepcii konflikta v sovremennoj amerikanskoj sociologii" (On the conceptions of conflict in contemporary American sociology), *Učen. Zap. (Moskovs. obl. pedag. Inst.)* 246(4), 1969 : 206-210.

2271   HAAS, M. "Three approaches to the study of war", *Int. J. comp. Sociol.* 10(1), mar 70 : 34-47.

2272   KELMAN, A. C. "The role of the individual in international relations: some conceptual and methodological considerations", *J. int. Aff.* 24(1), 1970 : 1-17.

2273   KONSTANTINOV, F. V. (ed.). *Sociologičeskie problemy meždunarodnyh otnošenij* (Sociological problems of international relations). Moskva, Nauka, 70, 326 p.

2274   KROES, R. "Conflict en radicalisme: een traps model" (Conflict and radicalism: a degree model), *Sociol. Gids* 17(1), jan-feb 70 : 1-18.

2275   KRONSJÖ, T. O. M. "Conflict and co-operation: aspects of the theory of war and peace", *Co-existence* 7(1), jan 70 : 51-62.

2276   KRYSMANSKI, H. J. "Sozialer Konflikt und Problem-lösungsprozesse" (Social conflict and problem-solving process), *Archiv Rechts- u. soz.-Philos.* 56(3), 1970 : 325-349.

2277   LEITES, N. C.; WOLF, C. Jr. *Rebellion and authority; an analytic essay on insurgent conflicts.* Chicago, Markham Publishing Co., 70, xii-174 p.

2278   MARTYNENKO, P. F. *Sociologija meždunarodnyh otnošenij* (Sociology of international relations). Kiev, 69, 98 p.

2279   MEGARGEE, E. I.; HOKANSON, J. E. (eds.). *The dynamics of aggression; individual, group, and international analyses.* New York, Harper and Row, 70, xiv-271 p.

2280   NIEZING, J. *Sociology, war and disarmament; studies in peace research.* Rotterdam, University Press, 70, xii-131 p.

2281   OTTERBEIN, K. F. *The evolution of war; a cross-cultural study.* Human Relations, Area Files Press, 70, 165 p.

2282   Bibl. XIX-1989. PRUITT, D. G.; SNYDER, R. C. (eds.). *Theory and research in the causes of war.* CR: J. REILING, *Amer. sociol. R.* 35(1), feb 70 : 151-152.

2283   RAPOPORT, A. "Is peace research applicable?", *J. Conflict Resol.* 14(2), jun 70 : 277-286.

2284   SEARA VÁZQUEZ, M. *Paz y conflicto en la sociedad internacional* (Peace and conflict in international society). México, Universidad Nacional Autónoma de Mexico, 69, viii-410 p.

2285   SOJAK, V. "Behaviorismus neboli teorie chováni ve vyzkumu mezinárodních vztahu" (Behaviorism or the theory of behavior in international relations research), *Mezin. Vztahy* 4(4), oct-dec 69 : 14-22.

2286   SWINGLE, P. G. *The structure of conflict.* New York, Academic Press, 70, x-305 p.

2287   TEITLER, G. "Conflict, militaire organisatie en samenleving" (Conflict, military organisation and society), *Int. Spectator* 24(13), jul 70 : 1231-1251.

2288   TEITLER, G. "Guerrilla en samenleving" (Guerrilla and society), *Men en Mij* 44(6), nov-dec 69 : 479-492.

2289   VALKENBURGH, P. *Anatomie van het conflict: een model theoretische benadering* (Anatomy of conflict: a theoretical approximation model). Alphen-aan-den-Rijn, Samson, 69, 179 p.

2290   WHITE, R. K. "Three not so obvious contributions of psychology to peace", *J. soc. Issues* 25(4), 1969 : 23-39.

2291   WIATR, J. J. "Nation, patrie et coexistence pacifique", *Tiers-Monde* 9(35-36), jul-dec 68 : 867-876.

2292 WILKENFIELD, J. "Some further findings regarding the domestic and foreign conflict behavior of nations", *J. Peace Res.* (2), 1969 : 147-156.

2293 ZILLER, R. C. *et al.* "The neutral in a communication network under conditions of conflict", *Amer. behav. Scientist* 13(2), nov-dec 69 : 265-282.

C.5 SOCIAL STRATIFICATION
STRATIFICATION SOCIALE

C.50 General studies
Études générales

[See also / Voir aussi: 1358, 1379, 1404, 1582, 1961, 2067, 2425, 2643, 2921, 3233, 4613, 4712, 5237]

2294 ADAMS, R. N. *Crucifixion by power; essays on Guatemalan national social structure, 1944-1966.* Austin, University of Texas Press, 70, xiv-553 p.

2295 ARDIGÒ, A. *La stratificazione sociale* (Social stratification). Bologna, R. Pàtron, 70, 192 p.

2296 BAGÚ, S. "La teoría de la estratificación social y el análisis de los sistemas estratigráficos en América latina" (The theory of social stratification and the analysis of stratigraphic systems in Latin America), *Bol. urug. Sociol.* 8(15-16-17), dec 69 : 44-57.

2297 BÉTEILLE, Z. *Social inequality—selected readings.* Harmondsworth, Penguin Books, 69, 397 p. CR: R. ERIKSON, *Acta sociol.* 13(3), 1970 : 200-201.

2298 CENTRE NATIONAL DE LA RECHERCHE SCIENTIFIQUE. *Les structures sociales de l'Aquitaine, du Languedoc et de l'Espagne au premier âge féodal.* Paris, Éditions du CNRS, 69, 282 p. [Les actes de ce colloque ont été publiés dans la revue *Annales du Midi*, tome 80, nº 89, 1968.]

2299 COELHO, R. G. DE A. *Estrutura social e dinâmica psicológica* (Social structure and psychological dynamics). São Paulo, Livraria Pioneira Editôra, 69, 222 p.

2300 COSTER, M. DE. "Le modèle de la société dualiste dans les sciences humaines", *C. int. Sociol.* 17(49), jul-dec 70 : 69-82.

2301 Bibl. XIX-2007. EVERS, H. D. (ed.). *Loosely structured social systems: Thailand in comparative perspective.* CR: E. H. VAJDA, *Amer. sociol. R.* 35(4), aug 70 : 784-785.

2302 FARARO, T. J. "Strictly stratified systems", *Sociology* 4(1), jan 70 : 85-104.

2303 GALKIN, A. A. "Social'no politiceskaja struktura kapitalisticeskogo obscestva i fasism" (The socio-political structure of capitalist society of fascism), *Vopr. Filos.* 23(2), feb 70 : 87-97.

2304 GUBBELS, R. "Les anti-élites ou de la lutte des classes en tant que type d'organisation", *R. Inst. Sociol.* 3, 1970 : 469-496.

2305 Bibl. XIX-2009. HELLER, C. S. (ed.). *Structured social inequality: a reader in comparative social stratification.* CR: I. KRAUSS, *Amer. sociol. R.* 35(1), feb 70 : 139-140.

2306 HEWITT, J. P. *Social stratification and deviant behavior.* New York, Random House, 70, viii-176 p.

2307 HOLLANDER, P. (ed.). *American and Soviet society; a reader in comparative sociology and perception.* Englewood Cliffs, N. J., Prentice Hall, 69, xviii-589 p. CR: V. N. DADRIAN, *Amer. sociol. R.* 35(4), aug 70 : 765-767.

2308 INGHAM, G. K. "Social stratification: individual attributes and social relationships", *Sociology* 4(1), jan 70 : 105-113.

2309 LARSON, M. S.; BERGMAN, A. I. *Social stratification in Peru.* Berkeley, Institute of International Studies, University of California, 69, ix-407 p.

2310 LAUMANN, E. O. (ed.). *Social stratification: research and theory for the 1970s.* Indianapolis, Bobbs-Merrill, 70, 280 p.

2311 MACHONIN, P. "Social stratification in contemporary Czechoslovakia", *Amer. J. Sociol.* 75(5), mar 70 : 725-741.

2312 OWEN, C. *Social stratification.* New York, Humanities Press, 69, 99 p. CR: R. G. DUMONT, *Amer. sociol. R.* 35(1), feb 70 : 137-138.

2313 PANCHANADIKAR, K. C.; PANCHANADIKAR, J. *Determinants of social structure and social change in India and other papers.* Bombay, Popular Prakashan, 70, xv-241 p.

2314 PAULSTON, R. G. "Estratificación social, poder y organización educacional: el caso peruano" (Social stratification, power and educational organization: the Peruvian case), *Aportes* 16, apr 70 : 91-111.

2315 PETRUSEK, M. "Sociální stratifikace československé společnosti" (Social stratification in Czechoslovak society), *Sociol. Čas.* 5(6), nov-dec 69 : 569-590.

2316 PLOTNICOV, L. (comp.). *Essays in comparative social stratification.* Ed. by L. PLOTNICOV and A. TUDEN. Pittsburgh, University of Pittsburgh Press, 70, vi-349 p.

2317 PRIETO ESCUDERO, G. "Estratificación social en la España balmesiana" (Social stratification in Balmes' Spain), *Riv. int. Sociol. (Madrid)* 28(111-112), mai-aug 70 : 21-38.

2318 RYTINA, J. H.; FORM, W. H.; PEASE, J. "Income and stratification ideology: beliefs about the American opportunity structure", *Amer. J. Sociol.* 75(4, *Part II*), jan 70 : 703-716.

2319 SAMUEL, E. *The structure of society in Israel.* New York, Random House, 69, 184 p. CR: Y. A. COHEN, *Amer. sociol. R.* 35(2), apr 70 : 392-393.

2320 SHARMA, K. N. "Resource networks and resource groups in the social structure", *East. Anthropol.* 22(1), jan-apr 69 : 13-27.

2321 SMITH, T. L. "A study of social stratification in the agricultural sections of the US: nature, data, procedures and preliminary results", *Rur. Sociol.* 34(4), dec 69 : 496-509.

2322 TUDEN, A.; PLOTNICOV, L. (eds.). *Social stratification in Africa.* New York, Free Press, 70, viii-392 p.

2323 TUDOR, A. "The dynamics of stratification systems", *Int. J. comp. Sociol.* 10(3-4), sep-dec 69 : 211-233.

2324 TUMIN, M. M. (comp.). *Readings on social stratification.* Englewood Cliffs, N. J., Prentice-Hall, 70, ix-454 p.

2325 WESOŁOWSKI, W. (ed.). *Zróżnicowanie społeczne* (Social differentiation). Wrocław, Zakład Narodowy im. Ossolińskich, 70, 400 p. [Poland.]

2326 WILLEMS, E. "Social differentiation in colonial Brazil", *Comp. Stud. Soc.* 12(1), jan 70 : 31-49.

C.51   Slavery
Esclavage

2327 ALPERS, E. A. "The French slave trade in East Africa, 1721-1810", *C. Ét. afr.* 10(1), 1970 : 80-124.

2328 CUCHÍ COLL, I. (comp.). *Historia de la esclavitud en Puerto Rico* (History of slavery in Puerto Rico). San Juan de Puerto Rico, Sociedad de Autores Puertorriqueños, 69, 171 p.

2329 DEGLER, C. N. "Slavery in Brazil and the United States: an essay in comparative history", *Amer. hist. R.* 75(4), apr 70 : 1004-1028.

2330 FONER, L.; GENOVESE, E. D. (eds.). *Slavery in the New World; a reader in comparative history.* Englewood Cliffs, N. J., Prentice-Hall, 69, xii-268 p.

2331 LISTON, R. A. *Slavery in America; the history of slavery.* New York, McGraw-Hill, 70, 128 p.

2332 MEILLASSOUX, C. "Le commerce précolonial et le développement de l'esclavage à Cubu du Sahel (Mali)", *Homme et Soc.* 15, jan-feb-mar 70 : 147-157.

2333 STAROBIN, R. S. *Industrial slavery in the Old South.* New York, Oxford University Press, 70, xiii-320 p. [USA.]

2334 UNGER, I.; REIMERS, D. *The slavery experience in the United States.* New York, Holt, Rinehart and Winston, 70, ix-234 p.

C.52   Caste

[See also / Voir aussi: 1113]

2335 BAVISKAR, B. S. "Co-operatives and caste in Maharashtra—a case study", *Sociol. B.* 18(2), sep 69 : 148-166.

2336 BETEILLE, A. *Castes: old and new; essays in social structure and social stratification.* Bombay-New York, Asia Publishing House, 69, viii-254 p.

2337 BHATTA, H. S. "Inter-caste relations and aspirational levels—an attitudinal study", *Ind. J. soc. Res.* 11(1), apr 70 : 43-48.

2338   Das, M. S.; Acuff, F. G. "The caste controversy in comparative perspective: India and the United States", *Int. J. comp. Sociol.* 11(1), mar 70 : 48-54.

2339   Fox, R. G. "*Varna* schemes and ideological integration in Indian society", *Comp. Stud. Soc. Hist.* 11(1), jan 69 : 27-45.

2340   Mathur, P. R. G. "Caste council among the Namputiri brahmans of Kerala", *East. Anthropol.* 22(2), mai-aug 69 : 207-224.

2341   Paranjpe, A. C. *Caste, prejudice and the individual.* Bombay, Lalvani Publishing House, 70, xvi-236 p.

2342   Patnaik, N. *Caste and social change; an anthropological study of three Orissa villages.* Hyderabad, India, National Institute of Community Development, 69, ii-76-1 p.

2343   Rittenberg, S. "Caste's role in Indian politics: a study in coalition formation", *Columb. Essays int. Aff.* 4, 1968 : 150-167.

2344   Rivière, C. "Guinée: la difficile émergence d'un artisanat casté", *C. Ét. afr.* 9(4), oct-dec 69 : 600-625.

2345   Sharma, K. L. "Caste and class consciousness in rural Rajasthan: some social and psychological expressions", *Sociol. soc. Res.* 54(3), apr 70 : 378-387.

2346   Singh, R. "The role of Bhagat movement in the inception of caste features in the Bhil tribe", *East. Anthropol.* 23(2), mai-aug 70 : 161-170.

C.53   Estates
États

2347   Bitton, D. *The French nobility in crisis, 1560-1640.* Stanford (Calif.), Stanford University Press, 69, xii-178 p.

2348   Elias, N. *Die höfische Gesellschaft; Untersuchungen zur Soziologie des Königtums und der höfischen Aristokratie, mit einer Einleitung; Soziologie und Geschichtswissenschaft* (Court society; surveys on sociology of court royalty and aristocracy; with an introduction: sociology and historical sciences). Neuwied, Luchterhand, 69, 456 p.

2349   Fourquin, G. *Seigneurie et féodalité au Moyen Age.* Paris, Presses universitaires de France, 70, 246 p.

2350   Vyas, R. P. *Role of nobility in Marwar, 1800-1873 A.D.* New Delhi, Jain Bros, 69, xv-266 p.

C.54   Social class and social status
Classe sociale, statut social

[See also / Voir aussi: 541, 590, 617, 718, 740, 819, 976, 987, 1366, 1400, 1418, 1604, 1608, 1874, 1970, 1978, 1993, 2186, 2304, 2465, 2467, 2525, 2539, 2628, 2684, 2833, 2870, 2936, 2941, 3045, 3048, 3085, 3105, 3316, 3317, 3725, 4185, 4206, 4245, 4248, 4272, 4294, 4316, 4321, 4324, 4684, 4701, 4710, 4979, 4983, 5005, 5035, 5184]

2351   Adam, A. "Les classes sociales urbaines au Maroc", *R. Occident musul. Méditerr.*, n° spéc., 1970 : 223-237.

2352   Aitov, N. A. "Obščee i soabennoe v klassovoj strukture stran socialističeskoj sistemy" (General and specific on the class-structure of socialist system countries), *Nauč. Dokl. vysš. Školy (ěkon. Nauki)* 3, 1970 : 81-88.

2353   Arpa, V. D'. "Classe sociale: da situazione oggettiva a concetto rivoluzionario" (Social class: from the objective situation to the revolutionary concept), *Crit. sociol. (Roma)* 13, 1970 : 93-127.

2354   Ataov, T. "The place of the worker in Turkish society and politics", *Turk. Yb. int. Relat.* 8(2), 1967 : 85-147.

2355   Barbulat, V. K. "Razvitie rabočego Klassa Moldavskoj SSR 1945-1955 gg." (Development of the Moldavian SSR working class, 1945-1955). Kišinev, Kartja moldovenjaske, 69, 179 p.

2356   Bertaux, D. "L'hérédité sociale en France", *Écon. et Statist.* 9, feb 70 : 37-47.

2357   Blishen, B. R. "Social class and opportunity in Canada", *Canad. R. Sociol. Anthropol.* 7(2), mai 70 : 110-127.

2358   Byrski, Z. "The communist 'middle class' in the USSR and Poland", *Survey* 73, 1969 : 80-92.

2359   CALAMAI, M. "Capitalismo e classe operaia in Spagna" (Capitalism and working class in Spain), *Probl. Social. (Milano)* 11(43), nov-dec 69 : 1123-1151.

2360   ČAPLYGIN, J. P. *Mif o 'edinom srednem klasse'* (The myth of the 'middle class'). Moskva, Politizdat, 70, 63 p.

2361   CARANDINI, G. "Il ruolo delle classi sociali nella rivoluzione inglese del XVII secolo" (The part played by social classes in the English revolution of the 17th century), *Quad. Sociol.* 19(2), apr-jun 70 : 182-214.

2362   CAREY, B. T. "Les changements dans la structure de la classe ouvrière d'Australie", *Nouv. R. int.* 13(9), sep 70 : 42-57.

2363   CASTILLO CASTILLO, J. "Las clases medias, ¿ mito o realidad ?" (Middle classes, myth or reality ?), *Estud. sindic. coop.* 3(9), jan-mar 69 : 61-80.

2364   CHKARATAN, O. "La classe ouvrière de la société socialiste à l'époque de la révolution scientifico-technique", *Sci. soc. aujourd.* 1, 1969 : 155-176.

2365   CICCHITTO, F. "Classe operaia, sindacati e partiti all'inizio degli anni settanta" (Working class, trade unions, parties at the beginning of the seventies), *Ponte* 26(1), jan 70 : 25-50. [Italy.]

2366   COHEN, F. "Situation de classes sociales en URSS", *Nouv. Crit.* 30, jan 70 : 24-31; 33, apr 70 : 36-41; 34, mai 70 : 20-27.

2367   CONGALTON, A. A. *Status and prestige in Australia.* Melbourne, Cheshire, 69, xv-160 p.

2368   CORNU, R.; LAGNEAU, J. *Hiérarchies et classes sociales.* Paris, A. Colin, 69, 320 p.

2369   CROZIER, M. *La société bloquée.* Paris, Éditions du Seuil, 70, 251 p. [France.]

2370   DENITCH, B. "La nouvelle gauche et la nouvelle classe ouvrière", *Homme et Soc.* 16, apr-mai-jun 70 : 43-54.

2371   DIERKES, M. *Der Beitrag des französischen Mittelstandes zum wirtschaftlichen Wachstum* (The contribution of French middle classes to economic growth). Köln-Opladen, Westdeutscher Verlag, 69, 365 p.

2372   DILIGUENSKI, G. "La conception marxiste de la conscience de classe et ses critiques", *Sci. soc. aujourd'.* 4, 1969 : 63-84.

2373   DILIGUENSKI, G. " 'La sociedad de consumo' y la conciencia de clase del proletariado" (Consumer society and class consciousness of the proletariat), *R. Inst. Sociol. boliv.* 9, 1969 : 51-75.

2374   DILIGUENSKIJ, G. G. *Rabočij na kapitalističeskom predprijatii. Issledovanija po social'noj psihologii francuzskogo rabočego klassa* (The worker in the capitalist enterprise. Researches on the social psychology of the French working class). Moskva, Nauka, 69, 410 p.

2375   DJILAS, M. *The unperfect society—beyond the new class.* London, Methuen, 69, x-192 p.

2376   DUFTY, N. F. *The sociology of the blue-collar worker.* Leiden, Brill, 69, 204 p.

2377   EISENSTADT, S. N. "Status segregation and class association in modern society", *Sociol. soc. Res.* 54(4), jul 70 : 425-440.

2378   ENCEL, S. *Equality and authority; a study of class, status and power in Australia.* Melbourne, Cheshire, 70, 492 p.

2379   FALABELLA, G. "Desarrollo del capitalismo y formación de clase: el torrante en la huella" (Development of capitalism and class formation: the 'Torrente in the trench'), *Bol. urug. Sociol.* 8(15-16-17), nov-dec 69 : 58-85. [Chile.]

2380   FORD, J. *Social class and the comprehensive school.* London, Routledge and Kegan Paul; New York, Humanities Press, 69, x-174 p. CR: D. HOLLY, *Brit. J. Sociol.* 21(2), jun 70 : 229-230. [UK.]

2381   FUKUSHIMA, M. "Katoki kaikyûtôsô no riron" (Theory of class struggle in the transitional period), *Tôyô Bunka Kenkyûjo Kiyô* 45, 1968 : 225-307.

2382   GALISSOT, R. "Les classes sociales en Algérie", *Homme et Soc.* 14, oct-nov-dec 69 : 207-225.

2383   GALLINO, L. "L'evoluzione della struttura di classe in Italia" (The evolution of class structure in Italy), *Quad. Sociol.* 19(2), apr-jun 70 : 115-154.

2384   GAUZNER, N. D. *Naučnotehničeskij progress i rabočij klass SSSR* (Scientific and technical progress and the USSR working class); Moskva, Nauka, 68, 310 p.

2385   GERNS, W. "Structure de la classe ouvrière en République fédérale", *Nouv. R. int.* 12(12), dec 69 : 145-160.

2386   GINTIS, H. "The new working class and revolutionary youth", *Social. Revol.* 1(3), mai-jun 70 : 13-43.

2387 HALPERN, M. "Egypt and the new middle class: reaffirmations and new explorations", *Comp. Stud. Soc. Hist.* 11(1), jan 69 : 97-108.

2388 HALPERN, M. "The problem of becoming conscious of a salaried new middle class", *Comp. Stud. Soc. Hist.* 12(1), jan 70 : 27-30. [UAR.]

2389 HESS, P. "Aktuelle Bezüge der leninschen Lehre von Klassenkampf und Revolution" (Current characteristics of the Leninist theory on class struggle and revolution), *Wirtsch.-Wiss.* 17(11), nov 69 : 1601-1621.

2390 HOROWITZ, I. L. (comp.). *Masses in Latin America.* New York, Oxford University Press, 70, 608 p.

2391 HUNT, A. "Class structure in Britain today", *Marxism today* 14(6), jun 70 : 167-172.

2392 ISKROV, M. V. "Žižnennost' leninskih idej ob istoričeskoj roli rabočego klassa" (Vitality of Lenin's ideas on the historical role of the working class), *Vopr. Ist. KPSS* 13(2), feb 70 : 3-17.

2393 ISRAEL, J. "Remarks concerning some problems of Marxist class theory", *Acta sociol.* 13(1), 1970 : 11-29. Also published in French in *Homme et Soc.* 15, jan-mar 70 : 269-294.

2394 IVANOV, M. S. *Rabočij klass sovremennogo Irana* (The working class in contemporary Iran). Moskva, Nauka, 69, 254 p.

2395 IZAGUIRRE, I. "Classes sociales et orientation professionnelle dans une université latino-américaine", *Éduc. perm.* 6, apr-mai-jun 70 : 77-105. [Argentina.]

2396 Bibl. XVIII-2076. JACKSON, B. *Working-class community: some general notions raised by a series of studies in Northern England.* CR: D. W. MINAR, *Amer. J. Sociol.* 75(5), mar 70 : 868-870.

2397 KALLOS, N. "Evoluția structurii de clasă a societătii și refléctarea ei în confruntările ideologice contemporane" (Evolution of the class structure society and its reflection in contemporary ideologies), *R. Filoz.* 17(5), 1970 : 491-500. [Rumania.]

2398 KEMÉNY, I. "Restratification of the working class", *New Hungar. Quart.* 11(38), 1970 : 26-37. [Hungary.]

2399 KENDALL, M. B.; SIBLEY, R. F. "Social class differences in the orientation: artifact", *J. soc. Psychol.* 82(2), dec 70 : 187-192.

2400 KOLBE, H.; RÖDER, K. H. *Staat und Klassenkampf; zur Machtsfrage in Westdeutschland* (State and class conflict; the problem of power in Western Germany). Berlin, Staatsverlag der Deutschen Demokratischen Republik, 69, 202 p.

2401 KUZEEV, R. G. *Rabočij klass—sozidatel'kommunizma (Rabočij klass Baškiri v 50-60é gody)* (The working class in the creation of communism. [Bachkiry working class in the 50's-60's]. Ufa, Bašknigoizdat, 69, 256 p.

2402 LABINI, P. S. "Produttori di ricchezze e produttori di servizi—classe operaia e classe media" (Producers of wealth and producers of services—working class and middle class), *Econ. e Lav.* 3(2), mar-apr 69 : 126-133.

2403 LAMATA, P. "Sobre las clases sociales" (On social classes), *Estud. sindic. coop.* 3(9), jan-mar 69 : 7-18.

2404 LAUMANN, E. O.; SIEGEL, P. M.; HODGE, R. W. (eds.). *The logic of social hierarchies.* Chicago, Markham Publishing Co., 70, xv-790 p.

2405 LAURENT, S. "À propos des classes sociales", *Écon. et Polit.* 186-187, jan-feb 70 : 125-134.

2406 LAURENT, S. "Les transformations en cours dans les classes et couches sociales", *Écon. et Polit.* 185, dec 69 : 15-46. Également publié dans la *Nouv. R. int.* 12(12), dec 69 : 131-144.

2407 LAWLOR, S. D. "Social class and achievement orientation", *Canad. R. Sociol. Anthropol.* 7(2), mai 70 : 148-153.

2408 Bibl. XVIII-2081. LEGGETT, J. C. *Class, race, and labor: working-class consciousness in Detroit.* CR: D. W. MINAR, *Amer. J. Sociol.* 75(5), mar 70 : 868-870.

2409 LEIK, R. K.; NAGASAWA, R. "A sociometric basis for measuring social status and social structure", *Sociometry* 33(1), mar 70 : 55-78.

2410 LINDER, S. B. *The harried leisure class.* New York, Columbia University Press, 70, viii-182 p. CR: T. SCITOVSKY, *J. econ. Liter.* 8(3), sep 70 : 884-885.

2411 LISSAK, M. "The class structure of Burma: continuity and change", *J. Southeast Asian Hist.* 1(1), mar 70 : 60-73.

2412 LOWY, M. "Structure de la conscience de classe ouvrière au Brésil", *C. int. Sociol.* 17(49), jul-dec 70 : 133-142.

2413   MACKENZIE, G. "The class situation of manual workers: the United States and Britain; review article", *Brit. J. Sociol.* 21(3), sep 70 : 333-342.

2414   MARAVALL, J. M. *El desarrollo económico y la clase obrera. (Un estudio sociólogico de los conflictos obreros en España)* (Economic development and the working class. A sociological study of labour conflicts in Spain). Caracas-Barcelona, Ariel, 70, 259 p.

2415   MARTÍN, A. *Marcuse y Venezuela. Se aburguesa la clase obrera en Venezuela?* (Marcuse and Venezuela. Is the Venezuelan working class becoming bourgeois ?). Caracas, Editorial, Cuadernos Rocinante, 69, 176 p.

2416   Bibl. XIX-2083. McDONALD, L. *Social class and delinquency* CR: J. F. SHORT, Jr., *Amer. J. Sociol.* 76(1), jul 70 : 186-188; E. SAGARIN, *Amer. sociol. R.* 35(4), aug 70 : 808-809.

2417   MEILLASSOUX, C. "A class analysis of the bureaucratic process in Mali", *J. Develop. Stud.* 6(2), jan 70 : 97-110.

2418   Bibl. XIX-2087. MILLER, S. M.; RIESSMAN, F. *Social class and social policy.* CR: P. MORRIS, *Amer. J. Sociol.* 75(4, *Part III*), jan 70 : 722-724.

2419   MOHIDDIN, A. "Socialism and class concept in African development", *Afr. Quart.* 9(2), jul-sep 69 : 83-94.

2420   MOROSINI, G. "Classi e potere in una comunità locale" (Classes and power in a local community), *A. Fond. Luigi Einaudi* 3, 1969 : 309-358. [Italy.]

2421   MORRIS, R. T.; JEFFRIES, V. "Class conflict: forget it!", *Sociol. soc. Res.* 54(3), apr 70 : 306-320. [USA.]

2422   MORTIMER, R. "Class, social cleavage and Indonesian communism", *Indonesia* 8, oct 69 : 1-20.

2423   MOSKOVSKIJ, A. S. *Formirovanie i razvitie rabočego klassa Sibirri v period stroitel'stva socializma* (Formation and development of the Siberian working class during the period of edification of socialism). Novosibirsk, Nauka, 68, 300 p.

2424   MOUSNIER, R. *Les hiérarchies sociales de 1450 à nos jours.* Paris, Presses universitaires de France, 69, 196 p. CR: J. LAUTMAN, *R. franç. Sociol.* 11(3), jul-sep 70 : 434.

2425   MUTAGIROV, D. Z. "Metodologičeskie voprosy izučenija social'noj struktury rabočego klassa" (Methodological questions on the study of the social structure of the working class), *Učen. Zap. (Leningr. gos. Univ. nauč.-issled. Inst. kompleks. sociol. Issled.)* (5), 1969 : 25-36.

2426   MYERS, F. E. "Social class and political change in Western industrial systems", *Comp. Polit.* 2(3), apr 70 : 389-412.

2427   "Myth and middle class", *Comp. Stud. soc. Hist.* 12(1), jan 70 : 14-49.

2428   NASH, G. B. *Class and society in early America.* Englewood Cliffs, N. J., Prentice Hall, 70, x-205 p.

2429   PALMIER, L. H. *Social status and power in Java.* London, Athlone Press; New York Humanities Press, 69, viii-171 p.

2430   PARKIN, F. "Class stratification in socialist societies", *Brit. J. Sociol.* 20(4), dec 69 : 355-374.

2431   PARRA, S. R. "Clases sociales y educación en el desarrollo de Colombia" (Social classes and education in Colombian development), *UN Rev. Dir. Divulg. cult.* 3, apr-aug 69 : 166-182.

2432   PERLMUTTER, A. "The myth of the myth of the new middle class: some lessons in social and political theory", *Comp. Stud. Soc. Hist.* 11(1), jan 70 : 14-26. [UAR.]

2433   PINARD, M. "Working class politics: an interpretation of the Quebec case", *Canad. R. Sociol. Anthropol.* 7(2), mai 70 : 87-109.

2434   POGOLOTTI, M. *La clase media y la cultura* (The middle class and culture). México, B. Costa-Amic, 70, 355 p.

2435   *Rabočij klass SSSR na sovremennom ětape* (The USSR working class in the contemporary era). Leningrad, 68, 168 p.

2436   RACHEL, C. "Der ideologische Klassenkampf in der nationalen Befreiungsbewegung Afrikas" (The ideological class struggle in national liberation movements), *Dtsche Z. Philos.* 18(1), 1970 : 32-56.

2437   RAYNOR, J. *The middle class.* New York, Humanities Press, 69, 125 p. CR: R. J. LAZAR, *Amer. sociol. R.* 35(4), aug 70 : 786-788.

2438   REISSMAN, L.; HALSTEAD, M. N. "The subject is class", *Sociol. soc. Res.* 54(3), apr 70 : 293-305.

2439 RIVIÈRE, C. "De l'objectivité des classes sociales, en Afrique noire", *C. int. Sociol.* 16(47), jul-dec 69 : 119-144.

2440 ROMEU ALFARO, F. *Las clases trabajadoras en España (1898-1930)* (Working classes in Spain, 1898-1930). Madrid, Taurus Ed., 70, 221 p.

2441 RUSHING, W. A. "Class differences in goal orientations and aspirations: rural patterns", *Rur. Sociol.* 35(3), sep 70 : 377-395.

2442 SCHREIBER, E. M.; NYGREEN, G. T. "Subjective social class in America: 1945-1948", *Soc. Forces* 48(3), mar 70 : 348-356.

2443 SEMENOV, V. S. *Kapitalizm i klassy. Issledovanie social'noj struktury kapitalističeskogo obščestiva* (Capitalism and classes. Research in the social structure of capitalist societies). Moskva, Nauka, 69, 399 p.

2444 SMITH, T. L. "The class structure in contemporary society in the USA", *Soc. Sci. (Winfield)* 45(3), jun 70 : 133-142.

2445 STAVENHAGEN, R. *Les classes sociales dans les sociétés agraires.* Paris, Anthropos, 69, 402 p. Publié aussi en espagnol, *Las clases sociales en las sociedades agrarias.* Mexico, Siglo Veintiuno Editores, 69, viii-292 p.

2446 STRAUS, M. A. "Social class and farm-city differencies in interaction with kin in relation to societal modernization", *Rur. Sociol.* 34(4), dec 69 : 476-495.

2447 SURPAT, G. "Transformări calitative ale clasei muncitoare în anni socialismului" (Qualitative transformations in the working class during the years of socialism), *Probl. econ. (București)* 22(12), dec 69 : 27-39. [Rumania.]

2448 SUSATO, S. "The white-collar strata in postwar Japan", *Develop. Econ.* 7(4), dec 69 : 451-470.

2449 TA-CHOU HUANG. "The process of social differentiation in Taiwanese communities", *Cornell J. soc. Relat.* 5(1), 1970 : 1-9.

2450 TORREGROSA, J. R. "Algunos datos y consideraciones sobre el autoritarismo de la clase trabajadora" (Data and thoughts on working class authoritarianism), *R. esp. Opin. públ.* 16, apr-jun 69 : 33-46.

2451 TUMANOV, L. K. *Formirovanie afrikanskoj buržuazii* (Formation of the African bourgeoisie). Moskva, Nauka, 69, 163 p.

2452 WALBERG, H. J. "Class size and the social environment of learning", *Hum. Relat.* 22(5), oct 69 : 465-475.

2453 WILLMOT, P. "Tendances de la société anglaise", *Anal. et Prévis.* 9(5), mai 70 : 279-294.

2454 WOOD, D. B. "Las relaciones revolucionarias de clase y los conflictos políticos en Cuba: 1868-1968" (Revolutionary class relations and political conflicts in Cuba: 1868-1968), *R. latinoamer. Sociol.* 5(1), 1969 : 30-79.

C.55 Elite
Élite

[See also / Voir aussi: **C.3121**; 1339, 1456, 1925, 1928, 1930, 2906, 3433, 3504, 3531, 3572, 4114, 4177, 4207, 4333, 4432, 4439, 5016]

2455 AGULLA, J. C. "Elites tradicionales, poder y desarrollo en Argentina" (Traditional elites, power and development in Argentina), *Sociol. int. (Berlin)* 8(2), 1970 : 129-166.

2456 AIBA, J. "Seiji shakai to erîto" (Political society and elite), *Jimbungaku* 103, 1968 : 19-37.

2457 BAIER, H. "Bewusstsein als Sozialphänomen. Zur Soziologie der Intellektuellen in der wissenschaftlichen Zivilisation" (Consciousness as a social phenomenon. About the sociology of intellectuals in scientific civilization), *Archiv Recht-u. soz.-Philos.* 56(2), 1970 : 163-179.

2458 BOESCH, E. E. *Zwiespältige Eliten. Eine sozialpsychologische Untersuchung über administrative Eliten in Thailand* (Divided elites; a socio-psychological survey on administrative elites in Thailand). Bern-Stuttgart-Wien, Hans Huber, 70, 333 p.

2459 BONILLA, F. "Les élites 'invisibles' " (Invisible elites), *R. mexic. Sociol.* 31(4), oct-dec 69 : 817-851.

2460 BONILLA, F. *The failure of elites.* Cambridge, Mass. MIT Press, 70, x-335 p.

2461 BOURNE, R. *Political leaders of Latin America.* New York, Knopf, 70, 310-x p.

2462   BRAVO-BRESANT, J. "Mythe et réalité de l'oligarchie péruvienne", *Tiers-Monde* 10(38), apr-jun 69 : 405-427.

2463   BRECHER, M. *Political leadership in India: an analysis of elite attitudes.* New York, Frederick Praeger and the Centre for Developing Area Studies, McGill, University, 69, 193 p. CR: R. S. ROBINS, *Amer. polit. Sci. R.* 64(1), mar 70 : 197-198.

2464   BUJRA, A. S. "Urban elites and colonialism: the nationalist elites of Aden and South Arabia", *Mid. East. Stud.* 6(2), mai 70 : 189-211.

2465   CASANOVA, A.; PRÉVOST, C.; METZGER, J. *Les intellectuels et les luttes de classes.* Paris, Éditions sociales, 70, 169 p. [France.]

2466   CATTERBER, E. R. "Los intelectuales latinoamericanos: su ubicación social y sus actitudes políticas e ideológicas" (Latin American intellectuals: their social situation and political attitudes and ideologies), *R. Inst. Cienc. soc.* (14), 1969 : 157-171.

2467   ČEŠKOV, M. " 'Élita' i klass v razvivajuščihsja stranah" (Elite and class in developing countries), *Mir. Ékon. meždun. Otnoš.* 13(1), jan 70 : 85-91.

2468   CHOPRA, S. L.; CHAUHAN, D. N. S. "Emerging pattern of political leadership in India", *J. constit. parl. Stud.* 4(1), jan-mar 70 : 119-127.

2469   CNUDDE, C. F. "Elite-mass relationships and democratic rules of the game", *Amer. behav. Scientist* 13(2), nov-dec 69 : 189-200.

2470   CORTEN, A. "Anatomie de l'oligarchie dominicaine", *Cult. et Dévelop.* 1(4), 1968 : 801-842.

2471   COSTER, M. DE. "Le pouvoir au Congo: approche d'une étude sur les élites congolaises", *R. franç. Ét. polit. afr.* 57, sep 70 : 26-61.

2472   DAALDER, H.; RUBÉE-BOONZAAIJER, S. "Sociale herkomst en politieke recrutering van Nederlandse kamerleden in 1968" (Social origin and political recruitment of Dutch parliamentarians in 1968), *Acta polit.* 5(3), apr 69-70 : 292-333.

2473   DEBBASCH, C. et al. *Pouvoir et administration au Maghreb; études sur les élites maghrébines.* Paris, Éditions du Centre national de la recherche scientifique, 70, 152 p.

2474   DOMES, J. "Chinas spätmaoistische Führungsgruppe. Die sozio-politische Struktur des IX. Zentralkomitees der Kommuninistischen Partei Chinas" (The late Maoist leadership group in China. The social-political structure of the IXth Central Committee of the Chinese Communist Party), *Polit. Vjschr.* 10(2-3), sep 69 : 191-219.

2475   DOMHOFF, G. W. *The higher circles; the governing class in America.* New York, Random House, 70, xii-367 p.

2476   "Elite e massa" (Elite and masses), *Vozes* 64(4), mai 70 : 253-319. [Brazil.]

2477   FRISCH, A. "Le rôle des minorités dans la société de masse", *Res publ.* 11(4), 1969 : 757-773.

2478   GALKINE, A. "L'élite au pouvoir du capitalisme moderne", *Sci. soc. aujourd.* 4, 1969 : 37-62.

2479   GENTILI, A. M. "Le elite africane a dieci anni dall'indipendenza" (African elites ten years after the independence), *Mulino* 19(9-10), sep-oct 70 : 255-279.

2480   GODOY, H. H. "La función de las elites en la integración de la América latina" (The function of elites in the integration of Latin America), *R. parag. Sociol.* 6(15), mai-aug 69 : 33-48.

2481   GOODE, J. G. "Responses of a traditional elite to modernization—lawyers in Colombia", *Hum. Org.* 29(1), 1970 : 70-80.

2482   HERZOG, H. H.; OEHLKE, P. *Intellektuelle Opposition im autoritären Sozialstaat* (Intellectual opposition in the authoritarian Social State), Neuwied, Luchterhand, 70, 216 p.

2483   HODARA, J. "Notas para una sociología de los intelectuales latinoamericanos" (Notes for a sociology of Latin American intellectuals), *Aportes* 18, oct 70 : 16-26.

2484   HUGHES, D. T. "Reciprocal influence of traditional and democratic leadership roles on Ponape", *Ethnology* 8(3), jul 69 : 278-291.

2485   IPPOLITO, D. S. "Stability and democratic elitism", *Soc. Sci. (Winfield)* 45(3), jun 70 : 143-148.

2486   JODL, M. *Teorie elity a problém elity* (Elite theory and problem of elites). Praha, Academia, 68, 226-2 p.

2487   KELNER, M. "Ethnic penetration into Toronto's elite structure", *Canad. R. Sociol. Anthropol.* 7(2), mai 70 : 128-137.

2488   KILSON, M. "Elite cleavages in African politics: the case of Ghana", *J. int. Aff.* 24(1), 1970 : 75-83.

2489 LACOUTURE, J. *Quatre hommes et leurs peuples; sur-pouvoir et sous-développement*. Paris, Éditions du Seuil, 69, 282 p. [Nasser, Bourguiba, Sihanouk, Nkrumah.]

2490 LEACH, E.; MUKHERJEE, S. N. (eds.). *Elites in South Asia*. Cambridge, Eng., University Press, 70, xiv-266 p.

2491 MARR, P. A. "Iraq's leadership dilemma: a study in leadership trends, 1948-1968", *Mid. East J.* 24(3), 1970 : 283-301.

2492 MARSAL, J. F. *El intelectual latinoamericano; um simposio sobre sociología de los intelectuales* (The Latin American intellectual: a symposium on intellectuals). Buenos Aires, Editorial del Instituto, Torcuato di Tella, 70, 253 p.

2493 MARSAL, J. F.; ARENT, M. J. "La derecha intelectual Argentina. Análisis de la ideología y la acción política de un grupo de intelectuales" (The intellectual-right in Argentina. Analysis of the ideology and political activity of a group of intellectuals), *R. latino-amer. Sociol.* 5(3), nov 69 : 486-519.

2494 MEL'NIKOV, A. "Intelligencija SŠA: čislennost', sostav social'naja differenciacija" (The intelligentsia in the United States: number, composition, social differentiation), *Mir. Ěkon. meždun. Otnoš.* 13(1), jan 70 : 102-111.

2495 MODELSKI, G. "The world's foreign ministers: a political elite", *J. Conflict Resol.* 14(2), jun 70 : 135-176.

2496 MOLINA PIÑEIRO, L. "Analisis sociológico-político de la estructura del poder en México y su funcionamiento" (Sociological-political analysis of the power structure in Mexico and its functioning), *Comunidades* 4(12), sep-dec 69 : 66-77.

2497 MURILO DE CARVALHO, J. "El papel de los intelectuales en la Révolución Mexicana" (The role of intellectuals in the Mexican Revolution), *R. latinoamer. Sociol.* 5(1), 1969 : 6-20.

2498 NATOLI, S. "L'intellettuale i un salariato o un privilegiato ?" (Is the intellectual a wage-earner or a privileged individual ?), *Crit. sociol. (Roma)* 14, 1970 : 143-155.

2499 NICHOLSON, N. K. "India's modernizing faction and the mobilization of power", *Int. J. compar. Sociol.* 9(3-4), sep-dec 68 : 302-317.

2500 OTLEY, C. B. "The social origins of British Army officers", *Sociol. R.* 18(2), jul 70 : 213-240.

2501 POMPER, P. *The Russian revolutionary intelligentsia*. New York, Crowell, 70, vii-216 p.

2502 PRAHL, H. W. "Intelligenz und Elitegruppen in der DDR-Gesellschaft" (Intelligentsia and elite groups in DDR society), *Deutschland Archiv* 3(2), feb 70 : 128-134.

2503 PUNNETT, R. M. "Selection of party leaders: a Canadian example", *J. Commonwealth polit. Stud.* 8(1), mar 70 : 54-69.

2504 RAUM, O. F. "Die Aufeinanderfolge afrikanischer Eliten" (Elite succession in Africa), *Int. Afr. Forum* 5(12), dec 69 : 763-772.

2505 RIEFF, P. (ed.). *On intellectuals: theoretical studies/Case studies*. Garden City, N. Y., Doubleday and Co., 69, 347 p. CR: L. W. SIRACUSE, *Amer. sociol. R.* 35(3), jun 70 : 551-552.

2506 RUSTOW, D. A. (comp.). *Philosophers and kings: studies in leadership*. New York, G. Braziller, 70, vii-526 p.

2507 SAHAY, B. N. *Dynamics of leadership*. New Delhi, Bookhive, 69, xi-227 p.

2508 SHAWNA, L.; KARUME, M. L. "Élites africaines et culture occidentale", *Tam-Tam* 17(4-5), 1969 : 14-19.

2509 SIMMS, L. M. Jr. "World War I and the American intellectual", *Soc. Sci. (Winfield)* 45(3), jun 70 : 157-162.

2510 SIQUEIRA, M. M. DE. "Elites politicas em Minas Gerais" (Political elites in Minas Gerais), *R. brasil. Estud. polit.* 29, jul 70 : 173-179. [Brazil.]

2511 SOULE, J. W. "Future political ambitions and the behavior of incumbent State legislators", *Midwest J. polit. Sci.* 13(3), aug 69 : 439-454. [USA.]

2512 STORER, N. "Le caractère international de la science et l'appartenance des savants à une nation", *R. int. Sci. soc.* 22(1), 1970 : 89-104.

2513 "Table ronde sur élite et peuple dans l'Afrique d'aujourd'hui, Paris, 11-12 avril 1969", *Présence afr.* 73, 1970 : 39-108.

2514 TELLA, T. S. DI.; HALPERIN DONGHI, T. (comps.). *Los fragmentos del poder de la oligarquía a la poliarquía argentina* (Fragments of power of the oligarchy and the polyarchy in Argentina). Buenos Aires, Editorial J. Alvarez, 69, 535 p.

2515　Tokumoto, M.; Kinugasa, T.; Saitô, F. "Toshika genshôka ni okeru chiiki shakai rîdā no seijiishiki" (Local leaders' political consciousness and urbanization), *Hôsei Kenkyû* 34(5-6), 1968 : 121-244.

2516　Valiev, A. K. *Sovetskaja nacional'naja intelligencija i eĕ social'naja rol'* (The Soviet national intelligentsia and its social role). Taškent, 69, 227 p.

2517　Waterbury, J. *The commander of the faithful: the Moroccan political elite—a study in segmented politics.* London, Weidenfeld and Nicolson, 70, xviii-368 p.

2518　Weaver, J. "La élite política de un régimen dominado por militares; el ejemplo de Guatemala" (The political elite of a military dominated regime: the Guatemalan example), *R. latinoamer. Sociol.* 5(1), mar 69 : 21-39.

2519　Bibl. xix-2191. Wilkinson, R. (ed.). *Governing elites: studies in training and selection.* CR: J. McEvoy III, *Amer. sociol. R.* 35(1), feb 70 : 131; C. Lacey, *Brit. J. Sociol.* 21(2), jun 70 : 232.

2520　Wriggins, W. H. *The ruler's imperative: strategies for political survival in Asia and Africa.* New York, Columbia University Press, 69, 275 p. CR: G. A. Almond, *Amer. polit. Sci. R.* 64(3), sep 70 : 909-910.

2521　Zahl, K. F. "Die Stellung der Bürokratie in der politischen Elite Japans nach dem zweiten Weltkrieg" (The position of the bureaucracy among the Japanese political elite after the Second World War), *Verwaltung* 2(1), 1969 : 47-64.

2522　Zanotti-Karp, A. "Elite theory and ideology", *Soc. Res.* 37(2), 1970 : 275-295.

C.56　　Social mobility
Mobilité sociale

[See also / Voir aussi: 3290]

2523　Ambannavar, J. P. "Upward occupational mobility through education and age", *Asian econ. R.* 11(3), mai 69 : 290-299.

2524　Barber, J. A. Jr. *Social mobility and voting behavior.* Chicago, Rand McNally, 70, xvi-280 p. [USA.]

2525　Bibl. xix-2198. Bell, C. *Middle class families. Social and geographical mobility.* CR: G. Albrecht, *Kölner Z. Soziol. u. soz.-Psychol.* 22(2), jun 70 : 408-413; J. T. Sprehe, *Amer. sociol. R.* 35(4), aug 70 : 788-789.

2526　Bertaux, D. "Sur l'analyse des tables de mobilité sociale", *R. franç. Sociol.* 10(4), oct-dec 69 : 448-490. [France.]

2527　Bode, J. G. "Status and mobility of Catholics vis-à-vis several Protestant denominations: more evidence", *Sociol. Quart.* 11(1), 1970 : 103-111.

2528　Bultena, G. L. "Career mobility of low-income farm operators", *Rur. Sociol.* 34(4), dec 69 : 563-569.

2529　Campion-Vincent, V. "Système d'enseignement et mobilité sociale au Sénégal", *R. franç. Sociol.* 11(2), apr-jun 70 : 164-178.

2530　Chekki, D. A. "Soziale Schichtung und Tendenzen sozialer Mobilität im zeitgenössischen Indien" (Social stratification and trends of social mobility in modern India), *Sociologus* 20(2), 1970 : 146-163.

2531　Cross, M.; Schwartzbaum, A. M. "Social mobility and secondary school selection in Trinidad and Tobago", *Soc. econ. Stud.* 18(2), jun 69 : 189-207.

2532　Davies, I. *Social mobility and political change.* New York, Praeger Publ., 70, 133 p.

2533　Ferge, Z. "Social mobility and the open character of society", *New Hungar. Quart.* 11(37), 1970 : 83-98.

2534　Fürstenberg, F. *Das Aufstiegsproblem in der modernen Gesellschaft* (Social promotion problem in modern society). 2nd rev. ed. Stuttgart, F. Enke Verlag, 69, 179 p. CR: K. M. Bolte, *Kölner Z. Soziol. u. soz.-Psychol.* 22(2), jun 70 : 406-407.

2535　Gibson, J. B. "Biological aspects of a high socio-economic group: IQ. education and social mobility", *J. biosoc. Sci.* 2(1), jan 70 : 1-16.

2536　Goodman, L. A. "On the measurement of social mobility: an index of status persistence", *Amer. sociol. R.* 34(6), dec 69 : 831-849.

2537　Gourdy, M. "Relaciones entre las profesiones de los padres y de los hijos" (Relations between the professions of fathers and sons), *Bol. Museo soc. argent.* 47(344), jul-sep 70 : 317-332. [Argentina.]

2538   GRUBER, U. *et al. Soziale Mobilität heute* (Social mobility today). Herford-Bonn, Maxmilian Verlag, 68, 64 p. CR: F. FÜRSTENBERG, *Kölner Z. Soziol. u. soz.-Psychol.* 22(2), jun 70 : 407-408.

2539   HUTCHINSON, B. A. *Social status and inter-generational social mobility in Dublin.* Dublin, Economic and Social Research Institute, 69, 37 p.

2540   INOUYE, A. "Les effets de la mobilité spatiale sur les communautés chrétiennes du centre de Tôkyô", *Soc. Compass* 17(1), 1970 : 97-118.

2541   KALLÓS, N. M. "The role of the school in social mobility", *Soc. Sci. (Winfield)* 45(2), apr 70 : 101-103.

2542   MCFARLAND, D. D. "Intragenerational social mobility as a Markov process: including a time-stationary Markovian model that explains observed declines in mobility rates", *Amer. sociol. R.* 35(3), jun 70 : 463-475.

2543   PARSLER, R. "Some economic aspects of embourgeoisement in Australia", *Sociology* 4(2), mai 70 : 165-179.

2544   PERTUCI, C. C.; PERRUCY, R. "Social origins, educational contexts, and career mobility", *Amer. sociol. R.* 35(3), jun 70 : 451-463.

2545   QUTUB, I. "The impact of industrialization on social mobility in Jordan", *Develop. and Change* 1(2), 1969-70 : 29-49.

2546   READ, P. B. "Migration and mobility: the myth of a Northern haven for Blacks", *Cornell J. soc. Relat.* 5(1), 1970 : 57-78. [USA.]

2547   RUSSELL-WOOD, A. J. R. "Mobilidade social na Bahia colonial" (Social mobility in colonial Bahia), *R. brasil. Estud. polít.* 27, jul 69 : 175-196. [Brazil.]

2548   SÁNCHEZ LÓPEZ, F. "Estructura y movilidad ocupacional-industrial. Noticia de una investigación sobre la movilidad social en la industria española: introducción" (Occupational-industrial structure and mobility. A report on a research study on social mobility in Spanish industry: introduction), *R. int. Sociol. (Madrid)* 27(107-108), jul-dec 69 : 15-43.

2549   SVALASTOGA, K.; WOLF, F. P. *Social rang og mobilited* (Social rank and mobility) by K. SVALASTOGA and P. WOLF. *Med et tillaeg om nyere bidrag til stratifikations-forskningen i Danmark* (With a new essay on stratification researches in Denmark) by R. RISHØJ. 2nd enl. ed. København, Gyldendal, 69, 228 p.

2550   SWEESTER, D. A. "The occupational mobility of sibling groups", *Acta sociol.* 13(3), 1970 : 189-197.

2551   TANAKA, T. "Koluin ni okeru kaisô idô kôsatsu" (Social mobility and civil servants), *Shakaigaku Ronsô* 42, 1968 : 51-59.

2552   TOMINAGA, K. "Trend analysis of social stratification and social mobility in contemporary Japan", *Develop. Econ.* 7(4), dec 69 : 471-498.

2553   TUGAULT, Y. "La mobilité géographique en France depuis un siècle: une étude par générations", *Population* 25(5), sep-oct 70 : 1019-1038.

2554   VORWALLER, D. J. "Social mobility and membership in voluntary associations", *Amer. J. Sociol.* 75(4, *Part I*), jan 70 : 481-495.

2555   WHITE, H. C. "Stayers and movers", *Amer. J. Sociol.* 76(2), sep 70 : 307-324.

C.6   MARRIAGE AND FAMILY
MARIAGE, FAMILLE

C.61   Sexual behaviour
Comportement sexuel

[See also / Voir aussi: **F.12**; 1977, 2592, 3797, 3975, 5281]

2556   BAROCHE, J. *Comportement sexuel de l'homme marié en France.* Paris, la Jeune Parque, 69, 240 p.

2557   BELLIVEAU, F.; BICHTER, L. *Understanding human sexual inadequacy.* New York, Bantam Books, 70, 242 p.

2558   BRINKMAN, W.; KOOMEN, W. "Sex in Nederland, een poging tot evaluatie" (Sex in the Netherlands; a tentative evaluation), *Mens en Mij*, 45(4), jul-aug 70 : 273-284. With a comment by G. A. KOOY : 285-288.

2559   CENTRE D'ÉTUDES LAËNNEC. *Sexualité humaine: histoire, ethnologie, sociologie, psychanalyse, philosophie.* Paris, Aubier-Montaigne, 70, 303 p.

2560   DIAMANT, L. "Premarital sexual behavior, attitudes, and emotional adjustment", *J. soc. Psychol.* 82(1), oct 70 : 75-80.

2561   FLAMAND, J. "Sexualité et religion", *Homme et Soc.* 17, jul-aug-sep 70 : 209-221.

2562   GOLDFARB, R. M. *Sexual repression and Victorian literature.* Lewisburg, Bucknell University Press, 70, 222 p.

2563   HARRISON, D. E.; BENNETT, W. H.; GLOBETTI, G. "Attitudes of rural youth toward premarital sexual permissiveness", *J. Marriage Family* 31(4), nov 69 : 83-787.

2564   HAUSER, R. M. "Context and consex: a cautionary tale", *Amer. J. Sociol.* 75(4, *Part II*), jan 70 : 645-664.

2565   HOLZER, H. "Sexualität und Herrschaft; Anmerkungen zum Problem der repressiven Entsublimierung" (Sexuality and domination; remarks on the problem of repressive desublimation), *Soz. Welt* 20(3), 1969 : 304-328.

2566   JOHNSON, C. E. (ed.). *Sex and human relationships.* Columbus, Ohio, Merrill, 70, 258 p.

2567   KON, I. "Seks, obščestvo, kul'tura" (Sex, society, culture), *Inostr. Lit.* (1), 1970 : 243-255.

2568   LUCKEY, E. B.; NASS, G. D. "A comparison of sexual attitudes and behavior in an international sample", *J. Marriage Family* 31(2), mai 69 : 364-379.

2569   MINTURN, L.; GROSSE, M.; HAIDER, S. "Cultural patterning of sexual beliefs and behavior", *Ethnology* 8(3), jul 69 : 301-318.

2570   MUNROE, R. L.; MUNROE, R. H. "A cross-cultural study of sex gender and social structure", *Ethnology* 8(2), apr 69 : 206-211.

2571   NIMMO, H. A. "Bajau sex and reproduction", *Ethnology* 9(3), jul 70 : 251-262.

2572   REISS, I. L. "Premarital sex as deviant behavior; an application of current approaches to deviance", *Amer. sociol. R.* 35(1), feb 70 : 78-87.

2573   ROSZAK, B.; ROSZAK, T. (eds.). *Masculine/feminine: readings in sexual mythology and the liberation of women.* New York, Harper and Rox, 69, xii-316 p.

2574   SIMONS, G. L. *A history of sex.* London, New English Library, 70, 188 p.

2575   SPREY, J. "On the institutionalization of sexuality", *J. Marriage Family* 31(3), aug 69 : 432-440.

2576   VAN USSEL, J. "Socio-economische grondslagen van de seksuele moraal" (Socio-economic foundations of sexual ethics), *Tijds. soc. Wetensch.* 14(2), 1969 : 155-206.

2577   WINICK, C. *The new people: desexualization in American life.* New York, Pegasus, 69, 384 p. CR: M. GORDON, *Amer. sociol. R.* 35(4), aug 70 : 802-803.

2578   WOHL, J.; DUNLOP, A. "Sexual attitudes of Thai students: an exploratory cross-cultural study", *Hum. Org.* 29(3), 1970 : 190-203.

2579   WRIGHT, H. *Sex and society.* Seattle, University of Washington Press, 69, 140 p.

C.62   Marriage
         Mariage

[See also / Voir aussi: 556, 669, 771, 807, 826, 871, 1929, 1965, 1968, 2004, 2225, 2556, 2633, 2710, 4223, 5306]

2580   AHMED, F. "Age at marriage in Pakistan", *J. Marriage Family* 31(4), nov 69 : 799-807.

2581   ARDIGO, A. "Introduzione all'analisi sociologica del divorzio" (Introduction to the sociological analysis of divorce), *Sociologia (Roma)* 4(1), jan 70 : 197-214. With a discussion : 215-250.

2582   BABB, L. A. "Marriage and malevolence: the uses of sexual opposition in a Hindu pantheon", *Ethnology* 9(2), apr 70 : 137-148.

2583   BAYER, A. E. "Life plans and marriage age: an application of path analysis", *J. Marriage Family* 31(3), aug 69 : 551-558.

2584   BELL, R. R. "Marriage and family differences among lower class Negro and East-Indian women in Trinidad", *Race* 12(1), jul 70 : 59-75.

2585   BERARDO, F. M. "Survivorship and social isolation: the case of the aged widower", *Family Coordinator* 19(1), jan 70 : 11-25.

2586   BIENVENU, M. J. "Measurement of marital communication", *Family Coordinator* 19(1), jan 70 : 26-31.

2587   BOHANNAN, P. (ed.). *Divorce and after.* Garden City, N. Y., Doubleday, 70, vi-301 p.

2588 BURMA, J. H.; CRESTER, G. A.; SEACREST, T. "A comparison of the occupational status of intramarrying and intermarrying couples: a research note", *Sociol. soc. Res.* 54(4), jul 70 : 508-519.

2589 CAMPOREALE, I.; VERDE, F. "Matrimonio e famiglia oggi in Italia" (Marriage and family today in Italy), *Vita soc.* 27(139), 1970 : 3-10.

2590 CARTER, H.; GLICK, P. C. *Marriage and divorce: a social and economic study.* Cambridge, Mass., Harvard University Press, 70, xxix-451 p.

2591 COOMBS, L. C. *et al.* "Premarital pregnancy and status before and after marriage", *Amer. J. Sociol.* 75(5), mar 70 : 800-820.

2592 DITZION, S. H. *Marriage, morals and sex in America; a history of ideas.* New York, Octagon Books, 69, 460 p.

2593 FERRISS, A. L. "An indicator of marriage dissolution by marriage cohort", *Soc. Forces* 48(3), mar 70 : 356-365.

2594 FESTINGER, G. "Conditions de symétrie des prohibitions lignagères de mariage: application au cas Omaha", *Homme* 10(2), apr-jun 70 : 109-115.

2595 GREELEY, A. M. "Religious intermarriage in a denominational society", *Amer. J. Sociol.* 75(6), mai 70 : 926-948.

2596 GREY, A. L. (ed.). *Man, woman and marriage: small group process in the family.* New York, Atherton Press, 70, 225 p.

2597 GULATI, S. C. "Impact of literacy, urbanization and sex-ratio on age at marriage in India", *Artha Vijnana* 11(4), dec 69 : 685-697.

2598 HARČEV, A. G.; GOLOD, S. I. "Molodež' i brak" (Youth and marriage), *Učen. Zap. (Leningr. gos. Univ. nauč. issled. Inst. kompleks. sociol. Issled.)* (6), 1969 : 78-88.

2599 HOÓŹ, I. "A házásságok stabilitásának hatása a házas nök termékenységére" (The influence of marital stability on the fecundity of married women), *Demográfia* 13(1-2), 1970 : 95-109. [Hungary.]

2600 HUBER, H. "Le principe de la réciprocité dans le mariage Nyende", *Africa (London)* 39(3), jul 69 : 260-274.

2601 HUDSON, J. W.; HENZE, L. F. "Campus values in mate selection: a replication", *J. Marriage Family* 31(4), nov 69 : 772-775.

2602 Bibl. XIX-2254. KAUPP, P. *Das Heiratsinserat im sozialen Wandel. Ein Beitrag zur Soziologie der Partnerwahl* (Social transformation of the marriage announcement. A contribution to the sociology of the choice of the partner). CR: H. JÜLKENBECK, *Kölner Z. Soziol. u. soz.-Psychol.* 22(3), sep 70 : 613-615.

2603 KELLEY, R. K. *Courtship, marriage, and the family.* New York, Harcourt, Brace and World, 69, 629 p. CR: D. P. IRISH, *Amer. sociol. R.* 35(1), feb 70 : 174-175.

2604 KENKEL, W. F. "Marriage and the family in modern science fiction", *J. Marriage Family* 31(1), feb 69 : 6-14.

2605 KLEMER, R. H. *Marriage and family relationships.* New York, Harper and Row, 70, xii-340 p.

2606 KOOY, G. A. *Het huwelijk in Nederland* (Marriage in the Netherlands). Utrecht, Spectrum, 69, 192 p.

2607 KUCERA, M. "Divortialité suivant la durée de l'existence du mariage", *Demosta* 2, 1969 : 150-157. [Tchécoslovaquie.]

2608 LIVELY, E. L. "Toward concept clarification: the case of marital interaction", *J. Marriage Family* 31(1), feb 69 : 108-115.

2609 MONAHAN, T. P. "Are interracial marriages really less stable ?", *Soc. Forces* 48(4), jun 70 : 461-473.

2610 MONTGOMERY, J. E. "Impact of housing patterns on marital interaction", *Family Coordinator* 19(3), jul 70 : 267-275.

2611 MORIOKA, K. "Préférence pour le mariage non-mixte parmi les Amidistes 'Shin' du bouddhisme japonais", *Soc. Compass* 17(1), 1970 : 9-20.

2612 MULHEARN, S. J. Interfaith marriage and adult religious practice", *Sociol. Anal.* 30(1), 1969 : 23-31.

2613 PAKRASI, K.; HALDER, A. "Polygynists of urban India, 1960-61", *Ind. J. soc. Res.* 11(1), apr 70 : 49-61.

2614 PEEL, J. "The Hull family survey. I. The survey couples, 1966", *J. biosoc. Sci.* 2(1), jan 70 : 45-70.

2615   PRAIS, S. J.; SCHMOOL, M. "Synagogue marriages in Great Britain, 1966-68", *Jew. J. Sociol.* 12(1), jun 70 : 21-28.

2616   ROUSSEL, L. "Les divorces et les séparations de corps en France (1936-1967)", *Population* 25(2), mar-apr 70 : 275-302.

2617   SAGANT, P. "Mariage par enlèvement chez les Limbu (Népal)", *C. int. Sociol.* 17(48), jan-jun 70 : 71-98.

2618   SAVIRANTA, J. "Avioitumisen alueellinen aspekti" (Spatial aspect of marriages), *Terra* 81(3), 1969 : 233-241. [Finland.]

2619   SCHMITT, R. C. "Age and race differences in divorce in Hawaii", *J. Marriage Family* 31(1), feb 69 : 48-50.

2620   SCHOENFELD, E. "Intermarriage and the small town: the Jewish case", *J. Marriage Family* 31(1), feb 69 : 61-64.

2621   SINGH, T. R. "Widow remarriage among Brahmans", *East. Anthropol.* 22(1), jan-apr 69 : 75-87.

2622   TETE, K. "La dot et sa signification dans la société Ngoli traditionnelle", *R. congol. Adm.* 2(4), 1969 : 178-183.

2623   VEROFF, J.; FELD, S. *Marriage and work in America; a study of motives and roles.* New York, Van Nostrand Reinhold Co., 70, x-404 p.

2624   WALLACE, B. J. "Pagan Gaddang spouse exchange", *Ethnology* 8(2), apr 69 : 183-188.

2625   WALSH, B. M. "A study of Irish country marriage rates, 1961-66", *Popul. Stud.* 24(2), jul 70 : 205-216.

2626   WALSH, B. M. "Marriage rates and population pressure: Ireland, 1871 and 1911", *Econ. Hist. R.* 23(1), apr 70 : 148-162.

2627   YOUNG, P. D. "A structural model of Ngawbe marriage", *Ethnology* 9(1), jan 70 : 85-95. [Panama.]

C.63   Family, kinship
**   Famille, parenté**

[See also / Voir aussi: F.211; 427, 492, 556, 653, 704, 738, 745, 877, 897, 901, 935, 966, 968, 1094, 1147, 1166, 1245, 1641, 1949, 1969, 1970, 2191, 2446, 2584, 2589, 2603, 2604, 2605, 2746, 2756, 2773, 2776, 4216, 4230, 4247, 4256, 4525, 4996, 5125, 5152, 5243]

2628   ALBERONI, F. "Famiglia e lotta di classe" (Family and class struggle), *Rass. ital. Sociol.* 11(1), jan-mar 70 : 29-48. [USA.]

2629   ALKIRE, A. A. "Social power and communication within families of disturbed and non-disturbed preadolescents", *J. Person. soc. Psychol.* 13(4), dec 69 : 335-349.

2630   AMMEN, A. *Die ausserhäusliche Berufstätigkeit des Vaters; eine empirische Untersuchung zur Familiensoziologie* (Father's outside occupation; an empirical research on family sociology). Stuttgart, F. Enke, 70, viii-177 p.

2631   "Aperçu sur l'organisation traditionnelle de la famille au Burundi", *Probl. soc. congol.* 86, sep 69 : 3-26.

2632   ARDIGO, A. "Problemi, tendenze, prospettive della famiglia nella società stratificata" (Problems, trends and prospects of the family in stratified society), *Quad. Sci. soc.* 9(1), 1970 : 3-35.

2633   BAILYN, L. "Career and family orientations of husbands and wives in relation to marital happiness", *Hum. Relat.* 23(2), apr 70 : 97-113.

2634   Bibl. XIX-2270. BENSON, L. *Fatherhood: a sociological perspective.* CR: B. E. SEGAL, *Amer. sociol. R.* 34(6), dec 69 : 1008-1009.

2635   BIE, P. DE; PRESVELOU, C. "Young families: a survey of facts and guiding images in the European and American literature", *J. Marriage Family* 31(2), mai 69 : 328-338.

2636   BILLER, H. B.; WEISS, S. D. "The father-daughter relationship and the personality development of the female", *J. genet. Psychol.* 116(1), mar 70 : 79-94.

2637   BJØRNDAL, I.; SCHJELDERUP, I.; SALOMONSEN, M. *Individ, familie, samfunn* (Individual, family, society). Stavanger, Nomi, 70, 138 p. + 2 l.

2638   CAMPANINI, G. "La contestazione nella famiglia e nella società" (Contestation in family and society), *Orientam. soc.* 26(4), apr 70 : 243-268.

2639 CAMPANINI, G. "La stabilità della famiglia come problema sociale" (Family stability as a social problem), *Civitas* 21(3-4), mar-apr 70 : 47-60.

2640 CASTELL, R. "Effect of familiar and unfamiliar environments on proximity behavior of young children", *J. exper. Child Psychol.* 9(3), jun 70 : 342-347.

2641 CHANG, K. H.-K. "The Inkyo system of Southwestern Japan: its functional utility in the household setting", *Ethnology* 9(4), oct 70 : 342-357. [The impact of father retirement practice on the household system.]

2642 CHRISTENSEN, H. T. "Normative theory derived from cross-cultural family research", *J. Marriage Family* 31(2), mai 69 : 209-222. With a note by R. R. BELL, 223-224.

2643 CHU, H. J.; HOLLINGSWORTH, J. S. "A cross-cultural study of the relationships between family types and social stratification", *J. Marriage Family* 31(2), mai 69 : 322-327.

2644 COHEN, M. L. "Agnatic kinship in South Taiwan", *Ethnology* 8(2), apr 69 : 167-182.

2645 CROCKETT, H. J.; BABCHUK, N.; BALLWEG, J. A. "Change in religious affiliation and family stability: a second study", *J. Marriage Family* 31(3), aug 69 : 464-468.

2646 CROSS, H. J. "The relation of parental training to conceptual structure in preadolescents", *J. genet. Psychol.* 116(2), jun 70 : 197-202.

2647 CUISENIER, J.; SEGALEN, M.; VIRVILLE, M. DE. "Pour l'étude de la parenté dans les sociétés européennes: le programme d'ordinateur ARCHIV", *Homme* 10(3), jul-sep 70 : 27-74.

2648 DELHEES, K. H.; CATTELL, R. B.; SWENEY, A. B. "The structure of parents' intrafamilial attitudes and sentiments measured by objective tests and a vector model", *J. soc. Psychol.* 82(2), dec 70 : 253-261.

2649 DIRKS, S. *La famille musulmane. Son évolution au 20è siècle.* Paris, Mouton, 69, 168 p.

2650 ECKHARDT, K. W.; SCHRINER, E. C. "Familial conflict, adolescent rebellion, and political expression", *J. Marriage Family* 31(3), aug 69 : 494-499.

2651 EDWARDS, J. N. "Familial behavior as social exchange", *J. Marriage Family* 31(3), aug 69 : 518-526.

2652 Bibl. XIX-2287. EDWARDS, J. N.; PAGE, C. H. (eds.). *The family and change.* CR: J. H. KAUFFMAN, *Amer. sociol. R.* 35(4), aug 70 : 782-783.

2653 EVANS, R. H.; SMITH, N. R. "A selected paradigm of family behavior", *J. Marriage Family* 31(3), aug 69 : 512-517.

2654 FARMER, M. E. *The family.* New York, Humanities Press, 70, vii-168 p.

2655 FERRISS, A. L. *Indicators of change in the American family.* New York, Russell Sage Foundation, 70, xii-145 p.

2656 FESTINGER, G. "Nouvelle analyse formelle de la terminologie de parenté seneca", *Homme* 10(1), jan-mar 70 : 77-93.

2657 FILESI, T. *L'istituto della famiglia nelle costituzioni degli stati africani* (The family institution in the constitution of the African States). Milano, A. Giufrè, 69, vii-318 p.

2658 FORTES, M. *Kinship and the social order: the legacy of Lewis Henry Morgan.* London, Routledge and K. Paul, 70, xii-347 p.

2659 GAULTHIER, J. P. "Sociologie et famille", *Pour la Vie* (3-4), 1969 : 259-284.

2660 GLASSER, P. H.; LOIS, N. (eds.). *Families in crisis.* New York, Harper and Row, 70, vi-405 p.

2661 GOODY, J. "Adoption in cross-cultural perspective", *Comp. Stud. Soc. Hist.* 11(1), jan 69 : 55-78.

2662 GOODY, J. R. *Comparative studies in kinship.* Stanford, Calif., Stanford University Press, 69, xvii-261 p.

2663 GORDON, D. N. "Societal complexity and kinship: family organization or rules of residence", *Pacific sociol. R.* 13(4), 1970 : 252-262.

2664 GRECO, G. "Potere e parentela nella Sicilia nuova" (Power and kinship in new Sicily), *Quad. Sociol.* 19(1), jan-mar 70 : 3-41.

2665 GURMAN, A. S. "The role of the family in underachievement", *J. School Psychol.* 8(1), 1970 : 48-53.

2666 HARRIS, C. C. (ed.). *Readings in kinship in urban society.* Oxford-New York, Pergamon Press, 70, x-397 p.

2667 HARRIS, C. C. *The family; an introduction.* New York, Praeger, 69, 212 p.

2668 HARRY, J. "Family localism and social participation", *Amer. J. Sociol.* 75(5), mar 70 : 821-827.

2669   HARTLEY, S. F. "Illegitimacy among 'married' women in England and Wales", *J. Marriage Family* 31(4), nov 69 : 793-798.

2670   HARTLEY, S. F. "Standardization procedures in the analysis of cross-national variations in illegitimacy measures", *J. biosoc. Sci.* 2(2), apr 70 : 95-110.

2671   HEINE, B. "Lingua franca und Familie in Afrika" (Lingua franca and the family in Africa), *Sociologus* 20(1), 1970 : 42-55.

2672   HEISKANEN, V. S. "Community structure and kinship ties: extended family relations in the Finnish communes", *Int. J. comp. Sociol.* 10(3-4), sep-dec 69 : 251-262.

2673   HENDERSHOT, G. E. "Familial satisfaction, birth order, and fertility values", *J. Marriage Family* 31(1), feb 69 : 27-33.

2674   HILL, R.; KÖNIG, R. (eds.). *Families in East and West; socialization process and kinship ties.* The Hague, Mouton, 70, xiv-630 p.

2675   HOPKINS, N. A. "A formal account of Chalchihuitán Tztozil kinship terminology", *Ethnology* 8(1), jan 69 : 85-102.

2676   HSIEN, J. C. "A note to utilizing Murdock's ethnographic survey materials for cross-cultural family research", *J. Marriage Family* 31(2), mai 69 : 311-314.

2677   HUNT, E. "The meaning of kinship in San Juan: genealogical and social models", *Ethnology* 8(1), jan 69 : 37-53.

2678   JACOBY, A. P. "Transition to parenthood: a reassessment", *J. Marriage Family* 31(4), nov 69 : 720-727.

2679   JACQUARD, A. "Panmixie et structure des familles", *Population* 25(1), jan-feb 70 : 69-76.

2680   JAFFE, E. D. "Adoption in Israel", *Jew. J. Sociol.* 12(2), dec 70 : 135-146.

2681   JAFFE, E. D. "Professional background and the utilization of institutional care of children as a solution to family crisis", *Hum. Relat.* 23(1), feb 70 : 15-21.

2682   JOLAS, T.; VERDIER, Y.; ZONABEND, F. " 'Parler famille' ", *Homme* 10(3), jul-sep 70 : 5-26.

2683   JUILLERAT, B. "Note sur trois relations de parenté chez les Muktelé (Nord Cameroun)", *C. Ét. afr.* 10(3), 1970 : 469-478.

2684   KENNETT, K. F.; CROPLEY, A. J. "Intelligence, family's size and socio-economic status", *J. biosoc. Sci.* 2(3), jul 70 : 227-236.

2685   KLEIN, J. F. *et al.* "Pilgrim's progress I: recent developments in family theory", *J. Marriage Family* 31(4), nov 69 : 677-687.

2686   KOCH, K.-F. "Structure and variability in the Jalé kinship terminology: a formal analysis", *Ethnology* 9(3), jul 70 : 263-301.

2687   KUČERA, M. "Změny ve vývoji rodíny v poslednich letech" (Changes in family dynamics over the last years), *Demografia* 11(4), oct-dec 69 : 289-302. [Czechoslovakia.]

2688   LAND, H. *Large families in London: a study of 86 families.* London, Bell, 69, 154 p.

2689   LAW, J. A. "Naua affinal kinship: a comparative study", *Ethnology* 8(1), jan 69 : 103-121.

2690   LeMASTERS, E. E. *Parents in modern America: a sociological analysis.* Homewood, Ill., Dorsey Press, 70, xiii-232 p.

2691   LIMA DOS SANTOS, M. DE. "Família e 'socialização': um aspecto da evolução social contemporânea" (Family and socialization: an aspect of contemporary social evolution), *Análise soc.* 7(25-26), 1969 : 67-84.

2692   LIU, W. T.; RUBEL, A. J.; YU, E. "The urban family of Cebu: a profile analysis", *J. Marriage Family* 31(2), mai 69 : 393-402.

2693   LUPRI, E. "Contemporary authority patterns in the West German family: a study in cross-national validation", *J. Marriage Family* 31(1), feb 69 : 134-144.

2694   LUPRI, E. "Social correlates for family authority patterns: the West German case", *Sociol. rur.* 10(2), 1970 : 99-119.

2695   MANTELL, D. M. "Die Bedeutung von Familienstruktur und Erziehung für das politische Verhalten" (The role of family structure and education in family behavior), *Polit. Stud. (München)* 21(191), mai-jun 70 : 277-285.

2696   MARMIER, M. P. *Sociologie de l'adoption: étude de sociologie juridique.* Paris, R. Pichon et R. Durand-Auzias, 69, iv-422 p.

2697   MARTIN, R. P. V. "Structure de la famille chez les Serer et les Wolof au Sénégal", *Population* 25(4), jul-aug 70 : 771-796.

2698   MARTINSON, F. M. *Family in society.* New York, Dodd, Mead, 70, xi-395 p.

2699   MATRAS, J.; ROSENFELD, J. M.; SALZBERGER, L. "On the predicaments of Jewish families in Jerusalem", *Int. J. comp. Sociol.* 10(3-4), sep-dec 69 : 235-250.

2700 MATSUBARA, H. "The family and Japanese society after World War II", *Develop. Econ.* 7(4), dec 69 : 499-526.

2701 McELHANON, K. A. "Komba kinship terminology", *Ethnology* 8(3), jul 69 : 273-277.

2702 MICHEL, A.; LAUTMAN FEYRABEND, F. "Real number of children and conjugal interaction in French urban families; a comparison with American families", *J. Marriage Family* 31(2), mai 69 : 359-363.

2703 MIRANDE, A. M. "Extended kinship ties, friendship relations, and community size: an exploratory inquiry", *Rur. Sociol.* 35(2), jun 70 : 262-266.

2704 MISHLER, E. G.; WAXLER, N. E. *Interaction in families: an experimental study of family processes and schizophrenia.* New York, J. Wiley, 68, 436 p. CR: F. L. STRODTBECK, *Amer. J. Sociol.* 75(5), mar 70 : 871-872; A. G. GERLING, *Amer. sociol. R.* 35(1), feb 70 : 173-174.

2705 MOGEY, J. M. "Research on the family. The search for world trends", *J. Marriage Family* 31(2), mai 69 : 225-232.

2706 MURDOCK, G. P. "Kin term patterns and their distribution", *Ethnology* 9(2), apr 70 : 165-207.

2707 NAFZIGER, E. W. "The effect of the Nigerian extended family on entrepreneurial activity", *Econ. Develop. cult. Change* 18(1, *Part I*), oct 69 : 25-33.

2708 NAMBOODIRI, N. K. "On the relation between economic status and family size preferences when status differentials in contraceptive instrumentalities are eliminated", *Popul. Stud.* 24(2), jul 70 : 233-239.

2709 NOBLE, T. "Family breakdown and social networks", *Brit. J. Sociol.* 21(2), jun 70 : 135-150.

2710 NUKUNYA, G. K. *Kinship and marriage among the Anlo Ewe.* London, University of London, Athlone Press; New York, Humanities Press, 69, x-217 p.

2711 OLSON, D. H. "The measurement of family power by self-report and behavioral methods", *J. Marriage Family* 31(3), aug 69 : 545-550.

2712 OSMOND, M. W. "A cross-cultural analysis of family organization", *J. Marriage Family* 31(2), mai 69 : 302-310.

2713 OTTO, H. A. (ed.). *The family in search of a future; alternate models for moderns.* New York, Appleton-Century-Crofts, 70, xiv-204 p.

2714 PAVALKO, R. M.; WALIZER, M. H. "Parental education: differences and the college plans of youth", *Sociol. soc. Res.* 54(1), oct 69 : 80-89.

2715 PETERSEN, K. K. "Kin network research: a plea for comparability", *J. Marriage Family* 31(2), mai 69 : 271-280.

2716 PINSENT, R. F. J. H. "Some characteristics of a family", *J. biosoc. Sci.* 2(3), jul 70 : 199-212.

2717 POPE, H. "Negro-white differences in decisions regarding illegitimate children", *J. Marriage Family* 31(4), nov 69 : 756-764.

2718 RADVANOVA, S. "Rapports juridiques entre parents et enfants dans le droit familial tchécoslovaque", *B. Dr. tchécosl.* 26(1-4), dec 68 : 16-29.

2719 RAU, M.; STOVER, L.; GUERNEY, B. G. Jr. "Relationship of socio-economic status, sex, and age to aggression of emotionally disturbed children in mothers' presence", *J. genet. Psychol.* 116(1), mar 70 : 95-100.

2720 REHBERG, R. A.; SINCLAIR, J.; SCHAFER, W. E. "Adolescent achievement behavior, family authority structure and parental socialization practices", *Amer. J. Sociol.* 75(6), mai 70 : 1012-1034.

2721 REISS, D.; SHERIFF, W. H. Jr. "A computer-automated procedure for testing some experiences of family membership", *Behav. Sci.* 15(5), sep 70 : 431-443.

2722 RIDINGTON, R. "Kin categories versus kin groups: a two-section system without sections", *Ethnology* 8(4), oct 69 : 460-467.

2723 ROHNER, R. P. "Parental rejection, food deprivation, and personality development: tests of alternative hypotheses", *Ethnology* 9(4), oct 70 : 414-427.

2724 ROSENTHAL, G. S. (ed.). *The Jewish family in a changing world.* New York, T. Yoseloff, 70, 367 p.

2725 RUANO, B. J.; BRUCE, J. D.; McDERMOTT, M. M. "Pilgrim's progress II: recent trends and prospects in family research", *J. Marriage Family* 31(4), nov 69 : 688-698.

2726 RÜBERG, R. "Autorität in der Familie" (Authority in the family), *Ehe* 6(6), 1969 : 145-163.

2727 SAFILIOS-ROTHSCHILD, C. "Family sociology or wives' family sociology? A cross-cultural examination of decision-making", *J. Marriage Family* 31(2), mai 69 : 290-301.

2728 SCHLESINGER, B.; STRAKHOVSKY, F. (eds.). *The one-parent family. Perspectives and annotated bibliography.* Toronto, University of Toronto Press, 69, xiv-132 p.

2730 SPREY, J. "The family as a system in conflict", *J. Marriage Family* 31(4), nov 69 : 699-706.

2731 STRAUS, M. A. *Family analysis: readings and replications of selected studies.* Chicago, Ill., Rand McNally and Co., 69, 222 p. CR: R. SENNETT, *Amer. sociol. R.* 35(3), jun 70 : 582.

2732 SUNDBERG, N. *et al.* "Family cohesiveness and autonomy of adolescents in India and the U.S.", *J. Marriage Family* 31(2), mai 69 : 403-407.

2733 SUSSMAN, M. B. "Cross-cultural family research: one view from the 'Catbird Seat' ", *J. Marriage Family* 31(2), mai 69 : 203-208.

2734 SWANSON, G. E. *Rules of descent; studies in the sociology of parentage.* Ann Arbor, University of Michigan, 69, v-108 p.

2735 SWEETSER, D. A. "The structure of sibling relationships", *Amer. J. Sociol.* 76(1), jul 70 : 47-58.

2736 TAYLOR, D. L. "The changing German family", *Int. J. comp. Sociol.* 10(3-4), sep-dec 69 : 299-302.

2737 TOMEH, A. K. "Birth order and kinship affiliation", *J. Marriage Family* 31(1), feb 69 : 19-26.

2738 TORRES, K. S. "Intra-family communication and juvenile delinquency", *Sociol. Quart.* 11(3), 1970 : 366-373.

2739 VATUK, S. "Reference, address, and fictive kinship in urban North India", *Ethnology* 8(3), jul 69 : 255-272.

2740 VINIČENKO, K. T. "Sem'ja kak ob'ekt i sub'ekt obščestvennogo soznanija" (Family as an object and a subject of social knowledge), *Izv. Tomsk. politehn. Inst.* 82, 1969 : 82-92.

2741 WICKE, C. E.; CHASE-SARDI, M. "Componential analysis of Chulupi (Asjluslay) kinship terminology", *Ethnology* 8(4), oct 69 : 484-493.

2742 WILLIE, C. V. (ed.). *The family life of Black people.* Columbus, Ohio, Merrill, 70, x-341 p.

2743 WYNN, M. *Family policy.* London, Joseph, 70, 355 p.

2744 YADAVA, J. S. "Kinship groups in a Haryana village", *Ethnology* 8(4), oct 69 : 494-502.

2745 ZGHAL, A. "Système de parenté et système coopératif dans les campagnes tunisiennes", *Civilisations* 19(4), 1969 : 483-497.

C.64   The social position of women
Statut social des femmes

[See also / Voir aussi: 1388, 1666, 1950, 1960, 1974, 2007, 2186, 2573, 2584, 2585, 2591, 3242, 3257, 3338, 4214, 5196, 5252, 5490]

2746 ALDOUS, J. "Wives' employment status and lower-class men as husband-fathers: support for the Moynihan thesis", *J. Marriage Family* 31(3), aug 69 : 468-476.

2747 ASTIN, H. S. *The woman doctorate in America: origins, career, and family.* New York, Russell Sage Foundation, 69, xii-196 p.

2748 BARCLAY, L. E. "A group approach to young unwed mothers", *Soc. Casewk* 50(7), 1970 : 379-384.

2749 BAYO, E. *Trabajos duros de la mujer* (Woman's hard labour). Barcelona, Ed. Plaza y Janes, 70, 257 p.

2750 BERENT, J. "Some demographic aspects of female employment in Eastern Europe and the USSR", *Int. Lab. R.* 101(2), feb 70 : 175-192.

2751 BEREŽNAJA, N. A. *Položenie i bor'ba trudjaščihsja ženščin stran Latinskoj Ameriki* (The situation and the struggle of working women in Latin American countries). Moskva, Nauka, 69, 192 p.

2752 BIRD, C.; BRILLER, S. W. *Born female; the high cost of keeping women down.* Rev. ed. New York, McKay, 70, xiv-392 p. [USA.]

2753 BOSERUP, E. *Woman's role in economic development.* London, Allen and Unwin; New York, St Martin Press, 70, 283 p.

2754 Bibl. XIX-2342. BROWN, D. R. (ed.). *The role and status of women in the Soviet Union.* CR: E. E. ELMER, *Amer. sociol. R.* 35(1), feb 70 : 182-183.

2755 BÜHRIG, M.; SCHMID-AFFOLTER, A. *Die Frau in der Schweiz* (Women in Switzerland). Bern, Haupt, 69, 131 p.

2756 CARISSE, C.; DUMAZEDIER, J. "Valeurs familiales de sujets féminins novateurs: perspectives d'avenir", *Sociol. et Soc.* 2(2), nov 70 : 265-281.

2757 "Condition féminine (La)", *Nef* 26(38), 1969 : 160 p.

2758 COSMELLI, M. E. M. "A mulher profissionalmente activa—sua vida familiar, seus interesses e aspirações" (The professionally active woman: her family life, her interests and aspirations), *Estud. polít.* 7(1), 1969 : 143-214. [Portugal.]

2759 DAVIS, A. E. "Women as a minority group in higher academics", *Amer. Sociologist* 4(2), mai 69 : 95-99.

2760 EPSTEIN, C. F. "Encountering the male establishment: sex-status limits on women's careers in the professions", *Amer. J. Sociol.* 75(6), mai 70 : 965-982.

2761 EPSTEIN, C. F. *Woman's place; options and limits in professional careers.* Berkeley, University of California Press, 70, x-221 p.

2762 "Femme à l époque de la science et de la technique (La)", *Impact* 20(1), jan-mar 70 : 112 p.

2763 FIRESTONE, S. *The dialectic of sex; the case for feminist revolution.* New York, Morrow, 70, 274 p.

2764 FREDRINSSON, I. "The future role of women", *Futures (Guildford)* 1(6), dec 69 : 532-540.

2765 FULLES, M. *Frauen in Partei und Parlament* (Women in parties and parliament). Köln, Verlag Wissenschaft und Politik, 69, 159 p.

2766 GENDELL, M.; ROSSELL, U. G. "The trends and patterns of the economic activity of women in Latin America during the 1950's", *Estadística (Washington)* 26(100), sep 68 : 561-576.

2767 HAAVIO-MANNILA, E. "Some consequences of women's emancipation", *J. Marriage Family* 31(1), feb 69 : 123-134.

2768 HAAVIO-MANNILA, E. "The position of Finnish women: regional and cross-national comparisons", *J. Marriage Family* 31(2), mai 69 : 339-347.

2769 HOCHSCHILD, A.; ROSSI, A. S. "Status of women in graduate departments of sociology, 1968-69", *Amer. Sociologist* 5(1), feb 70 : 1-12.

2770 KANOWITZ, L. *Women and the law: the unfinished revolution.* Albuquerque, N.M., University of New Mexico Press, 69, 312 p. CR: R. F. THOME, *Amer. sociol. R.* 35(4), aug 70 : 805.

2771 KNUDSEN, D. D. "The decline in status of women: popular myths and the failure of functionalist thought", *Soc. Forces* 48(2), dec 69 : 183-193.

2772 KURZYNOWSKI, A. "Czynniki warunkujące aktywność zawodową kobiet zamężnych" (Factors conditioning the professional activity of married women), *Biul. IGS* 13(2), 1970 : 37-62.

2773 LAMOUSÉ, A. "Family roles of women: a German example", *J. Marriage Family* 31(1), feb 69 : 145-152.

2774 LILAR, S.; GILBERT-DREYFUS. *Le malentendu du deuxième sexe.* Paris, Presses universitaires de France, 69, 306 p. CR: Y. BROUTIN, *C. int. Sociol.* 17(48), jan-jun 70 : 182-184.

2775 MEHTA, R. *The Western educated Hindu woman.* New York, Asia Publishing House, 70, viii-216 p.

2776 MICHEL, A. "Working wives and family interaction in French and American families", *Int. J. comp. Sociol.* 11(2), jun 70 : 157-165.

2777 MILLETT, K. *Sexual politics.* Garden City, N. Y., Doubleday, 70, xii-393 p.

2778 MIRZA, S. H. *Muslim women's role in the Pakistan movement.* Lahore, Research Society of Pakistan, University of the Punjab, 69, viii-166 p. [English or Urdu.]

2779 MONTANARI, A. "A proposito di sociologia e storia del lavoro femminile" (About the sociology and history of female labour), *Statistica (Bologna)* 29(4), oct-dec 69 : 803-821. [Italy.]

2780 OPPENHEIMER, V. K. *The female labor force in the United States: demographic and economic factors governing its growth and changing composition.* Berkeley, Institute of International Studies, University of California, 70, xii-197 p.

2781 PAULME, M. *et al. Femmes d'Afrique noire.* Paris, Mouton, 70, 280 p.

2782 PÉCHADRE, L.; ROUDY, Y. *La réussite de la femme.* Paris, Denoël, 70, 249-6 p.

2783 "Quelques aspects de la promotion de la femme en Belgique", *Textes et Doc. (Bruxelles)* 254, dec 69 : 1-65.

2784 RIEGEL, R. E. *American women; a story of social change.* Rutherford, Fairleigh Dickinson University Press, 70, 376 p.

2785 ROUX, C. "Tendances récentes de l'activité féminine en France", *Population* 25 (n° spec.), feb 70 : 179-194.

2786 RUNGE, E. *Frauen; Versuche zur Emanzipation* (Women; attempts at emancipation). Frankfurt am Main, Suhrkamp, 69, 268 p.

2787 SAFFIOTI, H. I. B. *A mulher na sociedade de classes; mito e realidade* (The woman in class society; myth and reality). São Paulo, Quatro Artes, 69, 404 p.

2788 SALAFF, J. W.; MERKELE, J. "Women in revolution: the lessons of the Soviet Union and China", *Berkeley J. Sociol.* 15, 1970 : 166-191.

2789 SALVIA, M. R. DE. "Il velo in Algeria: considerazioni sul valo della donna nei paesi arabi" (The veil in Algeria. Considerations on the woman's role in Arab countries), *Terzo Mondo* 3(7-8), mar-jun 70 : 97-107.

2790 SARACENO RUSCONI, C. "La maternità come responsabilità collettiva" (Maternity as a collective responsibility), *Crit. sociol. (Roma)* 15, 1970 : 69-87.

2791 SARACENO RUSCONI, C. "Condizione femminile come condizione di classe ?" (Female condition as a class condition), *Crit. sociol. (Roma)* 12, 1969-70 : 42-55.

2792 SHIMAZU, C. "Nihon ni okeru fujin kaihô undô to sono shisô" (Liberation of women in Japan: its theory and practice), *Shisô* 526, 1968 : 78-91.

2793 SIMON, R. J.; CROTTS, G.; MAHAN, L. "An empirical note about married women and their friends", *Soc. Forces* 48(4), jun 70 : 520-525.

2794 SOURIAU, C. "La société féminine en Libye", *R. Occident musul. Méditerr.* 6, 1969 : 127-155.

2795 TAE-YOUNG, L. "The legal status of Korean women", *Koreana Quart.* 11(4), 1969-70 : 31-48.

2796 TATARINOVA, N. I. *Women in the USSR, at home, at work, in society.* Moscow, Novosti Press Agency Publishing House, 69, 109 p.

2797 WARE, C. *Woman power: the movement for women's liberation.* New York, Tower Publications, 70, 176 p.

C.7   ETHNIC GROUPS
GROUPES ETHNIQUES

C.70   General studies
Études générales

2798 BARTH, F. (ed.). *Ethnic groups and boundaries. The social organization of culture difference.* Bergen, Universitetsforlaget; London, Allen and Unwin, 69, 153 p. CR: U. HANNERZ, *Acta sociol.* 13(2), 1970 : 132-133; M. FREEDMAN, *Brit. J. Sociol.* 21(2), jun 70 : 231.

2799 BATES, R. H. "Approaches to the study of ethnicity", *C. Ét. afr.* 10(4), 4 trim 70 : 546-561.

2800 BORHEK, J. T. "Ethnic-group cohesion", *Amer. J. Sociol.* 76(1), jul 70 : 33-46.

2801 SHEPHERD, G. W. Jr. *et al.* (ed.). *Race among nations: a conceptual approach.* Lexington, Mass., Heath Lexington Books, 70, xvii-238 p.

2802 STOCKING, G. W. Jr. *Race, culture and evolution: essays in the history of anthropology.* London, Collier-Macmillan, 69, 380 p. CR: D. G. MacRAE, *Brit. J. Sociol.* 20(4), dec 69 : 465.

2803 VAN DEN BERGHE, P. L. *Race and ethnicity; essays in comparative sociology.* New York, Basic Books, 70, viii-312 p.

2804 WITTERMANS, T. "The ethnic group as a matrix of social orientation", *Sociol. int. (Berlin)* 8(2), 1970 : 179-190.

C.71 Race relations
Relations raciales

C.711 *General works on racism and race relations*
Généralités sur le racisme et les relations raciales

[See also / Voir aussi: 1822, 2742]

2805 COLEMAN, H. D. "The problem of anti-semitism under the International Convention on the Elimination of all forms of Racial Discrimination", *R. Dr. Homme* 2(4), 1969 : 609-631.

2806 HUGHES, H. (comp.). *Racial and ethnic relations*. Boston, Allyn and Bacon, 70, xii-211 p.

2807 KORTE, C.; MILGRAM, S. "Acquaintance networks between racial groups: application of the small world method", *J. Person. soc. Psychol.* 15(2), jun 70 : 101-108.

2808 KUPER, L. "Continuities and discontinuities in race relations: evolutionary or revolutionary change", *C. Ét. afr.* 10(3), 3 trim 70 : 361-383.

2809 MALPASS, R. S.; KRAVITS, J. "Recognition for faces of own and other race", *J. Person. soc. Psychol.* 13(4), dec 69 : 330-334.

2810 MASON, P. *Race relations*. London-New York, Oxford University Press, 70, viii-181 p.

2811 PARAF, P. *Le racisme dans le monde*. 3e éd. mise à jour. Paris, Payot, 69, 223 p.

2812 REX, J. *Race relations in sociological theory*. London, Weidenfeld and Nicholson; New York, Schocken Books, 70, 169 p.

2813 RODINSON, M. "De l'histoire de l'antisémitisme à la sociologie du scandale", *C. int. Sociol.* 17(49), jul-dec 70 : 143-150.

2814 SCHERMERHORN, R. A. *Comparative ethnic relations; a framework for theory and research*. Consulting ed. P. I. ROSE. New York, Random House, 70, xviii-327 p.

2815 SHERMAN, R. B. (ed.). *The Negro and the city*. Englewood Cliffs, N. J., Prentice-Hall, 70, vi-182 p.

2816 SIMON, P.-J. "Ethnisme et racisme ou 'l'école de 1492' ", *C. int. Sociol.* 17(48), jan-jun 70 : 119-152.

C.712 *Descriptive studies by countries*
Études descriptives par régions

C.712(1) *Africa*
Afrique

[See also / Voir aussi: 1916, 2072]

2817 ARCHIBALD, D. "The Afrikaners as an emergent minority", *Brit. J. Sociol.* 20(4), dec 69 : 416-426.

2818 ASCHEIM, S. E. "The communal organization of South African Jewry", *Jew. J. Sociol.* 12(2), dec 70 : 201-232.

2819 BALLINGER, M. *From union to apartheid; a trek to isolation*. New York, Praeger, 69, 499 p.

2820 BECKERS, G. *Religiöse Faktoren in der Entwicklung der südafrikanischen Rassenfrage. Ein Beitrag zur Rolle des Kalvinismus in kolonialen Situationen* (Religious factors in evolution of the South African racial problem. A contribution on the role of Calvinism in a colonial situation). München, W. Fink, 69, 169 p.

2821 BERNUS, S. *Particularismes ethniques en milieu urbain: l'exemple de Niamey*. Paris, Musée de l'Homme, 69, 262 p. multigr.

2822 BHATTACHARYA, D. K. "Indians of African origin", *C. Ét. afr.* 10(4), 4 trim 70 : 579-582.

2823 HORRELL, M. *A survey of race relations*. Johannesburg, South African Institute of Race Relations, 69, xi-327 p. [South Africa.]

2824 HORRELL, M. *The African reserves of South Africa*. Johannesburg, South African Institute of Race Relations, 69, 142 p.

2825 JOHNSTONE, F. A. "White prosperity and white supremacy in South Africa today", *Afr. Aff.* 69(275), apr 70 : 124-140.

2826 GORODNOV, V. "Tribalizm kak instrument rasistskoj politiki" (Tribalism as an instrument of racial policy), *Mir. Èkon. meždun. Otnoš.* 10, oct 70 : 46-55. [South Africa.]

2827   KOOY, G. A.; ALBEDA, W.; KWANT, R. C. *Apartheid en arbeidsbestel in Zuid-Afrika*
        (Apartheid and motivation to work in South Africa). Bussum, Stichting Werkgroep
        2000, 69, 271 p.

2828   MAZRUI, A. A. "Violent contiguity and the politics of retribalization in Africa", *J. int.
        Aff.* 23(1), 1969 : 89-105.

2829   MISTROTIGO, L. " 'L'apartheid' nella società sud-africana" (Apartheid in the South
        African society), *Civitas* 21(5), mai 70 : 45-56.

2830   PARKIN, D. J. "Anti-tribalismus in Uganda" (Anti-tribalism in Uganda), *Int. Afr.
        Forum* 6(6), jun 70 : 369-374.

2831   RAUM, O. F. "Der Afrikaner in der südafrikanischen Industrie" (The African in South
        African industry), *Sociologus* 20(2), 1970 : 97-123.

2832   REINTANZ, G. *Apartheid in Südafrika* (Apartheid in South Africa). Berlin, Staatsverlag
        der DDR, 69, 111 p.

2833   SIMONS, H. J.; SIMONS, R. E. *Class and colour in South Africa, 1850-1950.* Harmonds-
        worth, Penguin, 69, 702 p.

2834   SMOCK, A. C.; SMOCK, D. R. "Ethnicity and attitudes toward development in Eastern
        Nigeria", *J. develop. Areas* 3(4), jul 69 : 499-512.

2835   "Tribalismus in Afrika" (Tribalism in Africa), *Int. Afr. Forum* 5(11), nov 69 : 664-710.

C.712(2)   *America*
               Amérique

[See also / Voir aussi: 729, 881, 882, 891, 903, 970, 1132, 1133, 1588, 1608, 1609, 1649,
1657, 1783, 2408, 2487, 2546, 2584, 3221, 3343, 3571, 3721, 3734, 3969, 3982, 4179,
4202, 4203, 4205, 4232, 4235, 4244, 4288, 5500]

2836   ALLEN, V. L. (ed.). "Ghetto riots", *J. soc. Issues* 26(1), 1970 : 1-239.

2837   ALLOWAY, D. N.; CORDASCO, F. *Minorities and the American city; a sociological primer
        for educators.* New York, McKay, 70, x-124 p.

2838   ALTSHULER, A. A. *Community control: the black demand for participation in large American
        cities.* New York, Pegasus, 70, 238 p.

2839   BARTLEY, N. V. *The rise of massive resistance; race and politics in the South during the
        1950's.* Baton Rouge, Louisiana State University Press, 69, ix-390 p. CR: M. H.
        JONES, *Amer. polit. Sci. R.* 64(3), sep 70 : 917-919.

2840   BEJAR NAVARRO, R. "Prejuicio y discriminación racial en México" (Racial prejudice
        and discrimination in Mexico), *R. mexic. Sociol.* 31(2), apr-jun 69 : 417-433.

2841   BLOCH, H. D. *The circle of discrimination; an economic and social study of the Black man
        in New York.* New York, New York University Press, 69, xiii-274 p.

2842   BOGART, L. (ed.). *Social research and the desegregation of the US Army: two original 1951
        field reports.* Chicago, Ill., Markham Publishing Co., 69, 393 p. CR: S. M. LYMAN,
        Amer. sociol. R. 35(3), jun 70 : 571-572.

2843   BYRNE, D.; IRVIN, C. R. "Attraction toward a Negro stranger as a function of prejudice,
        attitude similarity, and the stranger's evaluation of the subject", *Hum. Relat.* 22(5),
        oct 69 : 397-404.

2844   CANTY, D. *A single society: alternatives to urban apartheid.* New York, Praeger Publishers,
        69, ix-181 p.

2845   CONANT, R. W.; LEVY, S.; LEWIS, R. "Mass polarization. Negro and white attitudes on
        the pace of integration", *Amer. behav. Scientist* 13(2), nov-dec 69 : 247-263.

2846   DAVIDSON, D. "Black culture and liberal sociology", *Berkeley J. Sociol.* 14, 1969 : 164-
        175. With "Searching for White racism and Black culture: a comment on Davidson's
        critique", by S. W. KAPLAN, *ibid.*: 176-180, and "The dilemma of the White liberal:
        a rejoinder to Kaplan", by D. DAVIDSON, *ibid.*: 181-183.

2847   DRAKE, St. C.; CAYTON, H. R. *Black metropolis; a study of Negro life in a northern city.*
        Rev. and enl. ed. 2 vols. New York, Harcourt, Brace and World, 70, lxx-814 p. [USA.]

2848   ELDER, G. H. Jr. "Groups orientations and strategies in racial change", *Soc. Forces*
        48(4), jun 70 : 445-461.

2849   ETZKOWITZ, H.; SCHAFLANDER, G. M. *Ghetto crisis: riots or reconciliation?* Boston, Mass.,
        Little, Brown and Co., 69, 212 p. CR: N. GOLDNER, *Amer. sociol. R.* 35(1), feb 70 :
        148-149. [USA.]

2850 GARZA, J. M. "Race, the achievement syndrome and perception of opportunity", *Phylon* 30(4), 4 trim 69 : 338-354. [USA.]

2851 GOLDBERG, A. I. "Jews in the legal profession: a case of adjustment to discrimination", *Jew. soc. Stud.* 32(2), apr 70 : 148-161.

2852 GOLDSCHMID, M. L. (ed.). *Black Americans and white racism; theory and research.* New York, Holt, Rinehart and Winston, 70, xiii-434 p.

2853 GREEN, E. "Race, social status, and criminal arrest", *Amer. sociol. R.* 35(3), jun 70 : 476-490. [USA.]

2854 HAWKINS, B. W.; LORINSKAS, R. A. (eds.). *The ethnic factor in American politics.* Columbus, Ohio, Merrill, 70, xiv-197 p.

2855 HELM, J. (ed.). *Spanish speaking people in the United States.* Washington, University of Washington Press, 69, 215 p. CR: F. CORDASCO, *Amer. sociol. R.* 34(6), dec 69 : 975.

2856 HENDERSON, W. L.; LEDEBUR, L. C. *Economic disparity; problems and strategies for Black America.* New York, Free Press, 70, xiii-360 p.

2857 HIESTAND, D. L. *Discrimination in employment; an appraisal of the research.* Ann Arbor, Institute of Labor and Industrial Relations, University of Michigan-Wayne State University, 70, 68 p. [USA.]

2858 HOCHBAUM, J. "Change and challenge in Jewish community relations in the United States", *Jew. J. Sociol.* dec 70 : 181-186.

2859 HOLLOWAY, H. *The politics of the Southern Negro: from exclusion to big city organization.* New York, Random House, 69, 374 p. CR: T. JOHNSON, *Amer. polit. Sci. R.* 64(1), mar 70 : 196-197.

2860 HOWARD, J. R. (ed.). *Awakening minorities: American Indians, Mexican Americans, Puerto Ricans.* Chicago, Aldine, 70, 189 p.

2861 KOVEL, J. *White racism; a psychohistory.* New York, Pantheon Books, 70, vii-300 p.

2862 LOPREATO, J. *Italian Americans.* New York, Random House, 70, xiv-204 p.

2863 MASUDA, M.; MATSUMOTO, G. H.; MEREDITH, G. M. "Ethnic identity in three generations of Japanese Americans", *J. soc. Psychol.* 81(2), aug 70 : 199-207.

2864 McCONAHAY, J. B. "Attitudes of Negroes toward the Church following the Los Angeles riot", *Sociol. Anal.* 31(1), 1970 : 12-22.

2865 McCORD, W. et al. *Life styles in the Black ghetto.* New York, W. W. Norton, 69, 334 p. CR: E. E. HARRIS, *Amer. J. Sociol.* 75(4, Part II), jan 70 : 718-719.

2866 MEIER, A.; RUDWICK, E. (eds.). *Black protest in the sixties.* Chicago, Quadrangle Books, 70, xi-355 p.

2867 MELISH, I. H. "Attitudes toward the white minority on a black campus: 1966-1968", *Sociol. Quart.* 11(3), 1970 : 321-330.

2868 MOLOTCH, H. "Racial integration in a transition community", *Amer. sociol. R.* 34(6), dec 69 : 878-893.

2869 MOORE, J. W.; CUÉLLAR, A. *Mexican Americans.* Englewood Cliffs, N. J., Prentice-Hall, 70, xii-172 p.

2870 MÖRNER, M. (ed.). *Race and class in Latin America.* New York, Columbia University Press, 70, viii-309 p.

2871 NASH, G. B.; WEISS, R. (eds.). *The great fear: race in the mind of America.* New York, Holt, Rinehart and Winston, 70, ix-214 p.

2872 NELLI, H. S. *Italians in Chicago, 1880-1930; a study in ethnic mobility.* New York, Oxford University Press, 70, xx-300 p.

2873 NICHOLS, D. C.; MILLS, O. (eds.). *The campus and the racial crisis.* Washington, American Council on Education, 70, xv-309 p.

2874 NORTHRUP, H. R. et al. *Negro employment in basic industry; a study of racial policies in six industries.* Philadelphia, Industrial Research Unit, Wharton School of Finance and Commerce, University of Pennsylvania, 70, xvii-769 p. [USA.]

2875 PETERSEN, W. "The classification of subnations in Hawaii: au essay in the sociology of Knowledge", *Amer. sociol. R.* 34(6), dec 69 : 863-877.

2876 PICCONE STELLA, S. "Aggiornamento sulla situazione della popolazione negra in USA" (Updating on the situation of the black population in the USA), *Crit. sociol. (Roma)* 13, 1970 : 168-175.

2877 RAYMOND, R. "Regional differences in racial discrimination in education and employment", *West. econ. J.* 8(2), jun 70 : 190-208. [USA.]

117

2878   RIESTER, J. "Zur Integration des ostbolivischen Indianer" (The integration of the East-
        Bolivian Indian), *Sociologus* 20(2), 1970 : 172-185.
2879   ROCHE DE COPPENS, P. "The Negro religion in America", *R. int. Sociol. (Madrid)*
        28(109-110), jan-apr 70 : 45-71.
2880   ROSE, H. M. "The development of urban subsystems: the case of the Negro ghetto",
        A. Assoc. Amer. Geogr. 60(1), mar 70 : 1-17. [USA.]
2881   ROSE, P. U. (ed.). *The ghetto and beyond: essays on Jewish life in America.* New York,
        Random House, 69, 504 p. CR: J. N. PORTER, *Amer. J. Sociol.* 76(2), sep 70 : 350-
        351; J. R. MAPSTONE, *Amer. sociol. R.* 35(3), jun 70 : 574-575.
2882   ROSSI, P. H. (ed.). *Ghetto revolts.* Chicago, Aldine Publishing Co., 70, 171 p.
2883   SCHULZ, D. A. *Coming up black—patterns of ghetto socialization.* Englewood Cliffs,
        N. J., Prentice-Hall, 69, xiv-209 p. [USA.]
2884   SCHUMAN, H.; GRUENBERG, B. "The impact of city on racial attitudes", *Amer. J. Sociol.*
        76(2), sep 70 : 213-261. [USA.]
2885   SEELYE, N.; BREWER, M. B. "Ethnocentrism and acculturation of North Americans in
        Guatemala", *J. soc. Psychol.* 80(2), apr 70 : 147-155.
2886   SINGER, B. D.; OSBORN, R. W.; GESCHWENDER, J. A. *Black rioters; a study of social
        factors and communication in the Detroit riot.* Lexington, Mass., Heath Lexington
        Books, 70, ix-117 p.
2887   SMITH, M. W. "Measuring ethnocentrism in Hilo, Hawaii: a social distance scale",
        Sociol. soc. Res. 54(2), jan 70 : 220-236.
2888   SPILERMAN, S. "The causes of racial disturbances: a comparison of alternative ex-
        planations", *Amer. sociol. R.* 35(4), aug 70 : 627-649. [USA.]
2889   URIBE VILLEGAS, Ó. "La situación sociolingüística de México como marco de la condi-
        ción indígena" (The sociolinguistic situation of Mexico as a sign of the indigenous
        condition), *R. mexic. Sociol.* 31(4), oct-dec 69 : 1019-1025.
2890   VAN DER SLIK, J. R. (ed.). *Black conflict with white America; a reader in social and
        political analysis.* Columbus, Ohio, Merrill, 70, vii-344 p.
2891   WARREN, D. I. "Suburban isolation and race tension", *Soc. Probl.* 17(3), 1970 : 324-
        339. [USA.]
2892   WEATHERFORD, W. D.; JOHNSON, C. S. *Race relations; adjustment of whites and Negroes
        in the United States.* New York, Negro Universities Press, 69, x-590 p.
2893   YOUNG, R. P. (ed.). *Roots of rebellion; the evolution of Black politics and protest since
        World War II.* New York, Harper and Row, 70, xii-482 p.

C.712(3) *Asia*
              Asie

2894   ARASARATNAM, S. *Indians in Malaysia and Singapore.* Bombay, Institute of Race Re-
        lations; London, Oxford University Press, 70, xiii-214 p.
2895   ENLOE, C. H. "Issues and integration in Malaysia", *Pacific Aff.* 41(3), 1968 : 372-385.
2896   KHATENA, J. "Relative integration of selected ethnic groups in Singapore", *Sociol. soc.
        Res.* 54(4), jul 70 : 460-465.
2897   OKABE, T. "Shingaporu Kajin to Chugoku" (Chinese in Singapore and China), *Ajia
        Keizai* 9(4), 1968 : 14-37.
2898   RABUSHKA, A. "Affective, cognitive, and behavioral consistency of Chinese-Malay
        interracial attitudes", *J. soc. Psychol.* 82(1), oct 70 : 35-42.
2899   RABUSHKA, A. "The manipulation of ethnic politics in Malaya", *Polity* 2(3), 1970 :
        345-356.
2900   THOMPSON, V. McL.; ADLOFF, R. *Minority problems in Southeast Asia.* New York,
        Russell and Russell, 70, viii-295 p.
2901   WILLMOTT, W. E. "Congregations and associations: the political structure of the
        Chinese community in Phnom-Penh, Cambodia", *Comp. Stud. Soc. Hist.* 11(3),
        jun 69 : 282-301.
2902   ZAKARIA, R. *Rise of Muslims in Indian politics; an analysis of developments from 1885 to
        1906.* Bombay, Somaiya Publications, 70, xvi-427 p.

C.712(4) *Europe*

[See also / Voir aussi: 1089, 1714, 3717, 4129, 4240, 5228]

2903 BAGLEY, C. "Race relations and theories of status consistency", *Race* 11(3), jan 70 : 267-288. [UK.]

2904 BENSIMON, D.; VERDÈS-LEROUX, J. "Les Français et le problème juif. Analyse secondaire d'un sondage de l'IFOP", *Archiv. Sociol. Relig.* 15(29), jan-jun 70 : 53-91.

2905 BERMANT, C. I. *Troubled Eden; an anatomy of British Jewry.* New York, Basic Books, 70, 274 p.

2906 HELLER, C. S. " 'Anti-zionism' and the political struggle within the elite of Poland", *Jew. J. Sociol.* 11(2), dec 69 : 133-150.

2907 HOROWITZ, D. "The British conservatives and the racial issue in the debate on decolonization", *Race* 12(2), oct 70 : 169-188.

2908 JOWELL, R.; PRESCOTT-CLARKE, P. "Racial discrimination and white collar workers in Britain", *Race* 11(4), apr 70 : 397-417.

2909 KATZNELSON, I. "The politics of racial buffering in Nottingham, 1954-1968", *Race* 11(4), apr 70 : 431-446.

2910 KORCAZ, S. *Les Juifs de France et l'État d'Israël.* Paris, Denoël, 69, 213 p. CR: D. BENSIMON, *R. franç. Sociol.* 11(3), jul-sep 70 : 432.

2911 MARSH, A. "Awareness of racial differences in West African and British children", *Race* 11(3), jan 70 : 289-302.

2912 ROSE, F. J. B. *et al. Colour and citizenship: a report on British race relations.* London, Oxford University Press, 69, xxii-815 p. CR: A. PINKNEY, *Amer. J. Sociol.* 75(6), mai 70 : 1061-1064; B. A. INCE, *Amer. polit. Sci. R.* 64(3), sep 70 : 969-970.

2913 UNITED KINGDOM. Community Relations Commission. *Race relations in Britain: selected bibliography with emphasis on Commonwealth immigrants.* London, Community Relations Commission, 69, 14 p.

C.712(5) *Middle East*
Moyen-Orient

2914 HOFMAN, J. E. "The meaning of being a Jew in Israel: an analysis of ethnic identity", *J. Person. soc. Psychol.* 15(3), jul 70 : 196-203.

2915 KAPELIOUK, A. "L'état social, économique, culturel et juridique des Arabes chrétiens en Israël", *Asian Afr. Stud.* (5), 1969 : 51-95.

2916 PERES, Y.; EHRLICH, A.; YUVAL-DAVIS, N. "National education for Arab youth in Israel: a comparative analysis of curricula", *Jew. J. Sociol.* 12(2), dec 70 : 147-164.

2917 ROSHWALD, M. "Who is a Jew in Israel ?", *Jew. J. Sociol.* 12(2), dec 70 : 233-266.

2918 ZÛDÛ, L. *al-Masälat al-Kurdîyat wal-qawmíyat al-'ansârîyat fîl-Irâq* (The Kurdish question and racial nationalities in Iraq). Beirut, Sanâb, 69, 257 p.

C.712(6) *Pacific*
Pacifique

2919 COCHRANE, D. G. "Racialism in the Pacific—a descriptive analysis", *Oceania* 60(1), sep 69 : 1-12.

2920 TAFT, R.; GOLDLUST, J. "The current status of former Jewish refugees in Melbourne", *Austral. New Zeal. J. Sociol.* 6(1), apr 70 : 28-48.

C.712(7) *USSR*
URSS

2921 ŠKARATAN, O. I. "Ètno-social'naja struktura gorodskogo naselenija tatarskoj ASSR" (The ethnic and social structure of urban population in the Tatar Autonomous Republic), *Sov. Ètnogr.* 44(3), mai-jun 70 : 3-16.

2922 TADEVOSJAN, É. V. V. I. *Lenin o gosudarstvennyh rešenija nacional'nogo voprosa v SSSR* (V. I. Lenin and State ways of solving the national question in the USSR). Moskva, Moskovskij Universitet, 70, 212 p.

C.8 ECONOMIC INSTITUTIONS (SOCIOLOGICAL ASPECTS)
INSTITUTIONS ÉCONOMIQUES (ASPECTS SOCIOLOGIQUES)

C.80 General studies
Études générales

[See also / Voir aussi: **E.1**, **E.2**; 494, 534, 551, 570, 591, 598, 5317]

2923 ARONOFF, J. "Psychological needs as a determinant of the formation of economic structures: a confirmation", *Hum. Relat.* 23(2), apr 70 : 123-138.

2924 BASILOV, A. A. "Cennostnye storony truda i ih značenie v konkretno-sociologičeskih issledovanijah" (Monetary aspects of labour and their significance in concrete sociological studies), *Izv. Akad. Nauk SSR Ser. obšč. Nauk* (2), 1969 : 69-82.

2925 BLOCK, F. "Expanding capitalism: the British and American cases", *Berkeley J. Sociol.* 15, 1970 : 138-165.

2927 CUISENIER, J. "Sur l'action économique", *R. franç. Sociol.* 10, n° spécial, 1969 : 575-584.

2928 DUMONT, F. *La dialectique de l'objet économique.* Paris, Anthropos, 70, xiv-385 p.

2929 "Faits économiques (Les)", *R. franç. Sociol.* 10, n° spécial, 1969 : 575-743.

2930 GALBRAITH, J. K. "Economics as a system of belief", *Amer. econ. R.* 60(2), mai 70 *Pap. and Proc.*: 469-478. With a discussion by E. GOLDSTON and H. DEMSETZ: 479-484.

2931 GONZÁLEZ CASANOVA, P. *Sociología de la explotación* (Sociology of exploitation). México, Siglo Veintiuno Editores, 69, vi-291 p.

2932 HEINEMANN, K. *Grundzüge einer Soziologie des Geldes* (Foundations for a sociology of money). Stuttgart, Enke Verlag, 69, xiv-160 p.

2933 LASUK, L. P. "Učenie V. I. Lenina ob obščestvenno-ěkonomičeskih sistemah i problemy etnosociologii" (The Leninist doctrine of socio-economic systems and ethno-sociological problems), *Vestn. Moskovs. Univ. Ser. Ist.* 28(1), jan-feb 70 : 3-15.

2934 LOONE, E. N. "Metodologičeskie zametki o teorii obščestvenno-ěkonomičeskih formacij" (Methodological remarks on the theory of socio-economic formations), *Učen. Zap. (Tartusk. gos. Univ.) Trudy po Filos.* 225(12), 1969 : 141-184.

2935 MIHEEV, V. I. *Kapitalizm kak induztrial'noe obščestvo. Problemy sovremennogo kapitalizma i buržuaznaja sociologija* (Capitalism of industrial society. Problems of contemporary capitalism and bourgeois sociology). Moskva, Meždunarodnye otnošenija, 68, 207 p.

2936 MURMIS, M.; WAISMAN, C. "Monoproducción agroindustrial, crisis y clase obrera: la industria azucarera tucumana" (Agro-industrial monoproduction, crisis and working class: the Tucuman sugar industry), *R. latinoamer. Sociol.* 5(2), jul 69 : 344-383. [Argentina.]

2937 PASTORE, J. "As teorias psicosociais do desenvolvimento económico. Comentários críticos" (Social psychological theories of economic development. Critical comments), *R. Adm. Emprêsas* 10(1), jan-mar 70 : 79-94.

2938 PERPIÑA RODRÍGUEZ, A. *El capitalismo. Análisis sociológico* (Capitalism. A sociological analysis). Madrid, Consejo Superior de Investigaciones Científicas, Instituto Balmes, 70, 156 p.

2939 PETRONI, G. *La sociologia dei consumi* (The sociology of consumption). Milano, F. Angeli, 69, 102 p.

2940 ROBINEAU, C. "Surplus ou dynamique de groupe? Un exemple polynésien", *C. int. Sociol.* 17(49), jul-dec 70 : 111-132.

2941 STANESCU, N. S. "Determinări de clasă ale politicii economice a țărilor capitaliste dezvoltate" (Class determination of the economic policy of overdeveloped capitalist countries), *Probl. econ. (București)* 23(3), mar 70 : 118-127.

2942 VEGAS PÉREZ, A. "El aspecto sociológico del fenómeno económico" (The sociological aspect of the economic phenomenon), *R. int. Sociol. (Madrid)* 28(109-110), jan-apr 70 : 73-84.

2943 VUARIDEL, R. "Une définition des biens économiques", *Année sociol.* 19, 1968 : 133-170.

C.81 Property
Propriété

[See also / Voir aussi: 596]

2944 COLE, J. W. "Inheritance processes and their social consequences", *Sociologia (Roma)* 4(2), mai 70 : 133-146. Followed by an Italian translation: 147-157.

2945 DELPHY, C. "Le patrimoine et le double circulation des biens dans l'espace économique et le temps familial", *R. franç. Sociol.* 10, n° spécial 1969 : 664-686.

2946 ĔMEL'JANOV, A. "Due formy socialističeskoj sobstvennosti: tendencii i perspektivy razvitija" (Two forms of socialist property: trends and development perspectives), *Nauč. Dokl. vysš. Školy (ěkon. Nauki)* 13(7), jul 70 : 12-22.

2947 GREBEŠEČNIKOV, P. Ja. "V razvitii gosudarstvennoj sobstvennosti v SSSR" (On the development of State property in the USSR), *Učen. Zap. (Gor'kov. gos. Univ.) Ser. ist.* (94), 1968 : 67-79.

2948 NAITO, K. "Inheritance practices on a Catholic island: youngest-son inheritance (ultimogeniture) on Kuroshima, Nagasaki prefecture", *Soc. Compass* 17(1), 1970 : 21-36. [Japan.]

2949 OLSON, D. F. "Cooperative ownership experiences of Alaskan Eskimo reindeer herders", *Hum. Org.* 29(1), 1970 : 57-62.

2950 PETILLON, G. "Réflexions sur certains aspects sociologiques, économiques et juridiques du problème foncier", *Paysans* 14(81), jan-jul 70 : 62-71.

2951 ŠAFIEV, K. "Voprosy teorii socialističeskoj sobstvennosti" (Questions concerning the theory of socialist property), *Nauč. Dokl. vysš. Školy (ěkon. Nauki)* 13(10), oct 70 : 20-25.

2952 SDOBNOV, S. I. *Sobstvennost' i kommunizm* (Property and communism). Moskva, Mysl', 68, 328 p.

2953 SPORNIC, A. "Considerații privind perfecționarea relațiilor de proprietate in etapa actuala" (Considerations on property relations in the present stage), *Stud. Čerc. econ.* (1-2), 1969 : 13-22. [Rumania.]

2954 VALENTA, Z. "La propriété dans le socialisme et certains problèmes de la démocratie directe", *Autogestion* 11-12, mar-jun 70 : 71-97.

C.82 The organization of industry
Organisation industrielle

C.820 *General studies*
Études générales

[See also / Voir aussi: 44]

2955 BALCEREK, J. et al. *Materiały do studiowania socjologii pracy* (Materials for the study of labour sociology). Warszawa, Szkoła Główna Planowania i Statystyki, 70, 199 p.

2956 BIRNBAUM, N. *The crisis of industrial society*. New York, Oxford University Press, 69, xi-185 p. CR: B. GORMAN, *Amer. sociol. R.* 35(4), aug 70 : 762-763.

2957 BOLLE DE BAL, M. *Problèmes de sociologie du travail*. Bruxelles, Éditions de l'Institut de sociologie de l'Université libre de Bruxelles, 69, 307 p.

2958 BURNS, T. *Industrial man: selected readings*. Harmondsworth, Penguin, 69, 414 p. CR: R. LUND, *Acta sociol.* 13(3), 1970 : 204-205.

2959 CERNEA, M. "Industrial sociology and manpower fluctuation", *R. roum. Sci. soc. Sér. Philos. logique* 13(4), 1969 : 431-442.

2960 DAVIDJUK, G. P. *Kritika teorii 'edinogo industrial'nogo obščestva'* (Critiques of the theory of the one industrial society). Minsk, Nauka i tehnika, 68, 229 p.

2961 KOLÁŘ, J. *Sociologie podniku* (Industrial sociology). Praha, Práce, 68, 141-1 p.

2962 PADFIELD, H. "New industrial systems and cultural concepts of poverty", *Human Org.* 29(1), 1970 : 29-36.

2963 RUSHING, W. A.; DAVIES, V. "Note on the mathematical formalization of a measure of division of labour", *Soc. Forces* 48(3), mar 70 : 394-397.

2964 SALES, A. "L'entreprise et son environnement", *Sociol. et Soc.* 2(1), mai 70 : 107-122.

2965 WEINBERG, I. "The problem of the convergence of industrial societies: a critical look at the state of a theory", *Comp. Stud. Soc. Hist.* 11(1), jan 69 : 1-15.

C.821 *Entrepreneurship, personnel management and human relations in the field of work*
L'entrepreneur, l'administration du personnel et les relations humaines au sein de l'entreprise

[See also / Voir aussi: 1979]

2966 BALLON, R. J. (ed.). *The Japanese employee.* Tokyo, Sophia University; Rutland, Vt., C. E. Tuttle Co., 69, xvii-317 p.

2967 BARTÖLKE, K. *Überlegungen zu den Grundlagen der Planung von Betriebsorganisationen* (Considerations on the foundations of planning business organization). Berlin, Duncker und Humblot, 69, 223 p.

2968 BENGUIGUI, G. "L'évaluation de la bureaucratisation des entreprises", *Sociol. Trav.* 12(2), apr-jun 70 : 140-151.

2969 BHAR, B. K. *Personnel management, trade unions, and industrial adjudication in India.* Calcutta, Academic Publishers, 69, xi-195 p.

2970 BIASIO, S. *Entscheidung als Prozess. Methoden der Strukturanalyse von Entscheidungsverläufen. Ein Beitrag zur Psychologie der betrieblichen Entscheidung* (Decision as a process. Structural analysis methods of decision-making. Contribution to the psychology of decision in the enterprise). Bern-Stuttgart-Wien, Hans Huber, 69, 138 p.

2971 BOSETZKY, H. *Grundzüge einer Soziologie der Industrieverwaltung; Möglichkeiten und Grenzen der Betrachtung des industriellen Grossbetriebes als bürokratische Organisation* (Basic characteristics of a sociology of industrial administration; possibilities and limitations of viewing the large industrial enterprise as a bureaucratic organization). Stuttgart, F. Enke Verlag, 70, vii-342 p.

2972 BROWN, R.; BRANNEN, P. "Social relations and social perspectives amongst shipbuilding workers—a preliminary statement", *Sociology* 4(2), mai 70 : 197-211.

2973 BRUNO, S. *Partecipazione e sviluppo umano nell'impresa* (Participation and human development in the enterprise). Milano, F. Angeli, 69, 215 p.

2974 CARVELL, F. J. *Human relations in business.* New York, MacMillan, 70, ix-358 p.

2975 CUMMINGS, L. L.; ELSALMI, A. M. "The impact of role diversity, job level, and organizational size on managerial satisfaction", *Adm. Sci. Quart.* 15(1), mar 70 : 1-11.

2976 DARR, J. W. "A reflective analysis of management theory and practice", *Personnel J.* 48(10), oct 69 : 770-782.

2977 DESAI, K. G. *Human problems in Indian industries.* Bombay, Sindhu Publications, 69, viii-113 p.

2978 DRUMM, H. J. *Elemente und Strukturdeterminanten des informatorischen Kommunikationssystems industrieller Unternehmungen. Eine Möglichkeitsanalyse aus der Sicht der Organisationslehre* (Elements and structural determinants of the information system of communication in the industrial enterprise; analysis from the viewpoint of organisation theory). Berlin, Duncker und Humblot, 69, 176 p.

2979 DURAND, C.; TOURAINE, A. "Le rôle compensateur des agents de maîtrise", *Sociol. Trav.* 12(2), apr-jun 70 : 113-139.

2980 FUJIWARA, M. "Jinji gyôsei, Ei-Bei o chûshin to suru" (Personnel administration in Great Britain and the US), *Hôgaku Kenkyû* 41(11), 1968 : 1-41.

2981 GATTAZ, Y. *Les hommes en gris.* Paris, R. Laffont, 69, 244 p.

2982 GHOSH, P. *Personnel administration in India.* New Delhi, Sudha Publications, 69, xiv-408 p.

2983 GRAND, J. *Das Problem der Macht in der Unternehmung* (The problem of power in the enterprise). Zürich, Juris-Verlag, 70, xvi-189 p.

2984 GRANT, J. V.; SMITH, G. J. *Personnel administration and industrial relations.* Harlow, Longmans, 69, x-337 p.

2985 HAGBURG, E. C.; HELFRICH, M. L. "El trabajador industrial y la organización industrial. Examen de un complejo de interrelaciones" (The industrial worker and industrial organization. Examination of a complex of interrelations), *R. Cienc. soc. (Puerto-Rico)* 13(3), jul-sep 69 : 333-344.

2986 HAGE, J.; AIKEN, M. "Routine technology, social structure and organization goals", *Adm. Sci. Quart.* 14(3), sep 69 : 366-377.

2987 HILGENDORF, E. L.; IRVING, B. L. "Job attitude research: a new conceptual and analytical model", *Hum. Relat.* 22(5), oct 69 : 416-426.

2988 HORNADAY, J. A.; BUNKER, C. S. "The nature of the entrepreneur", *Personnel Psychol.* 23(1), 1970 : 47-54.

2989 INTERNATIONAL LABOR OFFICE. *Management development and personnel policies and practices in Asia; an account of the work of the Management Development Committee, Sixth Asian Regional Conference (Tokyo, 1969).* Geneva, ILO, 69, iv-125 p.

2990 KOHOUT, J.; KOLÁŘ, J. "Vúzkum pozice a role československých manažeru" (Research on the position and role of Czechoslovakian managers), *Sociol. Čas.* 5(6), nov-dec 69 : 608-617.

2991 KRAFT, R. H. P. "Manpower planning and its role in the age of automation", *R. educ. Res.* 40(4), oct 70 : 495-510.

2992 KUNZE, J. *Betriebsklima. Eine soziologische Studie zum System der sozialen Beziehungen in sozialistischen Industriebetrieb* (Enterprise atmosphere. A sociological study on the system of social relations in the socialist industrial enterprise). Berlin, Verlag Tribüne, 69, 193 p.

2993 Bibl. XIX-2552. LITWIN, G. L.; STRINGER, R. A. Jr. *Motivation and organizational climate.* CR: W. BENNIS, *Amer. J. Sociol.* 75(6), mai 70 : 1058-1060.

2994 LOEN, R. O. *Personnel management.* Washington, Small Business Administration, 69, 12 p.

2995 MILTON, C. R. *Ethics and expediency in personnel management; a critical history of personnel philosophy.* Columbia, University of South Carolina Press, 70, 252 p.

2996 MINER, J. B. *Personnel psychology.* London, Macmillan, 69, ix-310 p.

2997 MOŽINA, S. "Uspešnost kominiciranja v podjetju" (The efficiency of communication in enterprises), *Ekon. R. (Ljubljana)* 20(2), 1969 : 179-189.

2998 MUMFORD, E. "Job satisfaction: a new approach derived from an old theory", *Sociol. R.* 18(1), mar 70 : 71-101.

2999 MUNTERS, Q. J. "Rekrutering en rekruteringsvelden" (Recruitment and recruitment fields), *Mens en Mij* 45(3), mai-jun 70 : 194-203.

3000 NAFZIGER, A. W. "The relationship between education and entrepreneurship in Nigeria", *J. develop. Areas* 4(3), apr 70 : 349-368.

3001 NOČEVNIK, M. N. "Proizvodstvennyj kollektiv i sisteme socialističeskogo obščestva" (A productive collectivity in the socialist society system), *Sb. Trud. Vsesojuz. zaoč. politehn. Inst.* (57), 1969 : 75-88.

3002 PAMPALONI VIOLI, R. "Alcune osservazioni in merito alle implicazioni sociali del comportamento imprenditoriale" (Some observations on the social implications of the behaviour of firm managers), *Quad. Sci. soc.* 8(1-2), 1969 : 124-136.

3003 PODŽARKOV, V. G. *Social'nye problemy organizacii truda* (Social problems of labour organization). Moskva, Mysl', 69, 214 p.

3004 POUSSET, A. "Quelques types de modèles opératoires utilisés par les dirigeants dans la formulation et la résolution de leurs problèmes d'entreprises", *R. Inst. Sociol.* 4, 1969 : 709-760.

3005 RADŽJUKINAS, Ju. *Naučnaja organizacija truda: Rol' sociologičeskih issledovanij v naučnoj organizacii truda* (The scientific organization of labour: Role of sociological researches on scientific organization of labour). Viln'jus, 68, 108 p.

3006 RAGONE, G. "In margine ad una ricerca sulla imprenditorialità in Campania" (Marginal note on a research study of enterpreneurship in Campania), *Rass. econ. (Napoli)* 33(6), nov-dec 69 : 1389-1415.

3007 RITZER, G.; TRICE, H. M. *An occupation in conflict—a study of the personnel manager.* Ithaca, Cornell University, New York State School of Industrial and Labor Relations, 69, x-127 p. CR: D. F. ROY, *Amer. sociol. R.* 35(4), aug 70 : 814-815. [USA.]

3008 RUDRABASAVARAJ, M. N. *Personnel administration practices in India.* Poona, Vaikunth Mehta National Institute of Cooperative Management, 69, 467 p.

3009 RUSH, H. M. F. *Behavioral science; concepts and management application.* New York, National Industrial Conference Board, 69, ii-178 p.

3010 RYAVEC, K. W. "Soviet industrial managers, their superiors and the economic reform: a study of an attempt at planned behavioural change", *Sov. Stud.* 21(2), oct 69 : 208-229.

3011 SADLER, P. J. "Leadership style, confidence in management, and job satisfaction", *J. appl. behav. Sci.* 6(1), jan-feb-mar 70 : 3-19.

3012 SADLER, P. J. "Sociological aspects of skill", *Brit. J. industr. Relat.* 8(1), mar 70 : 22-31.

3013   SANCHEZ GIL, M. *Naturaleza y evolución de la función empresarial* (Nature and evolution
        of the entrepreneurial function). Madrid, Aguilar, 69, 562 p.
3014   STROHMER, A. F. Jr. *The skills of managing.* Reading, Mass., Addison-Wesley Publishing
        Co., 70, x-149 p.
3015   TOWLE, J. W. (ed.). *Human resources administration: problems of growth and change.*
        Boston, Houghton Mifflin, 70, x-426 p.
3016   WILLENER, A.; GAJDOS, C.; BENGUIGUI, G. *Les cadres en mouvement...* Paris, Éditions de
        l'Épi, 69, 284 p.

        C.822   *Labour organization: trade unions*
        Organisation du travail: syndicats

        [See also / Voir aussi: 939, 2365, 2969, 3196, 3540, 3720, 4293]

3017   AGOSTI, A.; ANDREASI, A.; BRAUO, G. M. *et al.* "Il movimento sindacale in Italia"
        (Trade union movement in Italy), *A. Fond. Luigi Einaudi* 3, 1969 : 151-284.
3018   ANANABA, W. *The trade union movement in Nigeria.* London, C. Hurst, 69, xii-336 p.
3019   AOKI, K. (ed.). *Nihon rôdô undô shi nempyô* (The chronology of the Japanese labor
        movement). Tokyo, Shinsei-sha, 68, 844 p.
3020   BAIN, G. S. *The growth of white-collar unionism.* Oxford, Clarendon Press, 70, xvi-233 p.
        [UK.]
3021   BERNSTEIN, I. *Turbulent years—a history of the American worker, 1933-1941.* Boston,
        Houghton Mifflin, 70, xiv-873 p.
3022   BLUM, A. A. *Teachers unions and associations—a comparative study.* Urbana, University
        of Illinois Press, 69, xi-353 p.
3023   BLUMLER, J. G.; EWBANK, A. J. "Trade unionists, the mass media and unofficial
        strikes", *Brit. J. industr. Relat.* 8(1), mar 70 : 32-54.
3024   BOK, D. C.; DUNLOP, J. T. *Labor and the American community.* New York, Simon and
        Schuster, 70, 542 p.
3025   CAMPBELL, D. V. A. "Trade unions and automation in Australia", *J. industr. Relat.*
        11(3), nov 69 : 223-230.
3026   CAPDEVIELLE, J.; MOURIAUX, R. (comps.). *Les syndicats ouvriers en France.* Paris, A.
        Colin, 70, 126 p.
3027   CARLSON, B. *Trade unions in Sweden.* Stockholm, Tiden, 69, 175-1 p.
3028   ČERKASOV, G. N. *Sociologija truda i profsojuzy* (Sociology of labour and trade unions).
        Moskva, Profizdat, 70, 192 p.
3029   "Confederation of Trade Unions of Yugoslavia (The)", *Yugosl. Surv.* 11(3), aug 70 :
        35-64.
3030   COULAND, J. *Le mouvement syndical au Liban, 1919-1946: son évolution pendant le mandat
        français : de l'occupation à l'évacuation et au Code du travail.* Paris, Éditions sociales,
        70, 453 p.
3031   DALE, L. A. *A bibliography of French labor, with a selection of documents on the French
        labor movement.* New York, A. M. Kelley, 69, xxxvii-317 p.
3032   DELON, P. *Les employés. De la plume d'oie à l'ordinateur. Un siècle de lutte. Origines et
        activité de la Fédération CGT.* Paris, Éditions sociales, 69, 224 p.
3033   ĐORDEVIĆ, J. "Načelni stavovi i pitanja o sindikatu" (Positions of principle and problems
        concerning trade unions), *Gledišta* 9(5), 1968 : 747-770. [Yugoslavia.]
3034   Bibl. XIX-2604. DUBIEF, H. *Le syndicalisme révolutionnaire.* CR: A. ROUX, *R. franç.
        Sociol.* 11(1), jan-mar 70 : 120.
3035   DUBOFSKY, M. *We shall be all—a history of the Industrial Workers of the World.* Chicago,
        Quadrangle Books, 69, xviii-557 p. [USA.]
3036   DUBOIS, P. "La résistance des délégués du personnel aux moyens de pressions patro-
        naux", *Sociol. Trav.* 12(1), jan-mar 70 : 15-32.
3037   DURAND, C.; CAZES, S. "La signification politique du mouvement de mai, analyse de
        tracts syndicaux et gauchistes", *Sociol. Trav.* 12(3), jul-sep 70 : 293-308.
3038   EDELSTEIN, J. D.; WARNER, M.; COOKE, W. F. "The pattern of opposition in British
        and American unions", *Sociology* 4(2), mai 70 : 145-163.
3039   ERRANDONEA, A.; COSTABILE, D. *Sindicato y sociedad en el Uruguay* (Trade union and
        society in Uruguay). Montevideo, Fundación de Cultura Universitaria, 69, 227 p.

3040 FABIANI, A. *Libertà sindacale e Stato* (Trade union freedom and State). L'Aquila, L. U. Japadre, 69, 139 p.

3041 FRIEDLAND, W. H. *Vuta kamba; the development of trade unions in Tanganyika.* Stanford, Calif., Hoover Institution Press, 69, xiii-280 p.

3042 GIOVANNINI, E. "Lotte operaie e democrazia sindacale" (Labour struggle and trade union democracy), *Probl. Social. (Milano)* 11(43), nov-dec 69 : 1030-1039. [Italy.]

3043 GIULLIANI, R.; PECORA, G. "Ricognizione sulle nuove forme della lotta operaia (Recognition of new forms of labour struggle), *Crit. sociol. (Roma)* 15, 1970 : 94-124.

3044 GOOD, J. W. *Irish unionism.* Port Washington, N. Y., Kennikat Press, 70, vii-240 p.

3045 IADAMSUREN, D. "Syndicats et classe ouvrière en Mongolie", *Nouv. R. int.* 13(7), jul 70 : 163-170.

3046 KAHN-FREUND, O. "Trade unions, the law and society", *Mod. Law R.* 33(3), mai 70 241-267. [UK.]

3047 KASSALOW, E. M. *Trade unions and industrial relations; an international comparison.* New York, Random House, 69, xvii-333 p.

3048 KRASUCKI, H. *Syndicats et lutte de classes.* Paris, Éditions sociales, 69, 124 p. [France.]

3049 LEEMAN, W. A. "Syndicalism in Yugoslavia", *Econ. Develop. cult. Change* 18(2), jan 70 : 230-239.

3050 LEFRANC, C. *Essais sur les problèmes socialistes et syndicaux.* Paris, Payot, 70, 264 p. [France.]

3051 LYON-CAEN, G. "Syndicats et partis politiques", *Dr. soc.* 33(2), feb 70 : 69-80.

3052 MALLET, S. "Contrôle ouvrier, parti et syndicat", *Crit. social. (Paris)* 1, mar-apr 70 : 57-71; 2, mai-jun 70 : 11-38. [France.]

3053 MARCANTONIO, A. DI. *Sindacati e certezza del diritto* (Trade unions and legal certainty). Milano, A. Giuffrè, 70, 290 p.

3054 MARTIN, R. *Communism and the British trade unions, 1924-1933—a study of the national minority movement.* Oxford, Clarendon Press, 69, xii-209 p.

3055 MARTIN, R. M. "The trade unions of colonial Africa", *Industr. R.* 7(2), jul 69 : 3-17.

3056 MARTIN, R. M. "Tribesmen into trade unionists—the African experience and the Papua-New Guinea prospect", *J. industr. Relat.* 11(2), jul 69 : 125-172.

3057 MUNRO, J. L. "Internal factors of control in USA labour union locals", *J. industr. Relat.* 11(2), jul 69 : 173-182.

3058 MUTHUCHIDAMBARAM, S. "Democracy as a goal of union organization—an interpretation of the United States experience", *Relat. industr.* 24(3), 1969 : 579-588.

3059 NEIRA, H. "Sindicalismo campesino y complejos regionales agrícolas. Perú 1960-1970" (Peasant trade-unionism and regional agricultural complexes), *Aportes* 18, oct 70 : 27-67. [Peru.]

3060 NYDEN, P. "Coal miners, 'their' union, and capital", *Sci. and Soc.* 34(2), 1970 : 194-223. [Appalachia, USA.]

3061 PAYNTER, W. *British trade unions and the problem of change.* London, George Allen and Unwin, 70, 172 p.

3062 PERLINE, M. M.; LORENZ, V. R. "Factors influencing member participation in trade union activities", *Amer. J. Econ. Sociol.* 29(4), oct 70 : 425-438.

3063 PIRKER, T. "Évolution des syndicats depuis 1945", *Documents (Cologne)* 25(2), mar-apr 70 : 5-26. [Allemagne, R. F.]

3064 POPPE, C. "Vormen en doelstellingen van vakbondsaktie" (Forms and aims of trade unions), *Mens en Mij* 45(2), mar-apr 70 : 9-27. [Netherlands.]

3065 RAMASWAMY, E. A. "Trade unions and politics", *Sociol. B.* 18(2), sep 69 : 137-147. [India.]

3066 ROBERGE, P. "Les conflits intersyndicaux au Québec (1957-1967)", *Relat. industr.* 24(3), 1969 : 521-558.

3067 SAINSAULIEU, R. "Fondements culturels de l'action syndicale dans l'entreprise", *Projet* 49, nov 70 : 1065-1076. [France.]

3068 SEIDMAN, J. (ed.). *Trade union government and collective bargaining: some critical issues.* New York, Praeger Publishers, 70, xxv-304 p. [USA.]

3069 *Sengo rôdôundô no tenkaikatei* (Labor movement in postwar Japan). Tokyo, Ochanomizu-shobô, 68, 210 p.

3070 SILVESTRE, P. *Le mouvement ouvrier jusqu'à la deuxième guerre mondiale.* Paris, A. Colin, 70, 96 p.

3071   SINGH, M. *History of Kenya's trade union movement to 1952.* Nairobi, East African Publishing House, 69, 332 p.

3072   SITO, N. "Occupational structure, development and unionism in Latin America", *Soziol. Inst. Univ. Zürich B.* 18, jul 70 : 1-46.

3073   SMITH, A. *The trade unions.* Edinburgh, Oliver and Boyd, 69, 7-119 p.

3074   SMOCK, D. R. *Conflict and control in an African trade union—a study of the Nigerian Coal Miners' Union.* Stanford, Calif., Hoover Institution Press, 69, x-170 p.

3075   SPADACCIA, G. "La nuova situazione sindacale in Italia" (The new trade union situation in Italy), *Tempi mod.* 12(2), 1970 : 33-36.

3076   SZÉPLÁBI, M. "Die Konkurrenz der Sozialideologien in den französischen Arbeitergewerkschaften" (The competition between social ideologies among French trade unions), *Schmollers Jb.* 90(4), 1970 : 385-418.

3077   TAVERNIER, Y. *Le syndicalisme paysan: F. N. S. E. A.; C. N. J. A.* Paris, A. Colin, 69, 227 p.

3078   TUMBO, N. S. K. *Towards NUTA: the search for permanent unity in Tanganyika's trade union movement.* Dar es Salaam, University College, 69, 31 p.

3079   URRUTIA, M. M. *Historia del sindicalismo en Colombia* (History of trade-unionism in Colombia). Bogotá, Ediciones Universidad de los Andes, 69, 275 p.

3080   URRUTIA, M. *The development of the Colombian labor movement.* New Haven, Yale University Press, 69, xi-297 p.

3081   VAN DE VALL, M. *Labor organizations—micro- and macro-sociological analysis on a comparative basis.* Cambridge, University Press, 70, xi-257 p.

3082   VIDAL, D. "Politique et conjugaison: revendications et groupes professionnels en mai-juin 1968", *Sociol. Trav.* 12(3), jul-sep 70 : 227-243.

3083   VIDALENC, G. *La classe ouvrière et le syndicalisme en France de 1789 à 1965.* Paris, Confédération Force Ouvrière, 69, 502 p.

3084   YARA, C. (ed.). *Okinawa kyôshokuin kumiai 16nen* (Teachers' union in Okinawa). Tôkyô, Rôdô Junpô-sha, 68, 285 p.

C.83   Labour relations
Relations du travail

C.830   *General studies*
Études générales

[See also / Voir aussi: 2424, 2984, 3047, 3326]

3085   AMETISTOV, É. M. *Meždunarodnoe trudovoe pravo i rabočij klass* (International labor laws and the working class). Moskva, Mezdunarodnye Otnošenija, 70, 184 p.

3086   BAIRSTOW, F. "A Canadian approach to the critical issues in industrial relations, with special relevance for Australia", *Austral. Quart.* 41(4), dec 69 : 101-112.

3087   BANKS, R. F. "The reform of British industrial relations—the Donovan Report and the Labour government's policy proposals", *Relat. industr.* 24(2), 1969 : 333-382.

3088   BLAIN, A. N. J.; GENNARD, J. "Industrial relations theory—a critical review", *Brit. J. industr. Relat.* 8(3), nov 70 : 389-407.

3089   CARBY-HALL, J. R. *Principles of industrial law.* London, Charles Knight, 69, lxiv-567 p.

3090   CARSON, W. G. "Some sociological aspects of strict liability and the enforcement of factory legislation", *Mod. Law R.* 33(4), jul 70 : 396-412. [UK.]

3091   CLEGG, H. A. *The system of industrial relations in Great Britain.* Oxford, Blackwell, 70, x-484 p.

3092   CHANDRASHEKAR, B. K. "Labour relations in India", *Brit. J. industr. Relat.* 8(3), nov 70 : 369-388.

3093   CÓRDOVA, E. "Collective labour relations in Latin American ports", *Int. Lab. R.* 100(4), oct 69 : 315-339.

3094   DASSA, S. "Le mouvement de mai et le système de relations professionnelles", *Sociol. Trav.* 12(3), jul-sep 70 : 244-261. [France.]

3095   DEMIRGIL, D. *Labor management relations in Turkey.* Istanbul, Economic Research Foundation, 69, 98 p.

3096   DRAKE, C. D. *Labour law.* London, Sweet and Maxwell, 69, xxiii-311 p.

3097 DUBOIS, P. "Un exemple d'analyse causale: l'activité du délégué du personnel dans l'entreprise", *R. franç. Sociol.* 11(2), apr-jun 70 : 197-210.

3098 EDDY, W. B.; SPOTTS, J. V. (comps.). *Behavioral science approaches to employee relations.* Chicago, Public Personnel Association, 70, 69 p.

3099 FLANDERS, A. D. *Management and unions: the theory and reform of industrial relations.* London, Faber and Faber, 70, 317 p. [UK.]

3100 FÜRSTENBERG, F. "Die Machtstruktur der industriellen Arbeitsbeziehungen" (Power structure in industrial labour relations). *Z. ges. Staatswiss.* 126(2), apr 70 : 309-322.

3101 GALENSON, W. *The Danish system of labour relations—a study in industrial peace.* New York, Russell and Russell, 69, xii-321 p.

3102 GASPARINI, G. *L'azienda industriale moderna e i problemi del lavore* (The modern industrial firm and labour problems). Milano, F. Angeli, 69, 189 p.

3103 GRANDI, M. *Studi sul diritto del lavoro inglese e nord-americano* (Studies on English and North American labour law). Milano, A. Giuffrè, 70, viii-451 p.

3104 "Industrial relations", *Scott. J. polit. Econ.* 17(2), jun 70 : 117-336. [A special issue. UK.]

3105 IVANOV, S. A. "Burzuaznoe trudovoe pravo: novye javlenija i klassovaja bor'ba' (Bourgeois labour legislation: new phenomenon and class struggle), *Sov. Gos. Pravo* 43(2), 1970 : 123-134.

3106 *Labor relations and the law in West Germany and the United States; a comparative study.* Ann Arbor, Bureau of Business Research, Graduate School of Business Administration, University of Michigan, 69, xxx-606 p.

3107 MALLES, P. *Trends in industrial relations systems of continental Europe.* Ottawa, Task Force on Labour Relations, 69, x-213 p.

3108 MAYER-MALY, T. *Österreichisches Arbeitsrecht* (Austrian labour law). Wien-New York, Springer, 70, vi-262 p.

3109 McLEOD, C. *All change: railway industrial relations in the sixties.* London, Gower Press, 70, xviii-222 p. [UK.]

3110 MERLI BRANDINI, P. *Le relazioni industriali* (Industrial relations). Milano, F. Angeli, 69, 181 p.

3111 MILLS, C. W. "The contribution of sociology to studies of industrial relations", *Berkeley J. Sociol.* 15, 1970 : 11-32.

3112 MORELLET, J. "The influence of international labour conventions on French legislation", *Int. Lab. R.* 101(4), apr 70 : 331-358.

3113 NASCIMENTO, A. M. *Fundamentos do direito do trabalho* (Fundamentals of labour law). São Paulo, LTr. Editôra, 70, 230 p.

3114 NIGRO, F. A. *Management-employee relations in the public service.* Chicago, Public Personnel Association, 69, xii-433 p. [USA and Canada.]

3115 NIHON RÔSHI-KANKEI KENKYÛ KYOKAI; NIHON RÔDÔ KYOKAI. *The changing patterns of industrial relations in Asian countries.* Tokyo, Japan Institute of Labour, 69, ii-308 p. [Asian Regional Conference on Industrial Relations, Tokyo, 1969.]

3116 RAHMAN, M. S. "Legal framework of industrial relations in East Pakistan", *East Pakistan Lab. J.* 21(3), sep 68 : 115-125.

3117 RENDON, G. *Le droit du travail en Amérique Latine, le contrat de travail.* Paris, Presses universitaires de France, 70, 72 p.

3118 RIZZO, N. *Struttura e durata del rapporto di lavoro* (Structure and duration of labour relation). Novara-Roma, PEM, 69, viii-551 p. [Italy.]

3119 ROMAGNOLI, U. "Temi e problemi di relazioni industriali" (Subjects and problems of industrial relations), *Mulino* 18(12), dec 69 : 1239-1251. [Italy.]

3120 ROSS, N. S. *Constructive conflict: an essay on employer-employee relations in contemporary Britain.* Edinburgh, Oliver and Boyd, 69, vii-98 p.

3121 SALVA, Z. "Izmenenija v trudovom zakonodatel'stve Pol'ši" (Changes in Polish labour legislation), *Sov. Gos. Pravo* 43(1), jan 70 : 103-110.

3122 SELZNICK, P.; NONET, P.; VOLLMER, H. M. *Law, society, and industrial justice.* New York, Russell Sage Foundation, 69, viii-282 p.

3123 SOMERS, G. G. *Essays in industrial relations theory.* Ames, Iowa State University Press, 69, xi-200 p.

3124 STURMTHAL, A. "Canadian industrial relations—the Task Force Report", *Relat. industr.* 24(3), 1969 : 289-497.

3125 TRIPIER, M. "La revendication des 'conseils d'unité' au Commissariat à l'Énergie Atomique en mai-juin 1968. Essai d'interprétation", *R. franç. Sociol.* 11(3), jul-sep 70 : 351-367. [France.]

3126 WALINE, P. *Cinquante ans de rapports entre patrons et ouvriers en Allemagne.* II. *Depuis 1945.* Paris, A. Colin, 70, 344 p. (Cahiers de la Fondation nationale des sciences politiques n⁰ 178). Voir pour le premier volume Bibl. XVIII-3322.

3127 WEBB, G. H.; BIANCO, T. C.; COURDIN, D. R. *Labor law and antitrust; analysis and explanation.* New York, Holt, Rinehart and Winston, 70, 158 p.

3128 WINDMULLER, J. P. "Perspectives in Dutch labor relations", *Mens en Onderneming* 24(2), mar 70 : 136-141.

C.831   *Collective bargaining and labour agreements*
             Contrats collectifs, conventions collectives

[See also / Voir aussi: 3068, 3185]

3129 BENACHENHOU, M. *Problèmes sociologiques de l'autogestion agricole en Mitidja.* Bordeaux, Université de Bordeaux, Faculté des Lettres et Sciences humaines, 69, x-371 p.

3130 BLAIR, T. L. *The land to those who work it—Algeria's experiment in workers' management.* New York, Doubleday, 69, viii-275 p.

3131 Bibl. XIX-2697. BLUMBERG, P. *Industrial democracy: the sociology of participation.* CR: D. S. RIDDELL, *Brit. J. Sociol.* 21(2), jun 70 : 234-235.

3132 BROEKMEYER, M. J.; CORNELISSEN, I. *Arbeidersraad of ondernemersstaat. Machten en machtsstrijd in Nederland en in Joegoslavië* (Workers council or entrepreneurship. Powers and power struggle in the Netherlands and Yugoslavia). Amsterdam, Van Gennep, 69, 215 p.

3133 BROEKMEYER, M. J. (ed.). *Yugoslav workers' self-management.* Proceedings of a symposium held in Amsterdam, 7-9 January, 1970. Dordrecht, Reidel, 70, 267 p.

3134 CARDIN, J. R. "La négociation collective par secteurs et le droit québecois du travail", *Relat. industr.* 24(3), 1969 : 467-488.

3135 "Conseils ouvriers en Tchécoslovaquie", *Autogestion* 11-12, mar-jun 70 : 252 p.

3136 CRISTOFARO, M. DE. *Le commissioni interne* (Workers councils). Padova, CEDAM, 70, xi-760 p. [Italy.]

3137 DESSEIGNE, G. "L'expérience des comités d'entreprise", *Polit. aujourd.* 12, dec 69 : 3-13.

3138 "Development of the self-managing organization of enterprises in Yugoslavia (The)", *Yugosl. Surv.* 11(3), aug 70 : 1-16.

3139 ESTIVIL, J. *et al.* La participatió dels treballadors a la gestió de l'empresa (Workers' participation to firm mangagement). Barcelona, Ed. Nova Terra, 70, 223 p.

3140 FISCHER, R. *Wirtschaftliche Mitbestimmung; Darstellung und Dokumentation* (Economic self-management; presentation and documentation). Neuwied, H. Luchterhand, 69, 224 p. [Germany, FR.]

3141 GLOBERSON, A. "Spheres and levels of employee participation in organizations", *Brit. J. industr. Relat.* 8(2), jul 70 : 252-262.

3142 HARTMAN, P. T. *Collective bargaining and productivity; the longshore mechanization agreement.* Berkeley, University of California Press, 69, xix-307 p.

3143 HELIE, D. "L'autogestion industrielle en Algérie", *R. Occident musul. Méditerr.* 6(1-2), 1969 : 113-126. Également publié dans *Autogestion (Paris)* (9-10), sep-dec 69 : 37-57.

3144 HONDRICH, K. O. *Mitbestimmung in Europa; ein Diskussionsbeitrag* (Joint management in Europe; a contribution to the discussion). Köln, Europa Union Verlag, 70, xi-119 p.

3145 INSTITUTE OF COLLECTIVE BARGAINING AND GROUP RELATIONS. *Collective bargaining today.* Washington, Bureau of National Affairs, 70, xvii-503 p.

3146 INTERNATIONAL LABOR OFFICE. *Participation of workers in decisions within undertakings; documents of a technical meeting (Geneva 20-29 November 1967).* Geneva, ILO, 69, iii-165 p.

3147 JAWORSKI, T.; STACHULSKI, R. "Samorzad robotniczy na obecym etapie rozwoju gospodarki" (Labour self-management in the current stage of economic development), *Nowe Drogi* 24(7), jul 70 : 59-70. [Poland.]

3148 KERGOAT, D. "Une expérience d'autogesion en mai 1968 (émergence d'un système d'action collective)", *Sociol. Trav.* 12(3), jul-sep 70 : 274-292.

3149 KOULYTCHIZKY, S. "Comment sont prises les décisions dans l'autogestion algérienne", *R. algér. Sci. jur. polit. écon.* 6(4), dec 69 : 1151-1194.

3150 KUDA, R. F. "Atypische Mitbestimmungsmodelle—Anpassungstaktik oder Reformstrategie" (Atypical models of self-management: adaptation tactic, or reform strategy), *Frankfurt. H.* 25(6), jun 70 : 419-426. [Germany, FR.]

3151 LEMAN, G. *Ungelöste Fragen im jugoslawischen System der Arbeiterselbstverwaltung* (Unsolved problems of the Yugoslavian system of worker self-management). Köln, Bundesinstitut für Ostwissenschaftliche und Internationale Studien, 69, 119 p.

3152 LEWIS, R. "The legal enforceability of collective agreements,,' *Brit. J. industr. Relat.* 8(3), nov 70 : 313-333.

3153 MAIONE, G. "Expérience d'autogestion en Italie (1919-1956)", *Autogestion* 9-10, sep-dec 69 : 89-119.

3154 MAREK, E. "Workers' participation in planning and management in Poland", *Int. Lab. R.* 101(3), mar 70 : 271-290.

3155 MARSHALL, R. "The impact of civil rights laws on collective bargaining in the construction industry", *Poverty hum. Resources Abstr.* 5(1), jan-feb 70 : 5-17.

3156 MASI, D. DE. "Lungo viaggio verso il classismo" (A long way towards classicism), *Rass. ital. Sociol.* 11(2), apr-jun 70 : 274-280. [An Italian experiment in joint management.]

3157 MEISTER, A. "Comment évolue l'autogestion yougoslave", *Écon. et Human.* 191, jan-feb 70 : 28-43. Voir aussi *Esprit* 38(9), sep 70 : 367-384; *Homme et Soc.* 17, jul-sep 70 : 91-96.

3158 MOSKOW, M. H.; LOEWENBERG, J. J.; KOZIARA, E. C. *Collective bargaining in public employment.* New York, Random House, 70, xiv-336 p.

3159 NAGELS, J. "Quelques problèmes économiques du socialisme et de l'autogestion" *C. écon. Bruxelles* 45, 1 trim 70 : 91-124; 46, 2 trim 70 : 253-280.

3160 OBRADOVIĆ, J.; FRENCH, J. R. P. Jr.; RODGERS, W. L. "Workers' councils in Yugoslavia", *Hum. Relat.* 23(5), oct 70 : 459-471.

3161 PANIKAR, P. G. K. "Worker-participation rates in Kerala", *Ind. J. Lab. Econ.* 10(3), oct 67 : 216-227.

3162 PAŠIČ, N. "L'autogestion—système social complet", *Quest. act. Social.* 96, dec 69 : 133-170.

3163 PETRONE, F. "L'esperienza dell' autogestione jugoslava" (The experience of Yugoslavian self management), *Crit. marx.* 8(4), jul-aug 70 : 50-62.

3164 RAINIO, K. "Valtasuhteet ja yritysdemokratia" (Industrial democracy and power relations), *Yritystalous* 13, 1969 : 58-63.

3165 "Réorganisation de l'autogestion agricole (La)", *Doss. docum. (Alger)* 2, dec 69 : 3-19. [Algerie.]

3166 RITTERSHAUS, J. "Konzeptionnelle Fragen der soziologischen Erforschung der sozialistischen Demokratie im Industriebetrieb" (Conceptual problems of sociological research on socialist democracy in the industrial enterprise), *Wirtsch.-Wiss.* 17(12), dec 69 : 1816-1824.

3167 ROSENFELD, K.; WOLF, H. "Einige Probleme der Weiterentwicklung des Betriebskollektivvertrages" (Some problems raised by the development collective agreements in enterprises), *Staat u. Recht* 19(3), mar 70 : 377-389.

3168 ROY, E. P. *Collective bargaining in agriculture.* Danville, Ill., Interstate Printers and Publishers, 70, 280 p. [USA.]

3169 SCHAD, W. *Le problème de la cogestion dans l'entreprise moyenne en Allemagne.* Genève, Éditions Médecine et Hygiène, 69, ix-211 p.

3170 SELSER, J. *Participación de los trabajadores en la gestión económica* (Workers participation in economic management). Buenos Aires, Ediciones Libera, 70, 179 p.

3171 SIEGEL, A. J. *The impact of computers on collective bargaining.* Cambridge, Mass., MIT Press, 69, xiv-294 p.

3172 SLEJŠKA, D. "Le modèle d'autogestion et ses conditions en Tchécoslovaquie après janvier 1968", *Homme et Soc.* 14, oct-nov-dec 69 : 157-178.

3173 SPECHT, G. "Mitbestimmung der Arbeitnehmer" (Worker joint management), *Polit. Stud. (München)* 21(193), sep-oct 70 : 566-576.

3174 SPRING, H. C. "Collective bargaining calendar for 1970", *Mthly Lab. R.* 93(1), jan 70 : 13-26. [USA.]

3175 STEGMANN, F. J. "Mitbestimmung: ja oder nein ?" (Joint management: yes or no ?),
      Polit. Stud. (München) 21(192), jul-aug 70 : 385-405. [Germany, FR.]
3176 SUPEK, R. "Problèmes et perspectives de l'autogestion ouvrière en Yougoslavie", *Homme
      et Soc.* 14, oct-nov-dec 69 : 127-138.
3177 TANIĆ, Ž. "Social composition of workers councils in Yugoslavia", *Ind. J. industr.
      Relat.* 3(1), jul 70 : 19-40.
3178 TANIĆ, Ž. *Workers' participation in management: ideal and reality in India.* New Delhi,
      Shri Ram Centre for Industrial Relations, 69, xi-132 p.
3179 THOMPSON, M. "Collective bargaining in the Mexican electrical industry", *Brit. J.
      industr. Relat.* 8(1), mar 70 : 55-68.
3180 TURNER, H. A. "Collective bargaining and the eclipse of incomes policy: retrospect,
      prospect and possibilities", *Brit. K. industr. Relat.* 8(2), jul 70 : 197-212. [UK.]
3181 VANEK, J. *The general theory of labor-managed market economies.* Ithaca, Cornell Universi-
      ty Press, 70, xiv-409 p.
3182 WOLFBEIN, S. L. (ed.). *Emerging sectors of collective bargaining.* Braintree, Mass., D. H.
      Mark Publishing Co., 70, viii-260 p.
3183 "Workers participation in management: an international comparison", *Industr. Relat.*
      9(2), feb 70 : 117-214.

C.832   *Mediation, arbitration*
         Médiation et arbitrage

3184 PALACIOS PIÑA, H. *Solución de los conflictos colectivos del trabajo; doctrina, legislación y
      jurisprudencia chilena* (Solution of collective labour conflicts; doctrine, legislation and
      Chilean jurisprudence). Santiago de Chile, Studium Chilena Editores, 70, 228 p.
3185 PRASOW, P.; PETERS, E. *Arbitration and collective bargaining: conflict resolution in labor
      relations.* New York, McGraw-Hill, 70, xix-426 p.
3186 WEILER, P. C. *Labour arbitration and industrial chance.* Ottawa, Task Force on Labour
      Relations, 69, vii-146 p.

C.833   *Conflicts*
         Conflits

      [See also / Voir aussi: **C.832;** 3023]

3187 ADAM, G. "Étude statistique des grèves de mai-juin 1968", *R. franç. Sci. polit.* 20(1),
      feb 70 : 105-118. [France.]
3188 BASTIN, M. "Les grèves", *Doss. Action soc. cath.* 47(1), jan-feb 70 : 1-12. [Belgique.]
3189 BAUMFELDER, E. "Les conflits et les enjeux à l'ORTF (revendication et contradiction)",
      Sociol. Trav. 12(3), jul-sep 70 : 262-273. [France.]
3190 BENTLEY, P. R. "Strike incidence in the Australian stevedoring industry—the govern-
      ment's search for a solution", *J. industr. Relat.* 11(2), jul 69 : 111-124.
3191 BRÉCY, R. *La grève générale en France.* Paris, Études et documentation internationales,
      69, x-102 p.
3192 CORNU, R.; MAURICE, M. "Revendications, orientations syndicales et participation de
      cadres à la grève", *Sociol. Trav.* 12(3), jul-sep 70 : 328-337.
3193 DÄUBLER, W. *Der Streik im öffentlichen Dienst* (The civil service strike). Tübingen, Mohr,
      70, xxii-293 p.
3194 DION, G. "La grève-sans-arrêt-de-travail", *Relat. industr.* 24(2), 1969 : 279-307. [USA.]
3195 DUBOIS, P. "Nouvelles pratiques de mobilisation dans la classe ouvrière", *Sociol. Trav.*
      12(3), jul-sep 70 : 338-344.
3196 ERBÈS-SEGUIN, S. "Le declenchement des grèves de mai: spontanéité des masses et rôle
      des syndicats", *Sociol. Trav.* 12(2), apr-jun 70 : 177-189.
3197 ERBÈS-SEGUIN, S. "Relations entre travailleurs dans l'entreprise en grève : le cas de mai-
      juin 1968", *R. franç. Sociol.* 11(3), jul-sep 70 : 339-350. [France.]
3198 GARCÍA ABELLÁN, J. *Derecho de conflictos colectivos de trabajo* (Law of collective labour
      conflicts). Madrid, Instituto de Estudios Políticos, 69, 404 p. [Spain.]

3199 JEROVŠEK, J. "Konflikti u radnim organizacijama" (Conflicts in work organisations), *Gledišta* 11(2), feb 70 : 201-215. [Yugoslavia.]

3200 JOSHI, N. K. "Industrial strikes", *Ind. Lab. J.* 10(11), nov 69 : 1519-1532.

3201 JOSHI, V. P. "Strikes in the Bombay cotton textile industry", *Artha Vijñāna* 11(3), sep 69 : 431-491.

3202 KOEHLER, K. "La grève des mineurs de Kiruna et son contexte politique", *Temps mod.* 26(285), apr 70 : 1666-1686. [Suède.]

3203 LAMMERS, C. J. "Strikes and mutinies: a comparative study of organizational conflicts between rulers and ruled", *Adm. Sci. Quart.* 14(4), dec 69 : 558-572.

3204 LEFRANC, G. *Grèves d'hier et d'aujourd'hui—histoire du travail et de la vie économique.* Paris, Aubier-Montaigne, 70, 302 p. [France.]

3205 MALLET, S. "L'après-mai 1968 : grèves pour le contrôle ouvrier", *Sociol. Trav.* 12(3), jul-sep 70 : 309-327. [France.]

3206 McCARTHY, W. E. J. "The nature of Britain's strike problem", *Brit. J. industr. Relat.* 8(2), jul 70 : 224-236.

3207 PENCAVEL, J. H. "An investigation into industrial strike activity in Britain',, *Economica (London)* 50(147), aug 70 : 239-255.

3208 "Sciopero (Lo)" (The strike), *Rass. sind.* 8(25), mar 70 : 3-159. [Italy.]

3209 TOURAINE, A. "Progrès et limites du traitement des conflits", *Projet* 49, nov 70 : 1056-1064. [France.]

3210 TURNER, H. A. *Is Britain really strike-prone? A review of the incidence, character and costs of industrial conflict.* Cambridge, Cambridge University Press, 69, 48 p.

3211 VANDERKAMP, J. "Economic activity and strikes in Canada", *Industr. Relat.* 9(2), feb 70 : 215-230.

3212 WEDDERBURN, K. W.; DAVIES, P. L. *Employment grievances and disputes procedures in Britain.* Berkeley, University of California Press, 69, xvi-301 p.

C.84   Occupational structure
Occupations, professions

[See also / Voir aussi: **A.81, C.64, F.223, F.224**; 816, 990, 1354, 1784, 1905, 1949, 1999, 2176, 2184, 2344, 2357, 2413, 2537, 2544, 2548, 2550, 2588, 2623, 2630, 2633, 2681, 2760, 2761, 2772, 2851, 2857, 2874, 3007, 3496, 3788, 4352]

3213 ADEBAHR, H. "Präferenztheorie und Wirklichkeit" (Preference theory and reality), *Schmollers Jb.* 90(4), 1970 : 419-437. [With regard to occupation.]

3214 ASHLEY, B. *et al.* "A sociological analysis of students' reasons for becoming teachers", *Sociol. R.* 18(1), mar 70 : 53-69.

3215 BARBAGLI, M.; DEI, M. *Le vestali della classe media; ricerca sociologica sugli insegnanti* (The vestals of the middle class. Sociological research on teachers). Bologna, Il Mulino, 69, 378 p.

3216 BERLINGUER, G. "Professione contro ruolo sociale: la figura del medico in Italia" (Profession versus social role: the image of the doctor in Italy), *Crit. sociol. (Roma)* 15, 1970 : 10-32.

3217 BIDOU, D.; GONTIER, G.; VRAIN, P. "Carrière universitaire et perspectives professionnelles; résultats d'une enquête sur les licenciés en lettres, en droit, en sciences économiques, et les diplomés des Instituts d'Études Politiques et des Grandes École de Commerce, de l'année 1966", *Population* 25 [nᵒ spéc.] feb 70 : 137-178. [France.]

3218 BOVY, L. "Responsabilité morale des cadres supérieurs, frustration sur le plan professionnel et compensation au sein de groupes sociaux", *Stato soc.* 13(9), sep 69 : 729-752.

3219 BUMAS, L. O. "Engineering occupational choice, 1950-1965", *Industr. Relat.* 9(2), feb 70 : 231-242.

3220 COE, R. M. "Processes in the development of established professions", *J. Health soc. Behav.* 11(1), mar 70 : 59-66.

3221 CRAIN, R. L. "School integration and occupational achievement of Negroes", *Amer. J. Sociol.* 75(4, *Part II*), jan 70 : 593-606.

3222 CRANE, D. "The academic marketplace revisited: a study of faculty mobility using the Cartter ratings", *Amer. J. Sociol.* 75(6), mai 70 : 953-964.

3223 DEMERS, G. "La fin des corporations professionnelles au Québec", _Sociol. et Soc._ 2(2), nov 70 : 317-326.

3224 DRAYER, A. M. _The teacher in a democratic society; an introduction to the field of education._ Columbus, Ohio, Merrill, 70, xii-449 p.

3225 ENGEL, G. V. "Professional autonomy and bureaucratic organization", _Adm. Sci. Quart._ 15(1), mar 70 : 12-21.

3226 Bibl. XIX-2771. ETZIONI, A. (ed.). _The semi-professions and their organization: teachers, nurses, social workers._ CR: R. THORNTON, _Amer. J. Sociol._ 75(6), mai 70 : 1068-1069.

3227 FELD, M. D. "Professionalism and politicization: notes on the military and civilian control", _Mens en Mij_ 45(6), nov-dec 70 : 409-415.

3228 FOLK, H. _The shortage of scientists and engineers._ Lexington, Mass., Heath Lexington Books, 70, xvii-364 p.

3229 FÜRSTENBERG, F. _et al._ _Die Soziallage der Chemiearbeiter—Industriesoziologische Untersuchungen in rationalisierten und automatisierten Chemiebetrieben_ (The social position of chemical industry workers—industrial sociology surveys on rationalized and automated chemical firms). Neuwied, Luchterhand, 69, vi-323 p.

3230 GEIST, H. "A comparison of vocation interest in Italy and the USA", _Boll. Psicol. appl._ (97-98-99), feb-apr-jun 70 : 81-85.

3231 GUILLON, R. "Le marché interne de l'emploi", _Sociol. Trav._ 12(2), apr-jun 70 : 208-213.

3232 HALL, D. T.; LAWLER, E. E. "Job characteristics and pressures and the organizational integration of professionals", _Adm. Sci. Quart._ 15(3), sep 70 : 271-281.

3233 HALL, R. H. _Occupations and the social structure._ Englewood Cliffs, N. J., Prentice-Hall, 69, 393 p. CR: B. GOLDSTEIN, _Amer. sociol. R._ 35(4), aug 70 : 812-813.

3234 HAUG, M. R.; SUSSMAN, M. B. "Professionalism and the public", _Sociol. Inquiry_ 39(1), 1969 : 57-64.

3235 Bibl. XVIII-3442. HESSE, H. A. _Berufe im Wandel—ein Beitrag zum Problem der Professionalisierung_ (Profession under change—a contribution to the problem of professionalization). CR: H. DAHEIM, _Amer. J. Sociol._ 75(5), mar 70 : 884-885.

3236 HOLT, B. W. G. "Social aspects in the emergence of chemistry as an exact science: the British chemical profession", _Brit. J. Sociol._ 21(2), jun 70 : 181-199.

3237 HUGHES, E. C. "The humble and the proud: the comparative study of occupations", _Sociol. Quart._ 11(2), 1970 : 147-156.

3238 HUGUES, P. D'; PESLIER, M. _Les professions en France, évolution et perspectives._ Paris, Presses universitaires de France, 69, xvi-473 p.

3239 JACEČKO, V. M. "Vybor special'nosti i ego motivy" (The choice of a profession and its motives), _Učen. Zap. (Gor'k. gos. Univ.) Ser. sociol. Sociol. vysš. Škola_ 100(2), 1970 : 30-44.

3240 JACKSÓN, É. F.; FOX, W. S.; CROCKETT, H. J. Jr. "Religion and occupational achievement" _Amer. sociol. R._ 35(1), feb 70 : 48-63.

3241 JONES, J. "The professions as inhibitors of socio-technical evolution", _Futures (Guildford)_ 2(1), mar 70 : 24-34.

3242 KLINGLER, J. "Wird der Lehrerberuf ein Frauenberuf?" (Is the teaching profession becoming a woman's profession?), _Kölner Z. Soziol. u. soz.-Psychol._ 22(1), 1970 : 39-59.

3243 LABOURIE, A. "Étude de l'évolution des métiers—l'exemple des métiers de la comptabilité", _R. franç Aff. soc._ 23(4), oct-dec 69 : 61-83.

3244 LELLI, M. "I tecnici come parte della classe operaia" (The technicians as a part of the working class), _Crit. sociol. (Roma)_ 12, 1969-1970 : 56-70.

3245 LEWIS, D. M. "Occupational aspiration and the occupational prestige structure", _Rur. Sociol._ 35(1), mar 70 : 92-96.

3246 LIEBHARDT, E. H. "Sozialisation im Beruf. Ergebnisse einer Panelbefragung von Studienreferendaren" (Socialization in occupation. Data of a panel survey on trained teachers), _Kölner Z. Soziol. u. soz.-Psychol._ 22(4), dec 70 : 715-736.

3247 LORENZO, C. _Situación del personal docente en América Latina_ (Situation of teaching personnel in Latin America). Santiago de Chile, Editorial Universitaria, 69, 322 p.

3248 MANNING, P. K.; HEARN, H. L. "Student actresses and their artistry: vicissitudes of learning a creative trade", _Soc. Forces_ 48(2), dec 69 : 202-213.

3249 MARQUART, F.; MONTLIBERT, C. DE. "Division du travail et concurrence en architecture", _R. franç. Sociol._ 11(3), jul-sep 70 : 368-389.

3250 McDONAGH, E. C.; SCHUERMAN, M. C.; SCHUERMAN, L. A. "Academic characteristics of presidents of major American universities", *Sociol. soc. Res.* 54(3), apr 70 : 356-370.

3251 McKINLAY, R. D. "Professionalization, politicization and civil-military relations", *Mens en Mij* 45(6), nov-dec 70 : 393-408.

3252 MOK, A. L. "Alte und neue Professionen" (Old and new professions), *Kölner Z. Soziol. u. soz.-Psychol.* 21(4), dec 69 : 770-780.

3253 MOORE, W. E. *The professions: roles and rules*. New York, Russell Sage Foundation, 70, xi-303 p.

3254 OLESEN, V. L.; WHITTAKER, E. W. *The silent dialogue. A study in the social psychology of professional socialization*. San Francisco, Jossey-Bass, Inc., 68, xii-312 p. CR: K. LÜSCHER, *Kölner Z. Soziol. u. soz.-Psychol.* 21(4), dec 69 : 908-910.

3255 PAGANI, A. *La professione del giudice. Ricerca sull'immagine della professione dei giudici a Milano* (The profession of judge. Research on the image of the judicial profession in Milan). Milano-Varese, Istituto editoriale cisalpino, 69, 173 p.

3256 PAPPALARDO, J. *Étude sociologique du personnel d'un centre de tri*. Paris, Librairie générale de droit et de jurisprudence, 69, viii-333 p. [France.]

3257 PARENT-LARDEUR, F. *Les demoiselles de magasin*. Paris, Éditions ouvrières, 70, 157 p.

3258 PEREZ DE GUZMAN MOORE, T.; LA CUEVA ALONSO, J. DE; HERRERO MURIEL, J. "Une tipología de los médicos españoles por estratos de residencia: rural, urbano y metropolitano" (A typology of Spanish doctors by residential areas: rural, urban, metropolitan), *Bol. Centro Estud. soc.* 9(1), 1969 : 5-13.

3259 RADOM, M. *The social scientist in American industry; self-perception of role, motivation, and career*. New Brunswick, N. J., Rutgers University Press, 70, xi-210 p.

3260 RIES, H. *Berufswahl in der modernen Industriegesellschaft—Beitrag zu einer Theorie der Berufswahl mit einer empirischen Untersuchung bei 320 Berufswahlschülern* (Choice of a profession in modern industrial society—contribution to a theory of occupational choice using an empirical survey among 320 students). Bern, Hans Huber, 70, 236 p. [Switzerland.]

3261 RIVALS, C. "L'instituteur produit de sa classe sociale et de son école", *Homo* 8 oct 69 : 141-164.

3262 RODGERS, W. B. "Developmental exposure and changing vocational preferences in the Out Island Bahamas", *Hum. Org.* 28(4), 1969 : 270-278.

3263 RONCERAY, H. DE. "La hiérarchie des occupations en Haïti", *Conjonction* 25(1), 1970 : 18-27.

3264 ROTHMAN, R. A.; PERRUCCI, R. "Organizational careers and professional expertise", *Adm. Sci. Quart.* 15(3), sep 70 : 282-294.

3265 SAINT-AMAND, A. "Problématique organisationnelle et projet social des ingénieurs syndiqués", *Sociol. et Soc.* 2(2), nov 70 : 203-225.

3266 SHIMBORI, M. "The academic marketplace in Japan", *Develop. Econ.* 7(4), dec 69 : 617-639.

3267 SIEBENS, H. "De accountant in Nederland" (The accountant in the Netherlands), *Econ. soc. Tijds.* 24(3), jun 70 : 193-209.

3268 SPAETH, J. L. "Occupational attainment among male college graduates", *Amer. J. Sociol.* 75(4, Part II), jan 70 : 632-645.

3269 STEBBINS, R. A. "Career: the subjective approach", *Sociol. Quart.* 11(1), 1970 : 32-49.

3270 VERY, P. S.; PRULL, R. W. "Birth order, personality development, and the choice of law as a profession", *J. genet. Psychol.* 116(2), jun 70 : 219-222.

3271 VODZINSKAJA, V. V. "Sociologičeskij aspekt problemy vybora professii" (The sociological aspects of the problems of choice of an occupation), *Učen. Zap. (Leningr. gos. Univ. nauč.-issled. Inst. sociol. Issled.)* (6), 1969 : 43-54.

3272 WALBERG, H. J. "Professional role discontinuities in educational careers", *R. educ. Res.* 40(3), jun 70 : 409-420.

3273 WHEELER, J. "Some effects of occupational status on work trips", *J. region. Sci.* 9(1), 1969 : 69-77.

3274 WHYTE, W. F. "The role of the US professor in developing countries", *Amer. Sociologist* 4(1), feb 69 : 19-28.

3275 WINDHAM, G. O. "Occupational aspirations of secondary school students in Sierra Leone", *Rur. Sociol.* 35(1), mar 70 : 40-53.

133

3276 YANOWITCH, M.; DODGE, N. T. "The social evaluation of occupations in the Soviet Union", *Slavic R.* (4), dec 69 : 619-643.

3277 ŽEMANOV, O. N. "Izmenenie professional'noj struktury socialističeskogo obščestva kak odno iz uslovij dostiženija polnogo social'nogo ravenstva" (Changes in the socialist society's professional structure as one of the conditions for complete social equality), *Trudy Ural'. politehn. Inst.* (178), 1970 : 44-54.

C.85 Work and leisure
Travail et loisir

C.851 *Human aspects of work*
Signification humaine du travail

[See also / Voir aussi: 1019, 2374, 2827, 2998, 3011, 3025, 3792, 3924, 4140, 4775]

3278 ANDREEVA, G. K. "Rol' socialističeskogo proizvodstvennogo kollektiva v izmenenii byta trudjaššihsja" (Role of socialist production complex in changes in workers habits), *Učen. Zap. (Moskovs. gos. pedag. Inst.)* (361), 1969 : 163-179.

3279 BURGHARDT, A. "Soziale Determinanten der beruflichen Lohnstruktur" (Social factors of the occupational wage structure), *Kölner Z. Soziol. u. soz.-Psychol.* 22(4), dec 70 : 679-692

3280 CERNEA, M. "A sociological survey of latent manpower fluctuation: size and motivation", *R. roum. Sci. soc. Sér. Sociol.* (14), 1970 : 41-57. [Rumania.]

3281 ČIŽOVA, L. S. "Izučenie voprosy material'nogo stimulirovanija s pomošč'ju sociologičeskih metodov" (A study on material stimulation questions using sociological methods), *Trud. i zarabot. Plata* (2), 1969 : 43-49.

3282 ČURSIN, A. I. "Trudovoj socialističeskij kollektiv kak social'naja osnova tovariščeskih otnošenij" (A socialist labour collectivity as a social basis of camaraderie relations), in: *Ličnost, kollektiv, obščestvo.* II. Krasnojarsk, 1968 : 46-58.

3283 DANEIL, W. W. "Industrial behaviour and orientation to work—a critique", *J.Manag. Stud.* 6(3), oct 69 : 366-375. [UK.]

3284 DEAGLIO, M. "La scelta tra maggior reddito e maggior tempo libero. Un'analisi del comportamento del lavoratore" (Choice between higher income and more leisure time. An analysis of worker behaviour), *Industria* 3, jul-sep 69 : 358-382.

3285 DZJUBALOV, V. A. "Vlijanie socialističeskogo proizvodstvennogo kollektiva na otnošenie rabočego k trudu" (Influence of socialist productive complex on workers relations to labour), *Učen. Zap. (Smolensk. pedag. Inst.)* (21), 1969 : 38-57.

3286 "Effects of task factors on job attitudes and behavior (a symposium)", *Personnel Psychol.* 22(4), 1969 : 415-444.

3287 FORD, R. N. *Motivation through the work itself.* New York, American Management Association, 69, 267 p. CR: W. J. JOKINEN, *Amer. sociol. R.* 35(3), jun 70 : 555-556.

3288 FRIDMAN, V. Š. "O ponjatii funkcii regulirovanija individual'nogo truda i ličnovo potreblenija" (On the notion of labour regulation and individual needs), *Vestn. Moskov. Univ. Ser. Pravo* 25(5), sep-oct 70 : 50-57.

3289 Bibl. XIX-2842. HACKMAN, R. C. *The motivated working adult.* CR. B. JACKSON, *Amer. J. Sociol.* 76(1), jul 70 : 193-196.

3290 HILL, A. B. "Motivation, satisfaction au travail et mobilité professionnelle parmi le personnel féminin de l'industrie électronique", *Trav. hum.* 32(3-4), jul-dec 69 : 199-216.

3291 HOWELLS, J. M.; WOODFIELD, A. E. "The ability of managers and trade union officers to predict worker's preferences", *Brit. J. industr. Relat.* 8(2), jul 70 : 237-251.

3292 JAQUES, E. *Work, creativity, and social justice.* New York, International Universities Press, 70, viii-262 p.

3293 JAVEAU, C. *Les vingt-quatre heures du Belge. L'enquête belge du Projet international budgets-temps.* Bruxelles, Éditions de l'Institut de sociologie de l'Université libre de Bruxelles, 70, 146 p.

3294 KALININ, A. I. *Rol' truda v razvitii ličnost· v uslovijah stroitel'stva kommunizma* (Role of labour in personality development in the condition of edification of communism). Čeboksary, Čuvašgoizdat, 69, 545 p.

3295 KOENE, G. B. M. L. "Industriele psychologie en ergonomie" (Industrial psychology and ergonomics), *Mens en Onderneming* 24(2), mar 70 : 90-102.

3296 KOSMO, R.; BEHLING, O. "Single continuum job satisfaction vs. duality—an empirical test" *Personnel Psychol.* 22(3), 1969 : 327-334.

3297 KRANZ, P. "What do people do all day ?", *Behav. Sci.* 15(3), mai 70 : 286-291. [Computer simulation of time budget.]

3298 MILLER, R. C. "The dockworker subculture and some problems in cross-cultural and cross-time generalizations", *Comp. Stud. Soc. Hist.* 11(3), jun 69 : 302-314.

3299 NICK, H.; WEIDING, R. "Mensch und Automatisierung im Sozialismus" (Man and automation in socialism), *Einheit* 25(9), 1970 : 1149-1161.

3300 ORLOV, V. V.; KRASNOV, G. S. "O social'noj prirode truda" (On the social nature of work), *Učen. Zap. (Perm. gos. Univ.) Filos. pogran. Probl. Nauki* 200(2), 1968 : 87-101.

3301 OSIPOV, G. V.; ŠČEPANSKIJ, Ja. *Social'nye problemy truda i proizvodstva. Sovetopol'skoe sravnitel'noe issledovanie* (Social problems of labour and production. A Soviet-Polish comparative study). Moskva, Mysl'; Varšava, Kziaška i Wiedza, 69, 511 p.

3302 PÜTZ, K. *Zeitbudgetforschung in der Sowjetunion; zur empirischen Sozialforschung in der UdSSR* (Time budget research in the Soviet Union; on empirical social research in the USSR). Meisenheim-am-Glan, A. Hain, 70, 102 p.

3303 ROSEMBLÜTH, G. "El empleo como barrera de la integración socio-económica" (Work as a barrier to socio-economic integration), *R. parag. Sociol.* 7(17), jan-mar 70 : 47-79.

3304 SANFORD, A. C. "A cross-culture study of industrial motivation", *South. Quart.* 8(2), jan 70 : 145-163. [Latin America.]

3305 SHEPARD, J. M. "Functional specialization, alienation, and job satisfaction", *Industr. Lab. Relat. R.* 23(2), jan 70 : 207-219.

3306 SOHN-RETHEL, A. "Travail intellectuel et travail manuel, essai d'une théorie matérialiste", *Homme et Soc.* 15, jan-feb-mar 70 : 317-343.

3307 STEEVES, A. D. "Dissatisfaction and the farm-nonfarm work context", *Soc. Forces* 48(2), dec 69 : 224-232.

3308 SUSLOV, V. Ja. "Sistema 'tehnika'—čelovek' kak sociologičeskaja problema" (Man-machine system as a sociological problem), *Učen. Zap. Kaf. obšč. Nauk Vuzov g. Leningr. Filos. filos. sociol. Issléd.* (9), 1968 : 156-168.

3309 ter HOEVEN, P. J. A. *Arbeiders tussen welvaart en onvrede* (Workers between welfare and dissension). Alphen-aan-den-Rijn, N. Samson, 69, 308 p. [Netherlands.]

3310 WEBER, K. "Ein Verfahren zur Erhebung von Zeitbudgets in Form von Tageslaufschilderungen" (An experience of composing a time-budget in the form of a description of daily activities), *Kölner Z. Soziol. u. soz. Psychol.* 22(1), mar 70 : 62-74.

3311 WILLEMS, P. J. "Ergonomische aspecten van de proces-industrie" (Ergonomic aspects of industrial process), *Mens en Onderneming* 24(2), mar 70 : 103-111.

3312 WILMAR, F. "Menschenwürde und Sachzwang in der Arbeitswelt" (Human dignity and constraints in the world of work), *Gegenwartskunde* 19(1), 1970 : 29-38.

C.852 Working conditions
La condition ouvrière

[See also / Voir aussi: 1779, 4201, 4217, 4513]

3313 ADAM, G. et al. *L'ouvrier français en 1970. Enquête nationale auprès de 1116 ouvriers d'industrie.* Paris, A. Colin, 70, 276 p. (Travaux et recherches de science politique, n° 13).

3314 Bibl. XIX-2872. BODIGUEL, J.-L. *La réduction du temps de travail. Enjeu de la lutte sociale.* CR: Y. LUCAS, *R. franç. Sociol.* 11(3), jul-sep 70 : 430-431.

3315 Bibl. XVIII-4336. GOLDTHORPE, J. H. et al. *The affluent worker: political attitudes and behaviour.* CR: B. JACKSON, *Amer. J. Sociol.* 71(6), jul 70 : 193-196; J. BRAND, *Amer. polit. Sci. R.* 64(1), mar 70 : 235-237; R. E. EDGAR, *Amer. sociol. R.* 35(1), feb 70 : 131-132; M. MAURICE; M. ARCIAUD, *Sociol. Trav.* 12(1), jan-mar 70 : 74-86. [See also Bibl. XVIII-4336.]

3316 GOLDTHORPE, J. H. et al. *The affluent worker in the class structure.* Cambridge, University Press, 69, viii-239 p.

3317   GOLDTHORPE, J. H. "L'image des classes chez les travailleurs manuels aisés", *R. franç. Sociol.* 11(3), jul-sep 70 : 311-338.

3318   GOMBERG, Ja. "Redukcija truda pri socializmae" (The reduction of work in the socialist system), *Vopr. Ékon.* 22(7), jul 70 : 83-96.

3319   GROSSIN, W. *Le travail et le temps, horaires, durées, rythmes, une enquête dans la construction mécanique et électrique de la région parisienne...* Paris, Éditions Anthropos, 69, xii-249 p.

3320   LEONS, W. "Modelos cambiantes de organización laboral en una comunidad boliviana" (Changing models of labour organization in a Bolivian community), *Estud. andinos* 1(2), 1970 : 49-60.

3321   MORSE, D. *The peripheral worker.* New York, Columbia University Press, 69, xvi-202 p. [Part time employment in the USA.]

3322   NIKIFOROVA, A. A. *Raboèee vremja i kapitalistièeskoe proizvodstvo* (Work time and capitalist production). Moskva, Mysl', 69, 127 p.

3323   RICHTER, H. *Gestaltung der Arbeits- und Lebensverhältnisse der LPG-Mitglieder. Rechtsfragen der Arbeits- und Sozialverhältnisse* (Development of living and working conditions of LPG members. Legal problems of social and work conditions). Berlin, Staatsverlag der Deutschen Demokratischen Republik, 70, 183 p.

3324   RUSTANT, M. "Les Français travaillent-ils trop ? Implications sociales et économiques de la réduction du temps de travail", *Anal. et Prévis.* 10(3), sep 70 : 535-553; 10(4), oct 70 : 609-628.

3325   SEMENOV, L. D. "Peremena truda i svobodnoe vremja" (The transformation of labour and leisure time), *Uèen. Zap. (Èit. gos. pedag. Inst.)* (20), 1969 : 103-118.

3326   WEISSENBERG, G.; CERNY, J. *Arbeitszeitgesetz* (The law on hours of labour). Wien, Verlag des Österreichisen Gewerkschaftsbundes, 70, xii-178 p. [Austria.]

C.853   *Leisure*
          Loisir

[See also / Voir aussi: 971, 3325, 3769]

3327   ALBERRO, A. "Les loisirs dans le région parisienne: le mode de transport joue un rôle déterminant", *Int. Mkting* 174, apr-mai 70 : 41-50.

3328   ANDREAE, C. A. *Ökonomik der Freizeit. Zur Wirtschaftstheorie a. modernen Arbeitswelt* (Economics of leisure. On the economic theory of the modern working world). Reinbek-bei-Hamburg, Rowohlt, 70, 247 p.

3329   BISHOP, D. W.; IKEDA, M. "Status and role factors in the leisure behavior of different occupations", *Sociol. soc. Res.* 54(2), jan 70 : 190-208.

3330   BREUSE, E. *Vers une pédagogie des loisirs juvéniles.* Bruxelles, Éditions de l'Institut de Sociologie, 69, 213 p.

3331   CRIBIER, F. *La grande migration d'été des citadins en France.* Paris, Éditions du Centre national de la recherche scientifique, 69, 403 p.

3332   DANECKI, J. *Jednoéæ podzielonego czasu. Czas wolny i czas pracy w spoleczeñstwach uprzemyslówionych* (The unity of divided time. Leasure-time and worktime in the industrial society). Warszawa, Ksi¹¿ka i Wiedza, 70, 356 p.

3333   DILIC, E. "Rural youth and leisure", *Soc. and Leisure* 1, 1970 : 66-76. [Yugoslavia.]

3334   DUMAZEDIER, J.; MARKIEWICZ-LAGNEAU, J. "Société soviétique, temps libre et loisir 1924-1964", *R. franç. Sociol.* 11(2), apr-jun 70 : 211-229.

3335   FILIPCOVA, B. "Sociologie volného casu a spoleèenská intervence" (Sociology of leisure and social intervention), *Sociol. Èas.* 6(1), jan-feb 70 : 1-9.

3336   FOURASTIÉ, J. FOURASTIÉ, F. *Des loisirs pour quoi faire ?* Tournai-Paris, Casterman, 70, 144 p.

3337   GEENS, V. "L'utilisation des loisirs pour l'éducation permanente des adultes", *Progr. soc.* 57(109), mai-jun 69 : 15-48.

3338   GOVAERTS, F. *Loisirs des femmes et temps libre.* Bruxelles, Éditions de l'Institut de Sociologie, 69, 312 p.

3339   GRUSHIN, B. A. *Problems of free time in the USSR; a sociological study.* Moscow, Novosti, 69, 87 p.

3340 HENTIG, H. VON. "Freizeit als Befreiungszeit" (Leisure time as a time of liberation), *Jb. krit. Aufklärung* 4, 1970 : 186-218.

3341 HIRSCHFELD, A. "L'utilisation des loisirs pour l'éducation permanente des adultes", *R. Ét. coop.* 49(161), 3 trim 70 : 263-284.

3342 JERBIC, V. "A factor analysis of leisure among children and youth", *Soc. and Leisure* 1, 1970 : 93-101.

3343 JONES, W. H. *Recreation and amusement among Negroes in Washington, D. C.; a sociological analysis of the Negro in an urban environment.* Westport, Conn., Negro Universities Press, 70, 216 p.

3344 "Leisure", *Convergence* 2(4), 1969 : 84 p.

3345 LE ROUX, P. "Les loisirs des Français", *Écon. et Statist.* 12, mai 70 : 45-49.

3346 LINDE, H,; HEINEMANN, K. *Leistungsengagement und Sportinteresse. Eine empirische Studie zur Stellung des Sports im betrieblichen und schulischen Leistungsfeld* (Commitment to performance and interests in sport. An empirical survey on the position of sports in the enterprise and the school). Schorndorf-bei-Stuttgart, Verlag K. Hofmann, 68, 114 p. CR: K. HAMMERICH, *Kölner Z. Soziol. u. soz.-Psychol.* 21(4), dec 69 : 912-915.

3347 LOY, J. W. Jr; KENYON, G. S. (eds.). *Sport, culture and society; a reader on the sociology of sport.* London, MacMillan, 69, xii-464 p. CR: G. TURBEVILLE, *Amer. sociol. R.* 35(4), aug 70 : 817-818.

3348 LYUBASEVSKIJ, J. "Svobodnoe vremja i obrazovanie vzroslyh" (Leisure and adult education), *Convergence* 3(2), 1970 : 64-71.

3349 MASSÉ, J. C. "Le travail du dimanche", *Social. et Soc.* 2(1), mai 70 : 145-161.

3350 MEYNAUD, J. "L'intervention de la politique dans le sport", *Écon. et Human.* 180, mar-apr 68 : 40-56.

3351 MILLONES, L. "Deportes y alienación en el Perú: el futbol en los barrios limeños" (Sports and alienation in Peru: soccer in the slums of Lima), *Estud. andinos* 1(2), 1970 : 87-95.

3352 ORTUÑO MEDINA, F. "Aspectos sociales de la caza" (Social aspects of hunting), *R. Estud. agro-soc.* 19(70), jan-mar 70 : 7-23.

3353 OWEN, J. D. *The price of leisure. An economic analysis of the demand for leisure time.* Montreal, McGill-Queen's University Press; Rotterdam, Rotterdam University Press, 69, x-169 p.

3354 PARKER, S. R. "Theory and practice of the work-leisure relationship", *Soc. and Leisure* 2, dec 69 : 29-49.

3355 PERRIN. "La réadaptation par le travail et les loisirs", *Vie soc.* (9), sep 69 : 471-478.

3356 PICHAULT, M. "L'utilisation des loisirs pour l'éducation permanente des adultes immigrés", *Progr. soc.* 57(109), mai-jun 69 : 49-64.

3357 RAYNOUARD, Y. "De l'industrie touristique au loisir", *Écon. et Human.* 191, jan-feb 70 : 44-53.

3358 RUVO, V. DE. "Il tempo libero e il dramma della società odierna" (Leisure time and drama of present society), *Rass. ital. Sociol.* 11(1), jan-mar 70 : 107-119.

3359 SHAFER, W. E.; REHBERG, R. A. "Athletic participation, college aspirations and college encouragement", *Pacific sociol. R.* 13(3), 1970 : 182-186.

3360 Bibl. XIX-2907. TIMM, A. *Verlust der Musse. Zur Geschichte der Freizeitgesellschaft* (Loss of obligation. History of the leisure society). CR: K. HAMMERICH, *Kölner Z. Soziol. u. soz.-Psychol.* 21(4), dec 69 : 915-916.

C.9   POLITICAL AND RELIGIOUS INSTITUTIONS (SOCIOLOGICAL ASPECTS)
       INSTITUTIONS POLITIQUES ET RELIGIEUSES (ASPECTS SOCIOLOGIQUES)

C.91   Political institutions
       Institutions politiques

C.910 *General studies*
       Études générales

[See also / Voir aussi: 183, 529, 3393, 4875]

3361   ALLARDT, E.; ROKKAN, S. (eds.). *Mass politics; studies in political sociology.* New York, Free Press, 70, xii-400 p.

3362   ANDRAIN, C. F. *Political life and social change: an introduction to political science.* Belmont, Calif., Wadsworth Publishing Co., 70, xi-306 p.

3363   DMITRIEV, A. V.; KETZEROV, N. M. "Predmet buržuaznoj političeskoj sociologii" (Object of bourgeois political sociology), *Učen. Zap. (Leningr. gos. Univ. nauč.-issled. Inst. kompleks. sociol. Issled.)* (5), 1969 : 15-24.

3364   FOTIA, M. "Structure du pouvoir et sociologie contemporaine aux États-Unis", *Homme et Soc.* 17, jul-sep 70 : 55-74.

3365   GOCKOWSKI, J. "Functions of literary work in the sociology of politics", *Polish sociol. B.* (1), 1968 : 59-64.

3366   LANG, F. "Politisches System und Organisation. Politische Wissenschaft als organisations-bezogene Wissenschaft" (Political system and organization. Political science as science of organization), *Z. Polit.* 16(3), sep 69 : 303-324.

3367   LIPSET, S. M. (ed.). *Politics and the social sciences.* New York, Oxford University Press, 69, xxii-328 p. CR: R. P. TAUB, *Amer. J. Sociol.* 76(1), jul 70 : 173-175; J. A. SCHLESINGER, *Amer. polit. Sci. R.* 64(3), sep 70 : 910-911.

3368   NARR, W. D. "Entwicklung der Politologie—Entwicklung der Gesellschaft; Bemerkung-en zum Stand der politischen Soziologie aus Anlass einiger Buchbesprechungen" (The evolution of political science and the evolution of society. Notes on the situation of political sociology on the occasion of various book reviews), *Kölner Z. Soziol. u. soz. Psychol.* 22(1), mar 70 : 98-120.

3369   NASSMACHER, K.-H. *Politikwissenschaft* (Political science). Düsseldorf, Werner, 70, 154 p. [Contents: I. *Politische Systeme und politische Soziologie* (Political systems and political sociology)].

3370   NORDLINGER, E. A. (ed.). *Politics and society; studies in comparative political sociology.* Englewood Cliffs, N. J., Prentice-Hall, 70, xii-351 p.

3371   SANI, G. "C'è davvero bisogno di una nuova sociologia politica ?" (Is a new political sociology really needed ?), *Rass. ital. Sociol.* 10(1), jan-mar 69 : 108-122.

3372   SARTORI, G. "Alla ricerca della sociologia politica" (In search of political sociology), *Rass. ital. Sociol.* 9(4), oct-dec 68 : 597-639.

3373   SOLAŘ, J. *Úvod do sociologie politiky* (Introduction to political sociology). Práha, SPN, rozmn. SČT, 69, 102 p.

3374   WINNER, L. "Cybernetic and political language", *Berkeley J. Sociol.* 14, 1969 : 1-17.

C.911 *Government and the State*
       Le gouvernement et l'État

[See also / Voir aussi: 541, 544, 608, 620, 1016, 1229, 1788, 1923, 2472, 2511, 2954, 3227, 3251, 3494, 3541, 3569, 3589, 3596, 4017, 4028, 4289, 4317, 4328, 4334, 4969, 5004, 5228, 5274, 5295]

3375   ADAMIAK, R. "The 'withering away' of the states: a reconsideration", *J. Polit.* 32(1), feb 70 : 3-18.

3376   AIKIN, C. "Two studies on representative government", *Jb. öff. Rechts Gegenwart* 17, 1968 : 1-22.

3377   ALDRUP, D. "Zu einer rationalen Theorie der Politik" (For a rational theory of politics), *Jb. soz.-Wiss.* 21(2), 1970 : 151-186.

3378 BARREA, J. *L'intégration politique externe. Notion globale et analyse sociologique. Avec références principales aux exemples de la formation des États-Unis d'Amérique, du Dominion du Canada, du Commonwealth d'Australie et de l'Union Sud-Africaine.* Louvain, Éditions Nauwelaerts; Paris, Béatrice-Nauwelaerts, 69, 335 p.

3379 BARTON, W. V. "Towards a policy science of democracy", *J. Polit.* 31(1), feb 69 : 32-51.

3380 BAY, C. "Behavioral research and the theory of democracy", *Berkeley J. Sociol.* 14, 1969 : 18-34.

3381 BERGERON, G. "Pouvoir, contrôle et régulation", *Sociol. et Soc.* 2(2), nov 70 : 227-248.

3382 BERKELEY, G. E. *The democratic policeman.* Boston, Beacon Press, 69, 232 p. CR: A. PINKNEY, *Amer. J. Sociol.* 76(2), sep 70 : 355-357. [USA.]

3383 BOURRICAUD, F. "Le modèle polyarchique et les conditions de sa survie", *R. franç. Sci. polit.* 20(5), oct 70 : 893-924.

3384 BRAGA, G. "Il problema dell'ordine pubblico visto da un sociologo" (The problem of public order seen by a sociologist), *Quad. Sci. soc.* 9(1), 1970 : 36-45.

3385 CHARLE, E. "Political systems and economic performance in some African societies", *Econ. Develop. cult. Change* 18(4, Part I), jul 70 : 575-616.

3386 CHEVIGNY, P. *Police power: police abuses in New York City.* New York, Pantheon Books, 69, 298 p. CR: P. K. MANNING, *Amer. sociol. R.* 34(6), dec 69 : 978-979.

3387 CORSI-OTÁLORA, L. *De la democracia al partido único; respuesta a la confusión ideológica actual* (From democracy to the single party; an answer to current ideological confusion). Bogotá, Ediciones Tercer Mundo, 69, 261 p.

3388 CRAIG, J. G.; GROSS, E. "The forum theory of organizational democracy: structural guarantees as time-related variables", *Amer. sociol. R.* 55(1), feb 70 : 19-33.

3389 CRUISE O'BRIEN, C.; VANEK, W. D. (eds.). *Power and consciousness.* London, University of London Press; New York, New York University Press, 69, 243 p.

3390 DIENES, C. T. "Judges, legislators and social change", *Amer. behav. Scientist* 13(4), mar-apr 70 : 511-521. [USA.]

3391 ECKSTEIN, H. "Authority relations and governmental performance: a theoretical framework", *Comp. polit. Stud.* 2(3), oct 69 : 269-326.

3392 EISENSTADT, S. N. "El Estado, la sociedad y la formación de centros. Algunos problemas en la evolución de la sociología política" (The State, society and center formation. Some problems in the evolution of political sociology), *R. esp. Opin. públ.* 18, oct-dec 69 : 9-40.

3393 FERRANDO BADÍA, J. "De la democracia política a la democracia social y económica" (From political democracy to social and economic democracy), *R. Estud. polít.* 168, nov-dec 69 : 73-120.

3394 FERNANDO BADÍA, J. "Dinâmica política e progresso político" (Political dynamics and political progress), *R. brasil. Estud. polit.* 27, jul 69 : 7-43.

3395 FÖLSING, G. H. "Demokratie und Evolution" (Democracy and evolution), *Polit. Stud. (München)* 186, jul-aug 69 : 389-399.

3396 FORBES, J. D. "Do tribes have rights? The question of self-determination", *J. hum. Relat.* 18(1), 1970 : 670-679.

3397 FRANKE, J. "Die Gesellschafts- und Staatskonzeption Ralf Dahrendorfs" (Conceptions of society and the State in Ralf Dahrendorf), *Dokum. Zeit* 14, jul 70 : 11-17.

3398 GREEN, P.; LEVINSON, S. (eds.). *Power and community; dissenting essays in political science.* New York, Pantheon Books, 70, ix-396 p.

3399 GROSSMAN, J. B. "The Supreme Court and social change: a preliminary inquiry", *Amer. behav. Scientist* 13(4), mar-apr 70 : 535-551. [USA.]

3400 GULIEV, V. E. *Demokratija i sovremennyj imperializm* (Democracy and contemporary imperialism). Moskva, Meždunarodnye Otnošenija, 70, 280 p.

3401 JANICKE, M. "Monopolismus und Pluralismus im kommunistischen Herrschaftssystem" (Monopolism and pluralism in communist governmental systems), *Z. Polit.* 14(2), jun 67 : 150-161.

3402 KANET, R. E. "The rise and fall of the 'all-people's State': recent changes in the Soviet theory of the State", *Sov. Stud.* 20(1), jul 68 : 81-93.

3403 KAPLAN, M. "Estado y sociedad" (State and society), *R. parag. Sociol.* 6(15), mai-aug 69 : 5-32.

3404 KASK, L. I. *Funkcii i struktura gosudarstva* (State functions and structure). Leningrad, Izdatel'stvo Leningradskogo Universiteta, 69, 65 p.

3405   KINSKY, R. *Der Staat der Zukunft. Eine Staatslehre auf naturgeschichtliche Grundlage* (The future State. A theory of the State based on natural history). München-Wien, Amalthea-Verlag, 69, 288 p.

3406   KLOKOČKA, V. *Volby v pluralitních demokraciích* (Elections in pluralist democracy). Praha, Svoboda, 68, 301-2 p.

3407   KROES, P. "Strategie en structuur in de Nederlandse politiek" (Strategy and structure in Dutch politics), *Sociol. Gids* 16(4), jul-aug 69 : 255-265. [A trend report on political sociology.]

3408   LEGUM, C. "Tribal survival in the modern African political system", *J. Asian Afr. Stud.* 5(1-2), jan-apr 70 : 102-112.

3409   LUCAS VERDÚ, P. "Análisis de la estructura política" (Analysis of political structure), *R. int. Sociol. (Madrid)* 26(103-104), jul-dec 68 : 5-30.

3410   LUCAS VERDÚ, P. "Contribución al estudio de la morfología política (las formas, elementos de la estructura política)" (A contribution to the study of political morphology [forms, elements of political structure]), *R. int. Sociol. (Madrid)* 27(105-106), jan-jun 69 : 5-49.

3411   LUHMANN, N. "Komplexität und Demokratie" (Complexity and democracy), *Polit. Vjschr.* 10(2-3), sep 69 : 314-325.

3412   MANKOFF, M. "Power in advanced capitalist society: a review essay on recent elitist and Marxist criticism of pluralist theory", *Soc. Probl.* 17(3), 1970 : 418-430.

3413   MANN, M. "The social cohesion of liberal democracy", *Amer. sociol. R.* 35(3), jun 70 : 423-439.

3414   Bibl. XIX-2965. McFARLAND, A. S. *Power and leadership in pluralist systems.* CR: P. HOLLANDER, *Amer. sociol. R.* 35(1), feb 70 : 129-131.

3415   MENDIETA Y NÚÑEZ, L. *Sociología del poder* (Sociology of power). México, Instituto de Investigaciones Sociales, Universidad Nacional Autónoma de México, 69, 127 p.

3416   MILIBAND, R. *The State in capitalist society: an analysis of the Western system of power.* New York, Basic Books Inc., 69, 292 p. CR: B. R. BARBER, *Amer. polit. Sci. R.* 64(3), sep 70 : 928-929.

3417   MOREIRA, A. "Sistemas políticos de la coyuntura" (Current political systems), *R. Estud. polít.* 167, sep-oct 69 : 5-67.

3418   NASCHOLD, F. "Demokratie und Komplexität. Thesen und Illustrationen zur Theoriediskussion in der Politikwissenschaft" (Democracy and complexity. Theses and illustrations of the theoretical discussion in political science), *Polit. Vjschr.* 9(4), dec 68 : 494-518.

3419   NEWTON, K. "A critique of the pluralist model", *Acta sociol.* 12(4), 1969 : 209-223.

3420   Bibl. XIX-2970. NIEDERHOFFER, A. *Behind the shield: the police in urban society.* CR: R. L. AKERS, *Amer. sociol. R.* 35(2), apr 70 : 406-407.

3421   OESTREICH, G. *Geist und Gestalt des frühmodernen Staates* (Spirit and form of the modern State). Berlin, Duncker und Humblot, 69, 355 p.

3422   OKE, M. "L'influence du tribalisme sur les régimes politiques africains", *R. franç. Ét. polit. afr.* 55, jul 70 : 63-69.

3423   OLIVEIRA TORRES, J. C. DE. "A transformação política moderna" (Modern political change), *R. brasil. Estud. polít.* 29, jul 70 : 51-61.

3424   OLSEN, M. E. (ed.). *Power in societies.* New York, Macmillan, 70, xii-451 p.

3425   OTT, G. M. *Frühe politische Ordnungsmodelle* (Ancient models of political organization). München, Kösel-Verlag, 70, 255-1 p.

3426   POCKLINGTON, T. "Protest, resistance and political obligation", *Canad. J. polit. Sci.* 3(1), mar 70 : 1-17.

3427   "Police and society", *Amer. behav. Scientist* 13(5-6), mai-jun/jul-aug 70 : 645-814.

3428   REJAI, M. "Toward the comparative study of political decision-makers", *Comp. polit. Stud.* 2(3), oct 69 : 349-360.

3429   SCHNEIDER, P. *Recht und Macht; Gedanken zum modernen Verfassungsstaat* (Law and power; thoughts on the modern constitutional State). Mainz, von Hase und Koehler, 70, 281 p.

3430   SCHOLTEN, G. H. "De fictie van de verantwoordelijkheid als grondslag voor democratisch bestuur" (The fiction of responsibility as the foundation of democratic management), *Acta polit.* 5(3), apr 69-70 : 237-253.

3431 SPANNRAFT, E. "Oligarchie oder Fundamentaldemokratisierung ?" (Oligarchy or fundamental democratisation ?), *Polit. Stud.* (*München*) 21(193), sep-oct 70 : 513-525.

3432 STRAUSZ-HUPÉ, R. "Social values and politics: the uninvited guests", *R. Polit.* 30(1), jan 68 : 59-78. [The integration of scientific-technological productivity into political development.]

3433 TADIC, L. "Le pouvoir, l'élite et la démocratie", *Homme et Soc.* 17, jul-sep 70 : 75-89.

3434 TARGINO LIMA, G. "Reflexóes sobre o poder constituinte" (On constituent power), *R. Ciênc. polit.* 2(3), jul-sep 68 : 46-58.

3435 TEITLER, G. "Rome, Byzantium en de Barbaren. Methodologische kanttekeningen bij de sociologie van de militaire organisatie" (Rome, Byzantium and the Barbarians. Methodological considerations on the sociology of military organization), *Mens en Mij* 45(4), jul-aug 70 : 258-265.

3436 THOMPSON, K. "Constitutional theory and political action", *J. Polit.* 31(3), aug 69 : 655-681.

3437 ZACHER, H. F. "Pluralität der Gesellschaft als rechtspolitische Aufgabe" (Social pluralism as a political-legal imperative), *Staat* 9(2), 1970 : 161-186.

3438 ZAMPETTI, P. L. *Democrazia e potere dei partiti. Il nuovo regime politico* (Democracy and party power. A new political regime). Milano, Rizzoli, 69, 147 p.

3439 ZAWADZKI, S. "Socjalna funkcja panstwa w okresie budownictwa socjalizmu" (The social function of the State in the edification period of communism), *Pán. i Prawo* 25(6), jun 70 : 849-862.

C.912 Public administration
L'administration publique

[See also / Voir aussi: **C.40**; 1564, 2171, 2417, 2521, 2551, 2971, 3811]

3440 "Administration (L')", *Esprit* 38(1), jan 70 : 1-195. [France.]

3441 ALBROW, M. *Bureaucracy.* New York, Praeger, 70, 157 p.

3442 ALFORD, R. R. *Bureaucracy and participation: political cultures in four Wisconsin cities.* Chicago, Rand McNally and Co., 69, 224 p. CR: J. Q. WILSON, *Amer. polit. Sci. R.* 64(1), mar 70 : 198-200.

3443 BADURA, P. "Die Verwaltung als soziales System" (Administration as a social system), *Öff. Verw.* 23(1-2), jan 70 : 18-22.

3444 BARNABAS, A. P. *Citizens' grievances and administration; a study in participation and alienation.* New Delhi, Indian Institute of Public Administration, 69, vi-163 p.

3445 BÉLANGER, F.; KHOURY, N. (eds.). *L'administration; principes et fonctions.* Montréal-New York, McGraw-Hill, 70, xiv-419 p.

3446 BENNIS, W. G. (ed.). *American bureaucracy.* Chicago, Aldine, 70, 187 p.

3447 BENVENISTE, G. *Bureaucracy and national planning; a sociological case study in Mexico.* New York, Praeger, 70, xiv-141 p.

3448 BODIGUEL, J.-L.; KESSLER, M.-C. *L'administration française.* Paris, A. Colin, 70, 80 p. (Bibliographies françaises de sciences sociales, Guides de recherches, n⁰ 1).

3449 BONJEAN, C. M.; GRIMES, M. D. "Bureaucracy and alienation: a dimensional approach", *Soc. Forces* 48(3), mar 70 : 365-373.

3450 BROWN, R. G. S. *The administrative process in Britain.* London, Methuen, 70, xiv-349 p.

3451 BURKE, F. G. "Public administration in Africa: the legacy of inherited colonial institutions", *J. comp. Adm.* 1(3), nov 69 : 345-378.

3452 CAIDEN, G. "Coping with turbulence: Israel's administrative experience", *J. comp. Adm.* 1(3), nov 69 : 259-280.

3453 CARNEY, T. F. "Two contemporary views of a traditional bureaucracy", *J. comp. Adm.* 1(4), feb 70 : 398-427.

3454 CATHERINE, R.; THUILLIER, G. *Introduction à une philosophie de l'administration.* Paris, Librairie Armand Colin, 69, 375 p.

3455 DARBEL, A.; SCHNAPPER, D. *Les agents du système administratif.* Paris, Mouton, 69, 163 p.

3456 DAVAL, R. "Bien public et service de l'État, enquête de psychologie sociale administrative", *B. Inst. int. Adm. publ.* 13, jan-mar 70 : 15-52.

3457 Bibl. XIX-3011. DEBBASCH, C. *L'administration au pouvoir. Fonctionnaires et politiques sous la Vᵉ République.* CR: R. DUCHAC, *R. franç. Sociol.* 11(2), apr-jun 70 : 266-269.

3458 DEMARCHI, F. "Autoriforma burocratica ?" (Bureaucratic self-reform), *Riv. Sociol.* 6(17), sep-dec 68 : 141-148.

3459 DENTON, C. F. "Bureaucracy in an immobilist society: the case of Costa Rica", *Adm. Sci. Quart.* 14(3), sep 69 : 418-425.

3460 DEUTSCHER, I. "Les racines de la bureaucratie", *Homme et Soc.* 14, oct-nov-dec 69 : 63-82.

3461 DEY, B. K. "Bureaucracy and development—some reflections", *Ind. J. publ. Adm.* 15(2), apr-jun 69 : 228-248.

3462 Bibl. XIX-3018. GAWTHROP, L. C. *Bureaucratic behavior in the executive branch: an analysis of organizational change.* CR: D. E. MILLER, *Amer. sociol. R.* 35(1), feb 70 : 167.

3463 GREENBERG, M. H. *Bureaucracy and development: a Mexican case study.* Lexington, Mass., Heath, 70, x-158 p.

3464 HOPKINS, J. W. "Comparative observations on Peruvian bureaucracy", *J. comp. Adm.* 1(3), nov 69 : 301-320.

3465 JACOBY, H. *Die Bürokratisierung der Welt; ein Beitrag zur Problemgeschichte* (Bureaucratization of the world; a contribution to the history of the problem). Neuwied, Luchterhand, 69, 340 p.

3466 JIMENEZ CASTRO, W. "Sistemas prioritarios para la administración del desarrollo" (Priorities systems for development administration), *Cienc. adm. (La Plata)* 12(29), mai-aug 69 : 91-112.

3467 KATZ, S. M. "A educação de administradores para o desenvolvimento: carácter, forma, contenido e currículo" (Education of administrators for development: character, form, content and curriculum), *R. Adm. públ. (Rio de Janeiro)* 3(1), jan-jun 69 : 27-54.

3468 KÖLBLE, J. "Grundprobleme einer Reform des öffentlichen Dienstes" (Basic problems of a public service reform), *Öff. Verw.* 23(13-14), jul 70 : 447-459.

3469 LA MORENA Y DE LA MORENA, L. DE. "Los servicios de inspección de la administración pública francesa y sus intentos de reforma" (Inspection services of French public administration and their attempts to reform), *Docum. adm.* 129, mai-jun 69 : 11-26.

3470 LÁZÁR, M. "A hivatalos személy fogalmának érvényesülése a gazdaságirányitás új rendszerének viszonyai között" (The current notion of the civil servant concept in the relations of the new economic management), *Jogtud. Közl.* 24(10), oct 69 : 516-523. [Hungary.]

3471 LEE, H. B. "Politischer Wandel und Entwicklung der öffentlichen Verwaltung in Korea seit 1945" (Political transformations and evolution of public administration in Korea since 1945), *Verwaltung* 1(3), 1968 : 333-357.

3472 LEGENDRE, P. *L'administration du 18e siècle à nos jours.* Paris, Presses universitaires de France, 69, 344 p. [France.]

3473 LEWIS, J. W. "Leader, Commissar and bureaucrat: the Chinese political system in the last days of the revolution", *J. int. Aff.* 24(1), 1970 : 48-74.

3474 LOURAU, R. *L'instituant contre l'institué...* Paris, Anthropos, 69, xii-197 p. CR: A. REVON, *R. franç. Sociol.* 11(3), jul-sep 70 : 432-433.

3475 LOUREIRO PINTO, A. "A institucionalizaçao organizacional como estratégia de desenvolvimento" (Organizational institutionalization as development strategy), *R. Adm. públ (Rio de Janeiro)* 3(1), jan-jun 69 : 7-25. [Brazil.]

3476 MALLET, S. "Bureaucracy and technocarcy in the socialist countries", *Sociol. Revol.* 1(3), mai-jun 70 : 44-75.

3477 MARUYAMA, M. "Toward non-hierarchical administration", *Sociol. int. (Berlin)* 8(2), 1970 : 233-243.

3478 MENZEL, E. "Parteienstaat und Beamtentum" (The Party State and the civil servants), *Öff. Verw.* 23(13-14), jul 70 : 433-447. [Germany, BR.]

3479 MEYER, P. "Derecho administrativo y administración pública (Noruega, Dinamarca y Suecia)" (Administrative law and public administration [Norway, Denmark and Sweden]), *R. Inst. Cienc. soc.* (11), 1968 : 225-234.

3480 Bibl. XIX-3046. MEYNAUD, J. *Technocracy.* CR: G. M. LYONS, *Amer. J. Sociol.* 75(6), mai 70 : 1050-1052; V. C. FERKISS, *Amer. polit. Sci. R.* 64(1), mar 70 : 238-239. [See also Bibl. XIII-1468.]

3481 MILNE, R. S. "Mechanistic and organic models of public administration in developing countries", *Adm. Sci. Quart.* 15(1), mar 70 : 57-67.

3482 MOLITOR, A. "Derecho administrativo y ciencias administrativas" (Administrative law and public administration), *R. Inst. Cienc. soc.* (11), 1968 : 109-133.

3483 MONTORO PUERTO, M. "La ciencia de la administración" (The science of public administration), *R. Inst. Cienc. soc.* (1), 1968 : 75-108.

3484 MYERS, P. *An introduction to public administration.* London, Butterworths, 70, ix-226 p. [UK.]

3485 NATERO CORDOBA, M. M. "Ciencias administrativas contemporáneas" (Contemporary administrative sciences), *Cienc. adm. (La Plata)* 13(32), mai-aug 70 : 100-129.

3486 RONNEBERGER, F. "Empirische Forschung in der Verwaltungswissenschaft" (Empirical research in administrative science), *Verwaltung* 1(3), 1968 : 257-274.

3487 ROOS, L. L. Jr.; ROOS, N. P. "Administrative change in a modernizing society", *Adm. Sci. Quart.* 15(1), mar 70 : 69-78.

3488 ROOS, L. L. Jr; ROOS, N. P. "Bureaucracy in the Middle East: some cross-cultural relationships", *J. comp. Adm.* 1(3), nov 69 : 281-299. [Egypt, Pakistan, Turkey.]

3489 SAMUEL, Y.; MANNHEIM, B. F. "A multidimensional approach toward a typology of bureaucracy", *Adm. Sci. Quart.* 15(2), jun 70 : 216-228.

3490 SBIH, M. *La fonction publique.* Paris, Hachette, 68, 256 p. [Algérie.]

3491 SCOTT, W. G. "Organization government: the prospects for a truly participative system", *Publ. Adm. R.* 29(1), jan-feb 69 : 43-53.

3492 SIMMONS, R. H. "Public administration: the enigma of definition", *Soc. Sci. (Winfield)* 45(4), oct 70 : 202-207.

3493 SMIGEL, E. O.; ROSS, H. L. *Crimes against bureaucracy.* New York, Van Nostrand Reinhold Co., 70, vii-142 p.

3494 SOBRINHO, M. DE O. F. "O poder político e o poder administrativo" (Political power and administrative power), *Cienc. adm. (La Plata)* 12(28), jan-apr 69 : 5-24.

3495 STACEY, F. "Derecho administrativo y administración pública en el Reino Unido" (Administrative law and public administration in Britain), *R. Inst. Cienc. soc.* (11), 1968 : 179-189.

3496 TONIX, J. L. *et al.* "La profesionalización del personal público" (The professionalisation of public personnel), *R. mexic. Cienc. polít.* 15(57), jul-sep 69 : 359-385. [Latin America.]

3497 WAHRLICH, B. M. DE S. "Uma reforma da administração de pessoal vinculado ao processo de desenvolvimento nacional" (A reform of personnel administration linked to the national development process), *R. Adm. públ. (Rio de Janeiro)* 4(1), jan-jun 70 : 7-31.

3498 WALDO, D. (ed.). *Temporal dimensions of development administration.* Durham, N. C., Duke University Press, 70, xiv-312 p.

3499 WILCOX, H. G. "Hierarchy, human nature, and the participative panacea", *Publ. Adm. R.* 29(1), jan-feb 69 : 53-64.

3500 WURZBURG, F. "Bureaucratic decay", *J. comp. Adm.* 1(4), feb 70 : 387-397.

3501 YAMANAKA, E. "Nihon kindai kokka to kanryôsei" (Modern Japan and bureaucracy), *Handai Hôgaku* (67), 1968 : 74-141; (68), 1968 : 1-66.

C.913 *Political groups, parties and movements*
Groupes politiques, partis, mouvements

[See also / Voir aussi: 1920, 2198, 2365, 2503, 3051, 3052, 3054, 3438, 3735, 4170, 4191, 4229, 4254, 4263, 4292, 4483, 4570]

3502 ALEXANDER, R. J. *The Communist Party of Venezuela.* Stanford, Calif., Stanford University, Hoover Institution on War, Revolution and Peace 69, xxi-245 p.

3503 ALEXANDER, R. J. "The communist parties of Latin America", *Probl. Communism* 19(4), jul-aug 70 : 37-46.

3504 ASTIZ, C. A. *Pressure groups and power elites in Peruvian politics.* Ithaca, Cornell University Press, 69, xviii-316 p. CR: R. D. TOMASEK, *Amer. polit. Sci. R.* 64(3), sep 70 : 953-954.

3505 BARJONET, A. *Le Parti communiste français.* Paris, J. Didier, 70, 236 p.

3506 BAYART, J.-F. "L'union nationale camerounaise", *R. franç. Sci. polit.* 20(4), aug 70 : 681-718.

3507   BEALEY, F. (ed.). *The social and political thought of the British Labour Party*. London, Weidenfeld and Nicolson, 70, xvi-233 p.

3508   BECK, R. "Politischer Pluralismus in Spanien ?" (Political pluralism in Spain ?), *Polit. Vjschr.* 9(4), dec 68 : 564-576.

3509   BELLOWS, T. J. *The People's Action Party of Singapore: emergence of a dominant party system*. New Haven, Conn.-Detroit, Cellar Book Shop, 70, xi-195 p.

3510   BÉRAUD, B. *La gauche révolutionnaire au Japon*. Paris, Éditions du Seuil, 70, 157 p.

3511   BERGER, D.; THIRARD, P.-L. "Un parti social-démocrate de type nouveau", *Temps mod.* 26(284), mar 70 : 1446-1471.

3512   BERNARD, A.; LEBLANC, G. "Le parti socialiste SFIO dans l'Isère", *R. franç. Sci. polit.* 20(3), jun 70 : 557-567.

3513   BERNSTEIN, S. "La vie du Parti radical: la fédération de Saône-et-Loire de 1919 à 1939", *R. franç. Sci. polit.* 20(6), dec 70 : 1136-1180.

3514   BERRY, D. R. *The sociology of grass roots politics: a study of party membership*. London, Macmillan; New York, St Martins Press, 70, 155 p.

3515   BESINEAU, J. "Les partis politiques", *Projet* 46, jun 70 : 668-675. [Japan.]

3516   BETTIN, G. "Partito e comunità locale. II. Partito o federazione di correnti ?" (Party and local community. II. Party or federation of currents ?), *Rass. ital. Sociol.* 10(4), oct-dec 69 : 651-677. [See for the first part Bibl. XIX-3088.]

3517   BEYME, K. VON. *Interessengruppen in der Demokratie* (Interest groups in democracy). München, R. Piper and Co., 69, 234 p. CR: J.-C. DARBOIS, *R. franç. Sociol.* 11(3), jul-sep 70 : 430.

3518   BIENEN, H. *Tanzania: party transformation and economic development*. Expanded ed. Princeton, N. J., Princeton University Press, 70, xxvii-506 p.

3519   BODENHEIMER, S. "La crisis del movimiento social demócrata en América Latina" (The crisis of the social democratic movement in Latin America), *Estud. int.* 12, jan-mar 70 : 544-567.

3520   BOURRICAUD, F. "Los militares: ¿ por qué y para qué ?" (The military: why and what for ?), *Aportes* 16, apr 70 : 13-55. [Peru.]

3521   BRIGUGLIO, L. *Il Partito Operaio Italiano e gli anarchici* (The Italian Labour Party and the anarchists). Roma, Edizioni di storia e letteratura, 69, xvi-304 p.

3522   BRUYN, L. P. J. DE. "Omvang van party-aanhang; een vergelijkend onderzoek" (The extent of party participation; a comparative survey), *Acta polit.* 5(3), apr 69-70 : 269-291.

3523   BUCHHOLZ, E. *Die Wirtschaftsverbände in der Wirtschaftsgesellschaft—eine Analyse ihres Ordnungs- und Selbsthilfesystems als Beitrag zu einer Theorie der Wirtschaftsverbände* (Economic associations in economic society. An analysis of their system of organization and self-defence as a contribution to the theory of economic associations). Tübingen, J. C. B. Mohr, 69, xiv-270 p.

3524   BURNETT, B. G. *Political groups in Chile; the dialogue between order and change*. Austin, University of Texas Press, 70, xiv-319 p.

3525   BÜSCHER, H. "Demokratisierung und Ansätze zur Parteienbildung in Afghanistan" (Democratization and the beginning of party formation in Afghanistan), *Vierteljahresberichte* 39, mar 70 : 1-32.

3526   CABOARA, L. "La partitocrazia cancrena dello stato" ("Partitocracy", the gangrene of the State), *Riv. int. Filos. polit. soc. Dir. comp.* (1), 1969 : 3-36.

3527   CAMPIGLIA, N. *Los grupos de presión y el proceso político: la experiencia uruguaya* (Pressure groups and the political process: the Uruguayan experience). Montevideo, Arca, 69, 230 p.

3528   CHAE-JIM LEE. "Factional politics in the Japan Socialist Party: the Chinese cultural revolution case", *Asian Sur* . 10(3), mar 70 : 230-243.

3529   COLE, G. D. H. *A history of the Labour Party from 1914*. London, Routledge and K. Paul, 69, x-517 p.

3530   COLLART, Y. *Le parti socialiste suisse et l'Internationale 1914-1915. De l'Union nationale à Zimmerwald*. Genève, Droz, 69, xii-375 p.

3531   COSTANTINI, E.; CRAIK, K. H. "Competing elites within a political party: a study of Republican leadership", *West. polit. Quart.* 22(4), dec 69 : 879-903. [USA.]

3532   COTLER, J. "Crisis política y populismo militar en el Perú" (Political crisis and military populism in Peru), *Estud. int.* 12, jan-mar 70 : 439-488.

3533 CROISAT, M. "Centralisation et décentralisation au sein des partis politiques canadiens", *R. franç. Sci. polit.* 20(3), jun 70 : 483-497.

3534 DEOL, G. S. *The role of the Ghadar Party in the national movement.* Delhi, Sterling Publishers, 69, xii-244 p.

3535 DESPRADEL, L. "Les fonctions des armées en Amérique latine et les causes de leurs interventions politiques", *R. Inst. Sociol.* 4, 1969 : 689-708.

3536 DOMHOFF, G. W. "Where a pluralist goes wrong", *Berkely J. Sociol.* 14, 1969 : 35-57.

3537 EBBINGHAUSEN, R. *Die Krise der Parteiendemokratie und die Parteiensoziologie. Eine Studie über Moisei Ostrogorski, Robert Michels und die neuere Entwicklung der Parteienforschung* (The crisis of party democracy and sociology of parties. A study on Moisei Ostrogorski, Robert Michels and recent developments in party research). Berlin, Duncker und Humblot, 69, 89 p.

3538 EXINGA, A. "Souveraineté populaire et parti unique en Afrique noire", *Présence afr.* 72, 4 trim 69 : 39-47.

3539 FARREL, B. "Labour and the Irish political party system: a suggested approach to analysis", *Econ. soc. R. (Dublin)* 1(4), jul 70 : 477-502.

3540 FEDOROV, R. P. "Predprinimatel'skie sojuzy i krah teorii 'pluralističeskogo obščestva' " (Employers unions and the "crack" in the theory of pluralist society), *Vopr. Filos.* 23(2), feb 70 : 98-108.

3541 FELDBERG, R. L. "Political systems and the role of the military", *Sociol. Quart.* 11(2), 1970 : 206-218.

3542 FLECHTHEIM, O. K. *Die KPD in der Weimarer Republik* (The German Communist Party in the Weimar Republic). Frankfurt-am-Main, Europäische Verlagsanstalt, 69, 359 p.

3543 FONER, E. *Free soil, free labor, free men: the ideology of the Republican Party before the Civil War.* New York, Oxford University Press, 70, xii-353 p. [USA.]

3544 "Fuerzas armadas y nación: subversión y revolución nacional" (Armed forces and nation: subversion and national revolution), *Estrategia* 1(2), jul-aug 69 : 7-136. [Latin America.]

3545 FUKUI, H. *Party in power; the Japanese Liberal-Democrats and policy-making.* Canberra, Australian National University Press; Berkeley, University of California Press, 70, 301 p.

3546 FURTAK, R. K. *Revolutionspartei und politische Stabilität in México* (Revolutionary Party and political stability in Mexico). Hamburg, Übersee Verlag, 69, 135 p.

3547 GÁRCES, J. E. "La continuidad del sistema a través del cambio: el sistema bipartidista en Colombia" (System continuity through change: the two-party system in Colombia), *R. latinoamer. Sociol.* 6(1), mar 70 : 7-59.

3548 GARCÍA MONTES, J.; ALONSO AVILA, A. *Historia del Partido Comunista de Cuba* (History of the Communist Party of Cuba). Miami, Fla., Ediciones Universal, 70, 559-7 p.

3549 GERBERDING, W. P.; SMITH, D. E. (eds.). *The radical left: the abuse of discontent.* Boston, Houghton Mifflin Co., 70, viii-366 p.

3550 GRUNER, E. *Die Parteien in der Schweiz* (Parties in Switzerland). Bern, Francke, 69, 278 p.

3551 GUERCI, L. *Il Partito Socialista Italiano dal 1919-al 1946* (The Italian Socialist Party from 1919 to 1946). Bologna, Cappelli, 69, 244 p.

3552 GUNLICKS, A. B. "Intraparty democracy in Western Germany: a look at the local level", *Comp. Polit.* 2(2), jan 70 : 229-249.

3553 HARASYMIW, B. "Nomenklatura: the Soviet Communist Party's leadership recruitment system", *Canad. J. polit. Sci.* 2(4), dec 69 : 493-512.

3554 HASELER, S. *The Gaitskellites: revisionism in the British Labour Party, 1951-1964.* London, Macmillan, 69, xiv-286 p.

3555 HURTIG, C. *De la SFIO au nouveau parti socialiste.* Paris, A. Colin, 70, 128 p. [France.]

3556 IZE, M. M. F. "La democracia cristiana en Chile. Análisis de una experiencia" (Christian Democracy in Chile. Analysis of an experiment), *Foro int.* 38(102), oct-dec 69 : 111-135.

3557 JAMES, J. L. *American political parties: potential and performance.* New York, Pegasus, 69, xii-205 p.

3558 JONES, C. O. *The minority party in Congress.* Boston, Little, Brown, 70, xvi-204 p.

3559 KALTEFLEITER, W. "The impact of the elections of 1969 and the formation of the new government on the German party system", *Comp. Polit.* 2(4), jul 70 : 593-604.

3560   KAMAL, K. L. *Party politics in an Indian state; a study of the main political parties in Rajasthan.* Delhi, S. Chand, 69, xv-270 p.

3561   KARPAT, K. H. "The military and politics in Turkey, 1960-1964: a socio-cultural analysis of a revolution", *Amer. hist. R.* 75(6), oct 70 : 1654-1683.

3562   KERNIG, C. D. (ed.). *Die kommunistischen Parteien der Welt* (Communist parties in the world). Freiburg, Herder, 69, xv-583-10 p.

3563   KING, A. "Political parties in Western democracies", *Polity* 2(2), 1969 : 111-141.

3564   KLUGMANN, J. *History of the Communist Party of Great Britain.* 2 vols. London, Lawrence and Wishart, 68, 381 p.; 69, 373 p. CR: M. CHARLOT, *R. franç. Sci. polit.* 20(4), aug 70 : 822-823.

3565   KRIEGEL, A. *Aux origines du communisme français. Contribution à l'histoire du mouvement ouvrier français.* Paris, Flammarion, 70, 442 p.

3566   Bibl. XIX-3142. KRIEGEL, A. *Les communistes français. Essai d'ethnographie politique.* CR: A. ROUX, *R. franç. Sociol.* 10(4), oct-dec 69 : 541-543.

3567   LADD, E. C. J. *American political parties; social change and political response.* New York, Norton, 70, xi-323 p.

3568   LAVAU, G. "Parti et société: les communistes français", *Critique* 25(271), dec 69 : 1083-1094.

3569   LEBEDEV, M. P. "Partija v političeskoj sisteme socializma" (The party in the political system of socialism), *Sov. Gos. Pravo* 43(2), 1970 : 3-13.

3570   LEIGH, M. "Party formation in Sarawak", *Indonesia* 9, apr 70 : 189-224.

3571   LESLIE, P. M. "The role of political parties in promoting the interests of ethnic minorities", *Canad. J. polit. Sci.* 2(4), dec 69 : 419-433.

3572   LIEBER, R. J. *British politics and European unity; parties, elites, and pressure groups.* Berkeley, University of California Press, 70, ix-317 p.

3573   LORENZO, C. M. *Les anarchistes espagnols et le pouvoir. 1868-1969.* Paris, Éditions du Seuil, 69, 431 p.

3574   MALLOY, J. M. "El MNR boliviano: estudio de un movimiento popular nacionalista en América latina", *Estud. andinos* 1(1), 1970 : 57-92.

3575   MEDDING, P. Y. "A framework for the analysis of power in political parties", *Polit. Stud. (Oxford)* 18(1), mar 70 : 1-17.

3576   MEYER, J. W.; ROTH, J. G. "A reinterpretation of American status politics", *Pacific sociol. R.* 13(2), 1970 : 95-102.

3577   MILLER, N. N. "The Rural African Party: political participation in Tanzania", *Amer. polit. Sci. R.* 64(2), jun 70 : 548-571.

3578   MILLER, S. M. "Socialist party decline and World War I: bibliography and interpretation", *Sci. and Soc.* 34(4), 1970 : 398-411.

3579   MORAIS, C. S. DE. "Grupos de presión del agro: movimientos y organizaciones de trabajadores agrícolas" (Agro pressure groups: movements and organizations of agricultural workers), *R. mexic. Sociol.* 31(3), jul-sep 69 : 489-511.

3580   MORENO, D. A. *Los partidos políticos del México contemporáneo (1926-1970)* (Political parties of contemporary Mexico, 1926-1970). México, B. Costa-Amic, 70, 289-6 p.

3581   NAGLE, J. D. *The National Democratic Party; right radicalism in the Federal Republic of Germany.* Berkeley, University of California Press, 70, 221 p.

3582   NAKAMURA, K. "Minshushakaitô no seiritsu" (The rise of the Democratic Socialist Party), *Hôgaku Kenkyû* 41(4), 1968 : 97-122. [Japan.]

3583   NAKANO, T.; IIZUKA, S. *Ninon o ugokasu soshiki, shakaitô, minshatô* (Important organizations in Japan: Japan Socialist Party, Japan Democratic Socialist Party). Tokyo, Sekka-sha, 68, 271 p.

3584   NEAL, A. G. (ed.). "Social movements today", *Sociol. Focus* 3(3), 1970 : 1-71.

3585   NIELSEN, H. J. "Forskelle mellem politiske partier ?" (Are there any differences between the political parties), *Økon. og Polit.* 43(2), 1969 : 156-165. [Denmark.]

3586   *Nihon no seitô* (Political parties in Japan). Tôkyô, Kôan Shiryô Chôsa-kai, 68, 373 p.

3587   NYHOLM, P. *Mångpartisystemet i ljuset av en mångdimensionell modell* (The multi-party system in the light of a multidimensional model). Helsinki, University of Helsinki, Institute of Political Science, 70, 39 p. Mimeo.

3588   OVERACKER, L. *Australian parties in a changing society: 1945-1967.* Melbourne-Canberra, Cheshire, 68, xi-337 p.

3589 PAES DE BARROS, S. F. "Os sistemas eleitorais e os partidos politicos: bipartidismo e multipartidismo" (Electoral systems and political parties: two-party system and multi-party system), *R. Ciênc. polít.* 3(1), jan-mar 69 : 82-100.

3590 PALMA, G. DI. "Disaffection and participation in Western democracies: the role of political oppositions", *J. Polit.* 31(4), nov 69 : 984-1010.

3591 PERCHERON, A. "A propos de l'application du cadre théorique d'Easton à l'étude du Parti Communiste Français", *R. franç. Sci. polit.* 20(1), feb 70 : 75-92.

3592 PERLMUTTER, A. *Military and politics in Israel: nation-building and role expansion.* New York, Frederick A. Praeger, 69, 161 p. CR: S. DECALO, *Amer. polit. Sci. R.* 64(2), jun 70 : 659-661.

3593 PESONEN, P. *Political parties and the Finnish eduskunta: voters' perspectives, party nominations, and legislative behavior.* Tampere, University of Tampere, Institute of Political Science, 70, 43 p.

3594 PHILLIPS, K. P. *The emerging Republican majority.* Garden City, N. Y., Anchor Books, 70, 482 p. [USA.]

3595 PIERCE, J. C. "Party identification and the changing role of ideology in American politics", *Midwest J. polit. Sci.* 14(1), feb 70 : 25-42.

3596 PLATKOVSKIJ, V. V. "Partija—rukovodjaščaja sila socialistićeskogo gosudarstva" (The party is the managerial form of the socialist State), *Sov. Gos. Pravo* 43(8), aug 70 : 3-12.

3597 RAM, M. *Indian communism: split within a split.* Delhi, Vikas Publications, 69, ix-293 p.

3598 RANGER, J. "Le parti communiste dans la société française en changement", *Projet* 45, mai 70 : 576-583.

3599 RAWSON, D. W. "The life-span of Labour parties", *Polit. Stud. (Oxford)* 17(3), sep 69 : 313-333.

3600 RIGBY, T. H. *Communist Party membership in the USSR, 1917-1967.* Princeton, N. J., Princeton University Press, 68, xvii-573 p. CR: V. V. ASPATURIAN, *Amer. polit. Sci. R.* 63(4), dec 69 : 1286-1287.

3601 ROBERTS, G. K. *Political parties and pressure-groups in Britain.* London, Weidenfeld and Nicolson, 70, 9-203 p.

3602 ROSA, G. DE. *Il Partito Popolare Italiano* (The Italian Peoples' Party). Bari, Laterza, 69, 339 p.

3603 ROSE, R. "The variability of party government: a theoretical and empirical critique", *Polit. Stud. (Oxford)* 17(4), dec 69 : 413-445.

3604 ROSE, R.; URWIN, P. W. "Persistence and change in party systems", *Polit. Stud. (Oxford)* 18(3), sep 70 : 287-319.

3605 RUIN, O. "Patterns of government composition in multi-party systems: the case of Sweden", *Scand. polit. Stud.* 4, 1969 : 71-87.

3606 SALISBURY, R. H. (comp.). *Interest group politics in America.* New York, Harper and Row, 70, vi-437 p.

3607 SANDOZ, G. *La gauche allemande de Karl Marx à Willy Brandt.* Paris, R. Julliard, 70, 256 p.

3608 *Seitô to habatsu* (Factions in Japanese political parties). Tôkyô, Asahi-Shinbun-sha, 68, 294 p.

3609 SEVORTJAN, R. "Armija i obščestvo v molodom gosudarstva'" (The army and society in a young state), *Mir. Ekon. meždun. Otnoš.* 13(6), jun 70 : 99-108.

3610 SHULGOVSKI, A. "El ejército en la vida política de los países latinoamericanos" (The army in political life in Latin American countries), *Doc. polít.* 88, jul-aug 70 : 44-63.

3611 SIMMONS, H. G. *French Socialists in search of a role, 1956-1967.* Ithaca, N. Y., Cornell University Press, 70, xi-313 p.

3612 SMITH, G. R. *The rise of the Labour Party in Great Britain.* London, Edward Arnold, 69, 64 p.

3613 STEPHAN, H. "Berufsverbände und Institutionen der französischen Demokratie in der Vierten und Fünften Republik" (Professional organizations and French democratic institutions under the 4th and the 5th Republics), *Jb. öff. Rechts Gegenwart* 18, 1969 : 95-150.

3614 STURM, H. J. "Éléments sociologiques et géographiques de la NPD", *R. Allem.* 1(4), oct-dec 69 : 484-501.

3615   TARROW, S. "Economic development and the transformation of the Italian party
        system", *Comp. Polit.* 1(2), jan 69 : 161-183. [See also Bibl. XVIII-2183.]
3616   TIBI, B. "Zum Verhältnis von Militär und kolonialem Nationalismus am Beispiel der
        arabischen Länder" (Relations between the military and colonial nationalism accord-
        ing to the example of the arab States), *Sozial. Polit.* 1(4), dec 69 : 4-19.
3617   TRISKA, J. *Communist party-states: comparative and international studies.* Indianapolis,
        Bobbs-Merrill, 69, 392 p. CR: R. BLACKWELL, *Amer. polit. Sci. R.* 64(3), sep 70 :
        949-951.
3618   TURNER, J. *Party and constituency; pressures on Congress.* Rev. ed. by E. SCHNEIDER, Jr.
        Baltimore, Johns Hopkins Press, 70, xvii-312 p.
3619   TURNER, R. H. "The theme of contemporary social movements", *Brit. J. Sociol.* 20(4),
        dec 69 : 390-405.
3620   URWIN, D. W. "Social cleavages and political parties in Belgium: problems of in-
        stitutionalization", *Polit. Stud. (Oxford)* 18(3), sep 70 : 320-340.
3621   VALIANI, L. "Le mouvement socialiste en Europe après 1914", *C. Vilfredo Pareto* 20,
        feb 70 : 93-119.
3622   VAN DER MAESEN, C. E. "Amsterdammers en hun politieke partijen" (Amsterdam
        citizens and their political parties), *Acta polit.* 5(3), apr 69-70 : 254-268.
3623   VÁZQUEZ CARRILLO, J. E. *El Partido Liberal Mexicano; ensayo socio-jurídico* (The
        Mexican Liberal Party; a socio-legal essay). México, B. Costa-Amic, 70, 146 p.
3624   VIDAL, D. "Formation sociale et mouvements sociaux", *Sociol. et Soc.* 2(2), nov 70 :
        167-188.
3625   VINOGRADOV, V. D. "Socialističeskaja partijnaja sistema i eě vidy" (The socialist party
        system and its forms), *Vestn. Leningrads. Univ. Ser. Ékon. Filos. Pravo* 24(4), dec
        69 : 72-79.
3626   WEIL, G. L. "La crise des partis politiques américains", *Res publ.* 11(2), 1969 : 251-371.
3627   Bibl. XIX-3307. YORBURG, B. *Utopia and reality: a collective portrait of American socialists.*
        CR: J. L. WALSH, *Amer. sociol. R.* 35(4), aug 70 : 768-769.
3628   YOUNG, W. D. *The anatomy of a party: the national CCF, 1932-1961.* Toronto, Uni-
        versity of Toronto Press, 69, 328 p. [Cooperative Commonwealth Federation in
        Canada.]
3629   ZEUNER, B. *Innerparteiliche Demokratie* (Internal party democracy). Berlin, Colloquium
        Verlag, 69, 158 p. [Germany, BR.]

C.92   **Religious institutions**
        Institutions religieuses

C.920   *General studies*
        Études générales

        [See also / Voir aussi: **D.13**; 194, 199, 206, 3862]

3630   "Bibliographie internationale de sociologie des religions/International bibliography of
        sociology of religion", *Soc. Compass* 16(4), 1969 : 509-516; 17(2), 1970 : 335-348;
        17(3), 1970 : 471-484.
3631   Bibl. XIX-3212. BIRNBAUM, N.; LENZER, G. *Sociology and religion: a book of readings.*
        CR: A. D. HAMMONDS, *Amer. sociol. R.* 35(4), aug 70 : 796-797.
3632   BOSSE, H. *Marx, Weber, Troeltsch. Religionssoziologie und marxistische Ideologiekritik*
        (Marx, Weber, Troeltsch. Religious sociology and Marxist ideological critique).
        München, Kaiser; Mainz, Matthias Grünewald Verlag, 70, 154 p.
3633   CENTRE NATIONAL DE LA RECHERCHE SCIENTIFIQUE. Groupe de sociologie des religions.
        Le Groupe de sociologie des religions. Paris, Éditions du CNRS, 69, 92 p.
3634   DECONCHY, J. P. "Du théorique au stratégique en psycho-sociologie des religions",
        Polit. aujourd. 2, feb 70 : 43-50.
3635   DEKKER, G. *Sociologie en kerk* (Sociology and church). Kampen, J. H. Kok, 69, 77 p.
3636   DHOOGHE, J. "Quelques problèmes posés par le dialogue entre sociologie et théologie
        pastorale", *Soc. Compass* 17(2), 1970 : 215-230.
3637   HILLER, H. H. "The new theology and the sociology of religion", *Canad. R. Sociol.
        Anthropol.* 6(3), aug 69 : 179-187.

3638 ISAMBERT, F. A. "The early days of French sociology of religion", *Soc. Compass* 16(4), 1969 : 435-452.

3639 KLJUGL', I. "K kritike strukturnogo funkcionalizma v buržuaznoj sociologii religii" (Critics of structural functionalism in the bourgeois sociology of religion), *Vopr. nauč. Ateizma* (7), 1969 : 168-191.

3640 LEMERCINIER, G. "L'incidence des sciences humaines sur la pensée théologique élaborée et enseignée dans le cadre de la Faculté de Théologie de l'Université catholique de Louvain", *Soc. Compass* 17(2), 1970 : 321-328.

3641 MAÎTRE, J. "Remarques sur l'analyse secondaire en sociologie des religions", *Archiv. Sociol. Relig.* 15(29), jan-jun 70 : 21-25.

3642 MORIOKA, K. "A bibliography on the sociology of Japanese religions", *Soc. Compass* 17(1), 1970 : 171-194.

3643 O'DEA, T. F. *Sociology and the study of religion; theory, research, interpretation.* New York, Basic Books, 70, x-307 p.

3644 OŠAKOV, Ž. "O metodologii i metodike konkretnogo sociologičeskogo issledovanija religii" (On the methodology and methods of concrete sociological studies of religion), *Vopr. nauč. Ateizma* (7), 1969 : 135-167.

3645 ROBERTSON, R. (comp.). *Sociology of religion: selected readings.* Baltimore, Penguin Books; Harmondsworth, Penguin, 69, 473 p. CR: W. S. SALISBURY, *Acta sociol.* 13(2), 1970 : 139-140.

3646 ROBERTSON, R. *The sociological interpretation of religion.* Oxford, Blackwell; New York, Schocken Books, 70, viii-256 p.

3647 ROUSSEAU, A. "Emploi du terme 'sociologie' dans les textiles du Magistère central de l'Église", *Soc. Compass* 17(2), 1970 : 309-320.

3648 RUSSO, A.; LANZONI, R. "Sociologie marxiste de la religion dans les pays de l'Est", *IDOC int.* 34, nov 15, 70 : 75-95.

3649 SAHER, P. J. *Eastern wisdom and Western thought; a comparative study in the modern philosophy of religion.* New York, N. Y., Barnes and Noble, 70, 292 p.

3650 Bibl. XIX-3221. SAVRAMIS, D. *Religionssoziologie. Eine Einführung* (Sociology of religion. An introduction). CR: G. KEHRER, *Kölner Z. Soziol. u. soz.-Psychol.* 22(3), sep 70 : 620-622.

3651 SCHNEIDER, L. *Sociological approach to religion.* New York, Wiley, 70, viii-188 p.

3652 SCHREUDER, O. "Trends in the sociology of religion in the Netherlands, 1960-1969", *Sociol. neerland.* 6(2), 1970 : 129-136.

3653 SCHREUDER, O. "Works on sociology and theology", *Soc. Compass* 17(2), 1970 : 329-334.

3654 SCHWEIKER, W. F. "Religion as a superordinate meaning system and sociopsychological integration", *J. scient. Study Relig.* 8(2), 1969 : 300-307.

3655 "Théologie et sciences sociales/Theology and social sciences", *Soc. Compass* 17(2), 1970 : 263-308.

3656 UCHIDA, Y. "Uêbâ shûkyô shakaigaku to chûgoku mondai" (China and Weber's theory of religion), *Shisô* 523, 1968 : 30-54.

3657 ZYBKOVEC, V. F. "Problema proizhoždenija religii v sovremennoj buržuaznoj istoriografii" (Problem of the origins of religions in contemporary bourgeois historiography), *Vopr. Ist.* 44(10), oct 70 : 56-69.

C.921 Morphology of religious groups
Morphologie des groupes religieux

C.9210 General studies
Études générales

3658 GIBBS, J. O.; EWER, P. A. "The external adaptation of religious organizations: church response to social issues", *Sociol. Anal.* 30(4), 1969 : 223-234.

3659 KALUSCHE, B. *Kirche wohin? Ein religions-demoskopische Beitrag zur Situationsanalyse der Institution Kirche* (Whither the Church? A religious-demoscopic contribution to the analysis of the situation of the Church as an institution). Bergen-Enkheim-bei-Frankfurt-am-Main, Kaffke, 69, 93 p.

3660   KUNZ, P. R.; BRINKERHOFF, M. B. "Growth in religious organizations: a comparative
        study", *Soc. Sci. (Winfield)* 45(4), oct 70 : 215-222.
3661   MILLETT, D. "A typology of religious organizations suggested by the Canadian census",
        Sociol. Anal. 30(2), 1969 : 108-119.
3662   SYKES, R. E. "An appraisal of the theory of functional-structural differentiation of
        religious collectivities", *J. scient. Study Relig.* 8(2), 1969 : 289-299.

        C.9211   *Group membership*
                      Appartenance au groupe

3663   WICKER, A. W. "Size of church membership and members' support of church behavior
        settings", *J. Person. soc. Psychol.* 13(3), nov 69 : 278-260.

        C.9212   *Authority leadership and role*
                      L'autorité et ses rôles

        [See also / Voir aussi: 1964]

3664   AUCAGNE, J. "Orient chrétien et célibat sacerdotal", *Trav. et Jours* 34, jan-mar 70 :
        75-86.
3665   BISSONNIER, H. *La religieuse de paroisse et le monde des inadaptés.* Paris, Éditions Fleurus,
        69, 175 p.
3666   BLANC, E. "La crise de l'autorité dans l'Église", *Prêtres aujourd.* 312, nov 69 : 514-522.
3667   BLUME, N. "Clergymen and social action", *Sociol. soc. Res.* 54(2), jan 70 : 237-248.
3668   CORGHI, C. "Clero in Bolivia. Risultati di una inchiesta" (Priest in Bolivia. Results of
        an investigation), *Vita soc.* 27(140), 1970 : 128-142.
3669   GUZMAN CAMPOS, G. "La révolte du clergé en Amérique latine", *Homme et Soc.* 17,
        jul-sep 70 : 183-208.
3670   HICKS, F. "Política, poder y el papél del cura de pueblo en el Paraguay" (Politics,
        power and role of the village priest in Paraguay), *R. Ateneo parag. Supl. antropol.*
        4(1), jun 69 : 35-44.
3671   JAROSZEWSKI, T. M. "Kryzys wladzy w kościele rzymsko-katolickim" (The power
        crisis in the Catholic Church), *Nowe Drogi* 24(3), mar 70 : 45-55.
3672   JOLSON, A. J. "The role of the priest and obstacles to priestly vocations in Oslo, Norway:
        a research note", *Sociol. Anal.* 31(2), 1970 : 115-117.
3673   KINNANE, J. F. *Career development for priests and religious; a framework for research and
        demonstration.* Washington, Center for Applied Research in the Apostolate, 70, vii-
        134 p.
3674   LE MAIRE, H. P. "Charismatic tension in the church", *Philippine Stud.* 17(4), oct 69 :
        739-755.
3675   MOHLER, J. A. *The origin and evolution of the priesthood; a return to the sources.* Staten
        Island, N. Y., Alba House, 70, xv-137 p.
3676   MOINGT, J. "Mutations du ministère sacerdotal", *Études (Paris)* apr 70 : 576-592.
3677   QUINZIO, S. "Monarchia e pluralismo nella Chiesa" (Monarchy and pluralism in the
        Church), *Ponte* 25(12), dec 69 : 1561-1572. [Catholic Church.]
3678   Bibl. XIX-3253. SAVRAMIS, D. *Die soziale Stellung der Priester in Griechenland* (The
        social position of the priest in Greece). CR: G. MENSCHING, *Kölner Z. Soziol. u.
        soz.-Psychol.* 22(3), sep 70 : 622-624.
3679   SIMONS, E.; SCHREUDER, O. *Revolution in der Kirche? Kritik der kirchlichen Amts-
        struktur* (Revolution in the Church. A critique of hierarchical structure). Düsseldorf,
        Patmos-Verlag, 69, 96 p.
3680   SMITH, A. *The parson in local government.* Ilfracombe, Stockwell, 69, 112 p.
3681   SNOOK, J. "The Protestant clergyman in America. The problem in analyzing his
        career", *Soc. Compass* 16(4), 1969 : 485-492.
3682   STEWART, J. H. "The changing role of the Catholic priest and his ministry in an inner
        city context", *Sociol. Anal.* 30(2), 1969 : 81-90. [USA.]
3683   STRUZZO, J. A. "Professionalism and the resolution of authority conflicts among the
        Catholic clergy", *Sociol. Anal.* 31(2), 1970 : 92-106.

3684 TUELL, J. M. *The organization of the United Methodist Church.* Nashville, Abingdon Press, 70, 190 p.

3685 ULIANICH, B. "Autorità e libertà nella chiesa: abbozzo di una problematica" (Authority and freedom in the church: outline of a problem), *Mulino* 19(1-2), jan-feb 70 : 60-94.

3686 VERSCHEURE, J. "Recherches sur le prêtre: problèmes méthodologiques", *Soc. Compass* 16(4), 1969 : 453-469.

C.9213 *Territorial organization*
Organisation territoriale

3687 BRUNETTA, G. "Le parrocchie in Italia" (Parishes in Italy), *Aggiorn. soc.* 21(2), feb 70 : 151-164.

3688 COMERIO DI VALENZA, A. "La realtà parrocchiale: riflessioni metodologiche" (Parish reality: methodological reflections), *Sociol. relig.* 11(17-18), 1968 : 133-142.

3689 DORE, N. "La parrochia nella realtà d'oggi" (The parish in contemporary reality), *Orientam. soc.* 26(7-8), jul-aug 70 : 483-567.

3690 FINDJI, M. T. "Images et fonctions du bâtiment-église dans la population urbaine française", *IDOC int.* 25, jun 1, 70 : 78-94.

3691 FUJII, M. "Un temple de grande ville et la population religieuse flottante", *Soc. Compass* 17(1), 1970 : 67-96. [Japon.]

3692 STODDARD, R. H. "Changing patterns of some rural churches", *Rocky Mountain soc. Sci. J.* 7(1), apr 70 : 61-68. [USA.]

3693 VENTURI, V. "Parrocchie e sacerdoti della diocesi di Pistoia" (Parishes and priesthood in Pistoia diocese), *Aggiorn. soc.* 21(7-8), jul-aug 70 : 567-572.

C.9214 *Religious communities (orders, brotherhoods, etc.)*
Communautés religieuses (ordres, confréries, etc.)

[See also / Voir aussi: **C.41**; 3665, 3673]

3694 ADAMS, R. L. "Conflict over charges of heresy in American Protestant seminaries", *Soc. Compass* 17(2), 1970 : 243-262.

3695 MOORHOUSE, G. *Against all reason.* London, Weidenfeld and Nicolson, 69, xiii-436 p. CR: M. HILL, *Brit. J. Sociol.* 20(4), dec 69 : 458-459. [On religious life.]

3696 MOULIN, L. "L'Assemblée, autorité souveraine dans l'Ordre des Chartreux", *Res publ.* 12(1), 1970 : 7-67.

3697 O'BRIEN, D. C. "Le talibé mouride: la soumission dans une confrérie religieuse sénégalaise", *C. Ét. afr.* 10(4), 4 trim 70 : 562-578.

3698 SY, C. T. *La confrérie sénégalaise des Mourides. Un essai sur l'Islam au Sénégal.* Paris, Présence africaine, 69, 354 p.

C.9215 *Relations between churches and religious groups*
Relations entre Églises et groupes religieux

3699 CARMAN, J. B. "Continuing tasks in inter-religious dialogue", *Ecumen. R.* 22(3), jul 70 : 199-209.

3700 DEVARAJA, N. K. *Hinduism and Christianity.* Bombay-New York, Asia Publishing House, 69, xi-126 p.

3701 REFOULE, F. (éd.). *Au bord du schisme? L'affaire d'Amsterdam et l'Église de Hollande.* Paris, Éditions du Cerf, 69, 144 p.

3702 RICHARDSON, P. *Israel in the apostolic Church.* London, Cambridge University Press, 69, xiii-257 p.

C.922 *Religious institutions: relations with social and political environment*
Institutions religieuses et milieu social

[See also / Voir aussi: 658, 3878, 4787]

3703 AARFLOT, A. *Kirke og stat i Norge* (Church and State in Norway). Stavanger, Nomi, 69, 130 p.

3704   ADAMS, J. L. *The growing church lobby in Washington,* Grand Rapids, Eerdmans, 70, xv-294 p.

3705   AHMAD, J.-u.-D. *Middle phase of Muslim political movement.* Lahore, Publishers United, 69, vi-202 p.

3706   ANTOINE, C. "L'épiscopat brésilien face au pouvoir (1962-1969)", *Études (Paris)* 333, jul 70 : 84-103.

3707   BENNETT, J. C. *Christianity and communism today.* New York, Association Press, 70, 192 p.

3708   BERGER, M. "The Mosque: aspects of governmental policy towards religion in Egypt today", *Mid. East. Stud.* 6(1), jan 70 : 3-34.

3709   BERMEO, A. *Relaciones entre la Iglesia y el Estado, en la República del Ecuador* (Relations between Church and State in the Republic of Ecuador). Guayaquil, Editorial Casa de la Cultura Ecuatoriana, 69, 257-v p.

3710   BETTEN, N. "Social catholicism and the emergence of Catholic radicalism in America", *J. hum. Relat.* 18(1), 1970 : 710-727.

3711   BIRNBAUM, E. *The politics of compromise: state and religion in Israel.* Rutherford, Fairleigh Dickinson University Press, 70, 348 p.

3712   BOISSEVAIN, J. *Saints and fireworks; religion and politics in rural Malta.* London, Athlone Press; New York, Humanities Press, 69, xii-162 p.

3713   BRIDSTON, K. R. *Church politics.* New York, World Publishing, 69, 173 p.

3714   BRUGAROLA, M. "Teología católica del desarrollo: su influjo en la misión" (Catholic theology of development: its influence on its missionary work), *R. int. Sociol. (Madrid)* 27(107-108), jul-dec 69 : 73-86; 28(111-112), mai-aug 70 : 39-50.

3715   COLEMAN, J. A. "Civil religion", *Sociol. Anal.* 31(2), 1970 : 67-77.

3716   DREIER, W. "Christliche verantwortete Politik und 'Politische Theologie'. Eine theo-logisch-politologische Grundsatzüberlegung" (The sentiment of Christian respon-sibility in politics and political theology. A theological political reflexion), *Jb. christ. soz. Wiss.* 10, 1969 : 235-258.

3717   EDINGTON, D. W. *Christians and colour in Britain.* London, Scripture Union, 70, 136 p.

3718   EINAUDI, L. *et al. Latin American institutional development: the changing Catholic Church.* Santa Monica, Calif., Rand Corporation, 69, xi-81 p.

3719   FISCHER, E. "Trennung von Staat und Kirche" (Separation of Church and State), *Jb. krit. Aufklärung* 4, 1970 : 231-249.

3720   GALLI, G. *I cattolici e il sindacato* (The Catholics and the union). Milano, Palazzi, 69, vii-366 p. [Italy.]

3721   GRIFFIN, J. H. *The Church and the black man.* Dayton, Ohio, Pflaum Press, 69, vii-132 p. [USA.]

3722   HADDEN, J. K. "Clergy involvement in civil rights", *A. Amer. Acad. polit. soc. Sci.* 387, jan 70 : 118-127.

3723   Bibl. XIX-3289. HADDEN, J. K. *The gathering storm in the churches: the widening gap between clergy and laymen.* CR: J. R. WOOD, *Amer. sociol. R.* 35(4), aug 70 : 797-798.

3724   HAYWARD, M.; FLETCHER, W. G. *Religion and the Soviet State: a dilemma of power.* New York, F. A. Praeger, 69, 200 p. CR: R. M. MILLS, *Amer. polit. Sci. R.* 64(3), sep 70 : 962-963.

3725   HAZELRIGG, L. E. "Religious and class bases of political conflict in Italy", *Amer. J. Sociol.* 75(4, Part I), jan 70 : 496-511.

3726   HESSEL, D. T. *Reconciliation and conflict; church controversy over social involvement.* Philadelphia, Westminster Press, 69, 172 p.

3727   HUDSON, W. S. (comp.). *Nationalism and religion in America: concepts of American identity and mission.* New York, Harper and Row, 70, xxxiii-211 p.

3728   ILLUMINATI, A.; TORO, C. DI. "Il ciclo capitalistico nell'Italia del dopoguerra: i cattolici tra integralismo e riformismo" (The capitalist cycle in Italy after the war: the catholics between integralism and reformism), *Crit. sociol. (Roma)* 12, 1969-1970 : 6-41.

3729   LANDSBERGER, H. A. (ed.). *The Church and social change in Latin America.* Notre Dame, University of Notre Dame Press, 70, xiii-240 p.

3730   LEONI, F. "El movimiento católico en la política italiana. Orígenes y evolución" (The Catholic movement in Italian politics. Origins and evolution), *R. Estud. polít.* 167, sept-oct 69 : 103-116.

3731　LOCHMAN, J. M. *Church in a Marxist society: a Czechoslovak view.* London, SCM Press, 70, 198 p.

3732　LODWICK, R. E. *The significance of the Church-State relationship to an evangelical program in Brazil.* Cuernavaca, Mexico, Centro Intercultural de Documentacíon, 69, 220 p.

3733　LOFF, W.; LOHSE, B. (eds.). *Christentum and Gesellschaft* (Christianity and society). Göttingen, Vandenhoeck und Ruprecht, 69, 267 p.

3734　LUCAS, L. *Black priest/White Church; Catholics and racism.* New York, Random House, 70, 270 p. [USA.]

3735　MAIER, H. *Revolution and church: the early history of Christian democracy, 1789-1901.* Notre Dame, University of Notre Dame Press, 69, 326 p. CR: G. LEWY, *Amer. polit. Sci. R.* 64(3), sep 70 : 929-930.

3736　METZ, J. B.; MOLTMANN, J.; OELMÜLLER, W. *Kirche im Prozess der Aufklärung, Aspekte einer neuen "politischen Theologie"* (The Church in the enlightenment process. Aspects of a new political theology). München, Kaiser, 70, 143 p.

3737　MOL, J. J. *Christianity in chains; a sociologist's interpretation of the churches' dilemma in a secular world.* Melbourne, Nelson, 69, vii-120 p.

3738　OLIVOS, L.; DELGADO, C. "Bibliografía sobre la Iglesia y el cambio social en América latina" (Bibliography in the Church and social change in Latin America), *Anu. Sociol. Pueblos ibér.* (5), 1969 : 52-109.

3739　PLONGERON, B. *Conscience religieuse en révolution. Regards sur l'historiographie religieuse de la Révolution française.* Paris, A.-J. Picard, 69, 352 p.

3740　QUINLEY, H. E. "The Protestant clergy and the war in Vietnam", *Publ. Opin. Quart.* 34(1), 1970 : 43-53. [USA.]

3741　"Religion and the public order", *Religion publ. Order* 5, 1969 : 3-178. [USA.]

3742　ROSSEL, R. D. "The great awakening: an historical analysis", *Amer. J. Sociol.* 75(6), mai 70 : 907-925.

3743　ROTER, Z. "Razvoj odnosov med latoliško cerkvijo in državo v socialistično Jugoslaviji" (Development of relations between the Catholic Church and the State in socialist Yugoslavia), *Teorija in Praksa* 7(8-9), sep 70 : 1273-1286.

3744　RÜPPEL, E. G. *Die Gemeinschaftsbewegung im Dritten Reich. Ein Beitrag zur Geschichte des Kirchenkampfes* (The community movement under the Third Reich. A contribution to the study of the Kirchenkampf). Göttingen, Vandenhoeck und Ruprecht, 69, 258 p.

3745　SCHLAICH, K. *Kollegialtheorie. Kirche, recht und Staat in der Aufklärung* (Collegial theory. Church, law and State in the enlightenment). München, Claudius Verlag, 69, 332 p.

3746　SMITH, D. E. *Religion and political development, an analytic study.* Boston, Little, Brown, 70, xvii-298 p.

3747　TOTH, J. "Les Églises et le nouvel ordre mondial. Commentaires sur l'assemblée d'Uppsala", *Justice dans le Monde* 11(2), dec 69 : 196-212.

3748　TURNER, F. C. "El protestantismo y el cambio social en Latinoamérica" (Protestantism and social change in Latin America), *R. parag. Sociol.* 7(17), jan-mar 70 : 5-27.

3749　VALLIER, I. *Catholicism, social control, and modernization in Latin America.* Englewood Cliffs, N. J., Prentice-Hall, 70, x-172 p.

3750　WIEBE, P. D. "Christianity and social change in South India", *Practic. Anthropol.* 17(3), mai-jun 70 : 128-136.

3751　WILLIAMS, E. J. "Latin American catholicism and political integration", *Comp. polit. Stud.* 2(3), oct 69 : 327-348.

D SOCIAL CONTROL AND COMMUNICATION
CONTRÔLE SOCIAL, COMMUNICATION SOCIALES

D.1 SOCIAL CONTROL
CONTRÔLE SOCIAL

D.10 General works: types of social control
Ouvrages généraux: types de contrôle social

[See also / Voir aussi: 1807, 1836, 2011, 2306, 2572, 4428, 5237, 5260, 5302]

3752 ABRAHAMSON, M.; SMITH, J. K. "Norms, deviance, and spatial location", *J. soc. Psychol.* 8(1), feb 70 : 95-101.

3753 Bibl. XIX-3325. DINITZ, S.; DYNES, R. R.; CLARKE, A. C. *Deviance: studies in the process of stigmatization and societal reaction.* CR: I. CHAPMAN, *Amer. sociol. R.* 35(1), feb 70 : 158-159.

3754 DOUGLAS, J. D. (ed.). *Deviance and respectability; the social construction of moral meanings.* New York, Basic Books, 70, xii-468 p.

3755 DOUGLAS, J. D. (ed.). *Observations of deviance.* New York, Random House, 70, viii-340 p.

3756 LANPHIER, C. M.; FAULKNER, J. E. "Deviance in a middle-class community", *Int. J. comp. Sociol.* 11(2), jun 70 : 146-156.

3757 Bibl. XIX-3328. LOFLAND, J. *Deviance and identity.* CR: M. K. OPLER, *Amer. J. Sociol.* 75(6), mai 70 : 1055-1056.

3758 NAUTA, A. P. N. "Sociale controle, sancties en referenties" (Social control, sanctions and references), *Soc. Wetensch.* 12(2), 1969 : 69-89.

3759 POLLIS, N. P.; POLLIS, C. A. "Sociological referents of social norms", *Sociol. Quart.* 11(2), 1970 : 230-242.

3760 SCHEFF, T.; SUNDSTROM, E. "The stability of deviant behavior over time: a reassessment", *J. Health soc. Behav.* 11(1), mar 70 : 37-43.

3761 SCHUMANN, K. F. *Zeichen der Unfreiheit. Zur Theorie und Messung sozialer Sanktionen* (The signs of lack of freedom. On the theory and nature of social sanctions). Freiburg, Rombach, 68, 181 p. CR: G. SPITTLER, *Kölner Z. Soziol. u. soz.-Psychol.* 21(4), dec 69 : 887-889.

3762 SEGAL, A. "Censorship, social control and socialization", *Brit. J. Sociol.* 21(1), mar 70 : 63-74. [Moral questions and censorship in socialization.]

3763 SUCHMAN, E. A. "Accidents and social deviance", *J. Health soc. Behav.* 11(1), mar 70 : 4-15.

3764 VERHOEVEN, J. *De sociologische verklaring van de sociale kontrole* (The sociological interpretation of social control). Mechelen, Sinfra, 69, 305 p.

3765 WINSLOW, R. W. *Society in transition; a social approach to deviancy.* New York, Free Press, 70, xiii-408 p.

D.11 Customs, mores, fashion
Coutumes, mœurs, modes

[See also / Voir aussi: 4474]

3766 DESPLANQUES, L. "Réflexions sur les incidences économiques de la mode", *Coopération* 40(3), mar 70 : 11-18.

3767 PISTOLESE, R.; HORSTING, R. *History of fashions.* New York, Wiley, 70, ix-340 p.

3768 RAGONE, G. "La moda come *craze* nella teoria del comportamento collettivo di N. J. Smelser" (Fashion as a "craze" in N. J. Smelser's theory of collective behaviour), *Rass. ital. Sociol.* 11(2), apr-jun 70 : 231-260.

D.12 Morals
Morale

[See also / Voir aussi: 498, 575, 1022, 1871, 2020, 2025, 2592, 2601, 3754, 4034, 4431, 4652, 4653, 5363]

3769 ANDERSON, N. "Measurement of values and future leisure", *Acta sociol.* 12(4), 1969 : 179-185.

3770 ATKINSON, R. F. *Conduct: an introduction to moral philosophy.* London, Macmillan, 69, 123 p.

3771 BALES, R. F.; COUCH, A. S. "The value profile: a factor analytic study of value statements", *Sociol. Inquiry* 39(1), 1969 : 3-18.

3772 BECK, R. N.; ORR, J. B. *Ethical choice; a case study approach.* New York, Free Press, 70, xix-444 p.

3773 COLIN, R.; MOLLET, A. "La participation face aux valeurs traditionnelles du Rwanda", *Dévelop. et Civilis.* 39-40, mar-jun 70 : 113-131.

3774 DAVIS, J. "Morals and backwardness", *Comp. Stud. Soc. Hist.* 12(3), jul 70 : 340-353. With a reply by J. DAVIS: 354-359.

3775 DRUCKMAN, D.; ZECHMEISTER, K. "Conflict of interest and value dissensus", *Hum. Relat.* 23(5), oct 70 : 431-438.

3776 ECKHARDT, W. "Communist value", *J. hum. Relat.* 18(1), 1970 : 778-788.

3777 FRIED, C. *An anatomy of values; problems of personal and social choice.* Cambridge, Harvard University Press, 70, xi-265 p.

3778 GAUTHIER, D. P. (ed.). *Morality and rational self-interest.* Englewood Cliffs, N. J., Prentice-Hall, 70, viii-184 p.

3779 GROSSER, A. *Au nom de quoi? Fondements d'une morale politique.* Paris, Éditions du Seuil, 69, 335 p.

3780 HENGSTENBERG, H. E. *Grundlegung der Ethik* (Foundations of ethics). Stuttgart-Berlin-Köln-Mainz, Kohlhammer, 69, 228 p.

3781 KAGITCIBASI, C. "Social norms and authoritarianism: a Turkish-American comparison", *J. Person. soc. Psychol.* 16(3), nov 70 : 444-451.

3782 KAWAGOE, J. "Value orientation innate to Japanese farmers", *Develop. Econ.* 7(4), dec 69 : 544-571.

3783 KAY, A. W. *Moral development: a psychological study of moral growth from childhood to adolescence.* New York, Schocken Books, 69, 270 p. CR: F. F. FÜRSTENBERG, Jr. *Amer. sociol. R.* 35(2), apr 70 : 399-400.

3784 Bibl. XIX-3357. KOLARI, R. *Über ideologische und nationale Werte: eine typologische Analyse mit ergänzender Betrachtung des Isomorphieproblems* (On ideological and national values. A typological analysis with a complementary consideration on the problem of isomorphism). CR: J. J. WIATR, *Acta sociol.* 13(1), 1970 : 58-59.

3785 KRIPPENDORFF, K. "The expression of value in political documents", *J-ism Quart.* 47(3), 1970 : 510-518.

3786 KRUTOVA, O. N. *Čelovek i moral': metodologiceskie problemy leninskogo analiza nravstvennosti* (Man and ethics: methodological problem of the Leninist analysis of ethics). Moskva, Izdatel'stvo politiceskoj literatury, 70, 221 p.

3787 KULTGEN, K. W. "The value of value judgments in sociology", *Sociol. Quart.* 11(2), 1970 : 181-193.

3788 LAZARI-PAWLOWSKA, I. "Professional ethics and conflicting social norms and roles", *Polish sociol. B.* (1), 1969 : 39-48.

3789 LEWIS, L. S. "The puritan ethic in universities and some worldly concerns of sociologists", *Amer. Sociologist* 4(3), aug 69 : 235-241. [USA.]

3790 MAHR, W. "Über eine Möglichkeit ontologischer Werturteile" (On the possibility of ontological value judgements), *Jb-r nat.-Ökon. u. Statist.* 184(4-5), sep 70 : 335-348.

3791 MEANS, R. L. *The ethical imperative: the crisis in American values.* Garden City, N. Y., Doubleday, 69, 277 p. CR: B. GORMAN, *Amer. sociol. R.* 35(4), aug 70 : 762-763.

3792 NESTEROV, V. G. *Trud i moral' v sovetskom obščestvo* (Labour and morals in Soviet society). Moskva, Mysl', 69, 189 p.

3793 NUNOKAWA, K. "Kinsei nômin rinri no keisei" (Japanese peasants and their ethical thought: a historical study), *Shisô* (528), 1968 : 95-108.

3794 OSSOWSKA, M. *Social determinants of moral ideas.* Philadelphia, University of Pennsylvania Press, 70, xiv-190 p.

3795 OSTROM, T. M.; BROCK, T. C. "Cognitive bonding to central values and resistance to a communication advocating change in policy orientation", *J. exper. Res. Personality* 4(1), jul 69 : 42-50.

3796 RAMIREZ, M. III. "Identification with Mexican-American values and psychological adjustment in Mexican-American adolescents", *Int. J. soc. Psychiatry* 15(2), 1969 : 151-156.

3797 RUBENSTEIN, R. L. *Morality and eros.* New York, McGraw-Hill, 70, vi-205 p.

3798 SATHAYE, S. G. "Morality and Parsons' model", *Archiv Rechts- u. soz.-Philos.* 55(4), 1969 : 541-565.

3799 SCHUFLETOWSKI, F. W.; REED, R. L. "Value structure: another dimension to attitude measurement", *J. soc. Psychol.* 82(1), oct 70 : 127-129.

3800 SCOTT, E. "Social value acquisition in preschool aged children. III. Internalization of institutionalized value expectation", *Sociol. Quart.* 11(1), 1970 : 14-31.

3801 SERRA ANDRADE, A. H. "Identificação e sistematização de valôres sociais. Estudo exploratório em dois núcleos rurais de Costa Rica" (Identification and systematization of social values. An exploratory study of two rural centers in Costa Rica), *R. brasil. Estatíst.* 30(119), jul-sep 69 : 259-276.

3802 SILVER, D. J. (comp.). *Judaism and ethics.* New York, Ktav Publishing House, 70, 338 p.

3803 SKVORCOV, L. V. "Krizis buržuaznyh cennostej i idealističeskaja filosofija" (The crisis of bourgeois values and idealist philosophy), *Vopr. Filos* 23(7), jul 70 : 3-13.

3804 SMITH, A. D. "L'homme moderne et la signification du mal", *Diogène* 71, jul-sep 70 : 69-86.

3805 STEPHENSON, G. M.; WHITE, J. H. "Privilege, deprivation and children's moral behavior: an experimental clarification of the role of investments", *J. exper. soc. Psychol.* 6(2), apr 70 : 167-176.

3806 SUNDBERG, N. D.; ROHILA, P. K.; TYLER, L. E. "Values of Indian and American adolescents", *J. Person. soc. Psychol.* 16(3), nov 70 : 374-397.

3807 TITARENKO, A. I. *Moral' i politika. Kritičeskie očerki sovremennyh predstavlenij o sootnošenii morali i politiki v buržuaznoj sociologii* (Ethics and politics. Critical study of contemporary notions on the interrelation between ethics and politics in bourgeois sociology). Moskva, Politizdat, 69, 264 p.

3808 TOMEH, A. K. "Cross-cultural differences in the structure of moral values: a factorial analysis", *Int. J. comp. Sociol.* 11(1), mar 70 : 18-33.

3809 UTZ, A. F.; STREITHOFEN, H. B. (eds.). *Ethik und Politik; aktuelle Grundfragen der Gesellschafts-, Wirtschafts- und Rechtsphilosophie* (Ethics and politics; current basic questions of social economic and legal philosophy). Stuttgart-Degerloch, Seewald, 70, 513 p.

3810 WALLACE, G.; WALKER, A. D. M. (eds.). *The definition of morality.* London, Methuen, 70, 262 p.

3811 WEAVER, J. L. "Value patterns of a Latin American bureaucracy", *Hum. Relat.* 23(3), jun 70 : 225-233.

3812 WEINSTEIN, M. A. "Politics and moral consciousness", *Midwest J. polit. Sci.* 14(2), mai 70 : 183-215.

D.13 Religion

[See also / Voir aussi: **C.92**]

D.130 *General studies*
Études générales

[See also / Voir aussi: 1765, 2561]

3813 BELLAH, R. N. *Beyond belief; essays on religion in a post-traditional world.* New York, Harper and Row, 70, xxi-298 p.

3814   Bibl. XIX-3374. BERGER, P. L. *A rumor of angels—modern society and rediscovery of the supernatural.* CR: S. BUDD, *Amer. J. Sociol.* 75(6), mai 70 : 1066-1068; G. L. GOLLIN, *Amer. sociol. R.* 35(3), jun 70 : 553-555.

3815   BERGER, P. L. *The social reality of religion.* London, Faber and Faber, 69, ooo p. CR: D. MARTIN, *Brit. J. Sociol.* 20(4), dec 69 : 457-458.

3816   BLISS, K. *The future of religion.* London, Watts, 69, xi-193 p.

3817   CRESPI, P. "Sacralizzazione e desacralizzazione" (Sacralization and desacralization), *Rass. ital. Sociol.* 10(4), oct-dec 69 : 523-536.

3818   Bibl. XIX-3375. DEMERATH, N. J. III; HAMMOND, P. E. *Religion in social context: tradition and transition.* CR: P. M. HARRISON, *Amer. sociol. R.* 34(6), dec 69 : 1004-1005.

3819   DESHEN, S. A. "On religious change: the situational analysis of symbolic action", *Comp. Stud. Soc. Hist.* 12(3), jul 70 : 260-274.

3820   GILKEY, L. B. *Religion and the scientific future; reflections on myth, science and theology.* New York, Harper and Row, 70, x-193 p.

3821   Bibl. XIX-3378. NELSON, G. K. *Spiritualism and society.* CR: S. BUDD, *Amer. J. Sociol.* 75(6), mai 70 : 1066-1068; F. FLIGELMAN, *Amer. sociol. R.* 35(4), aug 70 : 798.

3822   PEPPER, G. "Religion and evolution", *Sociol. Anal.* 31(2), 1970 : 78-91.

3823   SOUZA, A. DO. "The relevance of religion in modern society", *Soc. Action* 20(2), apr-jun 70 : 173-186.

D.131   *The religions of the world*
            Les religions dans le monde

D.1310   *General and comparative studies*
             Études générales et comparatives

3824   JURJI, E. J. (ed.). *Religious pluralism and world community. Interfaith and intercultural communication.* Leiden, E. J. Brill, 69, viii-314 p.

3825   LING, T. O. *A history of religion East and West; an introduction and interpretation.* New York, Harper and Row, 70, xxix-464 p.

D.1311   *Religion and magic in primitive societies*
             Religion et magie dans les sociétés primitives

[See also / Voir aussi: 3918, 3954]

3826   BOLT, J. W. DE. "Belief systems and evolution: a distinction between magic and religion and its implications for socio-cultural change", *Canad. R. Sociol. Anthropol.* 6(2), mai 69 : 80-91.

3827   CARNEIRO, R. L. "Hunting and hunting magic among the Amahuaca of the Peruvian Montaña", *Ethnology* 9(4), oct 70 : 331-341.

3828   COCKETT, M. *Magic and gold; tales from Northern Europe.* Oxford-New York, Pergamon Press, 70, 69 p.

3829   DEMOS, J. "Underlying themes in the witchcraft of seventeenth-century New England", *Amer. hist. R.* 75(5), jun 70 : 1311-1326.

3830   DOUGLAS, M. (ed.). *Witchcraft confessions and accusations.* London-New York, Tavistock Publications, 70, xxxviii-387 p.

3831   FABREGA, H. Jr.; SILVER, D. "Some social and psychological properties of Zinacanteco shamans", *Behav. Sci.* 15(6), nov 70 : 471-486.

3832   FAGET, E. *Folklore mágico del Uruguay* (Magic folklore in Uruguay). Montevideo, Tauro, 69, 126 p.

3833   FERGUSON, J. *The religions of the Roman Empire.* Ithaca, N. Y., Cornell University Press, 70, 296 p.

3834   FERNANDEZ, J. W. "Rededication and prophetism in Ghana", *C. Ét. afr.* 10(2), 2 trim 70 : 228-305.

3835   FIRTH, R. W. *Rank and religion in Tikopia; a study in Polynesian paganism and conversion to Christianity.* Boston, Beacon Press; London, Allen and Unwin, 70, 424 p.

3836   FROELICH, J. C. *Les nouveaux dieux d'Afrique...* Paris, Orante, 69, 128 p.

3837   GROTTANELLI, V. L. "Gods and morality in Nzema polytheism", *Ethnology* 8(4), oct
       69 : 370-405.

3838   HARWOOD, A. *Witchcraft, sorcery, and social categories among the Safwa.* London,
       Oxford University Press, 70, xvii-160 p.

3839   HEINTZE, B. *Besessenheits-Phänomene im mittleren Bantu-Gebiet* (Witchcraft phenomena
       in the middle Bantu region). Wiesbaden, F. Steiner, 70, 288 p.

3840   KENNEDY, J. G. "Psychosocial dynamics of witchcraft systems", *Int. J. soc. Psychiatry*
       15(3), 1969 : 165-178.

3841   MADSEN, W.; MADSEN, C. *A guide to Mexican witchcraft.* Mexico, Editorial Minutiae
       Mexicana, 69, 96 p.

3842   MARWICK, M. (ed.). *Witchcraft and sorcery; selected readings.* Harmondsworth, Eng.-
       Baltimore, Md., Penguin Books, 70, 416 p.

3843   MÉTAIS, P. "Contribution à une étude de la sorcellerie néo-calédonienne actuelle",
       Année sociol. 19, 1968 : 17-100. [Voir pour la première partie, *ibid.*, 18, 1967 : 111-
       220, et P. MÉTAIS, *La sorcellerie canaque actuelle. Étude de l'angoisse de mort et du
       mal-ajustement social dans une tribu.* Bibl. XVIII-4054.]

3844   MULHOLLAND, J. F. *Hawaii's religions.* Rutland, Vt., C. E. Tuttle Co., 70, 344 p.

3845   MUTHURAMAN, M. *Religion of Tirukkural.* Madras, Higginbothams, 69, viii-123-i p.

3846   Bibl. XIX-3395. PEEL, J. D. Y. *Aladura: a religious movement among the Yoruba.* CR:
       H. H. SMYTHE, *Amer. sociol. R.* 35(1), feb 70 : 171-172.

3847   "Shamanism", *Toyo Bunka* (46-47), mar 69 : 1-156. [Special issue on shamanism in
       Asia. In Japanese.]

3848   SHORTER, A. "Religious values in Kimbu historical charters", *Africa (London)* 39(3),
       jul 69 : 227-237.

3849   STEVENSON, I. "Characteristics of cases of the reincarnation type in Turkey and their
       comparison with cases in two other cultures", *Int. J. comp. Sociol.* 11(1), mar 60 :
       1-17.

3850   THOMAS, L.-V.; LUNEAU, R.; DONEUX, J.-L. *Les religions d'Afrique noire. Textes et
       traditions sacrés.* Paris, Fayard-Denoël, 69, 407 p. CR: C. RIVIÈRE, *C. int. Sociol.*
       17(49), jul-dec 70 : 184-187.

3851   TURNER, P. R. "Witchcraft as negative charisma", *Ethnology* 9(4), oct 70 : 366-372.

3852   Bibl. XVIII-4057. TURNER, V. W. *The drums of affliction. A study of religious process
       among the Ndembu of Zambia.* CR: F. FARAUT, *Homme* 10(1), jan-mar 70 : 100-101.

3853   VIG, L. *Charmes, spécimens et magie malgache.* Bergen, Oslo, Musée de l'Ethnographie,
       Université d'Oslo, 69, 179 p. CR: P. ORRINO, *Homme* 10(1), jan-mar : 110-111.

3854   WYLLIE, R. W. "Divination and face-work", *Brit. J. Sociol.* 21(1), mar 70 : 52-62.
       [West Africa.]

3855   ZIEGLER, J. "Une théocratie africaine au Brésil: le candomblé 'Ile Marôaialaje' (Salvador-
       Bahia)", *C. int. Sociol.* 17(48), jan-jun 70 : 99-118.

       D.1312   *Major religions in the world today*
                    Les grandes religions dans le monde actuel

       [See also / Voir aussi: 3802, 5448]

3856   ANSARI, A. H. *Islam.* Patiala, Punjab University, 69, ix-115 p.

3857   BELLAH, R. N. "Christianity and symbolic realism", *J. scient. Study Relig.* With com-
       ments by J. T. BURTCHAELL, S. Z. KLAUSNER, B. NELSON.

3858   GARDET, L. *L'Islam; religion et communauté.* Paris, Desclée, De Brouwer, 70, 496 p.

3859   LIVIERES BANKS, L. "Notas para la comprensión de la función socio-histórica de la
       Iglesia Católica Apostólica Romana en el Paraguay" (Notes for the understanding of
       the socio-historic function of the Roman Catholic Apostolic Church in Paraguay),
       R. parag. Sociol. 7(17), jan-mar 70 : 123-132.

3860   MALALGODA, K. "Millenialism in relation to Buddhism", *Comp. Stud. Soc. Hist.* 12(4),
       oct 70 : 424-441.

3861   O'DEA, T. F. "The Catholic crisis", *Sociol. Anal.* 30(2), 1969 : 121-123.

3862   POULAT, E. "Trois problèmes pour la sociologie du catholicisme", *Soc. Compass* 16(4),
       1969 : 471-483.

3863 SCHARF, B. R. "Durkheimian and Freudian theories of religion: the case of Judaism", *Brit. J. Sociol.* 21(2), jun 70 : 151-163.

3864 SILVA, S. P. DE. *A scientific rationalization of Buddhism.* Colombo, Metro Printers, 69, 187 p.

D.1313 *Characteristics of the religious situation in various countries*
Caractéristiques de la situation religieuse en divers pays

[See also / Voir aussi: 1197, 2088, 3835, 3964]

3865 ABE, K. "Protesutantizumu juyô no ichi keitai" (Reception of Protestantism in Japan), *Jimbun Gakuhô* (66), 1968 : 1-56.

3866 "Afrique chrétienne (L')", *Tam-Tam* 17(4-5), 1969 : 31-48.

3867 ALVES, R. A. "Protestantism in Latin America: its ideological function and utopian possibilities", *Ecumen. R.* 22(1), jan 70 : 1-15.

3868 ANDERSON, C. H. *White Protestant Americans: from national origins to religious group.* Englewood Cliffs, N. J., Prentice-Hall, 70, xx-188 p.

3869 BASTOS DE AVILA, F. "A Igreja católica no Brasil 1968" (The Catholic Church in Brazil in 1968), *Sintese polít. econ. soc.* 10(39-40), jul-dec 68 : 81-92.

3870 BERGER, M. *Islam in Egypt today; social and political aspects of popular religion.* Cambridge, Eng., University Press, 70, vii-138 p.

3871 BERNARD, G. "Diversité des nouvelles Églises congolaises", *C. Ét. afr.* 10(2), 2 trim 70 : 203-227.

3872 BERTHAUD, E. "Chrétiens d'Iran", *Orient* 12(45-46), 1-2 trim 68 : 23-36.

3873 BREMOND, A. "L'évolution des Églises en Suède", *Études (Paris)* aug-sep 70 : 287-303.

3874 "Catholicisme 1970", *Nef* 27(41), oct-dec 70 : 5-151.

3875 "Église catholique romaine et l'Afrique (L')", *R. franç. Ét. polit. afr.* 53, mai 70 : 33-99; 56, aug 70 : 10-61.

3876 FERNANDEZ, J. W. "Independent African Christianity: its study and its future", *J. Asian Afr. Stud.* 4(2), apr 69 : 132-147.

3877 GLEASON, P. (ed.). *Contemporary Catholicism in the United States.* Notre Dame, Ind., University of Notre Dame, 69, xviii-385 p.

3878 GUSTAFSON, J. M. (ed.). "The sixties: radical change in American religion", *A. Amer. Acad. polit. soc. Sci.* 387, jan 70 : 1-140.

3879 HOFFMANN, J. "Situation et problème du catholicisme allemand aujourd'hui", *R. Allem.* 2(2), apr-jun 70 : 194-230.

3880 HULICKA, K. "The battle against religion in the USSR", *Sociol. relig.* 11(17-18), 1968 : 75-90.

3881 KÁLDY, Z. "La situation de l'Église évangélique en Hongrie", *IDOC int.* 18, feb 15, 70 : 23-31.

3882 KUROKAWA, M. "Social characteristics of Japanese religion", *Sociol. int. (Berlin)* 8(1), 1970 : 97-114.

3883 LADANY, L. "Religious trends in China", *Soc. Action* 19(4), oct-dec 69 : 316-322.

3884 LIU, W. T.; PALLONE, N. J. (comps). *Catholics/USA; perspectives on social change.* New York, Wiley, 70, xi-529 p.

3885 MAHRENHOLZ, E. G. *Die Kirchen in der Gesellschaft der Bundesrepublik* (The Church in the society of the German Federal Republic). Hannover, Verlag für Literatur und Zeitgeschehen, 69, 192 p.

3886 MARTY, M. E. *Righteous empire; the Protestant experience in America.* New York, Dial Press, 70, 295 p.

3887 MAYOL, A.; HABEGGER, N.; ARMADA, A. G. *Los católicos posconciliares en la Argentina, 1963-1969* (Postconcilian Catholics in Argentina, 1963-1969). Buenos Aires, Editorial Galerna, 70, 407 p.

3888 MEHL, R. "Le protestantisme allemand d'aujourd'hui", *R. Allem.* 2(2), apr-jun 70 : 169-193.

3889 NORBECK, E. *Religion and society in modern Japan: continuity and change.* Houston, Tourmaline Press, 70, vii-232 p.

3890 ROCHE DE COPPENS, P. "The Negro religion in America", *R. inst. Sociol. (Madrid)* 28(109-110), sep-dec 70 : 45-72.

3891   SANDERS, T. G. "The Church in Latin America", *For. Aff.* 48(2), jan 70 : 285-299.
         [Catholic Church.]
3892   SASO, M. R. "The Taoïst tradition in Taiwan", *China Quart.* 41, jan-mar 70 : 83-102.
3893   STORRS, P. "The Church in South America", *Bank London South Amer. R.* 4(45), sep
         70 : 478-486.
3894   VITALIS, H. G. *The significance of changes in Latin American Catholicism since Chimbote,
         1953.* Cuernavaca, Mexico, Centro Intercultural de Documentacíon, 69, various
         pagings.
3895   WELCH, H. "Facades of religion in China", *Asian Sur* . 10(7), jul 70 : 614-626.
3896   WHITLEY, O. R. *The Church: mirror or window? Images of the Church in American
         society.* St. Louis, Mo., Bethany Press, 69, 189 p. CR: H. E. DICKINSON, *Amer.
         sociol. R.* 35(1), feb 70 : 171.

D.1314   *Minor differentiations, sects
               Différenciations mineures, sectes*

[See also / Voir aussi: 890, 2027, 2611]

3897   ANDERSON, C. H. "Denominational differences in white Protestant communality", *R.
         relig. Res.* 11(1), 1969-1970 : 66-72.
3898   ARON, M. *Ideas and ideals of the Hassidim.* New York, Citadel Press, 69, 350 p.
3899   DATOR, J. A. *Soka Gakkai, builders of the third civilization: Americans and Japanese
         members.* Seattle, Wash., University of Washington Press, 69, 171 p. CR: G. K.
         YAMAMOTO, *Amer. sociol. R.* 35(3), jun 70 : 594-595.
3900   EARHART, H. B. *A religious study of the Mount Haguro sect of Shugendô;* Tokyo, Sophia
         University, 70, xvi-212 p.
3901   EGGENBERGER, O. *Die Kirchen, Sondergruppen und religiösen Vereinigungen* (Churches,
         sects and religious associations). Zürich, EVZ-Verlag, 69, xii-156 p.
3902   JORSTAD, E. T. *The politics of doomsday; fundamentalists of the Far Right.* Nashville,
         Abingdon Press, 70, 190 p.
3903   KOSS, J. D. "Terapeútica del sistema de una secta en Puerto Rico" (System thera-
         peutics of a Puerto Rican sect), *R. Cienc. soc. (Puerto Rico)* 14(2), apr-jun 70 :
         295-278.
3904   MITCHELL, J. E. *The emergence of a Mexican church; the Associate Reformed Presbyterian
         Church of Mexico.* South Pasadena, Calif., William Carey Library, 70, 183 p.
3905   MURAKAMI, S. "Les religions nouvelles au Japon", *Soc. Compass* 17(1), 1970 : 137-152.
3906   NEEDLEMAN, J. *The new religions.* Garden City, N. Y., Doubleday, 70, xii-245 p.
3907   NICHOLS, W. W. "The Ismaili sect in East Africa", *Ufahamu* 1(1), 1970 : 34-51.
3908   POULAT, E. *Intégrisme et catholicisme intégral. Un réseau secret international antimoderniste:
         la "Sapinière" (1909-1921).* Paris, Casterman, 69, 627 p.
3909   RABINOWICZ, H. M. *The world of Hasdism.* Hartford, Hartmore House, 70, 271 p.
3910   RAHN, G. "Religiöser Nationalismus in Japan" (Religious nationalism in Japan),
         Verfassung u. Recht Übersee 3(3), 1970 : 335-348. [Soka Gakkai.]
3911   ROSS, J. L. "The establishment process in a middle-class sect", *Soc. Compass* 16(4),
         1969 : 500-507.
3912   SINGH, H. *Guru Nanak and origins of the Sikh faith.* Bombay-New York, Asia Publishing
         House, 69, 247 p.
3913   VANN, R. T. *The social development of English Quakerism, 1655-1755.* Cambridge, Mass.,
         Harvard University Press, 69, xiv-259 p.
3914   ZYGMUT, J. F. "Prophetic failure and chiliastic identity: the case of Jehovah's Witnesses",
         Amer. J. Sociol. 75(6), mai 70 : 926-948.

D.132   *Outward forms of religious life*
        Manifestations extérieures de la vie religieuse

D.1321 *Belief and representation, mythology*
        Croyance et représentation, mythologie

[See also / Voir aussi: 875]

3915   ALPERS, A. *Legends of the South Seas; the world of the Polynesians seen through their myths and legends, poetry, and art.* New York, Crowell, 70, xv-416 p.

3916   BELMONT, N. "Les croyances populaires comme récit mythologique", *Homme* 10(2), apr-jun 70 : 94-108.

3917   BHATTACHARJI, S. *The Indian theogony; a comparative study of Indian mythology from the Vedas to the Purāṇas.* London, Cambridge University Press, 70, xiii-396 p.

3918   BOYD, M. *Man, myth, and magic.* New York, Criterion Books, 69, 173 p.

3919   BRATTON, F. G. *Myths and legends of the ancient Near East.* New York, Crowell, 70, xv-188 p.

3920   DETIENNE, M. "La cuisine de Pythagore", *Archiv. Sociol. Relig.* 15(29), jan-jun 70 : 141-162.

3921   DOUGLAS, M. *Natural symbols: explorations in cosmology.* London, Barrie and Rockliff the Cresset Press; New York, Pantheon Books, 70, xvii-177 p.

3922   DUMÉZIL, G. *Heur et malheur du guérrier; aspects mythiques de la fonction guérrière chez les Indo-Européens.* Paris, Presses universitaires de France, 69, 148 p.

3923   GREELEY, A. "Superstition, ecstasy and tribal consciousness", *Soc. Res.* 37(2), 1970 : 203-211.

3924   HASSAN, R. "Glaubenssysteme und berufliche Befriedigung. Eine empirische Prüfung der Weberschen Hypotheses" (Belief systems and job satisfaction. An empirical test of the Weberian hypothesis), *Sociologus* 20(1), 1970 : 57-71.

3925   ICHON, A. *La religion des Totonaques de la Sierra.* Paris, Éditions du Centre national de la recherche scientifique, 69, 424 p.

3926   JACQUES, H. P. *Mythologie et psychanalyse; le châtiment des Danaïdes.* Montréal, Leméac, 69, 156 p.

3927   KIRK, G. S. *Myth: its meaning and functions in ancient and other cultures.* Cambridge, Eng., University Press; Berkeley, University of California Press, 70, xii-299 p.

3928   KITAGAWA, J. M.; LONG, C. H. (eds.). *Myths and symbols; studies in honor of Mircea Eliade.* Chicago, University of Chicago Press, 69, 438 p.

3929   KUTUDJIAN, G. "À propos de l'étude formelle du mythe", *Homme* 10(3), jul-sep 70 : 84-105.

3930   LA BARRE, W. *The ghost dance; origins of religion.* Garden City, N. Y., Doubleday, 70, xvi-677 p.

3931   MOON, S. *A magic dwells; a poetic and psychological study of the Navaho emergence myth.* Middletown, Conn., Wesleyan University Press, 70, 206 p.

3932   NORMAN, D. *The hero: myth, image, symbol.* New York, World Publishing Co., 69, xvii-238 p.

3933   ROBERTS, A.; MOUNTFORD, C. P. *The dawn of time; Australian aboriginal myths in paintings.* Adelaide, Rigby, 69, 79 p.

3934   RUNCIMAN, W. G. "The sociological explanation of 'religious' beliefs", *Archiv. europ. Sociol.* 10(2), 1969 : 149-191.

3935   STARK, R.; FOSTER, B. D. "In defence of orthodoxy: notes on the validity of an index", *Soc. Forces* 48(3), mar 70 : 383-394. [An empirical measure of religious belief: the Orthodoxy Index.]

3936   WILLIS, R. G. "Kaswa; oral tradition of a Fipa prophet", *Africa (London)* 11(3), jul 70 : 248-255.

3937   ZIÉGLER, J. *Sociologie et contestation, essai sur la société mythique.* Paris, Gallimard, 69, 256 p.

D.1322   *Rites and cults*
             Rites et cultes

[See also / Voir aussi: 3903]

3938   ALLEGRO, J. M. *The sacred mushroom and the cross; a study of the nature and origins of Christianity within the fertility cults of the ancient Near East.* London, Hodder and Stoughton, 70, xxii-349 p.

3939   BAHTI, T. *Southwestern Indian ceremonials.* Flagstaff, Ariz., KC Publications, 70, 64 p.

3940   BOCOCK, R. J. "Ritual: civic and religious", *Brit. J. Sociol.* 21(3), sep 70 : 285-297.

3941   BOMBART, J.-P. "Les cultes protestants dans une favela de Rio de Janeiro", *Amér. lat.* 12(3), jul-sep 69 : 127-136.

3942   CRUMRINE, N. R. "Ritual drama and culture change", *Comp. Stud. Soc. Hist.* 12(4), oct 70 : 361-372.

3943   FRUNDT, H. J. "Rite involvement and community formation", *Sociol. Anal.* 30(2), 1969 : 91-107.

3944   GOODMAN, F. D. "Phonetic analysis of glossalia in four cultural settings", *J. scient. Study Relig.* 8(2), 1969 : 227-239.

3945   KITZINGER, S. "Protest and mysticism: the Rastafari cult of Jamaica", *J. scient. Study Relig.* 8(2), 1969 : 240-262.

3946   LINE, V. H. "Pentecostal glossalia; toward a functional interpretation", *J. scient. Study Relig.* 8(2), 1969 : 211-226.

3947   OBEYESEKERE, G. "The ritual drama of the Sanni demons: collective representations of disease in Ceylon", *Comp. Stud. Soc. Hist.* 11(2), apr 69 : 175-216. With a comment by J. E. Levy: 217-226 and with a rejoinder by the author 12(3), jul 70 : 292-296.

3948   OSBORNE, K. B. "A Christian graveyard cult in the New Guinea Highlands", *Pacific. Anthropol.* 17(1), jan-feb 70 : 10-15.

3949   PAOLINI, J. "The Kabyle handling of grief", *Muslim Wld* 59(3-4), jul-oct 69 : 251-274. [Algeria.]

3950   PARKIN, D. "Politics of ritual syncretism: Islam among the non-Muslim Giriama of Kenya", *Africa (London)* 11(3), jul 70 : 217-233.

3951   POLLAK-ELTZ, A. "El culto de los gemelos en Africa occidental y en las Américas" (The "twins" cult in West Africa and the Americas), *Amér. lat.* 12(2), apr-jun 69 : 66-78.

3952   ROBBINS, T. "Eastern mysticism and the resocialization of drug users; the Meker Baba cult", *J. scient. Study Relig.* 8(2), 1969 : 308-317.

3953   SOUZA, J. R. DE. *O ritual africano e seus mistérios; grupos e figuras, orixás e voduns, lendas, provérbios, etc.* (Africa ritual and its mysteries: groups and figures, "orixás" and vodoos, legends, proverbs, etc). Rio de Janeiro, Editôra Espiritualista, 69, 156 p.

3954   SWANTZ, M.-L. *The religious and magical rites connected with the life cycle of the woman in some Bantu ethnic groups of Tanzania.* Dar es Salaam, Turku University, 69, 285 p.

3955   TAMBIAH, S. J. *Buddhism and the spirit cults in north-east Thailand.* Cambridge, Eng., University Press, 70, xi-388 p.

3956   TURNER, C. V. "The Sinasina stone bowl cult", *Amer. Anthropol.* 17(1), jan-feb 70 : 28-32.

D.1323   *Religious practice, and its evaluation*
             La pratique religieuse et sa mesure

[See also / Voir aussi: **C.9213;** 1574, 2612]

3957   AVER, E. *et al.* "Pratique religieuse et comportement électoral à travers les sondages d'opinion", *Archiv. Sociol. Relig.* 15(29), jan-jun 70 : 27-52.

3958   BOVY, L. "La vie religieuse à la périphéric de Paris", *Riv. Sociol.* 7(18), jan-mar 69 : 43-86.

3959   BURNHAM, K. E.; CONNORS, J. F.; LEONARD, R. C. "Religious affiliation, church attendance, religious education and student attitudes toward race", *Sociol. Anal.* 30(4), 1969 : 235-244.

3960   CARLOS, S. "Religious participation and the urban-suburban continuum", *Amer. J. Sociol.* 75(5), mar 70 : 742-759. [Canada.]

3961 HAERLE, R. K. Jr. "Church attendance patterns among intermarried Catholics: a panel study", *Sociol. Anal.* 30(4), 1969 : 204-216.

3962 POULAT, E. "Catholicisme urbaine et pratique religieuse", *Archiv. Sociol. Relig.* 15(29), jan-jun 70 : 97-116.

3963 "Sociologie et catéchèse/Sociology and religious education", *Soc. Compass* 17(3), 1970 : 359-490.

3964 SPENCER, A. E. C. W. *Report on the parish register, religious practice and population statistics of the Catholic Church in Scotland, 1967.* Harrow, Middlesex, Pastoral Research Centre, 69, 45 p.

D.1324 *Religious behaviour*
Attitudes et comportement

[See also / Voir aussi: 763, 1005, 1572, 2540, 2595, 2645, 2879, 3240, 3694, 4720, 4903]

3965 ANDERSON, C. H. "Religious communality and party preference", *Sociol. Anal.* 30(1), 1969 : 32-41.

3966 ANZAI, S. "The religious attitudes of university students", *Soc. Compass* 17(1), 1970 : 119-136.

3967 BALSWICK, J. O. "Theology and political attitudes among clergymen", *Sociol. Quart.* 11(3), 1970 : 397-404.

3968 BESNARD, P. *Protestantisme et capitalisme. La controverse post-weberienne.* Paris, A. Colin, 70, 427 p.

3969 BREWER, D. "Religious resistance to changing beliefs about race", *Pacific sociol. R.* 13(3), 1970 : 163-170.

3970 BURCHARD, W. W. "Denominational correlates and changing religious beliefs in college", *Sociol. Anal.* 31(1), 1970 : 36-45.

3971 CHANTELOUP, R. E. "Hawks and doves: an analysis of a Catholic attitude toward nuclear war", *Sociol. Anal.* 31(1), 1970 : 23-35.

3972 ESTUS, C. N.; OVERINGTON, M. A. "The meaning and end of religiosity", *Amer. J. Sociol.* 75(5), mar 70 : 760-781. With a comment by E. GOODE.

3973 FINNER, S. L.; GAMACHE, J. D. "The relation between religious commitment and attitudes towards induced abortion", *Sociol. Anal.* 30(1), 1969 : 1-12.

3974 GIBBS, J. O.; CRADER, K. W. "A criticism of two recent attempts to scale Glock and Stark's dimensions of religiosity: a research note", *Sociol. Anal.* 31(2), 1970 : 107-114.

3975 HELTSLEY, M. E.; BRODERICK, C. B. "Religiosity and premarital sexual permissiveness: reexamination of Reiss's traditionalism proposition", *J. Marriage Family* 31(3), aug 69 : 441-445.

3976 HINE, V. H. "Bridge Burners: commitment and participation in a religious movement", *Sociol. Anal.* 31(2), 1970 : 61-66.

3977 LAZERWITZ, B. "The association between religio-ethnic identification and fertility among 'contemporary' Protestants and Jews", *Sociol. Quart.* 11(3), 1970 : 307-320.

3978 LINDENTHAL, J. J. *et al.* "Mental status and religious behavior", *J. scient. Study Relig.* 9(2), 1970 : 143-149.

3979 MACDONALD, L. "Religion and voting: a study of the 1968 Canadian federal election in Ontario", *Canad. R. Sociol. Anthropol.* 6(3), aug 69 : 129-144.

3980 McHALE, V. E. "Religion and electoral politics in France: some recent observations", *Canad. J. polit. Sci.* 2(3), sep 69 : 292-311.

3981 MORIOKA, K. "The impact of suburbanization on Shinto belief and behavior", *Soc. Compass* 17(1), 1970 : 37-66.

3982 NELSEN, H. M.; YOKLEY, R. L. "Civil rights attitudes of rural and urban Presbyterians", *Rur. Sociol.* 35(2), jun 70 : 161-174. [USA.]

3983 PICCIOTTI, G. "Il voto dei cattolici" (The Catholic vote), *Nord e Sud* 17(126), jun 70 : 13-32. [Italy.]

3984 SHAW, B. W. "Religion and conceptual models of behaviour", *Brit. J. soc. clinic. Psychol.* 9(4), dec 70 : 320-327.

3985 SOUFFRANT, C. "Un catholicisme de résignation en Haïti. Sociologie d'un recueil de cantiques religieux", *Soc. Compass* 17(3), 1970 : 425-438.

3986   SPRAY, P. L.; MARX, J. H. "The origins and correlates of religious adherence and apostasy among mental health professionals", *Sociol. Anal.* 30(3), apr 69 : 132-150.

3987   WEIGERT, A. J.; THOMAS, D. L. "Socialization and religiosity: a cross-cultural analysis of Catholic adolescents", *Sociometry* 33(3), sep 70 : 305-326.

D.1325   *Religious dynamics: regression and expansion, religion and atheism*
       Dynamique religieuse: régression et expansion, religion et athéisme

3988   BOLLE, K. W. "Secularization as a problem for the history of religions", *Comp. Stud. Soc. Hist.* 12(3), jul 70 : 242-259.

3989   DELOOZ, P. "Église et société sécularisée, l'expérience scandinave", *IDOC int.* 15, jan 1, 70 : 79-94.

3990   FENN, R. K. "The process of secularization: a post-Parsonian view", *J. scient. Study Relig.* 9(2), 1970 : 117-136.

3991   HANSSLER, B. "La Iglesia ante la secularización y el progreso" (The Church facing secularization and progress), *Arbor* 76(295-296), jul-aug 70 : 303-317.

3992   HASSINGER, E. W.; HOLIK, J. S. "Changes in the number of rural churches in Missouri, 1952-1967", *Rur. Sociol.* 35(3), sep 70 : 364-366.

3993   HUNKE, S. *Europas andere Religion; die Überwindung der religiösen Krise* (Europe's other religion; victory over the religious crisis). Düsseldorf, Econ, 69, 558 p.

3994   MANDIĆ, O. "A marxist perspective on contemporary religious revivals", *Soc. Res.* 37(2), 1970 : 237-258.

3995   MARTIN, D. "Notes for a general theory of secularisation", *Archiv. europ. Sociol.* 10(2), 1969 : 192-201.

3996   Bibl. XIX-3560. MARTIN, D. *The religious and the secular—studies in secularization.* CR: S. BUDD, *Amer. J. Sociol.* 75(6), mai 70 : 1066-1068; P. L. BERG, *Amer. sociol. R.* 35(4), aug 70 : 795-796.

3997   NELEN, P. "Doodstrijd en groeikrisis binnen het latijns Amerikaanse Katholicisme" (Agony and crisis of growth of Catholicism in Latin America), *Int. Spectator* 24(6), mar 22, 70 : 537-547.

3998   PANCHAV, I. D. *Konkretno-sociologičeskoe izučenie sostojanija religioznosti i opyta atestičeskogo vospitanija* (A concrete sociological study on the religious content and experience of atheist education). Moskva, Moskovskij Universitet, 69, 282 p.

3999   REYBURN, W. D. "The helping relationship in missionary work", *Practic. Anthropol.* 17(2), mar-apr 70 : 49-59.

4000   RIEZU, J. "El contexto sociológico del ateismo actual" (The sociological context of current atheism), *Arbor* 74(287), nov 69 : 159-185.

4001   STOWE, D. M. "Changing patterns of missionary service in today's world", *Practic. Anthropol.* 17(3), mai-jun 70 : 107-118.

4002   VALLIER, I. "El 'desarrollo' de la Iglesia en América Latina: una comparación en cinco países" (The "development" of the Church in Latin America: a comparison of five countries), *R. parag. Sociol.* 7(17), jan-mar 70 : 28-46.

4003   WAMBUTDA, D. N. "An African Christian looks at Christian missions in Africa", *Practic. Anthropol.* 17(4), jul-aug 70 : 169-176.

D.14   **Law**
       Droit

[See also / Voir aussi: 1755, 2077, 2718, 4328, 4909, 4910, 5296]

4004   ALLOTT, A. N. *New essays in African law.* London, Butterworths, 70, xxxiv-348 p.

4005   AUBERT, V. *Sociology of law; selected readings.* Baltimore-Harmondsworth, Penguin Books, 69, 366 p. CR: B.-M. P. BLEGVAD, *Acta sociol.* 13(3), 1970 : 198-199.

4006   BIRMINGHAM, R. L. "The growth of the law: decision theory and the doctrine of consideration", *Archiv Rechts- u. soz.-Philos.* 55(4), 1969 : 467-491.

4007   BUCKNER, T. H. "Transformations of reality in the legal process", *Soc. Res.* 37(1), mar 70 : 88-101.

4008   COHEN, J. A. (ed.). *Contemporary Chinese law: research problems and perspectives.* Cambridge, Mass., Harvard University Press, 70, 380 p.

4009   CRABB, J. H. *The legal system of Congo-Kinshasa.* Charlottesville, Va., Michie Co., 70, xiii-233 p.

4010 DARLING, F. C. "The evolution of law in Thailand", *R. Polit.* 32(2), apr 70 : 197-218.

4011 DOMBEK, B. *Das Verhältnis der Tübinger Schule zur deutschen Rechtssoziologie* (Relations between the Tübingen school and the German sociology of law). Berlin, Duncker und Humblot, 69, 99 p.

4012 DROR, Y. "Law as a tool for directed social change: a framework for policy making", *Amer. behav. Scientist* 13(4), mar-apr 70 : 553-559.

4013 "Essor de la sociologie et la philosophie du droit (L')", *Archiv. Philos. Dr.* 14, 1969 : 211-264.

4014 GELARD, P. "Droit comparé et psychologie des peuples", *R. Psychol. Peuples* 25(1), 1 trim 70 : 18-45.

4015 GIL-CREMADES, J.-J. "Rechtstheorie und Rechtspraxis" (Legal theory and legal practice), *Archiv Rechts- u. soz.-Philos.* 56(1), 1970 : 1-42.

4016 GOYTISOLO, J. B. V. DE. *Sociedad de masa y derecho* (Mass society and law). Madrid, Taurus, 69, 658 p.

4017 HAZARD, J. N. *Communists and their law; a search for the common core of the legal systems of the Marxian socialist states.* Chicago, University of Chicago Press, 69, xvi-560 p.

4018 HAZARD, J. N. "Law and social change in Marxist Africa", *Amer. behav. Scientist* 13(4), mar-apr 70 : 575-584.

4019 IGLÉSIAS, A. M. "Derecho paraguayo y filosofía del derecho" (Paraguayan law and philosophy of law), *Verfassung u. Recht Übersee* 3(1), 1970 : 75-86.

4020 JOHNSON, E. L. *An introduction to the Soviet legal system.* London, Methuen, 69, xv-248 p.

4021 JØRGENSEN, S. *Ret of samfund* (Law and society). København, Berlingske, 70, 136 p.

4022 KULCSÁR, K. "A jogalkalmazás funkcionális elemzésének problémái" (Problems of functional analysis applied to international law), *Állam- és Jogtud.* 12(4), oct-dec 69 : 602-621.

4023 KWASNIEWSKI, J. "Motivation of declared conformity to a legal norm", *Polish sociol. B.* (1), 1969 : 74-82.

4024 LAZAR, L. "Legal centralism in South Africa", *Int. comp. Law Quart.* 19(3), jul 70 : 492-507.

4025 LEGRANDIĆ, R. "Über Rechtsdialektik" (On dialectic of law), *Archiv Rechts- u. soz.-Philos.* 56(4), 1970 : 485-492.

4026 MAYDA, J. "Quelques réflexions critiques sur le droit comparé contemporain", *R. int. Dr. comp.* 22(1), jan-mar 70 : 57-82.

4027 M'BAYE, K. "Le droit africain: ses voies et ses vertus", *R. sénég. Dr.* 4(7), mar 70 : 5-24.

4028 MENDELSON, W. "Law and the development of nations", *J. Polit.* 32(2), mai 70 : 223-238.

4029 MENSAH-BROWN, K. "Der Charakter des Akan-Eingeborenenrechts: eine kritische Analyse" (The nature of Akan native law: a critical analysis), *Sociologus* 20(2), 1970 : 123-146.

4030 MILLER, A. S. "Science challenges law: some interactions between scientific and legal changes", *Amer. behav. Scientist* 13(4), mar-apr 70 : 585-593.

4031 MINEMURA, T. "Dogmatic legal science and sociology of law", *Archiv Rechts- u. soz.-Philos.* 56(3), 1970 : 351-366.

4032 MÜLLER, F. "Thesen zur Struktur von Rechtsnormen" (Theses on the structure of legal norms), *Archiv Rechts- u. soz.-Philos.* 56(4), 1970 : 493-509.

4033 PAGEARD, R. *Le droit privé des Mossi. Tradition et évolution.* 2 vols. Paris, CNRS; Ouagadougou, CNRS, 69, 485 p. multigr.

4034 PODGÓRECKI, A. "Law and morals in theory and operation", *Polish sociol. B.* (1), 1969 : 26-38.

4035 POIRIER, J. "Situation actuelle et programme de travail de l'ethnologie juridique", *R. int. Sci. soc.* 22(3), 1970 : 509-527.

4036 POLICASTRI, C. "La sociologia giuridica nella *Rivista italiana di Sociologia*" (Legal sociology in the *Rivista Italiana di Sociologia*), *Riv. Sociol.* 7(18), jan-mar 69 : 145-170.

4037 RAGUIN, C. "Le droit naissant et les luttes de pouvoir", *Sociol. Trav.* 12(1), jan-mar 70 : 33-50.

4038 ROSA, F. A. DE M. *Sociologia do direito; o fenêmeno jurídico como fato social* (Sociology of law; a legal phenomenon as a social fact). Rio de Janeiro, Zahar Editores, 70, 202 p.

4039   SAROTTE, G. *Le matérialisme historique dans l'étude du droit.* Paris, Éditions du Pavillon, 69, 311 p.

4040   SAYAG, A. *Essai sur le besoin créateur de droit.* Paris, Librairie générale de droit et de jurisprudence, 69, 320 p. CR: C. RAGUIN, *R. franç. Sociol.* 11(3), jul-sep 70 : 435-437.

4041   SCHWARTZ, R. D.; SKOLNICK, J. H. (eds.). *Society and the legal order; cases and materials in the sociology of law.* New York, Basic Books, 70, xiv-652 p.

4042   SUMMERS, M. R.; BARTH, T. E. (eds.). *Law and order in a democratic society.* Columbus, Ohio, Merrill, 70, x-275 p.

4043   SUTTNER, R. S. "The study of 'Bantu law' in South Africa: a review article", *Acta jur. (Cape-Town)* 1968 : 147-156.

4044   "Tendances de la science juridique", *R. int. Sci. soc.* 22(3), 1970 : 403-499.

4045   TIEMEYER, J. *Zur Methodenfrage der Rechtssoziologie* (Method problems of sociology of law). Berlin, Duncker und Humblot, 69, 106 p. CR: F. ROTTNER, *Kölner Z. Soziol. u. soz.-Psychol.* 22(4), dec 70 : 824-826.

4046   TREVES, R. "I precursori della sociologia del diritto" (The precursors of the sociology of law), *Quad. Sociol.* 18(4), oct-dec 69 : 419-445.

4047   TREVES, R. *Sociologia del diritto* (Sociology of law). Milano, La goliardica, 70, 156 p.

4048   VERSELE, S.-C.; LEGROS, P.; ESTENNE, J. (eds.). "Actes du Colloque international de Sociologie du Droit et de la Justice, Bruxelles, 9-12 avril 1969", *R. Inst. Sociol.* (2), 1970 : 203-382.

D.2   **OPINION AND ATTITUDES**
        OPINION ET ATTITUDES

D.20   **General and methodological studies**
        Études générales et méthodologiques

[See also / Voir aussi: 584, 1834, 1985, 2001, 2887, 2987, 3760, 3799, 4373, 4420, 4497]

4049   AKUTO, H. "Shakaifuan to seijiishiki" (Social unrest and political attitude), *Nempô Shakai Shinrigaku* (9), 1968 : 3-26.

4050   ANDERSON, L. R. "Prediction of negative attitude from congruity, summation, and logarithm formulae for the evaluation of complex stimuli", *J. soc. Psychol.* 81(1), jun 70 : 37-48.

4051   BAGLEY, C.; WILSON, G. D.; BOSHIER, R. "The conservatism scale: a factor-structure comparison of English, Dutch, and New Zealand samples", *J. soc. Psychol.* 81(2), aug 70 : 267-268.

4052   BARRON, B. A.; HIRSCH, J.; GLUCKSMAN, M. "The construction and calibration of behavioral rating scales", *Behav. Sci.* 15(3), mai 70 : 220-226.

4053   BENC, M. "Politička kultura gradana i anketna istraživanja u Hrvatskoj" (Citizens political culture and sociological surveys in Croatia), *Polit. Misao* 7(1), 1970 : 23-33.

4054   BERLYNE, D. E. "Laughter, humor, and play", in: G. LINDZEY, E. ARONSON (eds.). *The handbook of social psychology.* 2nd ed. Vol. III. Reading, Mass., Addison-Wesley, 1968 : 795-852.

4055   CARTER, R. E. "La investigación social y las encuestas preelectorales" (Social research and pre-election surveys), *R. esp. Opin. públ.* 16, apr-jun 69 : 9-13.

4056   CHESON, B. D.; STRICKER, G.; FRY, C. L. "The repression-sensitization scale and measures of prejudice", *J. soc. Psychol.* 80(2), apr 70 : 197-200.

4057   CHOMBART DE LAUWE, P.-H. "Convergences et controverse sur la genèse des besoins", *C. int. Sociol.* 17(48), jan-jun 70 : 25-36.

4058   CHOMBART DE LAUWE, P.-H. "Dynamique des aspirations et changement des institutions", *Quad. Sci. soc.* 8(1-2), 1969 : 25-45.

4059   CHOMBART DE LAUWE, P.-H. *Pour une sociologie des aspirations. Éléments pour des perspectives nouvelles en sciences humaines.* Paris, Éditions Denoël, 69, 316 p. CR: J.-P. DECONCHY, *C. int. Sociol.* 17(49), jul-dec 70 : 182-184.

4060   CLORE, G. L.; BALDRIDGE, B. "The behavior of item weights in attitude-attraction research", *J. exper. soc. Psychol.* 6(2), apr 70 : 177-186.

4061   CONVERSE, P. E. "Alcune variabilidi fondamentali nelle ricerche elettorali comparate"

(Some basic variables in comparative voting research), *Rass. ital. Sociol.* 9(3), jul-sep 68 : 435-464.

4062 COOK, T. D.; BURD, J. R.; TALBERT, T. L. "Cognitive, behavioral and temporal effects of confronting a belief with its costly action implications", *Sociometry* 33(3), sep 70 : 358-369.

4063 CROOK, J. H. "Sources of cooperation in animals and man", *Soc. Sci. Inform./Inform. Sci. soc.* 9(1), feb 70 : 27-48. [Animal behaviour research.]

4064 DILLEHAY, R. C.; JERNIGAN, L. R. "The biased questionnaire as an instrument of opinion change", *J. Person. soc. Psychol.* 15(2), jun 70 : 144-150.

4065 DODDER, R. A. "A factor analysis of Dean's alienation scale", *Soc. Forces* 48(2), dec 69 : 252-255.

4066 EHRLICH, H. J. "Attitudes, behavior and the intervening variables", *Amer. Sociologist* 4(1), 1969 : 29-34.

4067 FRIEDMAN, P. H.; BUCK, R.; ALLEN, V. L. "Arousal, anxiety, aggression, and attitude change", *J. soc. Psychol.* 82(1), oct 70 : 99-108.

4068 GORMLY, A. V.; CLORE, G. L. "Attraction, dogmatism and attitude similarity-dissimilarity", *J. exper. Res. Personality* 4(1), jul 69 : 9-13.

4069 HARRY, J. "A by-product theory of primary behavior", *Pacific sociol. R.* 13(2), 1970 : 121-126.

4070 HAYES, L. D.; HEDLUND, R. D. (eds.). *The conduct of political inquiry; behavioral political analysis.* Englewood Cliffs, N. J., Prentice-Hall, 70, xi-255 p.

4071 HELMSTADTER, G. C. *Research concepts in human behavior: education, psychology, sociology.* New York, Appleton-Century-Crofts, 70, xv-448 p.

4072 HICKS, J. M. "Convergent-discriminant validation and factor analysis of five scales of liberalism-conservatism", *J. Person. soc. Psychol.* 14(2), feb 70 : 114-119.

4073 HOLMES, J. G.; STRICKLAND, L. H. "Choice freedom and confirmation of incentive expectancy as determinants of attitude change", *J. Person. soc. Psychol.* 14(1), jan 70 : 39-45.

4074 JOHNSON, C. E. (comp.). *Contemporary readings in behavior.* New York, McGraw-Hill, 70, xi-292 p.

4075 Bibl. XIX-3617. KIESLER, C. A.; COLLINS, B. E.; MILLER, N. *Attitude change: a critical analysis of theoretical approaches.* CR: S. J. SHERMAN, *Amer. sociol. R.* 35(2), apr 70 : 398-399.

4076 KOMURO, N. "Shakai kodoron no kiso" (A basis of behavioral theory), *Nempô Shakai Shinrigaku* (9), 1968 : 215-227.

4077 LEVY, L. H.; HOUSE, W. C. "Perceived origins of beliefs as determinants of expectancy for their change", *J. Person. soc. Psychol.* 14(4), apr 70 : 329-334.

4078 LINDGREN, H.; MARRASH, J. "A comparative study of international insight and empathy", *J. soc. Psychol.* 80(2), apr 70 : 135-141.

4079 MATALON, B.; PITROU, A. "L'utilisation des attitudes dans la recherche socio-éco-nomique", *R. franç. Sociol.* 10, n° spécial 1969 : 724-743.

4080 McFARLAND, S. G.; THISTLETHWAITE, D. L. "An analysis of a logical consistency model of belief change", *J. Person. soc. Psychol.* 15(2), jun 70 : 133-143.

4081 McGINNIES, E. *Social behavior: a functional analysis.* Boston, Houghton Miffin Co., 70, xi-459 p.

4082 McGUIRE, W. J. "The nature of attitudes and attitude change", in: G. LINDZEY, E. ARONSON (eds.). *The handbook of social psychology.* Vol. III. 2nd ed. Reading, Mass., Addison-Wesley, 1968 : 136-314.

4083 McKENNELL, A. "Attitude measurement: use of coefficient alpha with cluster or factor analysis", *Sociology* 4(2), mai 70 : 227-245.

4084 MEHRYAR, A. H. "A cross-cultural investigation of Eysenck's hypothesis regarding the relationship between personality and attitudes", *Brit. J. soc. clin. Psychol.* 9(3), sep 70 : 216-221.

4085 OSKAMP, S.; THOMPSON, G. "Internal inconsistency in the stereopathy-acquiscence scales: a warning note", *J. soc. Psychol.* 81(1), jun 70 : 73-77.

4086 PLOOG, D. "Neurological aspects of social behavior", *Soc. Sci. Inform./Inform. Sci. soc.* 9(3), jun 70 : 71-97.

4087 RAYNOLDS, D. R. "A spatial model for analyzing voting behavior", *Acta sociol.* 12(3), 1969 : 122-131.

4088   RHINE, R. J.; SEVERANCE, L. J. "Ego-involvement, discrepancy, source credibility, and attitude change", *J. Person. soc. Psychol.* 16(2), oct 70 : 175-190.

4089   RICHARDS, C. E. "Presumed behavior: modification of the ideal-real dichotomy", *Amer. Anthropol.* 71(6), dec 69 : 1115-1117.

4090   RIKER, W. H.; ZAVOINA, W. J. "Rational behavior in politics: evidence from a three person game", *Amer. polit. Sci. R.* 64(1), mar 70 : 48-60.

4091   ROBINSON, J. E.; INSKO, C. A. "Attributed belief similarity-dissimilarity versus race as determinants of prejudice; a further test of Rokeach's theory", *J. exper. Res. Personality* 4(1), jul 69 : 72-77.

4092   ROBINSON, J. P.; RUSK, J. G.; HEAD, K. B. *Measures of political attitudes.* Ann Arbor, Mich., Survey Research Center, Institute for Social Research, 68, iv-712 p. CR: G. M. MARANELL, *Amer. sociol. R.* 35(3), jun 70 : 566-567.

4093   ROGERS, R. W.; THISTLEWAITE, D. "Effects of fear arousal and reassurance on attitude change", *J. Person. soc. Psychol.* 15(3), jul 70 : 227-233.

4094   ROSNOW, R. L.; SULS, J. M. "Reactive effects of pretesting in attitude research", *J. Person. soc. Psychol.* 15(4), aug 70 : 338-343.

4095   ROSSOMANDO, N. P.; WEISS, W. "Attitude change effects of timing and amount of payment for counterattitudinal behavior", *J. Person. soc. Psychol.* 14(1), jan 70 : 32-38.

4096   SCHATTELES, F. "Un studiu formal al conditiilor şi limitelor previziunii ştiintifice a comportamentului social" (A formal study of conditions and limits of scientific forecasting of social behaviour), *R. Filoz.* 17(1), 1970 : 37-50. [Rumania.]

4097   SCOTT, W. A. "Attitude measurement", in: G. LINDZEY, E. ARONSON (eds.). *The handbook of social psychology.* Vol. II. 2nd ed. Reading, Mass., Addison-Wesley, 1968 : 204-273.

4098   SHERMAN, S. J. "Effects of choice and incentive on attitude change in a discrepant behavior situation", *J. Person. soc. Psychol.* 15(3), jul 70 : 245-252.

4099   SICINSKI, A. " 'Don't know' answers in cross-national surveys", *Publ. Opin. Quart.* 34(1), 1970 : 126-130.

4100   SILVERMAN, I.; SHULMAN, A. D. "A conceptual model of artifact in attitude change studies", *Sociometry* 33(1), mar 70 : 97-107.

4101   SUMMERS, G. F. (ed.). *Attitude measurement.* Chicago, Rand McNally, 70, xviii-568 p.

4102   SZALAY, L. B.; LYSNE, D. A. "Attitude research for intercultural communication and interaction", *J. Communication* 20(2), jun 70 : 180-200.

4103   SZALAY, L. B.; WINDLE, C.; LYSNE, D. A. "Attitude measurement by free verbal associations", *J. soc. Psychol.* 82(1), oct 70 : 43-55.

4104   TAJFEL, H. "Cognitive aspects of prejudice", *J. soc. Issues* 25(4), 1969 : 79-97.

4105   TUFTE, E. R. "A note of caution in using variables that have common elements", *Publ. Opin. Quart.* 33(4), 1970 : 622-626.

4106   VAN DINGENEN, F. "Application de la théorie mathématique des processus d'adaptation à l'étude d'un comportement politique", *R. Inst. Sociol.* 3, 1970 : 519-535.

4107   WARREN, D. I. "Dissonance, attitude change, and group structure: a preliminary analysis", *Pacific sociol. R.* 13(3), 1970 : 187-199.

4108   WICKER, A. W. "Attitudes versus actions: the relationship of verbal and overt behavioral responses to attitude objects", *J. soc. Issues* 25(4), 1969 : 41-78.

4109   WILSON, G. D. "Is there a general factor in social attitudes ? Evidence from a factor analysis of the conservatism scale", *Brit. J. soc. clin.* 9(2), jun 70 : 101-107.

4110   YOUNG, F. W. "Reactive subsystems", *Amer. sociol. R.* 35(2), apr 70 : 297-307.

4111   YUKL, G. "Leader LPG scores: attitude dimensions and behavioral correlates", *J. soc. Psychol.* 80(2), apr 70 : 207-212.

D.21   Public opinion and propaganda
Opinion publique et propagande

[See also / Voir aussi: 963, 4517, 4556]

4112   ABRAMS, M. "The opinion polls and the British election of 1970", *Publ. Opin. Quart.* 34(3), 1970 : 317-324.

4113   ANTAL, E. *Die Funktionen der Werbung im System der zentralen Wirtschaftslenkung* (The functions of advertising in a centralized economic system). Wiesbaden, O. Harrassowitz, 70, 170 p.

4114   BLECHA, K.; GEHMACHER, E. *Opinion-leaders in Österreich. Beiträge zur Erforschung der Meinungsbildung in Wirtschaft- und Währungsfragen* (Opinion leaders in Austria. A contribution to research in opinion formation on economic and monetary problems). Wien, Institut für Empirische Sozialforschung, 70, 68 p.

4115   BLOM, R. "Public opinion about the functioning of social institutions", *Acta sociol.* 13(2), 1970 : 110-126.

4116   BOUTHOUL, G. *et al. Opinions et motivations des étudiants français, 200 questions, 120 enquêteurs, 1216 étudiants, 250.000 réponses...* Paris, Presses universitaires de France, 69, 176 p.

4117   CHARLOT, M. (comp.). *La persuasion politique.* Paris, A. Colin, 70, 168 p.

4118   CROTTY, W. J. (comp.). *Public opinion and politics; a reader.* New York, Holt, Rinehart and Winston, 70, viii-431 p.

4119   EYDALIN, M. "La propaganda ideológica en el conjunto de la información" (Ideological propaganda and the information complex), *Estud. Inform.* 13, jan-mar 70 : 103-138.

4120   GLENN, N. D. "Problems of comparability in trend studies with opinion poll data", *Publ. Opin. Quart.* 34(1), 1970 : 82-91.

4121   GWYN, R. J. "Opinion advertising and the free market of ideas", *Publ. Opin. Quart.* 34(2), 1970 : 246-255.

4122   HENNESSY, B. C. "Public opinion and opinion change", *Polit. Sci. ann.* (1), 1966 : 243-296.

4123   IKUTA, M. "Seronkatei ni tsuite no ichi kôsatsu" (Problems of public opinion), *Hôgaku Kenkyû* 41(4), 1968 : 151-169.

4124   Bibl. XIX-3652. LAGNEAU, G. *Faire valoir. Une introduction à la sociologie des phénomènes publicitaires.* CR: J. MARCUS-STEIFF, *R. franç. Sociol.* 10(4), oct-dec 69 : 533-536.

4125   LONDON, H.; MELDMAN, P. J.; LANCKTON, A. VAN C. "The jury method: how the persuader persuades", *Publ. Opin. Quart.* 34(2), 1970 : 171-183.

4126   LUHMANN, N. "Öffentliche Meinung" (Public opinion), *Polit. Vjschr.* 11(1), mar 70 : 2-28.

4127   MOLES, A. A. *L'affiche dans la société urbaine.* Paris, Dunod, 70, iv-153 p.

4128   MÖLLER, C. *Gesellschaftliche Funktionen der Konsumwerbung* (Social function of consumer advertising). Stuttgart, C. E. Poeschel, 70, xi-147 p.

4129   MORIN, E. *La rumeur d'Orléans.* Paris, Éditions du Seuil, 69, 236 p. CR: B. STERNBERG-SAREL, *C. int. Sociol.* 17(48), jan-jun 70 : 189-190. [Opinion publique et racisme dans une ville française.]

4130   NIMMO, D. D. *The political persuaders; the techniques of modern election campaigns.* Englewood Cliffs, N. J., Prentice-Hall, 70, x-214 p.

4131   OIKONOMOU, D. P. *'É demosía gnômê* (Public opinion). 'Athênai, 'Ekdosis Bibliothêkês Théseis kai 'Idéai, 69, 64 p.

4132   POOL, I. DE S. "Public opinion in Czechoslovakia", *Publ. Opin. Quart.* 34(1), 1970 : 10-26.

4133   "Publicité dans la société contemporaine (La)", *Human. et Entr.* 62, aug 70 : 1-111.

4134   RENOUVIN, P. "L'étude historique de l'opinion publique", *R. Trav. Acad. Sci. mor. polit.* 121(4), 1 sem 68 : 123-143.

4135   RÖPKE, J. "Wettbewerb, Presse-Freiheit und öffentliche Meinung. Eine Analyse der Wirkungen" (Competition, freedom of the press and free opinions. An analysis of consequences), *Schmollers Jb.* 90(2), 1970 : 171-192.

4136   ROSENSTIEL, L. VON. *Psychologie der Werbung* (Advertising psychology). Rosenheim, Komar-Verlag, 69, 288 p.

4137   WEILBACHER, W. M. "What happens to advertisements when they grow up", *Publ. Opin. Quart.* 34(2), 1970 : 216-223.

D.22   Formation of attitudes and stereotypes
**   Formation des attitudes et stéréotypes**

[See also / Voir aussi: **C.31, C.40, C.71, D.132**; 581, 731, 886, 956, 1006, 1015, 1055, 1124, 1413, 1414, 1590, 1618, 1619, 1744, 1780, 1810, 1932, 1940, 1988, 1994, 2005, 2006, 2035, 2219, 2274, 2373, 2399, 2421, 2450, 2463, 2466, 2524, 2568, 2668, 2758, 2828, 2834, 2850, 2923, 2998, 3255, 3283, 3315, 3514, 3577, 3593, 3957, 3979, 3980, 4342, 4528, 4549, 4719, 4767, 4798, 4976, 5142]

4138   ADACHI, T. "Shôtengai ni okeru seijiishiki to tôhyô kôdô" (Political attitude and voting behaviour in a commercial district), *Hô to Seiji* 19(2), 1968 : 85-135. [Japan.]

4139   ADLER, N.; HARRINGTON, C. *The learning of political behavior.* Glenview, Ill., Scott, Foresman, 70, 208 p.

4140   ANDERSON, B.; SHELLY, R. K. "Reactions to inequity. II. A replication of the Adams experiment and a theoretical reformulation", *Acta sociol.* 13(1), 1970 : 1-10. [In a work situation, productivity and wages.]

4141   ARENDT, H. *On violence.* New York, Harcourt, Brace and World, 70, 106 p.

4142   ATKIN, C. K. "The impact of political poll reports on candidate and issue preferences", *J-ism Quart.* 46(3), 69 : 515-521.

4143   BAILES, D. W.; GULLER, I. B. "Dogmatism and attitudes toward the Vietnam war", *Sociometry* 33(2), jun 70 : 140-146.

4144   BARBIER, R. "L'attitude anti-sociologique des écrivains et des artistes", *Homme et Soc.* 16, apr-mai-jun 70 : 323-334.

4146   BARRESI, C. M.; LINDQUIST, J. H. "The urban community: attitudes toward neighborhood and urban renewal", *Urb. Aff.* 5(3), mar 70 : 278-290.

4147   BARTSCH, G. "Der Revolutionär als Typus" (The revolutionary as a type), *Polit. Stud. (München)* 186, jul-aug 69 : 400-407.

4148   BÄRWALD, H.; SCHEFFLER, H. *Der politische Radikalismus in der Bundesrepublik Deutschland* (Political radicalism in the Federal Republic of Germany). Bad Godesberg, Hohwacht-Verlag, 69, 235 p.

4149   BAX, M. "Patronage Irish style; Irish politicians as brokers", *Sociol. Gids* 17(3), mai-jun 70 : 179-191.

4150   BAXTER, C. *District voting trends in India; a research tool.* New York, Columbia University Press, 69, xxii-378 p.

4151   BECKER, C. "Einstellungen deutscher Schüler gegenüber Franzosen, Polen und Russen" (Stereotypes of the French, Polish and Russians among German pupils), *Kölner Z. Soziol. u. soz.-Psychol.* 22(4), dec 70 : 737-755.

4152   BERK, L. E.; ROSE, M. H.; STEWART, D. "Attitudes of English and American children toward their school experience", *J. educ. Psychol.* 61(1), feb 70 : 33-40.

4153   BERMAN, M. *The politics of authenticity; radical individualism and the emergence of modern society.* New York, Atheneum, 70, xxiv-325 p.

4154   BERNSTEIN, D. A. "The modification of smoking behavior: a search for effective variables", *Behav. Res. Therapy* 8(2), mai 70 : 133-146.

4155   BOCKLER, C. G. "Colonialismo, violencia y Universidad" (Colonialism, violence and university), *R. mexic. Sociol.* 31(4), oct-dec 69 : 1027-1040.

4156   BON, F.; MICHELAT, G. *Attitudes et comportements politiques à Boulogne-Billancourt. Enquête par panel.* Paris, A. Colin, 70, 140 p. (Travaux et recherches de science politique, n° 12).

4157   BONHAM, G. M. "Participation in regional parliamentary assemblies: effects on attitudes of Scandinavian parliamentarians", *J. Common Market Stud.* 8(4), jun 70 : 325-336.

4158   BOOTH, A. "Personal influence networks and participation in professional association activities", *Publ. Opin. Quart.* 33(4), 1970 : 611-614.

4159   BOURRICAUD, F. "Realidad y teorías sobre la 'violencia' en América Latina" (Reality and theories on "violence" in Latin America), *R. parag. Sociol.* 6(16), sep-oct 69 : 105-115.

4160   BOUSSARD, J. M. "Le comportement des agriculteurs en situation d'incertitude: étude de la valeur de différents critères de décision", *Rech. Écon. Sociol. rur.* 3, 1970 : 23-40.

4161 BUTLER, D. E.; STOKES, D. *Political change in Britain; forces shaping electoral choice.* New York, St Martin's Press, 69, xi-516 p.

4162 CAIN, E. R. "Conscientious objection in France, Britain and the United States", *Comp. Polit.* 2(2), jan 70 : 275-307.

4163 CALOT, G.; BOHLEY, P. "Die Wechselwähler in Hessen. Die Anwendung eines Regressionsmodells" (Floating voters in Hesse. The application of a regression model), *Z. ges. Staatswiss.* 126(1), jan 70 : 126-147.

4164 CARTER, R. D.; STUART, R. B. "Behavior modification theory and practice: a reply", *Soc. Wk* 15(1), jan 70 : 37-50.

4165 CHEYNE, W. M. "Stereotyped reactions to speakers with Scottish and English regional accents", *Brit. J. soc. clin. Psychol.* 9(1), feb 70 : 77-79.

4166 COCQ, G. A. DE. *Citizen participation—doomed to extinction or last foothold of democracy.* Leyden, A. W. Sijthoff, 69, 278 p.

4167 COURTHÉOUX, J. P. *Attitudes collectives et croissance économique...* Paris, M. Rivière et Cie, 69, xviii-241 p.

4168 COX, K. K. "Changes in stereotyping of negroes and whites in magazine advertisements", *Publ. Opin. Quart.* 33(4), 1970 : 603-606.

4169 COX, K. R. "Residential relocation and political behavior: conceptual model and empirical tests", *Acta sociol.* 13(1), 1970 : 40-53. [USA.]

4170 CUTLER, N. E. "Generation, maturation, and party affiliation: a cohort analysis", *Publ. Opin. Quart.* 33(4), 1970 : 583-592. With a reply by J. CRITTENDEN: 589-591, and a comment by N. E. CUTLER: 592.

4171 DAMJANOVIĆ, M. "Birač kao subjekt izborne participacije" (The voter as a subject of electoral participation), *Polit. Misao* 7(1), 1970 : 83-93. [Yugoslavia.]

4172 DAWSON, R. E. "Political socialization", *Polit. Sci. ann.* (1), 1966 : 1-84. [See also Bibl. XIX-1594.]

4173 DELSAUT, Y. "Les opinions politiques dans le système des attitudes: les étudiants en lettres et la politique", *R. franç. Sociol.* 11(1), jan-mar 70 : 45-64. [France.]

4174 DEVINE, D. J. *The attentive public; polyarchical democracy.* Chicago, Rand McNally, 70, xiii-146 p.

4175 DIAZ-PLAJA CONTESTI, G. *Los paraísos perdidos. La actitud "hippy" en la historia* (Lost paradises. "Hippy" attitude through history). Barcelona, Ed. Seix Barral, 70, 209 p.

4176 DISTEFANO, M. K. Jr; PRYER, M. W.; RICE, D. P. "Changes in success-failure attitudes during adolescence", *J. genet. Psychol.* 116(1), mar 70 : 11-14.

4177 DONLEY, R. E.; WINTER, D. G. "Measuring the motives of public officials at a distance: an exploratory study of American presidents", *Behav. Sci.* 15(3), mai 70 : 227-236.

4178 DRUCKMAN, D.; LUDWIG, L. D. "Consensus on evaluative description of one's own nation, its allies, and its enemies", *J. soc. Psychol.* 81(2), aug 70 : 223-234.

4179 DUBEY, S. "Black's preference for black professionals, businessmen, and religious bodies", *Publ. Opin. Quart.* 34(1), 1970 : 113-116. [USA.]

4180 DYNES, R. R. *Organized behavior in disaster.* Lexington, Mass., Heath Lexington Books, 70, vii-235 p.

4181 ECKHARDT, W.; ALCOCK, N. Z. "Ideology and personality in war/peace attitudes", *J. soc. Psychol.* 81(1), jun 70 : 105-116.

4182 ECKHARDT, W.; NEWCOMBE, A. G. "Militarism, personality, and other social attitudes", *J. Conflict Resol.* 13(2), jun 69 : 210-219.

4183 EPPS, E. G. (ed.). "Motivation and academic achievement of Negro Americans", *J. soc. Issues* 25(3), 1969 : 1-144.

4184 FAINI, U. C. G. "A classification of Italian regions according to the electoral behavior", *Quality and Quantity* 2(1-2), jan 68 : 116-123.

4185 FARIA, V. "Situaciones de clase, ideología y acción política" (Class situations, ideology and political action), *Bol. ELAS* 3(5), jun 70 : 47-75. [Latin American student's political behaviour.]

4186 FARQUAHRSON, R. *Theory of voting.* New Haven, Yale University Press; Oxford, Blackwell, 69, 83 p. CR: G. H. KRAMER, *Amer. polit. Sci. R.* 64(3), sep 70 : 914-916.

4187 FERROTTI, F. "La violenza come rifiuto della mediazione culturale" (Violence as the renunciation of cultural mediation), *Crit. sociol. (Roma)* 12, 1969-1970 : 137-148.

4188 FINIFTER, A. W. "Dimensions of political alienation", *Amer. polit. Sci. R.* 64(2), jun 70 : 389-410.

4189   FORTMANN, L. P. "Participation and collective action", *Cornell J. soc. Relat.* 5(1),
        1970 : 10-25.

4190   FRASER, J. "The mistrustful-efficacious hypothesis and political participation", *J.
        Polit.* 32(2), mai 70 : 4444-449.

4191   FUKUJU, Y. "The role of political parties and social groups in voting behavior", *Japan
        Inst. int. Aff. Ann. R.* 4, 1965-1968 : 170-186.

4192   FURSTENBERG, F. Jr; GORDIS, L.; MARKOWITZ, M. "Birth control knowledge and
        attitudes among unmarried pregnant adolescents: a preliminary report", *J. Marriage
        Family* 3(1), feb 69 : 34-42.

4193   GHINI, C. "Il voto delle campagne nelle elezioni politiche" (The rural vote in political
        elections), *Crit. marx. (Roma)* 8(1-2), jan-mar 70 : 343-354. [Italy.]

4194   GIROD, R.; RICQ, C. *Géographie de l'abstentionnisme à Genève. Analyses et documents.*
        Genève, Centre de sociologie, 69, 75 ff.

4195   GLASER, H. *Radikalität und Scheinradikalität. Zur Sozialpsychologie des jugendlichen
        Protests* (Radicalism and apparent radicalism. Social psychology of youth demon-
        stration). München, Manz, 70, 176 p.

4196   GOLD, J. A.; MODRICK, J. A. "Attitude toward the federal government", *J. soc. Psychol.*
        81(2), jun 70 : 25-30. [USA.]

4197   GONZALEZ-CASANOVA, P. "La violence latino-américaine dans les enquêtes empiriques
        nord-américaines", *Homme et Soc.* 15, jan-mar 70 : 159-177.

4198   GRAHAM, H. D.; GURR, T. R. *Violence in America: historical and comparative perspectives.*
        2 vols. Washington, United States Government Printing Office, 69, 644 p. CR: R. H.
        TURNER, *Amer. J. Sociol.* 75(5), mar 70 : 866-868; W. FLANIGAN, E. FOGELMAN,
        Amer. polit. Sci. R. 64(1), mar 70 : 191-192; L. A. COSER, *Amer. sociol. R.* 35(1), feb
        70 : 118-120.

4199   GREENBERG, E. S. "Children and the political community: a comparison across racial
        lines", *Canad. J. polit. Sci.* 2(4), dec 69 : 471-494.

4200   GREENBERG, E. S. (comp.). *Political socialization.* New York, Atherton Press, 70, x-199 p.

4201   GRETTON, J. *Students and workers—an analytical account of dissent in France, May-June
        1968.* London, Macdonald, 69, 320 p.

4202   GROVES, W. E.; ROSSI, P. H. "Police perceptions of a hostile ghetto: realism or pro-
        jection", *Amer. behav. Scientist.* 13(5-6), mai-jun/jul-aug 70 : 727-744. [USA.]

4203   GURIN, P. "Motivation and aspiration of Southern Negro college youth", *Amer. J.
        Sociol.* 75(4, Part II), jan 70 : 607-631.

4204   HAAVIO-MANNILA, E. *Sex roles in politics.* Helsinki, Institute of Sociology, University
        of Helsinki, 70, 46 p.

4205   HAHN, H. "Cops and rioters: ghetto perceptions of social conflict", *Amer. behav.
        Scientist* 13(5-6), mai-jun/jul-aug 70 : 761-780. [USA.]

4206   HAHN, H. "Ethos and social class", *Polity* 2(3), 1970 : 295-314.

4207   HAHN, H. "Leadership perceptions and voting behavior in a one-party legislative
        body", *J. Polit.* 32(1), feb 70 : 140-155.

4208   HARTMANN, H. "Institutional immobility and attitudinal change in West Germany",
        Comp. Polit. 2(4), jul 70 : 579-592.

4209   HERRMANN, R. O. (comp.). *The consumer behavior of children and teenagers: an annotated
        bibliography.* Chicago, American Marketing Association, 69, 160 p.

4210   HILL, D. "The attitudes of West Indian and English adolescents in Britain", *Race*
        11(3), jan 70 : 313-322.

4211   HOFSTADTER, R.; WALLACE, M. (eds.). *American violence; a documentary history.* New
        York, Knopf, 70, xiv-478-xiii p.

4212   IPPOLITO, D. S. "Motivational reorientation and change among party activists", *J.
        Polit.* 31(4), nov 69 : 1098-1101.

4213   JESSOR, R. *et al.* "Perceived opportunity, alienation, and drinking behavior among
        Italian and American youth", *J. Person. soc. Psychol.* 15(3), jul 70 : 215-222.

4214   JORIO, L. DE; ROSSI, S. "L'immagine della donna in un gruppo di studenti universitari"
        (The image of woman in a group of university students), *Sociologia (Roma)* 4(3),
        sep 70 : 137-152.

4215   KAASE, M. "Determinanten des Wahlverhaltens bei der Bundestagswahl 1969" (The
        determinants of electoral behaviorism in the 1969 Bundestag election), *Polit. Vjschr.*
        11(1), mar 70 : 46-110.

4216 KABAT, D.; BOSCO, S. E. "Marital status and ideology of the family size; case of young men in urban Brazil", *Amér. lat.* 12(2), apr-jun 69 : 17-34.

4217 Bibl. XIX-3734. KAES, R. *Images de la culture chez les ouvriers français.* CR: J. VERDÈS-LEROUX, *C. int. Sociol.* 17(48), jan-jun 70 : 186-189.

4218 KIM, C. L. "Political attitudes of defeated candidates in an American State election", *Amer. polit. Sci. R.* 64(3), sep 70 : 879-887.

4219 KIRBY, J. B. "Violence and the conflict of American values", *Rocky Mountain soc. Sci. J.* 4(2), oct 69 : 9-19.

4220 KIRKPATRICK, S. A. "Political attitudes and behavior: some consequences of attitudinal ordering", *Midwest J. polit. Sci.* 14(1), feb 70 : 1-24.

4221 KLOCKHAUS, R. "Ein Beitrag zur Analyse politischer Apathie" (An essay on the analysis of political apathy), *Kölner Z. Soziol. u. soz.-Psychol.* 22(3), sep 70 : 520-531.

4222 KORNBERG, A.; LINDER, D.; COOPER, J. "Understanding political behavior: the relevance of reactance theory", *Midwest J. polit. Sci.* 14(1), feb 70 : 131-138.

4223 KORSON, J. H. "Student attitudes toward mate selection in a Muslim society: Pakistan", *J. Marriage Family* 31(1), feb 69 : 153-165.

4224 KYÔGOKU, J. *Seiji ishiki no bunseki* (Analysis of political behaviour). Tôkyô, Tôkyô Daigaku Shuppan-kai, 68, 309 p.

4225 LAMMI, P.; SÄNKIAHO, R. "Opintosuunta, poliittisen kannan muuttuminen ja poliittiset asenteet" (Academic field, change in party affiliation and political attitudes among students), *Politiikka* 12(3), 1970 : 219-236.

4226 LARSON, C. J.; WASBURN, P. C. (eds.). *Power, participation and ideology: readings in the sociology of American political life.* New York, D. McKay, 69, 484 p. CR: A. BIRENBAUM, *Amer. sociol. R.* 35(4), aug 70 : 771-772.

4227 LeCOMPTE, W.; LeCOMPTE, G. "Effects of education and intercultural contact on traditional attitudes in Turkey", *J. soc. Psychol.* 80(1), feb 70 : 11-21.

4228 LEE, R. S. "Social attitudes and the computer revolution", *Publ. Opin. Quart.* 34(1), 1970 : 53-60.

4229 LEMIEUX, V. "La composition des préférences partisanes", *Canad. J. polit. Sci.* 2(4), dec 69 : 397-418.

4230 LIBBY, R. W. "Parental attitudes toward high school sex education programs", *Family Coordinator* 19(3), jul 70 : 234-247.

4231 LIGHT, H. L. "Attitudes of rural and urban adolescent girls toward selected concepts", *Family Coordinator* 19(3), jul 70 : 225-227.

4232 LIPSET, S. M. "Les préjugés et la politique dans l'Amérique d'hier et d'aujourd'hui", *Sociol. et Soc.* 1(1), mai 69 : 105-134.

4233 LOPREATO, J.; CHAFETZ, J. S. "The political orientation of skidders: a middle-range theory", *Amer. sociol. R.* 35(3), jun 70 : 440-451.

4234 LOUX, F. "Comportement économique d'ouvriers en milieu rural", *R. franç. Sociol.* 10, nᵒ spécial 1969 : 644-663. [France.]

4235 MALIK, Y. K. "Agencies of political socialization and East Indian ethnic identification in Trinidad", *Sociol. B.* 18(2), sep 69 : 101-121.

4236 MARANELL, G. M.; EITZEN, D. S. "The effect of discipline, region and rank on the political attitudes of college professors", *Sociol. Quart.* 11(1), 1970 : 112-118.

4237 MASOTTI, L. H.; BOWEN, D. R. *Riots and rebellion: civil violence in the urban community.* Beverly Hills, Sage Publications, 68, 459 p. CR: J. D. ABERBACH, *Amer. polit. Sci. R.* 64(1), mar 70 : 219-220.

4238 MAXWELL, J. W. "College students' attitudes toward abortion", *Family Coordinator* 19(3), jul 70 : 247-252.

4239 MAZRUI, A. A. *Violence and thought; essays on social tensions in Africa.* Harlow, Longmans; New York, Humanities Press, 69, vii-351 p.

4240 MEMMI, A. et al. "Differences and perception of differences among Jews in France", *Jew. J. Sociol.* 12(1), jun 70 : 7-19.

4241 MULLER, E. N. "Cross-national dimensions of political competence", *Amer. polit. Sci. R.* 64(3), sep 70 : 792-809.

4242 NATCHEZ, P. B. "Images of voting: the social psychologists", *Publ. Pol.* 18(4), 1970 : 553-588.

4243 NEVEL'ŠTEIN, V. S. "O social'no-psihologičeskom issledovanii nekotoryh social'nyh ustremlenij molodeži" (On socio-psychological researches on youth aspirations), *Učen. Zap. Kaf. obšč. Nauk Vuzov g. Leningr. Filos.* (10), 1969 : 87-93.

4244   OLSEN, M. E. "Social and political participation of Blacks", *Amer. sociol. R.* 35(4), aug 70 : 682-696. [USA.]

4245   ORUM, A. M.; McCRANIE, E. W. "Class, tradition and partisan alignments in a Southern urban electorate", *J. Polit.* 32(1), feb 70 : 156-176. [USA.]

4246   PABON, M. "La intolerancia social hacia los grupos políticos minoritarios en Puerto Rico" (Social intolerance towards minority political groups in Puerto Rico), *R. Cienc. soc. (Puerto Rico)* 14(2), apr-jun 70 : 173-202.

4247   PACAUD, S.; LAHALLE, M. O. *Attitudes, comportements, opinions des personnes âgées dans le cadre de la famille moderne.* Paris, CNRS, 69, 147 p. CR: M. PERIANEZ, *R. franç. Sociol.* 11(1), jan-mar 70 : 118-119.

4248   PAGANI, A. "L'immagine della struttura di classe nella popolazione italiana" (The image of class structure in the Italian population), *Quad. Sociol.* 19(2), apr-jun 70 : 155-181.

4249   PALMA, G. DI. *Apathy and participation; mass politics in Western societies.* New York, Free Press, 70, xix-263 p.

4250   PARRY, M. H. *Aggression on the road. A pilot study of behaviour in the driving situation.* London-New York-Sidney-Toronto-Wellington, Tavistock Publications, 68, 138 p. CR: G. KAISER, *Kölner Z. Soziol. u. soz.-Psychol.* 21(4), dec 69 : 918-920.

4251   PITKÄNEN, L. *A descriptive model of aggression and nonaggression with applications to children's behaviour.* Jyväskylä, Jyväskylän Yliopisto, 69, 208 p.

4252   "Political socialization", *Comp. polit. Stud.* 3(2), jul 70 : 140-263.

4253   "Politik und Psychologie" (Politics and psychology), *Polit. Stud. (München)* 21(191), mai-jun 70 : 257-333.

4254   QUITTER, J. H. "Image formation processes and foreign policy outcomes: American perceptions of the Italian Communist Party, 1946-1948", *Columb. Essays int. Aff.* 4, 1968 : 232-262.

4255   RANSFORD, H. E. "Isolation, powerlessness, and violence: a study of attitudes and participation in the Watts riot", *Amer. J. Sociol.* 72(5), mar 68 : 581-591.

4256   RODMAN, H.; NICHOLS, F. R.; VOYDANOFF, P. "Lower-class attitudes toward 'deviant' family patterns: a cross-cultural study", *J. Marriage Family* 31(2), mai 69 : 315-321.

4257   ROGERS, M. L. "Politization and political development in a rural Malay community", *Asian Surv.* 9(12), dec 69 : 919-933.

4258   ROSEN, B. C.; CROCKETT, H. J. Jr; NUNN, C. Z. (eds.). *Achievement in American society.* Cambridge, Mass., Schenkman, 69, 653 p. CR: H. D. SEIBEL, *Amer. J. Sociol.* 75(4, Part II), jan 70 : 717-718; H. D. SEIBEL, *Kölner Z. Soziol. u. soz.-Psychol.* 22(4), dec 70 : 822-824.

4259   ROSENTHAL, H.; SEN, S. "Candidate selection and voting behavior in France", *Publ. Choice* (6), 1969 : 71-92.

4260   ROSENTHAL, H.; SEN, S. "Participation électorale et conjoncture politique (application de la technique des régressions multiples aux élections de 1962)", *R. franç. Sci. polit.* 20(3), jun 70 : 545-556.

4261   SCHNEIDER, F. W.; SHAW, M. E. "Sanctioning behavior in Negro and in White populations", *J. soc. Psychol.* 81(1), jun 70 : 63-71.

4262   SCHROEDER, T. "Tolerance, a way of life", *J. hum. Relat.* 18(1), 1970 : 752-763.

4263   SEGAL, D. R.; KNOKE, D. "Political partisanship: its social and economic bases in the United States", *Amer. J. Econ. Sociol.* 29(3), jul 70 : 253-262.

4264   SEGAL, D. R.; WILDSTROM, S. H. "Community effects on political attitudes: partisanship and efficacy", *Sociol. Quart.* 11(1), 1970 : 67-85.

4265   SHORT, J. F. Jr; WOLFGANG, M. E. (eds.). "Collective violence", *A. Amer. Acad. polit. soc. Sci.* 391, sep 70 : viii-264 p.

4266   SICINSKI, A. "Stereotypes of countries and nations: survey results", *Polish sociol. B.* (1), 1968 : 79-85.

4267   SMITHERS, A. "Personality patterns and levels of dogmatism", *Brit. J. soc. clin. Psychol.* 9(2), jun 70 : 183-184.

4268   SMUCKER, J. "The impact of community prestige upon personal appraisals of life conditions: a comparative analysis", *Canad. R. Sociol. Anthropol.* 6(3), aug 69 : 145-161.

4269 SNYDER, E. F.; PERRY, J. B. "Farm employer attitudes toward Mexican-American migrant workers", *Rur. Sociol.* 35(2), jun 70 : 244-253.

4270 SPOCK, B. McL. *Decent and indecent; our personal and political behavior.* New York, McCall Publishing Co., 70, xiii-210 p.

4271 STEFFY, R. A.; MEICHENBAUM, D.; BEST, J. A. "Aversive and cognitive factors in the modification of smoking behaviour", *Behav. Res. Therapy* 8(2), mai 70 : 115-125.

4272 STEINER, J. "Participação política e estatuto social" (Political participation and social status), *R. Ciênc. polít.* 4(1), jan-mar 70 : 21-26.

4273 STEPHENS, W. N.; LONG, C. S. "Education and political behaviour", *Polit. Sci. ann.* 2, 1969-1970 : 3-33.

4274 STOLKA, S. M.; BARNETT, L. D. "Education and religion as factors in women's attitudes motivating childbearing", *J. Marriage Family* 31(4), nov 69 : 740-750.

4275 STRÜMPEL, B.; NOVY, K.; SCHWARTZ, S. "Consumer attitudes and outlays in Germany and North America", *Jb. soz.-Wiss.* 21(1), 1970 : 25-48.

4276 STRÜMPER, D. J. W. "Fear and affiliation during a disaster", *J. soc. Psychol.* 82(2), dec 70 : 263-268.

4277 SWEENEY, D. R.; TINLING, D. C.; SCHMALE, A. H. Jr. "Dimensions of affective expression in four expressive modes", *Behav. Sci.* 15(5), sep 70 : 393-407.

4278 TAJFEL, H. "Aspects of national and ethnic loyalty", *Soc. Sci. Inform./Inform. Sci. soc.* 9(3), jun 70 : 119-144.

4279 TANAKA, J. "Japanese attitudes toward nuclear arms", *Publ. Opin. Quart.* 34(1), 1970 : 26-43.

4280 TEDESCHI, J. T. *et al.* "Mythological ethnocentrism as a determinant of international attitudes", *J. soc. Psychol.* 80(1), feb 70 : 113-114.

4281 TOUKOMAA, P. "Isänmaallisuus ja poliittinen sosiaalistuminen" (Patriotism and political socialization), *Politiikka* 12(3), 1970 : 197-204.

4282 TOWNSEND, J. R. *Political participation in Communist China.* Berkeley, University of California Press, 69, xvi-233 p.

4283 TURNER, H. A.; SPAULDING, C. B. "Political attitudes and behaviour of selected academically-affiliated professional groups", *Polity* 1(3), 1969 : 309-336.

4284 TURNER, R. H. "The public perception of protest", *Amer. sociol. R.* 34(6), dec 69 : 815-831.

4285 VALKONEN, T. "Community context and politicization of individuals", *Acta sociol.* 12(3), 1969 : 144-155.

4286 VAN Es, J. C.; WHITTENBARGER, R. L. "Farm ownership, political participation, and other social participation in Central Brazil", *Rur. Sociol.* 35(1), mar 70 : 15-25.

4287 VERBA, S.; BRODY, R. "Participation, policy preferences, and the War in Vietnam", *Publ. Opin. Quart.* 34(3), 1970 : 325-332.

4288 WARNER, L. G.; DENNIS, R. M. "Prejudice versus discrimination: an empirical example and theoretical extension", *Soc. Forces* 48(4), jun 70 : 473-484.

4289 WESTLEY, W. A. *Violence and the police: a sociological study of law, custom, and morality.* Cambridge, Mass., MIT Press, 70, xxi-222 p.

4290 WILLIAMSON, R. C. "Modernism and related attitudes: an international comparison among university students", *Int. J. comp. Sociol.* 11(2), jun 70 : 130-145.

4291 WILSON, R. W. *Learning to be Chinese: the political socialization of children in Taiwan.* Cambridge, MIT Press, 70, xiii-203 p.

4292 WINHAM, G.; CUNNINGHAM, R. "Party leader images in the 1968 federal election", *Canad. J. polit. Sci.* 3(1), mar 70 : 37-55.

4293 WOLFE, A. C. "Trends in labor union voting behavior, 1948-1968", *Industr. Relat.* 9(1), oct 69 : 1-10. [USA.]

4294 ZEITLIN, M.; PETRAS, J. "The working-class vote in Chile: Christian Democracy versus Marxism", *Brit. J. Sociol.* 21(1), mar 70 : 6-29.

D.23   Ideologies
Idéologies

[See also / Voir aussi: **C.922**; 50, 250, 1072, 1344, 1404, 1823, 2303, 2339, 2397, 2436, 2522, 3076, 3595, 3616, 3727, 3776, 3784, 4051, 4072, 4181, 4185, 4226, 4360, 4483, 4491, 4550, 4581, 4899, 4988]

4295   ADER, E. B. *Communism; classic and contemporary.* Woodbury, N. Y., Barron's Educational Series, 70, vi-307 p.

4296   ADLER, L. K.; PATERSON, T. G. "Red fascism: the merger of Nazi Germany and Soviet Russia in the American image of totalitarianism, 1930's-1950's", *Amer. hist. R.* 75(4), apr 70 : 1046-1064.

4297   ALTHUSSER, L. "Idéologie et appareils idéologiques d'État. Notes pour une recherche", *Pensée* 151, mai-jun 70 : 3-38.

4298   "Anarchism today", *Gvt and Opposition* 5(4), 1970 : 397-554.

4299   ANSART, P. *Naissance de l'anarchisme; esquisse d'une explication sociologique du proudhonisme.* Paris, Presses universitaires de France, 70, 264 p.

4300   ARON, R. *Marxismes imaginaires; d'une sainte famille à l'autre.* Paris, Gallimard, 70, 377 p. [Voir aussi Bibl. XIX-3820.]

4301   BATAILLER-DEMICHEL, F. "L'individualisme politique et sa forme moderne: l'existentialisme", *A. Fac. Dr. Sci. écon. (Lyon)* 1, 1968 : 91-120.

4302   BENTON, W. A. *Whig-Loyalism. An aspect of political ideology in the American revolutionary era.* Rutherford, N. J., Fairleigh Dickinson University Press, 69, 231 p.

4303   BERTIER DE SAUVIGNY, G. DE. "Liberalism, nationalism, socialism: the birth of three words", *R. Polit.* 32(2), apr 70 : 147-166.

4304   BOTTOMORE, T. B. *Critics of society; radical thought in North America.* New York, Vintage Books, 69, 164 p. [Revised and enlarged edition of the author's *Social criticism in North America*, first published in 1966.]

4305   BROWN, S. R. "Consistency and the persistence of ideology: some experimental results", *Publ. Opin. Quart.* 34(1), 1970 : 60-69.

4306   COX, R. H. (comp.). *Ideology, politics, and political theory.* Belmont, Calif., Wadsworth Publishing Co., 69, 373 p.

4307   DELEU, P. "Idéologie, politique et polémologie", *R. Inst. Sociol.* 4, 1969 : 671-688.

4308   DIGGINS, J. P. "Ideology and pragmatism: philosophy or passion", *Amer. polit. Sci. R.* 64(3), sep 70 : 899-906.

4309   DOMIN, G.; MOCEK, R. (eds.). *Ideologie und Naturwissenschaft; Politik und Verkunft im Zeitalter des Sozialismus und der wissenschaftlich-technischen Revolution* (Ideology and natural sciences; policy and reason in the era of socialism and of scientific and technical revolution). Berlin, Deutscher Verlag der Wissenschaften, 69, 368 p.

4310   ELLIS, A. "Intellectual fascism", *J. hum. Relat.* 18(1), 1970 : 700-709.

4311   GARAUDY, R. *Le grand tournant du socialisme.* Paris, Gallimard, 69, 315 p.

4312   GOMEZ DE SOUZA, L. A. "The future of ideologies and the ideologies of the future", *Anticipation* (2), jun 70 : 10-26.

4313   GRANOV, V. "Le social-réformisme: l'idéologie d'un monde de classes", *Sci. soc. aujourd.* (7), 1969 : 47-64.

4314   Bibl. XIX-3849. GREGOR, A. J. *The ideology of fascism: the rationale of totalitarianism.* CR: D. GERMINO, *Amer. polit. Sci. R.* 64(2), jun 70 : 615-617.

4315   HASHIKAWA, B. *Nashonarizumu* (Nationalism). Tôkyô, Kinokuniya-shoten, 68, 190 p.

4316   HEISKANEN, V. S. "Ideologies, tension reduction and social structure. An application of Freudian principles to the analysis of reform movements", *Acta sociol.* 12(1), 1969 : 29-38.

4317   HELENIUS, R. *Demokraattisten kantaismien kuva. Demokraattisen sosialismin, liberalismin ja konservatismin luonteen sekä yhteisten ja erityisten uskomusten vertailu* (Picture of the primary democratic "isms": a comparison of the nature and common and special beliefs of democratic socialism, liberalism and conservatism). Helsinki, 70, 100 p. mimeo.

4318   HOWE, J. R. Jr. (ed.). *The role of ideology in the American Revolution.* New York, Holt, Rinehart and Winston, 70, 125 p.

4319   "Idéologies, sciences et pratiques sociales", *Écon. et Human.* 194, jul-aug 70 : 2-63.

4320   IONESCU, G.; GELLNER, E. *Populism, its meanings and national characteristics.* London,

Weidenfeld and Nicolson; New York, Macmillan, 69, 263 p. CR: G. C. ALROY, *Amer. polit. Sci. R.* 64(3), sep 70 : 968-969; J. L. WALSH, *Amer. sociol. R.* 35(4), aug 70 : 768-769.

4321 JUTGLAR, A. *Ideologías y clases en la España contemporánea. Aproximación a la historia social de las ideas* (Ideologies and classes in contemporary Spain. An approach to the history of social ideas). Madrid, Edicusa, 69, 329 p.

4322 KHADDURI, M. *Political trends in the Arab world; the role of ideas and ideals in politics.* Baltimore, Johns Hopkins Press, 70, xi-298 p.

4323 KIERNAN, V. G. "On the development of a Marxist approach to nationalism", *Sci. and Soc.* 34(1), 1970 : 92-98.

4324 LEBOVICS, H. *Social conservatism and the middle classes in Germany, 1914-1933.* Princeton, N. J., Princeton University Press, 69, xvi-248 p.

4325 LECA, J. "Ideologie et politique en Algérie", *Études (Paris)* mai 70 : 672-693.

4326 LOOMIS, C. P.; RYTINA, J. *Marxist theory and Indian Communism; a sociological interpretation.* East Lansing, Michigan State University Press, 70, vi-148 p.

4327 LYND, S. *Intellectual origins of American radicalism.* London, Faber, 69, viii-184 p.

4328 MAL'CEV, G. V. "Ideologija, politika i pravo" (Ideology, politics and law), *Sov. Gos. Pravo* 43(2), 1970 : 14-22.

4329 MANŠŮR, M. I. *al-Nužûm al-'ijtimâ'îyat wal-ishtirâkîyat* (Social systems and socialism). Iskenderîyat, Matba'at al-Mişrî, 69, 245 p.

4330 MILZA, P. *Fascismes et idéologies réactionnaires en Europe, 1919-1945.* Paris, A. Colin, 69, 96 p.

4331 MODELMOG, I. *Die andere Zukunft. Zur Publizistik und Soziologie der utopischen Kommunikation* (The other future. Literature and sociology of utopian communication). Düsseldorf, Bertelsmann Universitätsverlag, 70, 206 p.

4332 MOLINA PINEIRO, L. "Dos constantes en la ideología, la ciencia y la práctica política" (Two constants in ideology, science and political practice), *Anu. Sociol. Pueblos ibér.* (5), 1969 : 31-51.

4333 MUHLL, G. E. VON DER. "Marxism, ideologies and the intellectuals", *Ind. polit. Sci. R.* 2(3-4), apr-sep 68 : 121-131.

4334 NAUTA, R. "Military and pragmatism. Ideology as a phenomenon of style", *Mens en Mij* 45(6), nov-dec 70 : 416-424.

4335 PEČJAK, V. "Kognitivna struktura pojmov komunizem, socializem in kapitalizem" (Cognitive structure of concepts of communism, socialism and capitalism), *Teorija in Praksa* 7(6-7), jul 70 : 1022-1034.

4336 PIEPE, A.; PRIOR, R.; BOX, A. "The location of the proletarian and deferential worker", *Sociology* 3(2), mai 69 : 239-244. [The relationship between occupational and community structure and ideology.]

4337 RASMUSSEN, E. *Ideologi og politik* (Ideology and politics). København, Gyldendal, 69, 64 p.

4338 ROWLAND, W. S. "Das Wesen des Konservatismus und die Erscheinungsformen konservativen Denkens" (The essence of conservatism and the forms of conservative thought), *Staat* 8(3), 1969 : 349-361.

4339 RYTINA, J. H.; LOOMIS, C. P. "Marxist dialectic and pragmatism: power as knowledge", *Amer. sociol. R.* 35(2), apr 70 : 308-318.

4340 SAPOŽNIKOV, N. M. *Struktura političeskogo soznanija* (The structure of political consciousness). Minsk, Nauka i tehnika, 69, 163 p.

4341 SAUVY, A. *Le socialisme en liberté.* Paris, Denoël, 70, 408 p.

4342 SCHMIDT, H. D. "Nationalismus: einige psychologische Aspekte" (Nationalism: some psychological aspects), *Polit. Stud. (München)* 21(191), mai-jun 70 : 304-312.

4343 SIBLEY, M. Q. *Political ideas and ideologies; a history of political thought.* New York, Harper and Row, 70, xi-611 p.

4344 STROPPA, C. "L'ideologia sionista e i suoi rapporti con le cooperative israeliane" (Zionist ideology and its relation with Israeli cooperatives), *Rass. ital. Sociol.* 10(4), oct-dec 69 : 634-648.

4345 TERROW, E. *Sociedad e ideología en los orígenes de la España contemporánea* (Society and ideology in the origins of contemporary Spain). Barcelona, Ed. Peninsula, 69, 278 p.

4346 VIDAL, D. "Notes sur l'idéologie", *Homme et Soc.* 17, jul-sep 70 : 35-54.

4347 Bibl. XIX-3899. WAXMAN, C. I. (ed.). *The end of ideology debate.* CR: M. A. PAPE, *Amer. sociol. R.* 35(2), apr 70 : 359-360.

D.24   Sociology of knowledge
Sociologie de la connaissance

[See also / Voir aussi: **E.1, E.2**; 45, 50, 56, 146, 2195, 2875, 4410]

4348   AFANAS'EV, V. G. *Osnovy filosofskih zananij* (Foundations of philosophical knowledge). Moskva, Mysl', 69, 350 p.

4349   ARCHIBALD, K. A. "Alternative orientations to social science utilization", *Soc. Sci. Inform./Inform. Sci. soc.* 9(2), apr 70 : 7-34.

4350   BOLTANSKI, L. "Taxinomies populaires, taxinomies savantes: les objets de consommation et leur classement", *R. franç. Sociol.* 11(1), jan-mar 70 : 34-44.

4351   BOLTANSKI, L.; MALDIDIER, P. "Carrière scientifique, morale scientifique et vulgarisation", *Soc. Sci. Inform./Inform. Sci. soc.* 9(3), jun 70 : 99-118.

4352   COTGROVE, S. "The sociology of science and technology", *Brit. J. Sociol.* 21(1), mar 70 : 1-15.

4353   Bibl. XIX-3906. CRAWFORD, E. H.; BIDERMAN, A. D. (eds.). *Social scientists and international affairs: a case for a sociology of social science.* CR: N. C. MULLINS, *Amer. sociol. R.* 35(1), feb 70 : 136-137; L. SKLAIR, *Brit. J. Sociol.* 21(1), mar 70 : 112-114.

4354   CURTIS, J. E.; PETRAS, J. W. "The development of the sociology of sociology: some components in the US and Canadian cases", *Archiv Rechts- u. soz.-Philos.* 56(3), 1970 : 305-323.

4355   CURTIS, J. E.; PETRAS, J. W. (eds.). *The sociology of knowledge: a reader.* London, Duckworth; New York, Praeger, 70, vii-724 p.

4356   GOLIAT, I. "Probleme actuale de sociologia ştiintei" (Current problems of sociology of science), *Progr. Ştiin.* 5(8), aug 69 : 337-342.

4358   HILDAHL, S. H. "A note on '. . . A note on the sociology of knowledge' ", *Sociol. Quart.* 11(3), 1970 : 405-415.

4359   HOLL, A. "Max Scheler's sociology of knowledge and his position in relation to theology", *Soc. Compass* 17(2), 1970 : 231-242.

4360   JURDANT, B. "Vulgarisation scientifique et idéologique", *Communications* 14, 1969 : 150-161.

4361   KRUGER, M. "Sociology of knowledge and social theory", *Berkeley J. Sociol.* 14, 1969 : 152-163.

4362   "Making of modern science: biographical studies (The)", *Daedalus* 99(4), 1970 : 723-1120.

4363   ROSENTHAL, F. *Knowledge triumphant; the concept of knowledge in medieval Islam.* Leiden, Brill, 70, viii-358 p.

4364   RUSCONI, G. E. "Une riproposta della sociologia della conoscenza" (A reproposal of the sociology of knowledge), *Rass. ital. Sociol.* 10(4), oct-dec 69 : 625-633.

4365   SCHOLZ, H. (ed.). *Die Rolle der Wissenschaft in der modernen Gesellschaft* (The role of science in modern society). Berlin, Duncker und Humblot, 69, 406 p.

4366   Bibl. XIX-3913. SILVERT, K. H. (ed.). *The social reality of scientific myth: science and social change.* CR: B. HOLZNER, *Amer. sociol. R.* 35(3), jun 70 : 541-542.

4367   "Sociologie de la science", *R. int. Sci. soc.* 22(1), 1970 : 5-139.

4368   TONDL, L. "Die Wissenschaft als Planungsfaktor. Veränderungen der Nachdrucksmomente in der zeitgenössischen Wissenschaft" (Science as a planning factor. Change of reproduction periods in contemporary science), *Mens en Mij* 45(3), mai-jun 70 : 161-172.

4369   WANDERER, J. J. "An empirical study in the sociology of knowledge", *Sociol. Inquiry* 39(1), 1969 : 19-26.

4370   WEINGART, P. "Selbststeuerung der Wissenschaft und staatliche Wissenschaftspolitik" (Self-control of science and State science policy), *Kölner Z. Soziol. u. soz.-Psychol.* 22(3), sep 70 : 567-592.

4371   ZVORYKIN, A. A. "Sociologija nauki. Predmet, metod zakonomernosti novogo napravlenija" (Sociology of science. Object, and method of new tendencies laws), *Nauč. Org. Truda (Resp. Inst. nauč.-tehn. Inform. i Propagandy gos plan. Komissii Soveta Ministrov Lit. SSR)* (9), 1969 : 15-32.

D.3 COMMUNICATION
COMMUNICATIONS SOCIALES

D.30 General and methodological studies
Études générales et méthodologiques

[See also / Voir aussi: **B.33**; **B.34**; 248, 408, 497, 3795, 4705]

4372 "Analyse des images (L')", *Communications* 15, 1970 : 1-232. [Présentation par C. METZ: 1-10.]

4373 ARGYLE, M. *et al.* "The communication of inferior and superior attitudes by verbal and non-verbal signals", *Brit. J. soc. clin. Psychol.* 9(3), sep 70 : 222-231.

4374 BECKER, K.; SIEGEL, K.-A. (eds.). *Dynamik der Kommunikation* (Dynamics of communication). Frankfurt-am-Main, Verlag, J. Knecht, 68, 70 p. CR: A. SILBERMANN, *Kölner. Z. Soziol. u. soz.-Psychol.* 22(1), mar 70 : 213-216.

4375 BERCELLI, F. "Teoria dei segni e analisi del contenuto" (Theory of signs and content analysis), *Rass. ital. Sociol.* 11(3), jul-sep 70 : 371-400.

4376 BERLO, D. K. *et al.* "Dimensions for evaluating the acceptability of message sources", *Publ. Opin. Quart.* 33(4), 1970 : 563-576.

4377 BRAGA, G. "Il 'sistema delle comunicazioni' come costrutto mediatore fra società e linguaggio" (The "system of communication" as an intermediary structure between society and language), *Sociologia (Roma)* 4(2), mai 70 : 17-50.

4378 BRAGA, G. *La comunicazione sociale* (Social communication). Torino, ERI, 69, 212 p.

4379 BRÅTEN, S. "On the need and possible structure of a communication research information system in Scandinavia", *Acta sociol.* 13(3), 1970 : 149-160.

4380 BURLACKIJ, F. M. *Metody izučenija auditorii anglijskogo radio i televidenija* (Method of audience studies in English radio and television). Moskva, 69, 175 p.

4381 CAMARGO, N. DE. "Comunicação: uma nova perspectiva no campo das ciências do comportamento" (Communication: a new perspective in the behavioral sciences field), *R. Escola Comunic. cult.* 1(1), 1968 : 131-158.

4382 "Communication et culture de masse", *Diogène* 68, oct-dec 69 : 3-167.

4383 "Communicazione e comunità" (Communication and community), *Siprauno* 4, jul-aug 69 : 7-95.

4384 DAVIS, J. M.; FARINA, A. "Humor appreciation as social communication", *J. Person. soc. Psychol.* 15(2), jun 70 : 175-149.

4385 DENZIN, N. K. "Symbolic interactionism and ethno-methodology: a proposed synthesis", *Amer. sociol. R.* 34(6), dec 69 : 922-934.

4386 DORRA, H.; MILLET, G. *Les communications: l'entretien individuel.* Paris, Dunod, 70, viii-118 p.

4387 DRÖGE, F.; WEISSENBORN, R.; HAFT, H. *Wirkungen der Massenkommunikation* (Effects of mass communication). Münster, Regensberg, 69, 219 p. CR: A. SILBERMANN, *Kölner Z. Soziol. u. soz.-Psychol.* 22(3), sep 70 : 625-629.

4388 Bibl. XVIII-4525. DUNCAN, H. D. *Symbols and social theory.* CR: D. MARTINDALE, *Amer. J. Sociol.* 76(2), sep 70 : 359-361; R. A. HARDERT, *Amer. sociol. R.* 35(4), aug 70 : 764-765.

4389 Bibl. XIX-3927. DUNCAN, H. D. *Symbols in society.* CR: A. D. GRIMSHAW, *Amer. sociol. R.* 34(6), dec 69 : 959-960.

4390 Bibl. XIX-3930. FELDMAN, E. *Neue Studien zur Theorie der Massenmedien* (New studies in the theory of mass media). CR: A. SILBERMANN, *Kölner Z. Soziol. u. soz.-Psychol.* 22(3), sep 70 : 634-635.

4391 FUJITAKE, A. "Masur komyunikeishon katei ni okeru odiensu no ichi" (The place of the audience in mass communication), *Hôsôgaku Kenkyû* 18, 1968 : 83-125.

4392 GRITTI, J. *L'évènement, techniques d'analyse de l'évènement.* Paris, Éditions Fleurus, 69, 172 p.

4393 HARE, A. P. "Cultural differences in performance in communication networks in Africa, the United States, and the Philippines", *Sociol. soc. Res.* 54(1), oct 69 : 25-41.

4394 HASELOFF, O. W. (ed.). *Kommunikation* (Communication). Berlin, Colloquium Verlag, 69, 187 p. CR: A. SILBERMANN, *Kölner Z. Soziol. u. soz.-Psychol.* 22(3), sep 70 : 625-629.

4395 HOLSTI, O. R. "Content analysis", in: G. LINDZEY; E. ARONSON (eds.). *The handbook of social psychology.* Vol. II. 2nd ed. Reading, Mass., Addison-Wesley, 1968 : 596-692.

4396 HOLSTI, O. R. *Content analysis for the social sciences and humanities.* Reading, Mass., Addison-Wesley Publishing Co., 69, 235 p. CR: P. TORSVIK, *Acta sociol.* 13(2), apr 70 : 136-137; E. B. PARKER, *Amer. sociol. R.* 35(2), apr 70 : 356-357.

4397 JOHNSON, N. "Crisis in communications", *ETC Rev. gen. Semantics* 26(3), sep 69 : 358-367.

4398 JONES, R. A.; BREHM, J. W. "Persuasiveness of one- and two-sided communication as a function of awareness there are two sides", *J. exper. soc. Psychol.* 6(1), jan 70 : 47-56.

4399 LESCHNITZKÝ, V. "Systém vedeckej infirmácie vo vedecko technickej revolúcii" (The system of scientific information in the scientific and technical revolution), *Sociol. Čas.* 5(5), sep-oct 69 : 532-543. [Czechoslovakia.]

4400 LILLO, A. DE. "L'analisi dei messaggi nella prospettiva strutturalista" (The analysis of messages in the structuralist perspective), *Rass. ital. Sociol.* 11(3), jul-sep 70 : 401-438.

4401 LOHISSE, J. *La communication anonyme.* Louvain-Paris, Éditions universitaires, 69, 205 p.

4402 LUCAS, Y. "L'aire sémantique de l'automatisation", *C. int. Sociol.* 17(48), jan-jun 70 : 153-164.

4403 Bibl. XIX-3943. LUTHE, H. O. *Interpersonale Kommunikation und Beeinflussung. Beitrag zur einer soziologischen Theorie der Kommunikation* (Interpersonal communication and influence; contribution to a sociological theory of communication). CR: G. WIENDIECK, *Kölner Z. Soziol. u. soz.-Psychol.* 22(2), jun 70 : 435-436.

4404 LUTHE, H. O. "Omnipotencia o impotencia de los medios de comunicación de masas" (Omnipotence or impotence of mass communications media), *R. esp. Opin. públ. 20,* apr-mai 70 : 21-30.

4405 MELO, J. M. DE. *Comunicação social; teoria e pesquisa* (Social communication: theory and research). Petrópolis, Editôra Vozes, 70, 318 p.

4406 MEYERSOHN, R. "Les moyens d'information modernes et la sociologie: un dilemme", *Diogène* 68, oct-dec 69 : 147-165.

4407 MOLES, A. A. "El símbolo y la imagen en la civilización contemporánea" (The symbol and the image in contemporary civilization), *R. esp. Opin. públ.* 19, jan-mar 70 : 21-37.

4408 MOONMAN, E. *Communication in an expanding organization: a case study in action research.* London-New York, Tavistock Publications, 70, vii-182 p.

4409 PAGE, M. M. "Role of demand awareness in the communicator credibility effect", *J. soc. Psychol.* 82(1), oct 70 : 57-66.

4410 POWELL, L. S. *Communication and learning.* New York, American Elsevier Publishing Co., 69, xii-217 p.

4411 PRINZ, G. "Heterostereotype durch Massenkommunikation" (Heterostereotypes through mass communications), *Publizistik* 15(3), jul-sep 70 : 195-210.

4412 Bibl. XIX-3950. REIMANN, H. *Kommunikationssysteme. Umrisse einer Soziologie der Vermittlungs- und Mitteilungsprozesse* (Communication systems; lines of a sociology of transmission and communication). CR: A. SILBERMANN, *Kölner Z. Soziol. u. soz.-Psychol.* 22(1), mar 70 : 213-216.

4413 ROSEN, S.; TESSER, A. "On reluctance to communicate undesirable information: the MUM effect", *Sociometry* 33(3), sep 70 : 253-263.

4414 SAMOVAR, L. A.; BROOKS, R. D.; PORTER, R. E. "A survey of adult communication activities", *J. Communication* 19(4), dec 69 : 301-307.

4415 SOUCHON, M. "Diffusion de l'information et rapports d'autorité", *Études (Paris)*, mar 70 : 386-401.

4416 SUZUKI, H. "Settokuteki comyumikeishon no kôka kenkyû ni okeru ukete no haaku ni tsuite" (The effect of 'persuasive communication'), *Tôkyô Daigaku Shimbunkenkyûsho Kiyô* (17), 1968 : 139-186.

4417 VAN DEN ENDE, H. W. "Verslag van een inhoudsanalyse" (Report on a content analysis), *Mens en Mij* 44(6), nov-dec 69 : 510-519.

4418 VARDAMAN, G. T. *Effective communication of ideas.* New York, Van Nostrand Reinhold Co., 70, ix-255 p.

4419 WERSIG, G. *Inhaltsanalyse. Einführung in ihre Systematik und Literatur* (Content analysis. An introduction to its systematics and literature). Berlin, Verlag Volker Spiess, 68, 160 p. CR: O. HESSE-QUACK, *Kölner Z. Soziol. u. soz.-Psychol.* 22(2), jun 70 : 405-406.

4420 WORCHEL, S.; BREHM, J. W. "Effect of threats to attitudinal freedom as a function of agreement with the communicator", *J. Person. soc. Psychol.* 14(1), jan 70 : 13-22.

4421 WYER, R. S. Jr. "Information redundancy, inconsistency, and novelty and their role in impression formation", *J. exper. soc. Psychol.* 6(1), jan 70 : 111-127.

4422 YEOMANS, N. *et al.* "Measurement of conflicting communications in social networks", *Brit. J. soc. clin. Psychol.* 9(3), sep 70 : 275-281.

4423 ZANACCHI, A. *Potenza e prepotenza della comunicazione sociale* (Power and strength of social communication). Roma, Edizioni paoline, 69, 439 p.

4424 ZIEGLER, R. *Kommunikationsstruktur und Leistung sozialer Systeme* (Communication structure and realization of social systems). Meisenheim-am-Glan, Verlag Anton Hain, 68, x-255 p. CR: G. BÜSCHGES, *Kölner Z. Soziol. u. soz.-Psychol.* 21(4), dec 69 : 944-946.

D.31 Language
Langage

[See also / Voir aussi: 2059, 2656, 2671, 2675, 2686, 2701, 2706, 2741, 2889, 3374, 4103, 4372, 4377, 4542, 5126]

4425 BARDIS, P. D. "Aspetti sociali dell'onomastica personale fra gli antichi ebrei" (Social aspects of personal ononastics between ancient Hebrews), *Rass. ital. Sociol.* 11(1), jan-mar 70 : 81-98.

4426 BENJAMIN, R. L. *Semantics and language analysis.* Indianapolis, Bobbs-Merrill, 69, xvii-110 p.

4427 BENVENISTE, É.; LALLOT, J. *Le vocabulaire des institutions indo-européennes...* 2 vols. Paris, Éditions de Minuit, 69, 379 p.; 343 p.

4428 BERGSMA, H. M. "Tiv proverbs as a means of social control", *Africa (London)* 40(2), apr 70 : 151-163.

4429 BLUMENTAHL, A. L. *Language and psychology; historical aspects of psycholinguistics.* New York, Wiley, 70, x-248 p.

4430 BOLAFFI BENUZZI, S. "Studio sulla ricchezza di vocabulario e sulla complessità della frase nel linguaggio scritto di allievi bilingui nella classi secondarie della Scuola Europea di Varese" (Study on richness of vocabulary and on sentence complexity in the written language of bilingual students in secondary schools of the European School of Varese), *Riv. Psicol. soc.* 16(4), oct-dec 69 : 313-350.

4431 BOTHA, E. "The effect of language on values expressed by bilinguals", *J. soc. Psychol.* 80(2), apr 70 : 143-145.

4432 BRAGA, G. "Le percezioni del bilinguismo entro élites politiche e giovanili a Bolzano" (Perceptions of bilingualism by political elites and youth in Bolzano), *Quad. Sci. soc.* 8(3), 1969 : 259-277. [Italy.]

4433 BURLING, R. "Linguistics and ethnographic description", *Amer. Anthropol.* 71(5), oct 69 : 817-827.

4434 BURLING, R. *Man's many voices; language in its cultural context.* New York, Holt, Rinehart and Winston, 70, xi-222 p.

4435 BUTRON, M. J. "La mestización del lenguaje" (The mestization of language), *Temas soc.* 5, mar 70 : 47-54. [Bolivia.]

4436 CARDONA, G. R. "Sviluppo e linguaggio: problemi e prospettive" (Development and language: problems and prospects), *Futuribili* 4(20-21), mar-apr 70 : 85-92.

4437 COHEN, D. (comp.). *Mélanges Marcel Cohen; études de linguistique, ethnographie et sciences connexes offertes par ses amis et ses élèves à l'occasion de son 80 ème anniversaire.* The Hague, Mouton, 70, xxxix-461 p.

4438 COLLOQUE DE LEXICOLOGIE SUR LA FORMATION ET LES ASPECTS DU VOCABULAIRE POLITIQUE FRANCAIS DU XVIᵉ AU XXᵉ SIÈCLE. *Formation et aspects du vocabulaire politique français, XVIIᵉ-XXᵉ siècles...* Paris, Didier-Larousse, 69, [Saint-Cloud, 26-28 avril 1968.]

4439 COTTERET, J.-M.; MOREAU, R. *Le vocabulaire du Général de Gaulle.* Paris, A. Colin, 69, 252 p. (Travaux et recherches de science politique, nº 3).

4440 DASGUPTA, J. *Language conflict and national development; group politics and national language policy in India.* Berkeley, University of California Press, 70, viii-293 p.

4441 DENISON, N. "Sociolinguistic aspects of plurilingualism", *Soc. Sci. (Winfield)* 45(2), apr 70 : 98-101.

4442   DEUTSCHER, I. (ed.). "Language and conduct", *Sociol. Focus* 3(2), 1969-1970 : 1-85.

4443   DeVITO, J. A. *The psychology of speech and language; an introduction to psycholinguistics.* New York, Random House, 70, xi-308 p.

4444   DIECKMANN, W. *Sprache in der Politik; Einführung in die Pragmatik und Semantik der politischen Sprache* (The language of politics; introduction to the pragmatics and the language of politics). Heidelberg, C. Winter, 69, 132 p.

4445   FERRARIS, A. "Effetti del linguaggio dell'adulto sul linguaggio del fanciullo" (Effects of the language of a grown up person on the thought and the language of the child), *Riv. Psicol. soc.* 17(1), jan-mar 70 : 3-22.

4446   FISHMAN, J. A. *Sociolinguistics: a brief introduction.* Rowley, Mass., Newbury House, 70, xvi-126 p.

4447   FRIENDLY, M. L.; GLUCKSBERG, S. "On the description of subcultural lexicons: a multi-dimensional approach", *J. Person. soc. Psychol.* 14(1), jan 70 : 55-65.

4448   GREIMAS, A. J. *Du sens; essais sémiotiques.* Paris, Éditions du Seuil, 70, 313 p.

4449   GRIMSHAW, A. D. "Sociolinguistics and the sociologist", *Amer. Sociologist* 4(4), 1969 : 312-321.

4450   HARRIS, Z. S. *Papers in structural and transformational linguistics.* Dordrecht, Reidel, 70, x-850 p.

4451   HARWOOD, T. "Substantive significance of the linguistic relativity hypothesis when using translations of written personality measures", *J. soc. Psychol.* 81(1), jun 70 : 3-8.

4452   HEINE, B. *Status and use of African lingua francas.* München, Weltforum Verlag, 70, 206 p.

4453   HENDERSON, D. "Contextual specificity, discretion, and cognitive socialization: with special reference to language", *Sociology* 4(3), sep 70 : 311-338.

4454   JOYAUX, J. *Le langage, cet inconnu.* Paris, SGPP, 70, 318-2 p.

4455   KELLNER, H. "On the sociolinguistic perspective of the communicative situation", *Soc. Res.* 31(1), mar 70 : 71-87.

4456   KRISTEVA, J. *Recherches pour une sémanalyse.* Paris, Éditions du Seuil, 69, 381 p.

4457   LANG, W. *Probleme der allgemeinen Sprachtheorie* (Problems of the general theory of language). Stuttgart, Klett, 69, 124 p.

4458   LEVENTHAL, H.; FISCHER, K. "What reinforces in a social reinforcement situation, words or expressions ?", *J. Person. soc. Psychol.* 14(1), jan 70 : 83-94.

4459   LINDENFELD, J. "The social conditioning of syntactic variation in French", *Amer. Anthropol.* 71(5), oct 69 : 890-898.

4460   LOSTIA, M. "La lettura percettiva; formazione e condizionamento delle strutture" (Perceptive reading: formation and conditioning of structures), *Riv. Psicol. soc.* 16(4), oct-dec 69 : 351-368.

4461   LUMWAMU, F. "Sur les classes nominales et le nombre dans une langue bantu", *C. Ét. afr.* 10(4), 4 trim 70 : 489-529.

4462   MILLER, G. A.; McNEILL, D. "Psycholinguistics", in: G. LINDZEY, E. ARONSON (eds.). *The handbook of social psychology.* Vol. III. 2nd ed. Reading, Mass., Addison-Wesley, 1968 : 666-794.

4463   MORRA PELLEGRINO, M. L.; GARIBBO GIUGANINO, B. M. "Aspetti formali del linguaggio scritto e orale nei ragazzi" (Formal aspects of children's written and spoken language), *Riv. Psicol. soc.* 16(4), oct-dec 69 : 369-386.

4464   MORRA PELLEGRINO, M. L.; GARIBBO GIUGANINO, B. M. "Confronto di alcuni indici psicolinguistici applicabili al linguaggio scritto e orale in età evolutiva" (Confrontation of some psycholinguistic indexes applicable to written and oral language in developmental age), *Riv. Psicol. soc.* 17(2), jan-mar 70 : 99-108.

4465   MOULOUD, N. *Langage et structures; essais de logique et de sémiologie.* Paris, Payot, 69, 252 p.

4466   N'DIAYE, G. *Structure du dialecte basque de Maya.* The Hague, Mouton, 70, 249 p.

4467   PELLIZZI, C. "La dimensione filologica dell'empirismo" (Philological dimension of empirism), *Rass. ital. Sociol.* 11(2), apr-jun 70 : 159-168.

4468   "Plurilinguisme (Le). Colloque organisé par le Centre de Sociologie de l'Éducation", *R. Inst. Sociol.* (1), 1970 : 87-190.

4469   PORTER, J. "Bilingualism and the myths of culture", *Canad. R. Sociol. Anthropol.* 6(2), mai 69 : 111-119.

4470 RAEVSKIJ, M. V. *Lingvističeskie issledovanija* (Linguistic research). Tula, Tul'skij gos. pedag. Institut im L. N. Tolstoga, 69, 250 p.

4471 "Recherches rhétoriques", *Communications* (16), 1970 : 1-244.

4472 SAMARIN, W. J. "Language in resocialization", *Practic. Anthropol.* 17(6), nov-dec 70 : 269-279.

4473 SMITH, P. T. "Communication over noisy channels: applications to the statistical structure of English", *Brit. J. Psychol.* 61(2), mai 70 : 197-206.

4474 STUMPFE, O. *Die Symbolsprache der Märchen* (The symbolic language of folktales). 2nd rev. ed. Münster/Westfalen, Aschendorff, 69, 226 p.

4475 VACA-TOLEDO, F. "Fenomenología y política del lenguaje" (Language phenomenology and policy), *R. Inst. Sociol. boliv.* (9), 1969 : 76-88.

4476 WHITELEY, W. *Swahili. The rise of a national language.* London, Methuen, 69, x-150 p.

4477 WILLIAMS, J. E.; MORLAND, J. K.; UNDERWOOD, W. L. "Connotations of color names in the United States, Europe, and Asia", *J. soc. Psychol.* 82(2), oct 70 : 3-14.

D.32 Communication through art: the dance, music, drama, literature, painting
Communication au moyen de l'art: danse, musique, théâtre, littérature, peinture

[See also / Voir aussi: 1975, 2562, 3249, 5033]

4478 ACKERMAN, J. S. "The demise of the avant garde: notes on the sociology of recent American art", *Comp. Stud. Soc. Hist.* 11(4), oct 69 : 371-384.

4479 BERNARD, Y. "Faits sociaux et jugements de goût", *R. franç. Sociol.* 11(2), apr-jun 70 : 179-196.

4480 CANU, G. (comp.). *Contes mossi actuels; étude ethno-linguistique.* Dakar, IFAN, 69, 361 p.

4481 CASTELLNO, V. "Difficoltà, contenuto e limiti di una sociologie dell'arte" (Difficulty, content and limits of a sociology of art), *Ri . int. Sociol. (Madrid)* 28(111-112), mai-aug 70 : 5-20.

4482 CHILD, I. L. "Esthetics", in: G. LINDZEY, E. ARONSON (eds.). *The handbook of social psychology.* Vol. III. 2nd ed. Reading, Mass., Addison-Wesley, 1968 : 853-916.

4483 DENISOFF, R. S. "Folk music and the American left: a generational-ideological comparison", *Brit. J. Sociol.* 20(4), dec 69 : 427-442.

4484 ESCARPIT, R. *et al. Le littéraire et le social. Éléments pour une sociologie de la littérature.* Paris, Flammarion, 70, 319 p.

4485 FILHO, A. "Aspectos sociais do romance brasileiro" (Social aspects of the Brazilian novel), *R. brasil. Cultura* 2(3), jan-mar 70 : 147-162.

4486 Bibl. XIX-4035. FÜGEN, H. N. (ed.). *Wege der Literatursoziologie* (Trends in the sociology of literature). CR: A. SILBERMANN, *Kölner Z. Soziol. u. soz.-Psychol.* 22(3), sep 70 : 635-638.

4487 GOLDMANN, L. "Problèmes philosophiques et politiques dans le théâtre de Jean-Paul Sartre. L'intinéraire d'un penseur", *Homme et Soc.* 17, jul-aug-sep 70 : 5-34.

4488 Bibl. XIX-4024. GOLDMANN, L. (éd.). *Sociologie de la littérature. Recherches récentes et discussions.* CR: A. SILBERMANN, *Kölner Z. Soziol. u. soz.-Psychol.* 22(4), dec 70 : 809-813.

4489 GÖRÖG, V. "Littérature orale africaine: bibliographie analytique (périodiques)", *C. Ét. afr.* 10(4), 4 trim 70 : 583-631.

4490 GREEN, G. *The artists of Terezin.* New York, Hawthorne Books, 69, ix-191 p. CR: R. N. WILSON, *Amer. J. Sociol.* 76(6), mai 70 : 1060-1061.

4491 HADDAD, G. "La littérature dans l'idéologie", *Pensée* 151, mai-jun 70 : 88-99.

4492 HAFNER, A. M. "The new reality in art and science", *Comp. Stud. Soc. Hist.* 11(4), oct 69 : 385-397. With comments by G. KUBLER: 398-420 and T. S. KUHN: 403-412.

4493 HALE, S. "Arts in a changing society: Northern Sudan", *Ufahamu* 1(1), 1970 : 64-79.

4494 KASDAN, L.; APPLETON, J. H. "Tradition and change: the case of music", *Comp. Stud. Soc. Hist.* 12(1), jan 70 : 50-58.

4495 Bibl. XIX-4048. KAVOLIS, V. *Artistic expression: a sociological analysis.* CR: J. R. KRAMER, *Amer. sociol. R.* 35(3), jun 70 : 552-553.

4496   KNAPPERT, J. "Social and moral concepts in Swahili Islamic literature", *Africa (London)* 40(2), apr 70 : 125-136.

4497   LIEBERMAN, A. B. "The well-made play and the theatre of the absurd: a study of attitude change", *Sociol. Inquiry* 39(1), 1969 : 85-92.

4498   LIPMAN, A. "Architectural education and the social commitment of contemporary British architecture", *Sociol. R.* 18(1), mar 70 : 5-27.

4499   MARTIN, H.-J. *Livre, pouvoirs et société à Paris au XVIIᵉ siècle, 1598-1701.* 2 vols. Genève, Droz, 69, 1092 p.

4500   MAURY, C. *Folk origins of Indian art.* New York, Columbia University Press, 69, 245 p.

4501   MOULIN, R. "Art et société industrielle capitaliste. L'un et le multiple", *R. franç. Sociol.* 10, n° spécial 1969 : 687-702.

4502   OCAMPO LÓPEZ, J. *El folclor y su manifestación en las supervivencias musicales en Colombia* (Folklore and its manifestation in musical vestiges in Colombia). Tunja, Universidad Pedagogica y Tecnologia de Colombia, 70, 170 p.

4503   OL'DEROGGE, D. A. *Fol'klor i literatura narodov Afriki* (African popular folklore and literature). Moskva, Nauka, 70, 397 p.

4505   PRACHT, E.; NEUBERT, W. *Sozialistischer Realismus—Positionen, Probleme, Perspektiven* (Socialist realism - positions, problems, perspectives). Berlin, Dietz, 70, 342 p.

4506   Bibl. XIX-4058. ROSENGREN, K. E. *Sociological aspects of the literary system.* CR: J. H. BARNETT; W. KAESS, *Acta sociol.* 13(1), 1970 : 55-56; A. SILBERMANN, *Kölner Z. Soziol. u. soz.-Psychol.* 22(4), dec 70 : 809-813.

4507   SCHMALENBACH, W. *Kunst und Gesellschaft heute* (Art and contemporary society). Frankfurt-am-Main, Societäts-Verlag, 69, 37 p.

4508   SHEON, A. "Museums and cultural resources utilization", *J. develop. Areas* 3(4), jul 69 : 539-548.

4509   "Sociologie de la littérature: recherches récentes et discussions", *R. Inst. Sociol.* 3, 1969 : 335-368.

4510   TARRAB, G. "L'art permutationnel", *Sociol. et Soc.* 2(2), nov 70 : 283-296.

4511   YASIN, S. *al-Taḥlîl al-'ijtimâ'î lil-ädab* (The social analysis of literature). al-Qâḥiraṭ, Maktabaṭ al-Anjlû al-Miṣrîyaṭ, 70, 188 p.

D.33   **Mass media of communication: books, the press, radio, television, the cinema**
        Procédés de communication collective: livres, journaux, radiodiffusion, télévision, cinéma

[See also / Voir aussi: 658, 1963, 2237, 3023, 3785, 4135, 4168, 4380]

4512   ADAMSKI, F. "Press readers-studies to date and research needs", *Polish sociol. B.* (1), 1968 : 97-109.

4513   AGASSI, J. "The worker and the media", *Archiv. europ. Sociol.* 11(1), 1970 : 26-66.

4514   ALBRECHT, G. *Nationalsozialistische Filmpolitik. Eine soziologische Untersuchung über die Spielfilme des Dritten Reichs* (The National Socialist film policy. Sociological research on films of the Third Reich). Stuttgart, F. Enke, 69, 562 p. CR: C. GUINCHAT, *R. franç. Sociol.* 11(3), jul-sep 70 : 430.

4515   ALPER, W.; LEIDY, T. R. "The impact of information transmission through television", *Publ. Opin. Quart.* 33(4), 1969 : 556-562.

4516   AL-TIKRITI, M. B. *al-Ṣiḥâfaṭ al-'Irâqîyaṭ wal-tujâḥatîhâ al-sîyasîyaṭ wal-ijtima'îyaṭ wal-thaqâfîyaṭ min 1869-1921* (The press in Iraq, its political, social and cultural trends, 1869-1921). Baqhdâd, Maṭba'aṭ al-Irshâd, 69, 312 p.

4517   BAUER, H. *Die Presse und die öffentliche Meinung* (The press and public opinion). München-Wien, Günter Olzog Verlag, 68, 160 p. CR: A. SILBERMANN, *Kölner Z. Soziol. u. soz.-Psychol.* 21(4), dec 69 : 936-938.

4518   Bibl. XIX-4074. BLUMLER, J. G.; McQUAIL, D. *Television in politics: its uses and influence.* CR: H. MENDELSOHN, *Amer. J. Sociol.* 75(5), mar 70 : 882-884; W. H. HARLAN, *Amer. sociol. R.* 35(2), apr 70 : 388-389.

4519   BOGART, L. "Le contrôle des mass media", *Communications* 14, 1969 : 101-109.

4520   BONEU, J. "La televisión en las zonas rurales" (Television in rural zones), *Estud. Inform.* 13, jan-mar 70 : 59-79. [Spain.]

4521 BORRA, R. "Communication through television: Unesco adult education experiments in France, Japan and India", *J. Communication* 20(1), mar 70 : 65-83.

4522 BRIGANTI, A. "L'origine della terza pagina dei quotidiani italiani" (The origin of the third page of the Italian newspapers), *Crit. sociol. (Roma)* 12, 1969-1970 : 81-90.

4523 BURLACKIJ, F. M. *et al. Problemy sociologii pečati. I. Istorija, metodologija, metodika* (Problems of the sociology of the press. I. History, methodology, methods). Novosibirsk, Nauka, 69, 280 p.

4524 CHANEY, D. C. "Involvement, realism and the perception of aggression in television programmes", *Hum. Relat.* 23(5), oct 70 : 373-381.

4525 CHANEY, D. C. "Television dependency and family relationships amongst juvenile delinquents in the United Kingdom", *Sociol. R.* 18(1), mar 70 : 103-113.

4526 CHARTRAND, F.; McKENZIE, F. "La critique de la radio et de la télévision aux États-Unis et en Grande-Bretagne", *Communications* 14, 1969 : 185-198.

4527 DEBBASCH, C. *Le droit de la radio et de la télévision.* Paris, Presses universitaires de France, 69, 128 p. CR: A. REVON, *R. franç. Sociol.* 11(2), apr-jun 70 : 275-277.

4528 DION, L. "Information politique et participation", *Sociol. et Soc.* 2(1), mai 70 : 1-24.

4529 EHRENBERG, A. S. C.; GOODHART, G. J.; HALDANE, I. R. "The news in May", *Publ. Opin. Quart.* 33(4), 1970 : 546-555.

4530 ERDÉSZ, T.; FEKETE, I. "A tömegkommunikációs eszközök szerepe a népmüvelésben" (The role of mass communications media in popular culture), *Statiszt. Szle* 47(7), jul 69 : 691-704; 47(8-9), aug-sep 69 : 850-874.

4531 FAUCHER, J.-A.; JACQUEMART, N. *Le quatrième pouvoir. La presse française de 1830 à 1960.* Paris, Éditions Jacquemart, 69, 336 p.

4532 FISCHER, H. D.; MERRILL, J. *International communication; media, channels, functions.* New York, Hasting House, 70, xviii-508 p.

4533 FORD, C. *Caméra et "mass media"; la civilisation à l'âge des deux écrans.* Tours, Mame, 70, 157 p.

4534 FORE, W. F. *Image and impact; how man comes through in the mass media.* New York, Friendship Press, 70, 111 p.

4535 FORTIN, G. "La planification des mass media en vue du développement", *Communications* 14, 1969 : 129-136.

4536 GARCÍA FERNANDEZ, M. "El espectador cinematográfico en España" (The cinema spectator in Spain), *Estud. Inform.* 13, jan-mar 70 : 21-38.

4537 GLESSING, R. J. *The underground press in America.* Bloomington, Indiana University Press, 70, xvi-207 p.

4538 GONZÁLEZ PEDRERO, E. *et al. Los medios de comunicación de masas en México* (Mass communications media in Mexico). México, Universidad Nacional Autonóma de México, 69, 175 p.

4539 GREENBERG, B.; DERUIN, B. "Mass communication among the urban poor", *Publ. Opin. Quart.* 34(2), 1970 : 224-233. [USA.]

4540 HALLORAN, J. D.; BROWN, R. L.; CHANEY, D. C. *Television and delinquency.* Leicester, Leicester University Press, 70, 221 p.

4541 Bibl. XIX-4104. HALMOS, P. (ed.). *The sociology of mass-media communicators.* CR: J. M. LEWIS, *Amer. sociol. R.* 35(1), feb 70 : 153-154; A. SILBERMANN, *Kölner Z. Soziol. u. soz.-Psychol.* 22(3), sep 70 : 625-629.

4542 HESSE-QUACK, O. *Der Übertragungsprozess bei der Synchronisation von Filmen. Eine interkulturelle Untersuchung* (Transmission process through film synchronization. An intercultural research). München-Basel, Ernst Reinhardt Verlag, 69, 249 p. CR: J. H. KNOLL, *Kölner Z. Soziol. u. soz.-Psychol.* 22(3), sep 70 : 631-633.

4543 HOLZER, H. *Massenkommunikation und Demokratie in der Bundesrepublik Deutschland* (Mass communication and democracy in the German Federal Republic). Opladen, C. W. Leske, 69, 92 p. CR: A. SILBERMANN, *Kölner Z. Soziol. u. soz.-Psychol.* 22(3), sep 70 : 629-631.

4544 HOPKINS, M. W. *Mass media in the Soviet Union.* New York, Pegasus, 70, 384 p.

4545 JARVIE, I. C. *Movies and society.* New York, Basic Books, 70, xix-394 p. [London edition (Routledge and K. Paul) has title: *Towards a sociology: the cinema.*]

4546 JARVIE, I. C. (ed.). "Myths and mass media", *Archiv. europ. Sociol.* 10(2), 1969 : 205-291.

4547 KOSZYK, K. "The 'Illustrierten'—German reader's favourite glossies", *Gazette* 15(1), 1969 : 9-20.

4548   KRUGMAN, H. E.; HARTLEY, E. L. "Passive learning from television", *Publ. Opin.*
       Quart. 34(2), 1970 : 184-190.

4549   LANGE, D. L.; BAKER, R. K.; BALL, S. J. *Mass media and violence;* a report to the
       National Commission on the Causes and Prevention of Violence. Washington,
       United States Government Printing Office, 69, xxii-614 p.

4550   LEBEL, J. P. "Cinéma et idéologie. I. Invention 'idéologique' ou découverte scien-
       tifique ?", *Nouv. Crit.* 34, mai 70 : 67-73; 35, jun 70 : 60-67.

4551   LJUBIMOV, L. S. "Sociologija i pečat' " (Sociology and the press), *Žurnal Sibiri (Irkutsk.*
       gos. Univ.) (2), 1969 : 40-54.

4552   LOEVINGER, L. "Mass versus media—who controls", *ETC Rev. gen. Semantics* 26(3),
       sep 69 : 295-317.

4553   LUYKX, T. *Overzicht van de ontwikkeling der communicatiemedia* (Overview of the
       development of communication media). Brussel, Elsevier Sequoia, 70, 239-19 p.

4554   MARTINELLI, F. "Il consumo di libri in città" (Book consumption in cities), *Riv. Sociol.*
       7(18), jan-mar 69 : 87-144.

4555   MELON-MARTINEZ, E.; SALLERON, M.-A. *La télévision dans la famille et la société moderne.*
       Paris, Éditions sociales françaises, 69, 208 p.

4556   MENDELSOHN, H. A.; CRESPI, I. *Polls, television, and the new politics.* Scranton, Chandler
       Publishing Co., 70, xii-329 p.

4557   Bibl. XIX-4124. METZ, C. *Essais sur la signification au cinéma.* CR: A. SILBERMANN,
       Kölner Z. Soziol. u. soz.-Psychol. 22(3), sep 70 : 629-631.

4558   MISHRA, V. M. "Mass media use patterns in the Indian slums: a study of four vasties
       in greater Delhi", *Gazette* 15(1), 1970 : 27-38.

4559   MORIN, V. *L'écriture de presse.* Paris, Mouton, 69, 160 p.

4560   NAKANISHI, N. "Changes in living patterns brought about by television", *Develop.*
       Econ. 7(4), dec 69 : 572-589.

4561   NORDENSTRENG, K. "Consumption of mass media in Finland", *Gazette* 15(4), 1969 :
       249-259.

4562   PAKARINEN, E. (ed.). *Pressen i samhället* (The press in society). Borga, Söderström and
       Co., 70, 172 p.

4563   PIETILÄ, V. "Immediate versus delayed reward in newspaper reading", *Acta sociol.*
       12(4), 1969 : 199-208.

4564   RAZIK, T. A. "A study of American newspaper readability", *J. Communication* 19(4),
       dec 69 : 317-324.

4565   ROSENGREN, K. E. "International news: intra and extra media data", *Acta sociol.* 13(2),
       1970 : 96-109.

4566   SARKAR, C. *Challenge and stagnation: the Indian mass media.* New Delhi, Vikas Publi-
       cations, 69, vi-116 p.

4567   SELDES, G. V. *The great audience.* Westport, Conn., Greenwood Press, 70, viii-299 p.
       [Moving-picture, radio and television audiences.]

4568   SILBERMANN, A. (eds.). *Die Massenmedien und ihre Folgen. Kommunikationssoziologische*
       Studien (Mass media and their consequences. Studies on the sociology of communi-
       cation). München-Basel, E. Reinhardt, 70, 157 p. [Germany, BR.]

4569   SINGER, B. D. "Mass media and communication process in Detroit riot of 1967",
       Publ. Opin. Quart. 34(2), 1970 : 236-245.

4570   ŠIŠKOV, A. "Partija i sredstva massovoj informacii" (The party and mass communications
       media), *Kommunist (Moskva)* 46(4), mar 70 : 63-75. [USSR.]

4571   SOURIAU-HOEBRECHTS, C. *La presse maghrébine: Libye, Tunisie, Maroc, Algérie; évolution*
       historique, situation en 1965, organization et problèmes actuels. Paris, Éditions du
       Centre national de la recherche scientifique, 69, 369 p.

4572   STARCK, K. "Media credibility in Finland: a cross-national approach", *J-ism Quart.*
       46(4), 1969 : 790-795.

4573   STEINBERG, C. S. *The communicative arts; an introduction to mass media.* New York,
       Hastings House, 70, xii-371 p.

4574   TICHENOR, P. J.; DONOHUE, G. A.; OLIEN, C. N. "Mass media flow and differential
       growth in knowledge", *Publ. Opin. Quart.* 34(2), 1970 : 159-170.

4575   TUNSTALL, J. (comp.). *Media sociology; a reader.* London, Constable; Urbana University
       of Illinois Press, 70, ix-574 p.

4576   TYLER, P. *Magic and myth of the movies.* New York, Simon and Schuster, 70, xxix-283 p.

4577 VOOGLAJD, Ju. V. *Ličnost' i massovaja kommunikacija. Materialy vstreči sociologov* (Personality and mass communications. Materials for a meeting of sociologists). Tartu, 69, 274 p.

4578 WANDERER, J. J. "In defense of popular taste: film ratings among professionals and lay audiences", *Amer. J. Sociol.* 76(2), sep 70 : 262-272.

4579 WANGERMÉE, R. "Publics et culture en télévision", *Communications* (14), 1969 : 111-115.

4580 WIEBE, G. D. "Two psychological factors in media audience behavior", *Publ. Opin. Quart.* 33(4), 1970 : 523-536.

4581 YSMAL, C. "L'idéologie du *Canard enchaîné*", *R. polit. parl.* 72(808), mar 70 : 54-69.

4582 YU, F. T. C. "Persuasive communications during the cultural revolution", *Gazette* 16(2), 1970 : 73-87; 16(3), 1970 : 137-148.

4583 ZÖCHBAUER, F. "Der Unterhaltungsfilm in sozialpsychologischer und sozialhygenischer Sicht" (The entertaining films from the viewpoint of social psychology and hygiene), *Publizistik* 15(1), jan-mar 70 : 38-48.

4584 ZYGULSKI, K. "Radio and television in Japan", *Soc. Res* 37(1), mar 70 : 147-151.

D.34 Education
Éducation

D.340 *General studies*
Études générales

[See also / Voir aussi: 1753, 5008]

4585 ALAVI, S. M. Z. *An introduction to education.* Jullundur, Sterling Publishers, 69, ix-104 p.

4586 ALBRECHT, H. "Application of socio-psychological research in extension education", *Sociol. rur.* 10(3), 1970 : 237-252.

4587 ANDERSON, R. C. *et al.* (eds.). *Current research on instruction.* Englewood Cliffs, N. J., Prentice-Hall, 69, xiv-396 p.

4588 ASHLEY, B. J.; COHEN, H.; SLATTER, R. G. *An introduction to the sociology of education.* London, Macmillan, 69, 159 p.

4589 Bibl. XIX-4165. BANKS, O. *The sociology of education.* CR: W. E. SCHAFER, *Amer. sociol. R.* 34(6), dec 69 : 1002-1003.

4590 BEREDAY, G. Z. F. *Essays on world education—the crisis of supply and demand.* New York, Oxford University Press, 69, xiii-359 p.

4591 BOOLNOW, O. F. (comp.). *Erziehung in anthropologischer Sicht* (Education from an anthropological point of view). Zürich, Morgarten Verlag, 69, 266 p.

4592 BOURDIEU, P.; PASSERON, J.-C. *La reproduction. Éléments pour une théorie du système d'enseignement.* Paris, Éditions de Minuit, 70, 283 p.

4593 BOWDEN, E. "Creativity, education and democracy", *East Africa* 6(8), aug 68 : 19-29.

4594 CLARIZIO, H. F.; CRAIG, R. C.; MEHRENS, W. A. (eds.). *Contemporary issues in educational psychology.* Boston, Allyn and Bacon, 70, xv-747 p.

4595 CORDASCO, F. (ed.). *et al. The school in the social order; a sociological introduction to educational understanding.* Scranton, Pa., International Textbook Co., 70, xiv-425 p.

4596 DAVIES, I. "The management of knowledge: a critique of the use of typologies in educational sociology", *Sociology* 4(1), jan 70 : 1-22.

4597 DAVITZ, J. R.; BALL, S. (eds.). *Psychology of the educational process.* New York, McGraw-Hill, 70, xii-643 p.

4598 DEVILLE BICHOT, G. "L'éducation et les économistes", *Homo* 8, oct 69 : 109-125.

4599 DIECKMANN, J.; LORENZ, P. *Pädagogische Soziologie; zur Erziehungs- und Schulsoziologie* (Pedagogical sociology. On the sociology of education). Heidelberg, Quelle und Meyer, 70, 160 p.

4600 FISCHER, J. (ed.). *The social sciences and the comparative study of educational systems.* Scranton, Pa., International Textbook Co., 70, xiv-533 p.

4601 FOLGER, J. K.; ASTIN, H. S.; BAYER, A. E. *Human resources and higher education; staff report of the Commission on Human Resources and Advanced Education.* New York, Russell Sage Foundation, 70, xxxii-475 p.

4602 FRIEDENBERG, E. Z. "The function of the school in social homeostasis", *Canad. R. Sociol. Anthropol.* 7(1), fev 70 : 5-16.

4603 INLOW, G. M. *Education: mirror and agent of change; a foundations text.* New York, Holt, Rinehart and Winston, 70, xiii-542 p.

4604 JOHNSON, D. W. *The social psychology of education.* New York, Holt, Rinehart and Winston, 70, vi-314 p.

4605 KELLY, F. J.; CODY, J. C. *Educational psychology; a behavioral approach.* Columbus, Ohio, C. E. Merrill Publishing Co., 69, xi-339 p.

4606 KING, R. *Education.* Harlow-London, Longmans, 69, ix-138 p.

4607 LAENG, M. *L'educazione nella civiltà tecnologica* (Education in the technological civilization). Roma, A. Armando, 69, 319 p.

4608 LAWRENCE, E. S. *The origins and growth of modern education.* Baltimore, Penguin Books; Harmondsworth, Penguin, 70, 393 p.

4609 LEVIN, M. R.; SHANK, A. (eds.). *Education investment in an urban society: costs, benefits, and public policy.* New York, Teachers College Press, 70, 245 p.

4610 LINDQUIST, H. M. (ed.). *Education: readings in the processes of cultural transmission.* Boston, Houghton Mifflin, 70, xv-249 p.

4611 LIVELY, E. L. (ed.). "Education", *Sociol. Focus* 3(1), 1969 : 1-1110.

4612 LUTZ, F. W. (ed.). *Toward improved urban education.* Worthington, Ohio, C. A. Jones, 70, xvii-343 p.

4613 MARKIEWICZ-LAGNEAU, J. *Éducation, égalité et socialisme; théorie et pratique de la différenciation sociale en pays socialistes.* Paris, Éditions Anthropos, 69, xiii-172 p.

4614 Bibl. XIX-4179. MARTIN, D. (ed.). *Anarchy and culture: the problem of the contemporary university.* CR: D. H. KAMENS, *Amer. sociol. R.* 35(2), apr 70 : 375-376.

4615 MARTIN, W. B. *Conformity: standards and change in higher education.* San Francisco, Jossey-Bass, 69, xxii-264 p.

4616 MILES, M. B.; CHARTERS, W. W. Jr. *Learning in social settings; new readings in the social psychology of education.* Boston, Allyn and Bacon, 70, ix-751 p.

4617 MILLER, H. L.; WOOCK, R. R. *Social foundations of urban education.* Hinsdale, Ill., Dryden Press, 70, xiii-433 p.

4618 MOLLO, S. *L'école dans la société; psychosociologie des modèles éducatifs.* Paris, Dunod, 70, xi-306 p.

4619 MONSON, C. H. Jr. (ed.). *Education for what? Readings in the ends and means of education.* Boston, Houghton Mifflin, 70, xii-387 p.

4620 MORRISH, I. *Education since 1800.* London, Allen and Unwin; New York, Barnes and Noble, 70, xi-244 p.

4621 MUSGRAVE, P. W. (ed.). *Sociology, history and education: a reader.* London, Methuen, 70, viii-293 p.

4622 NATALIS, E. *Carrefours psychopédagogiques.* Bruxelles, C. Dessart, 70, 272 p.

4623 NELSON, J. L.; BESAG, F. P. *Sociological perspectives in education; models for analysis.* New York, Pitman Publishing Corporation, 70, x-230 p.

4624 NISBET, J. D.; ENTWISTLE, N. J. *Educational research methods.* London, University of London; New York, American Elsevier Publishing Co., 70, 192 p.

4625 OZMON, H. (comp.). *Contemporary critics of education.* Danville, Ill., Interstate Printers and Publishers, 70, 223 p.

4626 ROBBINS, F. G. *Educational sociology; a study in child, youth, school, and community.* New York, Greenwood Press, 69, xiv-529 p.

4627 RÖHRS, H. *Allgemeine Erziehungswissenschaft. Eine Einführung in die erziehungswissenschaftlichen Aufgaben und Methoden* (General education science. Introduction to its tasks and methods). Weinheim (Bergstr.)-Berlin-Basel, Beltz, 69, 487 p.

4628 SCHRÖDER, H. *Psychologie und Unterricht. Formen neuzeitlicher Unterrichtsgestaltung und ihre psychologischen Grundlagen* (Psychology and education. Forms of contemporary pedagogy and its psychological bases). Weinheim-Berlin-Basel, Beltz, 69, 185 p.

4629 SMITH, W. O. L. *Education: an introductory survey.* Rev. ed. reprinted with *revisions.* Harmondsworth, Penguin, 69, 248 p.

4630 STARR, B. D. (ed.). *The psychology of school adjustment.* New York, Random House, 70, xii-532 p.

4631 STIEGLITZ, H. *Soziologie und Erziehungswissenschaft. Wissenschaftstheoretische Grundzüge ihrer Erkenntnisstruktur und Zusammenarbeit* (Sociology and educational science. Basic scientific characteristics of their structure and co-operation). Stuttgart, Enke, 70, ix-608 p.

4632   STONES, E. *Readings in educational psychology: learning and teaching.* London, Methuen, 70, x-478 p.

4633   STREET, D. (ed.). *Innovation in mass education.* New York, J. Wiley and Sons, 69, 342 p. CR: E. P. WOLF, *Amer. J. Sociol.* 76(1), jul 70 : 179-182.

4634   TOSCANO, M. *Introdução a sociologia educacional* (Introduction to educational sociology). Pôrto Alegre, Edições Tabajara, 69, 173 p.

4635   TRAVERS, J. F. *Fundamentals of educational psychology.* Scranton, Pa., International Text Book Co., 70, vii-536 p.

4636   UNESCO. *Educational planning; a world survey of problems and prospects.* Paris, Unesco, 70, 195 p.

4637   "Università in un mondo in trasformazione (L')" (The university in a changing world), *Mulino* 19(7-8), jul-aug 70 : 27-171.

4638   VAN KEMENADE, J. A. "The situation and prospects of the sociology of education", *Sociol. neerland.* 6(2), 1970 : 148-154.

4639   VESTA, F. J. DI; THOMPSON, G. G. *Educational psychology; instruction and behavioral change.* New York, Appleton-Century-Crofts, 70, xii-718 p.

4640   VOGEL, A. W.; ZEPPER, J. T.; BACHELOR, D. L. (eds.). *Foundations of education; a social view.* Albuquerque, University of New Mexico Press, 70, xi-383 p.

4641   ZANOTTI, L. J. *La escuela y la sociedad en el siglo XX* (The school and society in the XXth century). Buenos Aires, A. Estrada, 70, 151 p.

D.341   *Methods and problems*
Méthodes et problèmes

[See also / Voir aussi: 866, 878, 887, 989, 1760, 1784, 1792, 1943, 2040, 2380, 2452, 3222, 3247, 4152, 4627]

4642   al-BAZZÂZ, Ĥ. 'A. *Taqyîm al-taftîsch al-ibtidâ'î fil-'Iraq* (Evaluation of supervision in primary schools in Iraq). Baghdâd, Maťba'ať al-Irshâd, 70, 332 p.

4643   ALSCHULER, A. S. "The effects of classroom structure on achievement motivation and academic performance", *Educ. Technol.* 9(8), aug 69 : 19-24.

4644   ANDREW, G. M.; MOIR, R. E. *Information-decision systems in education.* Itasca, Ill., F. E. Peacock, 70, xii-177 p.

4645   ARENA, T. "Social maturity in the prediction of academic achievement", *J. educ. Res.* 64(1), sep 70 : 21-22.

4646   ARMITAGE, P.; SMITH, C.; ALPER, P. *Decision models for educational planning.* London, Allen Lane, 69, ix-124 p.

4647   BARKER LUNN, J. C.; FERRI, E. *Streaming in the primary school : a longitudinal study of children in streamed and non-streamed junior schools.* Slough, National Foundation for Educational Research in England and Wales, 70, xxiii-508 p. [UK.]

4648   BASSETT, G. W. *Innovation in primary education; a study of recent developments in primary education in England and the USA.* London-New York, Wiley-Interscience, 70, x-209 p.

4649   BECCHI, E. *Problemi di sperimentalismo educativo* (Problems of educative experimentation). Roma, A. Armando, 69, 236 p.

4650   BELANGER, G. "L'université, une perspective économique", *Actual. écon.* 45(3), oct-dec 69 : 488-499.

4651   BILLETT, R. O. *Improving the secondary-school curriculum: a guide to effective curriculum planning.* New York, Atherton Press, 70, xxvii-364 p.

4652   Bibl. XIX-4203. BOLTANSKI, L. *Prime éducation et morale de classe.* CR: C. SUAUD, *R. franç. Sociol.* 11(1), jan-mar 70 : 91-93.

4653   BOURDIEU, P.; SAINT-MARTIN, M. DE. "L'excellence scolaire et les valeurs du système d'enseignement français", *Annales* 25(1), jan-feb 70 : 147-175.

4654   BRETON, R. "Academic stratification in secondary schools and the educational plans of students", *Canad. R. Sociol. Anthropol.* 7(1), feb 70 : 17-34. [Canada.]

4655   BROOKS, C. N. "Training system evaluation using mathematical models", *Éduc. Technol.* 9(6), jun 69 : 54-61.

4656   BROWN, D. J. *Appraisal procedures in the secondary schools.* Englewood Cliffs, N. J., Prentice-Hall, 70, ix-182 p.

4657 CERTEAU, M. DE. "L'université devant la culture de masse", *Projet* 47, jul-aug 70 : 843-855. [France.]

4658 CERVANTES, L. F.; HUSTED, G. P. *The dropout: causes and cures.* Ann Arbor, Mich., University of Michigan Press, 69, 244 p. CR: S. T. RICKSON, *Amer. sociol. R.* 35(2), apr 70 : 378-379.

4659 CHAN, A.; CHIU, A.; MUELLER, D. J. "An integrated approach to the modification of classroom failure and disruption: a case study", *J. School Psychol.* 8(2), 1970 : 114-121.

4660 CHESSWAS, J. D. *Methodologies of educational planning for developing countries.* 2 vols. Paris, Unesco, International Institute for Educational Planning, 69,

4661 CORREA, H. *Quantitative methods of educational planning.* Scranton, International Textbook Co., 69, xvii-242 p.

4662 CURLE, A. *The professional identity of the educational planner.* Paris, Unesco, International Institute for Educational Planning, 69, 49 p.

4663 DAYTON, C. M. *The design of educational experiments.* New York, McGraw-Hill, 70, xi-441 p.

4664 DENNY, T. (ed.). "Educational evaluation", *R. educ. Res.* 40(2), apr 70 : 181-320.

4665 DEUTSCH, S. E. *International education and exchange, a sociological analysis.* Cleveland, Press of Case Western Reserve University, 70, xviii-207 p.

4666 DINKMEYER, D. C.; CALDWELL, E. *Developmental counseling and guidance: a comprehensive school approach.* New York, McGraw-Hill, 70, ix-502 p.

4667 FANTINI, M. D.; GITTELL, M.; MAGAT, R. *Community control and the urban school.* New York, Praeger Publishers, 70, xix-268 p.

4668 FARGO, G. A.; BEHRNS, C.; NOLEN, P. (eds.). *Behavior modification in the classroom.* Belmont, Calif., Wadsworth Publishing Co., 70, xv-344 p.

4669 FOLLETT, M. P. "The teacher-student relation", *Adm. Sci. Quart.* 15(2), jun 70 : 137-149.

4670 FRANCIS, R. G. "Sociological awareness of the campus: a review article", *Sociol. Quart.* 11(2), 1970 : 255-264.

4671 GEORGE, F. H. "Educational technology and the systems approach", *Cybernetica* 13(2), 1970 : 105-114.

4672 GOOD, T. L.; BROPHY, J. E. "Teacher-child dyadic interactions: a new method of classroom observation", *J. School Psychol.* 8(2), 1970 : 131-138.

4673 GORDON, A. K. *Games for growth; educational games in the classroom.* Palo Alto, Calif., Science Research Associates, College Division, 70, 205 p.

4674 GORDON, E. W. (ed.). "Education for socially disadvantaged children", *R. educ. Res.* 40(1), feb 70 : 1-179.

4675 GOZZER, G. "Consideraciones sobre la 'inercia' de las estructuras educacionales" (Considerations on "inertia" in educational systems), *R. Educ. (Madrid)* 71(206), nov-dec 69 : 7-11.

4676 GRACIARENA, J. "Algunas hipótesis sobre la deserción y el retraso en los estudios universitarios en Uruguay" (Some hypotheses concerning dropping out and retardation in university studies in Uruguay), *R. mexic. Sociol.* 31(4), oct-dec 69 : 1041-1062.

4677 GRIFFITHS, D. E. (ed.). *Developing taxonomies of organizational behavior in education administration.* Chicago, Rand McNally, 69, viii-277 p.

4678 GRINDEA, D. "Considérations théoriques et pratiques sur la fonction productive de l'enseignement", *R. roum. Sci. soc. Sér. Sci. écon.* 14(2), 1970 : 167-176.

4679 Bibl. XIX-4215. GROSS, E.; GRAMBSCH, P. V. *University goals and academic power.* CR: R. M. PIKE, *Amer. sociol. R.* 35(4), aug 70 : 791-792.

4680 HAMILTON, V. "Non-cognitive factors in university students' examination performance", *Brit. J. Psychol.* 61(2), mai 70 : 229-242.

4681 HEDGES, W. D. *Evaluation in the elementary school.* New York, Holt, Rinehart and Winston, 69, iv-220 p.

4682 HEINEMANN, K. "Soziale Determinanten des Leistungserfolges in Gymnasien" (Social determination of success in high school), *Kölner Z. Soziol. u. soz.-Psychol.* 21(4), dec 69 : 830-846.

4683 HILFIKER, L. R. "Factors relating to the innovativeness of school systems", *J. educ. Res.* 64(1), sep 70 : 23-27.

4684 HONORÉ, S. *Adaptation scolaire et classes sociales.* Paris, Les Belles lettres, 70, 159 p.

4685 HORDLEY, I.; LEE, D. J. "The 'alternative route'—social change and opportunity in technical education", *Sociology* 4(1), jan 70 : 23-50.

4686 HOWES, V. M. (comp.). *Individualization of instruction; a teaching strategy.* New York, Macmillan, 70, ix-243 p.

4687 HUNT, J. McV. *The challenge of incompetence and poverty; papers on the role of early education.* Urbana University of Illinois Press, 69, xi-289 p.

4688 *Innovations and experiments in university teaching methods.* London, University of London, Institute of Education, 69, i-viii-191 p.

4689 ISAMBERT-JAMATI, V. "Extension du public et baisse de niveau dans l'enseignement du second degré", *R. franç. Sociol.* 11(2), apr-jun 70 : 151-163. [France.]

4690 JENSEN, S. *Bildungsplanung als Systemtheorie; Beiträge zum Problem gesellschaftlicher Planung im Rahmen der Theorie sozialer Systeme* (Educational planning as a systems theory: contribution to the problem of social planning in the framework of social systems theory). Bielefeld, Bertelsmann Universitätsverlag, 70, 134 p.

4691 JOYCE, W. W.; OANA, R. G.; HOUSTON, W. R. (eds.). *Elementary education in the seventies; implications for theory and practice.* New York, Holt, Rinehart and Winston, 70, xi-579 p.

4692 KARMEL, L. J. *Measurement and evaluation in the schools.* New York, Macmillan, 70, xx-492 p.

4693 KELLER, F. J. *The comprehensive high school.* Westport, Conn., Greenwood Press, 70, xv-302 p. [USA.]

4694 KEMENY, P. J. "Dualism in secondary technical education", *Brit. J. Sociol.* 21(1), mar 70 : 86-94. [UK.]

4695 KING, A. J. C.; RIPTON, R. A. "Teachers and students: a preliminary analysis of collective reciprocity", *Canad. R. Sociol. Anthropol.* 7(1), feb 70 : 35-48.

4696 LUCAS, N. C.; HARLESS, W. G.; THIES, R. E. "An experiment in learning behavior using computer-assisted instruction", *Behav. Sci.* 15(5), sep 70 : 447-451.

4697 LUNNEBORG, C. E.; LUNNEBORG, P. W. "Relations between aptitude changes and academic success during college", *J. educ. Psychol.* 61(3), jun 70 : 169-173.

4698 MADDOCK, J. "Selectivity and ability", *Sociology* 4(3), sep 70 : 339-351.

4699 MASSIALAS, B. G. *Education and the political system.* Reading, Mass., Addison-Wesley, 69, xvii-210 p. [USA.]

4700 METZGER, W. P. *et al. Dimensions of academic freedom.* Urbana, Ill., University of Illinois Press, 69, 121 p. CR: W. J. BOWERS, *Amer. sociol. R.* 35(2), apr 70 : 374-375. [USA.]

4701 MILLER, G. W. "Factors in school achievement and social class", *J. educ. Psychol.* 61(4, *Part I*), aug 70 : 260-269.

4702 MILLER, G. W. *Success, failure, and wastage in higher education—an overview of the problem derived from research and theory.* London, G. G. Harrap, 70, 264 p. [UK.]

4703 MINIUM, E. W. *Statistical reasoning in psychology and education.* New York, Wiley, 70, xx-465 p.

4704 MORRIS, R. N. *The sixth form and college entrance.* London, Routledge and K. Paul, 69, 223 p. CR: M. S. ARCHER, *Brit. J. Sociol.* 21(2), jun 70 : 236-237.

4705 MURRAY, F. B. "Credibility of information for educational innovation", *J. educ. Res* 64(1), sep 70 : 17-20.

4706 NEVES, I. DE G.; SIQUEIRA, O. K. *Dinâmica de orientação educacional* (Dynamics of educational guidance). Pôrto Alegre, Editôra Globo, 69, 285 p.

4707 NICOLOLSI, G. "Una soluzione alla crisi sociale contemporanea: la rivoluzione pedago-gico-resistenziale" (A solution to the contemporary social sciences: the pedagogical resistance revolution), *R. int. Sociol. (Madrid)* 27(105-106), jan-jun 69 : 89-98.

4708 ORGANISATION DE COOPÉRATION ET DE DÉVELOPPEMENT ÉCONOMIQUE. Groupe d'étude sur les aspects économiques de l'enseignement. *Objectifs sociaux et planification de l'enseignement.* Paris, OCDE, 69, 433 p.

4709 ORGANISATION DE COOPÉRATION ET DE DÉVELOPPEMENT ÉCONOMIQUE. *Quelques problèmes de développement de l'enseignement supérieur en Europe.* Paris, OCDE, 69, 369 p.

4710 PARSONS, T.; PLATT, G. M. "Age, social structure and socialization in higher education", *Sociol. Education* 43(1), 1970 : 1-37.

4711 PASSERON, J. C. "Sociologie des examens", *Éduc. et Gestion* 20, apr 70 : 6-16.

4712   PERRENOUD, P. "Stratification socio-culturelle et réussite scolaire: les défaillances de l'explication causale", *C. Vilfredo Pareto* 20, feb 70 : 5-75.

4713   PERRIAULT, J. "Domaines actuels d'utilisation des calculateurs dans l'enseignement", *Enseign. programmé* (1), mar 69 : 11-19.

4714   PFISTNER, H.-J. *Erziehungsbetragung. Psychologische Beiträge zur Erziehungs- und Bildungsberatung* (Educational guidance. Psychological essays on education and training orientation). Koblenz, K. Krieger Verlag, 68, 301 p. CR: M. MARKEFTA, *Kölner Z. Soziol. u. soz.-Psychol.* 22(1), mar 70 : 196-198.

4715   PILLET, J. "La mesure du retard scolaire en France et dans les pays africains d'expression française", *C. Ét. afr.* 9(4), 4 trim 69 : 546-569.

4716   POVEY, R. M. "Arts/science differences: their relationship to curriculum specialization", *Brit. J. Psychol.* 61(1), feb 70 : 55-64.

4717   *Recherche en enseignement programmé, tendances actuelles (La)/Programmed learning research, major trends*. Paris, Dunod, 69, xvi-360 p. [Actes d'un colloque OTAN, Nice, mai 1968.]

4718   REUCHLIN, M.; BACHER, F. *L'orientation à la fin du premier cycle secondaire, une enquête psycho-socio-pédagogique de l'Institut national d'étude du travail et d'orientation professionnelle*. Paris, Presses universitaires de France, 69, 392 p.

4719   REVERÓN, F. A. "Deserción estudiantil—causas y actitudes" (Student drop-outs—causes and attitudes), *Eduación* 30(132), mar 69 : 81-185. [Venezuela.]

4720   RHODES, A. L.; NAM, C. B. "The religious context of educational expectations", *Amer. sociol. R.* 35(2), apr 70 : 253-267. [USA.]

4721   ROBERTS, J. I. *Scene of the battle; group behavior in urban classrooms*. Garden City, N. Y., Doubleday, 70, xii-441 p.

4722   ROLFF, H.-G. *Bildungsplanung als rolende Reform. Eine soziologische Analyse der Zwecke, Mittel und Durchführungsformen einer reformbezogenen Planung des Bildungswesens* (Educational planning as a continuous reform. A sociological analysis of aims, means and ways of executing reformist educational planning). Frankfurt-am-Main-Berlin-München, Diesterweg, 70, xii-188 p.

4723   SILVA MICHELENA, J. A. "La construcción dentro de un sistema educativo de un mecanismo para la reforma y la innovación continuas" (The creation of a mechanism for continual reform and innovation, within an educational system), *R. Cienc. soc. (Puerto Rico)* 14(1), jan-mar 70 : 27-56.

4724   STEININGER, M. "Aptitude, dogmatism, and college press as codeterminants of academic achievement", *J. soc. Psychol.* 80(2), apr 70 : 229-230.

4725   TA-NGOC-CHÂU. *Les aspects démographiques de la planification de l'enseignement*. Paris, Unesco, Institut international de planification de l'éducation, 69, 89 p.

4726   ten HORN, L. A. "Selective voor het wetenschappelijk onderwijs" (Selections for scientific teaching), *Soc. Wetensch.* 12(2), 1969 : 106-125.

4727   "Theory in humanistic studies", *Daedalus* 99(2), 1970 : vii-530 p.

4728   TRONCHÈRE, J. *L'école d'aujourd'hui et la mutation des méthodes*. Paris, A. Colin, 70, 144 p. [France.]

4729   TUCKMAN, H. P. "Determinants of college student migration", *South. econ. J.* 37(2), oct 70 : 184-189. [USA.]

4730   WEGNER, E. L.; SEWELL, W. H. "Selection and context as factors affecting the probability of graduation from college", *Amer. J. Sociol.* 75(4, Part II), jan 70 : 665-679.

4731   WEINBERG, C. *Social foundations of education guidance*. New York, The Free Press, 69, 398 p. CR: H. M. REDBIRD, *Amer. sociol. R.* 35(1), feb 70 : 170-171.

4732   WIŚNIEWSKI, W. "Some factors affecting success at university", *Polish sociol. B.* (1), 1969 : 59-73.

4733   WITTROCK, M. C.; WILEY, D. E. (eds.). *The evaluation of instruction; issues and problems*. New York, Holt, Rinehart and Winston, 70, xiii-494 p.

4734   WOLCOTT, H. F. "An ethnographic approach to the study of school administration", *Hum. Org.* 29(2), 1970 : 115-122.

D.342 **Basic education. Adult education**
Éducation de base. Éducation des adultes

[See also / Voir aussi: 2395, 3348, 4521]

4735 ALENIŠKIN, G. F. "Vlijanie naučno-tehničeskogo progressa na rost oblazovatel'nogo urovnja tružhenikov sela" (Influence of scientific and technical progress on improvement in the education level of village workers), *Učen. Zap. (Mosko. gos. pedag. Inst.)* (361), 1969 : 117-131.

4736 ANDERSON, D.; NIEMI, J. A. *Adult education and the disadvantaged adult.* Syracuse, N. Y., ERIC Clearinghouse on Adult Education, 69, vi-96 p.

4737 BARRATT-BROWN, M. *Adult education for industrial workers: the contribution of Sheffield University Extramural Department.* London, National Institute of Adult Education (England and Wales), 69, 31 p.

4738 BASTIN, M. "Enseignement et éducation permanente: exigence de la participation des travailleurs", *Doss. Action soc. cath.* 47(2), mar-apr 70 : 99-117. [Belgique.]

4739 BEGASSAT, J. "Les exigences d'une véritable politique de formation permanente", *Confronter* 5, feb 70 : 43-50.

4740 BOUTIN, A. M. "Enseignement programmé et formation professionnelle dans les entreprises", *Enseign. programmé* (5), mar 69 : 9-42.

4741 CASPAR, P. *Formation des adultes; ou, Transformation des structures de l'entreprise. Une expérience du CUCES.* Paris, Éditions d'organisation, 70, 260 p.

4742 ČEBYSLEVA, V. V. *Psihologija trudivogo obučenija* (Psychology of professional training). Moskva, Proveščenie, 69, 303 p.

4743 COLES, E. T. *Adult education in developing countries.* Oxford, Pergamon Press, xiv-144 p.

4744 COTTAVE, R. "De la formation professionnelle à l'éducation permanente", *Éduc. perm.* 2, apr-jun 69 : 31-37.

4745 CROWLEY, D. W. (ed.). *The role of colleges of advanced education in Australian adult education.* Sydney, Australian Association of Adult Education, 69, 54 p.

4746 DAVID, M. "Universities and workers' education in France", *Int. Lab. R.* 101(2), feb 70 : 109-131.

4747 DIKAU, J. *Wirtschaft und Erwachsenenbildung. Ein kritischer Beitrag zur Geschichte der deutschen Volkshochschule* (Economy and education of adults. A critical contribution to history of the German People's University). Wienheim-Berlin-Basel, Beltz, 68, 420 p.

4748 FRITSCH, P. "Formateurs d'adultes et formation des adultes", *R. franç. Sociol.* 10(4), oct-dec 69 : 427-447.

4749 HUGHES, P. D'.; PETIT, G.; RÉRAT, F. "Premiers résultats d'une étude dans les entreprises sur l'évolution de la qualification ouvrière et les besoins en formation", *Population* 25(3), mai-jun 70 : 517-538.

4750 KELLY, T. *A history of adult education in Great Britain.* 2nd ed. rev. and *enl.* Liverpool, Liverpool University Press, 70, xii-420 p.

4751 KIIL, P. *Adult vocational training.* Copenhagen, Ministries of Labour and Social Affairs, International Relations Division, 69, 22 p.

4752 KRAFT, R. H. P. "Vocational-technical training and technological change", *Éduc. Technol.* 9(7), jul 69 : 12-18.

4753 LAWSON, K. H. "Universities and workers' education in Britain", *Int. Lab. R.* 101(1), jan 70 : 1-14.

4754 LEGRAND, P. "L'éducation des adultes et le concept de l'éducation permanente", *Convergence* 3(2), 1970 : 25-36.

4755 MENCARELLI, M. *Scuola di base e educazione permanente* (Basic school and continuing education). Brescia, La Scuola, 69, 317 p.

4756 NATIONAL INSTITUTE OF ADULT EDUCATION. "Adult education—adequacy of provision", *Adult. Educ. (London)* 42(6), mar 70 : 1-203.

4757 OTTO, C. P.; GLASER, R. O. *The management of training; a handbook for training and development personnel.* Reading, Mass., Addison-Wesley Publishing Co., 70, vi-410 p.

4758 PETERS, J. M. "Internal-external control, learning, and participation in occupational education", *Adult Educ. (Washington)* 20(1), 1969 : 23-43.

4759 PINE, G. J.; HORNE, P. J. "Principles and conditions for learning in adult education", *Adult Leadership* 18(4), oct 69 : 108-110, 126, 133-134.

4760   "Points de repère pour une alphabétisation fonctionnelle", *Hommes et Migr.* 114,
        [1970] : 25-102.

4761   ROHRINGER, J. *Die österreichische Berufsschule* (The Austrian professional school).
        Weinheim/(Bergstr.)-Berlin-Basel, Beltz, 70, 213 p.

4762   ROTH, R. M.; HERSCHENSON, D. B.; HILLIARD, T. (eds.). *The psychology of vocational
        development; readings in theory and research.* Boston, Allyn and Bacon, 70, xi-528 p.

4763   ROUX, B. *La formation permanente. Recyclage, promotion, reconversion, culture, perfection-
        nement, éducation sociale et politique.* Paris, Éditions du Centurion, 69, 192 p.

4764   ROUX, B. "Formation professionnelle et formation permanente", *Confronter* 5, feb 70 :
        29-37.

4765   SARÎYAᵵ, Ŝ. A. *Taîwîr al-ta'alîm al-ŝina'î fil-'Irâq* (Development of vocational training
        in Iraq). Baghdâd, Maᵵba'aᵵ Dâr al-Jâhâz, 69, 408 p.

4766   SCHADT, A. L. *Adult education in Germany; bibliography.* Syracuse, N. Y., ERIC
        Clearinghouse on Adult Education, 69, 40 p.

4767   SEAMAN, D. F.; SCHROEDER, W. L. "The relationship between extent of educative
        behavior by adults and their attitudes toward continuing education", *Adult. Educ.
        (Washington)* 20(2), 1970 : 99-105.

4768   SERRA, A. "Qualche riflessione sull'educazione permanente" (Some reflections on
        continuing education), *Riv. Sociol.* 6(17), sep-dec 68 : 161-166.

4769   SIEBERT, H. *Erwachsenenbildung in der Erziehungsgesellschaft der DDR. Zur Geschichte
        und Theorie der sozialistischen Erwachsenenbildung* (Adult education in the educational
        society of the German Democratic Republic. History and theory of adult education).
        Düsseldorf, Bertelsmann Universitätsverlag, 70, 334 p.

4770   SOLANO SAGARDE, N. *Educación rural boliviana* (Bolivian rural education). Tupiza,
        Bolivia Ediciones Rico, 69, 125 p.

4771   TIETGENS, H. "Entwicklungsländer als Thema der Erwachsenbildung" (Developing
        countries as a theme for adult education), *Off. Welt* 99-100, 1969 : 256-271.

4772   VANDENPUT, M. "La formation des adultes", *Synopsis* 12(123), jan-feb 70 : 39-48.

4773   VERMA, I. B. *Basic education; a reinterpretation.* Agra, Sri Ram Mehra, 69, viii-374 p.
        [India.]

4774   WARREN, V. B. (ed.). *The second treasury of techniques for teaching adults.* Washington,
        National Association for Public Continuing and Adult Education, 70, v-49 p.

4775   WEHNES, F. J. *Mensch und Arbeit; anthropologische Aspekte der Berufserziehung* (Man
        and work; anthropological aspects of vocational training). Trier, Spee-Verlag, 69,
        183 p.

4776   "Weiterbildung—objektives Erfordernis" (Continuing education: an objective demand),
        Hochschulwesen 17(7-8), jul-aug 69 : 453-580. [Germany, DR.]

D.343   *Educational systems and local realizations*
        Systèmes d'éducation et réalisations locales

        [See also / Voir aussi: 911, 913, 915, 920, 930, 940, 994, 1010, 1351, 2314, 2529, 2916,
        3250, 3789, 4986]

4777   ABERNETHY, D. B. *The political dilemma of popular education; an African case.* Stanford,
        Calif., Stanford University Press, 69, viii-357 p.

4778   AKENSON, D. H. *The Irisih education experiment; the national system of education in the
        nineteenth century.* London, Routledge and K. Paul, 70, x-430 p.

4779   al HAMER, A.-M. Y. *An analytical study of the system of education in Bahrain,* Bahrain,
        Oriental Press, 68, v-122 p.

4780   ALTBACH, P. G.; NYSTROM, B. *Higher education in developing countries: a select biblio-
        graphy.* Cambridge, Center for International Affairs, Harvard University, 70, 118 p.

4781   BARZUN, J. *The American university: how it runs, where it is going.* London, Oxford
        University Press, 69, xii-319 p.

4782   BESHIR, M. O. *Educational development in the Sudan, 1898-1956.* Oxford, Clarendon
        Press, 69, xi-276 p.

4783   BOCKSTAEL, E.; FEINSTEIN, O. *Higher education in the European community; reform and
        economics.* Lexington, Mass., Heath Lexington Books, 70, xii-154 p.

4784 BRAHAM, R. L. *Education in the Hungarian People's Republic.* Washington, United States Government Printing Office, 70, x-227 p.

4785 BRANDAUER, H. *Die Konzeption der österreichischen Hauptschule. Geschichtliche Entwicklung und Lehrplananalyse* (The Austrian conception of the University. Historical development and curriculum analysis). Wien, Ketterl, 70, 130 p.

4786 BROCH, H. *Zur Universitätreform* (The University reform). Frankfurt-am-Main, Suhrkamp, 69, 138 p. CR: M. KAASE, *Kölner Z. Soziol. u. soz.-Psychol.* 22(1), mar 70 : 194-196. [Germany, BR.]

4787 BUETOW, H. A. *Of singular benefit; the story of Catholic education in the United States.* New York, Macmillan, 70, xvii-526 p.

4788 CAIN, G. G.; WATTS, H. W. "Problems in making policy inferences from the Coleman Report", *Amer. sociol. R.* 35(2), apr 70 : 228-242. Followed by a reply by J. S. COLEMAN: 242-249 and another one by D. J. AIGNER: 249-252. [USA.]

4789 CALVET, G. "Quelques problèmes de scolarisation dans les campagnes", *Homo* 8, oct 69 : 167-187. [France.]

4790 CAMERON, J. *The development of education in East Africa.* New York, Teachers College Press, 70, ix-148 p.

4791 CARIOLA, P. "La enseñanza privada de nivel medio en algunos países de América Latina" (Private secondary education in some Latin American countries), *Educadores* 12(75), mai-jun 69 : 201-251.

4792 CHIAPPO, L. "Estructura y fines de la universidad peruana" (Structure and objectives of the Peruvian University), *Aportes* 16, apr 70 : 56-90.

4793 CHOUIKHA, A. "Conception et résultats de la réforme tunisienne de l'enseignement de 1958", *R. tunis. Sci. soc.* 6(19), dec 69 : 39-66.

4794 COWAN, L. G. *The cost of learning: the politics of primary education in Kenya.* New York, Teachers College Press, 70, xiii-106 p.

4795 CURLE, A. *Educational problems of developing societies; with case studies of Ghana and Pakistan.* New York, Praeger Publishers, 69, ix-170 p.

4796 DUBBELDAM, L. F. B. *The primary school and the community in Mwanza district, Tanzania.* Groningen, Wolters, 70, 200 p.

4797 "Embattled university (The)", *Daedalus* 99(1), 1970 : 1-221. [USA.]

4798 EULAU, H.; QUINLEY, H. *State officials and higher education; a survey of the opinions and expectations of policy makers in nine States.* New York, McGraw-Hill, 70, xiii-209 p. [USA.]

4799 FEKETE, J. "Public education in Hungary in the last 25 years", *New Hungar. Quart.* 11(38), 1970 : 94-106.

4800 FENLEY, W. J. (ed.). *Education in the 1970's and 1980's; continuity and change in Australian education.* Sydney, University of Sydney, Department of Education, 69, 179 p.

4801 FERRIS, A. L. *Indicators of trends in American education.* New York, Russel Sage Foundation, 69, xviii-454 p.

4802 FLERE, S. "Reforma visokog obrazovanja u nas" (The reform of our higher education), *Gledišta* 11(3), mar 70 : 371-381. [Yugoslavia.]

4803 FROESE, L. et al. *Aktuelle Bildungskritik und Bildungsreform in den USA* (Present critique of education and education reform in the USA). Heidelberg, Quelle und Meyer, 68, 258 p. CR: M. MARKEFTA, *Kölner Z. Soziol. u. soz.-Psychol.* 22(1), mar 70 : 196-198.

4804 GUDIJIGA, Z. G. C. "Maturation de l'enseignement supérieur et universitaire au Congo", *Congo-Afr.* 10(41), jan 70 : 15-32.

4805 GUTEK, G. L. *An historical introduction to American education.* New York, Crowell, 70, 246 p.

4806 HANDLIN, O.; HANDLIN, M. F. *The American college and American culture; socialization as a function of higher education.* New York, McGraw-Hill, 70, 104 p.

4807 HANF, T. *Erziehungswesen in Gesellschaft und Politik des Libanon* (Education in society and politics in Lebanon). Bielefeld, Bertelsmann Universitätsverlag, 69, 397 p.

4808 HARA, Y.; YANO, M. "Changes in education in postwar Japan: a graphic explanation", *Develop. Econ.* 7(4), dec 69 : 640-655.

4809 HERRIOTT, R. E.; HODGKINS, B. *Sociocultural context and the American school: an open-systems analysis of educational opportunity; final report.* Tallahassee, Center for the Study of Education, Florida State University, 69, 371 p.

4810 "Higher education in Spain", *Minerva* 8(2), 1970 : 268-283; 8(3), 1970 : 428-439.

4811   HOBART, C. W. "Eskimo education in the Canadian Arctic", *Canad. R. Sociol. Anthro-
        pol.* 7(1), feb 70 : 49-70.
4812   HODGKINSON, H. L. *Institutions in transition; a study of change in higher education.*
        Berkeley, Calif., Carnegie Commission on Higher Education, 70, v-169 p. [USA.]
4813   HOYLE, E. "Social theories of education in contemporary Britain", *Soc. Sci. Inform./In-
        form. Sci. soc.* 9(4), aug 70 : 169-186.
4814   HURWITZ, E.; MAIDMENT, R. (eds.). *Criticism, conflict, and change; readings in American
        education.* New York, Dodd, Mead, 70, xii-484 p.
4815   HYUNG-CHAN KIM. "Ideology and indoctrination in the development of North Korean
        education", *Asian Surv.* 9(11), nov 69 : 831-841.
4816   ITZKOFF, S. W. *Cultural pluralism and American education.* Scranton, Pa., International
        Textbook Co., 69, xi-202 p.
4817   JABEAU, C. "Essai sur la réforme administrative des établissements scolaires. De
        l'empirisme à la rationalité", *R. Inst. Sociol.* (3), 1970 : 537-585. [Belgique.]
4818   JOLLY, R. *Planning education for African development; economic and manpower perspec-
        tives.* Nairobi, East African Publishing House, 69, xxviii-168 p.
4819   KAEMPER, K. "L'enseignement en République démocratique allemande", *Allem.
        aujourd.* 20, nov-dec 69 : 77-92.
4820   KANDEL, I. L. (ed.). *Twenty-five years of American education.* New York, Arno Press,
        69, xvi-469 p.
4821   KAŠIN, M. P.; ČEHARIN, È. M. (eds.). *Narodnoe obrazovanie v RSFSR* (National
        education in the RFSFR). Moskva, Prosveščenie, 70, 352 p.
4822   KIRST, M. W. (ed.). *The politics of education at the local, State, and Federal levels.*
        Berekely, Calif., McCutchan Publishing Corporation, 70, xiii-406 p. [USA.]
4823   LABBENS, J. "Tradición y modernismo en la universidad de Chile" (Tradition and
        modernism in the Chilean university), *Aportes* 15, jan 70 : 13-27.
4824   MARQUARDT, W. F.; CORTRIGHT, R. W. "Education in Latin America", *Latin Amer.
        Res. R.* 3(3), 1968 : 47-69.
4825   MATEJKO, A. "Planning and tradition in Polish higher education", *Minerva* 7(4), 1969 :
        621-648
4826   MATTHIJSSEN, M. A.; VERVOORT, C. E. (eds.). *Education in Europe. Sociological research/
        L'éducation en Europe. Recherches sociologiques.* The Hague, Mouton, 70, xiv-317 p.
        [Proceedings of the European Seminar on Sociology of Education, Noordwijk aan
        Zee, 2-6 September 1968.]
4827   MILBERG, H. *Schulpolitik in der pluralistischen Gesellschaft. Die politischen und sozialen
        Aspekte der Schulreform in Hamburg 1890-1935* (School policy in a pluralist society.
        Social and political aspects of school reform in Hamburg, 1890 to 1935). Hamburg,
        Leibniz-Verlag, 70, 576 p.
4828   MILLER GUERRA, J. P.; SEDAS NUNEZ, A. "A crise da universidade em Portugal: reflexões
        e sugestões" (The crisis of the University in Portugal: reflections and suggestions),
        Análise soc. 7(25-26), 1969 : 5-49.
4829   ORFIELD, G. *The reconstruction of Southern education: the schools and the 1964 Civil
        Rights Act.* New York, Wiley-Interscience, 69, 376 p. CR: M. M. WILLEY, *Amer.
        sociol. R.* 35(4), aug 70 : 793-794. [USA.]
4830   ORGANIZATION FOR ECONOMIC CO-OPERATION AND DEVELOPMENT. *Reviews of national
        policies for education—Ireland.* Paris, OECD, 70, 140 p.
4831   ORGANIZATION FOR ECONOMIC CO-OPERATION AND DEVELOPMENT. *Reviews of national
        policies for education—Italy.* Paris, OECD, 69, 276 p.
4832   PRICE, R. F. *Education in Communist China.* London, Routledge and K. Paul, 70, xix-308 p.
4833   PROST, A. "Université et société dans la France contemporaine", *Écon. et Human.* 193,
        mai-jun 70 : 36-52.
4834   REIMANN, H. *Höhere Schule und Hochschule in den USA* (Secondary school and Uni-
        versity in the USA). Weinheim-Berlin-Basel, Beltz, 70, vii-379 p.
4835   RICOEUR, P.; CHAPUIS, R. "L'université, le pouvoir, la révolution", *Polit. aujourd.* 4,
        apr 70 : 12-25. [France.]
4836   "Riforma della scuola secondaria (La)" (The reform of secondary school), *Scuola e
        Città* 20(10), oct 69 : 467-532. [Europe.]
4837   "Rights and responsibilities: the university's dilemma", *Daedalus* 99(3), 1970 : xiv-
        531-721. [USA.]

4838   ROTHE, F. K. *Stammeserziehung und Schulerziehung. Eine Feldstudie zum Kulturwandel in der Republik Sudan* (Tribal education and school education. A study of the field of culture change in the Republic of Sudan). Braunschweig, Westermann, 69, 160 p.

4839   RUBIO, J. *La enseñanza superior en España* (Higher education in Spain). Madrid, Ed. Gredos, 69, 241 p.

4840   SCHIAVONE, M.; AVVEDUTO, S. "La diversificazione dell'insegnamento superiore". Il caso dell'Italia" (Diversification of higher education. The Italian case), *Quad. Sci. soc.* 8(3), 1969 : 278-309.

4841   SCHWARTZ, N. B. "Limited school progress and institutional incompatibility: a Guatemalan case", *Civilizations* 20(2), 1970 : 240-260.

4842   SILBERMAN, C. E. *Crisis in the classroom; the remaking of American education.* New York, Random House, 70, xiv-552 p.

4843   SILVA, G. B. *A educação secundária; perspectiva histórica e teoria* (Secondary education; an historical and theoretical perspective). São Paulo, Companhia Editôra Nacional, 69, 422 p. [Brazil.]

4844   SOULEZ, P. "Sociologie de la population scolaire en Côte d'Ivoire", *C. Ét. afr.* 9(4), oct-dec 69 : 527-545.

4845   TEIXEIRA, A. *Educação no Brasil* (Education in Brasil). São Paulo, Companhia Editora Nacional, 69, 385 p.

4846   THOMAS, T. M. *Indian educational reforms in cultural perspective.* Delhi, S. Chand, 70, xv-312 p.

4847   UNESCO. Regional Office for Education in Asia, Bangkok. *Progress of education in the Asia region: statistical review.* Bangkok, UNESCO, 69, 211 p.

4848   "University reform in France", *Minerva* 7(4), 1969 : 706-727.

4849   "University reform in Germany", *Minerva* 8(2), 1970 : 242-267.

4850   "University reform in Japan", *Minerva* 8(4), 1970 : 581-593.

4851   VOGT, H. *Bildung und Erziehung in der DDR; sozialistisch-industriegesellschaftliche Curriculum-Reform in Kindergarten, Schule und Berufsbildung* (Culture and education in the German Democratic Republic; the socialist, industrial societal curriculum reform of Kindergarten and professional formation). Stuttgart, E. Klett, 69, 313-1 p.

4852   VOSTER, W. "The structure of education in the Netherlands", *Planning Develop. Netherl.* 3(1-2), 1969 : 1-16.

4853   WALLERSTEIN, I. *University in turmoil: the politics of change.* New York, Atheneum, 69, 147 p. CR: W. C. RAMSHAW, *Amer. sociol. R.* 35(1), feb 70 : 168-169. [USA.]

4854   WARDLE, D. *English popular education 1780-1970.* Cambridge, Eng., University Press, 70, viii-182 p.

4855   WILSON, J. D.; STAMP, R. M.; AUDET, L. P. *Canadian education: a history.* Scarborough, Ont., Prentice-Hall of Canada, 70, xiv-528 p.

4856   WOLFF, J. H. *Bildungsplanung für Entwicklungsländer. Ein Modell und seine Anwendung auf den Kongo-Kinshasa* (Education planning in developing countries. A model and its application in Congo Kinshasa). Bielefeld, Bertelsmann Universitätsverlag, 69, 154 p.

4857   WYATT, D. K. *The politics of reform in Thailand education in the reign of King Chulalongkorn.* New Haven, Yale University Press, 69, xix-425 p.

E SOCIAL CHANGE
ÉVOLUTION SOCIALE

E.0 GENERAL STUDIES
ÉTUDES GÉNÉRALES

[See also / Voir aussi: 248, 288, 321, 612, 616, 1467, 1737, 1738, 1746, 1748, 3362, 3368, 3390, 3714, 4012, 4018, 4316, 4366, 5310, 5315]

4858 APPELBAUM, R. P. *Theories of social change*. Chicago, Markham Publishing Co., 70, 138 p.

4859 ATTESLANDER, P. "Soziologie und Planung" (Sociology and planning), *Mens en Mij* 44(6), nov-dec 69 : 469-478.

4860 AUJOULAT, L. P. *Action sociale et développement*. Paris, A. Colin, 69, 398 p.

4861 BAECHLER, J. *Les phénomènes révolutionnaires*. Paris, Presses universitaires de France, 70, 260 p.

4862 BEALS, C. *The nature of revolution*. New York, Crowell, 70, 296 p.

4863 BENNIS, W. G.; BENNE, K. D.; CHIN, R. (eds.). *The planning of change*. New York, Holt, Rinehart and Winston, 69, 627 p. CR: G. L. WILBER, *Amer. sociol. R.* 35(1), feb 70 : 142-143.

4864 BERGER, P. L.; NEUHAUS, J. *Movement and revolution*. Garden City, N. Y., Doubleday, 70, 240 p.

4865 BODENHEIMER, S. J. "The ideology of developmentalism: American political science's paradigm-surrogate for Latin American studies", *Berkeley J. Sociol.* 15, 1970 : 95-137.

4866 BOULDING, K. E. *A primer on social dynamics; history as dialectics and development*. New York, Free Press, 70, viii-153 p.

4867 BURGER, W. "Local initiative and the planning process in developing countries", *Sociol. rur.* 10(1), 1970 : 57-73.

4868 BURIN, F. S.; SHELL, K. L. (eds.). *Politics, law, and social change: selected essays of Otto Kirchheimer*. New York, Columbia University Press, 69, 483 p. CR: H. L. ROSS, *Amer. sociol. R.* 35(2), apr 70 : 350.

4869 CAMPBELL, D. T. "Variation and selective retention in socio-cultural evolution", *General System* (14), 1969 : 69-86.

4870 CAVALLI, L. *Il mutamento sociale. Sette ricerche sulla civiltà occidentale* (Social change. Seven researches on Western civilization). Bologna, Il Mulino, 70, xviii-626 p.

4871 DANCKWERTS, D. *et al. Die Sozialwissenschaften in der Strategie der Entwicklungspolitik* (The social sciences in the strategy of development policy). Frankfurt-am-Main, Suhrkamp, 70, 175 p.

4872 DARLINGTON, C. D. *The evolution of man and society*. New York, Simon and Schuster, 69, 753 p.

4873 DEUTSCH, M. "Organizational and conceptual barriers to social change", *J. soc. Issues* 25(4), 1969 : 5-18.

4874 DOVRING, F. "The principle of acceleration: a non dialectical theory of progress", *Comp. Stud. Soc. Hist.* 11(4), oct 69 : 413-425. With a comment by T. S. KUHN: 426-430 and a counter-comment by F. DOVRING: 431-432.

4875 EISENSTADT, S. N. "La sociologie politique et les expériences de modernisation des sociétés", *Sociol. Soc.* 2(1), mai 70 : 25-41.

4876 EISENSTADT, S. N. "Some observations on the dynamics of traditions", *Comp. Stud. Soc. Hist.* 11(4), oct 69 : 451-475.

4877 ELLUL, J. *Autopsie de la révolution*. Paris, Calmann-Lévy, 69, 356 p.

4878 FALS BORDA, O. "Algunos problemas prácticos de la sociología de la crísis" (Some practical problems of the sociology of crisis), *R. mexic. Sociol.* 31(4), oct-dec 69 : 767-793.

4879 FALS BORDA, O. "La crísis social y la orientación sociológica: una réplica" (The social crisis and its sociological orientation: a reply), *Aportes* 15, jan 70 : 62-76.

4880 GALIEV, G. S. "Marsistsko-leninsko učenie ob obščestvennom progresse" (The Marxist-Leninist teaching on social progress), *Učen. Zap. (Kujbyš. plan. Inst. Progress uslov kommun. Formacij)* (15), 1968 : 3-14.

4881 GALTUNG, J. "On the future of human society", *Futures (Guildford)* 2(2), jun 70 : 132-142.

4882 GALTUNG, J. "Pluralismo e futuro della società umana" (Pluralism and future of human society), *Futuribili* 4(23), jun 70 : 6-27.

4883 GALTUNG, J. "Sistemas feudales, violencia estructural y teoria estructural de las revoluciones" (Feudal systems, structural violence and structural theory of revolution), *R. latinoamer. Cienc. polit.* 1(1), apr 70 : 25-79.

4884 GERMANI, G. *Sociología de la modernización; estudios teóricos, metodológicos, y aplicados a América Latina* (Sociology of modernization; theoretical, methodological and applied studies in Latin America). Buenos Aires, Paidós, 69, 225 p.

4885 GLASTRA VAN LOON, J. "Social science and social change", *Develop. and Change* 1(1), 1969 : 35-49.

4886 GUTENSCHWAGER, A. C. "Social reality and social change", *Soc. Res.* 37(1), 1970 : 48-70.

4887 HAGE, J.; AIKEN, M. *Social change in complex organizations.* New York, Random House, 70, xvi-170 p.

4888 HOERNING, K. H. *Secondary modernization: societal changes of newly developing nations, a theoretical essay in comparative sociology.* Denver, University of Denver, 70, 46 p.

4889 ILCHMAN, W. F.; UPHOFF, N. T. *The political economy of change.* Berkeley, University of California Press, 69, 316 p. CR: K. E. BOULDING, *Amer. polit. Sci. R.* 64(2), jun 70 : 603-604.

4890 INKELES, A. "Making men modern: on the causes and consequences of individual change in six developing countries", *Amer. J. Sociol.* 75(2), sep 69 : 208-225.

4891 JOHNSON, C. *Revolutionary change.* London, University of London Press, 69, 191 p. CR: D. G. MacRAE, *Brit. J. Sociol.* 21(2), jun 70 : 229.

4892 KELLY, G. A.; BROWN, C. W. Jr. (eds.). *Struggles in the State: sources and patterns of world revolution.* New York, Wiley, 70, xi-511 p.

4893 KLAGES, H. "Measuring social innovations", *Sociol. int. (Berlin)* 8(1), 1970 : 69-77.

4894 KLOČKOV, V. M. "Razum mass i obščestvennoe razvitie" (Masses motives and social development), *Učen. Zap. (Kujbyš. gos. pedag. Inst.)* (62), 1969 : 3-30.

4895 KOVALEV, A. M. *Social'naja revoljucija* (Social revolution). Moskva, Vysšaja Škola, 69, 127 p.

4896 KUNKEL, J. H. *Society and economic growth; a behavioral perspective of social change.* New York, Oxford University Press, 70, xvi-368 p.

4897 LECRAMPE, S. *Le changement social.* Paris, Scodel, 69, 103 p.

4898 LEYS, C. (ed.). *Politics and change in developing countries: studies in the theory and practice of development.* London, Cambridge University Press, 69, xi-289 p.

4899 LOJKINE, J. "Pour une analyse marxiste du changement social", *Sociol. Trav.* 11(2), jul-sep 69 : 259-286.

4900 MACHIDA, T. "Kindaika no shinten to kindaikaron no tenkan" (Progress of modernization and theory conversion), *Shakai Kagaku Tokyû* 14(1), 1968 : 87-100.

4901 MANSÛR, M. I. *al-Thawrat wal-taqhayyur al-'ijtimâ'î* (The revolution and social change). Iskenderîyat Matba'at al-Mişrî, 69, 194 p.

4902 McCOLL, R. W. "The insurgent State: territorial bases of revolution", *A. Assoc. Amer. Geogr.* 59(4), dec 69 : 613-631.

4903 McCORMACK, T. "The Protestant ethic and the spirit of socialism", *Brit. J. Sociol.* 20(3), sep 69 : 266-276. [As instrument to modernization.]

4904 MENEZES, J. R. DE. *Filosofia social do desenvolvimento* (Social philosophy of development). Recife, Faculdade de Ciéncias da Administração de Pernambuco (da FESP), 69, 203 p.

4905 MISES, L. VON. *Theory and history; an interpretation of social and economic evolution.* New Rochelle, N. Y., Arlington House, 69, ix-384 p.

4906   Bibl. XIX-4443. MORSE, C. *et al. Modernization by design: social change in the twentieth century.* CR: R. W. BENJAMIN, *Amer. polit. Sci. R.* 64(1), mar 70 : 228-230; J. FORSTER, *Amer. sociol. R.* 35(2), apr 70 : 345-346.

4907   MUSTO, E. A. "Hacia el mensuramiento sociológico del desarrollo" (Towards the sociological measurement of development), *Anu. Sociol. Pueblos ibér.* (4), 1968 : 120-137.

4908   NAČKEBIJA, Ja. "Problema ponjatija obščestvennogo progressa" (Problem of the idea of social progress), *Trudy (Tbilis. gos. pedag. Inst.)* (22), 1969 : 25-48.

4909   NAGEL, S. S. "Overview of law and social change", *Amer. behav. Scientist* 13(4), mar-apr 70 : 485-491.

4910   NASCHITZ, A. M. "Les rapports entre le développement social et économique de la société et le développement du droit", *R. roum. Sci. soc. Sér. Sci. jur.* 14(1), 1970 : 3-16.

4911   NATALACIO, L. S.; HEREFORD, C. F.; NATALACIO, D. S. (eds.). *La contribución de las ciencias psicológicas y del comportamiento al desarrollo social y económico de los pueblos* (The contribution of psychological and behavioral sciences to economic and social development of peoples). 2 vols. México, Sociedad Interamericana de Psicología, 69, [Proceedings of the XIth Interamerican Congress of Psychology. México, decembre 17-22, 1967.]

4912   Bibl. XIX-4446. NISBET, R. A. *Social change and history: aspects of the Western theory of development.* CR: N. JACOBS, *Amer. J. Sociol.* 75(5), mar 70 : 874-876; J. C. DAVIES, *Amer. polit. Sci. R.* 64(2), jun 70 : 618-619; K. SYMMONS, *Amer. sociol. R.* 35(2), apr 70 : 343-344.

4913   Bibl. XIX-4447. NISBET, R. A. *Tradition and revolt: historical and sociological essays.* CR: H. ELSNER, Jr. *Amer. sociol. R.* 35(1), feb 70 : 122-123.

4914   PEREIRA, L. *Ensaios de sociologia do desenvolvimento* (Essays on sociology of development). São Paulo Livraria Pioneira Editôra, 70, 158 p.

4915   PEREIRA, L. (comp.). *Subdesenvolvimento e desenvolvimento* (Underdevelopment and development). Rio de Janeiro, Zahar Editores, Livrarias Editôras Reunidas, 69, 230 p.

4916   PERROUX, F. "L'innovation et l'économie de 'pleine innovation' ", *Écon. appl.* 23(2-3), 1970 : 181-216.

4917   PIERIS, R. *Studies in the sociology of development.* Rotterdam, Rotterdam University Press, 70, viii-222 p.

4918   PONSIOEN, J. A. *The analysis of social change reconsidered. A sociological study.* 3. print., rev., and enl. ed. The Hague, Mouton, 69, 215 p.

4919   REZSOHÁZY, R. *Temps social et développement.* Bruxelles, La Renaissance du Livre, 70, 248 p.

4920   RÖPKE, J. *Primitive Wirtschaft, Kulturwandel und Diffusion von Neureungen; Theorie und Realität der wirtschaftlichen Entwicklung aus ethnosoziologischer und kulturanthropologischer Sicht* (Primitive economy, cultural evolution and innovation diffusion; theory and reality of economic development from a viewpoint of ethno-sociology and cultural anthropology). Tübingen, Mohr, 70, ix-207 p.

4921   ROSZAK, T. *The making of a counter culture—reflections on the technocratic society and its youthful opposition.* London, Faber and Faber, 70, xiv-303 p. CR: J. KIRK, *Amer. J. Sociol.* 75(5), mar 70 : 893-896.

4922   SELSAM, H.; GOLDWAY, D.; MARTEL, H. (eds.). *Dynamics of social change; a reader in Marxist social science, from the writings of Marx, Engels and Lenin.* New York, International Publishers, 70, 416 p.

4923   SMITH, D. H. "The fate of personal adjustment in the process of modernization", *Int. J. comp. Sociol.* 11(2), jun 70 : 81-114.

4924   STREETEN, P. "An international critique of development concepts", *Archiv. europ. Sociol.* 11(1), 1970 : 69-80.

4925   VAN LEEUWEN, A. T. *Development through revolution.* New York, Scribner, 70, ix-310 p.

4926   WARNER, A. W.; MORSE, D.; COONEY, T. E. (eds.). *The environment of change.* New York, Columbia University Press, 69, 186 p. CR: P. A. THOMAS, *Amer. sociol. R.* 35(4), aug 70 : 777-778.

4927   ZIMMERMAN, G. *Sozialer Wandel und ökonomische Entwicklung* (Social change and economic development). Stuttgart, Enke Verlag, 69, xi-159 p. CR: H.-G. KRÜSSELBERG, *Kölner Z. Soziol. u. soz.-Psychol.* 22(4), dec 70 : 795-797.

E.1 INFLUENCE OF TECHNOLOGY ON SOCIAL CHANGE
INFLUENCE DE LA TECHNOLOGIE SUR L'ÉVOLUTION SOCIALE

[See also / Voir aussi: **C.851;** 576, 597, 3432, 4352, 4399, 4735]

4928 al-DAHIRI, A. W. M. *The introduction of technology into traditional societies and economies; using Iraq as a case study.* Baghdad, al-Ani Press, 69, vi-253 p.

4929 ARZUMANJAN, A. A. *Ėkonomičeskie problemy obščestvennogo razvitija* (Economic problems of social development). Moskva, Nauka, 68, 626 p.

4930 AVVEDUTO, S. "Natura, dimensioni e costi sociali del 'gap tecnologico' " (Nature, dimensions and social costs of the technological gap), *Quad. Sci. soc.* 8(1-2), 1969 : 5-11.

4931 BARANSON, J. "Role of science and technology, in advancing development of newly industrializing States", *Socio-econ. plan. Sci.* 3(4), dec 69 : 351-383.

4932 BECKER, M. H. "Sociometric location and innovativeness: reformulation and extension of the diffusion model", *Amer. sociol. R.* 35(2), apr 70 : 267-282.

4933 BURKS, R. V. *Technological innovation and political change in Communist Eastern Europe.* Santa Monica, Calif., Rand Corporation, 69, xiii-61 p.

4934 CALDER, N. *Technopolis: social control of the uses of science.* London, McGibbon and Kee; New York, Simon and Schuster, 69, 381 p.

4935 CHASZAR, E. *Science and technology in the theories of social and political alienation.* Washington, George Washington University, 69, 65 p.

4936 COLE, S. "Professional standing and the reception of scientific discoveries", *Amer. J. Sociol.* 76(2), sep 70 : 286-306.

4937 COTTRELL, W. F. *Energy and society; the relation between energy, social change, and economic development.* Westport, Conn., Greenwood Press, 70, xix-330 p.

4938 DOUGLAS, J. D. (ed.). *Freedom and tyranny; social problems in a technological society.* New York, Knopf, 70, xii-289 p.

4939 DRUCKER, P. F. *Technology, management and society; essays.* New York, Harper and Row, 70, x-209 p.

4940 EVANS, T. *The challenge of change; report of a conference on technological change and human development at Jerusalem, 1969.* Oxford-New York, Pergamon Press, 70, ix-190 p.

4941 GALAJ, P. "Industrializacja a procesy przemian spoleczno kulturalnych" (Industrialization and the socio-cultural change process), *Kult. i Społecz.* 14(1), jan-mar 70 : 155-163. [Poland.]

4942 GOUVERNEUR, J. "L'influence de la technologie sur la productivité du travail en pays sous-développé", *Cult. et Dévelop.* 1(4), 1968 : 883-892.

4943 GREGORI, T. R. DE. "Foreign investment and technological diffusion: the case of British colonial Africa", *J. econ. Issues* 2(4), dec 68 : 403-415.

4944 GREGORI, T. R. DE. *Technology and the economic development of the tropical African frontier.* Cleveland, Press of Case Western Reserve University, 69, viii-531 p.

4945 HETZLER, S. A. *Technological growth and social change—achieving modernization.* London, Routledge and Kegan Paul, 69, x-302 p.

4946 HODGES, W. L.; KELLY, M. A. (eds.). *Technological change and human development; an international conference, Jerusalem, April 14-18, 1969.* Ithaca, N. Y., New York State School of Industrial and Labor Relations, 70, xiv-388 p.

4947 IWAUCHI, R. "Adaptation to technological change", *Develop. Econ.* 7(4), dec 69 : 428-450.

4948 LAFFERTY, W. M. "Industrialization and labor response: notes toward the construction of a multi-level data structure", *Acta sociol.* 13(3), 1970 : 161-188.

4949 LEMNIJ, I. *Progresul tehnic și dezvoltarea economica* (Technical progress and economic development). Bucureşti, Academia Republicii Socialiste România, Institutul de Cercetşri Economice, 69, 196 p.

4950 LUCEY, D. I. F.; KALDOR, D. R. *Rural industrialization: the impact of industrialization on two rural communities in Western Ireland.* London, G. Chapman, 69, 208 p.

4951 MATSUSHITA, H. "Utilità sociale delle tecnologie" (Social utility of technology), *Futuribili* 6(24), jul 70 : 24-35.

4952 MBOYA, T. J. "La technique et le développement de l'Afrique: aperçu critique", *Impact* 19(4), oct-dec 69 : 371-377.

4953   MESTHENE, E. G. *Technological change: its impact on man and society.* Cambridge, Mass., Harvard University Press, 70, ix-127 p.

4954   MICHAEL, D. N. "Technologia e sviluppi sociali" (Technology and social developments), *Futuribili* 3(13-14), aug-sep 69 : 52-70.

4955   NALLO, A. R. DI. "Tecnomorfismo e progresso sociale. Riflessioni dalla tematica di Marshall McLuhan" (Technomorphism and social progress. Reflection on the central theme in Marshall McLuhan), *Sociologia (Roma)* 4(3), sep 70 : 5-60.

4956   NISKIER, A. *Ciência e tecnologia para o desenvolvimento* (Science and technology for development). Rio, Editorial Bruguera, 70, 200 p. [Brazil.]

4957   OMAROV, A. "Ékonomičeskij i social'nyj aspekty naučno-tehničeskogo progressa" (Economic and social aspects of scientific and technical progress), *Vopr. Ékon.* 22(9), sep 70 : 95-103.

4958   RATIONALISIERUNGS-KURATORIUM DER DEUTSCHEN WIRTSCHAFT. *Wirtschaftliche und soziale Aspekte des technischen Wandels in der Bundesrepublik Deutschland* (Economic and social aspects of technical changes in the German Federal Republic), Frankfurt-am-Main, Europäische Verlagsanstalt, 70, 387 p.

4959   RIHTA, R. "Naučno-tehničeskaja revoljucija i razvitie čeloveka" (The scientific and technical revolution and the fulfillment of the individual), *Vopr. Filos.* 23(2), feb 70 : 56-66.

4960   ROSE, J. *Technological injury—the effect of technological advances on environment, life, and society.* London-New York, Gordon and Breach Science Publishers, 69, xx-224 p.

4961   ROSENBERG, N. "The direction of technological change: inducement mechanisms and focusing devices", *Econ. Develop. cult. Change* 18(1, *Part I*), oct 69 : 1-24.

4962   RUGGIERINI, M. G. "Sviluppo tecnologico e progresso sociale" (Technological development and social progress), *Quad. Azione soc.* 21(6), jun 70 : 855-867.

4963   SVALASTOGA, K. "Differential rates of change and road accidents in Western Europe and North America", *Acta sociol.* 13(2), 1970 : 73-95.

4964   "Technologie et société", *Chron. soc. France* 77(6), dec 69 : 3-117.

4965   "Technologia e società" (Technology and society), *Form. e Lav.* (39), sep-oct 69 : 1-105.

4966   UNESCO. *Science and technology in Asian development.* Paris, Unesco, 70, 216 p.

4967   VALKONEK, T. "On the theory of diffusion of innovations", *Sociol. rur.* 10(2), 1970 : 162-179.

4968   VIDYARTHI, L. P. *Socio-cultural implications of industrialization in India; a case study of tribal Bihar.* Ranchi, Council of Social and Cultural Research, Bihar, Department of Anthropology, Ranchi University, 70, xxiii-552 p.

**E.2   SOCIAL FACTORS OF ECONOMIC DEVELOPMENT
FACTEURS SOCIAUX DU DÉVELOPPEMENT ÉCONOMIQUE**

[See also / Voir aussi: 663, 674, 675, 1105, 1125, 1144, 1146, 1391, 1396, 2431, 3056, 4167, 4535, 4818, 4987, 5093]

4969   BLEDEL, R. *Poder político y desarrollo económico* (Political power and economic development). Buenos Aires, Juárez Editor, 69, 308 p.

4970   BON ESPASANDÍN, M. "Tenencia, distribución y explotación de la tierra en el Uruguay. Sus implicaciones con el desarrollo" (Land tenure, distribution and exploitation in Uruguay. Its implication with development), *Bol. urug. Sociol.* 8(15-16-17), dec 69 : 3-34.

4971   BROKENSHA, D.; PEARSALL, M. (eds.). *The anthropology of development in sub-Saharan Africa.* Lexington, University Press of Kentucky, 69, 100 p.

4972   BRUCK, N. K. "Higher education and economic development in Central America", *R. soc. Econ.* 27(2), sep 69 : 160-180.

4973   CAPPELETTI VIDAL, R. "La marginalidad política como factor de innovación en áreas subdesarrolladas" (Political marginality as a factor of innovation in underdeveloped areas), *Foro int.* 10(4), apr-jun 70 : 425-435.

4974   CARDOSO, F. H. "Les obstacles structurels et institutionnels au développement", *Sociol. et Soc.* 2(2), nov 70 : 297-315.

4975   CARDOSO, F. H. *Sociologie du développement en Amérique latine*. Paris, Éditions Anthropos, 69, 264 p.

4976   CINTA, R. G. "Desarrollo económico, urbanización y radicalismo político" (Economic development, urbanization and political radicalism), *R. mexic. Sociol.* 31(3), jul-sep 69 : 643-688.

4977   COSTA PINTO, L. DE A. *Desenvolvimento económico e transição social* (Economic development and social change). 2nd enl. ed. Rio de Janeiro, Civilização Brasileira, 70, 156 p.

4978   "Éducation et développement", *Tiers-Monde* 11(41), jan-mar 70 : 1-218.

4979   FERNANDES, F. "Société de classes et sous-développement au Brésil", *Cult. et Dévelop.* 1(4), 1968 : 843-882.

4980   FERNANDES, F. "Universidad y desarrollo" (University and development), *Aportes* 17, jul 70 : 133-158.

4981   FROELICH, J. C. "Les structures sociales traditionnelles et le développement", *Genève-Afr.* 8(2), 1969 : 36-46.

4982   GALE, L. *Education and development in Latin America, with special reference to Colombia and some comparison with Guyana, South America*. London, Routledge and K. Paul, 69, xiv-178 p.

4983   GARCÍA, A. *Estructura social y desarrollo latinoamericanos* (Social structure and Latin American development). Santiago de Chile, Instituto de Capacitación e Investigación en Reforma Agraria, 69, 134 p.

4984   GLASSMAN, R. M. "The limiting social and structural conditions for Latin American modernization", *Soc. Res.* 36(2), 1969 : 182-205.

4985   GOSSELIN, G. "Travail, tradition et développement en pays Bisa", *Cah. ORSTOM Sér. Sci. hum.* 7(1), 1970 : 29-46.

4986   GOUVEIA, A. J.; HAVIGHURST, R. J. *Ensino médio e desenvolvimento* (Secondary education and development). São Paulo, Edições Melhoramentos, 69, 237 p. [Brazil.]

4987   HAVIGHURST, R. J.; GOUVEIA, A. J. *Brazilian secondary education and socio-economic development*. New York, Praeger Publishers, 69, xxvi-321 p.

4988   HOPKINS, N. S. "Socialism and social change in rural Mali", *J. mod. Afr. Stud.* 7(3), oct 69 : 457-467.

4989   KAMERSCHEN, D. R. "Population growth and economic development", *Schweizer. Z. Volkswirtsch. Statist.* 106(1), mar 70 : 79-88.

4990   KOTHARI, D. S. *Education, science, and national development*. Bombay-New York, Asia Publishing House, 70, xi-96 p.

4991   LORETO, S. "Reforma agrária no Brasil—implicações sociológicas" (Agrarian reform in Brazil—sociological implications), *R. brasil. Estud. polít.* 27, jul 69 : 95-150.

4992   MACHADO DE AMORIM, F. "Educação e desenvolvimento" (Education and development), *R. Adm. públ. (Rio de Janeiro)* (2), 1968 : 167-210.

4993   MACHLUP, F. *Education and economic growth*. Lincoln, University of Nebraska Press, 70, ix-106 p.

4994   McLEAN, D. (ed.). *It's people that matter; education for social change*. Sydney, Angus and Robertson, 69, xi-352 p. [Australia.]

4995   MEDELLÍN, R. A. "La dinámica de distanciamiento económico social de México" (The dynamics of socio-economic distanciation in Mexico), *R. mexic. Sociol.* 31(3), jul-sep 69 : 513-546.

4996   MEDINA, C. A. DE. "Família e desenvolvimento" (Family and development), *Amér. lat.* 12(2), apr-jun 69 : 53-65.

4997   MICKLIN, M. "Demographic, economic and social change in Latin America: an examination of causes and consequences", *J. develop. Areas* 4(2), jan 70 : 173-197.

4998   MITCHELL, J. C. "Tribe and social change in South Central Africa: a situation approach", *J. Asian Afr. Stud.* 5(1-2), jan-apr 70 : 83-101.

4999   MOXLEY, R. L.; WEIN, F. "Socio-economic inequalities, social rigidity and the relation to development", *Cornell J. soc. Relat.* 4(2), 1969 : 1-16.

5000   PITT, D. *Tradition and economic progress in Samoa—a case study of the role of traditional social institutions in economic development*. Oxford, Clarendon Press, 70, xi-295 p.

5001   REYNAUD, P.-L. *Seuils de modernisation et "Société de l'être". Étude de la psychologie économique du développement. France 1958-1959. URSS. Grèce. Turquie*. Paris, M.-Th. Génin, 69, 278 p.

5002   RUDEBECK, L. "Developmental pressure and political limits: a Tunisian example", *J. mod. Afr. Stud.* 8(2), jul 70 : 173-198.

5003   SECOMSKI, K. *Czynniki społeczne we współczesnym rozwoju gospodarczym* (Social factors and contemporary economic development). Warszawa, Wiedza Powszechna, 70, 115 p.

5004   SEGAL, D. R. "Differential institutional development in transitional society", *J. develop. Areas* 4(2), jan 70 : 157-173.

5005   SOARES, G. A. D. "Desarrollo económico y estructura de clase: notas para una teoría" (Economic development and class structure: notes for a theory), *R. parag. Sociol.* 6(15), mai-aug 69 : 49-82.

5006   URQUIDI, V. L. "El desarrollo económico y el crecimiento de la población" (Economic development and population growth), *R. Econ. (México)* 32(4), apr 69 : 117-122. [Latin America.]

5007   WIATR, J. J. "Społeczne czynnik rozwoju ekonomicznego" (Social factors of economic development), *Nowe Drogi* 24(5), 1970 : 120-134. [Poland.]

5008   ZEMAN, F. "Úloha vzdelania v ekonomickom raste" (The role of education in economic growth), *Plán. Hospod.* 23(3), mar 70 : 68-77. [Czechoslovakia.]

E.3   **HISTORY OF HUMAN SOCIETIES**
       HISTOIRE DES SOCIÉTÉS HUMAINES

[See also / Voir aussi: 36, 617, 943, 1121, 1151, 1247, 1455, 1456, 2110, 2313, 2481, 3399, 3518, 3561, 3729, 3738, 3748, 3750, 4857, 4944, 5468]

5009   ARANA, F. *Historia economíca y social argentina* (Argentine economic and social history). Buenos Aires, Editorial El Coloquio, 69, 373 p.

5010   ASIA-ETHNOS KENKYU-KAI (ed.). *Asia Kindai-ka no Kenkyu* (Study of modernization of Asia). Tokyo, Ochanomizu-shobo, 69, 413 p.

5011   AZAMKULOV, H. A. *Likvidacija tehniko-êkonomičeskoj otstalosti narodov sovetskogo vostoka* (Liquidation of technical and economic backwardness of Eastern Soviet peoples). Dušanbe, Irfon, 69, 180 p.

5012   BAER, G. *Studies in the social history of modern Egypt.* Chicago, University of Chicago Press, 69, xx-259 p.

5013   BANKS, J. A. (ed.). *Studies in British society.* London, Routledge and K. Paul, 69, 220 p. CR: M. LANE, *Acta sociol.* 13(1), 1970 : 57-58.

5014   BAUMANNS, H. L.; GROSSMANN, H. *Deformierte Gesellschaft? Soziologie der Bundesrepublik Deutschland* (Deformed society? Sociology of the German Federal Republic). Reinbek, Rowohlt, 69, 154 p.

5015   BETANCOURT ROA, G. "Revolución cubana y cambio social" (The Cuban Revolution and social change), *Bol. urug. Sociol.* 8(15-16-17), dec 69 : 119-128.

5016   BILL, J. A. "Modernization and reform from above: the case of Iran", *J. Polit.* 32(1), feb 70 : 19-40.

5017   BOBROWSKI, C. "Dix ans de planification dans les pays sous-développés", *Archiv. europ. Sociol.* 11(1), 1970 : 94-104.

5018   BOSE, A. B. "Directed social change in India", *Ind. J. soc. Wk* 29(4), jan 69 : 353-360.

5019   "Cambios en Bolivia" (Changes in Bolivia), *Aportes* 17, jul 70 : 31-132.

5020   Bibl. XIX-4584. CARD, B. Y. *Trends and change in Canadian society: their challenge to Canadian youth.* CR: P. C. PINEO, *Amer. sociol. R.* 35(3), jun 70 : 615.

5021   CARDOSO, F. H. "Les agents sociaux de changement et de conservation en Amérique latine", *Christ soc.* 77(9-12), sep-dec 69 : 441-469.

5022   CARDOSO, F. H. *Mudanças sociais na América Latina* (Social changes in Latin America). São Paulo, Difusão Européia do Livro, 69, 238 p.

5023   CARDOSO, F. H.; FALETTO, E. *Dependência e desenvolvimento na América Latina; ensaio de interpretação sociológica* (Dependence and development in Latin America; a tentative sociological interpretation). Rio de Janeiro, Livrarias Editôras Reunidas, 70, 143 p. [Also published in Spanish, Mexico, Siglo Veintiuno Editores, 69, 166 p.]

5024   CHARLES, G. P. "Haití: esencia y realidad del desarrollo" (Haiti: essence and reality of its development), *R. mexic. Sociol.* 31(3), jul-sep 69 : 589-608.

5025   COHN, E. J. *Turkish economic, social, and political change; the development of a more prosperous and open society.* New York, Praeger Publishers, 70, xiv-196 p.

5026   CORTÉS OBREGÓN, J. *et al. México, el dilema del desarrollo: democracia o autoritarismo* (Mexico, the dilemma of development: democracy or authoritarism). México, Academia Mexicana de Ciencias Humanas, 69, 32 p.

5027   COSTA PINTO, L. A.; COSTA PINTO, S. B. "La crísis latinoamericana. Fundamentación de un modelo teórico para su análisis sociológico" (The Latin American crisis. Creation of a theoretical model for its sociological analysis), *Aportes* 18, oct 70 : 7-15; *Cuad. Amer.* 170(3), mai-jun 70 : 90-100.

5028   CRIST, R. E. "Influences of some physical and cultural factors on the socio-political evolution of Colombia", *R. geogr. (Rio de Janeiro)* 68, jun 68 : 7-18.

5029   DOUTRELOUX, A. "Tradition et modernité dans le développement", *Cult. et Dévelop.* 2(1), 1969-1970 : 3-19. [Congo, Kinshasa.]

5030   DOWSE, R. E. *Modernization in Ghana and the USSR—a comparative study.* London, Routledge and Kegan Paul, 69, 107 p.

5031   EISENSTADT, S. N.; YOSEF, R. B.; ADLER, C. (eds.). *Integration and development in Israel.* New York, Praeger, 70, xv-703 p.

5032   FALS BORDA, O. *Subversion and social change in Colombia.* New York-London, Columbia University Press, 69, xiv-238 p. CR: E. WILLEMS, *Kölner Z. Soziol. u. soz.-Psychol.* 22(4), dec 70 : 801-803.

5033   FILMER, P. "The literary imagination and the explanation of socio-cultural change in modern Britain", *Archiv. europ. Sociol.* 10(2), 1969 : 271-291.

5034   FORSTER, J. *Social process in New Zealand; readings in sociology.* Auckland, Longman Paul, 69, viii-307 p.

5035   FRANK, A. G. "Dependencia económica, estructura de clases y política de subdesarrollo en Latinoamérica" (Economic dependency, class structure and politics of underdevelopment in Latin America), *Bol. urug. Sociol.* 8(15-16-17), dec 69 : 129-182.

5036   FRANK, A. G. *Latin America: underdevelopment of revolution; essays on the development for underdevelopment and the immediate enemy.* New York, Monthly Review Press, 70, xviii-409 p.

5037   FURTADO, C. "Desarrollo y estancamiento en América Latina—un enfoque estructuralista" (Development and stagnation in Latin America—a structuralist survey), *Invest. econ.* 29(113), jan-mar 70 : 43-73.

5038   FURTADO, C. "Planification et réformes de structure en Amérique latine", *Archiv. europ. Sociol.* 11(1), 1970 : 81-93.

5039   FUSE, T. "Religion and socio-economic development: the case of Japan. A study in the sociology of development", *Soc. Compass* 17(1), 1970 : 157-170.

5040   GARCÍA, A. *La estructura del atraso en América Latina* (The structure of backwardness in Latin America). Buenos Aires, Editorial Pleamar, 69, 382 p.

5041   GOTTHEIL, J. *El compromiso argentino; presente y futuro de una crísis de cambío en América Latina* (The Argentine compromise; present and future of a crisis of change in Latin America). Buenos Aires, Editorial Paidós, 69, 175 p.

5042   GOULD, P. R. "Tanzania 1920-1963: the spatial impress of the modernization process", *Wld Polit.* 22(2), jan 70 : 149-170.

5043   GRACIARENA, J. "La crísis latinoamericana y la investigación sociológica" (The Latin American crisis and sociological research), *R. parag. Sociol.* 6(16), sep-oct 69 : 5-31.

5044   GUZMÁN BÖCKLER, C.; HERBERT, J.-L. *Guatemala; una interpretación histórico-social* (Guatemala; a socio-historical interpretation). México, Siglo Veintiuno Editores, 70, vii-205 p.

5045   HARTMANN, H. "Sozialer Wandel und politische Stabilität in Indien" (Social change and political stability in India), *Z. Polit.* 15(1), mar 68 : 107-116.

5046   HAVENS, A. E.; FLINN, W. L. (eds.). *Internal colonialism and structural change in Colombia.* New York, Praeger Publishers, 70, xxi-250 p.

5047   HEINTZ, P. *Ein soziologisches Paradigma der Entwicklung mit besonderer Berücksichtigung Lateinamerikas* (A sociological paradigm of development with special consideration of Latin America). Stuttgart, F. Rnke, 69, viii-332 p. CR: S. SARIOLA, *Acta sociol.* 13(3), 1970 : 202-203.

5048   HULICKS, K. "The Soviet Union's future communist society", *Ind. sociol. B.* 6(4), jul 69 : 250-266.

5049   HYTTEN, E. *Esperienze di sviluppo sociale nel Mezzogiorno...* (Experience of social development in the South). Roma, Associazione per lo sviluppo dell'industria nel Mezzogiorno; Milano, Giuffrè, 69, viii-189 p.

5050   Bibl. XIX-4602. INKELES, A. *Social change in Soviet Russia.* CR: W. D. CONNOR, *Amer. sociol. R.* 35(3), jun 70 : 595-596.

5051   KIM, C. I. E.; CHEE, C. (eds.). *Aspects of social change in Korea.* Kalamazoo, Mich., Korea Research and Publication; Detroit, Cellar Book Shop, 69, x-272 p.

5052   KOVALEV, É. V. "Social'no-političeskie preobrazovanija v Meksike, 1930-1960 gg" (Socio-political transformations in Mexico, 1930-1960), *Vopr. Ist.* 44(6), jun 70 : 32-50.

5053   LABOVITZ, S.; PURDY, R. "Territorial differentiation and social change in the United States and Canada", *Amer. J. Econ. Sociol.* 29(2), apr 70 : 127-148.

5054   LABROUSSE, E. et al. *Des derniers temps de l'âge seigneurial aux préludes de l'âge industriel, 1660-1789.* Paris, Presses universitaires de France, 70, xvi-781 p. [*Histoire économique et sociale de la France.* Vol. II.]

5055   LANKFORD, J. E.; REIMSERS, D. (eds.). *Essays on American social history.* New York, Holt, Rinehart and Winston, 70, viii-408 p.

5056   LAURENT, S. "Formation, information et développement en Côte d'Ivoire", *C. Ét. afr.* 10(3), E trim 70 : 421-468.

5057   LING, D. L. "Tunisia: modernization and moderation", *Muslim Wld* 60(3), jul 70 : 247-253.

5058   LÜTGE, F. K. *Beiträge zur Sozial- und Wirtschaftsgeschichte* (Contributions to social and economic history). Ed. by E. SCHREMMER. Stuttgart, G. Fischer, 70, vii-305 p.

5059   MAURO MARINI, R. M. "Subdesarrollo y revolución en América latina" (Underdevelopment and revolution in Latin America), *Investig. econ.* 29(113), jan-mar 70 : 87-104.

5060   MONTOYA GÓMEZ, O. "La crísis del subdesarrollo en América latina" (The crisis of underdevelopment in Latin America), *R. Univ. Externado Colombia* 11(1), mai 70 : 17-60.

5061   MUKHERJI, P. N. "A study in induced social change: an Indian experiment", *Hum. Org.* 29(3), 1970 : 169-177.

5062   NAGAI, M. "Social change in postwar Japan", *Develop. Econ.* 7(4), dec 69 : 395-405.

5063   NGOMA, F. "Tradition et modernisme en milieux congolais", *C. congol. Rech. Dévelop.* mar-apr 70 : 87-99.

5064   ORGANISATION INTERNATIONAL DU TRAVAIL. *Transformations sociales et progrès social en Afrique.* Genève, Bureau International du Travail, 69, 123 p.

5065   OSBORNE, J. W. *The silent revolution; the industrial revolution in England as a source of cultural change.* New York, Scribner, 70, xi-232 p.

5066   PEREIRA PINTO, J. C. *Aspectos de la historia económica y social de los ultimos treinta años* (Aspects of social and economic history of the last 30 years). Buenos Aires, Editorial El Coloquio, 70, 139 p.

5067   PIEDRA, A. M. (ed.). *Socio-economic change in Latin America.* Washington, Catholic University of America Press, 70, xiii-271 p.

5068   PIERRE-CHARLES, G. "El proceso acumulativo del subdesarrollo: las sociedades en retroceso" (The accumulation process of underdevelopment: societies in retrogression), *Bol. urug. Sociol.* 8(15-16-17), dec 69 : 86-98. [Haiti.]

5069   PLATH, D. W. "Modernization and its discontents: Japan's little utopias", *J. Asian Afr. Stud.* 4(1), jan 69 : 1-17.

5070   PRASAD, N. *Change strategy in a developing society: India.* Meerut, Meenakshi Prakashan, 70, xi-344 p.

5071   RIDDELL, J. B. *The special dynamics of modernization in Sierra Leone; structure, diffusion, and response.* Evanston, Northwestern University Press, 70, xii-142 p.

5072   SERONDE, A.-M. et al. *Tradition et changement en Toscane.* Paris, A. Colin, 70, 448 p. (Cahiers de la Fondation nationale des sciences politiques, n° 176).

5073   SILVA SOLAR, J.; CHONCHOL, J. *El desarrollo de la nueva sociedad en América latina* (The development of the new society in Latin America). 2nd rev. ed. Santiago de Chile, Ed. universitaria, 69, 146 p.

5074   SMITH, T. L. *Studies of Latin American societies.* Garden City, N. Y., Anchor Books, 70, xvii-412 p.

5075   Suzuki, P. T. *Social change in Turkey since 1950; a bibliography of 866 publications.* Heidelberg, High Speed Press Center, 69, vi-108 p.

5076   Trappen, F.; Uschner, M. "Notwendigkeit und Möglichkeit sozialökonomischen Umgestaltungen in Lateinamerika" (Necessity for and possibility of socioeconomic transformations in Latin America), *Einheit* 25(1), 1970 : 89-100.

5077   Tsurumi, K. *Social change and the individual; Japan before and after defeat in World War II.* Princeton, N. J., Princeton University Press, 70, xiv-441 p.

5078   United Nations. Economic Commission for Latin America. *Social change and social development policy in Latin America.* New York, UN, 70, 318 p.

5079   Van Nieuwenhuijze, C. A. O. *Development, a challenge to whom? An essay on the present state and the next stage in development studies, with special reference to sociology and with examples from the Middle East.* The Hague, Mouton, 69, 203 p. CR: J. H. Turner, *Amer. sociol. R.* 35(4), aug 70 : 779-780.

5080   Watters, R. F. *Koro: economic development and social change in Fiji.* Oxford, Clarendon Press, 69, xvi-305 p.

F SOCIAL PROBLEMS AND SOCIAL POLICY
PROBLÈMES SOCIAUX ET POLITIQUE SOCIALE

F.1 SOCIAL PROBLEMS
PROBLÈMES SOCIAUX

F.10 General works
Ouvrages généraux

[See also / Voir aussi: 1200]

5081 DAVIS, F. J. *Social problems; enduring major issues in social change.* New York, Free Press, 70, xii-388 p.

5082 FREEMAN, H. E.; JONES, W. C. *Social problems: causes and controls.* Chicago, Rand McNally, 70, xiv-560 p.

5083 Bibl. XIX-4651. KAVOLIS, V. (ed.). *Comparative perspectives on social problems.* CR: B. J. COSNECK, *Amer. sociol. R.* 34(6), dec 69 : 1023.

5084 OFFENBACHER, D. I.; POSTER, C. H. (eds.). *Social problems and social policy.* New York, Appleton-Century-Crofts, 70, viii-331 p.

5085 ROSHA, A. M. *Social problems of Pakistan.* Hyderabad, Royal Book Depot, 69, 179 p.

5086 SCHAFFER, A. et al. *Understanding social problems.* Columbus, Ohio, Merrill, 70, vii-358 p.

5087 Bibl. XIX-4838. SIMEY, T. S. *Social science and social problems.* CR: A. L. COLEMAN, *Amer. sociol. R.* 35(3), jun 70 : 540-541.

5088 TUFTE, E. R. (ed.). *The quantitative analysis of social problems.* Reading, Mass., Addison-Wesley Publishing Co., 70, 449 p.

F.11 Poverty and unemployment
Pauvreté et chômage

[See also / Voir aussi: **F.213**; 1320, 1374, 1658, 1665, 1711, 2962, 4539, 5333]

5089 BAUVIR, L. "Évolution et situation actuelle du chômage dans les régions wallonnes", *R. Cons. écon. wallon* 94, jan-mar 70 : 12-43. [Belgique.]

5090 BHARDWAJ, R. C. *Employment and unemployment in India.* New York, Humanities Press, 69, 140 p.

5091 BHATIA, B. M. *India's food problem and policy since independence.* Bombay, Somaiya Publications, 70, ix-251 p.

5092 BLAIR, P. W. "The dimension of poverty", *Int. Org.* 23(3), 1969 : 683-704.

5093 BLANC, J. *Nutrition et développement; réflexion sur les aspects économiques de l'alimentation en Afrique de l'Ouest.* Grenoble, Institut de recherches et de planification de Grenoble, 69, 500-xii l.

5094 COATES, K.; SILBURN, R. *Poverty: the forgotten Englishmen.* Harmondsworth, Penguin, 70, 237 p.

5095 "Évolution du chômage des jeunes. Causes et remèdes", *R. Trav. (Bruxelles)* 70(9), sep 69 : 1273-1341. [Belgique.]

5096 FERMAN, L. A. (ed.). "Evaluating the war on poverty", *A. Amer. Acad. polit. soc. Sci.* 385, sep 69 : 1-251. [USA.]

5097 FERMAN, L. A. "The hard-core unemployed: myth and reality", *Poverty hum. Resources Abstr.* 4(6), nov-dec 69 : 5-12. [USA.]

5098 GATES, R. C. "Research on poverty in Queensland", *Econ. Activity* 13(1), jan 70 : 7-11.

5099 GUTTENTAG, M. (ed.). "The poor: impact on research and theory", *J. soc. Issues* 26(2), 1970 : 1-192.

5100   HANSEN, N. M. *Rural poverty and the urban crisis; a strategy for regional development.* Bloomington, Indiana University Press, 70, xv-352 p. [USA.]

5101   HOLMAN, R. (ed.). *Socially deprived families in Britain.* London, Bedford Square Press, 70, 4-235 p.

5102   KAPLAN, S. J.; LINDSTROM, D. E. (eds.). *Seeking more effective means to overcome poverty: proceedings of the Appalachia conference on research in poverty and development.* Blacksburg, Va., Virginia Polytechnic Institute Research and Extension Divisions, 69, 272 p. CR: W. L. YANCEY, *Amer. sociol. R.* 34(6), dec 69 : 976-977.

5103   KASTIER, O. "Une application de l'analyse de système au domaine social: la résorption du chômage", *R. franç. Aff. soc.* 24(1), jan-mar 70 : 87-114. [France.]

5104   KLANFER, J. *Die soziale Ausschliessung. Armut in reichen Ländern* (Social exclusion. The poor in rich countries). Wien-Frankfurt-Zürich, Europa Verlag, 69, 184 p.

5105   KOSA, J.; ANTONOVSKY, A.; ZOLA, I. K. (eds.). *Poverty and health: a sociological analysis.* Cambridge, Mass., Harvard University Press, 69, xvi-449 p.

5106   LABBENS, J. *Le quart-monde. La pauvreté dans la société industrielle: étude sur le sous-prolétariat français dans la région parisienne.* Pierrelaye, Éditions Science et Service, 69, 318 p.

5107   LISTON, R. A. *The American poor; a report on poverty in the United States.* New York, Delacorte Press, 70, 191 p.

5108   MASTERMAN, G. G. *Poverty in Australia—proceedings of the 35th Summer School, Canberra, 1969.* Sydney, Angus and Robertson, 69, 171 p.

5109   McCALL, J. J. "An analysis of poverty: a suggested methodology", *J. Busin.* 43(1), jan 70 : 31-43.

5110   MORSE, D. A. "Unemployment in developing countries", *Polit. Sci. Quart.* 85(1), mar 70 : 1-16.

5111   Bibl. XIX-4669. MOYNIHAN, D. P. (ed.). *On understanding poverty: perspectives from the social sciences.* CR: T. BLAU, *Amer. J. Sociol.* 76(2), sep 70 : 353-355; J. M. HUNNICUTT, *Amer. sociol. R.* 35(4), aug 70 : 800-802.

5112   MYRDAL, G. *The challenge of world poverty; a world anti-poverty program in outline.* New York, Pantheon Books, 70, xviii-518 p.

5113   Bibl. XVIII-5249. MYRDAL, G. *et al. Asian drama: an inquiry into the poverty of nations.* CR: K. NAIR, *Econ. Develop. cult. Change* 17(4), jul 69 : 449-459; D. KANTOWSKY, *Kölner Z. Soziol. u. soz.-Psychol.* 22(4), dec 70 : 797-799.

5114   OJHA, P. D. "A configuration of Indian poverty", *Soc. Action* 20(2), apr-jun 70 : 103-122.

5115   "Pauvres dans les sociétés riches (Les)", *Rech. soc.* 30, jul-aug 70 : 1-68.

5116   "Poverty and social disorder", *Hum. Org.* 29(1), 1970 : 1-80.

5117   SCHNITZER, M. *Regional unemployment and the relocation of workers—the experience of Western Europe, Canada, and the United States.* New York, Praeger, 70, xiii-253 p.

5118   Bibl. XIX-4679. SELIGMAN, B. B. (ed.). *Aspects of poverty.* CR: E. M. LARSON, *Amer. sociol. R.* 35(1), feb 70 : 144-146.

5119   SOCIOLOGICAL RESOURCES FOR THE SOCIAL STUDIES. *The incidence and effects of poverty in the United States.* Boston, Allyn and Bacon, 69, vii-57 p.

5120   SUNDQUIST, J. L. (ed.). *On fighting poverty: perspectives from experience.* New York, Basic Books, 69, 256 p. CR: J. M. HUNNICUTT, *Amer. sociol. R.* 35(4), aug 70 : 800-802. [Volume II of *Perspectives on poverty.*]

5121   THUROW, L. C. *Poverty and discrimination.* Washington, Brookings Institution, 69, viii-214 p. CR: M. BRONFENBRENNER, *J. econ. Liter.* 8(3), sep 70 : 882-883.

5122   TIFFANY, D. W.; COWAN, J. R.; TIFFANY, P. M. *The unemployed; a social-psychological portrait.* Englewood Cliffs, N. J., Prentice-Hall, 70, xii-180 p. [USA.]

5123   VANDEVILLE, V. "Les caractéristiques régionales du chômage en Belgique", *C. écon. Bruxelles* 46, 2 trim 70 : 281-291.

5124   VIENTOS GASTON, N. "Puerto Rico y la cultura de la pobreza" (Puerto Rico and the culture of poverty), *Cuad. amer.* 29(168), jan-feb 70 : 31-45.

5125   VISURI, E. "Köyhyys ja ei-toivotut lapset" (Poverty and unwanted children), *Sosiologia* 6(2), 1969 : 55-60.

5126   WILLIAMS, F. (ed.). *Language and poverty; perspectives on a theme.* Chicago, Markham Publishing Co., 70, xii-439 p.

F.12   Sexual abnormalities
Perversions sexuelles

[See also / Voir aussi: 5245]

5127   ALEXANDER, R. B. *Die Prostitution in Deutschland* (Prostitution in Germany). München, Lichtenberg, 69, 187 p.

5128   HARRIS, E. F.; BUMBALOUGH, E. *An evaluation of the legal, medical and psychological attitudes of homosexuality in contemporary American society*, n.p., 69, vi-109 l.

5129   HYDE, H. M. *The other love: an historical and contemporary survey of homosexuality in Britain.* London, Heinemann, 70, 8-323 p.

5130   MASTERS, W. H.; JOHNSON, V. E. *Human sexual inadequacy.* London, Churchill, 70, xi-467 p.

5131   SEPÚLVEDA NIÑO, S. *La prostitución en Colombia; una quiebra de las estructuras sociales* (Prostitution in Colombia; a fissure in social structures). Bogotá, Editorial Andes, 70, 204 p.

F.13   Drug addiction and alcoholism
Stupéfiants et alcoolisme

5132   ABDEL FATTAH, E.; GAUDREAU-TOUTANT, C.; TREMBLAY, R. *L'alcool chez les jeunes Québécois; modèles de consommation d'alcool chez un group de jeunes.* Québec, Presses de l'Université Laval, 70, 102 p.

5133   ARNDT, J. R.; BLOCKSTEIN, W. L. (eds.). *Problems in drug abuse.* Madison, University Extension, University of Wisconsin, Health Sciences Unit, 70, 176 p.

5134   BAHR, H. M. "Family size and stability as antecedents of homelessness and excessive drinking", *J. Marriage Family* 31(3), aug 69 : 477-483.

5135   BLACHY, P. H. (ed.). *Drug abuse: data and debate.* Springfield, Ill., Thomas, 70, xvi-322 p.

5136   Bibl. XIX-4703. BLUM, R. H. *et al. Society and drugs.* I. *Social and cultural observations.* CR: D. M. PETERSEN, *Amer. sociol. R.* 35(3), jun 70 : 606-607.

5137   BORGATTA, E. F.; EVANS, R. R. (eds.). *Smoking, health, and behavior.* Chicago, Aldine, 68, xii-288 p. CR: R. B. SMITH, *Amer. J. Sociol.* 75(5), mar 70 : 886-888.

5138   CHRISTIAENS, L.; SUSINI, J. "La drogue: désir ou refus de la société ?", *Études (Paris)*, mai 70 : 694-705.

5139   COOK, S. J. "Canadian narcotics legislation, 1908-1923: a conflict model interpretation", *Canad. R. Sociol. Anthropol.* 6(1), feb 69 : 36-46.

5140   EINSTEIN, S. *The use and misuse of drugs: a social dilemma.* Belmont, Calif., Wadsworth Publishing Co., 70, 86 p. [USA.]

5141   EVANS, R. E.; BORGATTA, E. F. "An experiment in smoking dissuasion among University freshmen: a followup", *J. Health soc. Behav.* 11(1), mar 70 : 30-36.

5142   GLASER, D. *et al. Public knowledge and attitudes on drug abuse in New York State.* Albany, Research Division, New York State Narcotic Addiction Control Commission, 69, ii-82 p.

5143   GOODE, E. (ed.). *Marijuana.* New York, Atherton Press, 69, 197 p. CR: H. SEBALD, *Amer. sociol. R.* 35(4), aug 70 : 809-810.

5144   HUDOLIN, V. "Alcoholism in Croatia", *Int. J. soc. Psychiatry* 15(2), 1969 : 85-91.

5145   KAPLAN, R. *Drug abuse: perspectives on drugs.* Dubuque, Iowa, W. C. Brown Co., 70, vii-67 p.

5146   LOMITZ, L. "Patterns of alcohol consumption among the Mapuche", *Hum. Org.* 28(4), 1969 : 287-296.

5147   MADDOX, G. L. (ed.). *The domesticated drug; drinking among collegians.* New Haven, Conn., College and University Press, 70, 479 p.

5148   McGRATH, J. H.; SCARPITTI, F. R. *Youth and drugs; perspectives on a social problem.* Glenview, Ill., Scott, Foresman, 70, 199 p.

5149   McKENNELL, A. C. "Smoking motivation factors", *Brit. J. soc. clin. Psychol.* 9(1), feb 70 : 8-22.

5150   REDLINGER, L. J.; MICHEL, J. B. "Ecological variations in heroin abuse", *Sociol. Quart.* 11(2), 1970 : 219-229.

5151 SCHAPS, E.; SANDERS, C. R. "Purposes, patterns, and protection in a campus drug using community", *J. Health soc. Behav.* 11(2), jun 70 : 135-145.

5152 SCOTT, E. M. *Struggles in an alcoholic family.* Springfield, Ill., Thomas, 70, xiii-265 p.

5153 SMITH, D. E. (ed.). *The new social drug: cultural, medical and legal perspectives on marijuana.* Englewood Cliffs, N. J., Prentice-Hall, 70, vi-186 p.

5154 SPRADLEY, J. P. *You owe yourself a drunk: an ethnography of urban nomads.* Boston, Little, Brown, 70, x-301 p.

5155 STEFFENHAGEN, R. A.; MCAREE, C. P.; ZHEUTLIN, L. S. "Social and academic factors associated with drug use on the University of Vermont campus", *Int. J. soc. Psychiatry* 15(2), 1969 : 92-96.

5156 STEFFENHAGEN, R. A.; MCAREE, C. P.; ZHEUTLIN, L. S. "Some social factors in college drug usage", *Int. J. soc. Psychiatry* 15(2), 1969 : 97-101.

5157 SZABADY, E. "Az alkoholizmus demográfiai vonatkozásai" (Demographic aspects of alcoholism), *Demográfia* 12(3), 1969 : 262-272. [Hungary.]

5158 UNITED STATES. National Center for Prevention and Control of Alcoholism. *Alcohol and alcoholism.* Rev. Chevy Chase, Md.-Washington, United States Government Printing Office, 69, xi-73 p.

5159 VALLES, J. *From social drinking to alcoholism.* Dallas, TANE Press, 69, vi-226 p.

5160 VAN DYKE, H. T. *Youth and the drug problem.* Boston, Ginn, 70, iv-140 p.

5161 WECHSLER, H. *et al.* "Religious-ethnic differences in alcohol consumption", *J. Health soc. Behav.* 11(1), mar 70 : 21-29.

5162 WIENER, R. S. P. *Drugs and schoolchildren.* Harlow, Longmans, 70, ix-238 p.

5163 WRIGHT, C. L. *Narcotics: background to a problem.* Frankfort, Ky., Legislative Research Commission, 69, iii-115 p.

F.14 **Social aspects of disease**
Aspects sociaux de la maladie

[See also / Voir aussi: **F.212, F.223, F.224**; 707, 869, 1863, 1964, 1970, 3947, 5236]

5164 ALLEN, R. M.; CORTAZZO, A. D. *Psychological and educational aspects and problems of mental retardation.* Springfield, Ill., C. C. Thomas, 70, xii-123 p.

5165 BLEULER, M. "Some results of research in schizophrenia", *Behav. Sci.* 15(3), mai 70 : 211-219.

5166 BLOOMBAUM, M.; GUGELYK, T. "Voluntary confinement among lepers", *J. Health soc. Behav.* 11(1), mar 70 : 16-20.

5167 BOON, R. A.; ROBERTS, D. F. "The social impact of haemophilia", *J. biosoc. Sci.* 2(3), jul 70 : 237-264.

5168 BUTLER, J. R. "Illness and the sick role: an evaluation in three communities", *Brit. J. Sociol.* 21(3), sep 70 : 241-261.

5169 DUFRANCATEL, C. "La sociologie des maladies mentales; tendances actuelles de la recherche et bibliographie, 1950-1967", *Curr. Sociol./Sociol. contemp.* 16(2), 1968 : 1-207.

5170 FERBER, C. VON. "Der Tod. Ein unbewältigtes Problem für Mediziner und Soziologen" (Death. An insoluble problem for doctors and sociologists), *Kölner Z. Soziol. u. soz.-Psychol.* 22(2), jun 70 : 237-250.

5171 GOVE, W. R. "Sleep deprivation: a cause of psychotic disorganization", *Amer. J. Sociol.* 75(5), mar 70 : 782-799.

5172 GRIGG, C. M.; HOLTMANN, A. G.; MARTIN, P. Y. *Vocational rehabilitation for the disadvantaged; an economic and sociological evaluation.* Lexington, Mass., Health Lexington Books, 70, xxi-275 p.

5173 HAAVIO, M. "Vajaamielisenä Suomessa" (The mentally deficient in Finland), *Sosiologia* 6(2), 1969 : 78-83.

5174 HANEY, C. A.; MILLER, K. S. "Definitional factors in mental incompetency", *Sociol. soc. Res.* 54(4), jul 70 : 520-532.

5175 HERZLICH, C. *Santé et maladie. Analyse d'une représentation sociale.* Paris, Mouton, 69, 211 p.

5176 HOENIG, J.; HAMILTON, M. W. *The de-segregation of the mentally ill.* London, Routledge and K. Paul, 1969. CR: B. MORGAN, *Brit. J. Sociol.* 21(2), jun 70 : 238.

5177   HULEK, A. *Teoria i praktyka rehabilitacji inwalidów. Analiza w aspekcie fizycznym, psychologicznym, społecznym i zawodowym* (Theory and practice of rehabilitation of disabled persons. Physical, psychological, social and professional aspects of analysis). Warszawa, Państwowe Zakłady Wydawnictw Lekarskich, 69, 447 p.

5178   JACKSON, H. M. "Social progress and mental health", *J. Conflict Resol.* 14(2), jun 70 : 265-276.

5179   KITANO, H. H. L. "Mental illness in four cultures", *J. soc. Psychol.* 80(2), apr 70 : 121-134.

5180   LYNCH, L. R. (ed.). *The cross-cultural approach to health behavior.* Rutherford, N. J., Fairleigh Dickinson University Press, 69, 463 p.

5181   MALIKIN, D.; RUSALEM, H. *Vocational rehabilitation of the disabled—an overview.* New York, New York University Press, 69, x-326 p.

5182   MATSUMOTO, Y. S. "Social stress and coronary heart disease in Japan: a hypothesis", *Milbank Memor. Fund Quart.* 48(1), jan 70 : 9-36.

5183   NEWMAN, P. "Malaria control and population growth", *J. Develop. Stud.* 6(2), jan 70 : 133-158. [Ceylon.]

5184   NUTTALL, R. L.; SOLOMON, L. F. "Prognosis in schizophrenia: the role of premorbid, social class, and demographic factors", *Behav. Sci.* 15(3), mai 70 : 255-264.

5185   OBEYESEKERE, G. "Ayurveda and mental illness", *Comp. Stud. soc. Hist.* 12(3), jul 70 : 292-296.

5186   PHILLIPS, D. L.; CLANCY, K. J. "Reponse biases in field studies of mental illness", *Amer. sociol. R.* 35(3), jun 70 : 503-514.

5187   "Preventive approaches to chronic diseases", *Milbank Memor. Fund Quart.* 47(3), jul 69 : 355 p. [USA.]

5188   ROSEN, H.; KOMORITA, S. S. "A decision paradigm for action research: problems of employing the physically handicapped", *J. appl. behav. Sci.* 5(4), oct-dec 69 : 509-518. [USA.]

5189   ROSENBAUM, C. P. *The meaning of madness; symptomatology, sociology, biology, and therapy of the schizophrenias.* New York, Science House, 70, xix-411 p.

5190   SAFILIOS-ROTSCHILD, C. *The sociology and social psychology of disability and rehabilitation.* New York, Random House, 70, xxii-326 p.

5191   SALES, S. M. "Organizational role as a risk factor in coronary disease", *Adm. Sci. Quart.* 14(3), sep 69 : 225-337.

5192   "Santé mentale, problème politique (La)", *Projet* 42, feb 70 : 143-200.

5193   SHAPIRO, S. *et al.* "Social factors in the prognosis of men following first myocardial infarction", *Milbank Memor. Fund Quart.* 48(1), jan 70 : 37-50.

5194   TESCHNER, J. *Krankheit und Gesellschaft. Erkenntnisse der Sozialmedizin* (Illness and society. Knowledge of social medicine). Reinbek-bei-Hamburg, Rowohlt, 69, 123 p.

5195   TIMSON, J. "Social factors in the incidence of spina bifida and anencephaly", *J. biosoc. Sci.* 2(1), jan 70 : 81-84.

F.15   **Crime and delinquency**
       Crime et délinquance

[See also / Voir aussi: 2000, 2416, 2853, 5298]

5196   AHUJA, R. *Female offenders in India.* Meerut, Meenakshi Prakashan, 69, xi-131 p.

5197   BLACK, D. J. "Production of crime rates", *Amer. sociol. R.* 35(4), aug 70 : 733-748.

5198   BONGER, W. *Criminality and economic conditions.* Abridged by A. T. TURK. Bloomington Ind., Indiana University Press, 69, 200 p. CR: R. L. HIGHTOWER, *Amer. sociol. R.* 35(3), jun 70 : 601-602.

5199   BREED, W. "The Negro and fatalistic suicide", *Pacific sociol. R.* 13(3), 1970 : 156-162.

5200   CARDOSO, O. B. *Psicologia do suicida* (Psychology of suicide). Rio de Janeiro, Conquista, 69, 221 p.

5201   CHESNEY, K. *The anti-society; an account of the Victorian underworld.* Boston, Gambit, 70, 398 p. [UK.] [London ed. (M. T. Smith) has title: *The Victorian underworld.*]

5202   CLARK, R. *Crime in America; observations on its nature, causes, prevention, and control.* New York, Simon and Schuster, 70, 346 p.

5203   DeSole, D. E. *et al.* "Suicide and role strain among physicians", *Int. J. soc. Psychiatry* 15(4), 1969 : 294-301.

5204   Drapkin, I. (ed.). *Studies in criminology.* Jerusalem, Magnes Press, Hebrew University, 69, 319 p.

5205   Duncan, D. F. "Stigma and delinquency", *Cornell J. soc. Relat.* 4(2), 1969 : 41-48.

5206   Enschedé, C. J. "Enkele beschouwingen over prioriteiten op het gebied van het criminologisch onderzoek" (Some considerations on priorities in the field of criminological research), *Mens en Mij* 45(1), jan-feb 70 : 1-8.

5207   Fabian, R. *The anatomy of crime.* London, Pelham, 70, 197 p.

5208   Bibl. xix-4747. Farber, M. L. *Theory of suicide.* CR: K. W. Goffman, *Amer. sociol. R.* 34(6), dec 69 : 1020.

5209   Gardiner, J. A. *The politics of corruption; organized crime in an American city.* New York, Russell Sage Foundation, 70, xi-129 p.

5210   Gershman, A. P. "Attempted suicide or inadequate defence mechanisms ?", *Brit. J. soc. Psychiatry* 3(4), 1969-1970 : 255-257.

5211   Giannell, A. S. "The role of internal inhibition in crime causation", *J. soc. Psychol.* 81(1), jun 70 : 31-36.

5212   Gibbons, D. C. *Delinquent behavior.* Englewood Cliffs, N. J., Prentice-Hall, 70, ix-276 p. [USA.]

5213   Gold, M. *Delinquent behavior in an American city.* Belmont, Calif., Brooks/Cole Publishing Co., 70, viii-150 p.

5214   Guenther, A. L. (ed.). *Criminal behavior and social systems; contributions of American sociology.* Chicago, Rand MacNally, 70, xi-561 p.

5215   Hackler, J. C.; Lautt, M. "Systematic bias in measuring self-reported delinquency", *Canad. R. Sociol. Anthropol.* 6(2), mai 69 : 92-106.

5216   Hartjen, C. A.; Gibbons, D. C. "An empirical investigation of a criminal typology", *Sociol. soc. Res.* 54(1), oct 69 : 56-62.

5217   Haskell, M. R.; Yablonsky, L. *Crime and delinquency.* Chicago, Rand McNally, 70, x-517 p.

5218   Healy, W.; Bronner, A. F. *New light on delinquency and its treatment.* Westport, Conn., Greenwood Press, 69, vii-226 p.

5219   Heppenstall, R. *A little pattern of French crime.* London, Hamilton, 69, ix-177 p.

5220   Hippler, A. E. "Fusion and frustration: dimensions in the cross-cultural ethnopsychology of suicide", *Amer. Anthropol.* 71(6), dec 69 : 1074-1087.

5221   Hirschi, T. *Causes of delinquency.* Berkeley, Calif., University of California Press, 69, 309 p. CR: E. Lemert, *Amer. J. Sociol.* 76(1), jul 70 : 188-191.

5222   Holyst, B. "Étude sur le problème des suicides en Pologne", *R. Inst. Sociol.* 4, 1969 : 597-610.

5223   Hughes, H. M. (comp.). *Delinquents and criminals: their social world.* Boston, Allyn and Bacon, 70, xii-211 p. [USA.]

5224   Jones, H. *Crime in a changing society.* Harmondsworth, Eng., Penguin Books, 69, 173 p.

5225   Klein, M. W. "On group context of delinquency", *Sociol. soc. Res.* 54(1), oct 69 : 63-71.

5226   Knudten, R. D. (ed.). *Crime, criminology, and contemporary society.* Homewood, Ill., Dorsey Press, 70, xiii-435 p.

5227   Knudten, R. D. *Crime in a complex society; an introduction to criminology.* Homewood, Ill., Dorsey Press, 70, xvii-758 p.

5228   Lambert, J. R.; Jenkinson, R. F. *Crime, police, and race relations: a study in Birmingham.* London-New York, Oxford University Press, 70, xxviii-308 p.

5229   Bibl. xix-4761. Maris, R. W. *Social forces in urban suicide.* CR: B. A. Kinsey, *Amer. sociol. R.* 35(2), apr 70 : 409.

5230   Martin, J. McC.; Fitzpatrick, J. P.; Gould, R. E. *The analysis of delinquent behavior; a structural approach.* New York, Random House, 70, x-208 p. [To be used in conjunction with *Delinquent behavior: a redefinition of the problem,* by the same authors, published in 1965.]

5231   McDonald, L. "Crime and punishment in Canada: a statistical test of the conventional wisdom", *Canad. R. Sociol. Anthropol.* 6(2), nov 69 : 212-236.

5232   McLennan, B. N. (ed.). *Crime in urban society.* New York, Dunellen, 70, xx-151 p.

213

5233   MELUK, A. *Etiología de la delincuencia en Colombia* (Etiology of delinquency in Colombia). Bogotá, Ediciones Tercer Mundo, 69, 169-2 p.

5234   MENDELWICZ, J. et al. "Les tentatives de suicide. Résultats d'une enquête à Bruxelles", *Population* 25(4), jul-aug 70 : 797-809.

5235   MIGUEL, J. M. DE. "El suicido en España" (Suicide in Spain), *R. esp. Opin. públ.* 18, oct-dec 69 : 195-231. See also *R. int. Sociol. (Madrid)* 28(109-110), sep-dec 70 : 21-44.

5236   MILLER, D. H. "Suicidal careers: case analysis of suicidal mental patients", *Soc. Wk* 15(1), jan 70 : 27-36.

5237   Bibl. XIX-4765. OPP, K.-D. *Kriminalität und Gesellschaftsstruktur. Eine kritische Analyse soziologischer Theorien abweichenden Verhaltens* (Criminality and social structure; a critical analysis of sociological theories on deviant behavior). CR: E. BLANKENBURG, *Kölner Z. Soziol. u. soz.-Psychol.* 22(2), jun 70 : 413-415.

5238   PICCA, G.; ROBERT, P. "Note sur une recherche prévisionnelle de l'évolution de la criminalité. Hypothèse, méthode et bibliographie critique", *R. franç. Sociol.* 11(3), jul-sep 70 : 390-405.

5239   PRADERVAND, P.; CARDIA, L. "Aspetti della delinquenza italiana a Ginevra" (Aspects of Italian delinquency in Geneva), *Studi Emigr.* 6(16), oct 69 : 283-305.

5240   QUINNEY, R. *Crime and justice in society.* Boston, Mass., Little, Brown and Co., 69, 535 p. CR: J. R. STRATTON, *Amer. sociol. R.* 35(2), apr 70 : 403.

5241   QUINNEY, R. *The problem of crime.* New York, Dodd, Mead, 70, viii-227 p.

5242   QUINNEY, R. *The social reality of crime.* Boston, Little, Brown, 70, x-339 p.

5243   RESNICK, P. J. "Child murder by parents: a psychiatric review of filicide", *Amer. J. Psychiatry* 126(3), sep 69 : 325-334.

5244   RETTERSTØL, N. *Long-term prognosis after attempted suicide, a personal follow-up examination.* Oslo, Universitetsforlaget, 70, 110 p.

5245   REYES, E. A. "Criminalidad femenina y prostitución" (Female criminality and prostitution), *R. Univ. Externado Colombia* 10(2), oct 69 : 173-193. [Colombia.]

5246   ROSENBERG, B.; SILVERSTEIN, H. *The varieties of delinquent experience.* Waltham, Blaisdell, 69, 165 p. CR: E. LEMERT, *Amer. J. Sociol.* 76(1), jul 70 : 188-191.

5247   ROUCEK, J. S. "Crime: the American way of life", *R. int. Sociol. (Madrid)* 26(103-104), jul-dec 68 : 41-48.

5248   ROUCEK, J. S. (ed.). *Sociology of crime.* New York, Greenwood Press, 69, 551 p.

5249   RUDESTAM, K. E. "Some cultural determinants of suicide in Sweden", *J. soc. Psychol.* 80(2), apr 70 : 225-227.

5250   RUŽIČKA, L. *Sebevraždednost v Československu z hlediska demografického a sociologického* (Suicide in Czechoslovakia from a demographic and sociological viewpoint). Praha, Academia, 68, 155-1 p.

5251   SALERNO, R. "Organized crime and criminal justice", *Fed. Probation* 33(2), jun 69 : 11-17.

5252   SANDHU, H. S.; ALLEN, D. E. "Female delinquency: goal obstruction and anomie", *Canad. R. Sociol. Anthropol.* 6(2), mai 69 : 107-110.

5253   SAUVY, A. "Quelques aspects économiques et démographiques de la criminalité", *Population* 25(4), jul-aug 70 : 759-769.

5254   SELLIN, T.; WOLFGANG, M. E. (eds.). *Delinquency: selected studies.* New York, John Wiley and Sons, 69, 161 p. CR: E. LEMERT, *Amer. J. Sociol.* 76(1), jul 70 : 188-191.

5255   SHNEIDMAN, E. S.; FARBEROW, N. L.; LITMAN, R. E. (comps.). *The psychology of suicide.* New York, Science House, 70, xvi-719 p.

5256   SHOHAM, S. *The mark of Cain; the stigma theory of crime and social deviation.* Jerusalem, Israel Universities Press; Dobbs Ferry, N. Y., Oceana Publications, 70, 282 p.

5257   SLATIN, G. T. "Ecological analysis of delinquency: aggregation effects", *Amer. sociol. R.* 34(6), dec 69 : 894-906.

5258   Bibl. XIX-4778. SPERGEL, I. A. *Community problem solving: the delinquency example.* CR: D. C. REITZES, *Amer. sociol. R.* 35(1), feb 70 : 158.

5259   SYKES, G. M.; DRABEK, T. E. *Law and the lawless; a reader in criminology.* New York, Random House, 69, 437 p. CR: R. A. BALL, *Amer. sociol. R.* 35(1), feb 70 : 157.

5260   SZABO, D.; NORMANDEAU, A. *Déviance et criminalité.* Paris, A. Colin, 70, 378 p.

5261   TÖRNUDD, P. "Syytutkimus—kriminologian umpikuja" (Study of reasons for crime in criminology), *Sosiologia* 6(3), 1969 : 119-129.

5262 Bibl. XIX-4787. TURK, A. T. *Criminality and legal order.* CR: R. D. HERMAN, *Amer. sociol. R.* 35(3), jun 70 : 599-600.

5263 VOSS, H. L. (ed.). *Society, delinquency, and delinquent behavior.* Boston, Little, Brown, 70, xiv-458 p.

5264 WEICHER, J. C. "The effect of income on delinquency: comment", *Amer. econ. R.* 60(1), mar 70 : 249-256.

5265 WEINSTOCK, N. "Een figuur die verdwijnt: de sociale bandiet" (A disappearing figure: the social bandit), *Tijds. soc. Wetensch.* 14(1), 1969 : 44-58.

5266 WEST, D. J. *Present conduct and future delinquency: first report of the Cambridge Study in Delinquent Development.* London, Heinemann Educational; New York, International University Press, 69, xvi-207 p. CR: E. LEMERT, *Amer. J. Sociol.* 76(1), jul 70 : 188-191.

F.151 *Juvenile delinquency*
Délinquance juvénile

[See also / Voir aussi: 1003, 1906, 2738, 4525, 4540, 5274, 5295, 5300, 5307]

5267 ABBOTT, K. A.; ABBOTT, E. L. "Juvenile delinquency in San Francisco's Chinese-American community: 1961-1966", *Nat. Taiwan Univ. J. Sociol.* 4, apr 68 : 45-56.

5268 ÁLVAREZ VILLAR, A. "Estudio psicométrica de la delincuencia juvenil" (A psychometric study of juvenile delinquency), *R. esp. Opin. públ.* 18, oct-dec 69 : 97-168. [Spain.]

5269 BARRENECHEA, J. J. "Las causas de la delincuencia juvenil" (Causes of juvenile delinquency), *R. Fomento soc.* 25(99), jul-sep 70 : 275-284.

5270 BOUDHIBA, A. "Quelques aspects de la délinquance juvénile en Tunisie", *R. tunis. Sci. soc.* 6(19), dec 69 : 67-87.

5271 CASSEL, R. N.; BLUM, L. P. "Computer assist counselling (COASCON) for the prevention of delinquent behavior among teenagers and youth", *Sociol. soc. Res.* 54(1), oct 69 : 72-79.

5272 CONNOR, W. D. "Juvenile delinquency in the USSR: some quantitative and qualitative indicators", *Amer. sociol. R.* 35(2), apr 70 : 283-297.

5273 Bibl. XIX-4797. EISNER, V. *The delinquency of label: the epidemiology of juvenile delinquency.* CR: M. M. McCUGGACE, *Amer. sociol. R.* 34(6), dec 69 : 983-984.

5274 FERDINAND, T. N.; LUCHTERHAND, E. G. "Inner-city youths, the police, the juvenile court, and justice", *Soc. Probl.* 17(4), 1970 : 510-526.

5275 FRANKENSTEIN, C. *Varieties of juvenile delinquency.* New York, Gordon and Breach Science Publishers, 70, 252 p.

5276 GLUECK, S.; GLUECK, E. "White delinquents in the core city: as boys and men", *Soc. Sci. (Winfield)* 45(2), apr 70 : 67-81. With a comment by M. MEAD: 82-83.

5277 HAIM, A. *Les suicides d'adolescents.* Paris, Payot, 69, 303 p.

5278 HEUYER, G. *La délinquance juvénile; étude psychiatrique.* Paris, Presses universitaires de France, 69, 312 p.

5279 JUNGER, J. *La délinquance juvénile au littoral.* Bruxelles, C.E.D.J., 69, 136 p.

5280 Bibl. XIX-4800. KORN, R. R. (ed.). *Juvenile delinquency.* CR: S. S. SANDHU, *Amer sociol. R.* 34(6), dec 69 : 980-981.

5281 LESTER, D. "Adolescent suicide and premarital sexual behavior", *J. soc. Psychol.* 82(1), oct 70 : 131-132.

5282 OREHOV, V. V.; SPIRIDONOV, L. I. "Junost' i voprosy predupreždenija pravonarusenij" (Youth and questions on crime prevention), *Učen. Zap. (Leningr. gos. nauč.-issled. Inst. kompleks. sociol. Issled.)* (5), 1969 : 130-138.

5283 PLATT, A. M. *The child savers: the invention of delinquency.* Chicago, Ill., University of Chicago Press, 69, 230 p. CR: R. L. AKERS, *Amer. sociol. R.* 35(4), aug 70 : 807-808.

5284 QUENSEL, S. *et al.* "Delinquenzbelastungsskalen für männliche Jugendliche" (Juvenile delinquency change scales), *Kölner Z. Soziol. u. soz.-Psychol.* 22(1), mar 70 : 75-97.

5285 SEMERARO, R. *Aggressività giovanile e immagionazione* (Juvenile aggressivity and imagination). Padova, Liviana, 69, vi-161 p.

5286 Bibl. XIX-4807. SHAW, C. R.; McKAY, H. D. *Juvenile delinquency and urban areas.* CR: J. WTULICH, *Amer. sociol. R.* 35(2), apr 70 : 407-408; P. E. ROCK, *Brit. J. Sociol.* 21(1), mar 70 : 117-118.

5287 STRZEMBOSZ, A. "Niektore zagadnienia pczestepczosci nieletnich w miescie i na wsi" (Certain problems posed by juvenile delinquency in cities and in the countryside based on police statistical data), *Pań. i Prawo* 24(11), nov 69 : 844-850. [Poland.]

5288 TEELE, J. E. (ed.). *Juvenile delinquency; a reader.* Itasca, Ill., F. E. Peacock, 70, ix-461 p.

5289 TORO-CALDER, J. "Algunos hallazgos sobre la delincuencia juvenil en Puerto Rico" (Some findings on juvenile delinquency in Puerto Rico), *R. Cienc. soc. (Puerto Rico)* 14(2), apr-jun 70 : 233-246.

5290 VAN DYKE, H. T. *Juvenile delinquency.* Boston, Ginn, 70, iii-119 p.

5291 VARMA, S. C. *The young delinquents; a sociological inquiry.* Lucknow, Pustak Kendra, 70, v-105 p. [India.]

5292 VEDDER, C. B.; SOMERVILLE, D. B. *The delinquent girl.* Springfield, Ill., Thomas, 70 xi-166 p.

F.16   Punishment and penal institutions
Mesures répressives et institutions pénitentiaires

[See also / Voir aussi: 5231, 5251]

5293 ARNOLD, W. R. *Juveniles on parole; a sociological perspective.* New York, Random House, 70, viii-177 p. [USA.]

5294 BITTNER, W. (ed.). *Verbrechen—Schuld oder Schicksal? Zur Reform des Strafwesens* (Crime—fault or fate? The reform of punishment). Stuttgart, E. Klett, 69, 265 p. CR: S. QUENSEL, *Kölner Z. Soziol. u. soz.-Psychol.* 22(2), jun 70 : 414-415.

5295 BLACK, D. J.; REISS, A. J. Jr. "Police control of juveniles", *Amer. sociol. R.* 35(1), feb 70 : 63-77.

5296 BLANKENBURG, E. "Die Selektivität rechtlicher Sanktionen; eine empirische Untersuchung von Ladendiebstählen" (The selectivity of legal sanctions: an empirical research on display shelf thefts), *Kölner Z. Soziol. u. soz.-Psychol.* 21(4), dec 69 : 805-829.

5297 COHEN, B. L. *Law without order; capital punishment and the liberals.* New Rochelle, N. Y., Arlington House, 70, 224 p.

5298 "Confrontation de la théorie générale de la responsabilité pénale avec les données de la criminologie", *A. Fac. Dr. Sci. écon. (Toulouse)* 17(1), 1969 : 198 p.

5299 EDWARDS, A. R. "Inmate adaptations and socialization in the prison", *Sociology* 4(2), mai 70 : 213-225.

5300 EMERSON, R. M. *Judging delinquents. Context and process in juvenile court.* Chicago, Aldine Publishing Co., 69, 278 p. CR: H. JACOB, *Amer. polit. Sci. R.* 64(3), sep 70 : 940-941.

5301 GAWAT, A. R. "A study of the correctional institution for women: needs for inmates and services rendered by the socio-civic and religious organizations", *Graduate Fac. Stud.* 19, 1968 : 222-232.

5302 GRAVENHORST, L. *Soziale Kontrolle abweichenden Verhaltens; Fallstudie an weiblichen Insassen eines Arbeitshauses* (Social control of deviant behaviour. A case study of women confined in a work house). Frankfurt-am-Main, Suhrkamp, 70, 142 p.

5303 HALL WILLIAMS, J. E. *The English penal system in transition.* London, Butterworths, 70, xix-388 p.

5304 HARTMANN, K. *Theoretische und empirische Beiträge zur Verwahrlosungsforschung* (Theoretical and empirical research on imprisonment). Berlin-New York, Springer Verlag, 70, x-149 p.

5305 HERRICK, J. E. *The social worker at the adult correctional institution.* Northbrook, Ill. Whitehall Co., 69, xii-249 p.

5306 HOPPER, C. B. *Sex in prison: the Mississippi experiment with conjugal visiting.* Baton Rouge, La., Louisiana State University Press, 69, 160 p. CR: W. NARDINI, *Amer. sociol. R.* 35(4), aug 70 : 806-807.

5307 LEMERT, E. McC. *Social action and legal change; revolution within the juvenile court.* Chicago, Aldine, 70, vi-248 p.

5308 McDONOUGH, J. N.; KING, D. B.; GARRETT, J. E. *Juvenile court handbook.* South Hackensack, N. J., F. B. Rothman, 70, 54 p.

5309 MILNER, A. (ed.). *African penal systems.* New York, F. A. Praeger, 69, 50 p. CR: L. C.
       KERCHER, *Amer. sociol. R.* 35(3), jun 70 : 597-598.
5310 ROBERTSON, A. "Penal policy and social change", *Hum. Relat.* 22(6), dec 69 : 547-563.
5311 Bibl. XIX-4810. WHEELER, S.; HUGHES, H. M. (eds.). *Controlling delinquents.* CR: J. F.
       SHORT, Jr. *Amer. J. Sociol.* 76(1), jul 70 : 186-188.
5312 WILKINS, L. T. *Evaluation of penal measures.* New York, Random House, 69, 177 p.
       CR: L. BRAITHWAITE, *Amer. sociol. R.* 35(2), apr 70 : 405-406.

F.2   SOCIAL POLICY
          POLITIQUE SOCIALE

F.20   General works
           Ouvrages généraux

F.200   *General studies*
            Études générales

5313 BOWER, J. L. "Systems analysis for social decisions", *Operations Res.* 17(6), nov-dec
       69 : 927-940.
5314 CAFFÈ, F. *Teorie e problemi di politica sociale* (Theories and problems of social policy).
       Bari, Laterza, 70, 177 p.
5315 ETZIONI, A. "Toward a theory of guided societal change", *Soc. Sci. Quart.* 50(3), dec
       69 : 749-754.
5316 EVANS, J. W. "Evaluating social action programs", *Soc. Sci. Quart.* 50(3), dec 69 :
       568-581.
5317 FRANK, J. "Wechselbeziehungen zwischen Sozialpolitik und Wirtschaftspolitik" (Re-
       ciprocal relations between social policy and economic policy), *Dtsche Versich.-Z.*
       24(1), jan 70 : 3-7.
5318 FREEMAN, H. E.; SHERWOOD, C. C. *Social research and social policy.* Englewood Cliffs,
       N. J., Prentice-Hall, 70, x-159 p.
5319 GIANNONI, M. "Lo sviluppo della tutela sociale rispetto al reddito" (The development
       of social protection with regard to income), *Probl. Sicur. soc.* 24(5), sep-oct 69 :
       857-880.
5320 GOEL, V. K. "A note on the role of social security in economic development", *Asian
       Tradeunion.* 6(4), dec 68 : 9-12.
5321 INTERNATIONAL LABOR OFFICE. *An introduction to social security.* Geneva, ILO, 70,
       vii-218 p.
5322 JENKINS, S. *Social security in international perspective—essays in honor of Eveline M.
       Burns.* New York, Columbia University Press, 69, xii-255 p.
5323 KAUFMANN, F. X. *Sicherheit als soziologisches und sozialpolitisches Problem* (Security as
       a sociological and social policy problem). Stuttgart, Enke, 70, xii-396 p.
5324 KLEINHENZ, G. *Probleme wissenschaftlicher Beschäftigung mit der Sozialpolitik* (Problems
       of scientific occupation with social policy). Berlin, Duncker und Humblot, 70, 142 p.
5325 NOBLE, J. H. Jr. "The uncertainty of evaluative research as a guide to social policy",
       Soc. Sci. Quart. 50(3), dec 69 : 589-597.
5326 PRELLER, L. *Praxis und Probleme der Sozialpolitik* (Practice and problems of social
       policy). Tübingen, Mohr (Siebeck); Zürich, Polygraphischer Verlag, 70, 2 vols.,
       xxviii-754 p.
5327 RYFFEL, H. "Soziale Sicherheit in der modernen Gesellschaft: Strukturen und Mass-
       stäbe" (Social security in modern society: structures and criteria), *Staat* 9(1), 1970 :
       1-19.
5328 SABATER, A. "Evaluación analítica del desarrollo dinámico de las instituciones de
       asistencia social y seguridad social" (Analytical evaluation of dynamic development
       of social assistance and social security institutions), *R. iberoamer. Segur. soc.* 19(3),
       mai-jun 70 : 447-461.
5329 "Social planning", *J. Develop. Stud.* 6(4), jul 70 : 162 p.
5330 YANCEY, W. L. "Intervention as a strategy of social inquiry: an exploratory study with
       unemployed Negro men", *Soc. Sci. Quart.* 50(3), dec 69 : 582-588.

F.201   *Local studies*
             Études localisées

[See also / Voir aussi: 8, 43, 447, 2418, 5078]

5331   ALBERTS, D. S. *A plan for measuring the performance of social programs; the application of operations research methodology.* New York, Praeger, 70, xix-157 p. [USA.]

5332   'ALÎ, M. K. M. *al-Rafâhîyaṭ al-'ijtima'îyaṭ, al-naẓarîyaṭ wal-taṭbiq* (Social welfare, theory and practice). al-Qâhiraṭ, Dâr el-Naḥdat al-'Arabîyaṭ, 70, 356 p. [UAR.]

5333   ATKINSON, A. B. *Poverty in Britain and the reform of social security.* London-Cambridge, University Press, 69, 224 p.

5334   BEER, S. H.; BARRINGER, R. E. (eds.). *The State and the poor.* Cambridge, Mass., Winthrop Publishers, 70, xi-329 p. [USA.]

5335   BELLINI, V. "I principi giuridici della providenza sociale nella loro evoluzione" (The legal principles of social assistance in evolution), *Probl. Sicur. soc.* 24(5), sep-oct 69 : 837-863. [Italy.]

5336   BEŠTER, M. "Prioritete in družbeni minimum na socialnem področju" (Priorities and social minimum in the social sphere), *Ekon. R. (Ljubljana)* 20(4), 1969 : 434-446. [Yugoslavia.]

5337   BORRAJO DACRUZ, E. "Los principios de la seguridad social y sus realizaciones en el sistema español" (Principles of social security and their realization in the Spanish system), *R. iberoamer. Segur. soc.* 19(2), mar-apr 70 : 219-230.

5338   CAMPBELL, C. D. "Social insurance in the United States: a program in search of exploration", *J. Law Econ.* 12(2), oct 69 : 249-265.

5339   CRAMPTON, H. M.; KEISER, K. K. *Social welfare: institution and process.* New York, Random House, 70, xii-308 p. [USA.]

5340   DELPERÉE, A. "La sécurité sociale: ses objectifs, son évolution, ses problèmes de demain", *R. belge Sécur. soc.* 12(1), jan 70 : 1-11.

5341   DIARRA, O. "La sécurité sociale en République du Mali", *C. afr. Sécur. soc.* (7), 1970 : 1-38.

5342   'EZ, 'A. A.-H. *al-Taäminât al-'ijtima'îyaṭ, al-mabâdy al-naẓarîyaṭ wal-taṭbîqîyaṭ al-'amalîyaṭ* (Social insurance, theoretical formulations and applications). al-Qâhiraṭ, Dâr al-Naḥdaṭ al-'Arabîyat, 69, 440 p. [UAR.]

5343   Bibl. XIX-4862. GEORGE, V. N. *Social security: Beveridge and after.* CR: P. S. GEORGE, *Brit. J. Sociol.* 20(4), dec 69 : 465-466. [UK.]

5344   GIORDANO, M. "Un progetto per la riforma dell'assistenza sociale" (A project for the reform of social assistance), *Orientam. soc.* 25(11-12), nov-dec 69 : 809-820. [Italy.]

5345   GRIFFO, D. "Un difficile cammino. Dalla previdenza sociale alle sicurezza sociale" (A difficult route. From social assistance to social security), *Quad. Sci. soc.* 8(1-2), 1969 : 158-166. [Italy.]

5346   HAGENSEN, K. "Det sociale tryghedssystem i England" (The social security system in England), *Soc. Tss.* 46(6), jun 70 : 217-227.

5347   Bibl. XIX-4867. HEIDT, S.; ETZIONI, A. (eds.). *Societal guidance: a new approach to social problems.* CR: G. W. SAMUELSON, *Amer. sociol. R.* 35(2), apr 70 : 372-373. [USA.]

5348   JAMBU-MERLIN, R. *La sécurité sociale.* Paris, A. Colin, 70, 373 p. [France.]

5349   KATZER, H. "Il bilancio sociale della V legislatura nella Repubblica federale tedesca" (The social balance sheet of the fifth legislature in the Federal Republic of Germany), *Previd. soc.* 25(5-6), sep-dec 69 : 1361-1367.

5350   KHANNA, R. L. *Social administration in India.* Chandigarh, Mohindra Capital Publishers, 70, ii-191 p.

5351   Bibl. XIX-4869. LOCHHEAD, A. V. S. (ed.). *A reader in social administration.* CR: R. SMITH, *Brit. J. Sociol.* 20(4), dec 69 : 468-469. [UK.]

5352   LOFFREDO, F. "La riforma del sistema previdenziale inglese" (The reform of the English social insurance system), *Probl. Sicur. soc.* 25(2), mar-apr 70 : 251-283.

5353   LOFFREDO, F. "Un esame critico della politica sociale in Germania" (Critical examination of the social policy in Germany), *Previd. soc.* 26(2), mar-apr 70 : 487-511.

5354   LOTAN, G. *National insurance in Israel.* Jerusalem, National Insurance Institute, 69, 162 p.

5355   MALLET, A. "Diversification or standardisation—two trends in Latin American social security", *Int. Lab. R.* 101(1), jan 70 : 49-83.

5356   Bibl. XIX-4874. MICHALE, D. N. *The unprepared society: planning for a precarious future.* CR: J. F. MURPHY, *Amer. sociol. R.* 34(6), dec 69 : 957. [USA.]

5357   MÓD, A. "Szociális programok és életszínvonal Magyarországon" (Social programs and standard of living in Hungary), *Statiszt. Szle* 48(1), jan 70 : 3-17.

5358   MOLES, R. R. "Relaciones entre la seguridad social y los servicios sociales", *R. mexic. Trab.* 16(2), apr-jun 69 : 147-172. [Latin America.]

5359   ORAM, C. A. *Social policy and administration in New Zealand.* Wellington, New Zealand University Press, Price Milburn, 69, 268 p.

5360   OSBORN, R. J. *Soviet social policies: welfare, equality, and community.* Homewood, Ill., Dorsey Press, 70, x-294 p.

5361   PETERS, H. "Die politische Funktionslosigkeit der Sozialarbeit und die 'pathologische' Definition ihrer Adressaten" (The absence of a political function in social aid and the "pathological" definition of its beneficiaries), *Jb. soz.-Wiss.* 20(3), 1969 : 405-416. [Germany, BR.]

5362   "Planned social intervention", *Soc. Sci. Quart.* 50(3), dec 69 : 437-758. [USA.]

5363   REGLI, F. J. A. *Soziale Sicherheit—Ein sozial- und wirtschaftsethische Untersuchung mit besonderer Berücksichtigung der Schweiz und der internationalen Solidarität* (Social security—a survey on social and economic ethics in light of the Swiss case and of international solidarity). Bern, Paul Haupt, 69, 244 p. [Switzerland.]

5364   REIN, M. *Social policy: issues of choice and change.* New York, Random House, 70, xvii-490 p.

5365   RIBARSKI, K.; VELCHEVSKA, L. *Social security in Bulgaria.* Sofia, Sofia Press, 69, 65 p.

5366   RIMLINGER, G. V. "Social security and society: an East-West comparison", *Soc. Sci. Quart.* 50(3), dec 69 : 494-506.

5367   ROHRLICH, G. F. "The place of social insurance in the pursuit of the general welfare", *J. Risk Insurance* 36(4), 1969 : 333-353. [USA.]

5368   SCHULZ, J. M. "Un régime dynamique de sécurité sociale pour les États-Unis. Analyse de simulation fondée sur le régime de la République fédérale d'Allemagne", *R. int. Sécur. soc.* 23(1), 1970 : 130-140.

5369   "Sécurité sociale aux Pays-Bas (La)", *R. int. Sécur. soc.* 23(1), 1970 : 3-63.

5370   SINGH, T. *Towards an integrated society; reflections on planning, social policy, and rural institutions.* Bombay, Orient Longmans, 69, xii-554 p. [India.]

5371   SINGHVI, L. M. (ed.). *Gandhi and social policy in India; a sociological analysis.* Delhi, National Publishing House, 70, xv-186 p.

5372   SMITH, R. E.; ZIETZ, D. *American social welfare institutions.* New York, Wiley, 70, xiii-363 p.

5373   "Social science and social policy: a written symposium", *Soc. Sci. Quart.* 50(3), dec 69 : 443-493. [USA.]

5374   TOMEŠ, I. *Ceskoslovenské právo sociálního zabezpečení* (Social security legislation in Czechoslovakia). Praha, Orbis, 68, 325 p.

5375   WHOLEY, J. S. *et al. Federal evaluation policy; analyzing the effects of public programs.* Washington, Urban Institute, 70, 134 p.

5376   Bibl. XIX-4899. WILCOX, C. *Toward social welfare: an analysis of programs and proposals attacking poverty, insecurity, and inequality of opportunity.* CR: G. GEISEL, *Amer. sociol. R.* 35(1), feb 70 : 144. [USA.]

5377   WINTERSTEIN, H. "Sozial Sicherung im Spannungsfeld von Freiheit und Bindung" (Social security torn between freedom and constraint), *Dtsche Versich.-Z.* 24(5), mai 70 : 101-110. [Germany, BR.]

5378   WOLF, K. H. "Entwicklungstendenzen der österreichischen Sozialversicherung" (Development trends of Austrian social security), *Soz. Sicherheit* 23(5), mai 70 : 142-150.

5379   YAZGAN, T. *Türkiye'de sosyal güvenlik sistemi* (Social security system in Turkey). Istanbul, Iktisadi Arastirmalar Vakfir, 69, iii-97 p.

F.21   Specific insurance systems
          Régimes particuliers d'assurance

F.211   *Family protection*
          Protection de la famille

5380   BIE, P. DE. "Images-guide et images induites de la politique des allocations familiales en Belgique", *Popul. et Famille* 18, jun-jul 69 : 19-35.
5381   GIORDANO, M. "La famiglia nella programmazione assistenziale" (The family in assistance planning), *Orientam. soc.* 26(6), jun 70 : 435-451. [Italy.]
5382   OUENSANGA, L. "Les prestations familiales aux Antilles", *Dr. soc.* 33(5), mai 70 : 247-254.
5383   TREVISI, V. "Aspetti giuridici evolutivi nella più recente legislazione sugli assegni familiari" (Legal and evolutive aspects in the most recent legislation on family allowances), *Previd. soc.* 26(1), jan-feb 70 : 67-92.

F.212   *Health insurance*
          Assurance-maladie

[See also / Voir aussi: **F.223**]

5384   "Assurance maladie des travailleurs non salariés des professions non agricoles (L')", *Dr. soc.* 33(3), mar 70 : 1-197. [France.]
5385   BELGIQUE. Ministère de la Prévoyance sociale. "L'assistance aux handicappés—législation, revalidation et reclassement social", *R. belge Sécur. soc.* 12(2), feb 70 : 155-346.
5386   BRYANT, J. *Health and the developing world.* Ithaca, N. Y., Cornell University Press, 69, xxvii-345 p.
5387   CITTERBART, K. "La nouvelle réglementation des soins apportés à la santé du peuple en République socialiste tchécoslovaque", *B. Dr. tchécosl.* 26(1-4), dec 68 : 30-44.
5388   HIRSHFIELD, D. S. *The lost reform; the campaign for compulsory health insurance in the United States from 1932-1943.* Cambridge, Mass., Harvard University Press, 70, xi-221 p.
5389   ILLUMINATI, F. *La tutela della salute e l'assicurazione di malattia* (Protection of health and health insurance). Firenze, Vallecchi, 70, 522 p.
5390   MARMOR, T. R.; MARMOR, J. S. *The politics of medicare.* London, Routledge and K. Paul, 70, xiii-146 p. [USA.]
5391   PETRONI, V. *Rapporto sull'assicurazione sociale di malattia* (Report on social health insurance). Milano, A. Giuffrè, 70, 136 p. [Italy.]
5392   ROCCARDI, G. "Il sistema dell'assicurazione malattia nel quadro della sicurezza sociale" (The system of health insurance in the framework of social security), *Probl. Sicur. soc.* 25(1), jan-feb 70 : 7-38. [Italy.]
5393   SCHÄFER, E. "Bestandsaufnahme und Fortentwicklung in der Krankenversicherung" (Inventory and evolution of health insurance), *Soz. Sicherheit* 23(2), feb 70 : 44-51. [Austria.]
5394   SELLIER, F. "Le rôle des organisations et des institutions dans le développement des besoins sociaux. Le cas du besoin de santé et de l'assurance-maladie", *Sociol. Trav.* 12(1), jan-mar 70 : 1-14. [France.]
5395   STANEK, F. "Die Gebarung der Krankenversicherungsträger im Jahre 1969" (The behaviour of social security recipients), *Soz. Sicherheit* 23(10), oct 70 : 346-356. [Austria.]

F.214   *Old age insurance*
          Assurance-vieillesse

5396   MERTENS, J. "Nouvelles perspectives pour une politique de la vieillesse", *R. belge Sécur. soc.* 12(3), mar 70 : 378-397. [Belgique.]
5397   ONESTI, G. "Per la difesa e il consolidamento della riforma pensionistica" (For the defence and consolidation of pension reform), *Assist. soc.* 23(6), nov-dec 69 : 642-658. [Italy.]

F.22 **Social work, social service**
Travail social, service social

F.220 *General studies*
Études générales

[See also / Voir aussi: 2166, 5084, 5284, 5358]

5398 ANDER-EGG, E. *Introducción a las técnicas de investigación social para trabajadores sociales* (Introduction to social research techniques for social workers). Buenos Aires, Editorial Humanitas, 69, 335 p.

5399 AUSTIN, D. M. "Social work's relation to national development in developing nations", *Soc. Wk* 15(1), jan 70 : 97-106.

5400 BARTLETT, H. M.; SAUNDERS, B. N. *The common base of social work practice*. New York, National Association of Social Workers, 70, 224 p.

5401 BRASNETT, M. *Voluntary social action: a history of the National Council of Social Service, 1919-1969*. London, National Council of Social Service, 69, ix-305 p. [UK.]

5402 BROWN, M. J. "Social work values in a developing country", *Soc. Wk* 15(1), jan 70 : 107-112.

5403 DASGUPTA, S. "Need reckoning in social work", *Ind. J. soc. Wk* 30(4), jan 70 : 277-284.

5404 DONATI, I. "Nuove prospettive del servizio sociale nello sviluppo integrato" (New prospects of social service in integrated development), *Quad. Sci. soc.* 9(1), 1970 : 62-72.

5405 EATON, J. W. "Reaching the hard-to-reach in Israel", *Soc. Wk* 15(1), jan 70 : 85-96.

5406 FORDER, A. (ed.). *Penelope Hall's social services of England and Wales*. London, Routledge and K. Paul, 69, 352 p. CR: M. JEFFREYS, *Brit. J. Sociol.* 20(4), dec 69 : 467-468.

5407 GUENEAU, P. "Réflexions sur l'animation sociale et culturelle, en quoi le service social est-il concerné ?", *Vie soc.* (12), dec 69 : 667-683.

5408 HANDLER, J. F.; HOLLINGSWORTH, E. J. "The administration of social services and the structure of dependency", *Soc. Serv. R.* 43(4), dec 69 : 406-420. [USA.]

5409 HEARUD, B. J. *Sociology and social work; perspectives and problems*. Oxford-New York, Pergamon Press, 70, xii-306 p.

5410 JAFFE, E. D. "The social work establishment and social change in Israel", *Soc. Wk* 15(2), apr 70 : 103-109.

5411 KATZ, A. H. "Self-help organizations and volunteer participation in social welfare", *Soc. Wk* 15(1), jan 70 : 51-60.

5412 KLENK, R. W.; RYAN, R. M. *The practice of social work*. Belmont, Calif., Wadsworth Publishing Co., 70, 373 p.

5413 McCORMICK, M. J. "Social advocacy: a new dimension in social work", *Soc. Casewk* 51(1), 1970 : 3-11.

5414 MEYER, C. H. *Social work practice: a response to the urban crisis*. New York, Free Press, 70, x-227 p.

5415 MUKUNDARAO, K. "Social work in India—indigenous cultural bases and the processes of modernization", *Int. soc. Wk* 12(3), 1969 : 29-39.

5416 ORO, P. L. DELL'. *Introduzione allo studio dell'organizzazione e amministrazione dei servizi sociali...* (Introduction to the study of the organization and administration of social services). Ed. by R. SELVA. Padova, A cura della Fondazione Emanuela Zancan, 69, 188 p.

5417 "Recherche et l'administration en service social (La)", *Serv. soc.* 17(1-2-3), jan-dec 68 : 1-111. [Canada.]

5418 SCHATZ, H. A. (ed.). *Social work administration: a resource book*. New York, Council on Social Work Education, 70, vii-397 p.

5419 "Service social dans la société de bien-être (Le)", *Socialisme* 16(96), nov 69 : 600-695. [Belgique.]

5420 SILVA, T. L. "The goals of social work practice in relation to national development", *Graduate Fac. Stud.* 18, 1967 : 126-138.

5421 TABER, M. "Clinical and social orientations in social work: an empirical study", *Soc. Serv. R.* 44(1), mar 70 : 34-43.

5422 TIMMS, N. *Social work: an outline for the intending student*. London, Routledge and K. Paul, 70, 5-170 p.

5423   ZALD, M. N. "The structure of society and social service integration", *Soc. Sci. Quart.*
        50(3), dec 69 : 557-567.

F.221   Social casework
Service social des cas individuels

5424   PLANT, R. *Social and moral theory in casework.* London, Routledge and K. Paul, 70, xi-99 p.

F.222   Social group work
Service social des groupes

5425   ALDERSON, J. J. (ed.). *Social work in schools: patterns and perspectives.* Northbrook, Ill.,
        Whitehall Co., 69, x-166 p.

5426   BATTEN, T. R.; BATTEN, M. *The human factor in youth work.* London-New York, Oxford
        University Press, 70, vi-170 p.

5427   CULVER, C. M. *et al.* "Community service workers and recipients: a combined middle
        class-lower class workshop", *J. appl. behav. Sci.* 5(4), oct-dec 69 : 519-535.

5428   DEPALMA, D. "A work group model for social work intervention", *Soc. Casewk* 51(2),
        1970 : 91-94.

5429   KLEIN, A. F. *Social work through group process.* Albany, School of Social Welfare, State
        University of New York, 70, 215 p.

5430   LEISSNER, A. *Street club work in Tel Aviv and New York.* London, Longmans, 69,
        xiv-316 p.

5431   "Service social et familles socialement handicapées", *Inform. soc. (Paris)* 23(11),
        nov 69 : 6-76.

5432   THOMPSON, S.; KAHN, J. H. *The group process as a helping technique; a textbook for social
        workers, psychologists, doctors, teachers, and other workers in community service.* Oxford-
        New York, Pergamon Press, 70, xvii-158 p.

F.223   Community organization and services: hospitals, asylums, ...
Service social des collectivités: hôpitaux, asiles, ...

        [See also / Voir aussi: 1024, 2681, 5495]

5433   BELL, N. W.; ZUCKER, R. A. "Family-hospital relationships in a hospital setting", *Int.
        J. soc. Psychiatry* 15(1), 1968-1969 : 73-80.

5434   BERKMAN, G. B.; REHR, H. "Unanticipated consequences of the case-finding system in
        hospital social service", *Soc. Wk* 15(2), apr 70 : 63-68.

5435   BORMAN, L. D. "The marginal route of a mental hospital innovation", *Hum. Org.* 29(1),
        1970 : 63-69.

5436   COE, R. M. (ed.). *Planned change in the hospital; case studies of organizational innovations.*
        New York, Praeger Publishers, 70, xxiv-260 p.

5437   CROSSLEY, B.; DENMARK, J. C. "Community care—a study of the psychiatric morbidity
        of a Salvation Army hospital", *Brit. J. Sociol.* 20(4), dec 69 : 443-449.

5438   DAMEN, P. C. "Organisatiestruktuur en sociaal milieu in zwakzinnigen-inrichtingen"
        (Organizational structure and social environment in psychiatric establishments),
        Soc. Wetensch. 12(3), 1969 : 175-213.

5439   FREEMAN, R. B. *Community health nursing practice.* Philadelphia, Saunders, 70, vii-414 p.

5440   "Hospitalisation privée en France (L')", *C. Laënnec* 30(2), jun 70 : 1-100.

5441   Bibl. XIX-4969. JONES, M. *Social psychiatry in practice: the idea of the therapeutic com-
        munity.* CR: C. P. RYSER, *Amer. sociol. R.* 35(1), feb 70 : 163.

5442   LASSWELL, H. D.; RUBENSTEIN, R. "An application of the policy sciences orientation:
        the sharing of power in a psychiatric hospital", *Polit. Sci. ann.* (1), 1966 : 191-241.
        [See Bibl. XVII-5475.]

5443   LEVINE, R. H. "Consumer participation in planning and evaluation of mental health
        services", *Soc. Wk* 15(2), apr 70 : 41-46.

5444   LILIENFELD, D. M. "Mental health information and moral values of lower class psy-
        chiatric clinic patients", *Int. J. soc. Psychiatry* 15(4), 1969 : 264-278.

5445   MOOS, R. H.; HOUTS, P. S. "Differential effects of the social atmosphere of human
        psychiatric wards", *Hum. Relat.* 23(1), feb 70 : 47-60.

5446 MORRIS, P. *Put away: a sociological study of institutions for the mentally retarded.* London, Routledge and K. Paul, 69, xxxiii-355 p. [UK.]

5447 POLSKY, H. W.; CLASTER, D. S.; GOLDBERG, C. (eds.). *Social system perspectives in residential institutions.* East Lansing, Michigan State University Press, 70, ix-802 p.

5448 REHM, K. E. *Die Rolle des Buddhismus in der indischen Medizin und das Spitalproblem* (The role of Buddhism in Hindu medicine and the hospital problem). Zürich, Juris-Verlag, 69, 57 p.

5449 ROCK, R. S.; JACOBSON, M. A.; JANOPAUL, R. M. *Hospitalisation and discharge of the mentally ill.* Chicago, University of Chicago Press, 69, xix-268 p. CR: L. TAYLOR, *Brit. J. Sociol.* 21(2), jun 70 : 237-238.

5450 ROUAN, G. G.; DOLLONE, J.; LE GAONACH, J. *La médecine du travail - organisation du service médical.* Paris, Dunod, 69, xi-115 p.

5451 SCHULMAN, J. *Remaking an organization: innovation in a specialized psychiatric hospital.* Albany, N. Y., State University of New York Press, 69, 255 p. CR: R. F. LARSON, *Amer. sociol. R.* 35(4), aug 70 : 813-814.

5452 SEGAL, B. E. "Hierarchy and work dissatisfaction in a Chilean hospital", *Soc. Forces* 48(2), dec 69 : 193-202.

5453 SOMERS, A. R. *Hospital regulation; the dilemma of public policy.* Princeton, N. J., Industrial Relations Section, Princeton University, 69, xxii-240 p.

5454 WING, J. K.; BROWN, G. W. *Institutionalism and schizophrenia; a comparative study of three mental hospitals, 1960-1968.* Cambridge, Eng. University Press, 70, xiii-260 p.

F.224 Social work and social medicine: the professional aspect
Service social, médecine sociale: aspect professionnel

[See also / Voir aussi: **F.212**; 1030, 3226, 5105, 5205, 5305]

5455 AICARDI, G. "Studi recenti di medicina sociale" (Recent studies of social medicine), *Quad. Sci. soc.* 9(1), 1970 : 56-61.

5456 BERARDI, A. "La professione di medico sociale" (The profession of social doctor), *Difesa soc.* 48(2), apr-jun 69 : 25-40.

5457 BESSELL, R. *Introduction to social work.* London, Batsford, 70, 2-142 p. [Social work as a profession.]

5458 BLISHEN, B. B. *Doctors and doctrines: the ideology of medical care in Canada.* Buffalo, N. Y., University of Toronto Press, 69, 202 p. CR: K. J. ROGHMANN, *Amer. sociol. R.* 35(4), aug 70 : 815-816.

5459 BROWN, R. G.; WHYTE, H. M. (eds.). *Medical practice and the community.* Canberra, Australian National University Press, 70, xvi-244 p.

5460 BUI DANG-HA-DOAN, J. "Évolutions récentes du corps médical français", *C. Sociol. Démogr. médic.* 10(2), apr-mai : 83-93.

5461 CHERUBINI, A. "Crisi della medicina, crisi della società" (Crisis of medicine, crisis of society), *Probl. Sicur. soc.* 24(4), jul-aug 69 : 687-710.

5462 CHEW, D. C. E. "Wastage patterns in the nursing profession in Singapore—a study of manpower utilisation", *Int. Lab. R.* 100(6), dec 69 : 583-594.

5463 COE, R. M. *Sociology of medicine.* New York, McGraw-Hill, 70, viii-388 p.

5464 CRISPINO, L. et al. "Medicina scolastica e medicina preventiva: un decennio di attività nel comune di Bergamo" (School medicine and preventive medicine. Ten years of activity in the municipality of Bergamo), *Dif. soc.* 47(3), jul-sep 68 : 47-75.

5465 EPSTEIN, I. "Professionalization, professionalism and social-worker radicalism", *J. Health soc. Behav.* 11(1), mar 70 : 67-77.

5466 FREIDSON, E. *Professional dominance: the social structure of medical care.* New York, Atherton Press, 70, 242 p.

5467 FREIDSON, E. *Profession of medicine; a study of the sociology of applied knowledge.* New York, Dodd, Mead, 70, xxi-409 p.

5468 GAVIRIA TRESPALACIOS, J.; GUERRERO GONZALEZ, P. "El médico y el desarrollo" (The doctor and development), *Doc. polít.* 85, jan-feb 70 : 22-39. [Colombia.)

5469 GROSSER, C.; HENRY, W. E.; KELLY, J. G. (eds.). *Nonprofessionals in the human services.* San Francisco, Jossey-Bass, 69, xxi-263 p. [Social workers, USA.]

5470   HART, E.; SECHRIST, W. (eds.). *Dynamics of wellness.* Belmont, Calif., Wadsworth
        Publishing Co., 70, 470 p.

5471   JACOBSON, V.; MONELLO, P. *Le travail social en équipe; la collaboration entre travailleurs
        sociaux de formation différente.* Toulouse, É. Privat, 70, 146 p.

5472   KAHN, A. J. "Perspectives on access to social services", *Soc. Wk* 15(2), apr 70 : 95-101.

5473   LAFITTE, V. "Démographie et sociologie de la médecine salariée", *Pensée* 151, mai-jun
        70 : 119-129 (France.]

5474   LEVY, C. S. "The social worker as agent of policy change", *Soc. Casewk* 51(2), 1970 :
        102-108.

5475   MANAHAN, L. "Perceived roles of volunteers in a community setting in Manila", *Gradua-
        te Fac. Stud.* 19, 1968 : 212-221.

5476   MARCOUX, F.; BEMRICH, D. "Démographie régionale des médecins spécialistes: l'im-
        portance du facteur âge", *C. Sociol. Démogr. médic.* 9(3), jul-sep 69 : 176-181.

5477   MECHANIC, D. "Correlates of frustration among British general practitioners", *J. Health
        soc. Behav.* 11(2), jun 70 : 87-103.

5478   "Médecins généralistes en France (Les)", *C. Sociol. Démogr. médic.* 9(3), jul-sep 69 :
        168-175.

5479   MORRIS, M. *Voluntary work in the welfare State.* London, Routledge and Kegan Paul, 69,
        xx-279 p. [Volunteer social workers in the UK.]

5480   NÉDÉLEC, M. *La médecine de groupe.* Paris, Éditions de Seuil, 70, 173 p.

5481   NOUVELOT, M. C.; BUI-DANG-HA-DOAN, J. "Dynamisme démo-géographique du corps
        médical (1965-1966)", *C. Sociol. Démogr. médic.* 9(3), jul-sep 69 : 137-152. [France.]

5482   NOUVELOT, M. C.; MONNIER, A. "Perspectives d'effectif de médecins en 1985", *C.
        Sociol. Démogr. médic.* 9(4), oct-dec 69 : 190-222. [France.]

5483   PÉQUIGNOT, H. "Le rendement économique de la profession médicale", *Vie soc.* (6),
        jun 70 : 323-334. [France.]

5484   PETERS, H. "Die misslungene Professionalisierung der Sozialarbeit: das Verhältnis von
        Rolle, Handlungsfeld und Methodik" (The unsuccessful professionalisation of social
        work: the relation between role, field of action and methodology), *Kölner Z. Soziol.
        u. soz.-Psychol.* 22(2), jun 70 : 335-355.

5485   "Pour une révision du secret médical", *C. Laënnec* 29(3), sep 69 : 3-73.

5486   PICHOT, F. "Premiers résultats d'une recherche sur le devenir professionnel des méde-
        cins", *B. Inst. nat. Santé Rech. médic.* 25(1), jan-feb 70 : 115-130. [France.]

5487   PREISS, E.; VRGA, D. J. "The patient-centered conference of nurses on a surgical ward",
        Ind. sociol. B. 6(4), jul 69 : 235-249. [Canada.]

5488   REIN, M. "Social work in search of a radical profession", *Soc. Wk* 15(2), apr 70 :
        13-28.

5489   SKIBA, E.-G. *Der Sozialarbeiter in der gegenwärtigen Gesellschaft. Empirische Unter-
        suchungen zum sozialen Fremdbild des Fürsorgers* (The social worker in contemporary
        society. Empirical surveys in the strange social image of the social assistant). Wein-
        heim-Berlin-Basel, Beltz, 69, 434 p.

5490   SPINDLER, O. "Contribution à l'étude des femmes médecins en France", *C. Sociol.
        Démogr. médic.* 10(1), jan-mar 70 : 3-22.

5491   TELLEGEN, E. *Medische sociologie; een literatuurverkenning* (Medical sociology: a literature
        review). Alphen-aan-den-Rijn, Samson, 70, 134 p.

5492   WEBER, A. A. "Effectifs du personnel de santé dans les pays de la région européenne de
        l'Organisation Mondiale de la Santé en 1965", *C. Sociol. Démogr. médic.* 10(2), apr-mai
        70 : 63-68.

5493   WILSON, R. N. *The sociology of health; an introduction.* New York, Random House, 70,
        xvii-134 p.

**F.225   Social work education
           Formation du personnel**

[See also / Voir aussi: 5398]

5494   "Innovations in medical education", *Milbank Memor. Fund Quart.* 47(4), oct 69 :
        343-476. [USA.]

5495   JAMOUS, H. *Sociologie de la décision. La réforme des études médicales et des structures hospitalières.* Paris, CNRS, 69, 257 p. CR: M. COORNAERT, *C. int. Sociol.* 17(49), jul-dec 70 : 187-190.

5496   MAYERS, F. "Differential use of group teaching in first-year field work", *Soc. Serv. R.* 44(1), mar 70 : 63-75.

5497   McCORMICK, M. J. "Dimensions of social work values in the United States—implications for social work education", *Int. soc. Wk* 12(3), 1969 : 14-28.

5498   MUNRO, A.; McCULLOCH, W. *Psychiatry for social workers.* Oxford-New York, Pergamon Press, 69, xvi-283 p.

5499   MURSÎ, K. I. *al-Tahalluf al-'aqlî wa-athar al-ri'âyaṯ wal tadrîb fîhi* (Mental retardation, care activities and training for it). al-Qâḥiraṯ, Dâr al-Naḥḍaṯ al-'Arabîyaṯ, 70, 451 p. [UAR.]

5500   SCOTT, C. (comp.). *Ethnic minorities in social work education; a collection of papers highlighting developments and issues concerning faculty, students and curriculum in social work education.* New York, Council on Social Work Education, 70, v-89 p. [USA.]

5501   YELAJA, S. A. "Schools of social work in India: historical development, 1936-1966", *Ind. J. soc. Wk* 29(4), jan 69 : 361-378.

AUTHOR INDEX
INDEX DES AUTEURS

Guinchat, C., 4514
Gulati, S. C., 2597
Guliev, V. E., 3400
Gullahorn, J. E., 448
Gullahorn, J. T., 448
Guller, I. B., 4143
Gulliver, P. H., 2065
Gunlicks, A. B., 3552
Gurin, P., 4203
Gurman, A. S., 2665
Gurr, T. R., 4198
Gustafson, J. M., 3878
Gutek, G. L., 4805
Gutenschwager, A. C., 4886
Guttentag, M., 5099
Guttmacher, A. F., 734
Guyer, M., 1850
Guzmán Böckler, C., 5044
Guzman Campos, G., 3669
Gwyn, R. J., 4121
Gyselings, R., 778

Haan, N., 917
Haas, M., 2271
Haavio, M., 5173
Haavio-Mannila, E., 2767, 2768, 4204
Habegger, N., 3887
Habenstreit, B., 1524
Hačaturjan, A. B., 1748
Hacker, S. L., 2220
Hackler, J. C., 5215
Hackman, J., 1936, 2221
Hackman, R. C., 3289
Haddad, G., 4491
Hadden, J. K., 3722, 3723
Haerle, R. K. Jr., 3961
Hafner, A. M., 4492
Haft, H., 4387
Hagburg, E. C., 2985
Hage, J., 2986, 4887
Hagensen, K., 5346
Hagstrom, W. O., 73
Hahn, H., 4205, 4206, 4207
Hahn, M., 518
Haider, S., 2569
Haim, A., 5277
Hair, P. E. H., 807
Haldane, I. R., 4529
Halder, A., 2613
Hale, B. M., 150
Hale, S., 4493
Halford, L. J., 380
Hall, C. S., 519
Hall, D. T., 2023, 3232
Hall, J., 2222
Hall, M. P., 731
Hall, R. H., 3233
Hall, R. L., 293
Halloran, J. D., 4540

Hall Williams, J. E., 5303
Halmos, P., 4541
Halperin Donghi, T., 2514
Halpern, M., 2387, 2388
Halpin, S. M., 449
Halstead, M. N., 2438
Hamilton, M. W., 5176
Hamilton, V., 4680
Hamm, B. C., 1989
Hamm, N. H., 883
Hammerich, K., 3360
Hammond, B., 1245
Hammond, P. E., 3818
Hammonds, A. D., 3631
Hammond-Tooke, W. D., 1442
Hampton, W. A., 1599
Hance, W. A., 709
Handler, J. F., 5408
Handlin, M. F., 4806
Handlin, O., 4806
Haney, C. A., 5174
Haney, G. A., 693
Hanf, T., 4807
Hanna, J. L., 1525
Hanna, W. J., 1525
Hannagen, R., 247
Hannerz, U., 2798
Hansen, N. M., 5100
Hanson, F. A., 1218
Hanssen, B., 357
Hanssler, B., 3991
Hara, Y., 4808
Harary, F., 1843
Harasawa, Y., 2147
Harasymiw, B., 3553
Harčev, A. G., 2598
Hardert, R. A., 4388
Hardgrave, R. L. Jr., 1219
Harding, T. G., 2115
Hardoy, J., 1443
Hardré, J., 2106
Hare, A. P., 4393
Harewood, J., 732
Hargous, S., 1220
Harless, W. G., 4696
Harloff, H. J., 1124
Harman, B. D., 1720
Harms, V., 595
Harp, J., 179
Harper, D. W., 911
Harrington, C., 4139
Harris, C., C., 2666, 2667
Harris, C. D., 1526
Harris, E. E., 2865
Harris, E. F., 5128
Harris, F. R., 43
Harris, J. R., 1125
Harris, M., 1749
Harris, Z. S., 4450

Turk, H., 1642
Turksma, L., 296
Turner, C. V., 3956
Turner, F. C., 3748
Turner, H. A., 3180, 3210, 4283
Turner, J., 3618
Turner, J. E., 319
Turner, J. H., 5079
Turner, P. R., 3851
Turner, R. H., 276, 3619, 4198, 4284
Turner, V. W., 3852
Tütengil, C. O., 350
Tyler, L. E., 3806
Tyler, P., 4576

Uchendu, V. C., 1256
Uchida, Y., 3656
Ucros, J., 1176
Ulianich, B., 3685
Underwood, W. L., 4477
Unger, I., 2334
Unkovic, C. M., 286
Uphoff, N. T., 4889
Urbanek, E., 69
Uribe Villegas, O., 2889
Urquidi, V. L., 5006
Urrutia, M. M., 3079, 3080
Urwin, D. W., 3620
Urwin, P. W., 3604
Uschner, M., 5076
Ustinov, V. A., 993
Utz, A. F., 3809

Vaca-Toledo, F., 4475
Vajda, E. H., 1362, 2301
Valabrègue, C., 1014
Valenta, Z., 2954
Valentey, D., 858
Valiani, L., 3621
Valiev, A. K., 2516
Valkenburgh, P., 2289
Valkonen, T., 4285, 4967
Valles, J., 5159
Vallier, I., 3749, 4002
Vallin, J., 676
Valsan, E. H., 1313
Van Bockstaele, J., 351
Vance, R. B., 222
Van Cleef, E., 1506
Van den Ban, A. W., 1898
Van den Berghe, P. L., 2803
Van den Ende, H. W., 471, 4417
Vandenput, M., 4772
Vanderkamp, J., 3211
Van der Maesen, C. E., 3622
Van der Slice, A., 561
Van der Slik, J. R., 2890
Van der Zwaan, A. H., 352
Van de Vall, M., 3081

Vandeville, V., 5123
Van Dingenen, F., 4106
Vandiver, J. S., 1471
Van Dycke, H. T., 5160, 5290
Vanek, J., 3181
Vanek, W. D., 3389
Van Es, J. C., 424, 4286
Van Hecke, E., 1427
Van Hoose, T., 1884
Van Houten, D. R., 295
Van Kemenade, J. A., 4638
Van Koolwijk, J., 425
Van Leeuwen, A. T., 4925
Vann, R. T., 3913
Van Nieuwenhuijze, C. A. O., 5079
Van Praag, P., 691
Van Praag, P. H., 2238
Van Rijswijk-Clerkx, L. E., 907
Van Rossum, W., 471
Van Ussel, J., 2576
Vapnarsky, C. A., 1507
Vaquero, P., 579
Vardaman, G. T., 4418
Varma, S. C., 5291
Vasconi, T. A., 617
Vatuk, S., 2739
Vaughan, G. M., 2016
Vaughan, T. R., 17
Vaujour, J., 1557
Vazjulin, V. A., 580
Vázquez Carrillo, J. E., 3623
Vedder, C. B., 5292
Vegas Pérez, A., 2942
Vejngol'd, Ju. Ju., 618
Velchevska, L., 5365
Veneckij, I., 859
Ventura, S., 692
Venturi, V., 3693
Verba, S., 4287
Verde, F., 2589
Verdes-Leroux, J., 2904, 4217
Verdier, Y., 2682
Verhoeve, J., 3764
Verma, I. B., 4773
Veroff, J., 2623
Vercheure, J., 3686
Versele, S.-C., 4048
Vervoort, C. E., 4826
Very, P. S., 3270
Vesta, F. J. di, 4639
Veyret-Verner, G., 1558
Victoroff, D., 104
Vidal, D., 3082, 3624, 4346
Vidal, J. L., 752
Vidalenc, G., 3083
Vidmar, N., 2221, 2251, 2252
Vidyarthi, L. P., 1559, 2101, 4968
Vientos Gaston, N., 5124
Viertler, R. B., 1257

SUBJECT INDEX

Abortion, 731, 788, 795, 853, 4238
Acculturation
    concept, 594
    see also Culture contacts
Aden, elites and urban living, 2464
Adjustment
    child, *see* Child, environment
    education, *see* Education, methods and problems
    family, *see* Family
    immigrants, *see* Immigrant absorption
    marital, *see* Marriage
    see also Group, adjustment and conformity
Adorno, T. W., 202, 568, 572
Advertising, 4113, 4121, 4124, 4128, 4133, 4136, 4137
Aesthetics, 4482
Afghanistan
    political parties and movements, 3525
    rural communities, 1288
Africa
    attitudes, 2828
    birth control, 698, 704, 705
    children, 2911
    communication, 4393
    community studies, 1195, 1227, 1228, 1233, 1253, 1256, 2065
    culture, 2059-2075, 4476
    delinquency, punishment, 5309
    disease, social aspects, 707
    economic development, social factors, 1125, 3056, 4818, 4971, 4998, 5093
    education, 4715; system, 4777, 4790, 4818
    elites, 2479, 2504, 2508, 2513, 2520
    family, 704, 2657, 2671, 2710
    fertility, 705
    food problem, 5093
    ideologies, 2436
    internal migrations, 709, 1117, 1125, 1153, 1168
    language, 2671, 4452, 4461, 4476
    law, sociology of, 4004, 4018, 4027
    literature, 4480, 4489, 4496, 4503
    marriage, 2600, 2710
    minorities, 2822
    mythology, 3936
    political parties and movements, 3538
    political power and government system, 3385, 3422

population 697-717
public administration, 3451
race relations, 2817-2835
refugee problems, 1076, 1079
religion: 3836, 3848, 3850, 3866, 3875, 3876; dynamics, 4003; minor differenciations, 3907; rites and cults, 3951
rural communities, 1278, 1294, 1304
rural population, 1330, 1334, 1352, 1357, 1361, 1363, 1368, 1389
rural-urban studies, 709, 1115, 1117, 1153, 1451
slavery, 2327
social change: 4018, 4017, 4944, 5064; and technology, 4943, 4944
social class, 2419, 2436, 2439, 2451
social sciences, bibliography, 154, 157, 4489
social stratification, 2067, 2322
sociology, current trends, 70
trade unions, 3055, 3056
urban communities, 1525, 1531
urban living, 1614, 2067
urbanism, 1729
violence, 4239
witchcraft, 3854
women, 2781
Age groups, 693, 860-868, 1379; *see also* Child; Old age; Youth
Aged workers, 1019
Aggressiveness, 1836, 2279
Agrarian reform, 1339, 1340, 1412
Albania, population, 832
Alcoholism, 5132, 5134, 5144, 5146, 5147, 5152, 5154, 5157-5159, 5161
Alienation, 921, 1091, 1400, 1779, 1783, 1785, 1794-1796, 1803, 1805, 1812, 1814, 1818, 1829, 3305, 3351, 3449, 4065, 4188, 4213, 4935
    concept, 524, 1808
Algeria
    birth control, 712
    emigration, 1044, 1060
    ideologies, 4325
    population, 716
    press, 4571
    public administration, 3490
    religion, rites and cults, 3949
    rural population, 3129, 3130, 3165
    self-management, 3129, 3143, 3149, 3165

Cult, religious, *see* Religions, cults and rites
Culture
 and personality, 572, 599, 1733-1776, 2434, 2567, 4382, 4451, 4714, 4921
 change, 1737-1739, 1742, 1748, 1768, 1774, 1920, 2074, 2080, 2087, 2093, 2097, 2099, 2118
 contacts, 594, 2107, 2120-2122, 2268, 2885, 4102, 4227, 4665
 descriptive and local studies, *see* Civilizations; National characteristics
Customs, 4478
Cybernetics, 334, 3374
Czechoslovakia
 communication, 4399
 community studies, 1208, 1254
 economic development, social factors, 5008
 education, 5008 .
 entrepreneurship, 2990
 family, 2687, 2718
 health insurance, 5387
 housing, 1655, 1656
 human aspect of work, 1019
 internal migrations, 1165
 law, sociology of, 2718
 marriage, 2607
 old age, 1019
 population, 5250
 public opinion, 4132
 religion, relations with social environment, 3731, 3743
 self-management, 3172
 social change and technology, 4399
 social policy, 5374
 social sciences, current trends, 2990
 social stratification, 2311, 2315
 sociology, current trends, 46, 69, 2990
 suicide, 5250
 workers'councils, 31315
 youth, 864, 945, 984

Dahrendorf, R., 543, 571, 582, 3397
Dances, folk
Data archives, 143, 148, 152, 156, 165, 170
Decision process, 2141, 2168, 2970; *see also* Group, decision process; Group, problem-solving
Delinquency, 2000, 2416, 2853, 5196-5266, 5298
 juvenile, 1003, 1906, 2738, 4525, 4540, 5274, 5267-5292, 5295, 5300, 5307
 punishment, 5231, 5251, 5293-5312
 sexual, *see* Sexual delinquency and perversions
Democracy, 3379, 3380, 3387, 3393, 3395, 3400, 3406, 3411, 3418, 3433, 3438
 concept, 605, 608
Demography
 and sociology, 26, 38, 287

 historical, 38, 659, 662, 724, 768, 770, 792, 801, 809, 813, 814, 817, 820, 1537, 2626,
 social, *see* Population
Denmark
 family, 966
 industrial relations, 3101
 political parties and movements, 3585
 public administration, 3479
 social mobility, 2549
 youth, 966
Dependency, concept, 617
Development, concept, 4924
Deviance, 1807, 2011, 2306, 2572, 3752-3757, 3760, 3763, 3765, 5237, 5260, 5302
Dialectics and sociology, 232
Dictatorship, 3431; *see also* Totalitarianism
Discrimination, racial, *see* Race problems; Race relations
Disease
 insurance, *see* Health insurance
 social aspects, 707, 869, 1863, 1964, 1970, 3947, 5164-5195, 5236
Divorce, 669, 871, 2581, 2587, 2590, 2593, 2607, 2616, 2619
Dogmatism, 4143, 4267
Dominican Republuc, elites, 2470
Drug addiction, 5133, 5135, 5136, 5138-5143, 5145, 5148, 5150, 5151, 5153, 5155, 5156, 5160, 5162, 5163
Durkheim, E., 492, 493, 502, 507, 511, 513, 516
Dwellings, *see* Rural dwellings; Urban housing

Ecology
 rural, *see* Rural sociology
 social, 1178-1194
 urban, *see* Urban sociology
Economic development, 2937, 4969, 4972, 4976, 4977, 4987, 4989, 4993, 5000, 5003, 5005-5007
 social factors, 663, 674, 675, 1105, 1125, 1144, 1146, 1391, 1396, 2431, 3056, 4167, 4535, 4818, 4969-5008, 5093
Economic life and moral order, 2995, 3792
Economy
 and society, 2933, 2934, 2942
 and sociology, 284, 291, 294, 551
Ecuador
 models, 1331
 religion, relations with social environment, 3709
 rural population, 1331
 sociology, current trends, 33
Education, 866, 878, 887, 911, 913, 915, 920, 930, 940, 989, 994, 1010, 1351, 1753, 1760, 1784, 1792, 1943, 2040, 2314, 2380, 2395, 2452, 2529, 2816, 3222, 3247, 3250, 3348, 3789, 4152, 4521, 4585-4857, 4986, 5008

Social surveys
  descriptive, 3260
  methods, 396, 399, 400, 406, 410, 414, 418,
    424, 429
Social system, concept, 616
Social will, concept, 618
Social work, 2166, 5084, 5284, 5358, 5398-
    5424, 5457
  education, 5398, 5494-5501
Social workers, 5465, 5471, 5474, 5479, 5484,
    5488, 5489
Socialism, 4303, 4311, 4317, 4335, 4341, 4988
  scientific, *see* Marxism
Socialization, 1777, 1784, 1786, 1788, 1792,
    1798, 1801, 1804, 1819, 1822, 1831, 2027,
    2691, 3246, 3254, 3760, 4172, 4200, 4453,
    4710, 4860
  concept, 610
Society
  evolution, *see* Social change
  individual, and, *see* Individual and society
  plural, *see* Plural society
  structure, *see* Social structure
Sociologists
  activities, 176-189, 2769, 4353
  biographies and obituaries, 190-218, 572
Sociology
  and other sciences, 281-296, 3640
  basic concepts, 421, 490, 541, 543, 555, 564,
    570, 571, 587-620, 648, 860, 919, 1194,
    1734, 1808, 2143, 2372, 2802, 3962, 4335,
    4363, 4753
  basic problems, 223-280
  current trends and activities, 21-70, 79, 109,
    115, 120, 168, 530, 750, 1265, 1267, 1735,
    2008, 2187, 2232, 2270, 2685, 2705, 2725,
    2990, 3302, 3364, 3407, 3537, 3638, 3652,
    4044, 4438, 4486, 4509, 4638, 4865, 5169
  economic, 494, 534, 551, 570, 591, 598,
    2923-2943, 5317; *see also* under specific
    subjects, for example: Economic develop-
    ment, social factors; Social change and
    technology; Underdevelopment, social
    aspects
  educational, *see* Education
  electoral, *see* Electoral sociology
  ethnic, *see* Race relations
  experimental, 432-476, 516, 603, 650, 655,
    893, 909, 1033, 1331, 1455, 1849, 1991,
    2230, 2274, 2721, 4022, 4907, 5284; *see
    also* Attitudes, research; Communication,
    research; Group experiments
  history, 1-10, 24, 61, 357, 1749, 3638, 4046;
    see also Sociology, theoretical systems
  industrial, *see* Industrial sociology
  Marxist, 28, 147, 484, 520, 527, 536, 538,
    548, 549, 558, 567, 579, 618, 2392
  medical, 1030, 3226, 5105, 5205, 5305, 5455-
    5493

meetings, 93-99, 684, 836, 1266, 1504, 3133,
    4048, 4468, 4826, 4940, 4946
method, *see* Methods
occupational, *see* Occupations
of art, 1975, 2562, 3249, 4478-4511, 5033
of knowledge, 45, 50, 56, 146, 2195, 2875,
    4348-4371, 4410
of law, *see* Law, sociology of
organization of research, 54, 71-92, 94, 148,
    161, 912, 3633, 4370
political, *see* Political sociology
reference books, 51, 60, 138-175, 289, 318,
    661, 1492, 1803, 2071, 2728, 2913, 3031,
    3578, 3630, 3642, 3728, 4036, 4489, 4766,
    4780, 5075, 5169, 5238
religious, *see* Religion, sociology
rural, *see* Rural sociology
teaching, 11-20, 30, 2082
textbooks, 100-137
theoretical systems, 4.28, 147, 193, 477-586,
    596, 614, 618, 1770, 1805, 2392, 2393,
    2415, 3397, 3632, 3798, 3968, 4359, 4487,
    4880, 4903, 4922
urban, *see* Urban sociology
Sociometric
  relations, *see* Group, small; Group psycho-
    therapy; Psychodrama
  techniques, *see* Group experiments; Me-
    thods, empirical
Sociometry, 441, 466, 2255; *see also* Group,
    small
Sociotherapy, 2212
Songs, folk, 4483, 4502
Sorokin, P. A., 498
South Africa (Republic of)
  attitudes, 1590
  authority, 1916, 1937
  community studies, 1260
  culture, 1937
  human aspect of work, 2827
  law, sociology of, 4024, 4043
  minorities, 2818
  political power and government system, 3378
  population, 714
  race relations, 1916, 2820, 2823-2827, 2829,
    2831-2833
  rural-urban studies, 1442
  social class, 2833
  urban living, 1590
  witchcraft, 3839
Sovereignty, State, *see* Political power and
    systems of government
Spain
  age groups, 1379
  culture: 2108; contacts, 594
  delinquency, juvenile, 1003, 5268
  education, system, 4810, 4839
  emigration, 1095
  family, 1147

Television, 4515, 4518, 4520, 4521, 4524-4527, 4540, 4548, 4555, 4556, 4560, 4579, 4584
Tensions, *see* Conflict; Relations
Terminology, 141, 147, 155, 162, 163, 169, 173
Tests, 439, 441, 456, 457, 460, 893, 2721
Thailand
  culture, 2095
  education, system, 4857
  elites, 2458
  fertility, 763
  internal migrations, 1160
  law, sociology of, 4010
  religion, attitudes, 763
  rural communities, 1284
  sexual behaviour, 2578
  social change, 4857
  social stratification, 2301
  youth, 2578
Theatre, 4487, 4497
Theory and verification in sociology, 331; *see also* Simulation techniques
Timasheff, N. S., 220
Time-budget, 3293, 3302, 3310, 3927
Time, concept, 588
Time study, *see* Work study
Togo
  culture, 1195
  rural population, 1343
Tönnies, F., 486, 493
Touraine, A., 530, 542
Tourism, 3357
Town planning, *see* Urbanism
Towns, *see* Urban communities
Trade unions, 939, 2365, 3017-3084, 3196, 3540, 3720, 4293
Tribalism, 2826, 2828, 2830, 2835, 3408, 3422
Trinidad and Tobago
  attitudes, 4235
  family, 2584
  marriage, 2584
  race relations, 2584, 4235
  social mobility, 2531
  women, 2584
Troeltsch, E., 3632
Tuberculosis, 707
Tunisia
  birth control, 703, 712
  co-operatives, 1422, 2745
  delinquency, juvenile, 5270
  economic development, social factors, 5002
  education, system, 4793
  elites, 2489
  internal migrations, 1155
  kinship, 2745
  modernization, 5057
  population, 702, 711
  press, 4571
  rural communities, 2745

  rural population, 1422
  urban living, 1155
Turkey
  attitudes, 4227
  authority, 3781
  culture: 2113; contacts, 4227
  economic development, social factors, 5001
  ethics, 3781
  industrial relations, 3095
  modernization, 1455
  political parties and movements, 3561
  population, 842
  public administration, 3488
  religion, 3859
  revolution, 3561
  rural population, 1358
  rural-urban studies, 1455, 1458, 1468
  social change, 5025, 5075
  social class, 2354
  social policy, 5379
  social sciences, computers, 1455
  social stratification, 1358
  sociology, bibliography, 172, 5075
  urban communities, 1458, 1535
Typological method, 306, 542

Uganda
  co-operatives, 2198
  political parties and movements, 2198
  race relations, 2830
  rural population, 1329
Underdevelopment, social aspects, *see* Community, organization and development; Economic development, social factors; Population, economic problems; Social change and technology
Unemployment, 5089, 5090, 5095, 5097, 5103, 5110, 5117, 5122, 5123
Union of Soviet Socialist Republics
  abortion, 853
  attitudes, 4151
  children, 4151
  community studies, 1197, 1198
  culture, 2119
  delinquency, juvenile, 5272
  economic development, social factors, 5001
  education, system, 4821
  elites, 2501, 2516
  entrepreneurship, 3010
  ethics, 3792
  fertility, 786
  human aspect of work, 3301, 3792
  ideologies, 50
  immigration, 1071
  internal migrations, 1156
  law, sociology of, 4020
  leadership, 1594
  leisure, 3334, 3339
  mass communication media, 4544, 4570

INDEX DES SUJETS

Communautés
de travail, *voir* Industrie, relations, Syndicats
ethniques, *voir* Relations raciales
études descriptives, 1195-1263, 1326, 2065, 2105, 2940; *voir aussi* Associations volontaires et communautés
familiales, *voir* Famille
juives, *voir* Juifs, communautés
nationales, *voir* Caractéristiques nationales
politiques, *voir* Partis et mouvements politiques
religieuses, *voir* Religion et institutions religieuses
rurales, 1275-1317, 4789
urbaines, 792, 838, 1174, 1458, 1510-1560, 2901, 3351
Communication
industrielle, *voir* Industrie, relations
moyens de, 658, 1963, 2237, 3023, 3785, 4135, 4168, 4380, 4512-4584
théorie et recherche, 248, 408, 497, 3795, 4372-4424, 4705; *voir aussi* Méthodes empiriques
Communisme, 4295, 4326
concept, 4335
voir aussi Marxisme
Comportement, électoral, *voir* Sociologie électorale
voir aussi Attitudes
Comte, A., 573
Condition ouvrière, *voir* Travail, conditions
Conflit
de classe, *voir* Classe, relations
de cultures, *voir* Cultures, contacts
de race, *voir* Relations raciales
de rôles, *voir* Rôle social
du travail, *voir* Travail, conflits
entre générations, 862, 864, 867, 868
entre groupes, *voir* Relations entre groupes
entre personnes, 1899
international, *voir* Guerre
Conformité sociale, *voir* Adaptation
Congo (Brazzaville), religion, 3871
Congo (Kinshasa)
charisme, 1920
communautés rurales, 1306
consensus, concept, 607
droit, sociologie du, 4009
éducation, système, 4804, 4856
élites, 2471
évolution sociale, 5063
habitat rural, 1427
mariage, 2622
modernisation, 5029
partis et mouvements politiques, 1920
paysannerie, 1336
population, 697, 715
vie urbaine, 715, 1632
Congruence des statuts, concept, 615

Conjoint, choix, 2601, 2602, 2611, 4223
Connaissance
concept, 4363
sociologie de, *voir* Sociologie de la connaissance
Conscience de classe, concept, 2372
Conservatisme, 4051, 4072, 4317, 4338
Contenu, analyse, *voir* Analyse du contenu
Contrôle social, 1807, 1836, 2011, 2306, 2572, 3752-3765, 4428, 5237, 5260, 5302; *voir aussi* Coutumes; Morale; Pouvoir politique; Religion
Conventions collectives, 3068, 3129-3183, 3185
Cooley, 561
Coopératives, 1366, 1417, 1422, 2178, 2193, 2198, 2745, 4344
Corée
administration publique, 3471
éducation, système, 4815
évolution sociale, 5051
femmes, 2795
logement, 1716
migrations intérieures, 1137
vie urbaine, 1137
Costa Rica
administration publique, 3459
paysannerie, 1399, 3801
valeurs, 3801
Côte d'Ivoire
éducation, système, 4844
évolution sociale, 5056
population, 4844
Coutumes, 4478
Créativité en groupe, *voir* Groupe, créativité
Crime, *voir* Délinquance
Criminologie, 5204, 5206, 5216, 5226, 5227, 5259, 5261, 5298; *voir aussi* Délinquance
Cuba
classe sociale, 2454
culture, 2084
partis et mouvements politiques, 3548
révolution, 5015
Cultes, *voir* Religions, rites et cultes
Culture
contacts, 594, 2107, 2120-2122, 2268, 2885, 4102, 4227, 4665
et personnalité, 572, 599, 1733-1776, 2434, 2567, 4382, 4451, 4714, 4921
études descriptives et localisées, *voir* Caractéristiques nationales; Civilisations
évolution, 1737-1739, 1742, 1748, 1768, 1774, 1920, 2074, 2080, 2087, 2093, 2097, 2099, 2118
Cybernétique, 334, 3374

Dahrendorf, R., 543, 571, 582, 3397
Danemark
administration publique, 3479
dépendance, concept, 617

Irlande [*suite*]
  paysannerie, 1413, 4950
  population, 839, 2626
  syndicats, 3044
  vie urbaine, 1413, 2539
  villes et campagnes, 1413
Islande
  communautés, études descriptives, 1244
  type idéal, concept, 564, 602
Israël
  adaptation publique, 3452
  adoption, 2680
  communautés, études descriptives, 1212
  communautés rurales, 4344
  éducation, système, 2916
  évolution sociale, 5031
  famille, 2191, 2699
  groupes d'âge, 864
  idéologies, 4344
  immigrants, absorption, 1085, 1086, 1101,
    1692
  immigration, 1063
  jeunesse, 1004, 5430
  kibboutz, 1417, 2191, 2192
  logement, 1692
  partis et mouvements politiques, 3592
  paysannerie, 1349, 1402, 1417
  politique sociale, 5354
  population, 843
  relations raciales, 2914-2917
  religion: relations avec l'environnement
    social, 3711; relations entre, 3702
  service social des groupes, 5430
  stratification sociale, 2319
  travail social, 5405, 5410
Italie
  aliénation, 4213
  assurance-maladie, 5389, 5392
  assurance-vieillesse, 5397
  attitudes, 3255, 4184, 4193, 4213, 4248
  autogestion, 3153
  classe sociale, 2365, 2383, 2420, 3725, 4248
  communautés rurales, 1293, 1309
  conseils ouvriers, 3136
  culture: 2102, 2107; contacts, 2107
  éducation, système, 4831, 4840
  élites, 4432
  entrepreneur, 3006
  évolution sociale, 5049, 5072
  famille: 2589; protection, 5381, 5383
  femmes, 1388, 2779
  idéologies, 1404
  jeunesse, 951, 983, 1009, 4213, 4432
  langage, 4432
  Mafia, 2188
  mariage, 826, 2589
  migrations intérieures, 1123, 1138, 1145,
    1150
  parenté, 2664

participation des ouvriers, 3156
partis et mouvements politiques, 2365, 3521,
  3551, 3602, 3615, 4254
paysannerie, 1338, 1388, 1404, 4193
politique sociale, 5335, 5344, 5345
population, 775, 782, 783, 787, 803, 806,
  815, 822, 825, 826, 829, 1434
presse, 4522
professions, 3215, 3216, 3230, 3255
relations industrielles, 3118, 3119
religion: attitudes, 3983; institutions, 3687,
  3689, 3693; relations avec l'environnement social, 3720, 3725, 3728, 3730
service social, aspect professionnel, 5464
sociologie: bibliographie, 168; tendances
  récentes, 168
stratification sociale, 1404
syndicats, 2365, 3040, 3042, 3075, 3720
travail, conflits, 3208
vie urbaine, 782, 1589, 1593, 1634
villes et campagnes, 1431, 1434

Jamaïque
  enfants, 894
  migrations intérieures, 1106
  religion, rites et cultes, 3945
Japon
  administration de personnel, 2966
  administration publique, 2521, 3501
  attitudes, 4138, 4279
  classe sociale, 2448
  communautés rurales, 1286
  communautés urbaines, 1532, 1550, 2540
  conformité, 2021
  culture, 2096, 2097
  éducation: de base, 4521; système, 4808, 4850
  élites, 2521
  éthique, 3782, 3793
  évolution sociale, 5039, 5062, 5077
  famille, 2700
  femmes, 2792
  jeunesse, 864, 934, 948, 967, 969, 991, 3967
  logement, 1131
  maladie, aspects sociaux, 5182
  mariage, 2611
  migrations intérieures, 1131, 1135
  mobilité sociale, 2540, 2552
  modernisation, 5069
  partis et mouvements, politiques, 3510,
    3515, 3528, 3545, 3582, 3583, 3586, 3608
  paysannerie, 3782
  pensée sociale, 5
  professions, 3266
  propriété, 2948
  radio, 4584
  religion: 3865, 3889; attitudes, 2540, 3967;
    différenciations mineures, 2611, 3899,
    3900, 3905, 3910; institutions, 3691;
    sociologie, 3642

Sartre, J. P., 4487
Satisfaction dans le travail, 2998, 3011, 3290, 3305, 3924
Scandinavie
attitudes, 4157
communautés, études descriptives, 2105
communication, 4379
culture, 2105
religion, dynamique, 3989
Scheler, M., 4359
Schumpeter, J., 551
Schutz, A., 552
Science, sociologie de, *voir* Sociologie de la connaissance
Science juridique et sociologie, *voir* Droit, sociologie
Science politique et sociologie, 40, 529; *voir aussi* Politique, sociologie
Sears, R. R., 892
Sectes religieuses, *voir* Religions, différenciations mineures
Sécurité sociale, *voir* Politique sociale
Ségrégation raciale, *voir* Relations raciales
Selsam, H., 204
Sémantique, *voir* Analyse du contenu; Langage
Sénégal
charisme, 1923
communautés, études descriptives, 1261
éducation, système, 2529
émigration, 1068
famille, 2697
mobilité sociale, 2529
population, 701, 713
pouvoir politique et système de gouvernement, 1923
religion, institutions, 3697, 3698
Service social, 2166, 5084, 5284, 5358, 5398-5424, 5457
formation du personnel, 5398, 5494-5501
groupes, 5425-5432
Services de santé, *voir* Hôpitaux, organisation
Sexualité, 1977, 2556-2579, 2592, 3797, 3975, 5281
délinquance et perversions, 5127-5131, 5245
Sierra-Léone
jeunesse, 3275
modernisation, 5071
professions, 3275
Similarité et relations entre personnes, 1859, 1875, 1886
Simmel, G., 485
Simulation, techniques, 432, 433, 445, 447, 448, 463, 1849, 3927
Singapour
immigrants, absorption, 1099
partis et mouvements politiques, 3509
population, 757
relations raciales, 2894, 2896, 2897
service social, aspect professionnel, 5462

Sionisme, 4344
Smelser, N. J., 3768
Socialisation, 1777, 1784, 1786, 1788, 1792, 1798, 1801, 1804, 1819, 1822, 1831, 2027, 2691, 3246, 3254, 3760, 4172, 4200, 4453, 4710, 4860
concept, 610
Socialisation politique, 4172, 4200, 4235, 4252, 4257, 4273, 4281, 4285, 4291
Socialisme, 4303, 4311, 4317, 4335, 4341, 4988
Socialisme scientifique, *voir* Marxisme
Société
évolution, 248, 288, 321, 612, 616, 1467, 1737, 1738, 1746, 1748, 3362, 3368, 3390, 3714, 4012, 4018, 4316, 4366, 4858-4927, 5310, 5315; *voir aussi* Culture, évolution; et technique, 576, 597, 3432, 4352, 4399, 4735, 4928-4968; *voir aussi* Automation
individu et, *voir* Individu et société
plurale, 3401, 3406, 3412, 3414, 3419, 3437, 3508, 3536, 3540
structure, *voir* Structure sociale
Sociologie
concepts fondamentaux, 421, 490, 541, 543, 555, 564, 570, 571, 587-620, 648, 860, 919, 1194, 1734, 1808, 2143, 2372, 2801, 3962, 4335, 4363, 4753
congrès, 93-99, 684, 836, 1266, 1504, 3133, 4048, 4468, 4826, 4940, 4946
de l'art, 1975, 2562, 3249, 4478-3511, 5033
de l'éducation, *voir* Éducation
de la connaissance, 45, 50, 56, 146, 2195, 2875, 4348-4371, 4410
de la profession, *voir* Professions
du droit, *voir* Droit, sociologie
économique, 494, 534, 551, 570, 591, 598, 2923-2943, 5317; *voir aussi* Les rubriques spéciales, par exemple: Développement économique, facteurs sociaux; Société, évolution et technologie
électorale, 4238, 4142, 4150, 4156, 4160, 4163, 4171, 4184, 4196, 4191, 4193, 4194, 4207, 4215, 4242, 4245, 4259, 4260, 4293, 4294
enseignement, 11-20, 30, 2082
ethnique, *voir* Relations raciales
expérimentale, 432-476, 516, 603, 650, 655, 893, 909, 1033, 1331, 1455, 1849, 1991, 2230, 2274, 2721, 4022, 4907, 5284; *voir aussi* Attitudes, recherches; Communications, recherches; Groupe, expérience
histoire, 1-10, 24, 61, 357, 1749, 3638, 4046; *voir aussi* Sociologie, systèmes théoriques
industrielle, *voir* Industrie, sociologie
manuels, 100-137
marxiste, 28, 147, 484, 520, 527, 536, 538, 548, 549, 558, 567, 579, 618, 2393
médicale, 1030, 3226, 5105, 5205, 5305, 5455-5493

Printed in Belgium.